EDUCATORS GUIDE TO FREE VIDEOS
Secondary Edition

*

Edited by
Kathleen Suttles Nehmer

*

Educational Consultant
Michael Belongie, B. S.
Curriculum Manager, Randolph Public Schools

*

SIXTY-FIFTH ANNUAL EDITION
2018-2019

EDUCATORS PROGRESS SERVICE, INC.
214 Center Street
Randolph, Wisconsin 53956

Published by

Educators Progress Service, Inc.

Randolph, Wisconsin 53956

Copyright EDUCATORS GUIDE TO FREE TAPES, SCRIPTS, AND TRANSCRIPTIONS
1955-1968 by Educators Progress Service

Copyright EDUCATORS GUIDE TO FREE TAPES, SCRIPTS, AND TRANSCRIPTIONS
1969-1976 by Educators Progress Service, Inc.

Copyright EDUCATORS GUIDE TO FREE AUDIO AND VIDEO MATERIALS
1977-1991 by Educators Progress Service, Inc.

Copyright EDUCATORS GUIDE TO FREE VIDEOTAPES
1992-1999 by Educators Progress Service, Inc.

Copyright EDUCATORS GUIDE TO FREE VIDEOTAPES–Secondary Edition
2000, 2001, 2002, 2003, 2004, 2005, 2006, 2007, 2008 by Educators Progress Service, Inc.

Copyright EDUCATORS GUIDE TO FREE VIDEOS–Secondary Edition
2009, 2010, 2011, 2012, 2013, 2014, 2015, 2016, 2017, 2018 by Educators Progress Service, Inc.

All rights reserved.

Reproduction of this work, in whole or in part,
without written permission of the publisher is prohibited.

Library of Congress Catalog Card Number 55-2784

Printed and Bound in the United States of America

International Standard Book Number 978-0-87708-639-0

TABLE OF CONTENTS

FROM THE PUBLISHER'S DESK	V
HOW TO USE THE EDUCATORS GUIDE TO FREE VIDEOTAPES–Secondary Edition	VI
ANALYSIS	VII
YOUR LETTERS OF REQUEST	VIII
HOW TO COOPERATE WITH THE SPONSORS	IX
EVALUATION OF INDUSTRY-SPONSORED EDUCATIONAL MATERIALS	X
AGRICULTURE	1
BUSINESS AND ECONOMICS	6
CAREER EDUCATION	16
ENTERTAINMENT	21
FAMOUS PEOPLE	28
FINE ARTS	
Art and Handwork	38
Music and Drama	62
GUIDANCE	72
HEALTH	76
HOME ECONOMICS	
Family Life Education	80
Foods	85
LANGUAGE ARTS	96
PHYSICAL EDUCATION AND RECREATION	100

RELIGION AND PHILOSOPHY	107
SCIENCE	
Environmental Education	119
General Science	135
Nature Study	137
SOCIAL STUDIES	
Geography–US	144
Geography–World	154
History	193
World Affairs	206
TITLE INDEX	221

Know the title of the material you want? These pages will help you find it.

SUBJECT INDEX   235

If you are interested in a certain subject, the "yellow pages" will lead you to appropriate materials.

SOURCE INDEX   261

Here are the names of the sponsoring sources listed in this edition, with page references.

FROM THE PUBLISHER'S DESK

In the sixty-five years that we have been publishing this guide–solely devoted to free educational videos–an explosion has occurred in both the quantity and quality of these free teaching aids. Slightly over 100 titles were listed in the first edition–this 65th edition lists more than 1,015 free videos, DVD, and even streaming video! In fact, you will find that a number of videos can be viewed INSTANTLY right over your Internet connection. Please note, that while You-tube videos and similar sites can be educational and definitely entertaining, these are not the types of streaming videos we have included. We've listed purely educational videos produced by known sources.

Teachers of high school students, college students, adult audiences and others will find that the trend of using free teaching aids–and specifically free videos–is waking students up in the classroom. Showing beats telling and students become more interested in the subject when they can visually appreciate the lesson. ALL TITLES listed in this edition are new–teaching with free videos has never been more convenient, easier, or more appropriate. This GUIDE lists well over 900 hours of videotape and DVD presentations!

As you might imagine, the process of revising the annual editions of the EDUCATORS GUIDES is a time consuming process (there are now sixteen titles in the series). In our efforts to find new materials every year, we write thousands of letters to companies inquiring about materials they are willing to offer free to educators and others. Each and every year these letters are written. If no response is received, no materials from that source are included. **No materials are included if we have not received permission from the source to list their availability.** All addresses are verified as well. Your requests for FREE educational aids WILL BE ANSWERED.

It's a lot of work but it is very rewarding. It really is a pleasure to be able to point educators to teaching aids that not only **save tight budgets** but **add to the educational environment**. We like to find materials that "help teachers teach," not only to make their jobs easier but to help students learn more. Any comments you may have regarding this GUIDE are welcomed–we like to learn from you, too.

Kathy Nehmer

P. S. Be sure to use only the 2018-2019 GUIDE for the current school year, as hundreds of titles available last year are no longer available!

HOW TO USE THE EDUCATORS GUIDE TO FREE VIDEOS–Secondary Edition

The 2018-2019 EDUCATORS GUIDE TO FREE VIDEOS–Secondary Edition provides busy (and cash-strapped) educators with information about more than 1,015 free videotapes, DVDs, and streaming video to help save money and enrich the classroom. Finding the materials you desire, and requesting them, is easy.

The **BODY** of the GUIDE (white pages) gives you full information on each of the 1,018 titles, **ALL of which are new in this edition**. These new titles dramatically illustrate one reason that it is so important to use only the most current edition of the GUIDE.

The **TITLE INDEX** (blue pages) is an alphabetical listing of all items appearing in the body of the GUIDE, with page references. This enables readers to locate any item whose title is known. The TITLE INDEX guides you directly to any specific item in the GUIDE, where you can read the description of the material and find all ordering information.

In the **SUBJECT INDEX** (yellow pages) all materials relating to topics of a more specific nature than the general subject headings in the body of the GUIDE are categorized. These "yellow pages" work like the familiar "yellow pages" of a telephone directory.

The **SOURCE INDEX** (green pages) provides an alphabetical list of the names of the organizations from which materials can be obtained. Also included in each entry are page numbers which indicate where the materials from that particular source appear in the body of the GUIDE. Use of this feature facilitates the ordering, with one letter, of more than one selection if a source offers several.

ANALYSIS OF EDUCATORS GUIDE TO FREE VIDEOS–
Secondary Edition–2018

	TOTAL ITEMS
Agriculture	19
Business and Economics	49
Career Education	21
Entertainment	33
Famous People	42
Fine Arts	
Art and Handwork	101
Music and Drama	52
Guidance	16
Health	19
Home Economics	
Family Life Education	17
Foods	45
Language Arts	18
Physical Education and Recreation	33
Religion and Philosophy	66
Science	
Environmental Education	78
General Science	10
Nature Study	34
Social Studies	
Geography–US	41
Geography–World	194
History	64
World Affairs	<u>66</u>
TOTALS	**1,018**

YOUR LETTERS OF REQUEST

When requesting materials, please make your letter of request clear. Identify yourself and your organization. Be sure to use any identifying numbers provided and **observe any restrictions** on distribution as indicated in the GUIDE.

Do not be alarmed if everything you request does not come. The list of materials changes; materials go out of date and are replaced by new items. We cannot tell at the time of printing how long each item will last. Sponsors are asked to assure us, with reasonable certainty, that their materials will be available for approximately one year. It is to meet this need that the GUIDE is revised annually.

There are 31 sources of free materials listed in the **2018-2019 EDUCATORS GUIDE TO FREE VIDEOTAPES–Secondary Edition.** Please make certain that the request you are making is to the proper company.

In writing for materials, the following form is suggested. The listing used as an example is selected from page 121.

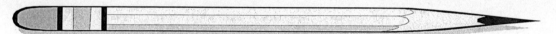

REGIONAL SCHOOL #7
Central Avenue
Winstead, Connecticut 06098

June 3, 2018

U. S. Environmental Protection Agency, Region 1
Customer Service Center
One Congress Street, Suite 1100
Boston, MA 02214

Dear Sponsor:

We would like to receive a copy of the following videotape as listed in the 2018 EDUCATORS GUIDE TO FREE VIDEOS–Secondary Edition:

Complete the Circle: How to Buy Recycled

I understand that we may keep the video. Thank you for your cooperation in assisting us to enrich the curriculum of our school.

Sincerely,

Stella Louise
High School Economics

VIII

HOW TO COOPERATE WITH THE SPONSORS

Subscribers to EPS services have frequently asked us for guidelines to follow in requesting sponsored materials. The following 14 questions are quoted from an address given by Thomas J. Sinclair, Ph.D., formerly Manager of Educational and Group Relations for the Association of American Railroads, at a convention of the National Science Teachers Association.

1. Poor handwriting, which you strive to correct in your pupils, often makes coupons and other requests useless. Is your handwriting distinct on requests?

2. Neither industry nor the U. S. Postal Service is omniscient. Do you include complete and accurate details of your address, including zip number?

3. Postcards, small social stationery, or slips of paper present filing problems and can easily be lost. Do you use standard sized stationery?

4. Remember that in big companies thousands of pieces of mail go in and out every day. Do you allow sufficient time for handling your request.

5. Most students advise businesses that they are studing a topic. Do you check your spelling?

6. If you were on the receiving end, you'd have a different view of mass classroom letter-writing projects to the same business organization. Do you make certain that only one request goes to a particular source from your classroom?

7. Instructions on a coupon, in a guide, or on an order form are there for a purpose. Do you read and follow these instructions?

8. Some organizations have dozens–sometimes hundreds–of different teaching aids. Specific needs should be outlined. Do you say "Send me everything you've got" or its equivalent?

9. Source lists and guides get out of date. Do you check to see if the list you are consulting is a recent one?

10. Sometimes aids are in limited supply or available only to teachers in single copies. Do you keep requests reasonable and show some respect for the costs of materials?

11. Sample copies are for examination, with the privilege of ordering quantities subsequently. Do you order classroom quantities blind–without first examining an item for suitability for your purpose?

12. Companies keep records and files. They frequently like to know precisely where their materials are going. Are you careful to mention your school connection?

13. Do you make a real effort to make certain the organization you are writing to is the correct one, and that it could reasonably have the material you are seeking?

14. Duplications and unnecessary correspondence only slow good service to the teaching profession. Do you consult your associates to see whether needed materials have already been supplied to your school?

These questions provide specific suggestions that should, in the long run, make for happier sponsors and better service to educators.

EVALUATION OF INDUSTRY-SPONSORED EDUCATIONAL MATERIALS

The business community has long recognized its obligation to support the agencies of the community that contribute to its security and well-being. In partial fulfillment of this obligation, industry trade associations and non-profit organizations have been producing supplementary materials for use in our nation's schools for some time. Properly planned, sponsored educational resources serve a valuable role and are particularly effective in giving information to students in an area where the sponsoring organization has achieved a high degree of specialization. When properly designed, sponsored materials can be used to motivate students and direct their energies into productive channels of growth.

Educational systems can respond more effectively to changes in technology, job structure, income, population, and manpower requirements with close support and involvement of industry. Both sectors have a common goal of strengthening the institutional programs at all levels in our schools. Operationally, this requires a strong industry-education alliance, particularly at the local level in preparing people for a productive role in the marketplace.

The National Association for Industry-Education Cooperation (NAIEC) was established in 1964 as a logical development out of the Business Industry Section of the National Science Teachers Association. Its purposes were (and still are) to bring about a better understanding between Education and the Business community and to mobilize the resources of education and industry to improve the relevance and quality of educational programs at all levels.

NAIEC members represent a variety of private and public organizations. Major trade associations, corporations, schools, and school districts are members. School superintendents, college presidents, curriculum and other education coordinators, business executives, industry-education coordinators, deans, department chairpersons, career education and job placement specialists, and faculty participate in the Association's programs.

The membership works together to identify problems of mutual interest, formulate plans and procedures, develop acceptable business-sponsored instructional materials, and communicate the advantages of industry-education cooperation.

The NAIEC membership has determined that the set of guiding principles (see below) for the preparation of materials for distribution to schools established by a study financed by American Iron and Steel Institute and carried out by the George Peabody Teachers College are valid and has found that materials embracing these criteria have usually found acceptance and use in the nation's schools and classrooms.

1. Work with a representative group of teachers and administrators to ensure meeting a curricular need.

2. Provide factual material desired by the schools. Include only that information which is significant to the study of particular problems or topics of concern to the teacher and student.

3. Exclude all advertising. A credit line naming the sponsor is enough; indeed schools need to know the publisher and the date of the material.

4. Materials must be written to the particular age level, reading level, interests, and maturity of the group for whom they are intended.

5. Keep the materials free of persuasion; avoid special pleading of the interests of any one point of view or group.

6. Make the materials available to educators only upon request.

X

In 1976 members of the NAIEC developed "A Guide for Evaluating Industry-Sponsored Educational Materials" which embodies the above listed criteria from the educator's viewpoint. This guide is an effort by the National Association for Industry-Education Cooperation (NAIEC) to present teachers with an instrument for evaluating sponsored education resources. These supplemental materials may take the form of teacher guides, filmstrips, games actually designed for the classroom, or pamphlets, reprinted articles, annual reports which may provide valuable background information but are not developed specifically for the teacher's use. (It is suggested that the Guide is more effective with the items actually designed for the classroom.)

If, after completing your evaluation of those items designed for the classroom, you have no further use for the instrument, the sponsoring organization providing the item would appreciate your evaluation with any comments you might have for guidance in the development of future materials. Hopefully this will foster closer industry-education cooperation.

A GUIDE FOR EVALUATING INDUSTRY-SPONSORED EDUCATIONAL MATERIALS

Title of material _____ Date produced, if available _____

Sponsor (name of organization)_____

Type of material: Audio _____ Audiovisual _____ Printed _____ Other _____

Type of instruction suitable for this material: Individual _____ Group _____

This evaluation is based on usage in _____ (grade level)

Evaluator _____ Date _____

Subject area/School _____

Address _____

_____

INSTRUCTIONS FOR USE:

Use the following scale by evaluating the material as it relates to your situation. Each of the descriptive statements is followed by a scale of (1), (2), (3), (4), (5). Indicate your assessment of the material by circling the appropriate number in the scale:

- (1) Definitely yes
- (2) Yes
- (3) No
- (4) Definitely no
- (5) Material cannot be evaluated on this concept

OBJECTIVES	SCALE
Identified outcomes may be obtained through use of the material.	1 2 3 4 5
The materials are representative of the curriculum involved; that is, they help further the objectives of the curriculum.	1 2 3 4 5

ABILITY RANGE	
The materials provide for the range of abilities and aptitudes of all pupils.	1 2 3 4 5

CONTENT	
The material is contemporary.	1 2 3 4 5
The material is controversial.	1 2 3 4 5
The material presents alternative views.	1 2 3 4 5
The material does not present a bias for a product, organization, or social cause.	1 2 3 4 5
The material does present a bias for a product, organization, or social cause.	1 2 3 4 5
If such a bias exists, it does not invalidate the material for my purposes.	1 2 3 4 5
The nature and scope of the material content is adequate to meet curriculum objectives.	1 2 3 4 5
The material is supplementary to the curriculum.	1 2 3 4 5
The material offers opportunity for integration of the subject within the existing curriculum.	1 2 3 4 5
The material correlates with a specific discipline area.	1 2 3 4 5
The material introduces experiences that would not otherwise be available in the classroom.	1 2 3 4 5
The material suggests other resources, supplementary and/or instructional.	1 2 3 4 5

UTILIZATION CHARACTERISTICS · SCALE

The anticipated time utilization is commensurate with anticipated value of outcome. 1 2 3 4 5

The material demands special conditions for use. 1 2 3 4 5

The material is appropriate for student's reading level. 1 2 3 4 5

The material is appropriate for student's interest level. 1 2 3 4 5

The material is attractive to students. 1 2 3 4 5

The material provides motivation for students. 1 2 3 4 5

PRESENTATION OF MATERIALS

Provisions are made for evaluating the material as it is used within the educational program. 1 2 3 4 5

Instructional procedures are outlined. 1 2 3 4 5

The style of the presentation is likely to lead students toward accomplishing basic goals. 1 2 3 4 5

Sample student activities and questions are included. 1 2 3 4 5

The instructions to teachers are clearly stated. 1 2 3 4 5

The intended use is easily understood. 1 2 3 4 5

The production quality of the materials is acceptable. 1 2 3 4 5

EVALUATION

The material provides for feedback to the user. 1 2 3 4 5

The material provides for self-evaluation. 1 2 3 4 5

AGRICULTURE

Acres of Oysters
Presents an overview of the oyster industry in Connecticut through interviews with oyster farmers and Connecticut Department of Agriculture, Aquaculture Division inspectors.
Availability: Staff at schools with NET, WIC, CSFP, FDPIR, CACFP, UMD or Child Nutrition Program food programs in the United States. Those not having such an affiliation should contact their library to place an interlibrary loan request.
Suggested Grade: 7-12
Order Number: NAL Video 1941
Production Date: 1992
Format: VHS videotape
Terms: Borrower pays return postage. RETURN the day after scheduled use. Book at least 4 weeks in advance. Requests must include your name, phone, mail address, eligibility program, title, NAL number, show date, and a statement, "I have read the warning on copyright restrictions and accept full responsibility for compliance." One title per request.
  Source: National Agricultural Library
  Document Delivery Services Branch
  4th Floor, Photo Lab
  10301 Baltimore Avenue
  Beltsville, MD 20705-2351
  Phone: 1-301-504-5994
  Fax: 1-301-504-5675
World Wide Web URL: http://www.nal.usda.gov/fnic
Email Address: lending@nal.usda.gov

Alabama, the Place for Aquaculture!
Profiles the size of the Alabama aquaculture industry and its infrastructure.
Availability: Staff at schools with NET, WIC, CSFP, FDPIR, CACFP, UMD or Child Nutrition Program food programs in the United States. Those not having such an affiliation should contact their library to place an interlibrary loan request.
Suggested Grade: 7-12
Order Number: NAL Video 2118
Production Date: 1991
Format: VHS videotape
Terms: Borrower pays return postage. RETURN the day after scheduled use. Book at least 4 weeks in advance. Requests must include your name, phone, mail address, eligibility program, title, NAL number, show date, and a statement, "I have read the warning on copyright restrictions and accept full responsibility for compliance." One title per request.
  Source: National Agricultural Library
  Document Delivery Services Branch
  4th Floor, Photo Lab
  10301 Baltimore Avenue
  Beltsville, MD 20705-2351
  Phone: 1-301-504-5994
  Fax: 1-301-504-5675
World Wide Web URL: http://www.nal.usda.gov/fnic
Email Address: lending@nal.usda.gov

Aquaculture and the Rural African Farmer/Pictorial Modelling
The first program illustrates how small-scale aquaculture using appropriate technology is being developed in rural Malawi. The second program describes how rural farmers can use flow charting as a planning tool to integrate the resources of aquaculture with other agricultural resources.
Availability: Staff at schools with NET, WIC, CSFP, FDPIR, CACFP, UMD or Child Nutrition Program food programs in the United States. Those not having such an affiliation should contact their library to place an interlibrary loan request.
Suggested Grade: 9-12
Order Number: NAL Video 1840
Production Date: 1990
Format: VHS videotape
Terms: Borrower pays return postage. RETURN the day after scheduled use. Book at least 4 weeks in advance. Requests must include your name, phone, mail address, eligibility program, title, NAL number, show date, and a statement, "I have read the warning on copyright restrictions and accept full responsibility for compliance." One title per request.
  Source: National Agricultural Library
  Document Delivery Services Branch
  4th Floor, Photo Lab
  10301 Baltimore Avenue
  Beltsville, MD 20705-2351
  Phone: 1-301-504-5994
  Fax: 1-301-504-5675
World Wide Web URL: http://www.nal.usda.gov/fnic
Email Address: lending@nal.usda.gov

Beekeeping in Northern Climates
Dr. Marla Spivak discusses basic principles of beekeeping.
Availability: Staff at schools with NET, WIC, CSFP, FDPIR, CACFP, UMD or Child Nutrition Program food programs in the United States. Those not having such an affiliation should contact their library to place an interlibrary loan request.
Suggested Grade: 7-12
Order Number: NAL Video 2509
Production Date: 1996
Format: VHS videotape
Special Notes: Includes a 68-page manual.
Terms: Borrower pays return postage. RETURN the day after scheduled use. Book at least 4 weeks in advance. Requests must include your name, phone, mail address, eligibility program, title, NAL number, show date, and a statement, "I have read the warning on copyright restrictions and accept full responsibility for compliance." One title per request.

*All materials listed in this 2018-2019 edition are **BRAND NEW**!*

AGRICULTURE

Source: National Agricultural Library
Document Delivery Services Branch
4th Floor, Photo Lab
10301 Baltimore Avenue
Beltsville, MD 20705-2351
Phone: 1-301-504-5994
Fax: 1-301-504-5675
World Wide Web URL: http://www.nal.usda.gov/fnic
Email Address: lending@nal.usda.gov

Biotechnology & Agriculture
Explains how biotechnology is allowing increased crop production in Japan.
Availability: Schools, libraries, homeschoolers, and nursing homes in Arizona and California (zipcodes beginning 900-931 and 935).
Suggested Grade: 6-Adult
Order Number: 132
Production Date: 1988
Format: VHS videotape
Terms: Borrower pays postage both ways; you may call the number below to learn how much postage costs. Return within two weeks of date borrowed. An individual may borrow 2 items at one time. For non-profit and educational use only.
Source: Consulate General of Japan, Los Angeles
350 South Grand Avenue, Suite 1700
Los Angeles, CA 90071-3459
Phone: 1-213-617-6700
Fax: 1-213-617-6727
World Wide Web URL: http://www.la.us.emb-japan.go.jp

Changing Attitude Toward Food, A
Discusses agriculture in Japan.
Availability: Schools, libraries, and nursing homes in Illinois, Indiana, Iowa, Kansas, Minnesota, Missouri, Nebraska, North Dakota, South Dakota, and Wisconsin.
Suggested Grade: All ages
Order Number: 01003
Production Date: 1999
Format: VHS videotape
Terms: Borrower pays return postage by U. S. Mail, UPS, or Federal Express, including insurance for "original" videos. Write, call, fax, or e-mail to request an application. An application form MUST be sent in one month in advance but not more than six months in advance. Include alternate titles and dates if provider can substitute titles. Send a SASE with request if you require confirmation. Return immediately after scheduled showing date. Videos may not be copied or broadcast without permission from the producer of the video. Borrower is responsible if video is lost or damaged.
Source: Consulate General of Japan at Chicago
Japan Information Center
Library
737 North Michigan Avenue, Suite 1000
Chicago, IL 60611
Phone: 1-312-280-0430
Fax: 1-312-280-6883
World Wide Web URL:
http://www.chicago.us.emb-japan.go.jp/jic.html
Email Address: jicchicago@webkddi.com

Day in Shrishnagar, A
Discusses a program in India that trains farmers to use new farming methods.
Availability: Schools and libraries in the United States.
Suggested Grade: 9-Adult
Order Number: SA3
Production Date: 1979
Format: VHS videotape
Terms: Borrower pays return postage. Return 3 days after showing via UPS. Book at least 2 weeks in advance.
Source: Syracuse University, South Asia Center
Video Library and Teaching Resources
346F Eggers Hall
The Maxwell School
Syracuse, NY 13244

Depending on Heaven: The Desert
Focuses on peasant families living on the edge of the expansive Mongolian desert. It shows farmers are applying modern agricultural techniques to combat erosion and to reclaim the land in China's Inner Mongolian region.
Availability: Schools, libraries, and nursing homes in the United States and Canada.
Suggested Grade: 6-12
Order Number: MV001
Format: VHS videotape
Terms: Borrower pays return postage. Return with 14 days after scheduled showing, via UPS or U. S. Mail. All requests must included an educational institution affiliation, a current address, and phone number. Order through web site only.
Source: Cornell University East Asia Program
World Wide Web URL:
http://eap.einaudi.cornell.edu/lending_library
Email Address: east_asia1@cornell.edu

Desert Agriculture
Reviews important research being carried out by the Sand Dune Research Institute of Tottori Prefecture and the Arid Land Agricultural Research Laboratory of Shizuoka University.
Availability: Schools, libraries, homeschoolers, and nursing homes in Arizona and California (zipcodes beginning 900-931 and 935).
Suggested Grade: 4-Adult
Order Number: 083
Production Date: 1984
Format: VHS videotape
Terms: Borrower pays postage both ways; you may call the number below to learn how much postage costs. Return within two weeks of date borrowed. An individual may borrow 2 items at one time. For non-profit and educational use only.

*All materials listed in this 2018-2019 edition are **BRAND NEW!***

AGRICULTURE

Source: Consulate General of Japan, Los Angeles
350 South Grand Avenue, Suite 1700
Los Angeles, CA 90071-3459
Phone: 1-213-617-6700
Fax: 1-213-617-6727
World Wide Web URL: http://www.la.us.emb-japan.go.jp

Farming in All Seasons
Fresh fruits, vegetables and flowers in all seasons of the year have been realized through improved techniques in hot house and vinyl tube agriculture. This video demonstrates the techniques for hydroponic farming.
Availability: Schools, libraries, homeschoolers, and nursing homes in Arizona and California (zipcodes beginning 900-931 and 935).
Suggested Grade: 4-Adult
Order Number: 083
Production Date: 1983
Format: VHS videotape
Terms: Borrower pays postage both ways; you may call the number below to learn how much postage costs. Return within two weeks of date borrowed. An individual may borrow 2 items at one time. For non-profit and educational use only.
Source: Consulate General of Japan, Los Angeles
350 South Grand Avenue, Suite 1700
Los Angeles, CA 90071-3459
Phone: 1-213-617-6700
Fax: 1-213-617-6727
World Wide Web URL: http://www.la.us.emb-japan.go.jp

Food and Agriculture in Contemporary Japan
Explains contemporary agricultural processes in Japan.
Availability: Schools, libraries, homeschoolers, and nursing homes in OREGON AND SOUTHERN IDAHO ONLY. Please make requests via the web site.
Suggested Grade: 4-12
Order Number: 414
Production Date: 1996
Format: VHS videotape
Terms: Borrower pays return postage. Return within three weeks after scheduled showing date. Book one month in advance if possible. Rewind the video and wrap securely for return. Be certain to indicate video number, date needed, name of your organization, and address to which video should be sent, along with phone number. Audience report enclosed with the video must be completed and returned.
Source: Consulate General of Japan, Oregon
Attn: Tamara, Video Library
1300 S. W. Fifth Avenue, Suite 2700
Portland, OR 97201
Phone: 1-503-221-1811, ext. 17
World Wide Web URL: http://www.portland.us.emb-japan.go.jp/en/index.html
Email Address: tamara@cgjpdx.org

Footholds
Filmed by the Canadian government's development research center, this video shows how rural people in Ecuador, Peru, Chile, Paraguay, and Colombia use technology in farming. It touches on geography, economies, and international development aid.
Availability: Schools in the United States.
Suggested Grade: 7-Adult
Order Number: order by title
Production Date: 1984
Format: VHS videotape
Terms: Borrower pays return postage. Return 14 days after receipt, via USPS including insurance. All borrowers must have a current lending agreement on file with the Outreach program. This agreement is available via the web site or may be requested via phone or fax.
Source: Center for Latin American Studies
University of Florida
319 Grinter Hall
P. O. Box 115530
Gainesville, FL 32611-5530
Phone: 1-352-392-0375
Fax: 1-352-392-7682
World Wide Web URL: http://www.latam.ufl.edu/outreach
Email Address: maryr@ufl.edu

Hamburger: Jungle Burger
While meat consumption drops, production rises, with detrimental results to the meat exports in Costa Rica. Graphic scenes of the slaughterhouse.
Availability: Schools, libraries, and nursing homes in the United States.
Suggested Grade: 6-12
Order Number: DEVCOS1-video
Production Date: 1985
Format: VHS videotape
Terms: Borrowers must have a User's Agreement on file with this source--available by mail or via the Internet. Return postage is paid by borrower; return 12 days after showing. Book at least three weeks in advance. All borrowers are limited to a total of ten items per semester.
Source: Latin American Resource Center
Stone Center for Latin American Studies
Tulane University
100 Jones Hall
New Orleans, LA 70118
Phone: 1-504-862-3143
Fax: 1-504-865-6719
World Wide Web URL: http://stonecenter.tulane.edu/pages/detail/48/Lending-Library
Email Address: crcrts@tulane.edu

Handling of Pigs
Discusses humane ways to handle pigs at the farm and at meat processing plants so that they are easier to handle.
Availability: Staff at schools with NET, WIC, CSFP, FDPIR, CACFP, UMD or Child Nutrition Program food programs in the United States. Those not having such an affiliation should

All materials listed in this 2018-2019 edition are BRAND NEW!

AGRICULTURE

Suggested Grade: 9-Adult
Order Number: DVD No. 8
Production Date: 2003
Format: DVD
Special Notes: Includes a CD.
Terms: Borrower pays return postage. RETURN the day after scheduled use. Book at least 4 weeks in advance. Requests must include your name, phone, mail address, eligibility program, title, NAL number, show date, and a statement, "I have read the warning on copyright restrictions and accept full responsibility for compliance." One title per request.
   Source: National Agricultural Library
   Document Delivery Services Branch
   4th Floor, Photo Lab
   10301 Baltimore Avenue
   Beltsville, MD 20705-2351
   Phone: 1-301-504-5994
   Fax: 1-301-504-5675
   World Wide Web URL: http://www.nal.usda.gov/fnic
   Email Address: lending@nal.usda.gov

Hollow Harvest
Outlines the history of farm families in Japan during the past fifty years. It provides insight into how major shifts in national agricultural policy, influenced by the global economy, end up affecting the lives of ordinary people.
Availability: Schools, libraries, and nursing homes in the United States and Canada.
Suggested Grade: 9-Adult
Order Number: JV035
Format: VHS videotape
Terms: Borrower pays return postage. Return with 14 days after scheduled showing, via UPS or U. S. Mail. All requests must included an educational institution affiliation, a current address, and phone number. Order through web site only.
   Source: Cornell University East Asia Program
   World Wide Web URL:
   http://eap.einaudi.cornell.edu/lending_library
   Email Address: east_asia1@cornell.edu

Introducing Mexico: Part One, The Land
Features a review of Mexico's geographical features and climates and discusses the relationship between these elements and the agricultural industry it permits.
Availability: Schools in the United States.
Suggested Grade: 7-12
Order Number: order by title
Format: VHS videotape
Terms: Borrower pays return postage. Return 14 days after receipt, via USPS including insurance. All borrowers must have a current lending agreement on file with the Outreach program. This agreement is available via the web site or may be requested via phone or fax.
   Source: Center for Latin American Studies
   University of Florida
   319 Grinter Hall
   P. O. Box 115530
   Gainesville, FL 32611-5530
   Phone: 1-352-392-0375
   Fax: 1-352-392-7682
   World Wide Web URL: http://www.latam.ufl.edu/outreach
   Email Address: maryr@ufl.edu

Japanese and Rice Cultivation, The
Explains how rice is cultivated in this country.
Availability: Schools, libraries, homeschoolers, and nursing homes in Arizona and California (zipcodes beginning 900-931 and 935).
Suggested Grade: 4-12
Order Number: 160
Production Date: 1996
Format: VHS videotape
Terms: Borrower pays postage both ways; you may call the number below to learn how much postage costs. Return within two weeks of date borrowed. An individual may borrow 2 items at one time. For non-profit and educational use only.
   Source: Consulate General of Japan, Los Angeles
   350 South Grand Avenue, Suite 1700
   Los Angeles, CA 90071-3459
   Phone: 1-213-617-6700
   Fax: 1-213-617-6727
   World Wide Web URL: http://www.la.us.emb-japan.go.jp

Japan's Leading Edge Agricultural Technology at Work in Biotechnology
Explains how biotechnology has benefitted agriculture in Japan.
Availability: Schools, libraries, homeschoolers, and nursing homes in Arizona and California (zipcodes beginning 900-931 and 935).
Suggested Grade: 6-12
Order Number: 271
Production Date: 1996
Format: VHS videotape
Terms: Borrower pays postage both ways; you may call the number below to learn how much postage costs. Return within two weeks of date borrowed. An individual may borrow 2 items at one time. For non-profit and educational use only.
   Source: Consulate General of Japan, Los Angeles
   350 South Grand Avenue, Suite 1700
   Los Angeles, CA 90071-3459
   Phone: 1-213-617-6700
   Fax: 1-213-617-6727
   World Wide Web URL: http://www.la.us.emb-japan.go.jp

Water for Agricultural Progress
Immense progress in recent years in better utilization of limited land resources and water reserves are shown.

AGRICULTURE

Availability: Schools, libraries, homeschoolers, and nursing homes in Arizona and California (zipcodes beginning 900-931 and 935).
Suggested Grade: 9-Adult
Order Number: 083
Production Date: 1974
Format: VHS videotape
Terms: Borrower pays postage both ways; you may call the number below to learn how much postage costs. Return within two weeks of date borrowed. An individual may borrow 2 items at one time. For non-profit and educational use only.

Source: Consulate General of Japan, Los Angeles
350 South Grand Avenue, Suite 1700
Los Angeles, CA 90071-3459
Phone: 1-213-617-6700
Fax: 1-213-617-6727
World Wide Web URL: http://www.la.us.emb-japan.go.jp

BUSINESS AND ECONOMICS

Against All the Odds
This program examines two controversial projects with environmental implications: a planned bypass around heavily populated Honshu Island and a series of nuclear power plants which the Japanese government constructed in its efforts to reduce Japan's dependency on foreign oil.
Availability: Schools, libraries, and nursing homes in the United States and Canada.
Suggested Grade: 9-Adult
Order Number: JV078
Format: VHS videotape
Terms: Borrower pays return postage. Return with 14 days after scheduled showing, via UPS or U. S. Mail. All requests must included an educational institution affiliation, a current address, and phone number. Order through web site only.
Source: Cornell University East Asia Program
World Wide Web URL:
http://eap.einaudi.cornell.edu/lending_library
Email Address: east_asia1@cornell.edu

Banana Split
Begins with Canadian consumers in a local fruit market and winds its way through the hustle and bustle of a major distribution center, to the daily challenges of everyday life in Honduras. Ends with a message about smallholder banana production as a potential vehicle for international development.
Availability: Schools and libraries in Iowa, Illinois, Michigan, Minnesota, and Wisconsin.
Suggested Grade: 9-12
Order Number: DEV/ECHONB22VHS
Production Date: 2002
Format: VHS videotape
Terms: Borrower pays return postage. Return 8 days after showing. Book 2 weeks in advance. Order may also be picked up for those near the Center.
Source: Center for Latin American and Caribbean Studies
UW-Milwaukee
P. O. Box 413
Milwaukee, WI 53201
Phone: 1-414-229-5987
World Wide Web URL: http://www.uwm.edu/Dept/CLACS
Email Address: audvis@usm.edu

Banking on Life and Debt
A documentary on the policy of the World Bank and the International Monetary Fund.
Availability: Schools in the United States.
Suggested Grade: 9-Adult
Order Number: order by title
Production Date: 1995
Format: VHS videotape
Terms: Borrower pays return postage. Return 14 days after receipt, via USPS including insurance. All borrowers must have a current lending agreement on file with the Outreach program. This agreement is available via the web site or may be requested via phone or fax.
Source: Center for Latin American Studies
University of Florida
319 Grinter Hall
P. O. Box 115530
Gainesville, FL 32611-5530
Phone: 1-352-392-0375
Fax: 1-352-392-7682
World Wide Web URL: http://www.latam.ufl.edu/outreach
Email Address: maryr@ufl.edu

Borderline Cases
Describes problems created by the maquiladoras, factories on the US-Mexico border, and promises for the future.
Availability: Schools, libraries, and nursing homes in the United States.
Suggested Grade: 6-12
Order Number: GEMEX12-video
Production Date: 1997
Format: VHS videotape
Terms: Borrowers must have a User's Agreement on file with this source--available by mail or via the Internet. Return postage is paid by borrower; return 12 days after showing. Book at least three weeks in advance. All borrowers are limited to a total of ten items per semester.
Source: Latin American Resource Center
Stone Center for Latin American Studies
Tulane University
100 Jones Hall
New Orleans, LA 70118
Phone: 1-504-862-3143
Fax: 1-504-865-6719
World Wide Web URL:
http://stonecenter.tulane.edu/pages/detail/48/Lending-Library
Email Address: crcrts@tulane.edu

Breaking Barriers: Foreign Companies That Succeed in Japan
Documents how several foreign companies have won places in the Japanese market.
Availability: Schools, libraries, homeschoolers, and nursing homes in Connecticut (except Fairfield County), Maine, Massachusetts, New Hampshire, Rhode Island, and Vermont.
Suggested Grade: 9-Adult
Order Number: 162
Format: VHS videotape
Special Notes: Tape 7 of the "Document Japan" series.
Terms: Borrower pays return postage, including insurance. Return two weeks after receipt.
Source: Consulate General of Japan, Boston
Federal Reserve Plaza, 14th Floor
600 Atlantic Avenue
Boston, MA 02210
Phone: 1-617-973-9772
Fax: 1-617-542-1329
World Wide Web URL:
http://www.boston.us.emb-japan.go.jp
Email Address: infocul@cgjbos.org

All materials listed in this 2018-2019 edition are BRAND NEW!

BUSINESS AND ECONOMICS

Breaking Barriers: Foreign Companies That Succeed in Japan
Documents how several foreign companies have won places in the Japanese market.
Availability: Schools, libraries, and nursing homes in Oklahoma and Texas.
Suggested Grade: 9-Adult
Order Number: C7
Production Date: 1988
Format: VHS videotape
Special Notes: Tape 7 of the "Document Japan" series.
Terms: Materials must be picked up in person. Under special circumstances, you may be able to have them shipped to you at your own expense (call for further details). Return within two weeks after scheduled showing. Videos must be registered with the U. S. Postal Service or returned by Priority Mail, Federal Express, or other registered shipping service.
    Source: Consulate General of Japan, Houston
    Cultural Affairs and Information Section
    909 Fannin Street, Suite 3000
    Houston, TX 77010
    Phone: 1-713-652-2977
    Fax: 1-713-651-7822
    World Wide Web URL: http://www.houston.us.emb-japan.go.jp/en/culture/page1.htm
    Email Address: info@cgjhouston.org

Breaking Barriers: Foreign Companies That Succeed in Japan
Documents how several foreign companies have won places in the Japanese market.
Availability: Schools, libraries, homeschoolers, and nursing homes in Arizona and California (zipcodes beginning 900-931 and 935).
Suggested Grade: 9-Adult
Order Number: 106
Format: VHS videotape
Special Notes: Tape 7 of the "Document Japan" series.
Terms: Borrower pays postage both ways; you may call the number below to learn how much postage costs. Return within two weeks of date borrowed. An individual may borrow 2 items at one time. For non-profit and educational use only.
    Source: Consulate General of Japan, Los Angeles
    350 South Grand Avenue, Suite 1700
    Los Angeles, CA 90071-3459
    Phone: 1-213-617-6700
    Fax: 1-213-617-6727
World Wide Web URL: http://www.la.us.emb-japan.go.jp

Breaking Barriers: Foreign Companies That Succeed in Japan
Documents how several foreign companies have won places in the Japanese market.
Availability: Schools, libraries, homeschoolers, and nursing homes in Nevada and northern California (zip codes beginning 932 and above, except 935).
Suggested Grade: 9-Adult
Order Number: order by title
Production Date: 1988
Format: Beta videotape; U-matic videotape; VHS videotape
Special Notes: Tape 7 of the "Document Japan" series.
Terms: Borrower pays return postage. Book two weeks in advance. Return within three weeks of date borrowed, via UPS, Federal Express or certified mail.
    Source: Consulate General of Japan, San Francisco
    50 Fremont Street, Suite 2300
    San Francisco, CA 94105-2236
    Phone: 1-415-356-2564
    Fax: 1-415-777-0518
World Wide Web URL: http://www.sf.us.emb-japan.go.jp/
    Email Address: infoav@cgjsf.org

Business Savvy
Made for both foreigners presently working in Japan and for those anticipating a leap into the Japanese corporate world, this video presents vital information regarding the structure of Japanese society, business manners and practices and many other special considerations which one cannot overlook when hoping to do business successfully in Japan.
Availability: Schools, libraries and homeschoolers in Alabama, Georgia, North Carolina, South Carolina, and Virginia.
Suggested Grade: 9-Adult
Order Number: 221
Format: VHS videotape
Terms: Borrower pays return postage. Two tapes may be borrowed at a time. Return within 7 days after receipt. Reservations may be made by filling the application found on the web site.
    Source: Consulate General of Japan, Atlanta
    Japan Information Center
    One Alliance Center
    3500 Lenox Road, Suite 1600
    Atlanta, GA 30326
    Phone: 1-404-365-9240
    Fax: 1-404-240-4311
    World Wide Web URL:
    http://www.atlanta.us.emb-japan.go.jp
    Email Address: info@cgjapanatlanta.org

Coffee: A Sack Full of Power
Takes a broad view of the influence of coffee through the ages. Explains the difference between the Brazilian and Costa Rican system of production, and why the Brazilian system has led to such poverty.
Availability: Schools and libraries in Iowa, Illinois, Michigan, Minnesota, and Wisconsin.
Suggested Grade: 9-Adult
Order Number: DEV/ECBRA/CRC65VH
Format: VHS videotape
Terms: Borrower pays return postage. Return 8 days after showing. Book 2 weeks in advance. Order may also be picked up for those near the Center.

*All materials listed in this 2018-2019 edition are **BRAND NEW!***

BUSINESS AND ECONOMICS

Source: Center for Latin American and Caribbean Studies
UW-Milwaukee
P. O. Box 413
Milwaukee, WI 53201
Phone: 1-414-229-5987
World Wide Web URL: http://www.uwm.edu/Dept/CLACS
Email Address: audvis@usm.edu

Commodities: Black Market
This video looks at the ways banks, corporations, governments, workers, and consumers are affected by such ordinary items as coffee, tea, and sugar.
Availability: Schools, libraries, and nursing homes in the United States and Canada.
Suggested Grade: 6-12
Order Number: CV003
Format: VHS videotape
Terms: Borrower pays return postage. Return with 14 days after scheduled showing, via UPS or U. S. Mail. All requests must included an educational institution affiliation, a current address, and phone number. Order through web site only.
Source: Cornell University East Asia Program
World Wide Web URL:
http://eap.einaudi.cornell.edu/lending_library
Email Address: east_asia1@cornell.edu

Communication Gap
Focuses upon the "communication gap" which exists between Japan and other industrial nations in a round table discussion.
Availability: Schools, libraries, and nursing homes in Hawaii.
Suggested Grade: 9-Adult
Order Number: BU-34
Production Date: 1981
Format: VHS videotape
Terms: Borrower pays return postage. A maximum of 3 videos may be borrowed per person. Return within one week of date borrowed.
Source: Consulate General of Japan, Honolulu
1742 Nuuanu Avenue
Honolulu, HI 96817-3294
Phone: 1-808-543-3111
Fax: 1-808-543-3170
World Wide Web URL:
http://www.honolulu.us.emb-japan.go.jp

Devil Gave Us Oil, The
Explores the oil industry in Mexico and follows the life of a typical farming family trying to survive in the shadow of an oil refinery.
Availability: Schools in the United States.
Suggested Grade: 10-Adult
Order Number: order by title
Production Date: 1987
Format: VHS videotape
Terms: Borrower pays return postage. Return 14 days after receipt, via USPS including insurance. All borrowers must have a current lending agreement on file with the Outreach program. This agreement is available via the web site or may be requested via phone or fax.
Source: Center for Latin American Studies
University of Florida
319 Grinter Hall
P. O. Box 115530
Gainesville, FL 32611-5530
Phone: 1-352-392-0375
Fax: 1-352-392-7682
World Wide Web URL: http://www.latam.ufl.edu/outreach
Email Address: maryr@ufl.edu

Earth: The Changing Environment
Describes how the impoverished nations of South America have begun a program of deforestation in the Amazon rain forest. Probes the ecological consequences of improper economic development.
Availability: Schools in the United States.
Suggested Grade: 9-12
Order Number: order by title
Production Date: 1987
Format: VHS videotape
Terms: Borrower pays return postage. Return 14 days after receipt, via USPS including insurance. All borrowers must have a current lending agreement on file with the Outreach program. This agreement is available via the web site or may be requested via phone or fax.
Source: Center for Latin American Studies
University of Florida
319 Grinter Hall
P. O. Box 115530
Gainesville, FL 32611-5530
Phone: 1-352-392-0375
Fax: 1-352-392-7682
World Wide Web URL: http://www.latam.ufl.edu/outreach
Email Address: maryr@ufl.edu

Economics
This four-part animated program examines economic systems and how they work. Shows how a system can be identified as a command, market, or mixed system. Examines the modified free enterprise economy, or mixed system, in detail. Covers the four partners and their roles, and how to determine prices according to supply and demand. Also looks at the business cycle, inflation, recession, depression, and economic growth.
Availability: Schools, libraries, and homeschoolers in the United States who serve the hearing impaired.
Suggested Grade: 10-Adult
Order Number: 13074
Production Date: 1993
Format: DVD
Special Notes: Produced by Films for the Humanities & Sciences.
Terms: Sponsor pays all transportation costs. Return one week after receipt. Participation is limited to deaf or hard of hearing Americans, their parents, families, teachers, counselors, or others whose use would benefit a deaf or

BUSINESS AND ECONOMICS

hard of hearing person. Only one person in the audience needs to be hearing impaired. You must register--which is free. These videos are all open-captioned--no special equipment is required for viewing.
**Source: Described and Captioned Media Program
National Association of the Deaf
4211 Church Street Ext.
Roebuck, SC 29376
Phone: 1-800-237-6213
Fax: 1-800-538-5636
World Wide Web URL: http://www.dcmp.org**

Economics Classroom, The: Growth & Entrepreneurship
Last in an eight-part series of professional development workshops designed to give high school teachers ideas about how to present economics in a way that will excite, inform, and entice students.
Availability: Schools, libraries, and homeschoolers in the United States who serve the hearing impaired.
Suggested Grade: Teacher Reference
Order Number: 10864
Production Date: 2002
Format: DVD
Special Notes: Also available as live streaming video over the Internet.
Terms: Sponsor pays all transportation costs. Return one week after receipt. Participation is limited to deaf or hard of hearing Americans, their parents, families, teachers, counselors, or others whose use would benefit a deaf or hard of hearing person. Only one person in the audience needs to be hearing impaired. You must register--which is free. These videos are all open-captioned--no special equipment is required for viewing.
**Source: Described and Captioned Media Program
National Association of the Deaf
4211 Church Street Ext.
Roebuck, SC 29376
Phone: 1-800-237-6213
Fax: 1-800-538-5636
World Wide Web URL: http://www.dcmp.org**

Economics Classroom, The: How Economists Think
First in an eight-part series of professional development workshops designed to give high school teachers ideas about how to present economics in a way that will excite, inform, and entice students.
Availability: Schools, libraries, and homeschoolers in the United States who serve the hearing impaired.
Suggested Grade: Teacher Reference
Order Number: 10865
Production Date: 2002
Format: DVD
Special Notes: Also available as live streaming video over the Internet.
Terms: Sponsor pays all transportation costs. Return one week after receipt. Participation is limited to deaf or hard of hearing Americans, their parents, families, teachers, counselors, or others whose use would be

benefit a deaf or hard of hearing person. Only one person in the audience needs to be hearing impaired. You must register--which is free. These videos are all open-captioned--no special equipment is required for viewing.
**Source: Described and Captioned Media Program
National Association of the Deaf
4211 Church Street Ext.
Roebuck, SC 29376
Phone: 1-800-237-6213
Fax: 1-800-538-5636
World Wide Web URL: http://www.dcmp.org**

Economics Classroom, The: Learning, Earning, Saving
Fourth in an eight-part series of professional development workshops designed to give high school teachers ideas about how to present economics in a way that will excite, inform, and entice students.
Availability: Schools, libraries, and homeschoolers in the United States who serve the hearing impaired.
Suggested Grade: Teacher Reference
Order Number: 10936
Production Date: 2002
Format: DVD
Special Notes: Also available as live streaming video over the Internet.
Terms: Sponsor pays all transportation costs. Return one week after receipt. Participation is limited to deaf or hard of hearing Americans, their parents, families, teachers, counselors, or others whose use would benefit a deaf or hard of hearing person. Only one person in the audience needs to be hearing impaired. You must register--which is free. These videos are all open-captioned--no special equipment is required for viewing.
**Source: Described and Captioned Media Program
National Association of the Deaf
4211 Church Street Ext.
Roebuck, SC 29376
Phone: 1-800-237-6213
Fax: 1-800-538-5636
World Wide Web URL: http://www.dcmp.org**

Economics Classroom, The: Monetary & Fiscal Policy
Seventh in an eight-part series of professional development workshops designed to give high school teachers ideas about how to present economics in a way that will excite, inform, and entice students.
Availability: Schools, libraries, and homeschoolers in the United States who serve the hearing impaired.
Suggested Grade: Teacher Reference
Order Number: 10907
Production Date: 2002
Format: DVD
Special Notes: Also available as live streaming video over the Internet.
Terms: Sponsor pays all transportation costs. Return one week after receipt. Participation is limited to deaf or hard of hearing Americans, their parents, families, teachers, counselors, or others whose use would benefit a deaf or

All materials listed in this 2018-2019 edition are BRAND NEW!

BUSINESS AND ECONOMICS

hard of hearing person. Only one person in the audience needs to be hearing impaired. You must register--which is free. These videos are all open-captioned--no special equipment is required for viewing.
**Source: Described and Captioned Media Program
National Association of the Deaf
4211 Church Street Ext.
Roebuck, SC 29376
Phone: 1-800-237-6213
Fax: 1-800-538-5636
World Wide Web URL: http://www.dcmp.org**

Economics Classroom, The: The Building Blocks of Macroeconomics
Sixth in an eight-part series of professional development workshops designed to give high school teachers ideas about how to present economics in a way that will excite, inform, and entice students.
Availability:	Schools, libraries, and homeschoolers in the United States who serve the hearing impaired.
Suggested Grade:	Teacher Reference
Order Number:	10827
Production Date:	2002
Format:	DVD
Special Notes:	Also available as live streaming video over the Internet.
Terms:	Sponsor pays all transportation costs. Return one week after receipt. Participation is limited to deaf or hard of hearing Americans, their parents, families, teachers, counselors, or others whose use would benefit a deaf or hard of hearing person. Only one person in the audience needs to be hearing impaired. You must register--which is free. These videos are all open-captioned--no special equipment is required for viewing.

**Source: Described and Captioned Media Program
National Association of the Deaf
4211 Church Street Ext.
Roebuck, SC 29376
Phone: 1-800-237-6213
Fax: 1-800-538-5636
World Wide Web URL: http://www.dcmp.org**

Economics Classroom, The: Trading Globally
Fifth in an eight-part series of professional development workshops designed to give high school teachers ideas about how to present economics in a way that will excite, inform, and entice students.
Availability:	Schools, libraries, and homeschoolers in the United States who serve the hearing impaired.
Suggested Grade:	Teacher Reference
Order Number:	10866
Production Date:	2002
Format:	DVD
Special Notes:	Also available as live streaming video over the Internet.
Terms:	Sponsor pays all transportation costs. Return one week after receipt. Participation is limited to deaf or hard of hearing Americans, their parents, families, teachers, counselors, or others whose use would benefit a deaf or hard of hearing person. Only one person in the audience needs to be hearing impaired. You must register--which is free. These videos are all open-captioned--no special equipment is required for viewing.

**Source: Described and Captioned Media Program
National Association of the Deaf
4211 Church Street Ext.
Roebuck, SC 29376
Phone: 1-800-237-6213
Fax: 1-800-538-5636
World Wide Web URL: http://www.dcmp.org**

Emerging Powers: Mexico
This Wall Street Journal video looks at the future of Mexico in wake of the economic collapse.
Availability:	Schools in the United States.
Suggested Grade:	9-12
Order Number:	order by title
Format:	VHS videotape
Terms:	Borrower pays return postage. Return 14 days after receipt, via USPS including insurance. All borrowers must have a current lending agreement on file with the Outreach program. This agreement is available via the web site or may be requested via phone or fax.

**Source: Center for Latin American Studies
University of Florida
319 Grinter Hall
P. O. Box 115530
Gainesville, FL 32611-5530
Phone: 1-352-392-0375
Fax: 1-352-392-7682
World Wide Web URL: http://www.latam.ufl.edu/outreach
Email Address: maryr@ufl.edu**

Global Assembly Line, The
Focusing on lives of women in manufacturing, from Tennessee to Mexico's Northern border, from Silicon Valley to the Philippines.
Availability:	Schools, libraries, and nursing homes in the United States.
Suggested Grade:	5-Adult
Order Number:	DEVMEX10-video
Format:	VHS videotape
Terms:	Borrowers must have a User's Agreement on file with this source--available by mail or via the Internet. Return postage is paid by borrower; return 12 days after showing. Book at least three weeks in advance. All borrowers are limited to a total of ten items per semester.

**Source: Latin American Resource Center
Stone Center for Latin American Studies
Tulane University
100 Jones Hall
New Orleans, LA 70118
Phone: 1-504-862-3143
Fax: 1-504-865-6719
World Wide Web URL:
http://stonecenter.tulane.edu/pages/detail/
48/Lending-Library
Email Address: crcrts@tulane.edu**

*All materials listed in this 2018-2019 edition are **BRAND NEW**!*

BUSINESS AND ECONOMICS

Human Geography: People, Places, Change
Draws attention to developments in the East that have potential consequences for the West and examines the role that overseas Chinese people play in the transnational business network.
Availability: Schools, libraries, and nursing homes in the United States and Canada.
Suggested Grade: 9-Adult
Order Number: CV018
Format: VHS videotape
Terms: Borrower pays return postage. Return with 14 days after scheduled showing, via UPS or U. S. Mail. All requests must included an educational institution affiliation, a current address, and phone number. Order through web site only.
Source: Cornell University East Asia Program
World Wide Web URL:
http://eap.einaudi.cornell.edu/lending_library
Email Address: east_asia1@cornell.edu

Human Relations in Japan
The clever use of animation and a well-directed presentation explain how relationships are formed among the Japanese. The two important concepts of "uchi" and "soto" are discussed, as viewers are shown how an American businessman can enter into an "uchi" relationship with his Japanese business associates.
Availability: Schools, libraries, homeschoolers, and nursing homes in OREGON AND SOUTHERN IDAHO ONLY. Please make requests via the web site.
Suggested Grade: 7-12
Order Number: 160
Production Date: 1978
Format: VHS videotape
Terms: Borrower pays return postage. Return within three weeks after scheduled showing date. Book one month in advance if possible. Rewind the video and wrap securely for return. Be certain to indicate video number, date needed, name of your organization, and address to which video should be sent, along with phone number. Audience report enclosed with the video must be completed and returned.
Source: Consulate General of Japan, Oregon
Attn: Tamara, Video Library
1300 S. W. Fifth Avenue, Suite 2700
Portland, OR 97201
Phone: 1-503-221-1811, ext. 17
World Wide Web URL:
http://www.portland.us.emb-japan.go.jp/en/index.html
Email Address: tamara@cgjpdx.org

Japan's Distribution System
Provides an analysis of Japan's distribution system, including the wholesale structure, trading practices, and human relations.
Availability: Schools, libraries, and nursing homes in Hawaii.
Suggested Grade: 9-Adult
Order Number: BU-32
Production Date: 1980
Format: VHS videotape
Terms: Borrower pays return postage. A maximum of 3 videos may be borrowed per person. Return within one week of date borrowed.
Source: Consulate General of Japan, Honolulu
1742 Nuuanu Avenue
Honolulu, HI 96817-3294
Phone: 1-808-543-3111
Fax: 1-808-543-3170
World Wide Web URL:
http://www.honolulu.us.emb-japan.go.jp

Japan Video Encyclopedia--Japanese Industry & Economy
This 10-segment video examines Japanese agriculture, fisheries, manufacturing, finance, international trade, and more.
Availability: Schools, libraries, homeschoolers, and nursing homes in Nevada and northern California (zip codes beginning 932 and above, except 935).
Suggested Grade: 4-Adult
Order Number: order by title
Format: VHS videotape
Terms: Borrower pays return postage. Book two weeks in advance. Return within three weeks of date borrowed, via UPS, Federal Express or certified mail.
Source: Consulate General of Japan, San Francisco
50 Fremont Street, Suite 2300
San Francisco, CA 94105-2236
Phone: 1-415-356-2564
Fax: 1-415-777-0518
World Wide Web URL: http://www.sf.us.emb-japan.go.jp/
Email Address: infoav@cgjsf.org

Keys to Success in the Japanese Market
Japan has been charged as not being open to foreign companies. Three executives are interviewed to find out the truth and how they have endeavored to become successful in the Japanese market.
Availability: Schools, libraries, and nursing homes in Hawaii.
Suggested Grade: 9-12
Order Number: BU-33
Production Date: 1981
Format: VHS videotape
Terms: Borrower pays return postage. A maximum of 3 videos may be borrowed per person. Return within one week of date borrowed.
Source: Consulate General of Japan, Honolulu
1742 Nuuanu Avenue
Honolulu, HI 96817-3294
Phone: 1-808-543-3111
Fax: 1-808-543-3170
World Wide Web URL:
http://www.honolulu.us.emb-japan.go.jp

All materials listed in this 2018-2019 edition are BRAND NEW!

BUSINESS AND ECONOMICS

Less Is More: Pollution Prevention Is Good Business
Looks at the ways in which industry is reducing its waste and eliminating pollution through the process of recycling and waste minimization.
- Availability: Schools, libraries, and homeschoolers in Connecticut, Maine, Massachusetts, New Hampshire, Rhode Island, and Vermont.
- Suggested Grade: Adult
- Order Number: VID 109
- Production Date: 1990
- Format: VHS videotape
- Terms: Borrower pays return postage. Return within three weeks of receipt. If the tape you request is available, it will be mailed within 5 business days. If not, you will be notified that this video is already out on loan. No more than three titles may be borrowed by one requestor at a time. No reservations for a specific date will be accepted. It is most efficient to order via the web site.
- Source: U. S. Environmental Protection Agency, Region 1
  Customer Service Center
  One Congress Street, Suite 1100
  Boston, MA 02214
  World Wide Web URL:
  http://yosemite.epa.gov/r1/videolen.nsf/

Maquila: A Tale of Two Mexicos
This documentary covers issues surrounding corporate globalization along the US-Mexico border. Candid interviews with maquila bosses and workers are given along with environmental and social points of view.
- Availability: Schools and libraries in Iowa, Illinois, Michigan, Minnesota, and Wisconsin.
- Suggested Grade: 9-Adult
- Order Number: DEV/ECMEXM32VHS
- Production Date: 2000
- Format: VHS videotape
- Terms: Borrower pays return postage. Return 8 days after showing. Book 2 weeks in advance. Order may also be picked up for those near the Center.
- Source: Center for Latin American and Caribbean Studies
  UW-Milwaukee
  P. O. Box 413
  Milwaukee, WI 53201
  Phone: 1-414-229-5987
  World Wide Web URL: http://www.uwm.edu/Dept/CLACS
  Email Address: audvis@usm.edu

One World, One Economy
Four-part video examining the economies of Mexico, Poland, Ghana, and the role of the IMF.
- Availability: Schools, libraries, and nursing homes in the United States.
- Suggested Grade: 6-12
- Order Number: DEV21-video
- Production Date: 1990
- Format: VHS videotape
- Special Notes: Includes 23-page instructor's guide.
- Terms: Borrowers must have a User's Agreement on file with this source--available by mail or via the Internet. Return postage is paid by borrower; return 12 days after showing. Book at least three weeks in advance. All borrowers are limited to a total of ten items per semester.
- Source: Latin American Resource Center
  Stone Center for Latin American Studies
  Tulane University
  100 Jones Hall
  New Orleans, LA 70118
  Phone: 1-504-862-3143
  Fax: 1-504-865-6719
  World Wide Web URL:
  http://stonecenter.tulane.edu/pages/detail/48/Lending-Library
  Email Address: crcrts@tulane.edu

Quality Control, An American Idea Takes Root in Japan
Quality control was born in the United States but has flowered in Japan. What are the preconditions for successful QC?
- Availability: Schools, libraries, homeschoolers, and nursing homes in Connecticut (except Fairfield County), Maine, Massachusetts, New Hampshire, Rhode Island, and Vermont.
- Suggested Grade: 9-Adult
- Order Number: 160
- Production Date: 1987
- Format: VHS videotape
- Special Notes: Tape 5 of the "Document Japan" series.
- Terms: Borrower pays return postage, including insurance. Return two weeks after receipt.
- Source: Consulate General of Japan, Boston
  Federal Reserve Plaza, 14th Floor
  600 Atlantic Avenue
  Boston, MA 02210
  Phone: 1-617-973-9772
  Fax: 1-617-542-1329
  World Wide Web URL:
  http://www.boston.us.emb-japan.go.jp
  Email Address: infocul@cgjbos.org

Quality Control, An American Idea Takes Root in Japan
Quality control was born in the United States but has flowered in Japan. What are the preconditions for successful QC?
- Availability: Schools, libraries, and nursing homes in Oklahoma and Texas.
- Suggested Grade: 9-Adult
- Order Number: C5
- Format: VHS videotape
- Special Notes: Tape 5 of the "Document Japan" series.
- Terms: Materials must be picked up in person. Under special circumstances, you may be able to have them shipped to you at your own expense (call for further details). Return within two weeks after scheduled showing. Videos must be registered with the U. S. Postal Service or returned by Priority Mail, Federal Express, or other registered shipping service.

BUSINESS AND ECONOMICS

Source: Consulate General of Japan, Houston
Cultural Affairs and Information Section
909 Fannin Street, Suite 3000
Houston, TX 77010
Phone: 1-713-652-2977
Fax: 1-713-651-7822
World Wide Web URL:
http://www.houston.us.emb-japan.go.jp/
en/culture/page1.htm
Email Address: info@cgjhouston.org

Quality Control, An American Idea Takes Root in Japan
Quality control was born in the United States but has flowered in Japan. What are the preconditions for successful QC?
- Availability: Schools, libraries, homeschoolers, and nursing homes in Arizona and California (zipcodes beginning 900-931 and 935).
- Suggested Grade: 9-Adult
- Order Number: 104
- Production Date: 1987
- Format: VHS videotape
- Special Notes: Tape 5 of the "Document Japan" series.
- Terms: Borrower pays postage both ways; you may call the number below to learn how much postage costs. Return within two weeks of date borrowed. An individual may borrow 2 items at one time. For non-profit and educational use only.

Source: Consulate General of Japan, Los Angeles
350 South Grand Avenue, Suite 1700
Los Angeles, CA 90071-3459
Phone: 1-213-617-6700
Fax: 1-213-617-6727
World Wide Web URL: http://www.la.us.emb-japan.go.jp

Quality Control, An American Idea Takes Root in Japan
Quality control was born in the United States but has flowered in Japan. What are the preconditions for successful QC?
- Availability: Schools, libraries, homeschoolers, and nursing homes in Nevada and northern California (zip codes beginning 932 and above, except 935).
- Suggested Grade: 9-Adult
- Order Number: order by title
- Production Date: 1987
- Format: Beta videotape; U-matic videotape; VHS videotape
- Special Notes: Tape 5 of the "Document Japan" series.
- Terms: Borrower pays return postage. Book two weeks in advance. Return within three weeks of date borrowed, via UPS, Federal Express or certified mail.

Source: Consulate General of Japan, San Francisco
50 Fremont Street, Suite 2300
San Francisco, CA 94105-2236
Phone: 1-415-356-2564
Fax: 1-415-777-0518
World Wide Web URL: http://www.sf.us.emb-japan.go.jp/
Email Address: infoav@cgjsf.org

Quality Control and the Q.C. Circle
Introduces the nature of quality control on the job in Japan.
- Availability: Schools, libraries, homeschoolers, and nursing homes in Arizona and California (zipcodes beginning 900-931 and 935).
- Suggested Grade: 9-Adult
- Order Number: 081
- Production Date: 1984
- Format: VHS videotape
- Terms: Borrower pays postage both ways; you may call the number below to learn how much postage costs. Return within two weeks of date borrowed. An individual may borrow 2 items at one time. For non-profit and educational use only.

Source: Consulate General of Japan, Los Angeles
350 South Grand Avenue, Suite 1700
Los Angeles, CA 90071-3459
Phone: 1-213-617-6700
Fax: 1-213-617-6727
World Wide Web URL: http://www.la.us.emb-japan.go.jp

Shacho, The--A Japanese President & His Company
Analyzes the power, salary, and duties of Japanese company presidents and helps to clarify the organization, labor relations and management systems of Japanese companies.
- Availability: Schools, libraries, homeschoolers, and nursing homes in Connecticut (except Fairfield County), Maine, Massachusetts, New Hampshire, Rhode Island, and Vermont.
- Suggested Grade: 9-Adult
- Order Number: 157
- Production Date: 1988
- Format: VHS videotape
- Special Notes: Tape 2 of the "Document Japan" series.
- Terms: Borrower pays return postage, including insurance. Return two weeks after receipt.

Source: Consulate General of Japan, Boston
Federal Reserve Plaza, 14th Floor
600 Atlantic Avenue
Boston, MA 02210
Phone: 1-617-973-9772
Fax: 1-617-542-1329
World Wide Web URL:
http://www.boston.us.emb-japan.go.jp
Email Address: infocul@cgjbos.org

Shacho, The--A Japanese President & His Company
Analyzes the power, salary, and duties of Japanese company presidents and helps to clarify the organization, labor relations and management systems of Japanese companies.
- Availability: Schools, libraries, and nursing homes in Oklahoma and Texas.
- Suggested Grade: 9-Adult
- Order Number: C2
- Production Date: 1988
- Format: VHS videotape

All materials listed in this 2018-2019 edition are BRAND NEW!

BUSINESS AND ECONOMICS

Special Notes: Tape 2 of the "Document Japan" series.
Terms: Materials must be picked up in person. Under special circumstances, you may be able to have them shipped to you at your own expense (call for further details). Return within two weeks after scheduled showing. Videos must be registered with the U. S. Postal Service or returned by Priority Mail, Federal Express, or other registered shipping service.
   Source: Consulate General of Japan, Houston
   Cultural Affairs and Information Section
   909 Fannin Street, Suite 3000
   Houston, TX 77010
   Phone: 1-713-652-2977
   Fax: 1-713-651-7822
   World Wide Web URL: http://www.houston.us.emb-japan.go.jp/en/culture/page1.htm
   Email Address: info@cgjhouston.org

Shacho, The--A Japanese President & His Company
Analyzes the power, salary, and duties of Japanese company presidents and helps to clarify the organization, labor relations and management systems of Japanese companies.
Availability: Schools, libraries, homeschoolers, and nursing homes in Arizona and California (zipcodes beginning 900-931 and 935).
Suggested Grade: 9-Adult
Order Number: 101
Production Date: 1988
Format: VHS videotape
Special Notes: Tape 2 of the "Document Japan" series.
Terms: Borrower pays postage both ways; you may call the number below to learn how much postage costs. Return within two weeks of date borrowed. An individual may borrow 2 items at one time. For non-profit and educational use only.
   Source: Consulate General of Japan, Los Angeles
   350 South Grand Avenue, Suite 1700
   Los Angeles, CA 90071-3459
   Phone: 1-213-617-6700
   Fax: 1-213-617-6727
   World Wide Web URL: http://www.la.us.emb-japan.go.jp

Shacho, The--A Japanese President & His Company
Analyzes the power, salary, and duties of Japanese company presidents and helps to clarify the organization, labor relations and management systems of Japanese companies.
Availability: Schools, libraries, homeschoolers, and nursing homes in Nevada and northern California (zip codes beginning 932 and above, except 935).
Suggested Grade: 9-Adult
Order Number: order by title
Production Date: 1988
Format: Beta videotape; U-matic videotape; VHS videotape
Special Notes: Tape 2 of the "Document Japan" series.
Terms: Borrower pays return postage. Book two weeks in advance. Return within three weeks of date borrowed, via UPS, Federal Express or certified mail.
   Source: Consulate General of Japan, San Francisco
   50 Fremont Street, Suite 2300
   San Francisco, CA 94105-2236
   Phone: 1-415-356-2564
   Fax: 1-415-777-0518
   World Wide Web URL: http://www.sf.us.emb-japan.go.jp/
   Email Address: infoav@cgjsf.org

South America: The Southern Plains
Examines the methods of transportation of the region, from the Rio de la Plata to the major highways of today, and how this has made it possible for production centers and trade to develop.
Availability: Schools in the United States.
Suggested Grade: 6-12
Order Number: order by title
Production Date: 1992
Format: VHS videotape
Terms: Borrower pays return postage. Return 14 days after receipt, via USPS including insurance. All borrowers must have a current lending agreement on file with the Outreach program. This agreement is available via the web site or may be requested via phone or fax.
   Source: Center for Latin American Studies
   University of Florida
   319 Grinter Hall
   P. O. Box 115530
   Gainesville, FL 32611-5530
   Phone: 1-352-392-0375
   Fax: 1-352-392-7682
   World Wide Web URL: http://www.latam.ufl.edu/outreach
   Email Address: maryr@ufl.edu

Story of Noriko, The
A 21-year-old redefines the role of women in Japan who aspire to ascend the ladder of business against formidable odds.
Availability: Schools, libraries, homeschoolers, and nursing homes in Connecticut (except Fairfield County), Maine, Massachusetts, New Hampshire, Rhode Island, and Vermont.
Suggested Grade: 9-Adult
Order Number: 169
Production Date: 1988
Format: VHS videotape
Special Notes: Part of the "Faces of Japan" series.
Terms: Borrower pays return postage, including insurance. Return two weeks after receipt.
   Source: Consulate General of Japan, Boston
   Federal Reserve Plaza, 14th Floor
   600 Atlantic Avenue
   Boston, MA 02210
   Phone: 1-617-973-9772
   Fax: 1-617-542-1329
   World Wide Web URL: http://www.boston.us.emb-japan.go.jp
   Email Address: infocul@cgjbos.org

*All materials listed in this 2018-2019 edition are **BRAND NEW**!*

BUSINESS AND ECONOMICS

Story of Noriko, The
A 21-year-old redefines the role of women in Japan who aspire to ascend the ladder of business against formidable odds.
Availability: Schools, libraries, and nursing homes in Oklahoma and Texas.
Suggested Grade: 9-Adult
Order Number: D1
Production Date: 1988
Format: VHS videotape
Special Notes: Part of the "Faces of Japan" series.
Terms: Materials must be picked up in person. Under special circumstances, you may be able to have them shipped to you at your own expense (call for further details). Return within two weeks after scheduled showing. Videos must be registered with the U. S. Postal Service or returned by Priority Mail, Federal Express, or other registered shipping service.
   Source: Consulate General of Japan, Houston
Cultural Affairs and Information Section
909 Fannin Street, Suite 3000
Houston, TX 77010
Phone: 1-713-652-2977
Fax: 1-713-651-7822
World Wide Web URL:
http://www.houston.us.emb-japan.go.jp/en/culture/page1.htm
Email Address: info@cgjhouston.org

Story of Noriko, The
A 21-year-old redefines the role of women in Japan who aspire to ascend the ladder of business against formidable odds.
Availability: Schools, libraries, homeschoolers, and nursing homes in Nevada and northern California (zip codes beginning 932 and above, except 935).
Suggested Grade: 9-Adult
Order Number: order by title
Production Date: 1988
Format: VHS videotape
Special Notes: Part of the "Faces of Japan" series.
Terms: Borrower pays return postage. Book two weeks in advance. Return within three weeks of date borrowed, via UPS, Federal Express or certified mail.
   Source: Consulate General of Japan, San Francisco
50 Fremont Street, Suite 2300
San Francisco, CA 94105-2236
Phone: 1-415-356-2564
Fax: 1-415-777-0518
World Wide Web URL: http://www.sf.us.emb-japan.go.jp/
Email Address: infoav@cgjsf.org

Tsukuba Academic New Town
A review of facilities in the planned community of Tsukuba is shown.
Availability: Schools, libraries, homeschoolers, and nursing homes in Arizona and California (zipcodes beginning 900-931 and 935).
Suggested Grade: 7-Adult
Order Number: 080
Production Date: 1982
Format: VHS videotape
Terms: Borrower pays postage both ways; you may call the number below to learn how much postage costs. Return within two weeks of date borrowed. An individual may borrow 2 items at one time. For non-profit and educational use only.
   Source: Consulate General of Japan, Los Angeles
350 South Grand Avenue, Suite 1700
Los Angeles, CA 90071-3459
Phone: 1-213-617-6700
Fax: 1-213-617-6727
World Wide Web URL: http://www.la.us.emb-japan.go.jp

U. S., Mexico, and NAFTA
Explores the economic and human rights ramifications of the implementation of NAFTA.
Availability: Schools in the United States.
Suggested Grade: 7-Adult
Order Number: order by title
Production Date: 1996
Format: VHS videotape
Terms: Borrower pays return postage. Return 14 days after receipt, via USPS including insurance. All borrowers must have a current lending agreement on file with the Outreach program. This agreement is available via the web site or may be requested via phone or fax.
   Source: Center for Latin American Studies
University of Florida
319 Grinter Hall
P. O. Box 115530
Gainesville, FL 32611-5530
Phone: 1-352-392-0375
Fax: 1-352-392-7682
World Wide Web URL: http://www.latam.ufl.edu/outreach
Email Address: maryr@ufl.edu

All materials listed in this 2018-2019 edition are BRAND NEW!

CAREER EDUCATION

Beauticians
Visit a typical beauty school and observe its classes.
- Availability: Schools, libraries, homeschoolers, and nursing homes in Arizona and California (zipcodes beginning 900-931 and 935).
- Suggested Grade: 4-Adult
- Order Number: 075
- Production Date: 1984
- Format: VHS videotape
- Terms: Borrower pays postage both ways; you may call the number below to learn how much postage costs. Return within two weeks of date borrowed. An individual may borrow 2 items at one time. For non-profit and educational use only.
- Source: Consulate General of Japan, Los Angeles
  350 South Grand Avenue, Suite 1700
  Los Angeles, CA 90071-3459
  Phone: 1-213-617-6700
  Fax: 1-213-617-6727
- World Wide Web URL: http://www.la.us.emb-japan.go.jp

Behavior Success
Teaches a simple message: A positive attitude coupled with great skills and a high-integrity work ethic leads to success on the job.
- Availability: Schools, libraries, and homeschoolers in the United States who serve the hearing impaired.
- Suggested Grade: 10-Adult
- Order Number: 11675
- Production Date: 2001
- Format: DVD
- Special Notes: Also available as live streaming video over the Internet.
- Terms: Sponsor pays all transportation costs. Return one week after receipt. Participation is limited to deaf or hard of hearing Americans, their parents, families, teachers, counselors, or others whose use would benefit a deaf or hard of hearing person. Only one person in the audience needs to be hearing impaired. You must register--which is free. These videos are all open-captioned--no special equipment is required for viewing.
- Source: Described and Captioned Media Program
  National Association of the Deaf
  4211 Church Street Ext.
  Roebuck, SC 29376
  Phone: 1-800-237-6213
  Fax: 1-800-538-5636
- World Wide Web URL: http://www.dcmp.org

Career Close-Ups: School Teacher
Profiles seven innovative and dedicated teachers who make a difference in the lives of their students. From kindergarten to high school, these teachers and thousands of their counterparts face often dangerous and crowded classrooms as they find creative ways to motivate their students to learn. These seven share their teaching philosophies. Encourages teaching as a profession as Whoopi Goldberg hosts.
- Availability: Schools, libraries, and homeschoolers in the United States who serve the hearing impaired.
- Suggested Grade: 9-Adult
- Order Number: 12359
- Production Date: 1994
- Format: DVD
- Special Notes: Produced by Aims Multimedia.
- Terms: Sponsor pays all transportation costs. Return one week after receipt. Participation is limited to deaf or hard of hearing Americans, their parents, families, teachers, counselors, or others whose use would benefit a deaf or hard of hearing person. Only one person in the audience needs to be hearing impaired. You must register--which is free. These videos are all open-captioned--no special equipment is required for viewing.
- Source: Described and Captioned Media Program
  National Association of the Deaf
  4211 Church Street Ext.
  Roebuck, SC 29376
  Phone: 1-800-237-6213
  Fax: 1-800-538-5636
- World Wide Web URL: http://www.dcmp.org

Communication Success
Presents basic communication components with examples to help people learn how to get a job.
- Availability: Schools, libraries, and homeschoolers in the United States who serve the hearing impaired.
- Suggested Grade: Adult
- Order Number: 11710
- Production Date: 2003
- Format: DVD
- Special Notes: Also available as live streaming video over the Internet. Signed in ASL with voice-over narration.
- Terms: Sponsor pays all transportation costs. Return one week after receipt. Participation is limited to deaf or hard of hearing Americans, their parents, families, teachers, counselors, or others whose use would benefit a deaf or hard of hearing person. Only one person in the audience needs to be hearing impaired. You must register--which is free. These videos are all open-captioned--no special equipment is required for viewing.
- Source: Described and Captioned Media Program
  National Association of the Deaf
  4211 Church Street Ext.
  Roebuck, SC 29376
  Phone: 1-800-237-6213
  Fax: 1-800-538-5636
- World Wide Web URL: http://www.dcmp.org

Cover Letter Training
Explains how to create a cover letter for your job application.
- Availability: Schools, libraries, and homeschoolers in the United States who serve the hearing impaired.
- Suggested Grade: Adult
- Order Number: 11709
- Format: DVD
- Special Notes: Also available as live streaming video over the Internet. Signed in ASL with voice-over narration.

All materials listed in this 2018-2019 edition are BRAND NEW!

CAREER EDUCATION

Terms: Sponsor pays all transportation costs. Return one week after receipt. Participation is limited to deaf or hard of hearing Americans, their parents, families, teachers, counselors, or others whose use would benefit a deaf or hard of hearing person. Only one person in the audience needs to be hearing impaired. You must register--which is free. These videos are all open-captioned--no special equipment is required for viewing.
Source: Described and Captioned Media Program
National Association of the Deaf
4211 Church Street Ext.
Roebuck, SC 29376
Phone: 1-800-237-6213
Fax: 1-800-538-5636
World Wide Web URL: http://www.dcmp.org

Dealing with Illegal Questions
Looks at sample questions that could be asked during a job interview.
Availability: Schools, libraries, and homeschoolers in the United States who serve the hearing impaired.
Suggested Grade: Adult
Order Number: 10798
Production Date: 2003
Format: DVD
Special Notes: Also available as live streaming video over the Internet. Signed in ASL with voice-over narration.
Terms: Sponsor pays all transportation costs. Return one week after receipt. Participation is limited to deaf or hard of hearing Americans, their parents, families, teachers, counselors, or others whose use would benefit a deaf or hard of hearing person. Only one person in the audience needs to be hearing impaired. You must register--which is free. These videos are all open-captioned--no special equipment is required for viewing.
Source: Described and Captioned Media Program
National Association of the Deaf
4211 Church Street Ext.
Roebuck, SC 29376
Phone: 1-800-237-6213
Fax: 1-800-538-5636
World Wide Web URL: http://www.dcmp.org

Diary of a Police Post
Credit goes to the police for making Tokyo the safest city in the world. Follow one police officer on a typical round and find how much he knows about the people he protects.
Availability: Schools, libraries, homeschoolers, and nursing homes in Connecticut (except Fairfield County), Maine, Massachusetts, New Hampshire, Rhode Island, and Vermont.
Suggested Grade: 9-Adult
Order Number: 172
Production Date: 1988
Format: VHS videotape
Special Notes: Part of the "Faces of Japan" series.
Terms: Borrower pays return postage, including insurance. Return two weeks after receipt.
Source: Consulate General of Japan, Boston
Federal Reserve Plaza, 14th Floor
600 Atlantic Avenue
Boston, MA 02210
Phone: 1-617-973-9772
Fax: 1-617-542-1329
World Wide Web URL: http://www.boston.us.emb-japan.go.jp
Email Address: infocul@cgjbos.org

Diary of a Police Post
Credit goes to the police for making Tokyo the safest city in the world. Follow one police officer on a typical round and find how much he knows about the people he protects.
Availability: Schools, libraries, and nursing homes in Oklahoma and Texas.
Suggested Grade: 9-Adult
Order Number: D4
Production Date: 1988
Format: VHS videotape
Special Notes: Part of the "Faces of Japan" series.
Terms: Materials must be picked up in person. Under special circumstances, you may be able to have them shipped to you at your own expense (call for further details). Return within two weeks after scheduled showing. Videos must be registered with the U. S. Postal Service or returned by Priority Mail, Federal Express, or other registered shipping service.
Source: Consulate General of Japan, Houston
Cultural Affairs and Information Section
909 Fannin Street, Suite 3000
Houston, TX 77010
Phone: 1-713-652-2977
Fax: 1-713-651-7822
World Wide Web URL: http://www.houston.us.emb-japan.go.jp/en/culture/page1.htm
Email Address: info@cgjhouston.org

Diary of a Police Post
Credit goes to the police for making Tokyo the safest city in the world. Follow one police officer on a typical round and find how much he knows about the people he protects.
Availability: Schools, libraries, homeschoolers, and nursing homes in Nevada and northern California (zip codes beginning 932 and above, except 935).
Suggested Grade: 9-Adult
Order Number: order by title
Production Date: 1988
Format: VHS videotape
Special Notes: Part of the "Faces of Japan" series.
Terms: Borrower pays return postage. Book two weeks in advance. Return within three weeks of date borrowed, via UPS, Federal Express or certified mail.
Source: Consulate General of Japan, San Francisco
50 Fremont Street, Suite 2300
San Francisco, CA 94105-2236
Phone: 1-415-356-2564

All materials listed in this 2018-2019 edition are BRAND NEW!

CAREER EDUCATION

Fax: 1-415-777-0518
World Wide Web URL: http://www.sf.us.emb-japan.go.jp/
Email Address: infoav@cgjsf.org

District Nurse, A
Presents the daily routine of a district nurse in the small farming town of Tamatsukuri.
Availability: Schools, libraries, homeschoolers, and nursing homes in Arizona and California (zipcodes beginning 900-931 and 935).
Suggested Grade: 6-Adult
Order Number: 084
Production Date: 1982
Format: VHS videotape
Terms: Borrower pays postage both ways; you may call the number below to learn how much postage costs. Return within two weeks of date borrowed. An individual may borrow 2 items at one time. For non-profit and educational use only.
Source: Consulate General of Japan, Los Angeles
350 South Grand Avenue, Suite 1700
Los Angeles, CA 90071-3459
Phone: 1-213-617-6700
Fax: 1-213-617-6727
World Wide Web URL: http://www.la.us.emb-japan.go.jp

Elementary School Teacher, An
Depicts the life and duties of Mrs. Yuki Nozawa, a 3rd grade teacher at the Takisato Elementary School in Chiboc Prefecture.
Availability: Schools, libraries, homeschoolers, and nursing homes in Arizona and California (zipcodes beginning 900-931 and 935).
Suggested Grade: 6-Adult
Order Number: 079
Production Date: 1982
Format: VHS videotape
Terms: Borrower pays postage both ways; you may call the number below to learn how much postage costs. Return within two weeks of date borrowed. An individual may borrow 2 items at one time. For non-profit and educational use only.
Source: Consulate General of Japan, Los Angeles
350 South Grand Avenue, Suite 1700
Los Angeles, CA 90071-3459
Phone: 1-213-617-6700
Fax: 1-213-617-6727
World Wide Web URL: http://www.la.us.emb-japan.go.jp

Job Search Preparation
Lists the steps that a job seeker needs to complete when preparing for a job search.
Availability: Schools, libraries, and homeschoolers in the United States who serve the hearing impaired.
Suggested Grade: 10-Adult
Order Number: 11708
Production Date: 2003
Format: DVD
Special Notes: Also available as live streaming video over the Internet. Signed in ASL with voice-over narration.
Terms: Sponsor pays all transportation costs. Return one week after receipt. Participation is limited to deaf or hard of hearing Americans, their parents, families, teachers, counselors, or others whose use would benefit a deaf or hard of hearing person. Only one person in the audience needs to be hearing impaired. You must register--which is free. These videos are all open-captioned--no special equipment is required for viewing.
Source: Described and Captioned Media Program
National Association of the Deaf
4211 Church Street Ext.
Roebuck, SC 29376
Phone: 1-800-237-6213
Fax: 1-800-538-5636
World Wide Web URL: http://www.dcmp.org

Learning a Trade
A vital part of Japan's education system--apart from the regular pattern of elementary, middle and high schools--is the vocational school which accepts and trains high school graduates for a wide variety of technical careers.
Availability: Schools, libraries, homeschoolers, and nursing homes in Arizona and California (zipcodes beginning 900-931 and 935).
Suggested Grade: 4-Adult
Order Number: 075
Production Date: 1980
Format: VHS videotape
Terms: Borrower pays postage both ways; you may call the number below to learn how much postage costs. Return within two weeks of date borrowed. An individual may borrow 2 items at one time. For non-profit and educational use only.
Source: Consulate General of Japan, Los Angeles
350 South Grand Avenue, Suite 1700
Los Angeles, CA 90071-3459
Phone: 1-213-617-6700
Fax: 1-213-617-6727
World Wide Web URL: http://www.la.us.emb-japan.go.jp

Rewarding Employment: How to Get a Really Good Job
Teenagers looking for work often don't know what to do first. Offers a step-by-step look at the employment process. Includes: balance between school, work, and free time; the importance of home support; researching the job and company; interview preparation dos and don'ts; and the timely follow-up. Encourages practicing possible responses and focuses on being relaxed and prepared.
Availability: Schools, libraries, and homeschoolers in the United States who serve the hearing impaired.
Suggested Grade: 10-Adult
Order Number: 12422
Production Date: 1996
Format: DVD
Special Notes: Produced by Film Ideas, Inc.

CAREER EDUCATION

Terms: Sponsor pays all transportation costs. Return one week after receipt. Participation is limited to deaf or hard of hearing Americans, their parents, families, teachers, counselors, or others whose use would benefit a deaf or hard of hearing person. Only one person in the audience needs to be hearing impaired. You must register--which is free. These videos are all open-captioned--no special equipment is required for viewing.
Source: Described and Captioned Media Program
National Association of the Deaf
4211 Church Street Ext.
Roebuck, SC 29376
Phone: 1-800-237-6213
Fax: 1-800-538-5636
World Wide Web URL: http://www.dcmp.org

So You Want to Be? Teacher/Make-Up Artist
Young interviewers ask a classroom teacher and a make-up artist about job and personal skill requirements for their two professions. Both adults also relate some personal experiences and observations. Gives contact addresses for further information.
Availability: Schools, libraries, and homeschoolers in the United States who serve the hearing impaired.
Suggested Grade: 6-10
Order Number: 12650
Format: DVD
Special Notes: Also available as live streaming video over the Internet.
Terms: Sponsor pays all transportation costs. Return one week after receipt. Participation is limited to deaf or hard of hearing Americans, their parents, families, teachers, counselors, or others whose use would benefit a deaf or hard of hearing person. Only one person in the audience needs to be hearing impaired. You must register--which is free. These videos are all open-captioned--no special equipment is required for viewing.
Source: Described and Captioned Media Program
National Association of the Deaf
4211 Church Street Ext.
Roebuck, SC 29376
Phone: 1-800-237-6213
Fax: 1-800-538-5636
World Wide Web URL: http://www.dcmp.org

Spirit of Edo Firemen, The--Alive in Tokyo Today
Known as "Tobi" or steeplejacks, the firemen of Edo organized in the late 1500s during the Tokugawa shogunate. This video explains the history and duties of the "Tobi" as well as their role in modern day Japan.
Availability: Schools, libraries, and nursing homes in Hawaii.
Suggested Grade: 6-12
Order Number: CU-97
Format: VHS videotape
Terms: Borrower pays return postage. A maximum of 3 videos may be borrowed per person. Return within one week of date borrowed.
Source: Consulate General of Japan, Honolulu
1742 Nuuanu Avenue
Honolulu, HI 96817-3294
Phone: 1-808-543-3111
Fax: 1-808-543-3170
World Wide Web URL:
http://www.honolulu.us.emb-japan.go.jp

Vocational Training
Review the wide range of training in fields such as automotive maintenance, machining, welding, mechanical drawing, etc.
Availability: Schools, libraries, homeschoolers, and nursing homes in Arizona and California (zipcodes beginning 900-931 and 935).
Suggested Grade: 4-Adult
Order Number: 075
Production Date: 1982
Format: VHS videotape
Terms: Borrower pays postage both ways; you may call the number below to learn how much postage costs. Return within two weeks of date borrowed. An individual may borrow 2 items at one time. For non-profit and educational use only.
Source: Consulate General of Japan, Los Angeles
350 South Grand Avenue, Suite 1700
Los Angeles, CA 90071-3459
Phone: 1-213-617-6700
Fax: 1-213-617-6727
World Wide Web URL: http://www.la.us.emb-japan.go.jp

Way of Life in Japan, The: Mastery of the Chef's Blade
Shows the life of an aspiring chef working at a restaurant in a major Japanese hotel. On the surface, the restaurant seems as modern as the hotel itself, but a look behind the scenes reveals the unchanging, traditional world of the Japanese chef.
Availability: Schools, libraries and homeschoolers in Alabama, Georgia, North Carolina, South Carolina, and Virginia.
Suggested Grade: 6-12
Order Number: 217
Format: VHS videotape
Special Notes: Part of the "Japan: Life and Nature" series.
Terms: Borrower pays return postage. Two tapes may be borrowed at a time. Return within 7 days after receipt. Reservations may be made by filling the application found on the web site.
Source: Consulate General of Japan, Atlanta
Japan Information Center
One Alliance Center
3500 Lenox Road, Suite 1600
Atlanta, GA 30326
Phone: 1-404-365-9240
Fax: 1-404-240-4311
World Wide Web URL:
http://www.atlanta.us.emb-japan.go.jp
Email Address: info@cgjapanatlanta.org

CAREER EDUCATION

Way of Life in Japan, The: Mastery of the Chef's Blade
Shows the life of an aspiring chef working at a restaurant in a major Japanese hotel. On the surface, the restaurant seems as modern as the hotel itself, but a look behind the scenes reveals the unchanging, traditional world of the Japanese chef.
Availability: Schools, libraries, homeschoolers, and nursing homes in Connecticut (except Fairfield County), Maine, Massachusetts, New Hampshire, Rhode Island, and Vermont.
Suggested Grade: 6-12
Order Number: 582
Format: VHS videotape
Special Notes: Part of the "Japan: Life and Nature" series.
Terms: Borrower pays return postage, including insurance. Return two weeks after receipt.
    Source: Consulate General of Japan, Boston
    Federal Reserve Plaza, 14th Floor
    600 Atlantic Avenue
    Boston, MA 02210
    Phone: 1-617-973-9772
    Fax: 1-617-542-1329
    World Wide Web URL:
    http://www.boston.us.emb-japan.go.jp
    Email Address: infocul@cgjbos.org

Way of Life in Japan, The: Mastery of the Chef's Blade
Shows the life of an aspiring chef working at a restaurant in a major Japanese hotel. On the surface, the restaurant seems as modern as the hotel itself, but a look behind the scenes reveals the unchanging, traditional world of the Japanese chef.
Availability: Schools, libraries, and nursing homes in Hawaii.
Suggested Grade: 6-12
Order Number: CU-131
Format: VHS videotape
Special Notes: Part of the "Japan: Life and Nature" series.
Terms: Borrower pays return postage. A maximum of 3 videos may be borrowed per person. Return within one week of date borrowed.
    Source: Consulate General of Japan, Honolulu
    1742 Nuuanu Avenue
    Honolulu, HI 96817-3294
    Phone: 1-808-543-3111
    Fax: 1-808-543-3170
    World Wide Web URL:
    http://www.honolulu.us.emb-japan.go.jp

Way of Life in Japan, The: Mastery of the Chef's Blade
Shows the life of an aspiring chef working at a restaurant in a major Japanese hotel. On the surface, the restaurant seems as modern as the hotel itself, but a look behind the scenes reveals the unchanging, traditional world of the Japanese chef.
Availability: Schools, libraries, homeschoolers, and nursing homes in OREGON AND SOUTHERN IDAHO ONLY. Please make requests via the web site.
Suggested Grade: 6-12
Order Number: 500
Production Date: 1994
Format: VHS videotape
Special Notes: Part of the "Japan: Life and Nature" series.
Terms: Borrower pays return postage. Return within three weeks after scheduled showing date. Book one month in advance if possible. Rewind the video and wrap securely for return. Be certain to indicate video number, date needed, name of your organization, and address to which video should be sent, along with phone number. Audience report enclosed with the video must be completed and returned.
    Source: Consulate General of Japan, Oregon
    Attn: Tamara, Video Library
    1300 S. W. Fifth Avenue, Suite 2700
    Portland, OR 97201
    Phone: 1-503-221-1811, ext. 17
    World Wide Web URL:
    http://www.portland.us.emb-japan.go.jp/en/index.html
    Email Address: tamara@cgjpdx.org

ENTERTAINMENT

Alias, La Gringa
Political drama where La Gringa finds himself in a prison situation beyond his control.
Availability: Schools and libraries in Iowa, Illinois, Michigan, Minnesota, and Wisconsin.
Suggested Grade: 6-1
LanguagesS Spanish with English subtitles
Order Number: FFPERA14VHS
Production Date: 1991
Format: VHS videotape
Terms: Borrower pays return postage. Return 8 days after showing. Book 2 weeks in advance. Order may also be picked up for those near the Center.
Source: **Center for Latin American and Caribbean Studies**
UW-Milwaukee
P. O. Box 413
Milwaukee, WI 53201
Phone: 1-414-229-5987
World Wide Web URL: http://www.uwm.edu/Dept/CLACS
Email Address: audvis@usm.edu

Alsino and the Condor
A boy's dream of flying above the madness of the world around him.
Availability: Schools and libraries in Iowa, Illinois, Michigan, Minnesota, and Wisconsin.
Suggested Grade: 6-12
Languages: Spanish with English subtitles
Order Number: FFNICAL7VHS
Production Date: 1982
Format: VHS videotape
Special Notes: Rated R.
Terms: Borrower pays return postage. Return 8 days after showing. Book 2 weeks in advance. Order may also be picked up for those near the Center.
Source: **Center for Latin American and Caribbean Studies**
UW-Milwaukee
P. O. Box 413
Milwaukee, WI 53201
Phone: 1-414-229-5987
World Wide Web URL: http://www.uwm.edu/Dept/CLACS
Email Address: audvis@usm.edu

Alsino and the Condor
A boy's dream of flying above the madness of the world around him.
Availability: Schools, libraries, and nursing homes in the United States.
Suggested Grade: 6-12
Languages: Spanish with English subtitles
Order Number: FFNIC1-video
Production Date: 1982
Format: VHS videotape
Special Notes: Rated R.
Terms: Borrowers must have a User's Agreement on file with this source--available by mail or via the Internet. Return postage is paid by borrower; return 12 days after showing. Book at least three weeks in advance. All borrowers are limited to a total of ten items per semester.
Source: **Latin American Resource Center**
Stone Center for Latin American Studies
Tulane University
100 Jones Hall
New Orleans, LA 70118
Phone: 1-504-862-3143
Fax: 1-504-865-6719
World Wide Web URL: http://stonecenter.tulane.edu/pages/detail/48/Lending-Library
Email Address: crcrts@tulane.edu

Apaissionata
Police scandal as a famous pianist is accused of a crime and tries to save her career.
Availability: Schools, libraries, and nursing homes in the United States.
Suggested Grade: 6-12
Language: Portuguese
Order Number: FFBRA23-video
Production Date: 1952
Format: VHS videotape
Terms: Borrowers must have a User's Agreement on file with this source--available by mail or via the Internet. Return postage is paid by borrower; return 12 days after showing. Book at least three weeks in advance. All borrowers are limited to a total of ten items per semester.
Source: **Latin American Resource Center**
Stone Center for Latin American Studies
Tulane University
100 Jones Hall
New Orleans, LA 70118
Phone: 1-504-862-3143
Fax: 1-504-865-6719
World Wide Web URL: http://stonecenter.tulane.edu/pages/detail/48/Lending-Library
Email Address: crcrts@tulane.edu

Asi es Mi Tierra
Mexican comedy about revolution.
Availability: Schools, libraries, and nursing homes in the United States.
Suggested Grade: 6-12
Language: Spanish
Order Number: FFMEX22-video
Format: VHS videotape
Terms: Borrowers must have a User's Agreement on file with this source--available by mail or via the Internet. Return postage is paid by borrower; return 12 days after showing. Book at least three weeks in advance. All borrowers are limited to a total of ten items per semester.
Source: **Latin American Resource Center**
Stone Center for Latin American Studies
Tulane University
100 Jones Hall
New Orleans, LA 70118
Phone: 1-504-862-3143
Fax: 1-504-865-6719
World Wide Web URL: http://stonecenter.tulane.edu/pages/detail/48/Lending-Library
Email Address: crcrts@tulane.edu

*All materials listed in this 2018-2019 edition are **BRAND NEW!***

ENTERTAINMENT

Black Orpheus
Mythic tale of Orpheus and his haunted lover Eurydice, retold with samba and Rio's Carnaval celebration serving as Hades.

Availability:	Schools and libraries in Iowa, Illinois, Michigan, Minnesota, and Wisconsin.
Suggested Grade:	6-12
Languages:	Portuguese with English subtitles
Order Number:	FFBRAB561DVD
Production Date:	1959
Format:	DVD
Terms:	Borrower pays return postage. Return 8 days after showing. Book 2 weeks in advance. Order may also be picked up for those near the Center.

Source: **Center for Latin American and Caribbean Studies**
UW-Milwaukee
P. O. Box 413
Milwaukee, WI 53201
Phone: 1-414-229-5987
World Wide Web URL: http://www.uwm.edu/Dept/CLACS
Email Address: audvis@usm.edu

Black Orpheus
Mythic tale of Orpheus and his haunted lover Eurydice, retold with samba and Rio's Carnaval celebration serving as Hades.

Availability:	Schools and libraries in Iowa, Illinois, Michigan, Minnesota, and Wisconsin.
Suggested Grade:	6-12
Languages:	Portuguese with English subtitles
Order Number:	FFBRAB561VHS
Production Date:	1959
Format:	VHS videotape
Terms:	Borrower pays return postage. Return 8 days after showing. Book 2 weeks in advance. Order may also be picked up for those near the Center.

Source: **Center for Latin American and Caribbean Studies**
UW-Milwaukee
P. O. Box 413
Milwaukee, WI 53201
Phone: 1-414-229-5987
World Wide Web URL: http://www.uwm.edu/Dept/CLACS
Email Address: audvis@usm.edu

Bolivar Soy Yo
"I am Bolivar" spoofs that distinctive Latin American genre, the telenovela.

Availability:	Schools, libraries, and nursing homes in the United States.
Suggested Grade:	6-12
Languages:	Spanish with English subtitles
Order Number:	FFCOL08-videoc02
Production Date:	2002
Format:	DVD
Terms:	Borrowers must have a User's Agreement on file with this source--available by mail or via the Internet. Return postage is paid by borrower; return 12 days after showing. Book at least three weeks in advance. All borrowers are limited to a total of ten items per semester.

Source: **Latin American Resource Center**
Stone Center for Latin American Studies
Tulane University
100 Jones Hall
New Orleans, LA 70118
Phone: 1-504-862-3143
Fax: 1-504-865-6719
World Wide Web URL: http://stonecenter.tulane.edu/pages/detail/48/Lending-Library
Email Address: crcrts@tulane.edu

Don Segundo Sombra
An old gaucho is mentor and model to his "pupil." Based on a novel of the same name.

Availability:	Schools and libraries in Iowa, Illinois, Michigan, Minnesota, and Wisconsin.
Suggested Grade:	6-12
Languages:	Spanish with English subtitles
Order Number:	FFARGD71.1VHS
Production Date:	1969
Format:	VHS videotape
Terms:	Borrower pays return postage. Return 8 days after showing. Book 2 weeks in advance. Order may also be picked up for those near the Center.

Source: **Center for Latin American and Caribbean Studies**
UW-Milwaukee
P. O. Box 413
Milwaukee, WI 53201
Phone: 1-414-229-5987
World Wide Web URL: http://www.uwm.edu/Dept/CLACS
Email Address: audvis@usm.edu

Dust to Dust
A gentle comedy about family and friendship.

Availability:	Schools, libraries, and nursing homes in the United States.
Suggested Grade:	6-12
Languages:	Spanish with subtitles
Order Number:	FFMEX75-videoc02
Production Date:	2000
Format:	DVD
Special Notes:	Winner of the 2001 Chicago Latino Film Festival's Audience Award.
Terms:	Borrowers must have a User's Agreement on file with this source--available by mail or via the Internet. Return postage is paid by borrower; return 12 days after showing. Book at least three weeks in advance. All borrowers are limited to a total of ten items per semester.

Source: **Latin American Resource Center**
Stone Center for Latin American Studies
Tulane University
100 Jones Hall
New Orleans, LA 70118
Phone: 1-504-862-3143
Fax: 1-504-865-6719
World Wide Web URL: http://stonecenter.tulane.edu/pages/detail/48/Lending-Library
Email Address: crcrts@tulane.edu

*All materials listed in this 2018-2019 edition are **BRAND NEW**!*

ENTERTAINMENT

El Norte
Two young Guatemalans flee political unrest in their homeland, dreaming of a utopian life in the U. S. Danger and frustration follow them constantly.
Availability: Schools and libraries in Iowa, Illinois, Michigan, Minnesota, and Wisconsin.
Suggested Grade: 6-12
Languages: Spanish with English subtitles
Order Number: FFGUAN74.1VHS
Production Date: 1984
Format: VHS videotape
Special Notes: Rated R.
Terms: Borrower pays return postage. Return 8 days after showing. Book 2 weeks in advance. Order may also be picked up for those near the Center.
Source: **Center for Latin American and Caribbean Studies**
UW-Milwaukee
P. O. Box 413
Milwaukee, WI 53201
Phone: 1-414-229-5987
World Wide Web URL: http://www.uwm.edu/Dept/CLACS
Email Address: audvis@usm.edu

El Peregrinaje de las Flores
Flower vendors retell ancient legends while traveling to market in brightly-decorated barges.
Availability: Schools, libraries, and nursing homes in the United States.
Suggested Grade: 6-12
Language: Spanish
Order Number: DFMEX14-video
Production Date: 1974
Format: VHS videotape
Terms: Borrowers must have a User's Agreement on file with this source--available by mail or via the Internet. Return postage is paid by borrower; return 12 days after showing. Book at least three weeks in advance. All borrowers are limited to a total of ten items per semester.
Source: **Latin American Resource Center**
Stone Center for Latin American Studies
Tulane University
100 Jones Hall
New Orleans, LA 70118
Phone: 1-504-862-3143
Fax: 1-504-865-6719
World Wide Web URL: http://stonecenter.tulane.edu/pages/detail/48/Lending-Library
Email Address: crcrts@tulane.edu

El Tango en Broadway
Musical comedy about exploits of Latin American artists in New York.
Availability: Schools and libraries in Iowa, Illinois, Michigan, Minnesota, and Wisconsin.
Suggested Grade: 9-12
Languages: Spanish with English subtitles
Order Number: FFMEXT15VHS
Production Date: 1934
Format: VHS videotape
Terms: Borrower pays return postage. Return 8 days after showing. Book 2 weeks in advance. Order may also be picked up for those near the Center.
Source: **Center for Latin American and Caribbean Studies**
UW-Milwaukee
P. O. Box 413
Milwaukee, WI 53201
Phone: 1-414-229-5987
World Wide Web URL: http://www.uwm.edu/Dept/CLACS
Email Address: audvis@usm.edu

Harder They Come, The
Ivan travels to the big city of Kingston, Jamaica, to make it big. Instead he kills a cop, and finds infamy is the fastest way to notoriety.
Availability: Schools and libraries in Iowa, Illinois, Michigan, Minnesota, and Wisconsin.
Suggested Grade: 9-12
Order Number: FFJAMH21DVD
Production Date: 1973
Format: DVD
Terms: Borrower pays return postage. Return 8 days after showing. Book 2 weeks in advance. Order may also be picked up for those near the Center.
Source: **Center for Latin American and Caribbean Studies**
UW-Milwaukee
P. O. Box 413
Milwaukee, WI 53201
Phone: 1-414-229-5987
World Wide Web URL: http://www.uwm.edu/Dept/CLACS
Email Address: audvis@usm.edu

Hour of the Star
Macabea, a young woman from the countryside moves to the sprawling city of Sao Paulo.
Availability: Schools and libraries in Iowa, Illinois, Michigan, Minnesota, and Wisconsin.
Suggested Grade: 9-12
Languages: Portuguese with English subtitles
Order Number: FFBRAH81VHS
Production Date: 1986
Format: VHS videotape
Special Notes: Won all twelve of the major film awards at the Brasilian Film Festival.
Terms: Borrower pays return postage. Return 8 days after showing. Book 2 weeks in advance. Order may also be picked up for those near the Center.
Source: **Center for Latin American and Caribbean Studies**
UW-Milwaukee
P. O. Box 413
Milwaukee, WI 53201
Phone: 1-414-229-5987
World Wide Web URL: http://www.uwm.edu/Dept/CLACS
Email Address: audvis@usm.edu

Jerico
Fictional account of a Dominican monk sent to the Amazon in the early 16th century as part of an expedition. He is captured by the Caribe tribe.

All materials listed in this 2018-2019 edition are **BRAND NEW!**

ENTERTAINMENT

Availability:	Schools and libraries in Iowa, Illinois, Michigan, Minnesota, and Wisconsin.
Suggested Grade:	6-12
Languages:	Spanish with English subtitles
Order Number:	FFVENJ47VHS
Production Date:	1991
Format:	VHS videotape
Terms:	Borrower pays return postage. Return 8 days after showing. Book 2 weeks in advance. Order may also be picked up for those near the Center.

Source: **Center for Latin American and Caribbean Studies**
UW-Milwaukee
P. O. Box 413
Milwaukee, WI 53201
Phone: 1-414-229-5987
World Wide Web URL: http://www.uwm.edu/Dept/CLACS
Email Address: audvis@usm.edu

Man Facing Southeast

A sci-fi parable of a saint-like stranger in a strange land--earth, who appears in a Buenos Airies psychiatric hospital.

Availability:	Schools and libraries in Iowa, Illinois, Michigan, Minnesota, and Wisconsin.
Suggested Grade:	6-12
Languages:	Spanish with English subtitles
Order Number:	FFARGM31.1VHS
Production Date:	1986
Format:	VHS videotape
Special Notes:	Rated R.
Terms:	Borrower pays return postage. Return 8 days after showing. Book 2 weeks in advance. Order may also be picked up for those near the Center.

Source: **Center for Latin American and Caribbean Studies**
UW-Milwaukee
P. O. Box 413
Milwaukee, WI 53201
Phone: 1-414-229-5987
Fax: 1-414-229-2879 (l Wide Web URL: http://www.uwm.edu/Dept/CLACS
Email Address: audvis@usm.edu

Maria Candelaria

A woman in her small village becomes an outcast because of her late mother's immoral behavior. Exploitation leads everyone into tragedy.

Availability:	Schools and libraries in Iowa, Illinois, Michigan, Minnesota, and Wisconsin.
Suggested Grade:	6-12
Languages:	Spanish with English subtitles
Order Number:	FFMEXM33VHS
Production Date:	1943
Format:	VHS videotape
Terms:	Borrower pays return postage. Return 8 days after showing. Book 2 weeks in advance. Order may also be picked up for those near the Center.

Source: **Center for Latin American and Caribbean Studies**
UW-Milwaukee
P. O. Box 413
Milwaukee, WI 53201
Phone: 1-414-229-5987
World Wide Web URL: http://www.uwm.edu/Dept/CLACS
Email Address: audvis@usm.edu

Martin Fierro

Dramatization of this beautiful and haunting epic of Argentina and the gaucho.

Availability:	Schools, libraries, and nursing homes in the United States.
Suggested Grade:	6-12
Language:	Spanish
Order Number:	LMARG10-video
Production Date:	1988
Format:	VHS videotape
Terms:	Borrowers must have a User's Agreement on file with this source--available by mail or via the Internet. Return postage is paid by borrower; return 12 days after showing. Book at least three weeks in advance. All borrowers are limited to a total of ten items per semester.

Source: **Latin American Resource Center**
Stone Center for Latin American Studies
Tulane University
100 Jones Hall
New Orleans, LA 70118
Phone: 1-504-862-3143
Fax: 1-504-865-6719
World Wide Web URL: http://stonecenter.tulane.edu/pages/detail/48/Lending-Library
Email Address: crcrts@tulane.edu

Missing

Political thriller about the disappearance of a young American writer during a South American coup, finally finds the painful truth.

Availability:	Schools and libraries in Iowa, Illinois, Michigan, Minnesota, and Wisconsin.
Suggested Grade:	6-12
Order Number:	FFUSAM68VHS
Production Date:	1982
Format:	VHS videotape
Special Notes:	Stars John Shea, Jack Lemmon, and Sissy Spacek.
Terms:	Borrower pays return postage. Return 8 days after showing. Book 2 weeks in advance. Order may also be picked up for those near the Center.

Source: **Center for Latin American and Caribbean Studies**
UW-Milwaukee
P. O. Box 413
Milwaukee, WI 53201
Phone: 1-414-229-5987
World Wide Web URL: http://www.uwm.edu/Dept/CLACS
Email Address: audvis@usm.edu

Miss Mary

Tale of English governess, the wealthy family, and the broad political events and personal dramas that carve their destinies.

Availability:	Schools and libraries in Iowa, Illinois, Michigan, Minnesota, and Wisconsin.

*All materials listed in this 2018-2019 edition are **BRAND NEW!***

ENTERTAINMENT

Suggested Grade: 6-12
Order Number: FFARGM68VHS
Production Date: 1986
Format: VHS videotape
Terms: Borrower pays return postage. Return 8 days after showing. Book 2 weeks in advance. Order may also be picked up for those near the Center.
Source: **Center for Latin American and Caribbean Studies**
UW-Milwaukee
P. O. Box 413
Milwaukee, WI 53201
Phone: 1-414-229-5987
World Wide Web URL: http://www.uwm.edu/Dept/CLACS
Email Address: audvis@usm.edu

On Top of the Whale

Team of linguists journey into the hinterlands of Pategonia to study a dying language. Stunning cinematography.
Availability: Schools, libraries, and nursing homes in the United States.
Suggested Grade: 6-12
Order Number: FFCHI5-video
Production Date: 1982
Format: VHS videotape
Terms: Borrowers must have a User's Agreement on file with this source--available by mail or via the Internet. Return postage is paid by borrower; return 12 days after showing. Book at least three weeks in advance. All borrowers are limited to a total of ten items per semester.
Source: **Latin American Resource Center**
Stone Center for Latin American Studies
Tulane University
100 Jones Hall
New Orleans, LA 70118
Phone: 1-504-862-3143
Fax: 1-504-865-6719
World Wide Web URL: http://stonecenter.tulane.edu/pages/detail/48/Lending-Library
Email Address: crcrts@tulane.edu

Para una Tumba sin Nombre

Dramatization of story which seeks the truth about a woman who died just before the story opens.
Availability: Schools, libraries, and nursing homes in the United States.
Suggested Grade: 6-12
Language: Spanish
Order Number: LMURU3-video
Production Date: 1988
Format: VHS videotape
Terms: Borrowers must have a User's Agreement on file with this source--available by mail or via the Internet. Return postage is paid by borrower; return 12 days after showing. Book at least three weeks in advance. All borrowers are limited to a total of ten items per semester.
Source: **Latin American Resource Center**
Stone Center for Latin American Studies
Tulane University
100 Jones Hall
New Orleans, LA 70118
Phone: 1-504-862-3143
Fax: 1-504-865-6719
World Wide Web URL: http://stonecenter.tulane.edu/pages/detail/48/Lending-Library
Email Address: crcrts@tulane.edu

Pixote

Award winning depiction of a homeless youth's descent into the criminal underworld.
Availability: Schools and libraries in Iowa, Illinois, Michigan, Minnesota, and Wisconsin.
Suggested Grade: 6-12
Languages: Portuguese with English subtitles
Order Number: FFBRAP68.1VHS
Production Date: 1981
Format: VHS videotape
Terms: Borrower pays return postage. Return 8 days after showing. Book 2 weeks in advance. Order may also be picked up for those near the Center.
Source: **Center for Latin American and Caribbean Studies**
UW-Milwaukee
P. O. Box 413
Milwaukee, WI 53201
Phone: 1-414-229-5987
World Wide Web URL: http://www.uwm.edu/Dept/CLACS
Email Address: audvis@usm.edu

Querido Diario

Animated story of a young girl who visits the ruins of Teotihuacan on a school trip, where she meets a pre-Columbian boy who shows her what life was like.
Availability: Schools, libraries, and nursing homes in the United States.
Suggested Grade: K-12
Language: Spanish
Order Number: APMEX40-video
Production Date: 1992
Format: VHS videotape
Special Notes: Recommended for language classes.
Terms: Borrowers must have a User's Agreement on file with this source--available by mail or via the Internet. Return postage is paid by borrower; return 12 days after showing. Book at least three weeks in advance. All borrowers are limited to a total of ten items per semester.
Source: **Latin American Resource Center**
Stone Center for Latin American Studies
Tulane University
100 Jones Hall
New Orleans, LA 70118
Phone: 1-504-862-3143
Fax: 1-504-865-6719
World Wide Web URL: http://stonecenter.tulane.edu/pages/detail/48/Lending-Library
Email Address: crcrts@tulane.edu

Quincas Berro D'Agua

Traces life of a minor civil servant who becomes a bohemian, after living an exemplary life.

*All materials listed in this 2018-2019 edition are **BRAND NEW**!*

ENTERTAINMENT

Availability: Schools, libraries, and nursing homes in the United States.
Suggested Grade: 6-12
Language: Portuguese
Order Number: FFBRA10-video
Production Date: 1980
Format: VHS videotape
Terms: Borrowers must have a User's Agreement on file with this source--available by mail or via the Internet. Return postage is paid by borrower; return 12 days after showing. Book at least three weeks in advance. All borrowers are limited to a total of ten items per semester.
**Source: Latin American Resource Center
Stone Center for Latin American Studies
Tulane University
100 Jones Hall
New Orleans, LA 70118
Phone: 1-504-862-3143
Fax: 1-504-865-6719**
World Wide Web URL: http://stonecenter.tulane.edu/pages/detail/48/Lending-Library
Email Address: crcrts@tulane.edu

Sugar Cane Alley
Story of Jose, an 11-year-old orphan, and his grandmother, who is determined to save him from the hard life of sugar plantations on French-occupied Martinique in the 1930's.
Availability: Schools and libraries in Iowa, Illinois, Michigan, Minnesota, and Wisconsin.
Suggested Grade: 6-12
Language: French with English subtitles
Order Number: FFMARU3VHS
Production Date: 1985
Format: VHS videotape
Terms: Borrower pays return postage. Return 8 days after showing. Book 2 weeks in advance. Order may also be picked up for those near the Center.
**Source: Center for Latin American and Caribbean Studies
UW-Milwaukee
P. O. Box 413
Milwaukee, WI 53201
Phone: 1-414-229-5987**
World Wide Web URL: http://www.uwm.edu/Dept/CLACS
Email Address: audvis@usm.edu

Tango Bar
An honest man discovers the woman he loves is a thief. She changes her life but he cannot believe in her ever again.
Availability: Schools and libraries in Iowa, Illinois, Michigan, Minnesota, and Wisconsin.
Suggested Grade: 6-12
Language: Spanish with English subtitles
Order Number: FFARGT15VHS
Production Date: 1987
Format: VHS videotape
Terms: Borrower pays return postage. Return 8 days after showing. Book 2 weeks in advance. Order may also be picked up for those near the Center.
**Source: Center for Latin American and Caribbean Studies
UW-Milwaukee
P. O. Box 413
Milwaukee, WI 53201
Phone: 1-414-229-5987**
World Wide Web URL: http://www.uwm.edu/Dept/CLACS
Email Address: audvis@usm.edu

Tango Bar
An honest man discovers the woman he loves is a thief. She changes her life but he cannot believe in her ever again.
Availability: Schools, libraries, and nursing homes in the United States.
Suggested Grade: 6-12
Language: Spanish with English subtitles
Order Number: FFARG21-video
Production Date: 1987
Format: VHS videotape
Terms: Borrowers must have a User's Agreement on file with this source--available by mail or via the Internet. Return postage is paid by borrower; return 12 days after showing. Book at least three weeks in advance. All borrowers are limited to a total of ten items per semester.
**Source: Latin American Resource Center
Stone Center for Latin American Studies
Tulane University
100 Jones Hall
New Orleans, LA 70118
Phone: 1-504-862-3143
Fax: 1-504-865-6719**
World Wide Web URL: http://stonecenter.tulane.edu/pages/detail/48/Lending-Library
Email Address: crcrts@tulane.edu

Viva Zapata
Marlon Brando stars as the peasant who fights his way to power and glory during the Mexican Revolution.
Availability: Schools, libraries, and nursing homes in the United States.
Suggested Grade: 6-12
Order Number: FFMEX31-video
Production Date: 1939
Format: VHS videotape
Special Notes: Stars Marlon Brando.
Terms: Borrowers must have a User's Agreement on file with this source--available by mail or via the Internet. Return postage is paid by borrower; return 12 days after showing. Book at least three weeks in advance. All borrowers are limited to a total of ten items per semester.
**Source: Latin American Resource Center
Stone Center for Latin American Studies
Tulane University
100 Jones Hall
New Orleans, LA 70118
Phone: 1-504-862-3143
Fax: 1-504-865-6719**
World Wide Web URL: http://stonecenter.tulane.edu/pages/detail/48/Lending-Library
Email Address: crcrts@tulane.edu

ENTERTAINMENT

Wuthering Heights
Adaptation of Bronte's work, where the Latin lovers throw themselves into their passion.
Availability: Schools and libraries in Iowa, Illinois, Michigan, Minnesota, and Wisconsin.
Suggested Grade: 6-12
Language: Spanish with English subtitles
Order Number: order by title
Production Date: 1953
Format: VHS videotape
Terms: Borrower pays return postage. Return 8 days after showing. Book 2 weeks in advance. Order may also be picked up for those near the Center.
Source: **Center for Latin American and Caribbean Studies**
UW-Milwaukee
P. O. Box 413
Milwaukee, WI 53201
World Wide Web URL: http://www.uwm.edu/Dept/CLACS
Email Address: audvis@usm.edu

Wuthering Heights
Adaptation of Bronte's work, where the Latin lovers throw themselves into their passion.
Availability: Schools, libraries, and nursing homes in the United States.
Suggested Grade: 6-12
Language: Spanish with English subtitles
Order Number: FFMEX16-video
Production Date: 1953
Format: VHS videotape
Terms: Borrowers must have a User's Agreement on file with this source--available by mail or via the Internet. Return postage is paid by borrower; return 12 days after showing. Book at least three weeks in advance. All borrowers are limited to a total of ten items per semester.
Source: **Latin American Resource Center**
Stone Center for Latin American Studies
Tulane University
100 Jones Hall
New Orleans, LA 70118
Phone: 1-504-862-3143
Fax: 1-504-865-6719
World Wide Web URL: http://stonecenter.tulane.edu/pages/detail/48/Lending-Library
Email Address: crcrts@tulane.edu

Zoot Suit
Actual Sleepy Lagoon murder case where the leader of a group of Mexican-Americans is sent to San Quentin without substantial evidence.
Availability: Schools and libraries in Iowa, Illinois, Michigan, Minnesota, and Wisconsin.
Suggested Grade: 6-12
Order Number: order by title
Production Date: 1981
Format: VHS videotape
Special Notes: Based on a real murder case. Stars Edward James Olmos and Tyne Daly.
Terms: Borrower pays return postage. Return 8 days after showing. Book 2 weeks in advance. Order may also be picked up for those near the Center.
Source: **Center for Latin American and Caribbean Studies**
UW-Milwaukee
P. O. Box 413
Milwaukee, WI 53201
Phone: 1-414-229-5987
World Wide Web URL: http://www.uwm.edu/Dept/CLACS
Email Address: audvis@usm.edu

*All materials listed in this 2018-2019 edition are **BRAND NEW!***

FAMOUS PEOPLE

Ana Mendieta: Fuego de Tierra
Presents the stunning work and life of Cuban Artist, Anna Mendieta.
- Availability: Schools in the United States.
- Suggested Grade: 9-Adult
- Languages: English and Spanish with English subtitles
- Order Number: order by title
- Production Date: 1987
- Format: VHS videotape
- Terms: Borrower pays return postage. Return 14 days after receipt, via USPS including insurance. All borrowers must have a current lending agreement on file with the Outreach program. This agreement is available via the web site or may be requested via phone or fax.
- Source: Center for Latin American Studies
  University of Florida
  319 Grinter Hall
  P. O. Box 115530
  Gainesville, FL 32611-5530
  Phone: 1-352-392-0375
  Fax: 1-352-392-7682
  World Wide Web URL: http://www.latam.ufl.edu/outreach
  Email Address: maryr@ufl.edu

Arruza
Greatest matador, Carlos Arruza, whose style and courage changed the art of bullfighting forever.
- Availability: Schools, libraries, and nursing homes in the United States.
- Suggested Grade: 6-12
- Order Number: DFMEX6-video
- Production Date: 1967
- Format: VHS videotape
- Terms: Borrowers must have a User's Agreement on file with this source--available by mail or via the Internet. Return postage is paid by borrower; return 12 days after showing. Book at least three weeks in advance. All borrowers are limited to a total of ten items per semester.
- Source: Latin American Resource Center
  Stone Center for Latin American Studies
  Tulane University
  100 Jones Hall
  New Orleans, LA 70118
  Phone: 1-504-862-3143
  Fax: 1-504-865-6719
  World Wide Web URL: http://stonecenter.tulane.edu/pages/detail/48/Lending-Library
  Email Address: crcrts@tulane.edu

Artist, The
During the Renaissance, the artist gradually achieved a new status and power in society and developed new forms of creative expression. Dramatic readings, historical reenactments, and interviews with historians and artists weave a portrait of Renaissance artists and their impact on art today. Includes Donatello, daVinci, Michelangelo, Raphael, Titian, Durer, and Caravaggio.
- Availability: Schools, libraries, and homeschoolers in the United States who serve the hearing impaired.
- Suggested Grade: 10-Adult
- Order Number: 12981
- Production Date: 1993
- Format: DVD
- Special Notes: Produced by Barr Media Group.
- Terms: Sponsor pays all transportation costs. Return one week after receipt. Participation is limited to deaf or hard of hearing Americans, their parents, families, teachers, counselors, or others whose use would benefit a deaf or hard of hearing person. Only one person in the audience needs to be hearing impaired. You must register--which is free. These videos are all open-captioned--no special equipment is required for viewing.
- Source: Described and Captioned Media Program
  National Association of the Deaf
  4211 Church Street Ext.
  Roebuck, SC 29376
  Phone: 1-800-237-6213
  Fax: 1-800-538-5636
  World Wide Web URL: http://www.dcmp.org

Benazir Bhutto: Walking the Tightrope
Explores the complex person of Benazir Bhutto, Prime Minister of Pakistan and the first woman to head a Muslim country, as well as Pakistan's political history.
- Availability: Schools, libraries, homeschoolers, and nursing homes in the southeastern United States.
- Suggested Grade: 7-12
- Order Number: order by title
- Production Date: 1995
- Format: VHS videotape
- Terms: Borrower pays return postage. Return 2 days after showing via United Parcel Service, insured. Book 2 weeks in advance.
- Source: Center for South Asian Studies
  University of Virginia
  Video Library Coordinator
  P. O. Box 400169, 110 Minor Hall
  Charlottesville, VA 22904-4169
  Phone: 1-434-924-8815
  Email Address: southasia@virginia.edu

Benedita da Silva
The life of Benedita da Silva, the first Black woman to be elected to the Brazilian national congress, touching on racism, feminism, ageism, politics and poverty.
- Availability: Schools, libraries, and nursing homes in the United States.
- Suggested Grade: 8-Adult
- Portuguese with English subtitles
- Order Number: SIBRA3-video
- Production Date: 1991
- Format: VHS videotape
- Terms: Borrowers must have a User's Agreement on file with this source--available by mail or via the Internet. Return postage is paid by borrower; return 12 days after showing. Book at least three weeks in advance. All borrowers are limited to a total of ten items per semester.

*All materials listed in this 2018-2019 edition are **BRAND NEW**!*

FAMOUS PEOPLE

Source: Latin American Resource Center
Stone Center for Latin American Studies
Tulane University
100 Jones Hall
New Orleans, LA 70118
Phone: 1-504-862-3143
Fax: 1-504-865-6719
World Wide Web URL: http://stonecenter.tulane.edu/pages/detail/48/Lending-Library
Email Address: crcrts@tulane.edu

Birth of an Empire

In the People's Republic of Mongolia, the reputation of Genghis Khan has undergone a dramatic transformation-- from despised enemy of the revolution to a virtual deity. This program examines how he emerged from obscurity, united the Mongol tribes under his banner, and transformed an obscure nomadic people into the most formidable fighting machine. It traces his spectacular campaigns through northern China, central Asia, Afghanistan, Georgia and Russia, which set down the foundations of a powerful empire.

Availability: Schools, libraries, and nursing homes in the United States and Canada.
Suggested Grade: 9-Adult
Order Number: MV003
Format: VHS videotape
Terms: Borrower pays return postage. Return with 14 days after scheduled showing, via UPS or U. S. Mail. All requests must included an educational institution affiliation, a current address, and phone number. Order through web site only.
Source: Cornell University East Asia Program
World Wide Web URL: http://eap.einaudi.cornell.edu/lending_library
Email Address: east_asia1@cornell.edu

Carlos Fuentes

Author, teacher, and diplomat offers perspective on current Latin American economics and prospects for political independence.

Availability: Schools, libraries, and nursing homes in the United States.
Suggested Grade: 6-12
Order Number: HCLA14-video
Production Date: 1988
Format: VHS videotape
Terms: Borrowers must have a User's Agreement on file with this source--available by mail or via the Internet. Return postage is paid by borrower; return 12 days after showing. Book at least three weeks in advance. All borrowers are limited to a total of ten items per semester.
Source: Latin American Resource Center
Stone Center for Latin American Studies
Tulane University
100 Jones Hall
New Orleans, LA 70118
Phone: 1-504-862-3143
Fax: 1-504-865-6719
World Wide Web URL: http://stonecenter.tulane.edu/pages/detail/48/Lending-Library
Email Address: crcrts@tulane.edu

Carmen Miranda: Bananas Is My Business

Traces Carmen Miranda's life from her birth in Portugal, to her childhood in Rio de Janeiro, and as a performer in the United States.

Availability: Schools and libraries in Iowa, Illinois, Michigan, Minnesota, and Wisconsin.
Suggested Grade: 6-12
Languages: English and Portuguese with English subtitles
Order Number: order by title
Production Date: 1994
Format: VHS videotape
Terms: Borrower pays return postage. Return 8 days after showing. Book 2 weeks in advance. Order may also be picked up for those near the Center.
Source: Center for Latin American and Caribbean Studies
UW-Milwaukee
P. O. Box 413
Milwaukee, WI 53201
Phone: 1-414-229-5987
World Wide Web URL: http://www.uwm.edu/Dept/CLACS
Email Address: audvis@usm.edu

Carmen Miranda: Bananas Is My Business

Traces Carmen Miranda's life from her birth in Portugal, to her childhood in Rio de Janeiro, and as a performer in the United States.

Availability: Schools, libraries, and nursing homes in the United States.
Suggested Grade: 6-12
Languages: English and Portuguese with English subtitles
Order Number: MUBRA10-video
Production Date: 1994
Format: VHS videotape
Terms: Borrowers must have a User's Agreement on file with this source--available by mail or via the Internet. Return postage is paid by borrower; return 12 days after showing. Book at least three weeks in advance. All borrowers are limited to a total of ten items per semester.
Source: Latin American Resource Center
Stone Center for Latin American Studies
Tulane University
100 Jones Hall
New Orleans, LA 70118
Phone: 1-504-862-3143
Fax: 1-504-865-6719
World Wide Web URL: http://stonecenter.tulane.edu/pages/detail/48/Lending-Library
Email Address: crcrts@tulane.edu

Columbus

Taking risks while building on an established base of knowledge is the thought processed in this program about Christopher Columbus.

All materials listed in this 2018-2019 edition are BRAND NEW!

FAMOUS PEOPLE

Availability: Schools, libraries, and nursing homes in the United States.
Suggested Grade: 6-12
Order Number: HLA17-video
Production Date: 1981
Format: VHS videotape
Terms: Borrowers must have a User's Agreement on file with this source--available by mail or via the Internet. Return postage is paid by borrower; return 12 days after showing. Book at least three weeks in advance. All borrowers are limited to a total of ten items per semester.
Source: Latin American Resource Center
Stone Center for Latin American Studies
Tulane University
100 Jones Hall
New Orleans, LA 70118
Phone: 1-504-862-3143
Fax: 1-504-865-6719
World Wide Web URL: http://stonecenter.tulane.edu/pages/detail/48/Lending-Library
Email Address: crcrts@tulane.edu

Compassion in Exile: The Story of the 14th Dalai Lama
Compassion in Exile is the first American feature documentary chronicling His Holiness the Dalai Lama's remarkable life and thirty-year exile from his homeland, Tibet.
Availability: Schools, libraries, and nursing homes in the United States and Canada.
Suggested Grade: 6-Adult
Order Number: TBV015
Format: VHS videotape
Terms: Borrower pays return postage. Return with 14 days after scheduled showing, via UPS or U. S. Mail. All requests must included an educational institution affiliation, a current address, and phone number. Order through web site only.
Source: Cornell University East Asia Program
World Wide Web URL: http://eap.einaudi.cornell.edu/lending_library
Email Address: east_asia1@cornell.edu

Dalai Lama: The Soul of Tibet
Details the life and struggles of the leader of a nation that exists only in exile.
Availability: Schools, libraries, and nursing homes in the United States and Canada.
Suggested Grade: 6-Adult
Order Number: TBV016
Format: VHS videotape
Terms: Borrower pays return postage. Return with 14 days after scheduled showing, via UPS or U. S. Mail. All requests must included an educational institution affiliation, a current address, and phone number. Order through web site only.
Source: Cornell University East Asia Program
World Wide Web URL: http://eap.einaudi.cornell.edu/lending_library
Email Address: east_asia1@cornell.edu

Dalda 13: A Talented Woman History Forgot
Profiles the career of Homai Vyarawalla, a photojournalist who is largely un-recognized for her powerful images of India.
Availability: Schools, libraries, homeschoolers, and nursing homes in the southeastern United States.
Suggested Grade: 7-12
Order Number: order by title
Production Date: 1997
Format: VHS videotape
Terms: Borrower pays return postage. Return 2 days after showing via United Parcel Service, insured. Book 2 weeks in advance.
Source: Center for South Asian Studies
University of Virginia
Video Library Coordinator
P. O. Box 400169, 110 Minor Hall
Charlottesville, VA 22904-4169
Phone: 1-434-924-8815
Email Address: southasia@virginia.edu

Dialogo Entre Augusto Roa Bastos y Fernando Alegria
Interview of Paraguayan poet laureate, Augusto Roa Bastos.
Availability: Schools, libraries, and nursing homes in the United States.
Suggested Grade: 6-12
Language: Spanish
Order Number: LMPAR1-video
Production Date: 1985
Format: VHS videotape
Terms: Borrowers must have a User's Agreement on file with this source--available by mail or via the Internet. Return postage is paid by borrower; return 12 days after showing. Book at least three weeks in advance. All borrowers are limited to a total of ten items per semester.
Source: Latin American Resource Center
Stone Center for Latin American Studies
Tulane University
100 Jones Hall
New Orleans, LA 70118
Phone: 1-504-862-3143
Fax: 1-504-865-6719
World Wide Web URL: http://stonecenter.tulane.edu/pages/detail/48/Lending-Library
Email Address: crcrts@tulane.edu

Dream Across Time and Place, A--The Legacy of Tsuda Umeko
Umeko traveled to the United States in 1871. At age six, she was the youngest of five young women sent to study there by the Japanese Government as part of its effort to modernize Japan. She spent a total of 14 years in two stays in America, returning home determined to create a school of higher learning for women so that other Japanese women benefit from education as she has done.
Availability: Schools, libraries, and nursing homes in the United States and Canada.

FAMOUS PEOPLE

Suggested Grade: 6-Adult
Language: Japanese
Order Number: JV104
Format: VHS videotape
Special Notes: An English text accompanies the production.
Terms: Borrower pays return postage. Return with 14 days after scheduled showing, via UPS or U. S. Mail. All requests must included an educational institution affiliation, a current address, and phone number. Order through web site only.
Source: Cornell University East Asia Program
World Wide Web URL:
http://eap.einaudi.cornell.edu/lending_library
Email Address: east_asia1@cornell.edu

Edouard Vuillard

Along with fellow post-impressionists, Edouard Vuillard helped change the course of French painting. This program chronicles his entire career.
Availability: Schools, community groups, homeschoolers and individuals in the United States.
Suggested Grade: 7-12
Order Number: VC 169
Format: VHS videotape
Special Notes: Programs may not be broadcast, reproduced, or transferred to another medium or format without special license from the National Gallery of Art. Closed captioned version also available as CC 169.
Terms: Borrower pays return postage. Return within 5 days of scheduled use. Book at least one month in advance, and provide alternate date. You will receive a confirmation noting our Shipping Date and your Return Date for each program. Large organizations that can provide programs to extensive audiences--such as school systems, instructional resource centers, museums, libraries, and public and instructional television stations--can arrange an Affiliate Loan for three years, with subsequent renewal to provide their audiences more immediate access to these free-loan extension programs.
Source: National Gallery of Art
Department of Education Resources
2000B South Club Drive
Landover, MD 20785
Phone: 1-202-842-6280
Fax: 1-202-842-6937
World Wide Web URL:
http://www.nga.gov/education/classroom/loanfinder/
Email Address: EdResources@nga.gov

Ernesto "Che" Guevara: Restless Revolutionary

"Che's" nanny, bodyguard, teacher, and friends offer unique background information and key life events that shaped the ideology of this revolutionary individual.
Availability: Schools in the United States.
Suggested Grade: 7-Adult
Order Number: order by title
Production Date: 2001
Format: VHS videotape
Terms: Borrower pays return postage. Return 14 days after receipt, via USPS including insurance. All borrowers must have a current lending agreement on file with the Outreach program. This agreement is available via the web site or may be requested via phone or fax.
Source: Center for Latin American Studies
University of Florida
319 Grinter Hall
P. O. Box 115530
Gainesville, FL 32611-5530
Phone: 1-352-392-0375
Fax: 1-352-392-7682
World Wide Web URL: http://www.latam.ufl.edu/outreach
Email Address: maryr@ufl.edu

Ernesto Che Guevara: The Bolivian Diary

Che Guevara's personal diary account of his 11-month attempt to foment revolution in Bolivia, before his execution in 1967.
Availability: Schools, libraries, and nursing homes in the United States.
Suggested Grade: 6-12
Order Number: HCBOL1-video
Production Date: 1998
Format: VHS videotape
Terms: Borrowers must have a User's Agreement on file with this source--available by mail or via the Internet. Return postage is paid by borrower; return 12 days after showing. Book at least three weeks in advance. All borrowers are limited to a total of ten items per semester.
Source: Latin American Resource Center
Stone Center for Latin American Studies
Tulane University, 100 Jones Hall
New Orleans, LA 70118
Phone: 1-504-862-3143
Fax: 1-504-865-6719
World Wide Web URL: http://stonecenter.tulane.edu/pages/detail/48/Lending-Library
Email Address: crcrts@tulane.edu

Evita: The Woman Behind the Myth

Examines the mix of myths and facts surrounding the life of Eva Duarte de Peron, from her minor actress days to her time of political power and prestige, ending with her tragic death from cancer at the age of 33.
Availability: Schools in the United States.
Suggested Grade: 7-Adult
Order Number: order by title
Production Date: 1996
Format: VHS videotape
Terms: Borrower pays return postage. Return 14 days after receipt, via USPS including insurance. All borrowers must have a current lending agreement on file with the Outreach program. This agreement is available via the web site or may be requested via phone or fax.
Source: Center for Latin American Studies
University of Florida, 319 Grinter Hall
P. O. Box 115530
Gainesville, FL 32611-5530

All materials listed in this 2018-2019 edition are BRAND NEW!

FAMOUS PEOPLE

Phone: 1-352-392-0375
Fax: 1-352-392-7682
World Wide Web URL: http://www.latam.ufl.edu/outreach
Email Address: maryr@ufl.edu

Evita: The Woman Behind the Myth
Explores the life of Eva Duarte de Peron, from her origins to her marriage to Juan Peron and her tragic death from cancer at age 33.
- Availability: Schools, libraries, and nursing homes in the United States.
- Suggested Grade: 6-12
- Order Number: HCARG2-video
- Production Date: 1996
- Format: VHS videotape
- Terms: Borrowers must have a User's Agreement on file with this source--available by mail or via the Internet. Return postage is paid by borrower; return 12 days after showing. Book at least three weeks in advance. All borrowers are limited to a total of ten items per semester.

**Source: Latin American Resource Center
Stone Center for Latin American Studies
Tulane University, 100 Jones Hall
New Orleans, LA 70118**
Phone: 1-504-862-3143
Fax: 1-504-865-6719
World Wide Web URL: http://stonecenter.tulane.edu/pages/detail/48/Lending-Library
Email Address: crcrts@tulane.edu

Eye of Thomas Jefferson, The
Thomas Jefferson was a man of remarkable achievements. Based on the National Gallery's bicentennial exhibition, this program is a survey of Jefferson's artistic interests and creative accomplishments. It traces Jefferson's journeys through Europe, where he found inspiration for many of his ideas on architecture and landscaping, as seen in his later designs for Monticello and the University of Virginia.
- Availability: Schools, community groups, homeschoolers and individuals in the United States.
- Suggested Grade: 4-12
- Order Number: VC 131
- Format: VHS videotape
- Special Notes: Programs may not be broadcast, reproduced, or transferred to another medium or format without special license from the National Gallery of Art. Closed captioned version also available as CC 131.
- Terms: Borrower pays return postage. Return within 5 days of scheduled use. Book at least one month in advance, and provide alternate date. You will receive a confirmation noting our Shipping Date and your Return Date for each program. Large organizations that can provide programs to extensive audiences--such as school systems, instructional resource centers, museums, libraries, and public and instructional television stations--can arrange an Affiliate Loan for three years, with subsequent renewal to provide their audiences more immediate access to these free-loan extension programs.

**Source: National Gallery of Art
Department of Education Resources
2000B South Club Drive
Landover, MD 20785**
Phone: 1-202-842-6280
Fax: 1-202-842-6937
World Wide Web URL: http://www.nga.gov/education/classroom/loanfinder/
Email Address: EdResources@nga.gov

Famous Deaf Americans--Part I
Focuses on the achievements of selected deaf Americans from a variety of careers.
- Availability: Schools, libraries, and homeschoolers in the United States who serve the hearing impaired.
- Suggested Grade: Adult
- Order Number: 2793
- Production Date: 1983
- Format: DVD
- Terms: Sponsor pays all transportation costs. Return one week after receipt. Participation is limited to deaf or hard of hearing Americans, their parents, families, teachers, counselors, or others whose use would benefit a deaf or hard of hearing person. Only one person in the audience needs to be hearing impaired. You must register--which is free. These videos are all open-captioned--no special equipment is required for viewing.

**Source: Described and Captioned Media Program
National Association of the Deaf
4211 Church Street Ext.
Roebuck, SC 29376**
Phone: 1-800-237-6213
Fax: 1-800-538-5636
World Wide Web URL: http://www.dcmp.org

Famous Deaf Americans--Part II
Focuses on the achievements of selected deaf Americans from a variety of careers.
- Availability: Schools, libraries, and homeschoolers in the United States who serve the hearing impaired.
- Suggested Grade: Adult
- Order Number: 2794
- Production Date: 1983
- Format: DVD
- Terms: Sponsor pays all transportation costs. Return one week after receipt. Participation is limited to deaf or hard of hearing Americans, their parents, families, teachers, counselors, or others whose use would benefit a deaf or hard of hearing person. Only one person in the audience needs to be hearing impaired. You must register--which is free. These videos are all open-captioned--no special equipment is required for viewing.

**Source: Described and Captioned Media Program
National Association of the Deaf
4211 Church Street Ext.
Roebuck, SC 29376**
Phone: 1-800-237-6213
Fax: 1-800-538-5636
World Wide Web URL: http://www.dcmp.org

*All materials listed in this 2018-2019 edition are **BRAND NEW!***

FAMOUS PEOPLE

Fidel Castro: El Comandante
Examines the life of the leader known as "El Comandante."
Availability: Schools in the United States.
Suggested Grade: 7-Adult
Order Number: order by title
Production Date: 1997
Format: VHS videotape
Terms: Borrower pays return postage. Return 14 days after receipt, via USPS including insurance. All borrowers must have a current lending agreement on file with the Outreach program. This agreement is available via the web site or may be requested via phone or fax.
Source: Center for Latin American Studies
University of Florida
319 Grinter Hall
P. O. Box 115530
Gainesville, FL 32611-5530
Phone: 1-352-392-0375
Fax: 1-352-392-7682
World Wide Web URL: http://www.latam.ufl.edu/outreach
Email Address: maryr@ufl.edu

Frida
On her deathbed, artist Frida Kahlo conjures up images and memories of her life as a revolutionary and one of the greatest painters of the 20th century. This film uses images and music to depict the life of this famous woman, and dialogue is used sparingly.
Availability: Schools in the United States.
Suggested Grade: Adult
Order Number: order by title
Production Date: 1984
Format: VHS videotape
Terms: Borrower pays return postage. Return 14 days after receipt, via USPS including insurance. All borrowers must have a current lending agreement on file with the Outreach program. This agreement is available via the web site or may be requested via phone or fax.
Source: Center for Latin American Studies
University of Florida
319 Grinter Hall
P. O. Box 115530
Gainesville, FL 32611-5530
Phone: 1-352-392-0375
Fax: 1-352-392-7682
World Wide Web URL: http://www.latam.ufl.edu/outreach
Email Address: maryr@ufl.edu

Frida Kahlo
Depicts the life and paintings of this artist who was ravaged with pain from the age of 16.
Availability: Schools and libraries in Iowa, Illinois, Michigan, Minnesota, and Wisconsin.
Suggested Grade: 7-12
Order Number: ART/FOLMEXK12.1VHS
Format: VHS videotape
Terms: Borrower pays return postage. Return 8 days after showing. Book 2 weeks in advance. Order may also be picked up for those near the Center.
Source: Center for Latin American and Caribbean Studies
UW-Milwaukee
P. O. Box 413
Milwaukee, WI 53201
Phone: 1-414-229-5987
World Wide Web URL: http://www.uwm.edu/Dept/CLACS
Email Address: audvis@usm.edu

Gabriel Garcia Marquez: Magic and Reality
Rare archival footage and appearances by the author and characters of "One Hundred Years of Solitude" and "The Autumn of the Patriarch."
Availability: Schools, libraries, and nursing homes in the United States.
Suggested Grade: 6-12
Order Number: LMCOL1-video
Production Date: 1981
Format: VHS videotape
Terms: Borrowers must have a User's Agreement on file with this source--available by mail or via the Internet. Return postage is paid by borrower; return 12 days after showing. Book at least three weeks in advance. All borrowers are limited to a total of ten items per semester.
Source: Latin American Resource Center
Stone Center for Latin American Studies
Tulane University
100 Jones Hall
New Orleans, LA 70118
Phone: 1-504-862-3143
Fax: 1-504-865-6719
World Wide Web URL: http://stonecenter.tulane.edu/pages/detail/48/Lending-Library
Email Address: crcrts@tulane.edu

Henry Moore: A Life in Sculpture
Depicts the life of this artist.
Availability: Schools, community groups, homeschoolers and individuals in the United States.
Suggested Grade: 6-12
Order Number: VC 164
Production Date: 2002
Format: VHS videotape
Special Notes: Programs may not be broadcast, reproduced, or transferred to another medium or format without special license from the National Gallery of Art. Closed captioned version also available as CC 164.
Terms: Borrower pays return postage. Return within 5 days of scheduled use. Book at least one month in advance, and provide alternate date. You will receive a confirmation noting our Shipping Date and your Return Date for each program. Large organizations that can provide programs to extensive audiences--such as school systems, instructional resource centers, museums, libraries, and public and instructional television stations--can arrange an Affiliate Loan for three years, with subsequent renewal to provide their audiences more immediate access to these free-loan extension programs.

All materials listed in this 2018-2019 edition are BRAND NEW!

FAMOUS PEOPLE

Source: National Gallery of Art
Department of Education Resources
2000B South Club Drive
Landover, MD 20785
Phone: 1-202-842-6280
Fax: 1-202-842-6937
World Wide Web URL:
http://www.nga.gov/education/classroom/loanfinder/
Email Address: EdResources@nga.gov

Hernan Cortes
Conflict when Cortes' army clashed with the forces of Montezuma, resulting in the birth of modern Mexico.
Availability: Schools, libraries, and nursing homes in the United States.
Suggested Grade: 6-12
Order Number: HMEX8-video
Production Date: 1970
Format: VHS videotape
Terms: Borrowers must have a User's Agreement on file with this source--available by mail or via the Internet. Return postage is paid by borrower; return 12 days after showing. Book at least three weeks in advance. All borrowers are limited to a total of ten items per semester.
Source: Latin American Resource Center
Stone Center for Latin American Studies
Tulane University
100 Jones Hall
New Orleans, LA 70118
Phone: 1-504-862-3143
Fax: 1-504-865-6719
World Wide Web URL: http://stonecenter.tulane.edu/pages/detail/48/Lending-Library
Email Address: crcrts@tulane.edu

Langston Hughes: The Dream Keeper
Biographers, friends, critics, and Hughes himself offer commentary on his life and work as a premier African-American poet and writer. Kansas-born Hughes was an influential voice for and about his race from the 1920s-1960s. Trips to Africa, Russia, and Spain enlarged his understanding of the universality of the beauty, dignity, and heritage of blacks in America. Performances of his work illustrate both his range and depth.
Availability: Schools, libraries, and homeschoolers in the United States who serve the hearing impaired.
Suggested Grade: 10-Adult
Order Number: 13130
Production Date: 1988
Format: DVD
Special Notes: Produced by Annenberg/CPB Project.
Terms: Sponsor pays all transportation costs. Return one week after receipt. Participation is limited to deaf or hard of hearing Americans, their parents, families, teachers, counselors, or others whose use would benefit a deaf or hard of hearing person. Only one person in the audience needs to be hearing impaired. You must register--which is free. These videos are all open-captioned--no special equipment is required for viewing.

Source: Described and Captioned Media Program
National Association of the Deaf
4211 Church Street Ext.
Roebuck, SC 29376
Phone: 1-800-237-6213
Fax: 1-800-538-5636
World Wide Web URL: http://www.dcmp.org

Last of the Khans, The
This program traces the life of the fifth Great Khan, Kublai Khan, who preferred to make his home in China, where he ruled as the first emperor of the Yuan dynasty.
Availability: Schools, libraries, and nursing homes in the United States and Canada.
Suggested Grade: 6-Adult
Order Number: MV004
Format: VHS videotape
Terms: Borrower pays return postage. Return with 14 days after scheduled showing, via UPS or U. S. Mail. All requests must included an educational institution affiliation, a current address, and phone number. Order through web site only.
Source: Cornell University East Asia Program
World Wide Web URL:
http://eap.einaudi.cornell.edu/lending_library
Email Address: east_asia1@cornell.edu

Legends of the American West: Part Two
Looks at legendary individuals whose brave actions shaped the history of the Old West during the time following the end of the American Civil War till the turn of the century. Uses archival photos, filmclips, classic Western art, and dramatic reenactments to tell about the lives and times of Billy the Kid, Wyatt Earp, Doc Holliday, and several well-known gunfighters. Also includes information about the struggle of Native Americans in the West.
Availability: Schools, libraries, and homeschoolers in the United States who serve the hearing impaired.
Suggested Grade: 10-Adult
Order Number: 11396
Production Date: 2004
Format: DVD
Special Notes: Also available as live streaming video over the Internet.
Terms: Sponsor pays all transportation costs. Return one week after receipt. Participation is limited to deaf or hard of hearing Americans, their parents, families, teachers, counselors, or others whose use would benefit a deaf or hard of hearing person. Only one person in the audience needs to be hearing impaired. You must register--which is free. These videos are all open-captioned--no special equipment is required for viewing.
Source: Described and Captioned Media Program
National Association of the Deaf
4211 Church Street Ext.
Roebuck, SC 29376
Phone: 1-800-237-6213
Fax: 1-800-538-5636
World Wide Web URL: http://www.dcmp.org

FAMOUS PEOPLE

Leo Tolstoy
Leo Tolstoy was born into wealth in Russia in 1828. After joining the army in 1851, he began writing. The Crimean War awoke his sense of patriotism, and his stories made him popular. He married, opened a school, and ultimately renounced his way of life, feeling the deep inequities between the social classes. Though authorities tried to discredit him, he remained a well-respected writer until his death in 1910.

- Availability: Schools, libraries, and homeschoolers in the United States who serve the hearing impaired.
- Suggested Grade: 11-Adult
- Order Number: 12342
- Production Date: 1991
- Format: DVD
- Special Notes: Produced by ACG/United Learning.
- Terms: Sponsor pays all transportation costs. Return one week after receipt. Participation is limited to deaf or hard of hearing Americans, their parents, families, teachers, counselors, or others whose use would benefit a deaf or hard of hearing person. Only one person in the audience needs to be hearing impaired. You must register--which is free. These videos are all open-captioned--no special equipment is required for viewing.

    Source: Described and Captioned Media Program
    National Association of the Deaf
    4211 Church Street Ext.
    Roebuck, SC 29376
    Phone: 1-800-237-6213
    Fax: 1-800-538-5636
    World Wide Web URL: http://www.dcmp.org

Mario Benedetti
Examines one of the most prolific writers in Latin America. Mario Benedetti was among the Latin writers who looked to the Cuban revolution for inspiration. In this interview Benedetti talks about politics now that the Cuban revolution is viewed by many as a failure.

- Availability: Schools in the United States.
- Suggested Grade: 10-Adult
- Order Number: order by title
- Format: VHS videotape
- Terms: Borrower pays return postage. Return 14 days after receipt, via USPS including insurance. All borrowers must have a current lending agreement on file with the Outreach program. This agreement is available via the web site or may be requested via phone or fax.

    Source: Center for Latin American Studies
    University of Florida
    319 Grinter Hall
    P. O. Box 115530
    Gainesville, FL 32611-5530
    Phone: 1-352-392-0375
    Fax: 1-352-392-7682
    World Wide Web URL: http://www.latam.ufl.edu/outreach
    Email Address: maryr@ufl.edu

Maysa Matarazzo
Documentary about a Brazilian popular singer/composer of the '50s and '60s, Maysa Matarazzo.

- Availability: Schools, libraries, and nursing homes in the United States.
- Suggested Grade: 6-12
- Language: Portuguese
- Order Number: MUBRA3-video
- Format: VHS videotape
- Terms: Borrowers must have a User's Agreement on file with this source--available by mail or via the Internet. Return postage is paid by borrower; return 12 days after showing. Book at least three weeks in advance. All borrowers are limited to a total of ten items per semester.

    Source: Latin American Resource Center
    Stone Center for Latin American Studies
    Tulane University
    100 Jones Hall
    New Orleans, LA 70118
    Phone: 1-504-862-3143
    Fax: 1-504-865-6719
    World Wide Web URL: http://stonecenter.tulane.edu/pages/detail/48/Lending-Library
    Email Address: crcrts@tulane.edu

Ocean of Wisdom
An intimate portrait of the Dalai Lama in his private and public life; includes footage of the Buddhist leader in his private religious practice and daily routine.

- Availability: Schools, libraries, homeschoolers, and nursing homes in the southeastern United States.
- Suggested Grade: 7-12
- Order Number: order by title
- Production Date: 1986
- Format: VHS videotape
- Terms: Borrower pays return postage. Return 2 days after showing via United Parcel Service, insured. Book 2 weeks in advance.

    Source: Center for South Asian Studies
    University of Virginia
    Video Library Coordinator
    P. O. Box 400169, 110 Minor Hall
    Charlottesville, VA 22904-4169
    Phone: 1-434-924-8815
    Email Address: southasia@virginia.edu

Pablo Neruda Present
A documentary about the life and works of this Chilean Nobel Prize winner.

- Availability: Schools and libraries in Iowa, Illinois, Michigan, Minnesota, and Wisconsin.
- Suggested Grade: 6-12
- Order Number: LITCHILEPA11DVD
- Production Date: 2004
- Format: DVD
- Terms: Borrower pays return postage. Return 8 days after showing. Book 2 weeks in advance. Order may also be picked up for those near the Center.

All materials listed in this 2018-2019 edition are BRAND NEW!

FAMOUS PEOPLE

Source: Center for Latin American and Caribbean Studies
UW-Milwaukee
P. O. Box 413
Milwaukee, WI 53201
Phone: 1-414-229-5987
World Wide Web URL: http://www.uwm.edu/Dept/CLACS
Email Address: audvis@usm.edu

Picasso and His Time
Pablo Picasso--individualist, artist, sculptor, designer, and more--was born in Spain in 1881. By age 16, he received the first of many honors. Reviews the lifelong influence Spain had on him and his work. Showing many of his artistic creations, follows the development of this prolific genius through his pink and blue periods, surrealism, cubism, sculpture, and ceramics. Interviews his oldest daughter. Picasso died in 1973.
Availability: Schools, libraries, and homeschoolers in the United States who serve the hearing impaired.
Suggested Grade: 10-Adult
Order Number: 12365
Production Date: 1994
Format: DVD
Special Notes: Produced by Films for the Humanities & Sciences.
Terms: Sponsor pays all transportation costs. Return one week after receipt. Participation is limited to deaf or hard of hearing Americans, their parents, families, teachers, counselors, or others whose use would benefit a deaf or hard of hearing person. Only one person in the audience needs to be hearing impaired. You must register--which is free. These videos are all open-captioned--no special equipment is required for viewing.
Source: Described and Captioned Media Program
National Association of the Deaf
4211 Church Street Ext.
Roebuck, SC 29376
Phone: 1-800-237-6213
Fax: 1-800-538-5636
World Wide Web URL: http://www.dcmp.org

Rotund World of Botero, The
A tribute to the popular painter and sculptor.
Availability: Schools and libraries in Iowa, Illinois, Michigan, Minnesota, and Wisconsin.
Suggested Grade: 6-12
Order Number: ART/FOLCOLR74VHS
Format: VHS videotape
Terms: Borrower pays return postage. Return 8 days after showing. Book 2 weeks in advance. Order may also be picked up for those near the Center.
Source: Center for Latin American and Caribbean Studies
UW-Milwaukee
P. O. Box 413
Milwaukee, WI 53201
Phone: 1-414-229-5987
World Wide Web URL: http://www.uwm.edu/Dept/CLACS
Email Address: audvis@usm.edu

Sokui-no-Rei, The
Shows the history of Emperor Akihito, his leisure activities, and his love of the environment. The full accession ceremony is shown with glimpses of the parade and court banquet.
Availability: Schools, libraries, homeschoolers, and nursing homes in Connecticut (except Fairfield County), Maine, Massachusetts, New Hampshire, Rhode Island, and Vermont.
Suggested Grade: 4-12
Order Number: 542
Production Date: 1992
Format: VHS videotape
Terms: Borrower pays return postage, including insurance. Return two weeks after receipt.
Source: Consulate General of Japan, Boston
Federal Reserve Plaza, 14th Floor
600 Atlantic Avenue
Boston, MA 02210
Phone: 1-617-973-9772
Fax: 1-617-542-1329
World Wide Web URL:
http://www.boston.us.emb-japan.go.jp
Email Address: infocul@cgjbos.org

Ten Who Dared - Alexander von Humboldt
Reenactment of travels of this famous explorer and geographer throughout Latin America.
Availability: Schools, libraries, and nursing homes in the United States.
Suggested Grade: 6-12
Order Number: HLA13-video
Production Date: 1980
Format: VHS videotape
Terms: Borrowers must have a User's Agreement on file with this source--available by mail or via the Internet. Return postage is paid by borrower; return 12 days after showing. Book at least three weeks in advance. All borrowers are limited to a total of ten items per semester.
Source: Latin American Resource Center
Stone Center for Latin American Studies
Tulane University
100 Jones Hall
New Orleans, LA 70118
Phone: 1-504-862-3143
Fax: 1-504-865-6719
World Wide Web URL:
http://stonecenter.tulane.edu/pages/detail/48/
Lending-Library
Email Address: crcrts@tulane.edu

Ten Who Dared: Francisco Pizzarro
Reenactment of adventures of the infamous Spanish conqueror of the Inca Empire.
Availability: Schools, libraries, and nursing homes in the United States.
Suggested Grade: 6-12
Order Number: HPER1-video
Production Date: 1980

FAMOUS PEOPLE

Format: VHS videotape
Terms: Borrowers must have a User's Agreement on file with this source--available by mail or via the Internet. Return postage is paid by borrower; return 12 days after showing. Book at least three weeks in advance. All borrowers are limited to a total of ten items per semester.

Source: Latin American Resource Center
Stone Center for Latin American Studies
Tulane University
100 Jones Hall
New Orleans, LA 70118
Phone: 1-504-862-3143
Fax: 1-504-865-6719
World Wide Web URL: http://stonecenter.tulane.edu/pages/detail/48/Lending-Library
Email Address: crcrts@tulane.edu

FINE ARTS--ART AND HANDWORK

American Impressionist, An: William Merritt Chase at Shinnecock
Highlights Chase's years at Shinnecock, on Long Island, New York, where in 1891 the artist established the first important outdoor summer school of art in America.
Availability: Schools, community groups, homeschoolers and individuals in the United States.
Suggested Grade: 7-12
Order Number: VC 150
Format: VHS videotape
Special Notes: Programs may not be broadcast, reproduced, or transferred to another medium or format without special license from the National Gallery of Art. Closed captioned version also available as CC 150.
Terms: Borrower pays return postage. Return within 5 days of scheduled use. Book at least one month in advance, and provide alternate date. You will receive a confirmation noting our Shipping Date and your Return Date for each program. Large organizations that can provide programs to extensive audiences--such as school systems, instructional resource centers, museums, libraries, and public and instructional television stations--can arrange an Affiliate Loan for three years, with subsequent renewal to provide their audiences more immediate access to these free-loan extension programs.
Source: National Gallery of Art
Department of Education Resources
2000B South Club Drive
Landover, MD 20785
Phone: 1-202-842-6280
Fax: 1-202-842-6937
World Wide Web URL:
http://www.nga.gov/education/classroom/loanfinder/
Email Address: EdResources@nga.gov

Ancient Chinese Paintings
Introducing the unique concepts and character of Chinese painting, this video presents a number of the finest works from the collection of the National Palace Museum in Taipei, Taiwan.
Availability: Schools, libraries, and nursing homes in the United States and Canada.
Suggested Grade: 6-Adult
Order Number: CV008
Format: VHS videotape
Terms: Borrower pays return postage. Return with 14 days after scheduled showing, via UPS or U. S. Mail. All requests must included an educational institution affiliation, a current address, and phone number. Order through web site only.
Source: Cornell University East Asia Program
World Wide Web URL:
http://eap.einaudi.cornell.edu/lending_library
Email Address: east_asia1@cornell.edu

Animation in the Classroom
Two artists explore simple ways to create animation without a camera. They demonstrate how to make early animation devices, including the thaumatrope, phenakistoscope, and zoetrope. Explaining "persistence of vision" as the eye's ability to blend images together, they show flip books and offer many helpful hints and suggestions for successful classroom animation. Brief summary at the end.
Availability: Schools, libraries, and homeschoolers in the United States who serve the hearing impaired.
Suggested Grade: 4-10
Order Number: 12376
Format: DVD
Special Notes: Produced by Crystal Productions.
Terms: Sponsor pays all transportation costs. Return one week after receipt. Participation is limited to deaf or hard of hearing Americans, their parents, families, teachers, counselors, or others whose use would benefit a deaf or hard of hearing person. Only one person in the audience needs to be hearing impaired. You must register--which is free. These videos are all open-captioned--no special equipment is required for viewing.
Source: Described and Captioned Media Program
National Association of the Deaf
4211 Church Street Ext.
Roebuck, SC 29376
Phone: 1-800-237-6213
Fax: 1-800-538-5636
World Wide Web URL: http://www.dcmp.org

Art and Meaning of Ikebana, The
The significance of Ikebana and the underlying thought and emotion of this unique art are shown through explanations of its historical development, theory, practice, and its relationship to modern daily life.
Availability: Schools, libraries, homeschoolers, and nursing homes in Arizona and California (zipcodes beginning 900-931 and 935).
Suggested Grade: 4-Adult
Order Number: order by title
Production Date: 1972
Format: VHS videotape
Terms: Borrower pays postage both ways; you may call the number below to learn how much postage costs. Return within two weeks of date borrowed. An individual may borrow 2 items at one time. For non-profit and educational use only.
Source: Consulate General of Japan, Los Angeles
350 South Grand Avenue, Suite 1700
Los Angeles, CA 90071-3459
Phone: 1-213-617-6700
Fax: 1-213-617-6727
World Wide Web URL: http://www.la.us.emb-japan.go.jp

Art and Revolution in Mexico
Abstract documentary deals with the art of the Mexican Revolution.
Availability: Schools and libraries in Iowa, Illinois, Michigan, Minnesota, and Wisconsin.
Suggested Grade: 6-12
Order Number: ART/FOLMEXAR7VHS
Production Date: 1982

All materials listed in this 2018-2019 edition are BRAND NEW!

FINE ARTS--ART AND HANDWORK

Format: VHS videotape
Terms: Borrower pays return postage. Return 8 days after showing. Book 2 weeks in advance. Order may also be picked up for those near the Center.
Source: Center for Latin American and Caribbean Studies
UW-Milwaukee
P. O. Box 413
Milwaukee, WI 53201
Phone: 1-414-229-5987
World Wide Web URL: http://www.uwm.edu/Dept/CLACS
Email Address: audvis@usm.edu

Art From Asia

Includes four programs made in conjunction with special exhibits on the art and cultures of Cambodia, China, Indonesia and Japan: Toyond the Yellow River: Recent Discoveries from Ancient China (20 minutes); Art of Indonesia (28 minutes); Sacred Art of Angkor (18 minutes); and, Daimyo (28 minutes).
Availability: Schools, community groups, homeschoolers and individuals in the United States.
Suggested Grade: 7-12
Order Number: DV334
Format: DVD
Terms: Borrower pays return postage. Return within 5 days of scheduled use. Book at least one month in advance, and provide alternate date. You will receive a confirmation noting our Shipping Date and your Return Date for each program. Large organizations that can provide programs to extensive audiences--such as school systems, instructional resource centers, museums, libraries, and public and instructional television stations--can arrange an Affiliate Loan for three years, with subsequent renewal to provide their audiences more immediate access to these free-loan extension programs.
Source: National Gallery of Art
Department of Education Resources
2000B South Club Drive
Landover, MD 20785
Phone: 1-202-842-6280
Fax: 1-202-842-6937
World Wide Web URL:
http://www.nga.gov/education/classroom/loanfinder/
Email Address: EdResources@nga.gov

Art: Ikebana--Flower Arrangement

Ikebana probably developed from the religious practice of making offerings of flowers to the Buddha. Today, it has an important role in modern life but still maintains its spiritual roots. This program presents a number of the basic forms of Ikebana.
Availability: Schools, libraries, homeschoolers, and nursing homes in OREGON AND SOUTHERN IDAHO ONLY. Please make requests via the web site.
Suggested Grade: 6-Adult
Order Number: 213
Production Date: 1985
Format: VHS videotape
Terms: Borrower pays return postage. Return within three weeks after scheduled showing date. Book one month in advance if possible. Rewind the video and wrap securely for return. Be certain to indicate video number, date needed, name of your organization, and address to which video should be sent, along with phone number. Audience report enclosed with the video must be completed and returned.
Source: Consulate General of Japan, Oregon
Attn: Tamara, Video Library
1300 S. W. Fifth Avenue, Suite 2700
Portland, OR 97201
Phone: 1-503-221-1811, ext. 17
World Wide Web URL:
http://www.portland.us.emb-japan.go.jp/en/index.html
Email Address: tamara@cgjpdx.org

Art of Haiti, The

Juxtaposes shots of contemporary Haiti with radiance of Haitian art. Examines the co-existence of Christian and voodoo beliefs.
Availability: Schools and libraries in Iowa, Illinois, Michigan, Minnesota, and Wisconsin.
Suggested Grade: 6-12
Order Number: ART/FOLHAIAR7VHS
Production Date: 1982
Format: VHS videotape
Terms: Borrower pays return postage. Return 8 days after showing. Book 2 weeks in advance. Order may also be picked up for those near the Center.
Source: Center for Latin American and Caribbean Studies
UW-Milwaukee
P. O. Box 413
Milwaukee, WI 53201
Phone: 1-414-229-5987
World Wide Web URL: http://www.uwm.edu/Dept/CLACS
Email Address: audvis@usm.edu

Art of Haiti, The

Juxtaposes shots of contemporary Haiti with radiance of Haitian art. Examines the co-existence of Christian and voodoo beliefs.
Availability: Schools, libraries, and nursing homes in the United States.
Suggested Grade: 6-12
Order Number: AMHAI2-video
Production Date: 1983
Format: VHS videotape
Terms: Borrowers must have a User's Agreement on file with this source--available by mail or via the Internet. Return postage is paid by borrower; return 12 days after showing. Book at least three weeks in advance. All borrowers are limited to a total of ten items per semester.
Source: Latin American Resource Center
Stone Center for Latin American Studies
Tulane University
100 Jones Hall
New Orleans, LA 70118
Phone: 1-504-862-3143

All materials listed in this 2018-2019 edition are BRAND NEW!

FINE ARTS--ART AND HANDWORK

Fax: 1-504-865-6719
World Wide Web URL: http://stonecenter.tulane.edu/pages/detail/48/Lending-Library
Email Address: crcrts@tulane.edu

Art of Romare Bearden, The
Narrated by Morgan Freeman with readings by Danny Glover, this film traces Bearden's career using new and archival footage to demonstrate the artistic impact of his memories and art historical models.
Availability:	Schools, community groups, homeschoolers and individuals in the United States.
Suggested Grade:	7-12
Order Number:	VC 170
Format:	VHS videotape
Special Notes:	Programs may not be broadcast, reproduced, or transferred to another medium or format without special license from the National Gallery of Art. Closed captioned version also available as CC 170.
Terms:	Borrower pays return postage. Return within 5 days of scheduled use. Book at least one month in advance, and provide alternate date. You will receive a confirmation noting our Shipping Date and your Return Date for each program. Large organizations that can provide programs to extensive audiences--such as school systems, instructional resource centers, museums, libraries, and public and instructional television stations--can arrange an Affiliate Loan for three years, with subsequent renewal to provide their audiences more immediate access to these free-loan extension programs.

Source: National Gallery of Art
Department of Education Resources
2000B South Club Drive
Landover, MD 20785
Phone: 1-202-842-6280
Fax: 1-202-842-6937
World Wide Web URL:
http://www.nga.gov/education/classroom/loanfinder/
Email Address: EdResources@nga.gov

Awareness Series: American Art
Short, evocative studies of the works of major artists represented in the collections of the National Gallery of Art: Copley, Catlin, Cassatt, and American Native painters. Programs are not intended as definitive studies of these artists; rather, each is designed as a starting point for group discussion of the art and artist. Segments may be used independently, in any order or combination.
Availability:	Schools, community groups, homeschoolers and individuals in the United States.
Suggested Grade:	7-12
Order Number:	VC 125
Format:	VHS videotape
Special Notes:	Programs may not be broadcast, reproduced, or transferred to another medium or format without special license from the National Gallery of Art. Closed captioned version also available as CC 125.
Terms:	Borrower pays return postage. Return within 5 days of scheduled use. Book at least one month in advance, and provide alternate date. You will receive a confirmation noting our Shipping Date and your Return Date for each program. Large organizations that can provide programs to extensive audiences--such as school systems, instructional resource centers, museums, libraries, and public and instructional television stations--can arrange an Affiliate Loan for three years, with subsequent renewal to provide their audiences more immediate access to these free-loan extension programs.

Source: National Gallery of Art
Department of Education Resources
2000B South Club Drive
Landover, MD 20785
Phone: 1-202-842-6280
Fax: 1-202-842-6937
World Wide Web URL:
http://www.nga.gov/education/classroom/loanfinder/
Email Address: EdResources@nga.gov

Awareness Series: Old Masters
Short, evocative studies of the works of major artists represented in the collections of the National Gallery of Art: Rembrandt, Rubens, El Greco, Fragonard, Goya, Blake, and Turner. Programs are not intended as definitive studies of these artists; rather, each is designed as a starting point for group discussion of the art and artist. Segments may be used independently, in any order or combination.
Availability:	Schools, community groups, homeschoolers and individuals in the United States.
Suggested Grade:	7-12
Order Number:	VC 115
Format:	VHS videotape
Special Notes:	Programs may not be broadcast, reproduced, or transferred to another medium or format without special license from the National Gallery of Art. Closed captioned version also available as CC 115.
Terms:	Borrower pays return postage. Return within 5 days of scheduled use. Book at least one month in advance, and provide alternate date. You will receive a confirmation noting our Shipping Date and your Return Date for each program. Large organizations that can provide programs to extensive audiences--such as school systems, instructional resource centers, museums, libraries, and public and instructional television stations--can arrange an Affiliate Loan for three years, with subsequent renewal to provide their audiences more immediate access to these free-loan extension programs.

Source: National Gallery of Art
Department of Education Resources
2000B South Club Drive
Landover, MD 20785
Phone: 1-202-842-6280
Fax: 1-202-842-6937
World Wide Web URL:
http://www.nga.gov/education/classroom/loanfinder/
Email Address: EdResources@nga.gov

FINE ARTS--ART AND HANDWORK

Beauty of Famous Paintings In the National Palace Museum, The
You'll come to appreciate 22 famous paintings from the National Palace Museum through five categories- brushstroke and ink, the collaboration of painting-calligraphy-poetry, color, the idea of creation, and seals and inscriptions.
- Availability: Schools, libraries, and nursing homes in the United States and Canada.
- Suggested Grade: All ages
- Languages: English, Chinese, and Japanese together
- Order Number: CD015
- Format: DVD
- Terms: Borrower pays return postage. Return with 14 days after scheduled showing, via UPS or U. S. Mail. All requests must included an educational institution affiliation, a current address, and phone number. Order through web site only.
- Source: **Cornell University East Asia Program**
  World Wide Web URL:
  http://eap.einaudi.cornell.edu/lending_library
  Email Address: east_asia1@cornell.edu

Cairo: 1001 Years of Art and Architecture
Divided into four sections, this presentation offers an introduction to the art and architecture of the medieval core of Cairo.
- Availability: Schools, libraries, homeschoolers, and nursing homes in the United States.
- Suggested Grade: 7-12
- Order Number: order by title
- Production Date: 1998
- Format: VHS videotape
- Terms: Borrower pays return postage via any carrier with $400 insurance per parcel. Videos are loaned for 14 days; may be retained longer if requested in advance. Borrowers must complete a lending agreement.
- Source: **Center for Middle Eastern Studies**
  Outreach Coordinator
  University of Texas at Austin
  1 University Station, F9400
  Austin, TX 78712-0527
  World Wide Web URL:
  http://www.utexas.edu/cola/depts/mes/center/outreach/library-catalog.php
  Email Address: crose@mail.utexas.edu

Cartoon Magic With Fran
Demonstrates step by step how to create cartoon figures. Also gives ideas for ways to use these figures in greeting cards, and others.
- Availability: Schools, libraries, and homeschoolers in the United States who serve the hearing impaired.
- Suggested Grade: All ages
- Order Number: 13209
- Production Date: 1996
- Format: DVD
- Terms: Sponsor pays all transportation costs. Return one week after receipt. Participation is limited to deaf or hard of hearing Americans, their parents, families, teachers, counselors, or others whose use would benefit a deaf or hard of hearing person. Only one person in the audience needs to be hearing impaired. You must register--which is free. These videos are all open-captioned--no special equipment is required for viewing.
- Source: **Described and Captioned Media Program**
  National Association of the Deaf
  4211 Church Street Ext.
  Roebuck, SC 29376
  Phone: 1-800-237-6213
  Fax: 1-800-538-5636
  World Wide Web URL: http://www.dcmp.org

Ceramics: Basic Throwing Skills with Alleghany Meadows
Learn how to make a cylinder and a bowl out of clay.
- Availability: Schools, libraries, and homeschoolers in the United States who serve the hearing impaired.
- Suggested Grade: Adult
- Order Number: 11694
- Production Date: 2001
- Format: DVD
- Special Notes: Also available as live streaming video over the Internet.
- Terms: Sponsor pays all transportation costs. Return one week after receipt. Participation is limited to deaf or hard of hearing Americans, their parents, families, teachers, counselors, or others whose use would benefit a deaf or hard of hearing person. Only one person in the audience needs to be hearing impaired. You must register--which is free. These videos are all open-captioned--no special equipment is required for viewing.
- Source: **Described and Captioned Media Program**
  National Association of the Deaf
  4211 Church Street Ext.
  Roebuck, SC 29376
  Phone: 1-800-237-6213
  Fax: 1-800-538-5636
  World Wide Web URL: http://www.dcmp.org

Ceramics Handbuilding: Pinch and Coil Construction with Mollie Favour
Shows how to create ceramic pinch pots and coil pots.
- Availability: Schools, libraries, and homeschoolers in the United States who serve the hearing impaired.
- Suggested Grade: 9-Adult
- Order Number: 10783
- Production Date: 1999
- Format: DVD
- Special Notes: Also available as live streaming video over the Internet.
- Terms: Sponsor pays all transportation costs. Return one week after receipt. Participation is limited to deaf or hard of hearing Americans, their parents, families, teachers, counselors, or others whose use would benefit a deaf or hard of hearing person. Only one person in the audience needs to be hearing impaired. You must register--which

All materials listed in this 2018-2019 edition are BRAND NEW!

FINE ARTS--ART AND HANDWORK

is free. These videos are all open-captioned--no special equipment is required for viewing.
Source: Described and Captioned Media Program
National Association of the Deaf
4211 Church Street Ext.
Roebuck, SC 29376
Phone: 1-800-237-6213
Fax: 1-800-538-5636
World Wide Web URL: http://www.dcmp.org

Chancay, the Forgotten Art
Famous pre-Columbian ceramics from Peru.
Availability: Schools, libraries, and nursing homes in the United States.
Suggested Grade: 6-12
Order Number: APPER1-video
Production Date: 1970
Format: VHS videotape
Terms: Borrowers must have a User's Agreement on file with this source--available by mail or via the Internet. Return postage is paid by borrower; return 12 days after showing. Book at least three weeks in advance. All borrowers are limited to a total of ten items per semester.
Source: Latin American Resource Center
Stone Center for Latin American Studies
Tulane University
100 Jones Hall
New Orleans, LA 70118
Phone: 1-504-862-3143
Fax: 1-504-865-6719
World Wide Web URL: http://stonecenter.tulane.edu/pages/detail/48/Lending-Library
Email Address: crcrts@tulane.edu

Chinese Folk Arts
Introduces shadow puppetry, silk embroidery, paper cutting, kite making and flying, lanterns, hand puppetry, and dragon and lion dances.
Availability: Schools, libraries, and nursing homes in the United States and Canada.
Suggested Grade: 6-Adult
Order Number: CV009
Format: VHS videotape
Terms: Borrower pays return postage. Return with 14 days after scheduled showing, via UPS or U. S. Mail. All requests must included an educational institution affiliation, a current address, and phone number. Order through web site only.
Source: Cornell University East Asia Program
World Wide Web URL:
http://eap.einaudi.cornell.edu/lending_library
Email Address: east_asia1@cornell.edu

Christmas Story in Art, The
The story of Christ from the Annunciation to the flight into Egypt is presented in paintings by Italian and Flemish masters of the Renaissance. Fine music accompanies the narrative which makes the presentation of the Christmas story even more beautiful.

Availability: Schools, community groups, homeschoolers and individuals in the United States.
Suggested Grade: 7-12
Order Number: VC 012
Format: VHS videotape
Special Notes: Programs may not be broadcast, reproduced, or transferred to another medium or format without special license from the National Gallery of Art. Closed captioned version also available as CC 012.
Terms: Borrower pays return postage. Return within 5 days of scheduled use. Book at least one month in advance, and provide alternate date. You will receive a confirmation noting our Shipping Date and your Return Date for each program. Large organizations that can provide programs to extensive audiences--such as school systems, instructional resource centers, museums, libraries, and public and instructional television stations--can arrange an Affiliate Loan for three years, with subsequent renewal to provide their audiences more immediate access to these free-loan extension programs.
Source: National Gallery of Art
Department of Education Resources
2000B South Club Drive
Landover, MD 20785
Phone: 1-202-842-6280
Fax: 1-202-842-6937
World Wide Web URL:
http://www.nga.gov/education/classroom/loanfinder/
Email Address: EdResources@nga.gov

City of Cathay, A
One of China's greatest art pieces is a 37-foot long scroll, the original of which dates back to the Sung dynasty (960-1279). While opening the scroll close-up to the viewer, the narrator of this video describes the everyday scenes in the ancient city of Cathay depicted by the more than 4,000 human figures, each only half an inch tall.
Availability: Schools, libraries, and nursing homes in the United States and Canada.
Suggested Grade: 9-Adult
Order Number: CV013
Format: VHS videotape
Terms: Borrower pays return postage. Return with 14 days after scheduled showing, via UPS or U. S. Mail. All requests must included an educational institution affiliation, a current address, and phone number. Order through web site only.
Source: Cornell University East Asia Program
World Wide Web URL:
http://eap.einaudi.cornell.edu/lending_library
Email Address: east_asia1@cornell.edu

Courtly Art of Ancient Maya
Presents the culture and society that created the most advanced civilization of ancient Mesoamerica. Filmed in the state of Chiapas in southern Mexico, the program focuses on the courts of the Maya kingdoms of Palenque, Tonina, and Bonampak.

FINE ARTS--ART AND HANDWORK

Availability: Schools, community groups, homeschoolers and individuals in the United States.
Suggested Grade: 7-12
Order Number: VC 171
Format: VHS videotape
Special Notes: Programs may not be broadcast, reproduced, or transferred to another medium or format without special license from the National Gallery of Art. Closed captioned version also available as CC 171.
Terms: Borrower pays return postage. Return within 5 days of scheduled use. Book at least one month in advance, and provide alternate date. You will receive a confirmation noting our Shipping Date and your Return Date for each program. Large organizations that can provide programs to extensive audiences--such as school systems, instructional resource centers, museums, libraries, and public and instructional television stations--can arrange an Affiliate Loan for three years, with subsequent renewal to provide their audiences more immediate access to these free-loan extension programs.
   Source: National Gallery of Art
   Department of Education Resources
   2000B South Club Drive
   Landover, MD 20785
   Phone: 1-202-842-6280
   Fax: 1-202-842-6937
   World Wide Web URL:
   http://www.nga.gov/education/classroom/loanfinder/
   Email Address: EdResources@nga.gov

Crafting in the USA: Appalachia Region
Shows how to create five crafts that represent this region.
Availability: Schools, libraries, and homeschoolers in the United States who serve the hearing impaired.
Suggested Grade: 5-12
Order Number: 11827
Production Date: 2003
Format: DVD
Special Notes: Also available as live streaming video over the Internet.
Terms: Sponsor pays all transportation costs. Return one week after receipt. Participation is limited to deaf or hard of hearing Americans, their parents, families, teachers, counselors, or others whose use would benefit a deaf or hard of hearing person. Only one person in the audience needs to be hearing impaired. You must register--which is free. These videos are all open-captioned--no special equipment is required for viewing.
   Source: Described and Captioned Media Program
   National Association of the Deaf
   4211 Church Street Ext.
   Roebuck, SC 29376
   Phone: 1-800-237-6213
   Fax: 1-800-538-5636
   World Wide Web URL: http://www.dcmp.org

Crafting in the USA: Folklore
Learn to make five easy crafts that represent some of the folklore and tall tale heroes of the United States.
Availability: Schools, libraries, and homeschoolers in the United States who serve the hearing impaired.
Suggested Grade: 5-12
Order Number: 11141
Production Date: 2003
Format: DVD
Special Notes: Also available as live streaming video over the Internet.
Terms: Sponsor pays all transportation costs. Return one week after receipt. Participation is limited to deaf or hard of hearing Americans, their parents, families, teachers, counselors, or others whose use would benefit a deaf or hard of hearing person. Only one person in the audience needs to be hearing impaired. You must register--which is free. These videos are all open-captioned--no special equipment is required for viewing.
   Source: Described and Captioned Media Program
   National Association of the Deaf
   4211 Church Street Ext.
   Roebuck, SC 29376
   Phone: 1-800-237-6213
   Fax: 1-800-538-5636
   World Wide Web URL: http://www.dcmp.org

Crafting in the USA: Hawaii
Enjoy making six crafts that represent the cultures and products of Hawaii.
Availability: Schools, libraries, and homeschoolers in the United States who serve the hearing impaired.
Suggested Grade: 5-12
Order Number: 11783
Production Date: 2003
Format: DVD
Special Notes: Also available as live streaming video over the Internet.
Terms: Sponsor pays all transportation costs. Return one week after receipt. Participation is limited to deaf or hard of hearing Americans, their parents, families, teachers, counselors, or others whose use would benefit a deaf or hard of hearing person. Only one person in the audience needs to be hearing impaired. You must register--which is free. These videos are all open-captioned--no special equipment is required for viewing.
   Source: Described and Captioned Media Program
   National Association of the Deaf
   4211 Church Street Ext.
   Roebuck, SC 29376
   Phone: 1-800-237-6213
   Fax: 1-800-538-5636
   World Wide Web URL: http://www.dcmp.org

Crafts in Less than 10 Minutes Vol. 1
Demonstrates step by step how to make numerous craft items which take very little time-bookmarks, garden gloves, lacy sun catchers, paper hearts, chenille bow, decorator mothballs, key ornaments, wine bottle covers, and oatmeal soothers.
Availability: Schools, libraries, and homeschoolers in the United States who serve the hearing impaired.

All materials listed in this 2018-2019 edition are BRAND NEW!

FINE ARTS--ART AND HANDWORK

Suggested Grade: All ages
Order Number: 13323
Format: DVD
Special Notes: Also available as live streaming video over the Internet.
Terms: Sponsor pays all transportation costs. Return one week after receipt. Participation is limited to deaf or hard of hearing Americans, their parents, families, teachers, counselors, or others whose use would benefit a deaf or hard of hearing person. Only one person in the audience needs to be hearing impaired. You must register--which is free. These videos are all open-captioned--no special equipment is required for viewing.
Source: Described and Captioned Media Program
National Association of the Deaf
4211 Church Street Ext.
Roebuck, SC 29376
Phone: 1-800-237-6213
Fax: 1-800-538-5636
World Wide Web URL: http://www.dcmp.org

Creating Abstract Art
Abstract art: taking a recognizable object, making it as simple as possible, and distorting it to fit the artist's purpose. Step-by-step, artist Gerald Brommer shows how to create abstraction, using five methods: simplification of shapes, distortion, overlapping and fracturing shapes, vertical displacement, and contour continuation.
Availability: Schools, libraries, and homeschoolers in the United States who serve the hearing impaired.
Suggested Grade: 6-Adult
Order Number: 12986
Production Date: 1994
Format: DVD
Special Notes: Produced by Crystal Productions.
Terms: Sponsor pays all transportation costs. Return one week after receipt. Participation is limited to deaf or hard of hearing Americans, their parents, families, teachers, counselors, or others whose use would benefit a deaf or hard of hearing person. Only one person in the audience needs to be hearing impaired. You must register--which is free. These videos are all open-captioned--no special equipment is required for viewing.
Source: Described and Captioned Media Program
National Association of the Deaf
4211 Church Street Ext.
Roebuck, SC 29376
Phone: 1-800-237-6213
Fax: 1-800-538-5636
World Wide Web URL: http://www.dcmp.org

Diego Rivera in the United States
Shows Rivera's work in Detroit, San Francisco, and his controversial mural at the Rockefeller Center in New York.
Availability: Schools, libraries, and nursing homes in the United States.
Suggested Grade: 6-12
Order Number: AMMEX18-video
Production Date: 1988
Format: VHS videotape
Terms: Borrowers must have a User's Agreement on file with this source--available by mail or via the Internet. Return postage is paid by borrower; return 12 days after showing. Book at least three weeks in advance. All borrowers are limited to a total of ten items per semester.
Source: Latin American Resource Center
Stone Center for Latin American Studies
Tulane University
100 Jones Hall
New Orleans, LA 70118
Phone: 1-504-862-3143
Fax: 1-504-865-6719
World Wide Web URL: http://stonecenter.tulane.edu/pages/detail/48/Lending-Library
Email Address: crcrts@tulane.edu

Doll Master and His Apprentice, The
Features the traditional Japanese art form of doll making by a master doll maker.
Availability: Schools, libraries, and nursing homes in Oklahoma and Texas.
Suggested Grade: All ages
Order Number: I3
Production Date: 1985
Format: VHS videotape
Terms: Materials must be picked up in person. Under special circumstances, you may be able to have them shipped to you at your own expense (call for further details). Return within two weeks after scheduled showing. Videos must be registered with the U. S. Postal Service or returned by Priority Mail, Federal Express, or other registered shipping service.
Source: Consulate General of Japan, Houston
Cultural Affairs and Information Section
909 Fannin Street, Suite 3000
Houston, TX 77010
Phone: 1-713-652-2977
Fax: 1-713-651-7822
World Wide Web URL:
http://www.houston.us.emb-japan.go.jp/en/culture/page1.htm
Email Address: info@cgjhouston.org

Doll Master and His Apprentice, The
Features the traditional Japanese art form of doll making by a master doll maker.
Availability: Schools, libraries, homeschoolers, and nursing homes in Arizona and California (zipcodes beginning 900-931 and 935).
Suggested Grade: All ages
Order Number: 058
Production Date: 1985
Format: VHS videotape
Terms: Borrower pays postage both ways; you may call the number below to learn how much postage costs. Return within two weeks of date borrowed. An individual may borrow 2 items at one time. For non-profit and educational use only.

All materials listed in this 2018-2019 edition are BRAND NEW!

FINE ARTS--ART AND HANDWORK

Source: Consulate General of Japan, Los Angeles
350 South Grand Avenue, Suite 1700
Los Angeles, CA 90071-3459
Phone: 1-213-617-6700
Fax: 1-213-617-6727
World Wide Web URL: http://www.la.us.emb-japan.go.jp

Drawing With Pastels

Artist Gail Price demonstrates the variety of pastels, including hard, soft, oil, iridescent, and pencil. She explains their properties and shows how they enhance a wide selection of subjects and backgrounds. Close-up photography allows a good view of drawing techniques.

- Availability: Schools, libraries, and homeschoolers in the United States who serve the hearing impaired.
- Suggested Grade: 4-Adult
- Order Number: 12339
- Production Date: 1994
- Format: DVD
- Special Notes: Produced by Crystal Productions.
- Terms: Sponsor pays all transportation costs. Return one week after receipt. Participation is limited to deaf or hard of hearing Americans, their parents, families, teachers, counselors, or others whose use would benefit a deaf or hard of hearing person. Only one person in the audience needs to be hearing impaired. You must register--which is free. These videos are all open-captioned--no special equipment is required for viewing.

Source: Described and Captioned Media Program
National Association of the Deaf
4211 Church Street Ext.
Roebuck, SC 29376
Phone: 1-800-237-6213
Fax: 1-800-538-5636
World Wide Web URL: http://www.dcmp.org

Dream Window: Reflections on the Japanese Garden

Reveals the rich beauty and artistry of the gardens of Japan which are truly works of art.

- Availability: Schools, libraries, homeschoolers, and nursing homes in Connecticut (except Fairfield County), Maine, Massachusetts, New Hampshire, Rhode Island, and Vermont.
- Suggested Grade: 4-12
- Order Number: 467
- Format: VHS videotape
- Special Notes: Part of the "Nippon the Land and Its People Series."
- Terms: Borrower pays return postage, including insurance. Return two weeks after receipt.

Source: Consulate General of Japan, Boston
Federal Reserve Plaza, 14th Floor
600 Atlantic Avenue
Boston, MA 02210
Phone: 1-617-973-9772
Fax: 1-617-542-1329
World Wide Web URL:
http://www.boston.us.emb-japan.go.jp
Email Address: infocul@cgjbos.org

From Impressionism to Modernism: The Chester Dale Collection

A shrewd business man, Chester Dale (1883-1962) started out as a Wall Street messenger in the early years of the twentieth century. By the mid 1920s, he had earned the fortune that enabled him and his wife Maud to assemble one of the finest art collections in America. Now you can see it.

- Availability: Schools, community groups, homeschoolers and individuals in the United States.
- Suggested Grade: 7-12
- Order Number: DV214
- Format: DVD
- Special Notes: Programs may not be broadcast, reproduced, or transferred to another medium or format without special license from the National Gallery of Art. Closed captioned version also available as CC 152.
- Terms: Borrower pays return postage. Return within 5 days of scheduled use. Book at least one month in advance, and provide alternate date. You will receive a confirmation noting our Shipping Date and your Return Date for each program. Large organizations that can provide programs to extensive audiences--such as school systems, instructional resource centers, museums, libraries, and public and instructional television stations--can arrange an Affiliate Loan for three years, with subsequent renewal to provide their audiences more immediate access to these free-loan extension programs.

Source: National Gallery of Art
Department of Education Resources
2000B South Club Drive
Landover, MD 20785
Phone: 1-202-842-6280
Fax: 1-202-842-6937
World Wide Web URL:
http://www.nga.gov/education/classroom/loanfinder/
Email Address: EdResources@nga.gov

Ginevra's Story

Ginevra de Benci, the first known portrait by Leonardo da Vinci, is both haunting and hypnotic. This film, narrated by Meryl Streep, unveils insights about the painting and about Ginevra and Leonardo.

- Availability: Schools, community groups, homeschoolers and individuals in the United States.
- Suggested Grade: 7-12
- Order Number: VC 201
- Format: VHS videotape
- Special Notes: Programs may not be broadcast, reproduced, or transferred to another medium or format without special license from the National Gallery of Art. Closed captioned version also available as CC 201.
- Terms: Borrower pays return postage. Return within 5 days of scheduled use. Book at least one month in advance, and provide alternate date. You will receive a confirmation noting our Shipping Date and your Return Date for each program. Large organizations that can provide programs to extensive audiences--such as school systems,

All materials listed in this 2018-2019 edition are BRAND NEW!

FINE ARTS--ART AND HANDWORK

instructional resource centers, museums, libraries, and public and instructional television stations--can arrange an Affiliate Loan for three years, with subsequent renewal to provide their audiences more immediate access to these free-loan extension programs.

Source: National Gallery of Art
Department of Education Resources
2000B South Club Drive
Landover, MD 20785
Phone: 1-202-842-6280
Fax: 1-202-842-6937
World Wide Web URL:
http://www.nga.gov/education/classroom/loanfinder/
Email Address: EdResources@nga.gov

Henri Rousseau: Jungles in Paris
Considers the art of this self-taught artist.

Availability:	Schools, community groups, homeschoolers and individuals in the United States.
Suggested Grade:	7-12
Order Number:	VC 173
Format:	VHS videotape
Terms:	Borrower pays return postage. Return within 5 days of scheduled use. Book at least one month in advance, and provide alternate date. You will receive a confirmation noting our Shipping Date and your Return Date for each program. Large organizations that can provide programs to extensive audiences--such as school systems, instructional resource centers, museums, libraries, and public and instructional television stations--can arrange an Affiliate Loan for three years, with subsequent renewal to provide their audiences more immediate access to these free-loan extension programs.

Source: National Gallery of Art
Department of Education Resources
2000B South Club Drive
Landover, MD 20785
Phone: 1-202-842-6280
Fax: 1-202-842-6937
World Wide Web URL:
http://www.nga.gov/education/classroom/loanfinder/
Email Address: EdResources@nga.gov

Images of Kingdoms
Analyzes the way photographers interpreted their world in the nineteenth century.

Availability:	Schools and libraries in Iowa, Illinois, Michigan, Minnesota, and Wisconsin.
Suggested Grade:	6-12
Order Number:	order by title
Production Date:	1985
Format:	VHS videotape
Terms:	Borrower pays return postage. Return 8 days after showing. Book 2 weeks in advance. Order may also be picked up for those near the Center.

Source: Center for Latin American and Caribbean Studies
UW-Milwaukee
P. O. Box 413
Milwaukee, WI 53201
Phone: 1-414-229-5987
World Wide Web URL: http://www.uwm.edu/Dept/CLACS
Email Address: audvis@usm.edu

Introduction to European Art in the National Gallery of Art
Offers a brief art historical overview and an introduction to the art of Europe.

Availability:	Schools, community groups, homeschoolers and individuals in the United States.
Suggested Grade:	7-12
Order Number:	VC 162
Format:	VHS videotape
Special Notes:	Programs may not be broadcast, reproduced, or transferred to another medium or format without special license from the National Gallery of Art. Closed captioned version also available as CC 162.
Terms:	Borrower pays return postage. Return within 5 days of scheduled use. Book at least one month in advance, and provide alternate date. You will receive a confirmation noting our Shipping Date and your Return Date for each program. Large organizations that can provide programs to extensive audiences--such as school systems, instructional resource centers, museums, libraries, and public and instructional television stations--can arrange an Affiliate Loan for three years, with subsequent renewal to provide their audiences more immediate access to these free-loan extension programs.

Source: National Gallery of Art
Department of Education Resources
2000B South Club Drive
Landover, MD 20785
Phone: 1-202-842-6280
Fax: 1-202-842-6937
World Wide Web URL:
http://www.nga.gov/education/classroom/loanfinder/
Email Address: EdResources@nga.gov

James McNeill Whistler: His Etchings
The nineteenth-century painter, James McNeill Whistler, also worked in the etching medium during his long career. This program shows the changes in Whistler's art and in his etching style over the years. Ruth Fine, curator of prints and drawings at the National Gallery, provides narration, pointing out how the artist achieved different effects in his etchings by exploring ways of drawing and by experimenting with inking and printing techniques.

Availability:	Schools, community groups, homeschoolers and individuals in the United States.
Suggested Grade:	7-12
Order Number:	VC 149
Format:	VHS videotape
Special Notes:	Programs may not be broadcast, reproduced, or transferred to another medium or format without special license from the National Gallery of Art. Closed captioned version also available as CC 149.

FINE ARTS--ART AND HANDWORK

Terms: Borrower pays return postage. Return within 5 days of scheduled use. Book at least one month in advance, and provide alternate date. You will receive a confirmation noting our Shipping Date and your Return Date for each program. Large organizations that can provide programs to extensive audiences--such as school systems, instructional resource centers, museums, libraries, and public and instructional television stations--can arrange an Affiliate Loan for three years, with subsequent renewal to provide their audiences more immediate access to these free-loan extension programs.

Source: National Gallery of Art
Department of Education Resources
2000B South Club Drive
Landover, MD 20785
Phone: 1-202-842-6280
Fax: 1-202-842-6937
World Wide Web URL:
http://www.nga.gov/education/classroom/loanfinder/
Email Address: EdResources@nga.gov

James McNeill Whistler: The Lyrics of Art

The painter and printmaker, James McNeill Whistler, was one of the most controversial and fascinating personalities of the nineteenth century. This program follows his life and career in America, London, Paris, and Venice. From his early realist paintings to his nearly abstract "Nocturnes," Whistler developed an aesthetic of refinement and pure harmony that influenced twentieth century innovations in art.

Availability: Schools, community groups, homeschoolers and individuals in the United States.
Suggested Grade: 7-12
Order Number: VC 157
Format: VHS videotape
Special Notes: Programs may not be broadcast, reproduced, or transferred to another medium or format without special license from the National Gallery of Art. Closed captioned version also available as CC 157.
Terms: Borrower pays return postage. Return within 5 days of scheduled use. Book at least one month in advance, and provide alternate date. You will receive a confirmation noting our Shipping Date and your Return Date for each program. Large organizations that can provide programs to extensive audiences--such as school systems, instructional resource centers, museums, libraries, and public and instructional television stations--can arrange an Affiliate Loan for three years, with subsequent renewal to provide their audiences more immediate access to these free-loan extension programs.

Source: National Gallery of Art
Department of Education Resources,
2000B South Club Drive
Landover, MD 20785
Phone: 1-202-842-6280
Fax: 1-202-842-6937
World Wide Web URL:
http://www.nga.gov/education/classroom/loanfinder/
Email Address: EdResources@nga.gov

Japan Arts and Crafts

Four short video stories, each of which explores an art form which continues to be practiced in Japan today.

Availability: Schools, libraries, and nursing homes in Illinois, Indiana, Iowa, Kansas, Minnesota, Missouri, Nebraska, North Dakota, South Dakota, and Wisconsin.
Suggested Grade: 6-Adult
Order Number: 03102
Production Date: 1999
Format: VHS videotape
Terms: Borrower pays return postage by U. S. Mail, UPS, or Federal Express, including insurance for "original" videos. Write, call, fax, or e-mail to request an application. An application form MUST be sent in one month in advance but not more than six months in advance. Include alternate titles and dates if provider can substitute titles. Send a SASE with request if you require confirmation. Return immediately after scheduled showing date. Videos may not be copied or broadcast without permission from the producer of the video. Borrower is responsible if video is lost or damaged.

Source: Consulate General of Japan at Chicago
Japan Information Center
Library
737 North Michigan Avenue, Suite 1000
Chicago, IL 60611
Phone: 1-312-280-0430
Fax: 1-312-280-6883
World Wide Web URL:
http://www.chicago.us.emb-japan.go.jp/jic.html
Email Address: jicchicago@webkddi.com

Korean Treasures

Shows most well-known examples of architectural, graphic, and plastic arts of traditional Korea.

Availability: Schools, libraries, and nursing homes in the United States and Canada.
Suggested Grade: 6-Adult
Order Number: KV012
Format: VHS videotape
Terms: Borrower pays return postage. Return with 14 days after scheduled showing, via UPS or U. S. Mail. All requests must included an educational institution affiliation, a current address, and phone number. Order through web site only.

Source: Cornell University East Asia Program
World Wide Web URL:
http://eap.einaudi.cornell.edu/lending_library
Email Address: east_asia1@cornell.edu

Landscape Gardener

Shows the beautiful art of landscape gardens through the filming of the actual construction of one type of garden.

All materials listed in this 2018-2019 edition are BRAND NEW!

FINE ARTS--ART AND HANDWORK

Availability: Schools, libraries, homeschoolers, and nursing homes in Arizona and California (zipcodes beginning 900-931 and 935).
Suggested Grade: 4-Adult
Order Number: 070
Production Date: 1984
Format: VHS videotape
Terms: Borrower pays postage both ways; you may call the number below to learn how much postage costs. Return within two weeks of date borrowed. An individual may borrow 2 items at one time. For non-profit and educational use only.
    Source: Consulate General of Japan, Los Angeles
    350 South Grand Avenue, Suite 1700
    Los Angeles, CA 90071-3459
    Phone: 1-213-617-6700
    Fax: 1-213-617-6727
World Wide Web URL: http://www.la.us.emb-japan.go.jp

Landscapes of Frederic Edwin Church, The
Traces Church's career from his early studies in the Hudson River Valley with Thomas Cole, through the later years.
Availability: Schools, community groups, homeschoolers and individuals in the United States.
Suggested Grade: 7-12
Order Number: VC 151
Format: VHS videotape
Special Notes: Programs may not be broadcast, reproduced, or transferred to another medium or format without special license from the National Gallery of Art. Closed captioned version also available as CC 151.
Terms: Borrower pays return postage. Return within 5 days of scheduled use. Book at least one month in advance, and provide alternate date. You will receive a confirmation noting our Shipping Date and your Return Date for each program. Large organizations that can provide programs to extensive audiences--such as school systems, instructional resource centers, museums, libraries, and public and instructional television stations--can arrange an Affiliate Loan for three years, with subsequent renewal to provide their audiences more immediate access to these free-loan extension programs.
    Source: National Gallery of Art
    Department of Education Resources
    2000B South Club Drive
    Landover, MD 20785
    Phone: 1-202-842-6280
    Fax: 1-202-842-6937
    World Wide Web URL:
http://www.nga.gov/education/classroom/loanfinder/
    Email Address: EdResources@nga.gov

Latino Artists: Pushing Artistic Boundaries
Explores lives of Puerto Rican poets and a group of performing artists in East Los Angeles.
Availability: Schools, libraries, and nursing homes in the United States.
Suggested Grade: 6-12
Order Number: HISP67-video
Production Date: 1995
Format: VHS videotape
Terms: Borrowers must have a User's Agreement on file with this source--available by mail or via the Internet. Return postage is paid by borrower; return 12 days after showing. Book at least three weeks in advance. All borrowers are limited to a total of ten items per semester.
    Source: Latin American Resource Center
    Stone Center for Latin American Studies
    Tulane University
    100 Jones Hall
    New Orleans, LA 70118
    Phone: 1-504-862-3143
    Fax: 1-504-865-6719
World Wide Web URL: http://stonecenter.tulane.edu/pages/detail/48/Lending-Library
    Email Address: crcrts@tulane.edu

L.E.A.R.: League of Revolutionary Artists and Writers
The L.E.A.R. was formed in Mexico in 1934 to combat imperialism and fascism. Interviews interspersed with murals, paintings, and poems.
Availability: Schools and libraries in Iowa, Illinois, Michigan, Minnesota, and Wisconsin.
Suggested Grade: 6-12
Order Number: ART/FOLMEXL47VHS
Production Date: 1988
Format: VHS videotape
Terms: Borrower pays return postage. Return 8 days after showing. Book 2 weeks in advance. Order may also be picked up for those near the Center.
    Source: Center for Latin American and Caribbean Studies
    UW-Milwaukee
    P. O. Box 413
    Milwaukee, WI 53201
    Phone: 1-414-229-5987
World Wide Web URL: http://www.uwm.edu/Dept/CLACS
    Email Address: audvis@usm.edu

Leonardo: To Know How to See
The genius and accomplishments of the Renaissance artist-inventor Leonardo da Vinci are depicted in this program. His best-known paintings are shown, including the "Mona Lisa" and the National Gallery's "Ginevra de' Benci," and notebooks of his drawings are examined. The narrator, Sir John Gielgud, introduces the viewer to Leonardo's contemporaries and to the Italian countryside, which the artist observed so keenly.
Availability: Schools, community groups, homeschoolers and individuals in the United States.
Suggested Grade: 7-12
Order Number: VC 107
Format: VHS videotape
Special Notes: Programs may not be broadcast, reproduced, or transferred to another medium or format without special license from the National Gallery of Art. Closed captioned version also available as CC 107.

FINE ARTS--ART AND HANDWORK

Terms: Borrower pays return postage. Return within 5 days of scheduled use. Book at least one month in advance, and provide alternate date. You will receive a confirmation noting our Shipping Date and your Return Date for each program. Large organizations that can provide programs to extensive audiences--such as school systems, instructional resource centers, museums, libraries, and public and instructional television stations--can arrange an Affiliate Loan for three years, with subsequent renewal to provide their audiences more immediate access to these free-loan extension programs.

Source: National Gallery of Art
Department of Education Resources
2000B South Club Drive
Landover, MD 20785
Phone: 1-202-842-6280
Fax: 1-202-842-6937
World Wide Web URL:
http://www.nga.gov/education/classroom/loanfinder/
Email Address: EdResources@nga.gov

Linnea In Monet's Garden

Linnea visits Mr. Bloom who shares his book about Claude Monet and his paintings. Linnea loves his art and they decide to visit Monet's garden. Going first to Paris, they visit a museum where Linnea learns about impressionism. They travel to Giverny and discover the real places which inspired their favorite paintings. Mixes animation and live action. Based on the book by Lena Anderson and Christina Bjork.

Availability: Schools, libraries, and homeschoolers in the United States who serve the hearing impaired.
Suggested Grade: 4-9
Order Number: 12363
Format: DVD
Special Notes: Produced by First Run Features.
Terms: Sponsor pays all transportation costs. Return one week after receipt. Participation is limited to deaf or hard of hearing Americans, their parents, families, teachers, counselors, or others whose use would benefit a deaf or hard of hearing person. Only one person in the audience needs to be hearing impaired. You must register--which is free. These videos are all open-captioned--no special equipment is required for viewing.

Source: Described and Captioned Media Program
National Association of the Deaf
4211 Church Street Ext.
Roebuck, SC 29376
Phone: 1-800-237-6213
Fax: 1-800-538-5636
World Wide Web URL: http://www.dcmp.org

Los Murales de la Cuidad de Mexico: El Muro de las Celebraciones

A blend of political and art history, this program charts the evolution of Mexican muralism through the masterpieces that decorate landmarks in and around Mexico City and in the U.S.

Availability: Schools in the United States.
Suggested Grade: 9-Adult
Order Number: order by title
Production Date: 1998
Format: VHS videotape
Terms: Borrower pays return postage. Return 14 days after receipt, via USPS including insurance. All borrowers must have a current lending agreement on file with the Outreach program. This agreement is available via the web site or may be requested via phone or fax.

Source: Center for Latin American Studies
University of Florida
319 Grinter Hall, P. O. Box 115530
Gainesville, FL 32611-5530
Phone: 1-352-392-0375
Fax: 1-352-392-7682
World Wide Web URL: http://www.latam.ufl.edu/outreach
Email Address: maryr@ufl.edu

Martin Chambi and the Heirs of the Incas

Chambi's documentary photographs of Peruvian Indians make a political as well as artistic statement.

Availability: Schools and libraries in Iowa, Illinois, Michigan, Minnesota, and Wisconsin.
Suggested Grade: 6-12
Order Number: order by title
Production Date: 1986
Format: VHS videotape
Terms: Borrower pays return postage. Return 8 days after showing. Book 2 weeks in advance. Order may also be picked up for those near the Center.

Source: Center for Latin American and Caribbean Studies
UW-Milwaukee
P. O. Box 413
Milwaukee, WI 53201
Phone: 1-414-229-5987
World Wide Web URL: http://www.uwm.edu/Dept/CLACS
Email Address: audvis@usm.edu

Masterpieces of Chinese Painting and Calligraphy at the National Palace Museum

Offers a multimedia presentation that features 30 masterpieces of ancient Chinese painting and calligraphy chosen from "Annual Special Exhibition of Treasured Paintings and Calligraphic Works."

Availability: Schools, libraries, and nursing homes in the United States and Canada.
Suggested Grade: All ages
Order Number: CD014
Format: DVD
Terms: Borrower pays return postage. Return with 14 days after scheduled showing, via UPS or U. S. Mail. All requests must included an educational institution affiliation, a current address, and phone number. Order through web site only.

Source: Cornell University East Asia Program
World Wide Web URL:
http://eap.einaudi.cornell.edu/lending_library
Email Address: east_asia1@cornell.edu

All materials listed in this 2018-2019 edition are BRAND NEW!

FINE ARTS--ART AND HANDWORK

Meinung's Oiled Paper Umbrellas
Features craftspeople at work preparing the bamboo and paper from start to finish, in exquisite detail.
- Availability: Schools, libraries, and nursing homes in the United States and Canada.
- Suggested Grade: All ages
- Order Number: TV005
- Format: VHS videotape
- Terms: Borrower pays return postage. Return with 14 days after scheduled showing, via UPS or U. S. Mail. All requests must included an educational institution affiliation, a current address, and phone number. Order through web site only.
- Source: Cornell University East Asia Program
  World Wide Web URL:
  http://eap.einaudi.cornell.edu/lending_library
  Email Address: east_asia1@cornell.edu

National Gallery of Art, A Treasury of Masterpieces
J. Carter Brown, the National Gallery's director from 1969 to 1992, tells the fascinating story of the museum's beginnings and of its growth.
- Availability: Schools, community groups, homeschoolers and individuals in the United States.
- Suggested Grade: 7-12
- Order Number: VC 208
- Format: VHS videotape
- Special Notes: Programs may not be broadcast, reproduced, or transferred to another medium or format without special license from the National Gallery of Art. Closed captioned version also available as CC 208.
- Terms: Borrower pays return postage. Return within 5 days of scheduled use. Book at least one month in advance, and provide alternate date. You will receive a confirmation noting our Shipping Date and your Return Date for each program. Large organizations that can provide programs to extensive audiences--such as school systems, instructional resource centers, museums, libraries, and public and instructional television stations--can arrange an Affiliate Loan for three years, with subsequent renewal to provide their audiences more immediate access to these free-loan extension programs.
- Source: National Gallery of Art
  Department of Education Resources
  2000B South Club Drive
  Landover, MD 20785
  Phone: 1-202-842-6280
  Fax: 1-202-842-6937
  World Wide Web URL:
  http://www.nga.gov/education/classroom/loanfinder/
  Email Address: EdResources@nga.gov

Neputa Painter, The
Tells the story of a Neputa painter preserving an ancient tradition.
- Availability: Schools, libraries and homeschoolers in Alabama, Georgia, North Carolina, South Carolina, and Virginia.
- Suggested Grade: 4-12
- Order Number: 402
- Production Date: 1988
- Format: VHS videotape
- Special Notes: Part of the "Faces of Japan" series.
- Terms: Borrower pays return postage. Two tapes may be borrowed at a time. Return within 7 days after receipt. Reservations may be made by filling the application found on the web site.
- Source: Consulate General of Japan, Atlanta
  Japan Information Center
  One Alliance Center
  3500 Lenox Road, Suite 1600
  Atlanta, GA 30326
  Phone: 1-404-365-9240
  Fax: 1-404-240-4311
  World Wide Web URL:
  http://www.atlanta.us.emb-japan.go.jp
  Email Address: info@cgjapanatlanta.org

Neputa Painter, The
Tells the story of a Neputa painter preserving an ancient tradition.
- Availability: Schools, libraries, homeschoolers, and nursing homes in Connecticut (except Fairfield County), Maine, Massachusetts, New Hampshire, Rhode Island, and Vermont.
- Suggested Grade: 4-12
- Order Number: 170
- Production Date: 1988
- Format: VHS videotape
- Special Notes: Part of the "Faces of Japan" series.
- Terms: Borrower pays return postage, including insurance. Return two weeks after receipt.
- Source: Consulate General of Japan, Boston
  Federal Reserve Plaza, 14th Floor
  600 Atlantic Avenue
  Boston, MA 02210
  Phone: 1-617-973-9772
  Fax: 1-617-542-1329
  World Wide Web URL:
  http://www.boston.us.emb-japan.go.jp
  Email Address: infocul@cgjbos.org

Neputa Painter, The
Tells the story of a Neputa painter preserving an ancient tradition.
- Availability: Schools, libraries, and nursing homes in Oklahoma and Texas.
- Suggested Grade: 4-12
- Order Number: D2
- Format: VHS videotape
- Special Notes: Part of the "Faces of Japan" series.
- Terms: Materials must be picked up in person. Under special circumstances, you may be able to have them shipped to you at your own expense (call for further details). Return within two weeks after scheduled showing. Videos must be registered with the U. S. Postal Service or returned by Priority Mail, Federal Express, or other registered shipping service.

FINE ARTS--ART AND HANDWORK

Source: **Consulate General of Japan, Houston**
Cultural Affairs and Information Section
909 Fannin Street, Suite 3000
Houston, TX 77010
Phone: 1-713-652-2977
Fax: 1-713-651-7822
World Wide Web URL:
http://www.houston.us.emb-japan.go.jp/
en/culture/page1.htm
Email Address: info@cgjhouston.org

Neputa Painter, The
Tells the story of a Neputa painter preserving an ancient tradition.
Availability: Schools, libraries, homeschoolers, and nursing homes in OREGON AND SOUTHERN IDAHO ONLY. Please make requests via the web site.
Suggested Grade: 4-12
Order Number: 515
Format: VHS videotape
Special Notes: Part of the "Faces of Japan" series.
Terms: Borrower pays return postage. Return within three weeks after scheduled showing date. Book one month in advance if possible. Rewind the video and wrap securely for return. Be certain to indicate video number, date needed, name of your organization, and address to which video should be sent, along with phone number. Audience report enclosed with the video must be completed and returned.
Source: **Consulate General of Japan, Oregon**
Attn: Tamara, Video Library
1300 S. W. Fifth Avenue, Suite 2700
Portland, OR 97201
Phone: 1-503-221-1811, ext. 17
World Wide Web URL:
http://www.portland.us.emb-japan.go.jp/en/index.html
Email Address: tamara@cgjpdx.org

Neputa Painter, The
Tells the story of a Neputa painter preserving an ancient tradition.
Availability: Schools, libraries, homeschoolers, and nursing homes in Nevada and northern California (zip codes beginning 932 and above, except 935).
Suggested Grade: 4-12
Order Number: order by title
Format: VHS videotape
Special Notes: Part of the "Faces of Japan" series.
Terms: Borrower pays return postage. Book two weeks in advance. Return within three weeks of date borrowed, via UPS, Federal Express or certified mail.
Source: **Consulate General of Japan, San Francisco**
50 Fremont Street, Suite 2300
San Francisco, CA 94105-2236
Phone: 1-415-356-2564
Fax: 1-415-777-0518
World Wide Web URL: http://www.sf.us.emb-japan.go.jp/
Email Address: infoav@cgjsf.org

Oaxacan Woodcarving: Innovation Meets Tradition
A woodcarver demonstrates the process of woodcarving and painting using techniques of the contemporary artisans in Oaxaca.
Availability: Schools and libraries in Iowa, Illinois, Michigan, Minnesota, and Wisconsin.
Suggested Grade: All ages
Languages: Spanish with English subtitles
Order Number: ARTMEXOAW9DVD
Production Date: 2003
Format: DVD
Special Notes: A teacher's guide is included.
Terms: Borrower pays return postage. Return 8 days after showing. Book 2 weeks in advance. Order may also be picked up for those near the Center.
Source: **Center for Latin American and Caribbean Studies**
UW-Milwaukee
P. O. Box 413
Milwaukee, WI 53201
Phone: 1-414-229-5987
World Wide Web URL: http://www.uwm.edu/Dept/CLACS
Email Address: audvis@usm.edu

Of Time, Tombs, and Treasure: The Treasures of Tutankhamun
This program takes the viewer on a journey to Egypt and the final resting place of a young king who ruled 3,000 years ago. Narrated by J. Carter Brown, the program tells the story of the tomb's discovery in 1922 by archaeologist Howard Carter and its fabulous treasure--objects which range from magnificent jewelry to furniture, alabaster vases, gilt figurines, and the famous gold burial mask. The beauty and detail of these objects is stunning.
Availability: Schools, community groups, homeschoolers and individuals in the United States.
Suggested Grade: 7-12
Order Number: VC 132
Format: VHS videotape
Special Notes: Programs may not be broadcast, reproduced, or transferred to another medium or format without special license from the National Gallery of Art. Closed captioned version also available as CC 132.
Terms: Borrower pays return postage. Return within 5 days of scheduled use. Book at least one month in advance, and provide alternate date. You will receive a confirmation noting our Shipping Date and your Return Date for each program. Large organizations that can provide programs to extensive audiences--such as school systems, instructional resource centers, museums, libraries, and public and instructional television stations--can arrange an Affiliate Loan for three years, with subsequent renewal to provide their audiences more immediate access to these free-loan extension programs.
Source: **National Gallery of Art**
Department of Education Resources
2000B South Club Drive
Landover, MD 20785
Phone: 1-202-842-6280

All materials listed in this 2018-2019 edition are BRAND NEW!

FINE ARTS--ART AND HANDWORK

Fax: 1-202-842-6937
World Wide Web URL:
http://www.nga.gov/education/classroom/loanfinder/
Email Address: EdResources@nga.gov

Origami

Origami, the centuries-old Japanese art of paper-folding, still enjoys great popularity among the young and old alike. Parents encourage this pastime at home, guiding their offspring in creating a wide variety of intricate figures. It's an invaluable aid in developing the creative imaginations of youngsters.

Availability: Schools, libraries, and nursing homes in Illinois, Indiana, Iowa, Kansas, Minnesota, Missouri, Nebraska, North Dakota, South Dakota, and Wisconsin.
Suggested Grade: 6-Adult
Order Number: 03403
Format: VHS videotape
Terms: Borrower pays return postage by U. S. Mail, UPS, or Federal Express, including insurance for "original" videos. Write, call, fax, or e-mail to request an application. An application form MUST be sent in one month in advance but not more than six months in advance. Include alternate titles and dates if provider can substitute titles. Send a SASE with request if you require confirmation. Return immediately after scheduled showing date. Videos may not be copied or broadcast without permission from the producer of the video. Borrower is responsible if video is lost or damaged.

Source: Consulate General of Japan at Chicago
Japan Information Center
Library
737 North Michigan Avenue, Suite 1000
Chicago, IL 60611
Phone: 1-312-280-0430
Fax: 1-312-280-6883
World Wide Web URL:
http://www.chicago.us.emb-japan.go.jp/jic.html
Email Address: jicchicago@webkddi.com

Past, Present and Future: Washi--Unique Japanese Paper Culture

Washi is introduced as an outstanding aspect of traditional culture. This video explores how this unique paper is incorporated into daily living in terms of production, wrapping, folding, art and other uses.

Availability: Schools, libraries, homeschoolers, and nursing homes in Connecticut (except Fairfield County), Maine, Massachusetts, New Hampshire, Rhode Island, and Vermont.
Suggested Grade: 4-12
Order Number: 561
Production Date: 1997
Format: VHS videotape
Terms: Borrower pays return postage, including insurance. Return two weeks after receipt.

Source: Consulate General of Japan, Boston
Federal Reserve Plaza, 14th Floor
600 Atlantic Avenue
Boston, MA 02210
Phone: 1-617-973-9772
Fax: 1-617-542-1329
World Wide Web URL:
http://www.boston.us.emb-japan.go.jp
Email Address: infocul@cgjbos.org

Past, Present and Future: Washi--Unique Japanese Paper Culture

Washi is introduced as an outstanding aspect of traditional culture. This video explores how this unique paper is incorporated into daily living in terms of production, wrapping, folding, art and other uses.

Availability: Schools, libraries, and nursing homes in Oklahoma and Texas.
Suggested Grade: 4-12
Order Number: A21
Production Date: 1997
Format: VHS videotape
Terms: Materials must be picked up in person. Under special circumstances, you may be able to have them shipped to you at your own expense (call for further details). Return within two weeks after scheduled showing. Videos must be registered with the U. S. Postal Service or returned by Priority Mail, Federal Express, or other registered shipping service.

Source: Consulate General of Japan, Houston
Cultural Affairs and Information Section
909 Fannin Street, Suite 3000
Houston, TX 77010
Phone: 1-713-652-2977
Fax: 1-713-651-7822
World Wide Web URL:
http://www.houston.us.emb-japan.go.jp/en/culture/page1.htm
Email Address: info@cgjhouston.org

Past, Present and Future: Washi--Unique Japanese Paper Culture

Washi is introduced as an outstanding aspect of traditional culture. This video explores how this unique paper is incorporated into daily living in terms of production, wrapping, folding, art and other uses.

Availability: Schools, libraries, homeschoolers, and nursing homes in Arizona and California (zipcodes beginning 900-931 and 935).
Suggested Grade: 4-12
Order Number: 250
Production Date: 1997
Format: VHS videotape
Terms: Borrower pays postage both ways; you may call the number below to learn how much postage costs. Return within two weeks of date borrowed. An individual may borrow 2 items at one time. For non-profit and educational use only.

FINE ARTS--ART AND HANDWORK

Source: Consulate General of Japan, Los Angeles
350 South Grand Avenue, Suite 1700
Los Angeles, CA 90071-3459
Phone: 1-213-617-6700
Fax: 1-213-617-6727
World Wide Web URL: http://www.la.us.emb-japan.go.jp

Past, Present and Future: Washi--Unique Japanese Paper Culture
Washi is introduced as an outstanding aspect of traditional culture. This video explores how this unique paper is incorporated into daily living in terms of production, wrapping, folding, art and other uses.
Availability: Schools, libraries, homeschoolers, and nursing homes in Nevada and northern California (zip codes beginning 932 and above, except 935).
Suggested Grade: 4-12
Order Number: order by title
Production Date: 1997
Format: VHS videotape
Terms: Borrower pays return postage. Book two weeks in advance. Return within three weeks of date borrowed, via UPS, Federal Express or certified mail.
Source: Consulate General of Japan, San Francisco
50 Fremont Street, Suite 2300
San Francisco, CA 94105-2236
Phone: 1-415-356-2564
Fax: 1-415-777-0518
World Wide Web URL: http://www.sf.us.emb-japan.go.jp/
Email Address: infoav@cgjsf.org

Picasso: The Early Years
A behind-the-scenes tour through the exhibition Picasso: The Early Years, 1892-1906, with the curator, conservator, and museum educators. From their varied perspectives, they explore Picasso's earliest works, from his days as a young student in Spain to the key paintings of his Blue and Rose periods. Discussion includes themes in Picasso's art and changes in his style as he matured and moved toward the groundbreaking innovations of cubism.
Availability: Schools, community groups, homeschoolers and individuals in the United States.
Suggested Grade: 7-12
Order Number: VC 212
Format: VHS videotape
Special Notes: Programs may not be broadcast, reproduced, or transferred to another medium or format without special license from the National Gallery of Art. Closed captioned version also available as CC 212.
Terms: Borrower pays return postage. Return within 5 days of scheduled use. Book at least one month in advance, and provide alternate date. You will receive a confirmation noting our Shipping Date and your Return Date for each program. Large organizations that can provide programs to extensive audiences--such as school systems, instructional resource centers, museums, libraries, and public and instructional television stations--can arrange an Affiliate Loan for three years, with subsequent renewal to provide their audiences more immediate access to these free-loan extension programs.
Source: National Gallery of Art
Department of Education Resources
2000B South Club Drive
Landover, MD 20785
Phone: 1-202-842-6280
Fax: 1-202-842-6937
World Wide Web URL: http://www.nga.gov/education/classroom/loanfinder/
Email Address: EdResources@nga.gov

Place to Be, A: The Construction of the East Building of the National Gallery of Art
Traces in the detail the creation of this impressive structure from idea to completion.
Availability: Schools, community groups, homeschoolers and individuals in the United States.
Suggested Grade: 7-12
Order Number: DV341
Format: DVD
Special Notes: Programs may not be broadcast, reproduced, or transferred to another medium or format without special license from the National Gallery of Art.
Terms: Borrower pays return postage. Return within 5 days of scheduled use. Book at least one month in advance, and provide alternate date. You will receive a confirmation noting our Shipping Date and your Return Date for each program. Large organizations that can provide programs to extensive audiences--such as school systems, instructional resource centers, museums, libraries, and public and instructional television stations--can arrange an Affiliate Loan for three years, with subsequent renewal to provide their audiences more immediate access to these free-loan extension programs.
Source: National Gallery of Art
Department of Education Resources
2000B South Club Drive
Landover, MD 20785
Phone: 1-202-842-6280
Fax: 1-202-842-6937
World Wide Web URL: http://www.nga.gov/education/classroom/loanfinder/
Email Address: EdResources@nga.gov

Place to Be, A: The Construction of the East Building of the National Gallery of Art
Traces in the detail the creation of this impressive structure from idea to completion.
Availability: Schools, community groups, homeschoolers and individuals in the United States.
Suggested Grade: 7-12
Order Number: VC 134
Format: VHS videotape
Special Notes: Programs may not be broadcast, reproduced, or transferred to another medium or format

FINE ARTS--ART AND HANDWORK

without special license from the National Gallery of Art. Closed captioned version also available as CC 134.

Terms: Borrower pays return postage. Return within 5 days of scheduled use. Book at least one month in advance, and provide alternate date. You will receive a confirmation noting our Shipping Date and your Return Date for each program. Large organizations that can provide programs to extensive audiences--such as school systems, instructional resource centers, museums, libraries, and public and instructional television stations--can arrange an Affiliate Loan for three years, with subsequent renewal to provide their audiences more immediate access to these free-loan extension programs.

Source: National Gallery of Art
Department of Education Resources
2000B South Club Drive
Landover, MD 20785
Phone: 1-202-842-6280
Fax: 1-202-842-6937
World Wide Web URL:
http://www.nga.gov/education/classroom/loanfinder/
Email Address: EdResources@nga.gov

Plunder
Looks at black market in stolen pre-Columbian antiquities.
Availability: Schools, libraries, and nursing homes in the United States.
Suggested Grade: 6-12
Order Number: APLA1-video
Production Date: 1990
Format: VHS videotape
Terms: Borrowers must have a User's Agreement on file with this source--available by mail or via the Internet. Return postage is paid by borrower; return 12 days after showing. Book at least three weeks in advance. All borrowers are limited to a total of ten items per semester.
Source: Latin American Resource Center
Stone Center for Latin American Studies
Tulane University, 100 Jones Hall
New Orleans, LA 70118
Phone: 1-504-862-3143
Fax: 1-504-865-6719
World Wide Web URL: http://stonecenter.tulane.edu/pages/detail/48/Lending-Library
Email Address: crcrts@tulane.edu

Popular Hispanic Culture
The cultural riches of art, literature, and music from centuries old Latin American countries bring us a treasury of beauty as shown here.
Availability: Schools in the United States.
Suggested Grade: 7-Adult
Order Number: order by title
Format: VHS videotape
Terms: Borrower pays return postage. Return 14 days after receipt, via USPS including insurance. All borrowers must have a current lending agreement on file with the Outreach program. This agreement is available via the web site or may be requested via phone or fax.

Source: Center for Latin American Studies
University of Florida
319 Grinter Hall
P. O. Box 115530
Gainesville, FL 32611-5530
Phone: 1-352-392-0375
Fax: 1-352-392-7682
World Wide Web URL: http://www.latam.ufl.edu/outreach
Email Address: maryr@ufl.edu

Pyramids of the Sun and Moon
Panorama of Teotihuacan and Aztec art filmed on location and at the Museum of Anthropology of Mexico City.
Availability: Schools, libraries, and nursing homes in the United States.
Suggested Grade: 6-12
Order Number: AZ8-video
Production Date: 1970
Format: VHS videotape
Terms: Borrowers must have a User's Agreement on file with this source--available by mail or via the Internet. Return postage is paid by borrower; return 12 days after showing. Book at least three weeks in advance. All borrowers are limited to a total of ten items per semester.
Source: Latin American Resource Center
Stone Center for Latin American Studies
Tulane University
100 Jones Hall
New Orleans, LA 70118
Phone: 1-504-862-3143
Fax: 1-504-865-6719
World Wide Web URL: http://stonecenter.tulane.edu/pages/detail/48/Lending-Library
Email Address: crcrts@tulane.edu

Quiet Collector, The: Andrew W. Mellon Remembered
A leader in finance and industry, Secretary of the Treasury through three administrations, U. S. Ambassador to the Court of St. James--Andrew W. Mellon was a man of numerous accomplishments. But his gift to the nation of the National Gallery of Art, with his own collection of masterpieces as its nucleus, ranks among his most enduring contributions. This program dramatizes Mellon's life as a collector and his single-minded pursuit of the finest works by such artists as Rembrandt, Vermeer, Titian, and Raphael. His dedication to his vision of an art gallery for the American people is shown here.
Availability: Schools, community groups, homeschoolers and individuals in the United States.
Suggested Grade: 7-12
Order Number: VC 142
Format: VHS videotape
Special Notes: Programs may not be broadcast, reproduced, or transferred to another medium or format without special license from the National Gallery of Art. Closed captioned version also available as CC 142.

FINE ARTS--ART AND HANDWORK

Terms: Borrower pays return postage. Return within 5 days of scheduled use. Book at least one month in advance, and provide alternate date. You will receive a confirmation noting our Shipping Date and your Return Date for each program. Large organizations that can provide programs to extensive audiences--such as school systems, instructional resource centers, museums, libraries, and public and instructional television stations--can arrange an Affiliate Loan for three years, with subsequent renewal to provide their audiences more immediate access to these free-loan extension programs.

Source: National Gallery of Art
Department of Education Resources
2000B South Club Drive
Landover, MD 20785
Phone: 1-202-842-6280
Fax: 1-202-842-6937
World Wide Web URL:
http://www.nga.gov/education/classroom/loanfinder/
Email Address: EdResources@nga.gov

Raphael and the American Collector

The work of the Renaissance master, Raphael, was much admired as a model of perfection in his own time and in succeeding centuries. In this program, Raphael's art is surveyed briefly as a background for understanding the quest for Raphael's paintings in the early twentieth century by such collectors as Isabella Stewart Gardner, J. P. Morgan, Andrew W. Mellon, and P. A. B. Widener. The pictures these individuals purchased are now to be seen in distinguished American museums, particularly the National Gallery of Art, whose holdings include five paintings by Raphael--among them, Saint George and the Dragon and the Alba Madonna.

Availability: Schools, community groups, homeschoolers and individuals in the United States.
Suggested Grade: 7-12
Order Number: VC 145
Format: VHS videotape
Special Notes: Programs may not be broadcast, reproduced, or transferred to another medium or format without special license from the National Gallery of Art. Closed captioned version also available as CC 145.
Terms: Borrower pays return postage. Return within 5 days of scheduled use. Book at least one month in advance, and provide alternate date. You will receive a confirmation noting our Shipping Date and your Return Date for each program. Large organizations that can provide programs to extensive audiences--such as school systems, instructional resource centers, museums, libraries, and public and instructional television stations--can arrange an Affiliate Loan for three years, with subsequent renewal to provide their audiences more immediate access to these free-loan extension programs.

Source: National Gallery of Art
Department of Education Resources
2000B South Club Drive
Landover, MD 20785
Phone: 1-202-842-6280
Fax: 1-202-842-6937
World Wide Web URL:
http://www.nga.gov/education/classroom/loanfinder/
Email Address: EdResources@nga.gov

Reflections: The Story of "The Treasure Houses of Britain"

Tells the behind-the-scenes story of the creation of the most ambitious exhibitions at the National Gallery of Art. Former Gallery Director J. Carter Brown guides the viewer through the exhibition, highlighting key themes and exploring the show's history, planning, and design. Commentary by the curator and designers, along with documentary footage of the installation, provide insight into the making of an exhibition.

Availability: Schools, community groups, homeschoolers and individuals in the United States.
Suggested Grade: 7-12
Order Number: VC 203
Format: VHS videotape
Special Notes: Programs may not be broadcast, reproduced, or transferred to another medium or format without special license from the National Gallery of Art. Closed captioned version also available as CC 203.
Terms: Borrower pays return postage. Return within 5 days of scheduled use. Book at least one month in advance, and provide alternate date. You will receive a confirmation noting our Shipping Date and your Return Date for each program. Large organizations that can provide programs to extensive audiences--such as school systems, instructional resource centers, museums, libraries, and public and instructional television stations--can arrange an Affiliate Loan for three years, with subsequent renewal to provide their audiences more immediate access to these free-loan extension programs.

Source: National Gallery of Art
Department of Education Resources
2000B South Club Drive
Landover, MD 20785
Phone: 1-202-842-6280
Fax: 1-202-842-6937
World Wide Web URL:
http://www.nga.gov/education/classroom/loanfinder/
Email Address: EdResources@nga.gov

Rimpa School Crosses the Ocean

The Rimpa school of decorative design flourished during the Edo Period, and made a lasting mark on European art at the Paris Exhibition of 1878. Handicrafts, prints, and screens emphasized arrangement of natural forms into a visual rhythm.

Availability: Schools, libraries, homeschoolers, and nursing homes in Connecticut (except Fairfield County), Maine, Massachusetts, New Hampshire, Rhode Island, and Vermont.
Suggested Grade: 7-12

All materials listed in this 2018-2019 edition are BRAND NEW!

FINE ARTS--ART AND HANDWORK

Order Number: 192
Production Date: 1989
Format: VHS videotape
Special Notes: No. 5 in the "Japan: Spirit and Form" series.
Terms: Borrower pays return postage, including insurance. Return two weeks after receipt.
Source: Consulate General of Japan, Boston
Federal Reserve Plaza, 14th Floor
600 Atlantic Avenue
Boston, MA 02210
Phone: 1-617-973-9772
Fax: 1-617-542-1329
World Wide Web URL:
http://www.boston.us.emb-japan.go.jp
Email Address: infocul@cgjbos.org

Rimpa School Crosses the Ocean
The Rimpa school of decorative design flourished during the Edo Period, and made a lasting mark on European art at the Paris Exhibition of 1878. Handicrafts, prints, and screens emphasized arrangement of natural forms into a visual rhythm.
Availability: Schools, libraries, and nursing homes in Oklahoma and Texas.
Suggested Grade: 7-12
Order Number: E5
Production Date: 1989
Format: VHS videotape
Special Notes: No. 5 in the "Japan: Spirit and Form" series.
Terms: Materials must be picked up in person. Under special circumstances, you may be able to have them shipped to you at your own expense (call for further details). Return within two weeks after scheduled showing. Videos must be registered with the U. S. Postal Service or returned by Priority Mail, Federal Express, or other registered shipping service.
Source: Consulate General of Japan, Houston
Cultural Affairs and Information Section
909 Fannin Street, Suite 3000
Houston, TX 77010
Phone: 1-713-652-2977
Fax: 1-713-651-7822
World Wide Web URL:
http://www.houston.us.emb-japan.go.jp/en/culture/page1.htm
Email Address: info@cgjhouston.org

Rimpa School Crosses the Ocean
The Rimpa school of decorative design flourished during the Edo Period, and made a lasting mark on European art at the Paris Exhibition of 1878. Handicrafts, prints, and screens emphasized arrangement of natural forms into a visual rhythm.
Availability: Schools, libraries, homeschoolers, and nursing homes in Arizona and California (zipcodes beginning 900-931 and 935).
Suggested Grade: 7-12
Order Number: 121
Production Date: 1989
Format: VHS videotape
Special Notes: No. 5 in the "Japan: Spirit and Form" series.
Terms: Borrower pays postage both ways; you may call the number below to learn how much postage costs. Return within two weeks of date borrowed. An individual may borrow 2 items at one time. For non-profit and educational use only.
Source: Consulate General of Japan, Los Angeles
350 South Grand Avenue, Suite 1700
Los Angeles, CA 90071-3459
Phone: 1-213-617-6700
Fax: 1-213-617-6727
World Wide Web URL: http://www.la.us.emb-japan.go.jp

Rimpa School Crosses the Ocean
The Rimpa school of decorative design flourished during the Edo Period, and made a lasting mark on European art at the Paris Exhibition of 1878. Handicrafts, prints, and screens emphasized arrangement of natural forms into a visual rhythm.
Availability: Schools, libraries, homeschoolers, and nursing homes in Nevada and northern California (zip codes beginning 932 and above, except 935).
Suggested Grade: 7-12
Order Number: order by title
Production Date: 1989
Format: Beta videotape; U-matic videotape; VHS videotape
Special Notes: No. 5 in the "Japan: Spirit and Form" series.
Terms: Borrower pays return postage. Book two weeks in advance. Return within three weeks of date borrowed, via UPS, Federal Express or certified mail.
Source: Consulate General of Japan, San Francisco
50 Fremont Street, Suite 2300
San Francisco, CA 94105-2236
Phone: 1-415-356-2564
Fax: 1-415-777-0518
World Wide Web URL: http://www.sf.us.emb-japan.go.jp/
Email Address: infoav@cgjsf.org

Rivera: Portrait of an Artist
Archival footage explores the great beauty and political expression in Rivera's most extensive body of work--murals created for the Ford Motor Company.
Availability: Schools and libraries in Iowa, Illinois, Michigan, Minnesota, and Wisconsin.
Suggested Grade: 6-12
Order Number: ART/FOLMEXR52VHS
Format: VHS videotape
Terms: Borrower pays return postage. Return 8 days after showing. Book 2 weeks in advance. Order may also be picked up for those near the Center.
Source: Center for Latin American and Caribbean Studies
UW-Milwaukee, P. O. Box 413
Milwaukee, WI 53201
Phone: 1-414-229-5987
World Wide Web URL: http://www.uwm.edu/Dept/CLACS
Email Address: audvis@usm.edu

*All materials listed in this 2018-2019 edition are **BRAND NEW!***

FINE ARTS--ART AND HANDWORK

Roji Koie-Potter
Koie makes not only traditional everyday ware, but also avant-garde works which are esteemed internationally.
Availability: Schools, libraries, homeschoolers, and nursing homes in Connecticut (except Fairfield County), Maine, Massachusetts, New Hampshire, Rhode Island, and Vermont.
Suggested Grade: 9-Adult
Order Number: 425
Production Date: 1990
Format: VHS videotape
Special Notes: No. 9 of the "Nippon Life" series.
Terms: Borrower pays return postage, including insurance. Return two weeks after receipt.
Source: Consulate General of Japan, Boston
Federal Reserve Plaza, 14th Floor
600 Atlantic Avenue
Boston, MA 02210
Phone: 1-617-973-9772
Fax: 1-617-542-1329
World Wide Web URL: http://www.boston.us.emb-japan.go.jp
Email Address: infocul@cgjbos.org

Roji Koie-Potter
Koie makes not only traditional everyday ware, but also avant-garde works which are esteemed internationally.
Availability: Schools, libraries, homeschoolers, and nursing homes in Arizona and California (zipcodes beginning 900-931 and 935).
Suggested Grade: 9-Adult
Order Number: 145
Production Date: 1990
Format: VHS videotape
Special Notes: No. 9 of the "Nippon Life" series.
Terms: Borrower pays postage both ways; you may call the number below to learn how much postage costs. Return within two weeks of date borrowed. An individual may borrow 2 items at one time. For non-profit and educational use only.
Source: Consulate General of Japan, Los Angeles
350 South Grand Avenue, Suite 1700
Los Angeles, CA 90071-3459
Phone: 1-213-617-6700
Fax: 1-213-617-6727
World Wide Web URL: http://www.la.us.emb-japan.go.jp

Roji Koie-Potter
Koie makes not only traditional everyday ware, but also avant-garde works which are esteemed internationally.
Availability: Schools, libraries, homeschoolers, and nursing homes in Nevada and northern California (zip codes beginning 932 and above, except 935).
Suggested Grade: 9-Adult
Order Number: order by title
Production Date: 1990
Format: Beta videotape; U-matic videotape; VHS videotape
Special Notes: No. 9 of the "Nippon Life" series.
Terms: Borrower pays return postage. Book two weeks in advance. Return within three weeks of date borrowed, via UPS, Federal Express or certified mail.
Source: Consulate General of Japan, San Francisco
50 Fremont Street, Suite 2300
San Francisco, CA 94105-2236
Phone: 1-415-356-2564
Fax: 1-415-777-0518
World Wide Web URL: http://www.sf.us.emb-japan.go.jp/
Email Address: infoav@cgjsf.org

Sabina Sanchez - The Art of Embroidery
Life and work of a Zapotec woman in Oaxaca who makes the embroidered blouses of her traditional village costume.
Availability: Schools, libraries, and nursing homes in the United States.
Suggested Grade: 6-12
Order Number: FAMEX11-video
Production Date: 1976
Format: VHS videotape
Terms: Borrowers must have a User's Agreement on file with this source--available by mail or via the Internet. Return postage is paid by borrower; return 12 days after showing. Book at least three weeks in advance. All borrowers are limited to a total of ten items per semester.
Source: Latin American Resource Center
Stone Center for Latin American Studies
Tulane University, 100 Jones Hall
New Orleans, LA 70118
Phone: 1-504-862-3143
Fax: 1-504-865-6719
World Wide Web URL: http://stonecenter.tulane.edu/pages/detail/48/Lending-Library
Email Address: crcrts@tulane.edu

Seeing Color: Object, Light, Observer
Focusing on works by Titian, Turner, Monet, and Matisse, this film asks "what is color?" and turns for answers to artists, curators, conservation scientists, and science students. Filmed in studios, laboratories, and museum galleries, this film looks at its subject as both an aesthetic and physical phenomenon.
Availability: Schools, community groups, homeschoolers and individuals in the United States.
Suggested Grade: 7-12
Order Number: VC 165
Format: VHS videotape
Special Notes: Programs may not be broadcast, reproduced, or transferred to another medium or format without special license from the National Gallery of Art. Closed captioned version also available as CC 165.
Terms: Borrower pays return postage. Return within 5 days of scheduled use. Book at least one month in advance, and provide alternate date. You will receive a confirmation noting our Shipping Date and your Return Date for each program. Large organizations that can provide programs to extensive audiences--such as school systems,

FINE ARTS--ART AND HANDWORK

instructional resource centers, museums, libraries, and public and instructional television stations--can arrange an Affiliate Loan for three years, with subsequent renewal to provide their audiences more immediate access to these free-loan extension programs.

    Source: National Gallery of Art
    Department of Education Resources
    2000B South Club Drive
    Landover, MD 20785
    Phone: 1-202-842-6280
    Fax: 1-202-842-6937
    World Wide Web URL:
    http://www.nga.gov/education/classroom/loanfinder/
    Email Address: EdResources@nga.gov

Shaw Memorial, The: The Power and Glory of Public Art

Tells about the history, literary connections, and artistic significance of this sculpture as an artwork and a national monument.

Availability:	Schools, community groups, homeschoolers and individuals in the United States.
Suggested Grade:	7-12
Order Number:	VC 213
Format:	VHS videotape
Special Notes:	Programs may not be broadcast, reproduced, or transferred to another medium or format without special license from the National Gallery of Art. Closed captioned version also available as CC 213.
Terms:	Borrower pays return postage. Return within 5 days of scheduled use. Book at least one month in advance, and provide alternate date. You will receive a confirmation noting our Shipping Date and your Return Date for each program. Large organizations that can provide programs to extensive audiences--such as school systems, instructional resource centers, museums, libraries, and public and instructional television stations--can arrange an Affiliate Loan for three years, with subsequent renewal to provide their audiences more immediate access to these free-loan extension programs.

    Source: National Gallery of Art
    Department of Education Resources
    2000B South Club Drive
    Landover, MD 20785
    Phone: 1-202-842-6280
    Fax: 1-202-842-6937
    World Wide Web URL:
    http://www.nga.gov/education/classroom/loanfinder/
    Email Address: EdResources@nga.gov

Shingo Kojima--Cabinetmaker

As Kojima makes his furniture he engages in a struggle between the direction of his creativity and the very nature of trees. He tells us about his feelings and life.

Availability:	Schools, libraries, homeschoolers, and nursing homes in Connecticut (except Fairfield County), Maine, Massachusetts, New Hampshire, Rhode Island, and Vermont.
Suggested Grade:	9-Adult
Order Number:	428
Production Date:	1990
Format:	VHS videotape
Special Notes:	No. 12 of the "Nippon Life" series.
Terms:	Borrower pays return postage, including insurance. Return two weeks after receipt.

    Source: Consulate General of Japan, Boston
    Federal Reserve Plaza, 14th Floor
    600 Atlantic Avenue
    Boston, MA 02210
    Phone: 1-617-973-9772
    Fax: 1-617-542-1329
    World Wide Web URL:
    http://www.boston.us.emb-japan.go.jp
    Email Address: infocul@cgjbos.org

Shingo Kojima--Cabinetmaker

As Kojima makes his furniture he engages in a struggle between the direction of his creativity and the very nature of trees. He tells us about his feelings and life.

Availability:	Schools, libraries, and nursing homes in Oklahoma and Texas.
Suggested Grade:	9-Adult
Order Number:	F12
Production Date:	1990
Format:	VHS videotape
Special Notes:	No. 12 of the "Nippon Life" series.
Terms:	Materials must be picked up in person. Under special circumstances, you may be able to have them shipped to you at your own expense (call for further details). Return within two weeks after scheduled showing. Videos must be registered with the U. S. Postal Service or returned by Priority Mail, Federal Express, or other registered shipping service.

    Source: Consulate General of Japan, Houston
    Cultural Affairs and Information Section
    909 Fannin Street, Suite 3000
    Houston, TX 77010
    Phone: 1-713-652-2977
    Fax: 1-713-651-7822
    World Wide Web URL:
    http://www.houston.us.emb-japan.go.jp/en/culture/page1.htm
    Email Address: info@cgjhouston.org

Shingo Kojima--Cabinetmaker

As Kojima makes his furniture he engages in a struggle between the direction of his creativity and the very nature of trees. He tells us about his feelings and life.

Availability:	Schools, libraries, homeschoolers, and nursing homes in Arizona and California (zipcodes beginning 900-931 and 935).
Suggested Grade:	9-Adult
Order Number:	148
Production Date:	1990
Format:	VHS videotape
Special Notes:	No. 12 of the "Nippon Life" series.

*All materials listed in this 2018-2019 edition are **BRAND NEW**!*

FINE ARTS--ART AND HANDWORK

Terms: Borrower pays postage both ways; you may call the number below to learn how much postage costs. Return within two weeks of date borrowed. An individual may borrow 2 items at one time. For non-profit and educational use only.
Source: Consulate General of Japan, Los Angeles
350 South Grand Avenue, Suite 1700
Los Angeles, CA 90071-3459
Phone: 1-213-617-6700
Fax: 1-213-617-6727
World Wide Web URL: http://www.la.us.emb-japan.go.jp

Shingo Kojima--Cabinetmaker
As Kojima makes his furniture he engages in a struggle between the direction of his creativity and the very nature of trees. He tells us about his feelings and life.
Availability: Schools, libraries, homeschoolers, and nursing homes in Nevada and northern California (zip codes beginning 932 and above, except 935).
Suggested Grade: 9-Adult
Order Number: order by title
Production Date: 1990
Format: Beta videotape; U-matic videotape; VHS videotape
Special Notes: No. 12 of the "Nippon Life" series.
Terms: Borrower pays return postage. Book two weeks in advance. Return within three weeks of date borrowed, via UPS, Federal Express or certified mail.
Source: Consulate General of Japan, San Francisco
50 Fremont Street, Suite 2300
San Francisco, CA 94105-2236
Phone: 1-415-356-2564
Fax: 1-415-777-0518
World Wide Web URL: http://www.sf.us.emb-japan.go.jp/
Email Address: infoav@cgjsf.org

Shogyo Ohba's Challenge--Lacquerer
Ohba, an authority on Japanese lacquer, completes an epoch-making work combining traditions of Japan and France, lacquer and glass with passionate creativity.
Availability: Schools, libraries, and nursing homes in Illinois, Indiana, Iowa, Kansas, Minnesota, Missouri, Nebraska, North Dakota, South Dakota, and Wisconsin.
Suggested Grade: 9-Adult
Order Number: 03007
Production Date: 1990
Format: VHS videotape
Special Notes: No. 13 of the "Nippon Life" series.
Terms: Borrower pays return postage by U. S. Mail, UPS, or Federal Express, including insurance for "original" videos. Write, call, fax, or e-mail to request an application. An application form MUST be sent in one month in advance but not more than six months in advance. Include alternate titles and dates if provider can substitute titles. Send a SASE with request if you require confirmation. Return immediately after scheduled showing date. Videos may not be copied or broadcast without permission from the producer of the video. Borrower is responsible if video is lost or damaged.
Source: Consulate General of Japan at Chicago
Japan Information Center
Library
737 North Michigan Avenue, Suite 1000
Chicago, IL 60611
Phone: 1-312-280-0430
Fax: 1-312-280-6883
World Wide Web URL:
http://www.chicago.us.emb-japan.go.jp/jic.html
Email Address: jicchicago@webkddi.com

Toulouse-Lautrec and Montmartre
Traces the relationship between Toulouse-Lautrec and Montmartre's avant-garde culture, using works by the artists and his colleagues, rare archival footage and sound records, period photographs, and interviews with contemporary scholars.
Availability: Schools, community groups, homeschoolers and individuals in the United States.
Suggested Grade: 7-12
Order Number: VC 172
Format: VHS videotape
Special Notes: Programs may not be broadcast, reproduced, or transferred to another medium or format without special license from the National Gallery of Art. Closed captioned version also available as CC 172.
Terms: Borrower pays return postage. Return within 5 days of scheduled use. Book at least one month in advance, and provide alternate date. You will receive a confirmation noting our Shipping Date and your Return Date for each program. Large organizations that can provide programs to extensive audiences--such as school systems, instructional resource centers, museums, libraries, and public and instructional television stations--can arrange an Affiliate Loan for three years, with subsequent renewal to provide their audiences more immediate access to these free-loan extension programs.
Source: National Gallery of Art
Department of Education Resources
2000B South Club Drive
Landover, MD 20785
Phone: 1-202-842-6280
Fax: 1-202-842-6937
World Wide Web URL:
http://www.nga.gov/education/classroom/loanfinder/
Email Address: EdResources@nga.gov

Tour of the Prado, A
Tour of European and Spanish paintings housed in Madrid's Prado Museum.
Availability: Schools, libraries, and nursing homes in the United States.
Suggested Grade: 6-12
Order Number: ASPA2-video
Production Date: 1982

All materials listed in this 2018-2019 edition are BRAND NEW!

FINE ARTS--ART AND HANDWORK

Format: VHS videotape
Terms: Borrowers must have a User's Agreement on file with this source--available by mail or via the Internet. Return postage is paid by borrower; return 12 days after showing. Book at least three weeks in advance. All borrowers are limited to a total of ten items per semester.
Source: **Latin American Resource Center**
Stone Center for Latin American Studies
Tulane University
100 Jones Hall
New Orleans, LA 70118
Phone: 1-504-862-3143
Fax: 1-504-865-6719
World Wide Web URL: http://stonecenter.tulane.edu/pages/detail/48/Lending-Library
Email Address: crcrts@tulane.edu

Visiones del Pueblo: The Folk Art of Latin America
Presents examples of Latin American folk art within its cultural context of daily life, ritual and celebration.
Availability: Schools and libraries in Iowa, Illinois, Michigan, Minnesota, and Wisconsin.
Suggested Grade: 6-12
Order Number: ART/FOLMEXV82VHS
Production Date: 1992
Format: VHS videotape
Terms: Borrower pays return postage. Return 8 days after showing. Book 2 weeks in advance. Order may also be picked up for those near the Center.
Source: **Center for Latin American and Caribbean Studies**
UW-Milwaukee
P. O. Box 413
Milwaukee, WI 53201
Phone: 1-414-229-5987
World Wide Web URL: http://www.uwm.edu/Dept/CLACS
Email Address: audvis@usm.edu

Women in Ukiyo-E
Ukiyo-e (pictures of the floating world) is a style of painting on woodblock as well as prints and cards depicting a wide variety of characters.
Availability: Schools, libraries, homeschoolers, and nursing homes in Connecticut (except Fairfield County), Maine, Massachusetts, New Hampshire, Rhode Island, and Vermont.
Suggested Grade: 7-12
Order Number: 194
Production Date: 1989
Format: VHS videotape
Special Notes: No. 7 in the "Japan: Spirit and Form" series.
Terms: Borrower pays return postage, including insurance. Return two weeks after receipt.
Source: **Consulate General of Japan, Boston**
Federal Reserve Plaza, 14th Floor
600 Atlantic Avenue
Boston, MA 02210
Phone: 1-617-973-9772
Fax: 1-617-542-1329
World Wide Web URL: http://www.boston.us.emb-japan.go.jp
Email Address: infocul@cgjbos.org

Women in Ukiyo-E
Ukiyo-e (pictures of the floating world) is a style of painting on woodblock as well as prints and cards depicting a wide variety of characters.
Availability: Schools, libraries, and nursing homes in Oklahoma and Texas.
Suggested Grade: 7-12
Order Number: E7
Production Date: 1989
Format: VHS videotape
Special Notes: No. 7 in the "Japan: Spirit and Form" series.
Terms: Materials must be picked up in person. Under special circumstances, you may be able to have them shipped to you at your own expense (call for further details). Return within two weeks after scheduled showing. Videos must be registered with the U. S. Postal Service or returned by Priority Mail, Federal Express, or other registered shipping service.
Source: **Consulate General of Japan, Houston**
Cultural Affairs and Information Section
909 Fannin Street, Suite 3000
Houston, TX 77010
Phone: 1-713-652-2977
Fax: 1-713-651-7822
World Wide Web URL: http://www.houston.us.emb-japan.go.jp/en/culture/page1.htm
Email Address: info@cgjhouston.org

Women in Ukiyo-E
Ukiyo-e (pictures of the floating world) is a style of painting on woodblock as well as prints and cards depicting a wide variety of characters.
Availability: Schools, libraries, homeschoolers, and nursing homes in Arizona and California (zipcodes beginning 900-931 and 935).
Suggested Grade: 7-12
Order Number: 123
Production Date: 1989
Format: VHS videotape
Special Notes: No. 7 in the "Japan: Spirit and Form" series.
Terms: Borrower pays postage both ways; you may call the number below to learn how much postage costs. Return within two weeks of date borrowed. An individual may borrow 2 items at one time. For non-profit and educational use only.
Source: **Consulate General of Japan, Los Angeles**
350 South Grand Avenue, Suite 1700
Los Angeles, CA 90071-3459
Phone: 1-213-617-6700
Fax: 1-213-617-6727
World Wide Web URL: http://www.la.us.emb-japan.go.jp

Women in Ukiyo-E
Ukiyo-e (pictures of the floating world) is a style of painting

FINE ARTS--ART AND HANDWORK

on woodblock as well as prints and cards depicting a wide variety of characters.
Availability: Schools, libraries, homeschoolers, and nursing homes in Nevada and northern California (zip codes beginning 932 and above, except 935).
Suggested Grade: 7-12
Order Number: order by title
Production Date: 1989
Format: Beta videotape; U-matic videotape; VHS videotape
Special Notes: No. 7 in the "Japan: Spirit and Form" series.
Terms: Borrower pays return postage. Book two weeks in advance. Return within three weeks of date borrowed, via UPS, Federal Express or certified mail.

Source: Consulate General of Japan, San Francisco
50 Fremont Street, Suite 2300
San Francisco, CA 94105-2236
Phone: 1-415-356-2564
Fax: 1-415-777-0518
World Wide Web URL: http://www.sf.us.emb-japan.go.jp/
Email Address: infoav@cgjsf.org

Yaro Civilization, The
Among the civilizations conquered by the Inca, the Yaro empire is still impressive, with five-story houses and huge silos to store supplies.
Availability: Schools, libraries, and nursing homes in the United States.
Suggested Grade: 6-12
Order Number: APAND2-video
Production Date: 1989
Format: VHS videotape
Terms: Borrowers must have a User's Agreement on file with this source--available by mail or via the Internet. Return postage is paid by borrower; return 12 days after showing. Book at least three weeks in advance. All borrowers are limited to a total of ten items per semester.

Source: Latin American Resource Center
Stone Center for Latin American Studies
Tulane University
100 Jones Hall
New Orleans, LA 70118
Phone: 1-504-862-3143
Fax: 1-504-865-6719
World Wide Web URL: http://stonecenter.tulane.edu/pages/detail/48/Lending-Library
Email Address: crcrts@tulane.edu

FINE ARTS--MUSIC AND DRAMA

Bellas Damas, Las
A collection of the top Latin American music videos by women.
- Availability: Schools in the United States.
- Suggested Grade: 7-Adult
- Language: Spanish
- Order Number: order by title
- Production Date: 1990
- Format: VHS videotape
- Terms: Borrower pays return postage. Return 14 days after receipt, via USPS including insurance. All borrowers must have a current lending agreement on file with the Outreach program. This agreement is available via the web site or may be requested via phone or fax.
- Source: Center for Latin American Studies
  University of Florida
  319 Grinter Hall
  P. O. Box 115530
  Gainesville, FL 32611-5530
  Phone: 1-352-392-0375
  Fax: 1-352-392-7682
- World Wide Web URL: http://www.latam.ufl.edu/outreach
- Email Address: maryr@ufl.edu

Between Heaven and Earth: The Temple of Taiwan
Ornately decorated halls, an array of stalls selling delicious snacks, harmonious and skilled movements of performers-- people in Taiwan pull out all the stops when putting on temple shows. This presentation shows this to be true.
- Availability: Schools and libraries in Connecticut, New Jersey, New York, and Pennsylvania.
- Suggested Grade: 6-12
- Order Number: order by title
- Production Date: 2006
- Format: DVD
- Terms: Borrower pays return postage. Return 7 days after showing. Book at least 21 days in advance and provide alternate showing date.
- Source: Taipei Economic and Cultural Office in New York
  Press Division
  1 East 42nd Street, 11th Floor
  New York, NY 10017
  Phone: 1-212-317-7343
  Fax: 1-212-557-3043
- World Wide Web URL: http://www.taipei.org
- Email Address: roctaiwan@taipei.org

Between Heaven and Earth: The Temple of Taiwan
Ornately decorated halls, an array of stalls selling delicious snacks, harmonious and skilled movements of performers-- people in Taiwan pull out all the stops when putting on temple shows. This presentation shows this to be true.
- Availability: Schools and libraries in Connecticut, New Jersey, New York, and Pennsylvania.
- Suggested Grade: 6-12
- Order Number: order by title
- Production Date: 2006
- Format: VHS videotape
- Terms: Borrower pays return postage. Return 7 days after showing. Book at least 21 days in advance and provide alternate showing date.
- Source: Taipei Economic and Cultural Office in New York
  Press Division
  1 East 42nd Street, 11th Floor
  New York, NY 10017
  Phone: 1-212-317-7343
  Fax: 1-212-557-3043
- World Wide Web URL: http://www.taipei.org
- Email Address: roctaiwan@taipei.org

Brazilian Music
Various Brazilian musicians taped from a TV broadcast.
- Availability: Schools, libraries, and nursing homes in the United States.
- Suggested Grade: 6-12
- Language: Portuguese
- Order Number: MUBRA4-video
- Format: VHS videotape
- Terms: Borrowers must have a User's Agreement on file with this source--available by mail or via the Internet. Return postage is paid by borrower; return 12 days after showing. Book at least three weeks in advance. All borrowers are limited to a total of ten items per semester.
- Source: Latin American Resource Center
  Stone Center for Latin American Studies
  Tulane University
  100 Jones Hall
  New Orleans, LA 70118
  Phone: 1-504-862-3143
  Fax: 1-504-865-6719
- World Wide Web URL: http://stonecenter.tulane.edu/pages/detail/48/Lending-Library
- Email Address: crcrts@tulane.edu

Buena Vista Social Club
Director Wim Wenders reveals the astonishing life stories, vibrant personalities and unforgettable music of the brilliantly talented but long overlooked performers who collaborated on the Buena Vista Social Club, a now-legendary recording of Cuban folk music.
- Availability: Schools in the United States.
- Suggested Grade: 7-Adult
- Languages: Spanish with English subtitles
- Order Number: order by title
- Production Date: 1999
- Format: VHS videotape
- Terms: Borrower pays return postage. Return 14 days after receipt, via USPS including insurance. All borrowers must have a current lending agreement on file with the Outreach program. This agreement is available via the web site or may be requested via phone or fax.
- Source: Center for Latin American Studies
  University of Florida, 319 Grinter Hall
  P. O. Box 115530
  Gainesville, FL 32611-5530
  Phone: 1-352-392-0375
  Fax: 1-352-392-7682

*All materials listed in this 2018-2019 edition are **BRAND NEW!***

FINE ARTS--MUSIC AND DRAMA

World Wide Web URL: http://www.latam.ufl.edu/outreach
Email Address: maryr@ufl.edu

Bunraku Puppet Theatre of Japan
Explains in detail the art of the Japanese Bunraku theater, including a description of the craft of making the large puppets and the long arduous training undergone by traditional Bunraku puppeteers.
Availability: Schools, libraries, homeschoolers, and nursing homes in Arizona and California (zipcodes beginning 900-931 and 935).
Suggested Grade: 7-Adult
Order Number: 078
Production Date: 1966
Format: VHS videotape
Terms: Borrower pays postage both ways; you may call the number below to learn how much postage costs. Return within two weeks of date borrowed. An individual may borrow 2 items at one time. For non-profit and educational use only.
Source: Consulate General of Japan, Los Angeles
350 South Grand Avenue, Suite 1700
Los Angeles, CA 90071-3459
Phone: 1-213-617-6700
Fax: 1-213-617-6727
World Wide Web URL: http://www.la.us.emb-japan.go.jp

Chinese Musical Instruments: Parts I and II
Bowed string instruments followed by wind instruments.
Availability: Schools, libraries, and nursing homes in the United States and Canada.
Suggested Grade: All ages
Languages: Chinese; subtitled in English
Order Number: CV010
Format: VHS videotape
Terms: Borrower pays return postage. Return with 14 days after scheduled showing, via UPS or U. S. Mail. All requests must included an educational institution affiliation, a current address, and phone number. Order through web site only.
Source: Cornell University East Asia Program
World Wide Web URL:
http://eap.einaudi.cornell.edu/lending_library
Email Address: east_asia1@cornell.edu

Chinese Musical Instruments: Parts III and IV
Percussion instruments followed by plucked string instruments.
Availability: Schools, libraries, and nursing homes in the United States and Canada.
Suggested Grade: All ages
Languages: Chinese; subtitled in English
Order Number: CV011
Format: VHS videotape
Terms: Borrower pays return postage. Return with 14 days after scheduled showing, via UPS or U. S. Mail. All requests must included an educational institution affiliation, a current address, and phone number. Order through web site only.
Source: Cornell University East Asia Program
World Wide Web URL:
http://eap.einaudi.cornell.edu/lending_library
Email Address: east_asia1@cornell.edu

Chulas Fronteras
An introduction to Norteno (Texas-Mexican border) music.
Availability: Schools in the United States.
Suggested Grade: 9-Adult
Order Number: order by title
Production Date: 1976
Format: VHS videotape
Terms: Borrower pays return postage. Return 14 days after receipt, via USPS including insurance. All borrowers must have a current lending agreement on file with the Outreach program. This agreement is available via the web site or may be requested via phone or fax.
Source: Center for Latin American Studies
University of Florida
319 Grinter Hall
P. O. Box 115530
Gainesville, FL 32611-5530
Phone: 1-352-392-0375
Fax: 1-352-392-7682
World Wide Web URL: http://www.latam.ufl.edu/outreach
Email Address: maryr@ufl.edu

Ennosuke Ichikawa III: Kabuki Actor
Features a famous Japanese Kabuki actor in several performances. The Kabuki theater dates from the early 17th century and is still popular today.
Availability: Schools, libraries, homeschoolers, and nursing homes in Connecticut (except Fairfield County), Maine, Massachusetts, New Hampshire, Rhode Island, and Vermont.
Suggested Grade: All ages
Order Number: 112
Production Date: 1985
Format: VHS videotape
Terms: Borrower pays return postage, including insurance. Return two weeks after receipt.
Source: Consulate General of Japan, Boston
Federal Reserve Plaza, 14th Floor
600 Atlantic Avenue
Boston, MA 02210
Phone: 1-617-973-9772
Fax: 1-617-542-1329
World Wide Web URL:
http://www.boston.us.emb-japan.go.jp
Email Address: infocul@cgjbos.org

Ennosuke Ichikawa III: Kabuki Actor
Features a famous Japanese Kabuki actor in several performances. The Kabuki theater dates from the early 17th century and is still popular today.
Availability: Schools, libraries, and nursing homes in Oklahoma and Texas.
Suggested Grade: All ages
Order Number: 19

All materials listed in this 2018-2019 edition are BRAND NEW!

FINE ARTS--MUSIC AND DRAMA

Production Date: 1985
Format: VHS videotape
Terms: Materials must be picked up in person. Under special circumstances, you may be able to have them shipped to you at your own expense (call for further details). Return within two weeks after scheduled showing. Videos must be registered with the U. S. Postal Service or returned by Priority Mail, Federal Express, or other registered shipping service.
Source: Consulate General of Japan, Houston
Cultural Affairs and Information Section
909 Fannin Street, Suite 3000
Houston, TX 77010
Phone: 1-713-652-2977
Fax: 1-713-651-7822
World Wide Web URL:
http://www.houston.us.emb-japan.go.jp/en/culture/page1.htm
Email Address: info@cgjhouston.org

Ennosuke Ichikawa III: Kabuki Actor
Features a famous Japanese Kabuki actor in several performances. The Kabuki theater dates from the early 17th century and is still popular today.
Availability: Schools, libraries, homeschoolers, and nursing homes in Arizona and California (zipcodes beginning 900-931 and 935).
Suggested Grade: All ages
Order Number: 056
Production Date: 1985
Format: VHS videotape
Terms: Borrower pays postage both ways; you may call the number below to learn how much postage costs. Return within two weeks of date borrowed. An individual may borrow 2 items at one time. For non-profit and educational use only.
Source: Consulate General of Japan, Los Angeles
350 South Grand Avenue, Suite 1700
Los Angeles, CA 90071-3459
Phone: 1-213-617-6700
Fax: 1-213-617-6727
World Wide Web URL: http://www.la.us.emb-japan.go.jp

Gagaku: The Court Music of Japan
This video allows the viewer to experience the haunting sounds of the Japanese court orchestra and to see the magnificent costumes and masks of its stately dances.
Availability: Schools, libraries, and nursing homes in the United States and Canada.
Suggested Grade: 6-Adult
Order Number: JV067
Format: VHS videotape
Terms: Borrower pays return postage. Return with 14 days after scheduled showing, via UPS or U. S. Mail. All requests must included an educational institution affiliation, a current address, and phone number. Order through web site only.
Source: Cornell University East Asia Program
World Wide Web URL:
http://eap.einaudi.cornell.edu/lending_library
Email Address: east_asia1@cornell.edu

Grupo Corpo--Brazilian Dance Theatre
A performance by this Brazilian dance company featuring Brazilian music and folk songs.
Availability: Schools and libraries in Iowa, Illinois, Michigan, Minnesota, and Wisconsin.
Suggested Grade: All ages
Order Number: DANBRAGRU92DVD
Production Date: 1996
Format: DVD
Terms: Borrower pays return postage. Return 8 days after showing. Book 2 weeks in advance. Order may also be picked up for those near the Center.
Source: Center for Latin American and Caribbean Studies
UW-Milwaukee
P. O. Box 413
Milwaukee, WI 53201
Phone: 1-414-229-5987
World Wide Web URL: http://www.uwm.edu/Dept/CLACS
Email Address: audvis@usm.edu

Hajari Bhand of Rajasthan: Jester Without Court
Hajari Bhand of Chittorgarh, Rajasthan is renowned in the nearby courts, towns, and villages of Mewar for his skill as a bahurupiya, a wandering mimic performing mostly comic routines. This video highlights twenty different disguises and his performance of various routines interspersed with interviews with the artist.
Availability: Schools, libraries, homeschoolers, and nursing homes in the southeastern United States.
Suggested Grade: 7-12
Order Number: order by title
Production Date: 1985
Format: VHS videotape
Terms: Borrower pays return postage. Return 2 days after showing via United Parcel Service, insured. Book 2 weeks in advance.
Source: Center for South Asian Studies
University of Virginia
Video Library Coordinator
P. O. Box 400169, 110 Minor Hall
Charlottesville, VA 22904-4169
Phone: 1-434-924-8815
Email Address: southasia@virginia.edu

Harvesting New Songs - Brazil
Folkloric group Sotavento describes instruments, rhythms, and social influences of the music of Brazil, and performs three selections.
Availability: Schools, libraries, and nursing homes in the United States.
Suggested Grade: 6-12
Order Number: MUBRA7-video

All materials listed in this 2018-2019 edition are **BRAND NEW!**

FINE ARTS--MUSIC AND DRAMA

Production Date: 1986
Format: VHS videotape
Terms: Borrowers must have a User's Agreement on file with this source--available by mail or via the Internet. Return postage is paid by borrower; return 12 days after showing. Book at least three weeks in advance. All borrowers are limited to a total of ten items per semester.
Source: Latin American Resource Center
Stone Center for Latin American Studies
Tulane University, 100 Jones Hall
New Orleans, LA 70118
Phone: 1-504-862-3143
Fax: 1-504-865-6719
World Wide Web URL: http://stonecenter.tulane.edu/pages/detail/48/Lending-Library
Email Address: crcrts@tulane.edu

Heated Competition: Jonkara-Bushi

A contest to appoint the national champion of young players of Tsugaru Jamisen, a traditional banjo-like musical instrument.
Availability: Schools, libraries, homeschoolers, and nursing homes in Connecticut (except Fairfield County), Maine, Massachusetts, New Hampshire, Rhode Island, and Vermont.
Suggested Grade: 4-12
Order Number: 472
Production Date: 1991
Format: VHS videotape
Special Notes: Part of the "Nippon Life II" series.
Terms: Borrower pays return postage, including insurance. Return two weeks after receipt.
Source: Consulate General of Japan, Boston
Federal Reserve Plaza, 14th Floor, 600 Atlantic Avenue
Boston, MA 02210
Phone: 1-617-973-9772
Fax: 1-617-542-1329
World Wide Web URL: http://www.boston.us.emb-japan.go.jp
Email Address: infocul@cgjbos.org

Heated Competition: Jonkara-Bushi

A contest to appoint the national champion of young players of Tsugaru Jamisen, a traditional banjo-like musical instrument.
Availability: Schools, libraries, and nursing homes in Oklahoma and Texas.
Suggested Grade: 4-12
Order Number: G3
Production Date: 1991
Format: VHS videotape
Special Notes: Part of the "Nippon Life II" series.
Terms: Materials must be picked up in person. Under special circumstances, you may be able to have them shipped to you at your own expense (call for further details). Return within two weeks after scheduled showing. Videos must be registered with the U. S. Postal Service or returned by Priority Mail, Federal Express, or other registered shipping service.
Source: Consulate General of Japan, Houston
Cultural Affairs and Information Section
909 Fannin Street, Suite 3000
Houston, TX 77010
Phone: 1-713-652-2977
Fax: 1-713-651-7822
World Wide Web URL: http://www.houston.us.emb-japan.go.jp/en/culture/page1.htm
Email Address: info@cgjhouston.org

Heated Competition: Jonkara-Bushi

A contest to appoint the national champion of young players of Tsugaru Jamisen, a traditional banjo-like musical instrument.
Availability: Schools, libraries, homeschoolers, and nursing homes in Arizona and California (zipcodes beginning 900-931 and 935).
Suggested Grade: 4-12
Order Number: 163
Production Date: 1991
Format: VHS videotape
Special Notes: Part of the "Nippon Life II" series.
Terms: Borrower pays postage both ways; you may call the number below to learn how much postage costs. Return within two weeks of date borrowed. An individual may borrow 2 items at one time. For non-profit and educational use only.
Source: Consulate General of Japan, Los Angeles
350 South Grand Avenue, Suite 1700
Los Angeles, CA 90071-3459
Phone: 1-213-617-6700
Fax: 1-213-617-6727
World Wide Web URL: http://www.la.us.emb-japan.go.jp

Heated Competition: Jonkara-Bushi

A contest to appoint the national champion of young players of Tsugaru Jamisen, a traditional banjo-like musical instrument.
Availability: Schools, libraries, homeschoolers, and nursing homes in Nevada and northern California (zip codes beginning 932 and above, except 935).
Suggested Grade: 4-12
Order Number: order by title
Production Date: 1991
Format: Beta videotape; U-matic videotape; VHS videotape
Special Notes: Part of the "Nippon Life II" series.
Terms: Borrower pays return postage. Book two weeks in advance. Return within three weeks of date borrowed, via UPS, Federal Express or certified mail.
Source: Consulate General of Japan, San Francisco
50 Fremont Street, Suite 2300
San Francisco, CA 94105-2236
Phone: 1-415-356-2564
Fax: 1-415-777-0518
World Wide Web URL: http://www.sf.us.emb-japan.go.jp/
Email Address: infoav@cgjsf.org

All materials listed in this 2018-2019 edition are BRAND NEW!

FINE ARTS--MUSIC AND DRAMA

Jongara Bushi Competition--The Tsugaru Jamisen National Contest
A contest to appoint the national champion of young players of Tsugaru Jamisen, a traditional banjo-like musical instrument.
- Availability: Schools, libraries, and nursing homes in Hawaii.
- Suggested Grade: 4-12
- Order Number: CU-50
- Format: VHS videotape
- Terms: Borrower pays return postage. A maximum of 3 videos may be borrowed per person. Return within one week of date borrowed.
- Source: Consulate General of Japan, Honolulu
  1742 Nuuanu Avenue
  Honolulu, HI 96817-3294
  Phone: 1-808-543-3111
  Fax: 1-808-543-3170
  World Wide Web URL:
  http://www.honolulu.us.emb-japan.go.jp

Journey Within a Journey, A
A documentation of some of the powerful folkloric art forms of India--ritualistic dances, shadow puppetry, martial arts--as viewed through the eyes of Chitra Neogy, a traveler returning to the villages of Kerala in India after the death of her father, in search of inner renewal.
- Availability: Schools, libraries, homeschoolers, and nursing homes in the southeastern United States.
- Suggested Grade: 7-12
- Order Number: order by title
- Production Date: 1996
- Format: VHS videotape
- Terms: Borrower pays return postage. Return 2 days after showing via United Parcel Service, insured. Book 2 weeks in advance.
- Source: Center for South Asian Studies
  University of Virginia
  Video Library Coordinator
  P. O. Box 400169, 110 Minor Hall
  Charlottesville, VA 22904-4169
  Phone: 1-434-924-8815
  Email Address: southasia@virginia.edu

Kabuki: Classic Theater of Japan/Noh, Drama, Bunraku: The Puppet Theater of Japan
The unique theatrical art form of Kabuki combines dance, music, and acting skills. The Noh drama, one of Japan's finest art forms is presented. Also the art of Japanese Bunraku theatre, including a description of the craft of making the large puppets.
- Availability: Schools, libraries, and nursing homes in Hawaii.
- Suggested Grade: 6-12
- Order Number: CU-14
- Production Date: 1964
- Format: VHS videotape
- Special Notes: Quite dated but the information is still pertinent.
- Terms: Borrower pays return postage. A maximum of 3 videos may be borrowed per person. Return within one week of date borrowed.
- Source: Consulate General of Japan, Honolulu
  1742 Nuuanu Avenue
  Honolulu, HI 96817-3294
  Phone: 1-808-543-3111
  Fax: 1-808-543-3170
  World Wide Web URL:
  http://www.honolulu.us.emb-japan.go.jp

Kabuki: Classic Theater of Japan/Noh, Drama, Bunraku: The Puppet Theater of Japan
The unique theatrical art form of Kabuki combines dance, music, and acting skills. The Noh drama, one of Japan's finest art forms is presented with the accompaniment of musicians and chorus. Also the art of Japanese Bunraku theatre, including a description of the craft of making the large puppets.
- Availability: Schools, libraries, homeschoolers, and nursing homes in OREGON AND SOUTHERN IDAHO ONLY. Please make requests via the web site.
- Suggested Grade: 6-12
- Order Number: 123
- Production Date: 1985
- Format: VHS videotape
- Special Notes: Quite dated but the information is still pertinent.
- Terms: Borrower pays return postage. Return within three weeks after scheduled showing date. Book one month in advance if possible. Rewind the video and wrap securely for return. Be certain to indicate video number, date needed, name of your organization, and address to which video should be sent, along with phone number. Audience report enclosed with the video must be completed and returned.
- Source: Consulate General of Japan, Oregon
  Attn: Tamara, Video Library
  1300 S. W. Fifth Avenue, Suite 2700
  Portland, OR 97201
  Phone: 1-503-221-1811, ext. 17
  World Wide Web URL:
  http://www.portland.us.emb-japan.go.jp/en/index.html
  Email Address: tamara@cgjpdx.org

Kings, Lovers, and Thieves
Documents the changing fate of two traditional forms of folk opera: Nautanki and Kyal, in relation to current socio-political and cultural influences in "modernizing" India.
- Availability: Schools, libraries, homeschoolers, and nursing homes in the southeastern United States.
- Suggested Grade: 7-12
- Order Number: order by title
- Production Date: 1997
- Format: VHS videotape

FINE ARTS--MUSIC AND DRAMA

Terms: Borrower pays return postage. Return 2 days after showing via United Parcel Service, insured. Book 2 weeks in advance.
Source: Center for South Asian Studies
University of Virginia
Video Library Coordinator
P. O. Box 400169, 110 Minor Hall
Charlottesville, VA 22904-4169
Phone: 1-434-924-8815
Email Address: southasia@virginia.edu

Kings, Lovers, and Thieves
Documents the changing fate of two traditional forms of folk opera: Nautanki and Kyal, in relation to current socio-political and cultural influences in "modernizing" India.
Availability: Schools and libraries in the United States.
Suggested Grade: 7-12
Order Number: 98
Production Date: 1997
Format: VHS videotape
Terms: Borrower pays return postage. Return 3 days after showing via UPS. Book at least 2 weeks in advance.
Source: Syracuse University, South Asia Center
Video Library and Teaching Resources
346F Eggers Hall
The Maxwell School
Syracuse, NY 13244

Mountain Music in Peru
Documentary portrait of the centuries-old musical culture of the Andes.
Availability: Schools, libraries, and nursing homes in the United States.
Suggested Grade: 6-12
Languages: Spanish, Quechua and Aymara with English subtitles
Order Number: MUPER1-video
Production Date: 1984
Format: VHS videotape
Terms: Borrowers must have a User's Agreement on file with this source--available by mail or via the Internet. Return postage is paid by borrower; return 12 days after showing. Book at least three weeks in advance. All borrowers are limited to a total of ten items per semester.
Source: Latin American Resource Center
Stone Center for Latin American Studies
Tulane University
100 Jones Hall
New Orleans, LA 70118
Phone: 1-504-862-3143
Fax: 1-504-865-6719
World Wide Web URL: http://stonecenter.tulane.edu/pages/detail/48/Lending-Library
Email Address: crcrts@tulane.edu

Music of Bunraku
Allows the viewer to experience the exotic drama of Bunraku, the puppet theater of Japan, and to understand its music.
Availability: Schools, libraries, and nursing homes in the United States and Canada.
Suggested Grade: 6-Adult
Order Number: JV068
Format: VHS videotape
Terms: Borrower pays return postage. Return with 14 days after scheduled showing, via UPS or U. S. Mail. All requests must included an educational institution affiliation, a current address, and phone number. Order through web site only.
Source: Cornell University East Asia Program
World Wide Web URL: http://eap.einaudi.cornell.edu/lending_library
Email Address: east_asia1@cornell.edu

Music of Latin America
Roots of Indian music, with wind and percussion, and proceeds through development of string instruments in Latin America.
Availability: Schools, libraries, and nursing homes in the United States.
Suggested Grade: 6-12
Order Number: MULA9-video
Production Date: 1987
Format: VHS videotape
Terms: Borrowers must have a User's Agreement on file with this source--available by mail or via the Internet. Return postage is paid by borrower; return 12 days after showing. Book at least three weeks in advance. All borrowers are limited to a total of ten items per semester.
Source: Latin American Resource Center
Stone Center for Latin American Studies
Tulane University
100 Jones Hall
New Orleans, LA 70118
Phone: 1-504-862-3143
Fax: 1-504-865-6719
World Wide Web URL: http://stonecenter.tulane.edu/pages/detail/48/Lending-Library
Email Address: crcrts@tulane.edu

Music of Modern Japan/Kitaro, Synthesizer Musician
Representative examples of the broad variety of music in modern Japan is matched with visual images. Also, Kitaro--poet, musician, composer, artist--is shown at his home and studio.
Availability: Schools, libraries, homeschoolers, and nursing homes in Nevada and northern California (zip codes beginning 932 and above, except 935).
Suggested Grade: 9-Adult
Order Number: order by title
Format: VHS videotape
Special Notes: Tape 2 of a series.
Terms: Borrower pays return postage. Book two weeks in advance. Return within three weeks of date borrowed, via UPS, Federal Express or certified mail.

All materials listed in this 2018-2019 edition are BRAND NEW!

FINE ARTS--MUSIC AND DRAMA

Source: Consulate General of Japan, San Francisco
50 Fremont Street, Suite 2300
San Francisco, CA 94105-2236
Phone: 1-415-356-2564
Fax: 1-415-777-0518
World Wide Web URL: http://www.sf.us.emb-japan.go.jp/
Email Address: infoav@cgjsf.org

Noh Drama, Kabuki, Bunraku--Classical Theater in Japan
The unique theatrical art form of Kabuki combines dance, music, and acting skills. The Noh drama, one of Japan's finest art forms is presented. Also the art of Japanese Bunraku theatre, including a description of the craft of making the large puppets.
Availability: Schools, libraries, homeschoolers, and nursing homes in Arizona and California (zipcodes beginning 900-931 and 935).
Suggested Grade: 6-12
Order Number: 078
Production Date: 1964
Format: VHS videotape
Terms: Borrower pays postage both ways; you may call the number below to learn how much postage costs. Return within two weeks of date borrowed. An individual may borrow 2 items at one time. For non-profit and educational use only.
Source: Consulate General of Japan, Los Angeles
350 South Grand Avenue, Suite 1700
Los Angeles, CA 90071-3459
Phone: 1-213-617-6700
Fax: 1-213-617-6727
World Wide Web URL: http://www.la.us.emb-japan.go.jp

Our Mexican-American Musical Heritage
Explores pre-Columbian and Spanish antecedents of Mexican music and their effect on contemporary forms.
Availability: Schools, libraries, and nursing homes in the United States.
Suggested Grade: 6-12
Order Number: HISP39-video
Format: VHS videotape
Special Notes: Includes study questions.
Terms: Borrowers must have a User's Agreement on file with this source--available by mail or via the Internet. Return postage is paid by borrower; return 12 days after showing. Book at least three weeks in advance. All borrowers are limited to a total of ten items per semester.
Source: Latin American Resource Center
Stone Center for Latin American Studies
Tulane University
100 Jones Hall
New Orleans, LA 70118
Phone: 1-504-862-3143
Fax: 1-504-865-6719
World Wide Web URL: http://stonecenter.tulane.edu/pages/detail/48/Lending-Library
Email Address: crcrts@tulane.edu

Raices Del Pueblo: Cantos y Danzas de Veracruz
Ballet Folklorico de la Universidad Veracruzana performs traditional regional dances.
Availability: Schools, libraries, and nursing homes in the United States.
Suggested Grade: 6-12
Language: Spanish
Order Number: DFMEX18-video
Production Date: 1990
Format: VHS videotape
Terms: Borrowers must have a User's Agreement on file with this source--available by mail or via the Internet. Return postage is paid by borrower; return 12 days after showing. Book at least three weeks in advance. All borrowers are limited to a total of ten items per semester.
Source: Latin American Resource Center
Stone Center for Latin American Studies
Tulane University
100 Jones Hall
New Orleans, LA 70118
Phone: 1-504-862-3143
Fax: 1-504-865-6719
World Wide Web URL: http://stonecenter.tulane.edu/pages/detail/48/Lending-Library
Email Address: crcrts@tulane.edu

Roots of Rhythm
Harry Belafonte hosts this critically acclaimed documentary of Latin music that aired on PBS. Viewers visit tribal celebrations in African jungles which trace the roots of Latin music, Cuba's wild carnivals and the packed dance floors of New York's hottest nightspots on this musical odyssey.
Availability: Schools in the United States.
Suggested Grade: 7-Adult
Order Number: order by title
Format: Set of 3 videotapes
Terms: Borrower pays return postage. Return 14 days after receipt, via USPS including insurance. All borrowers must have a current lending agreement on file with the Outreach program. This agreement is available via the web site or may be requested via phone or fax.
Source: Center for Latin American Studies
University of Florida
319 Grinter Hall
P. O. Box 115530
Gainesville, FL 32611-5530
Phone: 1-352-392-0375
Fax: 1-352-392-7682
World Wide Web URL: http://www.latam.ufl.edu/outreach
Email Address: maryr@ufl.edu

Roots, Rock, Reggae: Inside the Jamaican Music Scene
A street-level tour of the Kingston, Jamaica, music scene records a peak year in the social history of reggae, that began in the post-Independence Sixties. Connections to Jamaican politics, urban ghetto life, and to the Rastafari religion are shown.

FINE ARTS--MUSIC AND DRAMA

Availability: Schools in the United States.
Suggested Grade: 7-Adult
Order Number: order by title
Production Date: 1988
Format: VHS videotape
Terms: Borrower pays return postage. Return 14 days after receipt, via USPS including insurance. All borrowers must have a current lending agreement on file with the Outreach program. This agreement is available via the web site or may be requested via phone or fax.
Source: Center for Latin American Studies
University of Florida
319 Grinter Hall
P. O. Box 115530
Gainesville, FL 32611-5530
Phone: 1-352-392-0375
Fax: 1-352-392-7682
World Wide Web URL: http://www.latam.ufl.edu/outreach
Email Address: maryr@ufl.edu

Routes of Rhythm--Part II
History of popular music in Cuba.
Availability: Schools, libraries, and nursing homes in the United States.
Suggested Grade: 6-12
Order Number: MULA11-video
Format: VHS videotape
Terms: Borrowers must have a User's Agreement on file with this source--available by mail or via the Internet. Return postage is paid by borrower; return 12 days after showing. Book at least three weeks in advance. All borrowers are limited to a total of ten items per semester.
Source: Latin American Resource Center
Stone Center for Latin American Studies
Tulane University
100 Jones Hall
New Orleans, LA 70118
Phone: 1-504-862-3143
Fax: 1-504-865-6719
World Wide Web URL: http://stonecenter.tulane.edu/pages/detail/48/Lending-Library
Email Address: crcrts@tulane.edu

Routes of Rhythm--Part III
History of Latin American music in the United States.
Availability: Schools, libraries, and nursing homes in the United States.
Suggested Grade: 6-12
Order Number: MULA11-video
Format: VHS videotape
Terms: Borrowers must have a User's Agreement on file with this source--available by mail or via the Internet. Return postage is paid by borrower; return 12 days after showing. Book at least three weeks in advance. All borrowers are limited to a total of ten items per semester.
Source: Latin American Resource Center
Stone Center for Latin American Studies
Tulane University
100 Jones Hall
New Orleans, LA 70118
Phone: 1-504-862-3143
Fax: 1-504-865-6719
World Wide Web URL: http://stonecenter.tulane.edu/pages/detail/48/Lending-Library
Email Address: crcrts@tulane.edu

Selected Songs by Famous Singers
A selection of songs from the Beijing Opera.
Availability: Schools, libraries, and nursing homes in the United States and Canada.
Suggested Grade: All ages
Language: Mandarin
Order Number: CD019
Production Date: 2003
Format: DVD
Terms: Borrower pays return postage. Return with 14 days after scheduled showing, via UPS or U. S. Mail. All requests must included an educational institution affiliation, a current address, and phone number. Order through web site only.
Source: Cornell University East Asia Program
World Wide Web URL: http://eap.einaudi.cornell.edu/lending_library
Email Address: east_asia1@cornell.edu

Shadows of Turkey/The Witches
This documentary features a performance and explanation of the shadow puppets of Turkey.
Availability: Schools, libraries, homeschoolers, and nursing homes in the United States.
Suggested Grade: 7-12
Order Number: order by title
Production Date: 1996
Format: VHS videotape
Terms: Borrower pays return postage via any carrier with $400 insurance per parcel. Videos are loaned for 14 days; may be retained longer if requested in advance. Borrowers must complete a lending agreement.
Source: Center for Middle Eastern Studies
Outreach Coordinator
University of Texas at Austin
1 University Station, F9400
Austin, TX 78712-0527
World Wide Web URL: http://www.utexas.edu/cola/depts/mes/center/outreach/library-catalog.php
Email Address: crose@mail.utexas.edu

Taking Blessings Door to Door
Ise Dai Kagura are known for their performances in front of people's houses. This art form has become rare, due to lack of successors. Efforts are being made to preserve the tradition.
Availability: Schools, libraries, homeschoolers, and nursing homes in Connecticut (except Fairfield County), Maine, Massachusetts, New Hampshire, Rhode Island, and Vermont.
Suggested Grade: 9-Adult
Order Number: 419

All materials listed in this 2018-2019 edition are BRAND NEW!

FINE ARTS--MUSIC AND DRAMA

Production Date: 1990
Format: VHS videotape
Special Notes: No. 3 of the "Nippon Life" series.
Terms: Borrower pays return postage, including insurance. Return two weeks after receipt.
Source: Consulate General of Japan, Boston
Federal Reserve Plaza, 14th Floor
600 Atlantic Avenue
Boston, MA 02210
Phone: 1-617-973-9772
Fax: 1-617-542-1329
World Wide Web URL:
http://www.boston.us.emb-japan.go.jp
Email Address: infocul@cgjbos.org

Taking Blessings Door to Door
Ise Dai Kagura are known for their performances in front of people's houses. This art form has become rare, due to lack of successors. Efforts are being made to preserve the tradition.
Availability: Schools, libraries, and nursing homes in Oklahoma and Texas.
Suggested Grade: 9-Adult
Order Number: F3
Production Date: 1990
Format: VHS videotape
Special Notes: No. 3 of the "Nippon Life" series.
Terms: Materials must be picked up in person. Under special circumstances, you may be able to have them shipped to you at your own expense (call for further details). Return within two weeks after scheduled showing. Videos must be registered with the U. S. Postal Service or returned by Priority Mail, Federal Express, or other registered shipping service.
Source: Consulate General of Japan, Houston
Cultural Affairs and Information Section
909 Fannin Street, Suite 3000
Houston, TX 77010
Phone: 1-713-652-2977
Fax: 1-713-651-7822
World Wide Web URL:
http://www.houston.us.emb-japan.go.jp/en/culture/page1.htm
Email Address: info@cgjhouston.org

Taking Blessings Door to Door
Ise Dai Kagura are known for their performances in front of people's houses. This art form has become rare, due to lack of successors. Efforts are being made to preserve the tradition.
Availability: Schools, libraries, homeschoolers, and nursing homes in Nevada and northern California (zip codes beginning 932 and above, except 935).
Suggested Grade: 9-Adult
Order Number: order by title
Production Date: 1990
Format: Beta videotape; U-matic videotape; VHS videotape
Special Notes: No. 3 of the "Nippon Life" series.
Terms: Borrower pays return postage. Book two weeks in advance. Return within three weeks of date borrowed, via UPS, Federal Express or certified mail.
Source: Consulate General of Japan, San Francisco
50 Fremont Street, Suite 2300
San Francisco, CA 94105-2236
Phone: 1-415-356-2564
Fax: 1-415-777-0518
World Wide Web URL: http://www.sf.us.emb-japan.go.jp/
Email Address: infoav@cgjsf.org

Tale of the Heike, The: Biwa Concern at Cornell University
Tsutomu Imai, the last active performer in a historic guild of blind musicians, performs the traditional Tale of the Heike.
Availability: Schools, libraries, and nursing homes in the United States and Canada.
Suggested Grade: 6-Adult
Language: Japanese
Order Number: JV052
Format: VHS videotape
Terms: Borrower pays return postage. Return with 14 days after scheduled showing, via UPS or U. S. Mail. All requests must included an educational institution affiliation, a current address, and phone number. Order through web site only.
Source: Cornell University East Asia Program
World Wide Web URL:
http://eap.einaudi.cornell.edu/lending_library
Email Address: east_asia1@cornell.edu

Tango Is Also History
Development of the tango in Argentina, and its role in political and cultural history.
Availability: Schools and libraries in Iowa, Illinois, Michigan, Minnesota, and Wisconsin.
Suggested Grade: 6-12
Order Number: DANARGT15.VHS
Production Date: 1983
Format: VHS videotape
Terms: Borrower pays return postage. Return 8 days after showing. Book 2 weeks in advance. Order may also be picked up for those near the Center.
Source: Center for Latin American and Caribbean Studies
UW-Milwaukee
P. O. Box 413
Milwaukee, WI 53201
Phone: 1-414-229-5987
World Wide Web URL: http://www.uwm.edu/Dept/CLACS
Email Address: audvis@usm.edu

Tango: Our Dance
Captures the sensuality and rituals of the complex art form of the tango, Argentina's national dance.
Availability: Schools, libraries, and nursing homes in the United States.
Suggested Grade: 6-12

*All materials listed in this 2018-2019 edition are **BRAND NEW!***

FINE ARTS--MUSIC AND DRAMA

Languages: Spanish with English subtitles
Order Number: DFARG6-video
Production Date: 1987
Format: VHS videotape
Terms: Borrowers must have a User's Agreement on file with this source--available by mail or via the Internet. Return postage is paid by borrower; return 12 days after showing. Book at least three weeks in advance. All borrowers are limited to a total of ten items per semester.
Source: **Latin American Resource Center**
Stone Center for Latin American Studies
Tulane University
100 Jones Hall
New Orleans, LA 70118
Phone: 1-504-862-3143
Fax: 1-504-865-6719
World Wide Web URL: http://stonecenter.tulane.edu/pages/detail/48/Lending-Library
Email Address: crcrts@tulane.edu

Theater Lives, The
Shows the Japanese puppet theater, theater in the outlying rural areas, and the lifestyles of the people in these areas. Also shows the creation of puppets and their customs.
Availability: Schools, libraries, homeschoolers, and nursing homes in Connecticut (except Fairfield County), Maine, Massachusetts, New Hampshire, Rhode Island, and Vermont.
Suggested Grade: 6-Adult
Order Number: 114
Production Date: 1985
Format: VHS videotape
Terms: Borrower pays return postage, including insurance. Return two weeks after receipt.
Source: **Consulate General of Japan, Boston**
Federal Reserve Plaza, 14th Floor
600 Atlantic Avenue
Boston, MA 02210
Phone: 1-617-973-9772
Fax: 1-617-542-1329
World Wide Web URL: http://www.boston.us.emb-japan.go.jp
Email Address: infocul@cgjbos.org

Umm Kulthum: A Voice Like Egypt
This documentary details the life of the legendary Egyptian singer and actress, placing the events of her life in the context of the story of 20th century Egypt.
Availability: Schools, libraries, homeschoolers, and nursing homes in the United States.
Suggested Grade: 7-12
Order Number: order by title
Format: VHS videotape
Special Notes: English subtitles.
Terms: Borrower pays return postage via any carrier with $400 insurance per parcel. Videos are loaned for 14 days; may be retained longer if requested in advance. Borrowers must complete a lending agreement.
Source: **Center for Middle Eastern Studies**
Outreach Coordinator
University of Texas at Austin
1 University Station, F9400
Austin, TX 78712-0527
World Wide Web URL: http://www.utexas.edu/cola/depts/mes/center/outreach/library-catalog.php
Email Address: crose@mail.utexas.edu

Voice from Heaven, A: Nusrat Fateh Ali Khan
Filmed in Pakistan, India, Canada, and the United States, this is a tribute to a beautiful singing voice.
Availability: Schools, libraries, homeschoolers, and nursing homes in the southeastern United States.
Suggested Grade: 7-12
Order Number: order by title
Production Date: 2001
Format: DVD
Terms: Borrower pays return postage. Return 2 days after showing via United Parcel Service, insured. Book 2 weeks in advance.
Source: **Center for South Asian Studies**
University of Virginia
Video Library Coordinator
P. O. Box 400169, 110 Minor Hall
Charlottesville, VA 22904-4169
Phone: 1-434-924-8815
Email Address: southasia@virginia.edu

Waiapi Instrumental Music
Waiapi wind instruments are made of wood, reed, and bone.
Availability: Schools, libraries, and nursing homes in the United States.
Suggested Grade: 6-12
Order Number: INDBRA4-video
Production Date: 1987
Format: VHS videotape
Terms: Borrowers must have a User's Agreement on file with this source--available by mail or via the Internet. Return postage is paid by borrower; return 12 days after showing. Book at least three weeks in advance. All borrowers are limited to a total of ten items per semester.
Source: **Latin American Resource Center**
Stone Center for Latin American Studies
Tulane University
100 Jones Hall
New Orleans, LA 70118
Phone: 1-504-862-3143
Fax: 1-504-865-6719
World Wide Web URL: http://stonecenter.tulane.edu/pages/detail/48/Lending-Library
Email Address: crcrts@tulane.edu

GUIDANCE

Ethics in America

This series uses the Socratic method to build analytical skills and examine ethical questions. The programs aim to sharpen moral reasoning without favoring a particular position by exploring ethical dilemmas in legal, political, medical, corporate, and military arenas.

Availability: All requesters
Suggested Grade: 9-Adult
Order Number: not applicable
Production Date: 1989
Format: Streaming Video
Terms: A simple FREE registration is required to view videos.
    Source: Annenberg Media
    World Wide Web URL:
    http://www.learner.org/resources/browse.html

Goal Away: Setting and Achieving Goals: Turning Dreams Into Reality

Covers barriers to achieving goals and practical advice on setting and achieving goals.

Availability: Schools, libraries, and homeschoolers in the United States who serve the hearing impaired.
Suggested Grade: 8-Adult
Order Number: 13489
Production Date: 2001
Format: DVD
Terms: Sponsor pays all transportation costs. Return one week after receipt. Participation is limited to deaf or hard of hearing Americans, their parents, families, teachers, counselors, or others whose use would benefit a deaf or hard of hearing person. Only one person in the audience needs to be hearing impaired. You must register--which is free. These videos are all open-captioned--no special equipment is required for viewing.
    Source: Described and Captioned Media Program
    National Association of the Deaf
    4211 Church Street Ext.
    Roebuck, SC 29376
    Phone: 1-800-237-6213
    Fax: 1-800-538-5636
    World Wide Web URL: http://www.dcmp.org

Growing Old in a New Age

Video instructional series that challenges common misconceptions about aging.

Availability: All requesters
Suggested Grade: 9-Adult
Order Number: not applicable
Production Date: 1993
Format: Streaming Video
Terms: A simple FREE registration is required to view videos.
    Source: Annenberg Media
    World Wide Web URL:
    http://www.learner.org/resources/browse.html

How to Deal With the "Jerks" In Your Life and Earn the Respect of Your Friends

High school and junior high students created and dramatized five skits that demonstrate three typical responses to familiar school situations. The responses--passive, aggressive, and assertive--are first defined and then compared. After each response, instant replay offers discussion opportunities. The school situations include harassment; peer pressure to drink, steal, and smoke; and dating.

Availability: Schools, libraries, and homeschoolers in the United States who serve the hearing impaired.
Suggested Grade: 7-12
Order Number: 13126
Production Date: 1994
Format: DVD
Special Notes: Produced by SI Video Sales Group.
Terms: Sponsor pays all transportation costs. Return one week after receipt. Participation is limited to deaf or hard of hearing Americans, their parents, families, teachers, counselors, or others whose use would benefit a deaf or hard of hearing person. Only one person in the audience needs to be hearing impaired. You must register--which is free. These videos are all open-captioned--no special equipment is required for viewing.
    Source: Described and Captioned Media Program
    National Association of the Deaf
    4211 Church Street Ext.
    Roebuck, SC 29376
    Phone: 1-800-237-6213
    Fax: 1-800-538-5636
    World Wide Web URL: http://www.dcmp.org

Leaving School

Canadian teenagers tell why they left school before graduating and how that decision impacted their lives. They share experiences of trying to find work, how the real world is different than imagined, the loss of friends, loneliness, and what they've learned. They compare the school environment with the harsh reality of the world of work. Their advice: stay in school; education pays off.

Availability: Schools, libraries, and homeschoolers in the United States who serve the hearing impaired.
Suggested Grade: 8-12
Order Number: 12362
Production Date: 1993
Format: DVD
Special Notes: Produced by Films For the Humanities & Sciences.
Terms: Sponsor pays all transportation costs. Return one week after receipt. Participation is limited to deaf or hard of hearing Americans, their parents, families, teachers, counselors, or others whose use would benefit a deaf or hard of hearing person. Only one person in the audience needs to be hearing impaired. You must register--which is free. These videos are all open-captioned--no special equipment is required for viewing.
    Source: Described and Captioned Media Program
    National Association of the Deaf
    4211 Church Street Ext.
    Roebuck, SC 29376
    Phone: 1-800-237-6213

GUIDANCE

Fax: 1-800-538-5636
World Wide Web URL: http://www.dcmp.org

Loosening the Mold
Explores the range of human emotions conveyed through the faces and words of a Shinto priest, an elderly woman, the headmaster of a tea school, and others.
Availability: Schools, libraries, homeschoolers, and nursing homes in Connecticut (except Fairfield County), Maine, Massachusetts, New Hampshire, Rhode Island, and Vermont.
Suggested Grade: 9-Adult
Order Number: 510
Production Date: 1995
Format: VHS videotape
Special Notes: No. 11 of the "Nihon No Kokoro" series.
Terms: Borrower pays return postage, including insurance. Return two weeks after receipt.
Source: Consulate General of Japan, Boston
Federal Reserve Plaza, 14th Floor
600 Atlantic Avenue
Boston, MA 02210
Phone: 1-617-973-9772
Fax: 1-617-542-1329
World Wide Web URL:
http://www.boston.us.emb-japan.go.jp
Email Address: infocul@cgjbos.org

Loosing the Mold
Explores the range of human emotions conveyed through the faces and words of a Shinto priest, an elderly woman, the headmaster of a tea school, and others.
Availability: Schools, libraries, and nursing homes in Oklahoma and Texas.
Suggested Grade: 9-Adult
Order Number: K11
Production Date: 1995
Format: VHS videotape
Special Notes: No. 11 of the "Nihon No Kokoro" series.
Terms: Materials must be picked up in person. Under special circumstances, you may be able to have them shipped to you at your own expense (call for further details). Return within two weeks after scheduled showing. Videos must be registered with the U. S. Postal Service or returned by Priority Mail, Federal Express, or other registered shipping service.
Source: Consulate General of Japan, Houston
Cultural Affairs and Information Section
909 Fannin Street, Suite 3000
Houston, TX 77010
Phone: 1-713-652-2977
Fax: 1-713-651-7822
World Wide Web URL:
http://www.houston.us.emb-japan.go.jp/en/culture/page1.htm
Email Address: info@cgjhouston.org

Loosing the Mold
Explores the range of human emotions conveyed through the faces and words of a Shinto priest, an elderly woman, the headmaster of a tea school, and others.
Availability: Schools, libraries, homeschoolers, and nursing homes in Nevada and northern California (zip codes beginning 932 and above, except 935).
Suggested Grade: 9-Adult
Order Number: order by title
Production Date: 1995
Format: VHS videotape
Special Notes: No. 11 of the "Nihon No Kokoro" series.
Terms: Borrower pays return postage. Book two weeks in advance. Return within three weeks of date borrowed, via UPS, Federal Express or certified mail.
Source: Consulate General of Japan, San Francisco
50 Fremont Street, Suite 2300
San Francisco, CA 94105-2236
Phone: 1-415-356-2564
Fax: 1-415-777-0518
World Wide Web URL: http://www.sf.us.emb-japan.go.jp/
Email Address: infoav@cgjsf.org

Real People Coping with Eating Disorders
This program documents the stories of three young people recovering from the eating disorders bulimia and anorexia nervosa.
Availability: Staff at schools with NET, WIC, CSFP, FDPIR, CACFP, UMD or Child Nutrition Program food programs in the United States. Those not having such an affiliation should contact their library to place an interlibrary loan request.
Suggested Grade: 7-12
Order Number: NAL Video 778
Production Date: 1989
Format: VHS videotape
Terms: Borrower pays return postage. RETURN the day after scheduled use. Book at least 4 weeks in advance. Requests must include your name, phone, mail address, eligibility program, title, NAL number, show date, and a statement, "I have read the warning on copyright restrictions and accept full responsibility for compliance." One title per request.
Source: National Agricultural Library
Document Delivery Services Branch
4th Floor, Photo Lab
10301 Baltimore Avenue
Beltsville, MD 20705-2351
Phone: 1-301-504-5994
Fax: 1-301-504-5675
World Wide Web URL: http://www.nal.usda.gov/fnic
Email Address: lending@nal.usda.gov

R-E-S-P-E-C-T
Dramatic vignettes examine four basic issues of respect: for authority, for rules, for others' opinions, and for oneself. Each real-life situation challenges teenagers to recognize disrespect and to think critically about their own behaviors. Pertinent discussion questions between segments encourage

GUIDANCE

understanding and dialogue.
- Availability: Schools, libraries, and homeschoolers in the United States who serve the hearing impaired.
- Suggested Grade: 9-12
- Order Number: 13088
- Production Date: 1996
- Format: DVD
- Special Notes: Produced by Sunburst Communications.
- Terms: Sponsor pays all transportation costs. Return one week after receipt. Participation is limited to deaf or hard of hearing Americans, their parents, families, teachers, counselors, or others whose use would benefit a deaf or hard of hearing person. Only one person in the audience needs to be hearing impaired. You must register--which is free. These videos are all open-captioned--no special equipment is required for viewing.
- Source: **Described and Captioned Media Program**
  National Association of the Deaf
  4211 Church Street Ext.
  Roebuck, SC 29376
  Phone: 1-800-237-6213
  Fax: 1-800-538-5636
  World Wide Web URL: http://www.dcmp.org

Student Workshop: All About Respect

This four-part presentation dramatizes different kinds of respect: for feelings, for rules and authority, for differences, and for self. Each scene illustrates a different issue and challenges young teenagers to analyze the situation. The host asks pertinent questions for discussion and encourages critical thinking about the role of respect.
- Availability: Schools, libraries, and homeschoolers in the United States who serve the hearing impaired.
- Suggested Grade: 6-9
- Order Number: 13093
- Production Date: 1998
- Format: DVD
- Special Notes: Produced by Sunburst Communications.
- Terms: Sponsor pays all transportation costs. Return one week after receipt. Participation is limited to deaf or hard of hearing Americans, their parents, families, teachers, counselors, or others whose use would benefit a deaf or hard of hearing person. Only one person in the audience needs to be hearing impaired. You must register--which is free. These videos are all open-captioned--no special equipment is required for viewing.
- Source: **Described and Captioned Media Program**
  National Association of the Deaf
  4211 Church Street Ext.
  Roebuck, SC 29376
  Phone: 1-800-237-6213
  Fax: 1-800-538-5636
  World Wide Web URL: http://www.dcmp.org

To Live in a Multi-Cultural World

An adaptation of Youth for Understanding's training materials, here are nine lesson plans focusing on counteracting stereotypes and learning about other cultures.
- Availability: Schools and libraries in Iowa, Illinois, Michigan, Minnesota, and Wisconsin.
- Suggested Grade: 5-12
- Order Number: CI/URMEXN86VHS
- Production Date: 1992
- Format: VHS videotape
- Terms: Borrower pays return postage. Return 8 days after showing. Book 2 weeks in advance. Order may also be picked up for those near the Center.
- Source: **Center for Latin American and Caribbean Studies**
  UW-Milwaukee
  P. O. Box 413
  Milwaukee, WI 53201
  Phone: 1-414-229-5987
  World Wide Web URL: http://www.uwm.edu/Dept/CLACS
  Email Address: audvis@usm.edu

Wake Up Call

Young people being sexually harassed and exploited is a serious issue today, particularly if the relationship is with someone in a trusted role, such as a teacher or boss. Lizzie finds a flexible, well-paying job, but her boss makes inappropriate and unwanted sexual overtures and innuendoes. She must decide whether to compromise her values for the chance to earn money for college.
- Availability: Schools, libraries, and homeschoolers in the United States who serve the hearing impaired.
- Suggested Grade: 8-Adult
- Order Number: 12401
- Production Date: 1996
- Format: DVD
- Special Notes: Produced by Aims Multimedia.
- Terms: Sponsor pays all transportation costs. Return one week after receipt. Participation is limited to deaf or hard of hearing Americans, their parents, families, teachers, counselors, or others whose use would benefit a deaf or hard of hearing person. Only one person in the audience needs to be hearing impaired. You must register--which is free. These videos are all open-captioned--no special equipment is required for viewing.
- Source: **Described and Captioned Media Program**
  National Association of the Deaf
  4211 Church Street Ext.
  Roebuck, SC 29376
  Phone: 1-800-237-6213
  Fax: 1-800-538-5636
  World Wide Web URL: http://www.dcmp.org

Win-Win

Because people interact with each other, conflict exists. Five scenarios present a true-to-life look at familiar, relevant topics: violence, prejudice/discrimination, student-parent conflict, peer pressure, and sexual harassment. Each scene sets up a conflict situation, then stops to allow viewers to answer and discuss specific related questions.
- Availability: Schools, libraries, and homeschoolers in the United States who serve the hearing impaired.
- Suggested Grade: 7-Adult

GUIDANCE

Order Number: 1814
Production Date: 1994
Format: DVD
Special Notes: Produced by Film Ideas, Inc.
Terms: Sponsor pays all transportation costs. Return one week after receipt. Participation is limited to deaf or hard of hearing Americans, their parents, families, teachers, counselors, or others whose use would benefit a deaf or hard of hearing person. Only one person in the audience needs to be hearing impaired. You must register--which is free. These videos are all open-captioned--no special equipment is required for viewing.
Source: Described and Captioned Media Program
National Association of the Deaf
4211 Church Street Ext.
Roebuck, SC 29376
Phone: 1-800-237-6213
Fax: 1-800-538-5636
World Wide Web URL: http://www.dcmp.org

Women in Dental Research

Exciting career possibilities in dental research are illustrated by following three amazing women.
Availability: All requesters
Suggested Grade: 6-12
Order Number: not applicable
Format: Streaming Video
Special Notes: You may request DVD via the web site. This link brings you to a general page, please search for this title.
Source: National Institutes of Health, Office of Science Education
World Wide Web URL:
http://www.nidcr.nih.gov/EducationalResources/

Women Scientists with Disabilities

This video depicts three women scientists with disabilities who followed their dreams and, despite physical challenges, forged unique paths into their chosen specialties.
Availability: All requesters
Suggested Grade: 6-12
Order Number: not applicable
Format: Streaming Video
Special Notes: You may request DVD via the web site. This link brings you to a general page, please search for this title.
Source: National Institutes of Health, Office of Science Education
World Wide Web URL:
http://www.nidcr.nih.gov/EducationalResources/

All materials listed in this 2018-2019 edition are BRAND NEW!

HEALTH

Anemia: The Silent Shadow
Discusses iron deficiency and folic acid, identifies groups at risk, provides nutrition guidelines for prevention, and offers recipes and cooking tips.
Availability: Staff at schools with NET, WIC, CSFP, FDPIR, CACFP, UMD or Child Nutrition Program food programs in the United States. Those not having such an affiliation should contact their library to place an interlibrary loan request.
Suggested Grade: 7-12
Language: English; Spanish
Order Number: English NAL Video 2295; Spanish NAL Video 3243
Production Date: 1995
Format: VHS videotape
Terms: Borrower pays return postage. RETURN the day after scheduled use. Book at least 4 weeks in advance. Requests must include your name, phone, mail address, eligibility program, title, NAL number, show date, and a statement, "I have read the warning on copyright restrictions and accept full responsibility for compliance." One title per request.
Source: National Agricultural Library
Document Delivery Services Branch
4th Floor, Photo Lab
10301 Baltimore Avenue
Beltsville, MD 20705-2351
Phone: 1-301-504-5994
Fax: 1-301-504-5675
World Wide Web URL: http://www.nal.usda.gov/fnic
Email Address: lending@nal.usda.gov

Battle Against Disease, The
Looks at the efforts of the Japanese government and the Japan Medical Association in their battle against infectious disease.
Availability: Schools, libraries, homeschoolers, and nursing homes in Arizona and California (zipcodes beginning 900-931 and 935).
Suggested Grade: 6-Adult
Order Number: 084
Production Date: 1982
Format: VHS videotape
Terms: Borrower pays postage both ways; you may call the number below to learn how much postage costs. Return within two weeks of date borrowed. An individual may borrow 2 items at one time. For non-profit and educational use only.
Source: Consulate General of Japan, Los Angeles
350 South Grand Avenue, Suite 1700
Los Angeles, CA 90071-3459
Phone: 1-213-617-6700
Fax: 1-213-617-6727
World Wide Web URL: http://www.la.us.emb-japan.go.jp

Covert Bailey's Fit or Fat
A series of programs on fitness and how to get fit.
Availability: Staff at schools with NET, WIC, CSFP, FDPIR, CACFP, UMD or Child Nutrition Program food programs in the United States. Those not having such an affiliation should contact their library to place an interlibrary loan request.
Suggested Grade: 4-12
Order Number: NAL Video 1757
Production Date: 1993
Format: Set of 4 VHS videotapes
Terms: Borrower pays return postage. RETURN the day after scheduled use. Book at least 4 weeks in advance. Requests must include your name, phone, mail address, eligibility program, title, NAL number, show date, and a statement, "I have read the warning on copyright restrictions and accept full responsibility for compliance." One title per request.
Source: National Agricultural Library
Document Delivery Services Branch
4th Floor, Photo Lab
10301 Baltimore Avenue
Beltsville, MD 20705-2351
Phone: 1-301-504-5994
Fax: 1-301-504-5675
World Wide Web URL: http://www.nal.usda.gov/fnic
Email Address: lending@nal.usda.gov

Eating Disorders
Profiles four young people and their experiences with an eating disorder.
Availability: Schools, libraries, and homeschoolers in the United States who serve the hearing impaired.
Suggested Grade: Teacher Reference
Order Number: 2517
Production Date: 2000
Format: Streaming video
Terms: Sponsor pays all transportation costs. Return one week after receipt. Participation is limited to deaf or hard of hearing Americans, their parents, families, teachers, counselors, or others whose use would benefit a deaf or hard of hearing person. Only one person in the audience needs to be hearing impaired. You must register--which is free. These videos are all open-captioned--no special equipment is required for viewing.
Source: Described and Captioned Media Program
National Association of the Deaf
4211 Church Street Ext.
Roebuck, SC 29376
Phone: 1-800-237-6213
Fax: 1-800-538-5636
World Wide Web URL: http://www.dcmp.org

Fetal Alcohol Syndrome: Prenatal Drug and Alcohol Use and Its Effects
Discusses the effects of drugs, alcohol, and smoking on the fetus.

HEALTH

Availability: Staff at schools with NET, WIC, CSFP, FDPIR, CACFP, UMD or Child Nutrition Program food programs in the United States. Those not having such an affiliation should contact their library to place an interlibrary loan request.
Suggested Grade: 7-Adult
Language: English; Spanish
Order Number: English Video 3251; Spanish Video 2352
Production Date: 1999
Format: VHS videotape
Terms: Borrower pays return postage. RETURN the day after scheduled use. Book at least 4 weeks in advance. Requests must include your name, phone, mail address, eligibility program, title, NAL number, show date, and a statement, "I have read the warning on copyright restrictions and accept full responsibility for compliance." One title per request.
Source: National Agricultural Library
Document Delivery Services Branch
4th Floor, Photo Lab, 10301 Baltimore Avenue
Beltsville, MD 20705-2351
Phone: 1-301-504-5994
Fax: 1-301-504-5675
World Wide Web URL: http://www.nal.usda.gov/fnic
Email Address: lending@nal.usda.gov

Guide to Your Healthy Heart

Explains what coronary heart disease is and how it develops.
Availability: Staff at schools with NET, WIC, CSFP, FDPIR, CACFP, UMD or Child Nutrition Program food programs in the United States. Those not having such an affiliation should contact their library to place an interlibrary loan request.
Suggested Grade: 9-12
Order Number: NAL Video 2157
Production Date: 1994
Format: VHS videotape
Special Notes: Produced by the American Medical Association
Terms: Borrower pays return postage. RETURN the day after scheduled use. Book at least 4 weeks in advance. Requests must include your name, phone, mail address, eligibility program, title, NAL number, show date, and a statement, "I have read the warning on copyright restrictions and accept full responsibility for compliance." One title per request.
Source: National Agricultural Library
Document Delivery Services Branch
4th Floor, Photo Lab, 10301 Baltimore Avenue
Beltsville, MD 20705-2351
Phone: 1-301-504-5994
Fax: 1-301-504-5675
World Wide Web URL: http://www.nal.usda.gov/fnic
Email Address: lending@nal.usda.gov

Hepatitis-The Silent Epidemic

Covers the three types of hepatitis, their symptoms, and the functions of the liver, and a hepatitis patient relates his experience. Suggests further sources of information, a book on hepatitis C and the Internet.
Availability: Schools, libraries, and homeschoolers in the United States who serve the hearing impaired.
Suggested Grade: 7-Adult
Order Number: 13347
Format: Streaming Video
Terms: Sponsor pays all transportation costs. Return one week after receipt. Participation is limited to deaf or hard of hearing Americans, their parents, families, teachers, counselors, or others whose use would benefit a deaf or hard of hearing person. Only one person in the audience needs to be hearing impaired. You must register--which is free. These videos are all open-captioned--no special equipment is required for viewing.
Source: Described and Captioned Media Program
National Association of the Deaf
4211 Church Street Ext.
Roebuck, SC 29376
Phone: 1-800-237-6213
Fax: 1-800-538-5636
World Wide Web URL: http://www.dcmp.org

How to Read the New Food Label

Explains the features of the new label and helps consumers learn to use it.
Availability: Staff at schools with NET, WIC, CSFP, FDPIR, CACFP, UMD or Child Nutrition Program food programs in the United States. Those not having such an affiliation should contact their library to place an interlibrary loan request.
Suggested Grade: 6-Adult
Language: English; Spanish
Order Number: English--NAL Video 1480; Spanish--NAL Video 1643
Format: VHS videotape
Terms: Borrower pays return postage. RETURN the day after scheduled use. Book at least 4 weeks in advance. Requests must include your name, phone, mail address, eligibility program, title, NAL number, show date, and a statement, "I have read the warning on copyright restrictions and accept full responsibility for compliance." One title per request.
Source: National Agricultural Library
Document Delivery Services Branch
4th Floor, Photo Lab
10301 Baltimore Avenue
Beltsville, MD 20705-2351
Phone: 1-301-504-5994
Fax: 1-301-504-5675
World Wide Web URL: http://www.nal.usda.gov/fnic
Email Address: lending@nal.usda.gov

Introduction to Diabetes: The Game Plan

Explains managing diabetes through lifestyle changes--better nutrition, daily medication, regular exercise, and monitoring blood sugar levels.

All materials listed in this 2018-2019 edition are BRAND NEW!

HEALTH

Availability: Staff at schools with NET, WIC, CSFP, FDPIR, CACFP, UMD or Child Nutrition Program food programs in the United States. Those not having such an affiliation should contact their library to place an interlibrary loan request.
Suggested Grade: 9-12
Order Number: NAL Video 1875
Production Date: 1994
Format: VHS videotape
Terms: Borrower pays return postage. RETURN the day after scheduled use. Book at least 4 weeks in advance. Requests must include your name, phone, mail address, eligibility program, title, NAL number, show date, and a statement, "I have read the warning on copyright restrictions and accept full responsibility for compliance." One title per request.

Source: National Agricultural Library
Document Delivery Services Branch
4th Floor, Photo Lab, 10301 Baltimore Avenue
Beltsville, MD 20705-2351
Phone: 1-301-504-5994
Fax: 1-301-504-5675
World Wide Web URL: http://www.nal.usda.gov/fnic
Email Address: lending@nal.usda.gov

Lo Que Comes: Por Ti Y Tu Bebe

This program uses the novella format to teach young pregnant women about healthy eating habits during pregnancy. It includes information about weight gain and WIC (Women, Infants & Children).

Availability: Staff at schools with NET, WIC, CSFP, FDPIR, CACFP, UMD or Child Nutrition Program food programs in the United States. Those not having such an affiliation should contact their library to place an interlibrary loan request.
Suggested Grade: 6-Adult
Language: Spanish
Order Number: NAL Video 1797
Production Date: 1993
Format: VHS videotape
Special Notes: This Philadelphia Department of Health and Ethnovision production includes a discussion guide and an English script.
Terms: Borrower pays return postage. RETURN the day after scheduled use. Book at least 4 weeks in advance. Requests must include your name, phone, mail address, eligibility program, title, NAL number, show date, and a statement, "I have read the warning on copyright restrictions and accept full responsibility for compliance." One title per request.

Source: National Agricultural Library
Document Delivery Services Branch
4th Floor, Photo Lab, 10301 Baltimore Avenue
Beltsville, MD 20705-2351
Phone: 1-301-504-5994
Fax: 1-301-504-5675
World Wide Web URL: http://www.nal.usda.gov/fnic
Email Address: lending@nal.usda.gov

Mirror in My Mind, The: Body Image & Self-Esteem

Discusses how personal body image develops during the teen yeas and how it can lead to unacceptable, unhealthy behavior.

Availability: Schools, libraries, and homeschoolers in the United States who serve the hearing impaired.
Suggested Grade: 7-12
Order Number: 10939
Production Date: 2002
Format: DVD
Special Notes: Also available as live streaming video over the Internet.
Terms: Sponsor pays all transportation costs. Return one week after receipt. Participation is limited to deaf or hard of hearing Americans, their parents, families, teachers, counselors, or others whose use would benefit a deaf or hard of hearing person. Only one person in the audience needs to be hearing impaired. You must register--which is free. These videos are all open-captioned--no special equipment is required for viewing.

Source: Described and Captioned Media Program
National Association of the Deaf
4211 Church Street Ext.
Roebuck, SC 29376
Phone: 1-800-237-6213
Fax: 1-800-538-5636
World Wide Web URL: http://www.dcmp.org

Rockin' Hand Washin' Report, The

Through the use of humor, this video tells how to wash your hands properly to prevent spreading disease.

Availability: Staff at schools with NET, WIC, CSFP, FDPIR, CACFP, UMD or Child Nutrition Program food programs in the United States. Those not having such an affiliation should contact their library to place an interlibrary loan request.
Suggested Grade: 6-12
Order Number: NAL Video 2490
Production Date: 1989
Format: VHS videotape
Terms: Borrower pays return postage. RETURN the day after scheduled use. Book at least 4 weeks in advance. Requests must include your name, phone, mail address, eligibility program, title, NAL number, show date, and a statement, "I have read the warning on copyright restrictions and accept full responsibility for compliance." One title per request.

Source: National Agricultural Library
Document Delivery Services Branch
4th Floor, Photo Lab
10301 Baltimore Avenue
Beltsville, MD 20705-2351
Phone: 1-301-504-5994
Fax: 1-301-504-5675
World Wide Web URL: http://www.nal.usda.gov/fnic
Email Address: lending@nal.usda.gov

HEALTH

Teenage Nutrition: Prevention of Obesity
More teenagers than ever are overweight, and the problem may lead to a lifetime of obesity. Focuses on several practical tools in a total health plan. Explains the 80/20 concept and the food pyramid, the Hunger Scale, the F.A.T.S. formula, and nutrition labels. Also stresses exercise, attitude, and avoiding high-risk situations and how these will produce a healthy body without dieting.

- Availability: Schools, libraries, and homeschoolers in the United States who serve the hearing impaired.
- Suggested Grade: 7-12
- Order Number: 12852
- Production Date: 1997
- Format: DVD
- Special Notes: Produced by Film Ideas, Inc. Also available as streaming video.
- Terms: Sponsor pays all transportation costs. Return one week after receipt. Participation is limited to deaf or hard of hearing Americans, their parents, families, teachers, counselors, or others whose use would benefit a deaf or hard of hearing person. Only one person in the audience needs to be hearing impaired. You must register--which is free. These videos are all open-captioned--no special equipment is required for viewing.

Source: Described and Captioned Media Program
National Association of the Deaf
4211 Church Street Ext.
Roebuck, SC 29376
Phone: 1-800-237-6213
Fax: 1-800-538-5636
World Wide Web URL: http://www.dcmp.org

Wash Those Hands!
Presents concise information about basic personal hygiene, including a look at germs and how they make people sick.

- Availability: Staff at schools with NET, WIC, CSFP, FDPIR, CACFP, UMD or Child Nutrition Program food programs in the United States. Those not having such an affiliation should contact their library to place an interlibrary loan request.
- Suggested Grade: All ages
- Order Number: NAL Video 2370
- Production Date: 1996
- Format: VHS videotape
- Special Notes: Closed-captioned.
- Terms: Borrower pays return postage. RETURN the day after scheduled use. Book at least 4 weeks in advance. Requests must include your name, phone, mail address, eligibility program, title, NAL number, show date, and a statement, "I have read the warning on copyright restrictions and accept full responsibility for compliance." One title per request.

Source: National Agricultural Library
Document Delivery Services Branch
4th Floor, Photo Lab
10301 Baltimore Avenue
Beltsville, MD 20705-2351
Phone: 1-301-504-5994
Fax: 1-301-504-5675
World Wide Web URL: http://www.nal.usda.gov/fnic
Email Address: lending@nal.usda.gov

Weight: Maintaining a Healthy Balance
Teaches viewers a variety of skills to help them control their weight.

- Availability: Staff at schools with NET, WIC, CSFP, FDPIR, CACFP, UMD or Child Nutrition Program food programs in the United States. Those not having such an affiliation should contact their library to place an interlibrary loan request.
- Suggested Grade: 6-12
- Order Number: NAL Video 2294
- Production Date: 1996
- Format: VHS videotape
- Terms: Borrower pays return postage. RETURN the day after scheduled use. Book at least 4 weeks in advance. Requests must include your name, phone, mail address, eligibility program, title, NAL number, show date, and a statement, "I have read the warning on copyright restrictions and accept full responsibility for compliance." One title per request.

Source: National Agricultural Library
Document Delivery Services Branch
4th Floor, Photo Lab
10301 Baltimore Avenue
Beltsville, MD 20705-2351
Phone: 1-301-504-5994
Fax: 1-301-504-5675
World Wide Web URL: http://www.nal.usda.gov/fnic
Email Address: lending@nal.usda.gov

You're in Charge: Teens With Asthma
Teens talk about their experiences with asthma and the use of peak flow meters as well as prescribed medications. Animated graphics illustrate how asthma acts in the body.

- Availability: Schools, libraries, and homeschoolers in Connecticut, Maine, Massachusetts, New Hampshire, Rhode Island, and Vermont.
- Suggested Grade: 4-12
- Order Number: VID 167
- Format: VHS videotape
- Terms: Borrower pays return postage. Return within three weeks of receipt. If the tape you request is available, it will be mailed within 5 business days. If not, you will be notified that this video is already out on loan. No more than three titles may be borrowed by one requestor at a time. No reservations for a specific date will be accepted. It is most efficient to order via the web site.

Source: U. S. Environmental Protection Agency, Region 1
Customer Service Center
One Congress Street, Suite 1100
Boston, MA 02214
World Wide Web URL:
http://yosemite.epa.gov/r1/videolen.nsf/

All materials listed in this 2018-2019 edition are BRAND NEW!

HOME ECONOMICS--FAMILY LIFE EDUCATION

Baby Shower for Betsy, A
Betsy's friends try to convince her that breastfeeding is the best way to feed her baby.
- Availability: Staff at schools with NET, WIC, CSFP, FDPIR, CACFP, UMD or Child Nutrition Program food programs in the United States. Those not having such an affiliation should contact their library to place an interlibrary loan request.
- Suggested Grade: 9-Adult
- Order Number: Videocassette No. 2351(E)
- Production Date: 1994
- Format: VHS videotape
- Terms: Borrower pays return postage. RETURN the day after scheduled use. Book at least 4 weeks in advance. Requests must include your name, phone, mail address, eligibility program, title, NAL number, show date, and a statement, "I have read the warning on copyright restrictions and accept full responsibility for compliance." One title per request.

  Source: National Agricultural Library
  Document Delivery Services Branch
  4th Floor, Photo Lab, 10301 Baltimore Avenue
  Beltsville, MD 20705-2351
  Phone: 1-301-504-5994
  Fax: 1-301-504-5675
  World Wide Web URL: http://www.nal.usda.gov/fnic
  Email Address: lending@nal.usda.gov

Body Image for Boys
Discusses how young men see themselves and examines the growing phenomena of increasing gym memberships, exercise addiction, and more.
- Availability: Schools, libraries, and homeschoolers in the United States who serve the hearing impaired.
- Suggested Grade: 6-12
- Order Number: 11648
- Format: DVD
- Special Notes: Also available as live streaming video over the Internet.
- Terms: Sponsor pays all transportation costs. Return one week after receipt. Participation is limited to deaf or hard of hearing Americans, their parents, families, teachers, counselors, or others whose use would benefit a deaf or hard of hearing person. Only one person in the audience needs to be hearing impaired. You must register--which is free. These videos are all open-captioned--no special equipment is required for viewing.

  Source: Described and Captioned Media Program
  National Association of the Deaf
  4211 Church Street Ext.
  Roebuck, SC 29376
  Phone: 1-800-237-6213
  Fax: 1-800-538-5636
  World Wide Web URL: http://www.dcmp.org

Eating, Teens and Calcium
Explains why pregnant teens need more calcium to build strong bones for themselves and their baby.
- Availability: Staff at schools with NET, WIC, CSFP, FDPIR, CACFP, UMD or Child Nutrition Program food programs in the United States. Those not having such an affiliation should contact their library to place an interlibrary loan request.
- Suggested Grade: 9-12
- Order Number: NAL Video 2610
- Production Date: 1997
- Format: VHS videotape
- Terms: Borrower pays return postage. RETURN the day after scheduled use. Book at least 4 weeks in advance. Requests must include your name, phone, mail address, eligibility program, title, NAL number, show date, and a statement, "I have read the warning on copyright restrictions and accept full responsibility for compliance." One title per request.

  Source: National Agricultural Library
  Document Delivery Services Branch
  4th Floor, Photo Lab
  10301 Baltimore Avenue
  Beltsville, MD 20705-2351
  Phone: 1-301-504-5994
  Fax: 1-301-504-5675
  World Wide Web URL: http://www.nal.usda.gov/fnic
  Email Address: lending@nal.usda.gov

First Foods: Lily Feeds Her Baby
Explains the dietary needs of infants and how these needs change drastically within a baby's first year. Discusses the importance of a baby's balanced diet, introducing new foods, watching for allergic reactions, food preparation, and dealing with the infant's emotional reaction toward eating.
- Availability: Staff at schools with NET, WIC, CSFP, FDPIR, CACFP, UMD or Child Nutrition Program food programs in the United States. Those not having such an affiliation should contact their library to place an interlibrary loan request.
- Suggested Grade: 7-12
- Order Number: NAL Video 1546
- Production Date: 1991
- Format: VHS videotape
- Terms: Borrower pays return postage. RETURN the day after scheduled use. Book at least 4 weeks in advance. Requests must include your name, phone, mail address, eligibility program, title, NAL number, show date, and a statement, "I have read the warning on copyright restrictions and accept full responsibility for compliance." One title per request.

  Source: National Agricultural Library
  Document Delivery Services Branch
  4th Floor, Photo Lab
  10301 Baltimore Avenue
  Beltsville, MD 20705-2351
  Phone: 1-301-504-5994
  Fax: 1-301-504-5675
  World Wide Web URL: http://www.nal.usda.gov/fnic
  Email Address: lending@nal.usda.gov

HOME ECONOMICS--FAMILY LIFE EDUCATION

14 Steps to Better Breastfeeding
Provides information for new mothers on how to breastfeed successfully.
- Availability: Staff at schools with NET, WIC, CSFP, FDPIR, CACFP, UMD or Child Nutrition Program food programs in the United States. Those not having such an affiliation should contact their library to place an interlibrary loan request.
- Suggested Grade: Adult
- Languages: English; Spanish
- Order Number: English NAL Video 2955; Spanish NAL Video 2956
- Production Date: 2000
- Format: VHS videotape
- Terms: Borrower pays return postage. RETURN the day after scheduled use. Book at least 4 weeks in advance. Requests must include your name, phone, mail address, eligibility program, title, NAL number, show date, and a statement, "I have read the warning on copyright restrictions and accept full responsibility for compliance." One title per request.

    Source: National Agricultural Library
    Document Delivery Services Branch
    4th Floor, Photo Lab
    10301 Baltimore Avenue
    Beltsville, MD 20705-2351
    Phone: 1-301-504-5994
    Fax: 1-301-504-5675
    World Wide Web URL: http://www.nal.usda.gov/fnic
    Email Address: lending@nal.usda.gov

Health During Pregnancy: Lily Looks Back
Main character Lily looks back at her pregnancy and tells her sister about prenatal care, good nutrition for pregnancy, the Food Guide Pyramid, the importance of breakfast, exercise during pregnancy, and substances to avoid during pregnancy.
- Availability: Staff at schools with NET, WIC, CSFP, FDPIR, CACFP, UMD or Child Nutrition Program food programs in the United States. Those not having such an affiliation should contact their library to place an interlibrary loan request.
- Suggested Grade: 9-Adult
- Languages: English; Spanish
- Order Number: NAL Video 1887
- Production Date: 1993
- Format: VHS videotape
- Special Notes: This program was produced by the Altschul Group Corporation, Evanston, IL.
- Terms: Borrower pays return postage. RETURN the day after scheduled use. Book at least 4 weeks in advance. Requests must include your name, phone, mail address, eligibility program, title, NAL number, show date, and a statement, "I have read the warning on copyright restrictions and accept full responsibility for compliance." One title per request.

    Source: National Agricultural Library
    Document Delivery Services Branch
    4th Floor, Photo Lab
    10301 Baltimore Avenue
    Beltsville, MD 20705-2351
    Phone: 1-301-504-5994
    Fax: 1-301-504-5675
    World Wide Web URL: http://www.nal.usda.gov/fnic
    Email Address: lending@nal.usda.gov

Healthy Eating for a Healthy Baby
Expectant mothers are taught about proper weight gain and good nutrition practices using the food guide pyramid.
- Availability: Staff at schools with NET, WIC, CSFP, FDPIR, CACFP, UMD or Child Nutrition Program food programs in the United States. Those not having such an affiliation should contact their library to place an interlibrary loan request.
- Suggested Grade: 9-Adult
- Languages: English; Spanish
- Order Number: English NAL Video 2765; Spanish NAL Video 2844
- Production Date: 1995
- Format: VHS videotape
- Terms: Borrower pays return postage. RETURN the day after scheduled use. Book at least 4 weeks in advance. Requests must include your name, phone, mail address, eligibility program, title, NAL number, show date, and a statement, "I have read the warning on copyright restrictions and accept full responsibility for compliance." One title per request.

    Source: National Agricultural Library
    Document Delivery Services Branch
    4th Floor, Photo Lab
    10301 Baltimore Avenue
    Beltsville, MD 20705-2351
    Phone: 1-301-504-5994
    Fax: 1-301-504-5675
    World Wide Web URL: http://www.nal.usda.gov/fnic
    Email Address: lending@nal.usda.gov

Healthy Foods, Healthy Baby
In a novella format, two young teens, one Black-American, one Hispanic, learn about good nutrition during pregnancy.
- Availability: Staff at schools with NET, WIC, CSFP, FDPIR, CACFP, UMD or Child Nutrition Program food programs in the United States. Those not having such an affiliation should contact their library to place an interlibrary loan request.
- Suggested Grade: 6-Adult
- Order Number: NAL Video 1426
- Production Date: 1992
- Format: VHS videotape
- Special Notes: Produced by the Philadelphia Department of Health.
- Terms: Borrower pays return postage. RETURN the day after scheduled use. Book at least 4 weeks in advance. Requests must include your name, phone, mail address,

*All materials listed in this 2018-2019 edition are **BRAND NEW!***

HOME ECONOMICS--FAMILY LIFE EDUCATION

eligibility program, title, NAL number, show date, and a statement, "I have read the warning on copyright restrictions and accept full responsibility for compliance." One title per request.
    Source: National Agricultural Library
    Document Delivery Services Branch
    4th Floor, Photo Lab
    10301 Baltimore Avenue
    Beltsville, MD 20705-2351
    Phone: 1-301-504-5994
    Fax: 1-301-504-5675
World Wide Web URL: http://www.nal.usda.gov/fnic
    Email Address: lending@nal.usda.gov

Inside My Mom
A cartoon fetus talks to his mom about how to feed him during pregnancy.
- Availability: Staff at schools with NET, WIC, CSFP, FDPIR, CACFP, UMD or Child Nutrition Program food programs in the United States. Those not having such an affiliation should contact their library to place an interlibrary loan request.
- Suggested Grade: 9-Adult
- Languages: English; Spanish
- Order Number: NAL Video 933
- Production Date: 1990
- Format: VHS videotape
- Special Notes: Produced by the March of Dimes Birth Defects Foundation.
- Terms: Borrower pays return postage. RETURN the day after scheduled use. Book at least 4 weeks in advance. Requests must include your name, phone, mail address, eligibility program, title, NAL number, show date, and a statement, "I have read the warning on copyright restrictions and accept full responsibility for compliance." One title per request.
    Source: National Agricultural Library
    Document Delivery Services Branch
    4th Floor, Photo Lab
    10301 Baltimore Avenue
    Beltsville, MD 20705-2351
    Phone: 1-301-504-5994
    Fax: 1-301-504-5675
World Wide Web URL: http://www.nal.usda.gov/fnic
    Email Address: lending@nal.usda.gov

Look Who's Eating
Explains what signs to look for when your baby is ready for solid foods and includes feeding tips for baby.
- Availability: Staff at schools with NET, WIC, CSFP, FDPIR, CACFP, UMD or Child Nutrition Program food programs in the United States. Those not having such an affiliation should contact their library to place an interlibrary loan request.
- Suggested Grade: 7-12
- Languages: English; Spanish
- Order Number: English NAL Video 2972; Spanish IPM001204404
- Production Date: 1999
- Format: VHS videotape
- Terms: Borrower pays return postage. RETURN the day after scheduled use. Book at least 4 weeks in advance. Requests must include your name, phone, mail address, eligibility program, title, NAL number, show date, and a statement, "I have read the warning on copyright restrictions and accept full responsibility for compliance." One title per request.
    Source: National Agricultural Library
    Document Delivery Services Branch
    4th Floor, Photo Lab
    10301 Baltimore Avenue
    Beltsville, MD 20705-2351
    Phone: 1-301-504-5994
    Fax: 1-301-504-5675
World Wide Web URL: http://www.nal.usda.gov/fnic
    Email Address: lending@nal.usda.gov

Pregnant Teens Taking Care
Discusses the importance of nutrition and early medical care during pregnancy, and describes the ways in which the mother's eating habits affect the fetus as well as the risk of "casual" use of drugs, alcohol and cigarettes during pregnancy.
- Availability: Staff at schools with NET, WIC, CSFP, FDPIR, CACFP, UMD or Child Nutrition Program food programs in the United States. Those not having such an affiliation should contact their library to place an interlibrary loan request.
- Suggested Grade: 9-Adult
- Order Number: NAL Video 743
- Format: VHS videotape
- Terms: Borrower pays return postage. RETURN the day after scheduled use. Book at least 4 weeks in advance. Requests must include your name, phone, mail address, eligibility program, title, NAL number, show date, and a statement, "I have read the warning on copyright restrictions and accept full responsibility for compliance." One title per request.
    Source: National Agricultural Library
    Document Delivery Services Branch
    4th Floor, Photo Lab
    10301 Baltimore Avenue
    Beltsville, MD 20705-2351
    Phone: 1-301-504-5994
    Fax: 1-301-504-5675
World Wide Web URL: http://www.nal.usda.gov/fnic
    Email Address: lending@nal.usda.gov

Reproductive Systems
Learn about the male and female reproductive systems. Explains each system, its hormonal effect on maturation, and its part in creating a baby. With animation and medical photography, watch a baby developing from the initial fertilization of egg and sperm as it becomes a zygote, an embryo with a beating heart, a fetus, and finally a newborn child. Shows a baby being born.

HOME ECONOMICS--FAMILY LIFE EDUCATION

Availability:	Schools, libraries, and homeschoolers in the United States who serve the hearing impaired.
Suggested Grade:	6-10
Order Number:	12821
Format:	DVD
Special Notes:	Produced by National Geographic Society.
Terms:	Sponsor pays all transportation costs. Return one week after receipt. Participation is limited to deaf or hard of hearing Americans, their parents, families, teachers, counselors, or others whose use would benefit a deaf or hard of hearing person. Only one person in the audience needs to be hearing impaired. You must register--which is free. These videos are all open-captioned--no special equipment is required for viewing.

      Source: Described and Captioned Media Program
      National Association of the Deaf
      4211 Church Street Ext.
      Roebuck, SC 29376
      Phone: 1-800-237-6213
      Fax: 1-800-538-5636
      World Wide Web URL: http://www.dcmp.org

Sound Nutrition for Teenage Mothers-to-Be

Designed to be used in teen parenting classes to promote quality nutrition throughout pregnancy.

Availability:	Staff at schools with NET, WIC, CSFP, FDPIR, CACFP, UMD or Child Nutrition Program food programs in the United States. Those not having such an affiliation should contact their library to place an interlibrary loan request.
Suggested Grade:	7-12
Order Number:	NAL Video RG556.5.S68-1991
Production Date:	1991
Format:	VHS videotape
Terms:	Borrower pays return postage. RETURN the day after scheduled use. Book at least 4 weeks in advance. Requests must include your name, phone, mail address, eligibility program, title, NAL number, show date, and a statement, "I have read the warning on copyright restrictions and accept full responsibility for compliance." One title per request.

      Source: National Agricultural Library
      Document Delivery Services Branch
      4th Floor, Photo Lab, 10301 Baltimore Avenue
      Beltsville, MD 20705-2351
      Phone: 1-301-504-5994
      Fax: 1-301-504-5675
      World Wide Web URL: http://www.nal.usda.gov/fnic
      Email Address: lending@nal.usda.gov

Starting Solid Foods: Lily Helps Ana

Helps new mothers determine when and how to start feeding their babies solid foods.

Availability:	Staff at schools with NET, WIC, CSFP, FDPIR, CACFP, UMD or Child Nutrition Program food programs in the United States. Those not having such an affiliation should contact their library to place an interlibrary loan request.
Suggested Grade:	7-12
Languages:	English; Spanish
Order Number:	English NAL Video 2978; Spanish NAL Video 2978
Production Date:	2000
Format:	VHS videotape
Terms:	Borrower pays return postage. RETURN the day after scheduled use. Book at least 4 weeks in advance. Requests must include your name, phone, mail address, eligibility program, title, NAL number, show date, and a statement, "I have read the warning on copyright restrictions and accept full responsibility for compliance." One title per request.

      Source: National Agricultural Library
      Document Delivery Services Branch
      4th Floor, Photo Lab
      10301 Baltimore Avenue
      Beltsville, MD 20705-2351
      Phone: 1-301-504-5994
      Fax: 1-301-504-5675
      World Wide Web URL: http://www.nal.usda.gov/fnic
      Email Address: lending@nal.usda.gov

Teen Breastfeeding: The Natural Choice

A diverse group of breastfeeding teen mothers present their own experiences of fitting breastfeeding into an active teen lifestyle.

Availability:	Staff at schools with NET, WIC, CSFP, FDPIR, CACFP, UMD or Child Nutrition Program food programs in the United States. Those not having such an affiliation should contact their library to place an interlibrary loan request.
Suggested Grade:	9-12
Order Number:	Video 2758
Production Date:	1998
Format:	VHS videotape
Special Notes:	Includes a facilitator's guide. Two parts are included.
Terms:	Borrower pays return postage. RETURN the day after scheduled use. Book at least 4 weeks in advance. Requests must include your name, phone, mail address, eligibility program, title, NAL number, show date, and a statement, "I have read the warning on copyright restrictions and accept full responsibility for compliance." One title per request.

      Source: National Agricultural Library
      Document Delivery Services Branch
      4th Floor, Photo Lab
      10301 Baltimore Avenue
      Beltsville, MD 20705-2351
      Phone: 1-301-504-5994
      Fax: 1-301-504-5675
      World Wide Web URL: http://www.nal.usda.gov/fnic
      Email Address: lending@nal.usda.gov

Well Baby Check Ups: From Infants to Tots

Gives advice to parents and expectant parents on the recommended schedule of well-baby visits.

All materials listed in this 2018-2019 edition are BRAND NEW!

HOME ECONOMICS--FAMILY LIFE EDUCATION

Availability: Schools, libraries, and homeschoolers in the United States who serve the hearing impaired.
Suggested Grade: Adult
Order Number: 12483
Production Date: 1995
Format: DVD
Terms: Sponsor pays all transportation costs. Return one week after receipt. Participation is limited to deaf or hard of hearing Americans, their parents, families, teachers, counselors, or others whose use would benefit a deaf or hard of hearing person. Only one person in the audience needs to be hearing impaired. You must register--which is free. These videos are all open-captioned--no special equipment is required for viewing.
Source: **Described and Captioned Media Program**
National Association of the Deaf
4211 Church Street Ext.
Roebuck, SC 29376
Phone: 1-800-237-6213
Fax: 1-800-538-5636
World Wide Web URL: http://www.dcmp.org

Young Family, A
The contemporary Japanese lifestyle mixes modernity and tradition. Topics in this video include arranged marriages, the high cost of living, the problem of husbands working away from home, and the efforts being made to encourage Japanese men to take more time off in order to be with their families.
Availability: Schools, libraries, homeschoolers, and nursing homes in Nevada and northern California (zip codes beginning 932 and above, except 935).
Suggested Grade: 9-Adult
Order Number: order by title
Format: VHS videotape
Terms: Borrower pays return postage. Book two weeks in advance. Return within three weeks of date borrowed, via UPS, Federal Express or certified mail.
Source: **Consulate General of Japan, San Francisco**
50 Fremont Street, Suite 2300
San Francisco, CA 94105-2236
Phone: 1-415-356-2564
Fax: 1-415-777-0518
World Wide Web URL: http://www.sf.us.emb-japan.go.jp/
Email Address: infoav@cgjsf.org

HOME ECONOMICS--FOODS

Deep Fat Frying and Pan Frying
Describes deep fat frying and lists items which are commonly prepared this way. Also demonstrates pan frying and tells which items are best suited for this method of preparation.
- Availability: Staff at schools with NET, WIC, CSFP, FDPIR, CACFP, UMD or Child Nutrition Program food programs in the United States. Those not having such an affiliation should contact their library to place an interlibrary loan request.
- Suggested Grade: 6-12
- Order Number: NAL Video 2309
- Production Date: 1989
- Format: VHS videotape
- Terms: Borrower pays return postage. RETURN the day after scheduled use. Book at least 4 weeks in advance. Requests must include your name, phone, mail address, eligibility program, title, NAL number, show date, and a statement, "I have read the warning on copyright restrictions and accept full responsibility for compliance." One title per request.
    Source: National Agricultural Library
    Document Delivery Services Branch
    4th Floor, Photo Lab
    10301 Baltimore Avenue
    Beltsville, MD 20705-2351
    Phone: 1-301-504-5994
    Fax: 1-301-504-5675
World Wide Web URL: http://www.nal.usda.gov/fnic
Email Address: lending@nal.usda.gov

Dinner's Served: A Food Safety Program
Explains the proper way to shop and prepare food at home to prevent E. coli infection.
- Availability: Staff at schools with NET, WIC, CSFP, FDPIR, CACFP, UMD or Child Nutrition Program food programs in the United States. Those not having such an affiliation should contact their library to place an interlibrary loan request.
- Suggested Grade: 6-12
- Order Number: NAL Video 2697
- Production Date: 1996
- Format: VHS videotape
- Terms: Borrower pays return postage. RETURN the day after scheduled use. Book at least 4 weeks in advance. Requests must include your name, phone, mail address, eligibility program, title, NAL number, show date, and a statement, "I have read the warning on copyright restrictions and accept full responsibility for compliance." One title per request.
    Source: National Agricultural Library
    Document Delivery Services Branch
    4th Floor, Photo Lab
    10301 Baltimore Avenue
    Beltsville, MD 20705-2351
    Phone: 1-301-504-5994
    Fax: 1-301-504-5675
World Wide Web URL: http://www.nal.usda.gov/fnic
Email Address: lending@nal.usda.gov

Eating for Life
Covers healthy lifestyle changes that will improve health and help prevent heart disease, steps for changing eating habits, the value of vitamin and mineral supplements, and how to eat healthy in restaurants.
- Availability: Schools, libraries, and homeschoolers in the United States who serve the hearing impaired.
- Suggested Grade: 9-Adult
- Order Number: 12907
- Production Date: 2000
- Format: DVD
- Special Notes: Also available as live streaming video over the Internet.
- Terms: Sponsor pays all transportation costs. Return one week after receipt. Participation is limited to deaf or hard of hearing Americans, their parents, families, teachers, counselors, or others whose use would benefit a deaf or hard of hearing person. Only one person in the audience needs to be hearing impaired. You must register--which is free. These videos are all open-captioned--no special equipment is required for viewing.
    Source: Described and Captioned Media Program
    National Association of the Deaf
    4211 Church Street Ext.
    Roebuck, SC 29376
    Phone: 1-800-237-6213
    Fax: 1-800-538-5636
World Wide Web URL: http://www.dcmp.org

Eating Well, Increasing Fiber
This cooking program demonstrates how to prepare stir-fry and a high-fiber dessert. The cooks discuss the five fiber groups, their roles in a well-balanced diet, how much fiber is too much and examples of the categories of foods containing fiber.
- Availability: Staff at schools with NET, WIC, CSFP, FDPIR, CACFP, UMD or Child Nutrition Program food programs in the United States. Those not having such an affiliation should contact their library to place an interlibrary loan request.
- Suggested Grade: 6-12
- Order Number: NAL Video 765
- Production Date: 1989
- Format: VHS videotape
- Terms: Borrower pays return postage. RETURN the day after scheduled use. Book at least 4 weeks in advance. Requests must include your name, phone, mail address, eligibility program, title, NAL number, show date, and a statement, "I have read the warning on copyright restrictions and accept full responsibility for compliance." One title per request.
    Source: National Agricultural Library
    Document Delivery Services Branch
    4th Floor, Photo Lab, 10301 Baltimore Avenue
    Beltsville, MD 20705-2351

All materials listed in this 2018-2019 edition are BRAND NEW!

HOME ECONOMICS--FOODS

Phone: 1-301-504-5994
Fax: 1-301-504-5675
World Wide Web URL: http://www.nal.usda.gov/fnic
Email Address: lending@nal.usda.gov

Fats of Life, The
A calculator, quiz reviews, tips for reading food labels, study sheets, and a healthy heart poster all accompany this video designed to teach about fats before hardened habits and hardened arteries set in. Saturated, unsaturated, polyunsaturated fats, cholesterol, fat-heart disease and controlling fat in the diet are the topics.

- Availability: Staff at schools with NET, WIC, CSFP, FDPIR, CACFP, UMD or Child Nutrition Program food programs in the United States. Those not having such an affiliation should contact their library to place an interlibrary loan request.
- Suggested Grade: 7-12
- Order Number: NAL Video 308
- Production Date: 1989
- Format: VHS videotape
- Terms: Borrower pays return postage. RETURN the day after scheduled use. Book at least 4 weeks in advance. Requests must include your name, phone, mail address, eligibility program, title, NAL number, show date, and a statement, "I have read the warning on copyright restrictions and accept full responsibility for compliance." One title per request.

Source: National Agricultural Library
Document Delivery Services Branch
4th Floor, Photo Lab, 10301 Baltimore Avenue
Beltsville, MD 20705-2351
Phone: 1-301-504-5994
Fax: 1-301-504-5675
World Wide Web URL: http://www.nal.usda.gov/fnic
Email Address: lending@nal.usda.gov

Food: A Multi-Cultural Feast
Discusses how the food we eat in the United States is multi-cultural in its origin. The origins of a number of foods are illustrated.

- Availability: Staff at schools with NET, WIC, CSFP, FDPIR, CACFP, UMD or Child Nutrition Program food programs in the United States. Those not having such an affiliation should contact their library to place an interlibrary loan request.
- Suggested Grade: 4-12
- Order Number: NAL Video 2865
- Production Date: 1998
- Format: VHS videotape
- Terms: Borrower pays return postage. RETURN the day after scheduled use. Book at least 4 weeks in advance. Requests must include your name, phone, mail address, eligibility program, title, NAL number, show date, and a statement, "I have read the warning on copyright restrictions and accept full responsibility for compliance." One title per request.

Source: National Agricultural Library
Document Delivery Services Branch
4th Floor, Photo Lab
10301 Baltimore Avenue
Beltsville, MD 20705-2351
Phone: 1-301-504-5994
Fax: 1-301-504-5675
World Wide Web URL: http://www.nal.usda.gov/fnic
Email Address: lending@nal.usda.gov

Great Food Mixes You Can Make at Home
Tells how to make substitute food mixes right in your own kitchen instead of spending money on prepared mixes.

- Availability: Staff at schools with NET, WIC, CSFP, FDPIR, CACFP, UMD or Child Nutrition Program food programs in the United States. Those not having such an affiliation should contact their library to place an interlibrary loan request.
- Suggested Grade: 7-Adult
- Order Number: Video 2845
- Production Date: 1994
- Format: VHS videotape
- Terms: Borrower pays return postage. RETURN the day after scheduled use. Book at least 4 weeks in advance. Requests must include your name, phone, mail address, eligibility program, title, NAL number, show date, and a statement, "I have read the warning on copyright restrictions and accept full responsibility for compliance." One title per request.

Source: National Agricultural Library
Document Delivery Services Branch
4th Floor, Photo Lab
10301 Baltimore Avenue
Beltsville, MD 20705-2351
Phone: 1-301-504-5994
Fax: 1-301-504-5675
World Wide Web URL: http://www.nal.usda.gov/fnic
Email Address: lending@nal.usda.gov

Healthy Dividends: A Plan for Balancing Your Fat Budget
This video is designed to help adults lower fat to 30% or less of their total calories and to lower saturated fat to 10% of total calories. It emphasizes the importance of eating nutrient-dense foods from all four food groups for optimum nutritional health. The plan offers a do-it-yourself approach to calculate your individual fat budget and to lower dietary fat without deprivation or prohibition.

- Availability: Staff at schools with NET, WIC, CSFP, FDPIR, CACFP, UMD or Child Nutrition Program food programs in the United States. Those not having such an affiliation should contact their library to place an interlibrary loan request.
- Suggested Grade: 10-Adult
- Order Number: NAL Video 683
- Production Date: 1990
- Format: VHS videotape

*All materials listed in this 2018-2019 edition are **BRAND NEW**!*

HOME ECONOMICS--FOODS

Terms: Borrower pays return postage. RETURN the day after scheduled use. Book at least 4 weeks in advance. Requests must include your name, phone, mail address, eligibility program, title, NAL number, show date, and a statement, "I have read the warning on copyright restrictions and accept full responsibility for compliance." One title per request.
Source: National Agricultural Library
Document Delivery Services Branch
4th Floor, Photo Lab
10301 Baltimore Avenue
Beltsville, MD 20705-2351
Phone: 1-301-504-5994
Fax: 1-301-504-5675
World Wide Web URL: http://www.nal.usda.gov/fnic
Email Address: lending@nal.usda.gov

Healthy Japanese Diet, The
Introduces healthy Japanese dishes that can be prepared with ingredients that can easily be obtained.
Availability: Schools, libraries and homeschoolers in Alabama, Georgia, North Carolina, South Carolina, and Virginia.
Suggested Grade: 4-12
Order Number: 321
Production Date: 1997
Format: VHS videotape
Terms: Borrower pays return postage. Two tapes may be borrowed at a time. Return within 7 days after receipt. Reservations may be made by filling the application found on the web site.
Source: Consulate General of Japan, Atlanta
Japan Information Center
One Alliance Center
3500 Lenox Road, Suite 1600
Atlanta, GA 30326
Phone: 1-404-365-9240
Fax: 1-404-240-4311
World Wide Web URL:
http://www.atlanta.us.emb-japan.go.jp
Email Address: info@cgjapanatlanta.org

Healthy Japanese Diet, The
Introduces healthy Japanese dishes that can be prepared with ingredients that can easily be obtained.
Availability: Schools, libraries, homeschoolers, and nursing homes in Connecticut (except Fairfield County), Maine, Massachusetts, New Hampshire, Rhode Island, and Vermont.
Suggested Grade: 4-12
Order Number: 563
Production Date: 1997
Format: VHS videotape
Terms: Borrower pays return postage, including insurance. Return two weeks after receipt.
Source: Consulate General of Japan, Boston
Federal Reserve Plaza, 14th Floor
600 Atlantic Avenue
Boston, MA 02210
Phone: 1-617-973-9772
Fax: 1-617-542-1329
World Wide Web URL:
http://www.boston.us.emb-japan.go.jp
Email Address: infocul@cgjbos.org

Healthy Japanese Diet, The
Introduces healthy Japanese dishes that can be prepared with ingredients that can easily be obtained.
Availability: Schools, libraries, and nursing homes in Hawaii.
Suggested Grade: 4-12
Order Number: CU-129
Production Date: 1997
Format: VHS videotape
Terms: Borrower pays return postage. A maximum of 3 videos may be borrowed per person. Return within one week of date borrowed.
Source: Consulate General of Japan, Honolulu
1742 Nuuanu Avenue
Honolulu, HI 96817-3294
Phone: 1-808-543-3111
Fax: 1-808-543-3170
World Wide Web URL:
http://www.honolulu.us.emb-japan.go.jp

Healthy Japanese Diet, The
Introduces healthy Japanese dishes that can be prepared with ingredients that can easily be obtained.
Availability: Schools, libraries, and nursing homes in Oklahoma and Texas.
Suggested Grade: 4-12
Order Number: A23
Production Date: 1997
Format: VHS videotape
Terms: Materials must be picked up in person. Under special circumstances, you may be able to have them shipped to you at your own expense (call for further details). Return within two weeks after scheduled showing. Videos must be registered with the U. S. Postal Service or returned by Priority Mail, Federal Express, or other registered shipping service.
Source: Consulate General of Japan, Houston
Cultural Affairs and Information Section
909 Fannin Street, Suite 3000
Houston, TX 77010
Phone: 1-713-652-2977
Fax: 1-713-651-7822
World Wide Web URL: http://www.houston.us.emb-japan.go.jp/
en/culture/page1.htm
Email Address: info@cgjhouston.org

Healthy Japanese Diet, The
Introduces healthy Japanese dishes that can be prepared with ingredients that can easily be obtained.
Availability: Schools, libraries, homeschoolers, and nursing homes in Arizona and California (zipcodes beginning 900-931 and 935).
Suggested Grade: 4-12

All materials listed in this 2018-2019 edition are BRAND NEW!

HOME ECONOMICS--FOODS

Order Number: 252
Production Date: 1997
Format: VHS videotape
Terms: Borrower pays postage both ways; you may call the number below to learn how much postage costs. Return within two weeks of date borrowed. An individual may borrow 2 items at one time. For non-profit and educational use only.
Source: Consulate General of Japan, Los Angeles
350 South Grand Avenue, Suite 1700
Los Angeles, CA 90071-3459
Phone: 1-213-617-6700
Fax: 1-213-617-6727
World Wide Web URL: http://www.la.us.emb-japan.go.jp

Healthy Japanese Diet, The
Introduces healthy Japanese dishes that can be prepared with ingredients that can easily be obtained.
Availability: Schools, libraries, homeschoolers, and nursing homes in OREGON AND SOUTHERN IDAHO ONLY. Please make requests via the web site.
Suggested Grade: 4-12
Order Number: 422
Production Date: 1997
Format: VHS videotape
Terms: Borrower pays return postage. Return within three weeks after scheduled showing date. Book one month in advance if possible. Rewind the video and wrap securely for return. Be certain to indicate video number, date needed, name of your organization, and address to which video should be sent, along with phone number. Audience report enclosed with the video must be completed and returned.
Source: Consulate General of Japan, Oregon
Attn: Tamara, Video Library
1300 S. W. Fifth Avenue, Suite 2700
Portland, OR 97201
Phone: 1-503-221-1811, ext. 17
World Wide Web URL:
http://www.portland.us.emb-japan.go.jp/en/index.html
Email Address: tamara@cgjpdx.org

Healthy Japanese Diet, The
Introduces healthy Japanese dishes that can be prepared with ingredients that can easily be obtained.
Availability: Schools, libraries, homeschoolers, and nursing homes in Nevada and northern California (zip codes beginning 932 and above, except 935).
Suggested Grade: 4-12
Order Number: order by title
Production Date: 1997
Format: VHS videotape
Terms: Borrower pays return postage. Book two weeks in advance. Return within three weeks of date borrowed, via UPS, Federal Express or certified mail.
Source: Consulate General of Japan, San Francisco
50 Fremont Street, Suite 2300
San Francisco, CA 94105-2236
Phone: 1-415-356-2564
Fax: 1-415-777-0518
World Wide Web URL: http://www.sf.us.emb-japan.go.jp/
Email Address: infoav@cgjsf.org

High Five: Nutrition Program for High School Youth
Teens get together and discuss such topics as preparing quick, healthy snacks, eating disorders, and other topics.
Availability: Staff at schools with NET, WIC, CSFP, FDPIR, CACFP, UMD or Child Nutrition Program food programs in the United States. Those not having such an affiliation should contact their library to place an interlibrary loan request.
Suggested Grade: 9-12
Order Number: NAL Video 2230
Production Date: 1996
Format: VHS videotape
Terms: Borrower pays return postage. RETURN the day after scheduled use. Book at least 4 weeks in advance. Requests must include your name, phone, mail address, eligibility program, title, NAL number, show date, and a statement, "I have read the warning on copyright restrictions and accept full responsibility for compliance." One title per request.
Source: National Agricultural Library
Document Delivery Services Branch
4th Floor, Photo Lab
10301 Baltimore Avenue
Beltsville, MD 20705-2351
Phone: 1-301-504-5994
Fax: 1-301-504-5675
World Wide Web URL: http://www.nal.usda.gov/fnic
Email Address: lending@nal.usda.gov

Home Plate
This program was developed to help parents develop healthy eating patterns for their children. It covers topics such as snacking, trying new foods, food safety and pesticides, and getting a nutritious dinner on the table in a short time.
Availability: Staff at schools with NET, WIC, CSFP, FDPIR, CACFP, UMD or Child Nutrition Program food programs in the United States. Those not having such an affiliation should contact their library to place an interlibrary loan request.
Suggested Grade: Adult
Order Number: NAL Video 2151
Production Date: 1994
Format: VHS videotape
Terms: Borrower pays return postage. RETURN the day after scheduled use. Book at least 4 weeks in advance. Requests must include your name, phone, mail address, eligibility program, title, NAL number, show date, and a statement, "I have read the warning on copyright restrictions and accept full responsibility for compliance."

*All materials listed in this 2018-2019 edition are **BRAND NEW**!*

HOME ECONOMICS--FOODS

Source: National Agricultural Library
Document Delivery Services Branch
4th Floor, Photo Lab
10301 Baltimore Avenue
Beltsville, MD 20705-2351
Phone: 1-301-504-5994
Fax: 1-301-504-5675
World Wide Web URL: http://www.nal.usda.gov/fnic
Email Address: lending@nal.usda.gov

How Safe Is Your Food?
A CNN presentation on food safety, this program covers issues such as handling of chicken and beef from the slaughterhouse to the table.
- Availability: Staff at schools with NET, WIC, CSFP, FDPIR, CACFP, UMD or Child Nutrition Program food programs in the United States. Those not having such an affiliation should contact their library to place an interlibrary loan request.
- Suggested Grade: 7-Adult
- Order Number: Video 2866
- Production Date: 1997
- Format: VHS videotape
- Terms: Borrower pays return postage. RETURN the day after scheduled use. Book at least 4 weeks in advance. Requests must include your name, phone, mail address, eligibility program, title, NAL number, show date, and a statement, "I have read the warning on copyright restrictions and accept full responsibility for compliance." One title per request.

Source: National Agricultural Library
Document Delivery Services Branch
4th Floor, Photo Lab
10301 Baltimore Avenue
Beltsville, MD 20705-2351
Phone: 1-301-504-5994
Fax: 1-301-504-5675
World Wide Web URL: http://www.nal.usda.gov/fnic
Email Address: lending@nal.usda.gov

How to Lower Your Cholesterol: A Simple Dietary Approach
Discusses what cholesterol is and what the dietary sources of cholesterol are. Suggestions are given for low fat meals and what foods may be substituted for saturated fat. Lists of substitutes are provided. Methods of lowering cholesterol in the diet are discussed.
- Availability: Staff at schools with NET, WIC, CSFP, FDPIR, CACFP, UMD or Child Nutrition Program food programs in the United States. Those not having such an affiliation should contact their library to place an interlibrary loan request.
- Suggested Grade: 7-12
- Order Number: NAL Video 452
- Production Date: 1988
- Format: VHS videotape
- Terms: Borrower pays return postage. RETURN the day after scheduled use. Book at least 4 weeks in advance. Requests must include your name, phone, mail address, eligibility program, title, NAL number, show date, and a statement, "I have read the warning on copyright restrictions and accept full responsibility for compliance." One title per request.

Source: National Agricultural Library
Document Delivery Services Branch
4th Floor, Photo Lab
10301 Baltimore Avenue
Beltsville, MD 20705-2351
Phone: 1-301-504-5994
Fax: 1-301-504-5675
World Wide Web URL: http://www.nal.usda.gov/fnic
Email Address: lending@nal.usda.gov

How to Read the New Food Label for Persons with Diabetes
Explains how the new food label expands available information to enable diabetics to make better food choices.
- Availability: Staff at schools with NET, WIC, CSFP, FDPIR, CACFP, UMD or Child Nutrition Program food programs in the United States. Those not having such an affiliation should contact their library to place an interlibrary loan request.
- Suggested Grade: 9-12
- Order Number: NAL Video 1764
- Production Date: 1994
- Format: VHS videotape
- Terms: Borrower pays return postage. RETURN the day after scheduled use. Book at least 4 weeks in advance. Requests must include your name, phone, mail address, eligibility program, title, NAL number, show date, and a statement, "I have read the warning on copyright restrictions and accept full responsibility for compliance." One title per request.

Source: National Agricultural Library
Document Delivery Services Branch
4th Floor, Photo Lab
10301 Baltimore Avenue
Beltsville, MD 20705-2351
Phone: 1-301-504-5994
Fax: 1-301-504-5675
World Wide Web URL: http://www.nal.usda.gov/fnic
Email Address: lending@nal.usda.gov

I Love Sushi
An instruction program on how to make sushi with ingredients readily available at local American supermarkets.
- Availability: Schools, libraries and homeschoolers in Alabama, Georgia, North Carolina, South Carolina, and Virginia.
- Suggested Grade: 6-Adult
- Order Number: 206
- Production Date: 1992
- Format: VHS videotape

HOME ECONOMICS--FOODS

Terms: Borrower pays return postage. Two tapes may be borrowed at a time. Return within 7 days after receipt. Reservations may be made by filling the application found on the web site.
Source: Consulate General of Japan, Atlanta
Japan Information Center
One Alliance Center
3500 Lenox Road, Suite 1600
Atlanta, GA 30326
Phone: 1-404-365-9240
Fax: 1-404-240-4311
World Wide Web URL:
http://www.atlanta.us.emb-japan.go.jp
Email Address: info@cgjapanatlanta.org

Japanese Cooking--A Taste for All Seasons
Focuses on the Japanese diet and the preparation of Japanese foods.
Availability: Schools, libraries, homeschoolers, and nursing homes in Connecticut (except Fairfield County), Maine, Massachusetts, New Hampshire, Rhode Island, and Vermont.
Suggested Grade: 4-12
Order Number: 109
Production Date: 1984
Format: VHS videotape
Terms: Borrower pays return postage, including insurance. Return two weeks after receipt.
Source: Consulate General of Japan, Boston
Federal Reserve Plaza, 14th Floor
600 Atlantic Avenue
Boston, MA 02210
Phone: 1-617-973-9772
Fax: 1-617-542-1329
World Wide Web URL:
http://www.boston.us.emb-japan.go.jp
Email Address: infocul@cgjbos.org

Japanese Cooking--A Taste for All Seasons
Focuses on the Japanese diet and the preparation of Japanese foods.
Availability: Schools, libraries, and nursing homes in Hawaii.
Suggested Grade: 4-12
Order Number: CU-9
Production Date: 1984
Format: VHS videotape
Terms: Borrower pays return postage. A maximum of 3 videos may be borrowed per person. Return within one week of date borrowed.
Source: Consulate General of Japan, Honolulu
1742 Nuuanu Avenue
Honolulu, HI 96817-3294
Phone: 1-808-543-3111
Fax: 1-808-543-3170
World Wide Web URL:
http://www.honolulu.us.emb-japan.go.jp

Japanese Cooking--A Taste for All Seasons
Focuses on the Japanese diet and the preparation of Japanese foods.
Availability: Schools, libraries, and nursing homes in Oklahoma and Texas.
Suggested Grade: 4-12
Order Number: I7
Production Date: 1985
Format: VHS videotape
Terms: Materials must be picked up in person. Under special circumstances, you may be able to have them shipped to you at your own expense (call for further details). Return within two weeks after scheduled showing. Videos must be registered with the U. S. Postal Service or returned by Priority Mail, Federal Express, or other registered shipping service.
Source: Consulate General of Japan, Houston
Cultural Affairs and Information Section
909 Fannin Street, Suite 3000
Houston, TX 77010
Phone: 1-713-652-2977
Fax: 1-713-651-7822
World Wide Web URL:
http://www.houston.us.emb-japan.go.jp/en/culture/page1.htm
Email Address: info@cgjhouston.org

Japanese Cooking--A Taste for All Seasons
Focuses on the Japanese diet and the preparation of Japanese foods.
Availability: Schools, libraries, homeschoolers, and nursing homes in Arizona and California (zipcodes beginning 900-931 and 935).
Suggested Grade: 4-12
Order Number: 046
Production Date: 1984
Format: VHS videotape
Terms: Borrower pays postage both ways; you may call the number below to learn how much postage costs. Return within two weeks of date borrowed. An individual may borrow 2 items at one time. For non-profit and educational use only.
Source: Consulate General of Japan, Los Angeles
350 South Grand Avenue, Suite 1700
Los Angeles, CA 90071-3459
Phone: 1-213-617-6700
Fax: 1-213-617-6727
World Wide Web URL: http://www.la.us.emb-japan.go.jp

Japanese Cooking--A Taste for All Seasons
Focuses on the Japanese diet and the preparation of Japanese foods.
Availability: Schools, libraries, homeschoolers, and nursing homes in OREGON AND SOUTHERN IDAHO ONLY. Please make requests via the web site.
Suggested Grade: 4-12
Order Number: 209
Production Date: 1985

HOME ECONOMICS--FOODS

Format: VHS videotape
Terms: Borrower pays return postage. Return within three weeks after scheduled showing date. Book one month in advance if possible. Rewind the video and wrap securely for return. Be certain to indicate video number, date needed, name of your organization, and address to which video should be sent, along with phone number. Audience report enclosed with the video must be completed and returned.
    Source: Consulate General of Japan, Oregon
    Attn: Tamara, Video Library
    1300 S. W. Fifth Avenue, Suite 2700
    Portland, OR 97201
    Phone: 1-503-221-1811, ext. 17
    World Wide Web URL:
    http://www.portland.us.emb-japan.go.jp/en/index.html
    Email Address: tamara@cgjpdx.org

Knife Skills: Vegetables
Demonstrates the various techniques of cutting vegetables for cooking.
Availability: Staff at schools with NET, WIC, CSFP, FDPIR, CACFP, UMD or Child Nutrition Program food programs in the United States. Those not having such an affiliation should contact their library to place an interlibrary loan request.
Suggested Grade: 6-12
Order Number: NAL Video 2313
Production Date: 1987
Format: VHS videotape
Terms: Borrower pays return postage. RETURN the day after scheduled use. Book at least 4 weeks in advance. Requests must include your name, phone, mail address, eligibility program, title, NAL number, show date, and a statement, "I have read the warning on copyright restrictions and accept full responsibility for compliance." One title per request.
    Source: National Agricultural Library
    Document Delivery Services Branch
    4th Floor, Photo Lab
    10301 Baltimore Avenue
    Beltsville, MD 20705-2351
    Phone: 1-301-504-5994
    Fax: 1-301-504-5675
    World Wide Web URL: http://www.nal.usda.gov/fnic
    Email Address: lending@nal.usda.gov

La Piramide de la Alimentacion
Describes the Food Guide Pyramid and discusses the reason for the Pyramid design.
Availability: Staff at schools with NET, WIC, CSFP, FDPIR, CACFP, UMD or Child Nutrition Program food programs in the United States. Those not having such an affiliation should contact their library to place an interlibrary loan request.
Suggested Grade: 7-12
Language: Spanish
Order Number: NAL Video 1783
Production Date: 1994
Format: VHS videotape
Terms: Borrower pays return postage. RETURN the day after scheduled use. Book at least 4 weeks in advance. Requests must include your name, phone, mail address, eligibility program, title, NAL number, show date, and a statement, "I have read the warning on copyright restrictions and accept full responsibility for compliance." One title per request.
    Source: National Agricultural Library
    Document Delivery Services Branch
    4th Floor, Photo Lab
    10301 Baltimore Avenue
    Beltsville, MD 20705-2351
    Phone: 1-301-504-5994
    Fax: 1-301-504-5675
    World Wide Web URL: http://www.nal.usda.gov/fnic
    Email Address: lending@nal.usda.gov

Masters of the Wok
Introduces Chinese cuisine from peasant fare to highly refined imperial cooking.
Availability: Schools, libraries, and nursing homes in the United States and Canada.
Suggested Grade: 6-Adult
Order Number: CV023
Format: VHS videotape
Terms: Borrower pays return postage. Return with 14 days after scheduled showing, via UPS or U. S. Mail. All requests must included an educational institution affiliation, a current address, and phone number. Order through web site only.
    Source: Cornell University East Asia Program
    World Wide Web URL:
    http://eap.einaudi.cornell.edu/lending_library
    Email Address: east_asia1@cornell.edu

Meal Planning: Eating Right for People with Diabetes
Provides a sensible approach to meal planning and good eating for people with diabetes; follows the Food Guide Pyramid.
Availability: Staff at schools with NET, WIC, CSFP, FDPIR, CACFP, UMD or Child Nutrition Program food programs in the United States. Those not having such an affiliation should contact their library to place an interlibrary loan request.
Suggested Grade: 9-12
Order Number: NAL Video 1927
Production Date: 1994
Format: VHS videotape
Terms: Borrower pays return postage. RETURN the day after scheduled use. Book at least 4 weeks in advance. Requests must include your name, phone, mail address, eligibility program, title, NAL number, show date, and a statement, "I have read the warning on copyright restrictions and accept full responsibility for compliance." One title per request.

*All materials listed in this 2018-2019 edition are **BRAND NEW!***

HOME ECONOMICS--FOODS

Source: National Agricultural Library
Document Delivery Services Branch
4th Floor, Photo Lab
10301 Baltimore Avenue
Beltsville, MD 20705-2351
Phone: 1-301-504-5994
Fax: 1-301-504-5675
World Wide Web URL: http://www.nal.usda.gov/fnic
Email Address: lending@nal.usda.gov

Poaching and Steaming
Discusses these methods of food preparation for fish.
Availability: Staff at schools with NET, WIC, CSFP, FDPIR, CACFP, UMD or Child Nutrition Program food programs in the United States. Those not having such an affiliation should contact their library to place an interlibrary loan request.
Suggested Grade: 6-12
Order Number: NAL Video 2310
Production Date: 1989
Format: VHS videotape
Special Notes: Produced by the Culinary Institute of America.
Terms: Borrower pays return postage. RETURN the day after scheduled use. Book at least 4 weeks in advance. Requests must include your name, phone, mail address, eligibility program, title, NAL number, show date, and a statement, "I have read the warning on copyright restrictions and accept full responsibility for compliance." One title per request.
Source: National Agricultural Library
Document Delivery Services Branch
4th Floor, Photo Lab
10301 Baltimore Avenue
Beltsville, MD 20705-2351
Phone: 1-301-504-5994
Fax: 1-301-504-5675
World Wide Web URL: http://www.nal.usda.gov/fnic
Email Address: lending@nal.usda.gov

Producer Through Consumer--Partners to a Safe Food Supply
A curriculum that teaches major food safety issues.
Availability: Staff at schools with NET, WIC, CSFP, FDPIR, CACFP, UMD or Child Nutrition Program food programs in the United States. Those not having such an affiliation should contact their library to place an interlibrary loan request.
Suggested Grade: All ages
Order Number: NAL Kit 328
Production Date: 1992
Format: VHS videotape
Special Notes: Includes a number of supplementary teaching aids. Available in an adult version as well as a youth version--please specify.
Terms: Borrower pays return postage. RETURN the day after scheduled use. Book at least 4 weeks in advance. Requests must include your name, phone, mail address, eligibility program, title, NAL number, show date, and a statement, "I have read the warning on copyright restrictions and accept full responsibility for compliance." One title per request.
Source: National Agricultural Library
Document Delivery Services Branch
4th Floor, Photo Lab
10301 Baltimore Avenue
Beltsville, MD 20705-2351
Phone: 1-301-504-5994
Fax: 1-301-504-5675
World Wide Web URL: http://www.nal.usda.gov/fnic
Email Address: lending@nal.usda.gov

Recreating Taste in Low Fat Cooking
Shows how to create low-fat meals through demonstrating hands-on cooking and presentation techniques.
Availability: Staff at schools with NET, WIC, CSFP, FDPIR, CACFP, UMD or Child Nutrition Program food programs in the United States. Those not having such an affiliation should contact their library to place an interlibrary loan request.
Suggested Grade: 7-12
Order Number: NAL Video 2056
Production Date: 1994
Format: VHS videotape
Special Notes: Includes a teacher's guide.
Terms: Borrower pays return postage. RETURN the day after scheduled use. Book at least 4 weeks in advance. Requests must include your name, phone, mail address, eligibility program, title, NAL number, show date, and a statement, "I have read the warning on copyright restrictions and accept full responsibility for compliance." One title per request.
Source: National Agricultural Library
Document Delivery Services Branch
4th Floor, Photo Lab
10301 Baltimore Avenue
Beltsville, MD 20705-2351
Phone: 1-301-504-5994
Fax: 1-301-504-5675
World Wide Web URL: http://www.nal.usda.gov/fnic
Email Address: lending@nal.usda.gov

Roasting
Describes the roasting method of cooking, which is used for large or whole multi-portion cuts of meat.
Availability: Staff at schools with NET, WIC, CSFP, FDPIR, CACFP, UMD or Child Nutrition Program food programs in the United States. Those not having such an affiliation should contact their library to place an interlibrary loan request.
Suggested Grade: 6-12
Order Number: NAL Video 2311
Production Date: 1989
Format: VHS videotape
Special Notes: Produced by the Culinary Institute of America.

HOME ECONOMICS--FOODS

Terms: Borrower pays return postage. RETURN the day after scheduled use. Book at least 4 weeks in advance. Requests must include your name, phone, mail address, eligibility program, title, NAL number, show date, and a statement, "I have read the warning on copyright restrictions and accept full responsibility for compliance." One title per request.
    Source: National Agricultural Library
    Document Delivery Services Branch
    4th Floor, Photo Lab
    10301 Baltimore Avenue
    Beltsville, MD 20705-2351
    Phone: 1-301-504-5994
    Fax: 1-301-504-5675
World Wide Web URL: http://www.nal.usda.gov/fnic
    Email Address: lending@nal.usda.gov

Safe Food, Healthy Children
Deals with problems of foodborne illness and its possible devastating effects on children.
Availability: Staff at schools with NET, WIC, CSFP, FDPIR, CACFP, UMD or Child Nutrition Program food programs in the United States. Those not having such an affiliation should contact their library to place an interlibrary loan request.
Suggested Grade: Teacher Reference
Order Number: NAL Kit 340
Production Date: 1995
Format: VHS videotape
Terms: Borrower pays return postage. RETURN the day after scheduled use. Book at least 4 weeks in advance. Requests must include your name, phone, mail address, eligibility program, title, NAL number, show date, and a statement, "I have read the warning on copyright restrictions and accept full responsibility for compliance." One title per request.
    Source: National Agricultural Library
    Document Delivery Services Branch
    4th Floor, Photo Lab
    10301 Baltimore Avenue
    Beltsville, MD 20705-2351
    Phone: 1-301-504-5994
    Fax: 1-301-504-5675
World Wide Web URL: http://www.nal.usda.gov/fnic
    Email Address: lending@nal.usda.gov

Shopping for Health: Smart Choices at the Supermarket
Features five guidelines for making smart choices at the supermarket as well as tips for moving toward a healthier, plant-based eating style.
Availability: Staff at schools with NET, WIC, CSFP, FDPIR, CACFP, UMD or Child Nutrition Program food programs in the United States. Those not having such an affiliation should contact their library to place an interlibrary loan request.
Suggested Grade: 7-Adult
Order Number: NAL Video 2614
Production Date: 1997
Format: VHS videotape
Terms: Borrower pays return postage. RETURN the day after scheduled use. Book at least 4 weeks in advance. Requests must include your name, phone, mail address, eligibility program, title, NAL number, show date, and a statement, "I have read the warning on copyright restrictions and accept full responsibility for compliance." One title per request.
    Source: National Agricultural Library
    Document Delivery Services Branch
    4th Floor, Photo Lab
    10301 Baltimore Avenue
    Beltsville, MD 20705-2351
    Phone: 1-301-504-5994
    Fax: 1-301-504-5675
World Wide Web URL: http://www.nal.usda.gov/fnic
    Email Address: lending@nal.usda.gov

Shopping for Heart Health: Lower Your Blood Cholesterol and Reduce Your Risk of Coronary Artery Disease
Features five guidelines for making smart choices at the supermarket and tips for moving toward a healthier, plant-based eating style.
Availability: Staff at schools with NET, WIC, CSFP, FDPIR, CACFP, UMD or Child Nutrition Program food programs in the United States. Those not having such an affiliation should contact their library to place an interlibrary loan request.
Suggested Grade: 7-12
Order Number: NAL Video 2621
Production Date: 1997
Format: VHS videotape
Terms: Borrower pays return postage. RETURN the day after scheduled use. Book at least 4 weeks in advance. Requests must include your name, phone, mail address, eligibility program, title, NAL number, show date, and a statement, "I have read the warning on copyright restrictions and accept full responsibility for compliance." One title per request.
    Source: National Agricultural Library
    Document Delivery Services Branch
    4th Floor, Photo Lab
    10301 Baltimore Avenue
    Beltsville, MD 20705-2351
    Phone: 1-301-504-5994
    Fax: 1-301-504-5675
World Wide Web URL: http://www.nal.usda.gov/fnic
    Email Address: lending@nal.usda.gov

Taste of Japan, The: A Tradition of Hospitality
Introduces the culinary cultural traditions of various regions, styles and people, all through Japan's seasonal changes, as well as the peoples way of living.

All materials listed in this 2018-2019 edition are BRAND NEW!

HOME ECONOMICS--FOODS

Availability: Schools, libraries, homeschoolers, and nursing homes in Connecticut (except Fairfield County), Maine, Massachusetts, New Hampshire, Rhode Island, and Vermont.
Suggested Grade: 4-12
Order Number: 459
Production Date: 1991
Format: VHS videotape
Special Notes: No. 4 of the "Nippon the Land and Its People" series.
Terms: Borrower pays return postage, including insurance. Return two weeks after receipt.
Source: Consulate General of Japan, Boston
Federal Reserve Plaza, 14th Floor
600 Atlantic Avenue
Boston, MA 02210
Phone: 1-617-973-9772
Fax: 1-617-542-1329
World Wide Web URL: http://www.boston.us.emb-japan.go.jp
Email Address: infocul@cgjbos.org

Taste of Japan, The: A Tradition of Hospitality
Introduces the culinary cultural traditions of various regions, styles and people, all through Japan's seasonal changes, as well as the peoples way of living.
Availability: Schools, libraries, and nursing homes in Oklahoma and Texas.
Suggested Grade: 4-12
Order Number: B4
Production Date: 1991
Format: VHS videotape
Special Notes: No. 4 of the "Nippon the Land and Its People" series.
Terms: Materials must be picked up in person. Under special circumstances, you may be able to have them shipped to you at your own expense (call for further details). Return within two weeks after scheduled showing. Videos must be registered with the U. S. Postal Service or returned by Priority Mail, Federal Express, or other registered shipping service.
Source: Consulate General of Japan, Houston
Cultural Affairs and Information Section
909 Fannin Street, Suite 3000
Houston, TX 77010
Phone: 1-713-652-2977
Fax: 1-713-651-7822
World Wide Web URL: http://www.houston.us.emb-japan.go.jp/en/culture/page1.htm
Email Address: info@cgjhouston.org

Taste of Japan, The: A Tradition of Hospitality
Introduces the culinary cultural traditions of various regions, styles and people, all through Japan's seasonal changes, as well as the peoples way of living.
Availability: Schools, libraries, homeschoolers, and nursing homes in Arizona and California (zipcodes beginning 900-931 and 935).
Suggested Grade: 4-12
Order Number: 173
Production Date: 1991
Format: VHS videotape
Special Notes: No. 4 of the "Nippon the Land and Its People" series.
Terms: Borrower pays postage both ways; you may call the number below to learn how much postage costs. Return within two weeks of date borrowed. An individual may borrow 2 items at one time. For non-profit and educational use only.
Source: Consulate General of Japan, Los Angeles
350 South Grand Avenue, Suite 1700
Los Angeles, CA 90071-3459
Phone: 1-213-617-6700
Fax: 1-213-617-6727
World Wide Web URL: http://www.la.us.emb-japan.go.jp

Taste of Japan, The: A Tradition of Hospitality
Introduces the culinary cultural traditions of various regions, styles and people, all through Japan's seasonal changes, as well as the peoples way of living.
Availability: Schools, libraries, homeschoolers, and nursing homes in Nevada and northern California (zip codes beginning 932 and above, except 935).
Suggested Grade: 4-12
Order Number: order by title
Production Date: 1991
Format: VHS videotape
Special Notes: No. 4 of the "Nippon the Land and Its People" series.
Terms: Borrower pays return postage. Book two weeks in advance. Return within three weeks of date borrowed, via UPS, Federal Express or certified mail.
Source: Consulate General of Japan, San Francisco
50 Fremont Street, Suite 2300
San Francisco, CA 94105-2236
Phone: 1-415-356-2564
Fax: 1-415-777-0518
World Wide Web URL: http://www.sf.us.emb-japan.go.jp/
Email Address: infoav@cgjsf.org

Traditional Japanese Culture: Japanese Cuisine
Japanese cuisine uses a wide range of seasonings. This program looks at the traditional protection methods of some of the commonly used seasonings such as bean paste, soy sauce, salt, and vinegar.
Availability: Schools, libraries, homeschoolers, and nursing homes in Connecticut (except Fairfield County), Maine, Massachusetts, New Hampshire, Rhode Island, and Vermont.
Suggested Grade: 6-12
Order Number: 590
Production Date: 2001
Format: VHS videotape
Terms: Borrower pays return postage, including insurance. Return two weeks after receipt.

HOME ECONOMICS--FOODS

Source: Consulate General of Japan, Boston
Federal Reserve Plaza, 14th Floor
600 Atlantic Avenue
Boston, MA 02210
Phone: 1-617-973-9772
Fax: 1-617-542-1329
World Wide Web URL:
http://www.boston.us.emb-japan.go.jp
Email Address: infocul@cgjbos.org

Traditional Japanese Culture: Japanese Cuisine
Japanese cuisine uses a wide range of seasonings. This program looks at the traditional protection methods of some of the commonly used seasonings such as bean paste, soy sauce, salt, and vinegar.

- Availability: Schools, libraries, and nursing homes in Oklahoma and Texas.
- Suggested Grade: 6-12
- Order Number: A28
- Production Date: 2001
- Format: VHS videotape
- Terms: Materials must be picked up in person. Under special circumstances, you may be able to have them shipped to you at your own expense (call for further details). Return within two weeks after scheduled showing. Videos must be registered with the U. S. Postal Service or returned by Priority Mail, Federal Express, or other registered shipping service.

Source: Consulate General of Japan, Houston
Cultural Affairs and Information Section
909 Fannin Street, Suite 3000
Houston, TX 77010
Phone: 1-713-652-2977
Fax: 1-713-651-7822
World Wide Web URL:
http://www.houston.us.emb-japan.go.jp/en/culture/page1.htm
Email Address: info@cgjhouston.org

Traditional Japanese Culture: Japanese Cuisine
Japanese cuisine uses a wide range of seasonings. This program looks at the traditional protection methods of some of the commonly used seasonings such as bean paste, soy sauce, salt, and vinegar.

- Availability: Schools, libraries, homeschoolers, and nursing homes in Nevada and northern California (zip codes beginning 932 and above, except 935).
- Suggested Grade: 6-12
- Order Number: order by title
- Production Date: 2001
- Format: VHS videotape
- Terms: Borrower pays return postage. Book two weeks in advance. Return within three weeks of date borrowed, via UPS, Federal Express or certified mail.

Source: Consulate General of Japan, San Francisco
50 Fremont Street, Suite 2300
San Francisco, CA 94105-2236
Phone: 1-415-356-2564
Fax: 1-415-777-0518
World Wide Web URL: http://www.sf.us.emb-japan.go.jp/
Email Address: infoav@cgjsf.org

Your Body, Your Diet, and Cholesterol
This program on cardiovascular disease discusses the risk factors associated with the disease, the role of diet (particularly fats and cholesterol), and stresses the importance of having your blood cholesterol and blood pressure checked regularly.

- Availability: Staff at schools with NET, WIC, CSFP, FDPIR, CACFP, UMD or Child Nutrition Program food programs in the United States. Those not having such an affiliation should contact their library to place an interlibrary loan request.
- Suggested Grade: 7-12
- Order Number: NAL Video 441
- Production Date: 1989
- Format: VHS videotape
- Terms: Borrower pays return postage. RETURN the day after scheduled use. Book at least 4 weeks in advance. Requests must include your name, phone, mail address, eligibility program, title, NAL number, show date, and a statement, "I have read the warning on copyright restrictions and accept full responsibility for compliance." One title per request.

Source: National Agricultural Library
Document Delivery Services Branch
4th Floor, Photo Lab
10301 Baltimore Avenue
Beltsville, MD 20705-2351
Phone: 1-301-504-5994
Fax: 1-301-504-5675
World Wide Web URL: http://www.nal.usda.gov/fnic
Email Address: lending@nal.usda.gov

*All materials listed in this 2018-2019 edition are **BRAND NEW!***

LANGUAGE ARTS

Adelante
Spanish for mastery video program where Spanish words and phrases are linked to authentic cultural proficiency.
- Availability: Schools, libraries, and nursing homes in the United States.
- Suggested Grade: 6-12
- Order Number: LANSPA12-video
- Production Date: 1984
- Format: Set of 4 VHS videotapes
- Special Notes: 4 cassettes, 4 videos, and two reference guides.
- Terms: Borrowers must have a User's Agreement on file with this source--available by mail or via the Internet. Return postage is paid by borrower; return 12 days after showing. Book at least three weeks in advance. All borrowers are limited to a total of ten items per semester.

Source: **Latin American Resource Center**
Stone Center for Latin American Studies
Tulane University
100 Jones Hall
New Orleans, LA 70118
Phone: 1-504-862-3143
Fax: 1-504-865-6719
World Wide Web URL: http://stonecenter.tulane.edu/pages/detail/48/Lending-Library
Email Address: crcrts@tulane.edu

Anuncios Comerciales
Spanish language commercials for the North American and Mexico markets provide language practice while showing slices of another culture.
- Availability: Schools in the United States.
- Suggested Grade: All ages Spanish
- Order Number: order by title
- Production Date: 1989
- Format: VHS videotape
- Terms: Borrower pays return postage. Return 14 days after receipt, via USPS including insurance. All borrowers must have a current lending agreement on file with the Outreach program. This agreement is available via the web site or may be requested via phone or fax.

Source: **Center for Latin American Studies**
University of Florida
319 Grinter Hall
P. O. Box 115530
Gainesville, FL 32611-5530
Phone: 1-352-392-0375
Fax: 1-352-392-7682
World Wide Web URL: http://www.latam.ufl.edu/outreach
Email Address: maryr@ufl.edu

Expanding Canon, The: Teaching Multicultural Literature in High School
This professional development workshop for high school teachers is an exploration of the richness of multicultural literature shown through four pedagogical approaches to teaching it: reader response, inquiry, cultural studies, and critical pedagogy.
- Availability: All requesters
- Suggested Grade: Teacher Reference
- Order Number: not applicable
- Format: Streaming on Video
- Terms: A simple FREE registration is required to view videos.

Source: **Annenberg Media**
World Wide Web URL: http://www.learner.org/resources/browse.html

Good Earth, The
This documentary tells part of the story of Sukyung Lim, a South Korean student leader who was charged with violating the National Security Act in 1989 for traveling to North Korea and imprisoned for three and a half years.
- Availability: Schools, libraries, and nursing homes in the United States and Canada.
- Suggested Grade: 6-Adult
- Order Number: CV036
- Format: VHS videotape
- Terms: Borrower pays return postage. Return with 14 days after scheduled showing, via UPS or U. S. Mail. All requests must included an educational institution affiliation, a current address, and phone number. Order through web site only.

Source: **Cornell University East Asia Program**
World Wide Web URL: http://eap.einaudi.cornell.edu/lending_library
Email Address: east_asia1@cornell.edu

Introduction to Let's Learn Japanese Basic I
Basic language lessons for learning Japanese.
- Availability: Schools, libraries, homeschoolers, and nursing homes in Connecticut (except Fairfield County), Maine, Massachusetts, New Hampshire, Rhode Island, and Vermont.
- Suggested Grade: 6-Adult
- Order Number: 607
- Production Date: 1999
- Format: VHS videotape
- Terms: Borrower pays return postage, including insurance. Return two weeks after receipt.

Source: **Consulate General of Japan, Boston**
Federal Reserve Plaza, 14th Floor
600 Atlantic Avenue
Boston, MA 02210
Phone: 1-617-973-9772
Fax: 1-617-542-1329
World Wide Web URL: http://www.boston.us.emb-japan.go.jp
Email Address: infocul@cgjbos.org

Introduction to Let's Learn Japanese Basic II
Basic language lessons for learning Japanese.
- Availability: Schools, libraries, homeschoolers, and nursing homes in Connecticut (except Fairfield County), Maine, Massachusetts, New Hampshire, Rhode Island, and Vermont.
- Suggested Grade: 6-Adult
- Order Number: 608

LANGUAGE ARTS

Production Date: 1999
Format: VHS videotape
Terms: Borrower pays return postage, including insurance. Return two weeks after receipt.
Source: Consulate General of Japan, Boston
Federal Reserve Plaza, 14th Floor
600 Atlantic Avenue
Boston, MA 02210
Phone: 1-617-973-9772
Fax: 1-617-542-1329
World Wide Web URL:
http://www.boston.us.emb-japan.go.jp
Email Address: infocul@cgjbos.org

Kaguya Hime: Princess of the Moon
Animated version and folktale, useful in language classes.
Availability: Schools, libraries, homeschoolers, and nursing homes in Arizona and California (zipcodes beginning 900-931 and 935).
Suggested Grade: 2-12
Language: Japanese
Order Number: 085
Production Date: 1994
Format: VHS videotape
Terms: Borrower pays postage both ways; you may call the number below to learn how much postage costs. Return within two weeks of date borrowed. An individual may borrow 2 items at one time. For non-profit and educational use only.
Source: Consulate General of Japan, Los Angeles
350 South Grand Avenue, Suite 1700
Los Angeles, CA 90071-3459
Phone: 1-213-617-6700
Fax: 1-213-617-6727
World Wide Web URL: http://www.la.us.emb-japan.go.jp

Let's Learn Japanese: Basic I
Basic language lessons for learning Japanese.
Availability: Schools, libraries, and nursing homes in Oklahoma and Texas.
Suggested Grade: 6-Adult
Order Number: N6
Format: VHS videotape
Terms: Materials must be picked up in person. Under special circumstances, you may be able to have them shipped to you at your own expense (call for further details). Return within two weeks after scheduled showing. Videos must be registered with the U. S. Postal Service or returned by Priority Mail, Federal Express, or other registered shipping service.
Source: Consulate General of Japan, Houston
Cultural Affairs and Information Section
909 Fannin Street, Suite 3000
Houston, TX 77010
Phone: 1-713-652-2977
Fax: 1-713-651-7822
World Wide Web URL:
http://www.houston.us.emb-japan.go.jp/en/culture/page1.htm
Email Address: info@cgjhouston.org

Mexican Sign Language
Instructional video demonstrating more than one thousand words in Mexican Sign Language. The manual alphabet and number signs are shown. Each word is voiced and captioned in both Spanish and English and is signed twice. The instruction is divided into 10 lessons.
Availability: Schools, libraries, and homeschoolers in the United States who serve the hearing impaired.
Suggested Grade: All ages
Language: Spanish
Order Number: 12879
Format: DVD
Special Notes: Produced by Signing Fiesta.
Terms: Sponsor pays all transportation costs. Return one week after receipt. Participation is limited to deaf or hard of hearing Americans, their parents, families, teachers, counselors, or others whose use would benefit a deaf or hard of hearing person. Only one person in the audience needs to be hearing impaired. You must register--which is free. These videos are all open-captioned--no special equipment is required for viewing.
Source: Described and Captioned Media Program
National Association of the Deaf
4211 Church Street Ext.
Roebuck, SC 29376
Phone: 1-800-237-6213
Fax: 1-800-538-5636
World Wide Web URL: http://www.dcmp.org

Molly's Pilgrim
A young, Russian-Jewish immigrant, Molly, is teased by her classmates because of her accent and mannerisms. The teasing stops and an appreciation begins due to a Thanksgiving assignment on Pilgrims. The students realize that it takes all kinds of pilgrims to make a Thanksgiving. Based on the book by Barbara Cohen.
Availability: Schools, libraries, and homeschoolers in the United States who serve the hearing impaired.
Suggested Grade: 4-12
Order Number: 31294
Production Date: 1985
Format: DVD
Special Notes: Also available as live streaming video.
Terms: Sponsor pays all transportation costs. Return one week after receipt. Participation is limited to deaf or hard of hearing Americans, their parents, families, teachers, counselors, or others whose use would benefit a deaf or hard of hearing person. Only one person in the audience needs to be hearing impaired. You must register--which is free. These videos are all open-captioned--no special equipment is required for viewing.
Source: Described and Captioned Media Program
National Association of the Deaf
4211 Church Street Ext.
Roebuck, SC 29376
Phone: 1-800-237-6213
Fax: 1-800-538-5636
World Wide Web URL: http://www.dcmp.org

All materials listed in this 2018-2019 edition are BRAND NEW!

LANGUAGE ARTS

Narrative Writing 1: Structures--What is a Narrative?
Discusses the three-act structure of a classical narrative with examples.
- Availability: Schools, libraries, and homeschoolers in the United States who serve the hearing impaired.
- Suggested Grade: 8-Adult
- Order Number: 11610
- Production Date: 2002
- Format: DVD
- Special Notes: Also available as live streaming video over the Internet.
- Terms: Sponsor pays all transportation costs. Return one week after receipt. Participation is limited to deaf or hard of hearing Americans, their parents, families, teachers, counselors, or others whose use would benefit a deaf or hard of hearing person. Only one person in the audience needs to be hearing impaired. You must register--which is free. These videos are all open-captioned--no special equipment is required for viewing.
- Source: Described and Captioned Media Program
  National Association of the Deaf
  4211 Church Street Ext.
  Roebuck, SC 29376
  Phone: 1-800-237-6213
  Fax: 1-800-538-5636
- World Wide Web URL: http://www.dcmp.org

Popol Vuh: The Creation Myth of the Maya
Portrays the creation myth of the Quiche Maya of Guatemala. Animated using actual Maya artwork found on pottery and in murals.
- Availability: Schools, libraries, and nursing homes in the United States.
- Suggested Grade: All ages
- Order Number: MY24-video
- Production Date: 1986
- Format: VHS videotape
- Special Notes: Specify short or long version.
- Terms: Borrowers must have a User's Agreement on file with this source--available by mail or via the Internet. Return postage is paid by borrower; return 12 days after showing. Book at least three weeks in advance. All borrowers are limited to a total of ten items per semester.
- Source: Latin American Resource Center
  Stone Center for Latin American Studies
  Tulane University
  100 Jones Hall
  New Orleans, LA 70118
  Phone: 1-504-862-3143
  Fax: 1-504-865-6719
- World Wide Web URL: http://stonecenter.tulane.edu/pages/detail/48/Lending-Library
- Email Address: crcrts@tulane.edu

Punctuation: Program 6--Introduction to Punctuation and the End Marks
Gives clear rules and examples of how to use punctuation.
- Availability: Schools, libraries, and homeschoolers in the United States who serve the hearing impaired.
- Suggested Grade: 6-12
- Order Number: 11622
- Production Date: 2000
- Format: DVD
- Special Notes: Also available as live streaming video over the Internet.
- Terms: Sponsor pays all transportation costs. Return one week after receipt. Participation is limited to deaf or hard of hearing Americans, their parents, families, teachers, counselors, or others whose use would benefit a deaf or hard of hearing person. Only one person in the audience needs to be hearing impaired. You must register--which is free. These videos are all open-captioned--no special equipment is required for viewing.
- Source: Described and Captioned Media Program
  National Association of the Deaf
  4211 Church Street Ext.
  Roebuck, SC 29376
  Phone: 1-800-237-6213
  Fax: 1-800-538-5636
- World Wide Web URL: http://www.dcmp.org

Voices of Latin America
Explores the cultural identity of Latin America through its writers and literature.
- Availability: Schools in the United States.
- Suggested Grade: 7-Adult
- Order Number: order by title
- Production Date: 1987
- Format: VHS videotape
- Terms: Borrower pays return postage. Return 14 days after receipt, via USPS including insurance. All borrowers must have a current lending agreement on file with the Outreach program. This agreement is available via the web site or may be requested via phone or fax.
- Source: Center for Latin American Studies
  University of Florida
  319 Grinter Hall
  P. O. Box 115530
  Gainesville, FL 32611-5530
  Phone: 1-352-392-0375
  Fax: 1-352-392-7682
- World Wide Web URL: http://www.latam.ufl.edu/outreach
- Email Address: maryr@ufl.edu

William Wordsworth
Poet Tobias Hill examines the poetry of William Wordsworth as he treks in the Lake District of England, Wordsworth's home. Hill dialogs with others about what influenced Wordsworth and what kind of poet he was. Notes his poetry is concerned with nature, humans, and society. Excerpts from "The Rainbow," "The Prelude," "Lucy Gray," and others illustrate some of his themes. Addresses Wordsworth's poetry, not his life.
- Availability: Schools, libraries, and homeschoolers in the United States who serve the hearing impaired.
- Suggested Grade: 10-Adult
- Order Number: 12433
- Production Date: 1998

All materials listed in this 2018-2019 edition are BRAND NEW!

LANGUAGE ARTS

Format: DVD
Special Notes: Produced by Benchmark Media.
Terms: Sponsor pays all transportation costs. Return one week after receipt. Participation is limited to deaf or hard of hearing Americans, their parents, families, teachers, counselors, or others whose use would benefit a deaf or hard of hearing person. Only one person in the audience needs to be hearing impaired. You must register--which is free. These videos are all open-captioned--no special equipment is required for viewing.

Source: Described and Captioned Media Program
National Association of the Deaf
4211 Church Street Ext.
Roebuck, SC 29376
Phone: 1-800-237-6213
Fax: 1-800-538-5636
World Wide Web URL: http://www.dcmp.org

PHYSICAL EDUCATION AND RECREATION

Budo: The Martial Arts/The Art of Karate
Introduces the art and philosophy of the representative martial arts of Japan: Judo, Karate, and Aikido.
- Availability: Schools, libraries and homeschoolers in Alabama, Georgia, North Carolina, South Carolina, and Virginia.
- Suggested Grade: 6-Adult
- Order Number: 102
- Production Date: 1982
- Format: VHS videotape
- Terms: Borrower pays return postage. Two tapes may be borrowed at a time. Return within 7 days after receipt. Reservations may be made by filling the application found on the web site.

Source: Consulate General of Japan, Atlanta
Japan Information Center
One Alliance Center, 3500 Lenox Road, Suite 1600
Atlanta, GA 30326
Phone: 1-404-365-9240
Fax: 1-404-240-4311
World Wide Web URL:
http://www.atlanta.us.emb-japan.go.jp
Email Address: info@cgjapanatlanta.org

Budo: The Martial Arts/The Art of Karate
Introduces the art and philosophy of the representative martial arts of Japan: Judo, Karate, and Aikido.
- Availability: Schools, libraries, homeschoolers, and nursing homes in Connecticut (except Fairfield County), Maine, Massachusetts, New Hampshire, Rhode Island, and Vermont.
- Suggested Grade: 6-Adult
- Order Number: 138
- Production Date: 1982
- Format: VHS videotape
- Terms: Borrower pays return postage, including insurance. Return two weeks after receipt.

Source: Consulate General of Japan, Boston
Federal Reserve Plaza, 14th Floor
600 Atlantic Avenue
Boston, MA 02210
Phone: 1-617-973-9772
Fax: 1-617-542-1329
World Wide Web URL:
http://www.boston.us.emb-japan.go.jp
Email Address: infocul@cgjbos.org

Budo: The Martial Arts/The Art of Karate
Introduces the art and philosophy of the representative martial arts of Japan: Judo, Karate, and Aikido.
- Availability: Schools, libraries, and nursing homes in Hawaii.
- Suggested Grade: 6-Adult
- Order Number: SP-2
- Production Date: 1982
- Format: VHS videotape
- Terms: Borrower pays return postage. A maximum of 3 videos may be borrowed per person. Return within one week of date borrowed.

Source: Consulate General of Japan, Honolulu
1742 Nuuanu Avenue
Honolulu, HI 96817-3294
Phone: 1-808-543-3111
Fax: 1-808-543-3170
World Wide Web URL:
http://www.honolulu.us.emb-japan.go.jp

Budo: The Martial Arts/The Art of Karate
Introduces the art and philosophy of the representative martial arts of Japan: Judo, Karate, and Aikido.
- Availability: Schools, libraries, homeschoolers, and nursing homes in OREGON AND SOUTHERN IDAHO ONLY. Please make requests via the web site.
- Suggested Grade: 6-Adult
- Order Number: 109
- Production Date: 1982
- Format: VHS videotape
- Terms: Borrower pays return postage. Return within three weeks after scheduled showing date. Book one month in advance if possible. Rewind the video and wrap securely for return. Be certain to indicate video number, date needed, name of your organization, and address to which video should be sent, along with phone number. Audience report enclosed with the video must be completed and returned.

Source: Consulate General of Japan, Oregon
Attn: Tamara, Video Library
1300 S. W. Fifth Avenue, Suite 2700
Portland, OR 97201
Phone: 1-503-221-1811, ext. 17
World Wide Web URL:
http://www.portland.us.emb-japan.go.jp/en/index.html
Email Address: tamara@cgjpdx.org

Budo: The Martial Arts/The Art of Karate
Introduces the art and philosophy of the representative martial arts of Japan: Judo, Karate, and Aikido.
- Availability: Schools, libraries, homeschoolers, and nursing homes in Nevada and northern California (zip codes beginning 932 and above, except 935).
- Suggested Grade: 6-Adult
- Order Number: order by title
- Production Date: 1982
- Format: VHS videotape
- Terms: Borrower pays return postage. Book two weeks in advance. Return within three weeks of date borrowed, via UPS, Federal Express or certified mail.

Source: Consulate General of Japan, San Francisco
50 Fremont Street, Suite 2300
San Francisco, CA 94105-2236
Phone: 1-415-356-2564
Fax: 1-415-777-0518
World Wide Web URL: http://www.sf.us.emb-japan.go.jp/
Email Address: infoav@cgjsf.org

PHYSICAL EDUCATION AND RECREATION

Christian Laettner: The Power Forward
This basketball play shows how to play the power forward position. He reveals his conditioning program and positive mental approach to the game.
    Availability: Schools, libraries, and homeschoolers in the United States who serve the hearing impaired.
    Suggested Grade: Adult
    Order Number: 10826
    Production Date: 1998
    Format: DVD
    Special Notes: Also available as live streaming video over the Internet.
    Terms: Sponsor pays all transportation costs. Return one week after receipt. Participation is limited to deaf or hard of hearing Americans, their parents, families, teachers, counselors, or others whose use would benefit a deaf or hard of hearing person. Only one person in the audience needs to be hearing impaired. You must register--which is free. These videos are all open-captioned--no special equipment is required for viewing.
    Source: Described and Captioned Media Program
    National Association of the Deaf
    4211 Church Street Ext.
    Roebuck, SC 29376
    Phone: 1-800-237-6213
    Fax: 1-800-538-5636
    World Wide Web URL: http://www.dcmp.org

Eddie's Last Fight: The Old Trainer/19 Year Old Champion
An endearing portrait of Edward Townsend Jr., known as Eddie, who raised six world champion boxers in Japan.
    Availability: Schools, libraries, homeschoolers, and nursing homes in Connecticut (except Fairfield County), Maine, Massachusetts, New Hampshire, Rhode Island, and Vermont.
    Suggested Grade: 7-12
    Order Number: 168
    Production Date: 1988
    Format: VHS videotape
    Special Notes: Tape 13 of the "Document Japan" series.
    Terms: Borrower pays return postage, including insurance. Return two weeks after receipt.
    Source: Consulate General of Japan, Boston
    Federal Reserve Plaza, 14th Floor
    600 Atlantic Avenue
    Boston, MA 02210
    Phone: 1-617-973-9772
    Fax: 1-617-542-1329
    World Wide Web URL:
    http://www.boston.us.emb-japan.go.jp
    Email Address: infocul@cgjbos.com

Eddie's Last Fight: The Old Trainer/19 Year Old Champion
An endearing portrait of Edward Townsend Jr., known as Eddie, who raised six world champion boxers in Japan.
    Availability: Schools, libraries, and nursing homes in Oklahoma and Texas.
    Suggested Grade: 7-12
    Order Number: C13
    Production Date: 1988
    Format: VHS videotape
    Special Notes: Tape 13 of the "Document Japan" series.
    Terms: Materials must be picked up in person. Under special circumstances, you may be able to have them shipped to you at your own expense (call for further details). Return within two weeks after scheduled showing. Videos must be registered with the U. S. Postal Service or returned by Priority Mail, Federal Express, or other registered shipping service.
    Source: Consulate General of Japan, Houston
    Cultural Affairs and Information Section
    909 Fannin Street, Suite 3000
    Houston, TX 77010
    Phone: 1-713-652-2977
    Fax: 1-713-651-7822
    World Wide Web URL:
    http://www.houston.us.emb-japan.go.jp/en/culture/page1.htm
    Email Address: info@cgjhouston.org

Eddie's Last Fight: The Old Trainer/19 Year Old Champion
An endearing portrait of Edward Townsend Jr., known as Eddie, who raised six world champion boxers in Japan.
    Availability: Schools, libraries, homeschoolers, and nursing homes in Nevada and northern California (zip codes beginning 932 and above, except 935).
    Suggested Grade: 7-12
    Order Number: order by title
    Production Date: 1988
    Format: Beta videotape; U-matic videotape; VHS videotape
    Special Notes: Tape 13 of the "Document Japan" series.
    Terms: Borrower pays return postage. Book two weeks in advance. Return within three weeks of date borrowed, via UPS, Federal Express or certified mail.
    Source: Consulate General of Japan, San Francisco
    50 Fremont Street, Suite 2300
    San Francisco, CA 94105-2236
    Phone: 1-415-356-2564
    Fax: 1-415-777-0518
    World Wide Web URL: http://www.sf.us.emb-japan.go.jp/
    Email Address: infoav@cgjsf.org

Fervor! The Giant Kite Battle of Ensyu
For three days Hamamatsu city was full of the excitement of a Kite Competition with 1,500 kites and 2.7 million participants. Three towns take part in the competition and flies a kite with a unique design of the town, and competitions to cut other's string are held.
    Availability: Schools, libraries and homeschoolers in Alabama, Georgia, North Carolina, South Carolina, and Virginia.
    Suggested Grade: 7-Adult
    Order Number: 702

All materials listed in this 2018-2019 edition are BRAND NEW!

PHYSICAL EDUCATION AND RECREATION

Production Date: 1991
Format: VHS videotape
Special Notes: No. 2 of the "Nippon Life II" series.
Terms: Borrower pays return postage. Two tapes may be borrowed at a time. Return within 7 days after receipt. Reservations may be made by filling the application found on the web site.
Source: Consulate General of Japan, Atlanta
Japan Information Center
One Alliance Center
3500 Lenox Road, Suite 1600
Atlanta, GA 30326
Phone: 1-404-365-9240
Fax: 1-404-240-4311
World Wide Web URL:
http://www.atlanta.us.emb-japan.go.jp
Email Address: info@cgjapanatlanta.org

Fervor! The Giant Kite Battle of Ensyu
For three days Hamamatsu city was full of the excitement of a Kite Competition with 1,500 kites and 2.7 million participants. Three towns take part in the competition and flies a kite with a unique design of the town, and competitions to cut other's string are held.
Availability: Schools, libraries, homeschoolers, and nursing homes in Connecticut (except Fairfield County), Maine, Massachusetts, New Hampshire, Rhode Island, and Vermont.
Suggested Grade: 7-Adult
Order Number: 471
Production Date: 1991
Format: VHS videotape
Special Notes: No. 2 of the "Nippon Life II" series.
Terms: Borrower pays return postage, including insurance. Return two weeks after receipt.
Source: Consulate General of Japan, Boston
Federal Reserve Plaza, 14th Floor
600 Atlantic Avenue
Boston, MA 02210
Phone: 1-617-973-9772
Fax: 1-617-542-1329
World Wide Web URL:
http://www.boston.us.emb-japan.go.jp
Email Address: infocul@cgjbos.org

Fervor! The Giant Kite Battle of Ensyu
For three days Hamamatsu city was full of the excitement of a Kite Competition with 1,500 kites and 2.7 million participants. Three towns take part in the competition and flies a kite with a unique design of the town, and competitions to cut other's string are held
Availability: Schools, libraries, and nursing homes in Hawaii.
Suggested Grade: 7-Adult
Order Number: Cu-51
Format: VHS videotape
Terms: Borrower pays return postage. A maximum of 3 videos may be borrowed per person. Return within one week of date borrowed.

Source: Consulate General of Japan, Honolulu
1742 Nuuanu Avenue
Honolulu, HI 96817-3294
Phone: 1-808-543-3111
Fax: 1-808-543-3170
World Wide Web URL:
http://www.honolulu.us.emb-japan.go.jp

Fervor! The Giant Kite Battle of Ensyu
For three days Hamamatsu city was full of the excitement of a Kite Competition with 1,500 kites and 2.7 million participants. Three towns take part in the competition and flies a kite with a unique design of the town, and competitions to cut other's string are held.
Availability: Schools, libraries, and nursing homes in Oklahoma and Texas.
Suggested Grade: 6-12
Order Number: G2
Production Date: 1991
Format: VHS videotape
Special Notes: No. 2 of the "Nippon Life II" series.
Terms: Materials must be picked up in person. Under special circumstances, you may be able to have them shipped to you at your own expense (call for further details). Return within two weeks after scheduled showing. Videos must be registered with the U. S. Postal Service or returned by Priority Mail, Federal Express, or other registered shipping service.
Source: Consulate General of Japan, Houston
Cultural Affairs and Information Section
909 Fannin Street, Suite 3000
Houston, TX 77010
Phone: 1-713-652-2977
Fax: 1-713-651-7822
World Wide Web URL:
http://www.houston.us.emb-japan.go.jp/
en/culture/page1.htm
Email Address: info@cgjhouston.org

Fervor! The Giant Kite Battle of Ensyu
For three days Hamamatsu city was full of the excitement of a Kite Competition with 1,500 kites and 2.7 million participants. Three towns take part in the competition and flies a kite with a unique design of the town, and competitions to cut other's string are held.
Availability: Schools, libraries, homeschoolers, and nursing homes in OREGON AND SOUTHERN IDAHO ONLY. Please make requests via the web site.
Suggested Grade: 6-12
Order Number: 172
Production Date: 1991
Format: VHS videotape
Special Notes: No. 2 of the "Nippon Life II" series.
Terms: Borrower pays return postage. Return within three weeks after scheduled showing date. Book one month in advance if possible. Rewind the video and wrap securely for return. Be certain to indicate video number, date needed, name of your organization, and address to

PHYSICAL EDUCATION AND RECREATION

which video should be sent, along with phone number. Audience report enclosed with the video must be completed and returned.
Source: Consulate General of Japan, Oregon
Attn: Tamara, Video Library
1300 S. W. Fifth Avenue, Suite 2700
Portland, OR 97201
Phone: 1-503-221-1811, ext. 17
World Wide Web URL:
http://www.portland.us.emb-japan.go.jp/en/index.html
Email Address: tamara@cgjpdx.org

Fervor! The Giant Kite Battle of Ensyu
For three days Hamamatsu city was full of the excitement of a Kite Competition with 1,500 kites and 2.7 million participants. Three towns take part in the competition and flies a kite with a unique design of the town, and competitions to cut other's string are held.
Availability: Schools, libraries, homeschoolers, and nursing homes in Nevada and northern California (zip codes beginning 932 and above, except 935).
Suggested Grade: 7-Adult
Order Number: order by title
Production Date: 1991
Format: Beta videotape; U-matic videotape; VHS videotape
Special Notes: No. 2 of the "Nippon Life II" series.
Terms: Borrower pays return postage. Book two weeks in advance. Return within three weeks of date borrowed, via UPS, Federal Express or certified mail.
Source: Consulate General of Japan, San Francisco
50 Fremont Street, Suite 2300
San Francisco, CA 94105-2236
Phone: 1-415-356-2564
Fax: 1-415-777-0518
World Wide Web URL: http://www.sf.us.emb-japan.go.jp/
Email Address: infoav@cgjsf.org

Flexibility
Looks at the definition of flexibility and how it is assessed.
Availability: Schools, libraries, and homeschoolers in the United States who serve the hearing impaired.
Suggested Grade: 7-12
Order Number: 11025
Format: DVD
Special Notes: Also available as streaming video.
Terms: Sponsor pays all transportation costs. Return one week after receipt. Participation is limited to deaf or hard of hearing Americans, their parents, families, teachers, counselors, or others whose use would benefit a deaf or hard of hearing person. Only one person in the audience needs to be hearing impaired. You must register--which is free. These videos are all open-captioned--no special equipment is required for viewing.
Source: Described and Captioned Media Program
National Association of the Deaf
4211 Church Street Ext.
Roebuck, SC 29376
Phone: 1-800-237-6213
Fax: 1-800-538-5636
World Wide Web URL: http://www.dcmp.org

Kendo
History of martial arts leading to the present-day Kendo, with scenes of training and contests, as well as the moral instruction that accompanies this art.
Availability: Schools, libraries, and nursing homes in Illinois, Indiana, Iowa, Kansas, Minnesota, Missouri, Nebraska, North Dakota, South Dakota, and Wisconsin.
Suggested Grade: All ages
Order Number: 18003
Production Date: 1994
Format: VHS videotape
Terms: Borrower pays return postage by U. S. Mail, UPS, or Federal Express, including insurance for "original" videos. Write, call, fax, or e-mail to request an application. An application form MUST be sent in one month in advance but not more than six months in advance. Include alternate titles and dates if provider can substitute titles. Send a SASE with request if you require confirmation. Return immediately after scheduled showing date. Videos may not be copied or broadcast without permission from the producer of the video. Borrower is responsible if video is lost or damaged.
Source: Consulate General of Japan at Chicago
Japan Information Center
Library
737 North Michigan Avenue, Suite 1000
Chicago, IL 60611
Phone: 1-312-280-0430
Fax: 1-312-280-6883
World Wide Web URL:
http://www.chicago.us.emb-japan.go.jp/jic.html
Email Address: jicchicago@webkddi.com

Kendo
History of martial arts leading to the present-day Kendo, with scenes of training and contests, as well as the moral instruction that accompanies this art.
Availability: Schools, libraries and homeschoolers in Alabama, Georgia, North Carolina, South Carolina, and Virginia.
Suggested Grade: All ages
Order Number: 201
Production Date: 1984
Format: VHS videotape
Terms: Borrower pays return postage. Two tapes may be borrowed at a time. Return within 7 days after receipt. Reservations may be made by filling the application found on the web site.
Source: Consulate General of Japan, Atlanta
Japan Information Center
One Alliance Center
3500 Lenox Road, Suite 1600
Atlanta, GA 30326

PHYSICAL EDUCATION AND RECREATION

Phone: 1-404-365-9240
Fax: 1-404-240-4311
World Wide Web URL:
http://www.atlanta.us.emb-japan.go.jp
Email Address: info@cgjapanatlanta.org

Kendo
History of martial arts leading to the present-day Kendo, with scenes of training and contests, as well as the moral instruction that accompanies this art.
Availability: Schools, libraries, and nursing homes in Hawaii.
Suggested Grade: All ages
Order Number: SP-5
Production Date: 1997
Format: VHS videotape
Terms: Borrower pays return postage. A maximum of 3 videos may be borrowed per person. Return within one week of date borrowed.
Source: Consulate General of Japan, Honolulu
1742 Nuuanu Avenue
Honolulu, HI 96817-3294
Phone: 1-808-543-3111
Fax: 1-808-543-3170
World Wide Web URL:
http://www.honolulu.us.emb-japan.go.jp

Kendo
History of martial arts leading to the present-day Kendo, with scenes of training and contests, as well as the moral instruction that accompanies this art.
Availability: Schools, libraries, homeschoolers, and nursing homes in OREGON AND SOUTHERN IDAHO ONLY. Please make requests via the web site.
Suggested Grade: All ages
Order Number: 441
Production Date: 1997
Format: VHS videotape
Terms: Borrower pays return postage. Return within three weeks after scheduled showing date. Book one month in advance if possible. Rewind the video and wrap securely for return. Be certain to indicate video number, date needed, name of your organization, and address to which video should be sent, along with phone number. Audience report enclosed with the video must be completed and returned.
Source: Consulate General of Japan, Oregon
Attn: Tamara, Video Library
1300 S. W. Fifth Avenue, Suite 2700
Portland, OR 97201
Phone: 1-503-221-1811, ext. 17
World Wide Web URL:
http://www.portland.us.emb-japan.go.jp/en/index.html
Email Address: tamara@cgjpdx.org

Naginata
In the Middle Ages, the "naginata," a long-handled sword, was the weapon of the infantry. Interestingly, this martial art is practiced today mainly by women. This video shows more about this sport.
Availability: Schools, libraries, and nursing homes in Illinois, Indiana, Iowa, Kansas, Minnesota, Missouri, Nebraska, North Dakota, South Dakota, and Wisconsin.
Suggested Grade: 6-Adult
Order Number: 18005
Production Date: 1999
Format: VHS videotape
Terms: Borrower pays return postage by U. S. Mail, UPS, or Federal Express, including insurance for "original" videos. Write, call, fax, or e-mail to request an application. An application form MUST be sent in one month in advance but not more than six months in advance. Include alternate titles and dates if provider can substitute titles. Send a SASE with request if you require confirmation. Return immediately after scheduled showing date. Videos may not be copied or broadcast without permission from the producer of the video. Borrower is responsible if video is lost or damaged.
Source: Consulate General of Japan at Chicago
Japan Information Center
Library
737 North Michigan Avenue, Suite 1000
Chicago, IL 60611
Phone: 1-312-280-0430
Fax: 1-312-280-6883
World Wide Web URL:
http://www.chicago.us.emb-japan.go.jp/jic.html
Email Address: jicchicago@webkddi.com

Naginata
In the Middle Ages, the "naginata," a long-handled sword, was the weapon of the infantry. Interestingly, this martial art is practiced today mainly by women. This video shows more about this sport.
Availability: Schools, libraries, and nursing homes in Hawaii.
Suggested Grade: 6-Adult
Order Number: SP-11
Production Date: 1999
Format: VHS videotape
Terms: Borrower pays return postage. A maximum of 3 videos may be borrowed per person. Return within one week of date borrowed.
Source: Consulate General of Japan, Honolulu
1742 Nuuanu Avenue
Honolulu, HI 96817-3294
Phone: 1-808-543-3111
Fax: 1-808-543-3170
World Wide Web URL:
http://www.honolulu.us.emb-japan.go.jp

Sumo
Presents a guide to appreciate the finer points of sumo and life in a sumo training stable.

*All materials listed in this 2018-2019 edition are **BRAND NEW!***

PHYSICAL EDUCATION AND RECREATION

Availability: Schools, libraries, and nursing homes in Illinois, Indiana, Iowa, Kansas, Minnesota, Missouri, Nebraska, North Dakota, South Dakota, and Wisconsin.
Suggested Grade: 4-Adult
Order Number: 18006
Production Date: 1994
Format: VHS videotape
Terms: Borrower pays return postage by U. S. Mail, UPS, or Federal Express, including insurance for "original" videos. Write, call, fax, or e-mail to request an application. An application form MUST be sent in one month in advance but not more than six months in advance. Include alternate titles and dates if provider can substitute titles. Send a SASE with request if you require confirmation. Return immediately after scheduled showing date. Videos may not be copied or broadcast without permission from the producer of the video. Borrower is responsible if video is lost or damaged.
Source: Consulate General of Japan at Chicago
Japan Information Center
Library
737 North Michigan Avenue, Suite 1000
Chicago, IL 60611
Phone: 1-312-280-0430
Fax: 1-312-280-6883
World Wide Web URL:
http://www.chicago.us.emb-japan.go.jp/jic.html
Email Address: jicchicago@webkddi.com

Traditional Sports: Karatedo
The Japanese form of self-defense, Karatedo has developed into a major sport.
Availability: Schools, libraries, homeschoolers, and nursing homes in Nevada and northern California (zip codes beginning 932 and above, except 935).
Suggested Grade: All ages
Order Number: order by title
Production Date: 1997
Format: VHS videotape
Terms: Borrower pays return postage. Book two weeks in advance. Return within three weeks of date borrowed, via UPS, Federal Express or certified mail.
Source: Consulate General of Japan, San Francisco
50 Fremont Street, Suite 2300
San Francisco, CA 94105-2236
Phone: 1-415-356-2564
Fax: 1-415-777-0518
World Wide Web URL: http://www.sf.us.emb-japan.go.jp/
Email Address: infoav@cgjsf.org

Traditional Sports: Kendo
History of martial arts leading to the present-day Kendo, with scenes of training and contests, as well as the moral instruction that accompanies this art.
Availability: Schools, libraries, homeschoolers, and nursing homes in Nevada and northern California (zip codes beginning 932 and above, except 935).
Suggested Grade: All ages
Order Number: order by title
Production Date: 1997
Format: VHS videotape
Terms: Borrower pays return postage. Book two weeks in advance. Return within three weeks of date borrowed, via UPS, Federal Express or certified mail.
Source: Consulate General of Japan, San Francisco
50 Fremont Street, Suite 2300
San Francisco, CA 94105-2236
Phone: 1-415-356-2564
Fax: 1-415-777-0518
World Wide Web URL: http://www.sf.us.emb-japan.go.jp/
Email Address: infoav@cgjsf.org

Traditional Sports: Sumo
Reports on the popular and traditional Japanese sport of Sumo wrestling.
Availability: Schools, libraries, homeschoolers, and nursing homes in Nevada and northern California (zip codes beginning 932 and above, except 935).
Suggested Grade: All ages
Order Number: order by title
Production Date: 1997
Format: VHS videotape
Terms: Borrower pays return postage. Book two weeks in advance. Return within three weeks of date borrowed, via UPS, Federal Express or certified mail.
Source: Consulate General of Japan, San Francisco
50 Fremont Street, Suite 2300
San Francisco, CA 94105-2236
Phone: 1-415-356-2564
Fax: 1-415-777-0518
World Wide Web URL: http://www.sf.us.emb-japan.go.jp/
Email Address: infoav@cgjsf.org

Young Baseball Heroes
A high school team prepares for a great tournament at Koshen Stadium.
Availability: Schools, libraries and homeschoolers in Alabama, Georgia, North Carolina, South Carolina, and Virginia.
Suggested Grade: 6-Adult
Order Number: 403
Format: VHS videotape
Special Notes: Part of the "Faces of Japan" series.
Terms: Borrower pays return postage. Two tapes may be borrowed at a time. Return within 7 days after receipt. Reservations may be made by filling the application found on the web site.
Source: Consulate General of Japan, Atlanta
Japan Information Center
One Alliance Center
3500 Lenox Road, Suite 1600
Atlanta, GA 30326

All materials listed in this 2018-2019 edition are BRAND NEW!

PHYSICAL EDUCATION AND RECREATION

Phone: 1-404-365-9240
Fax: 1-404-240-4311
World Wide Web URL:
http://www.atlanta.us.emb-japan.go.jp
Email Address: info@cgjapanatlanta.org

Young Baseball Heroes
A high school team prepares for a great tournament at Koshen Stadium.
Availability: Schools, libraries, homeschoolers, and nursing homes in Connecticut (except Fairfield County), Maine, Massachusetts, New Hampshire, Rhode Island, and Vermont.
Suggested Grade: 6-Adult
Order Number: 171
Format: VHS videotape
Special Notes: Part of the "Faces of Japan" series.
Terms: Borrower pays return postage, including insurance. Return two weeks after receipt.
Source: Consulate General of Japan, Boston
Federal Reserve Plaza, 14th Floor
600 Atlantic Avenue
Boston, MA 02210
Phone: 1-617-973-9772
Fax: 1-617-542-1329
World Wide Web URL:
http://www.boston.us.emb-japan.go.jp
Email Address: infocul@cgjbos.org

Young Baseball Heroes
A high school team prepares for a great tournament at Koshen Stadium.
Availability: Schools, libraries, and nursing homes in Oklahoma and Texas.
Suggested Grade: 6-Adult
Order Number: D3
Format: VHS videotape
Special Notes: Part of the "Faces of Japan" series.
Terms: Materials must be picked up in person. Under special circumstances, you may be able to have them shipped to you at your own expense (call for further details). Return within two weeks after scheduled showing. Videos must be registered with the U. S. Postal Service or returned by Priority Mail, Federal Express, or other registered shipping service.
Source: Consulate General of Japan, Houston
Cultural Affairs and Information Section
909 Fannin Street, Suite 3000
Houston, TX 77010
Phone: 1-713-652-2977
Fax: 1-713-651-7822
World Wide Web URL: http://www.houston.us.emb-japan.go.jp/en/culture/page1.htm
Email Address: info@cgjhouston.org

Young Baseball Heroes
A high school team prepares for a great tournament at Koshen Stadium.
Availability: Schools, libraries, homeschoolers, and nursing homes in OREGON AND SOUTHERN IDAHO ONLY. Please make requests via the web site.
Suggested Grade: 6-Adult
Order Number: 516
Format: VHS videotape
Special Notes: Part of the "Faces of Japan" series.
Terms: Borrower pays return postage. Return within three weeks after scheduled showing date. Book one month in advance if possible. Rewind the video and wrap securely for return. Be certain to indicate video number, date needed, name of your organization, and address to which video should be sent, along with phone number. Audience report enclosed with the video must be completed and returned.
Source: Consulate General of Japan, Oregon
Attn: Tamara, Video Library
1300 S. W. Fifth Avenue, Suite 2700
Portland, OR 97201
Phone: 1-503-221-1811, ext. 17
World Wide Web URL:
http://www.portland.us.emb-japan.go.jp/en/index.html
Email Address: tamara@cgjpdx.org

Young Baseball Heroes
A high school team prepares for a great tournament at Koshen Stadium.
Availability: Schools, libraries, homeschoolers, and nursing homes in Nevada and northern California (zip codes beginning 932 and above, except 935).
Suggested Grade: 6-Adult
Order Number: order by title
Format: VHS videotape
Special Notes: Part of the "Faces of Japan" series.
Terms: Borrower pays return postage. Book two weeks in advance. Return within three weeks of date borrowed, via UPS, Federal Express or certified mail.
Source: Consulate General of Japan, San Francisco
50 Fremont Street, Suite 2300
San Francisco, CA 94105-2236
Phone: 1-415-356-2564
Fax: 1-415-777-0518
World Wide Web URL: http://www.sf.us.emb-japan.go.jp/
Email Address: infoav@cgjsf.org

RELIGION AND PHILOSOPHY

Altar of Fire
Records the Agnicayana, the Vedic sacrifice to the fire-god Agni, as performed in 1975 in a village in Kerala, South India. The 12-day rite had never been seen by outsiders.
- Availability: Schools, libraries, homeschoolers, and nursing homes in the southeastern United States.
- Suggested Grade: 7-12
- Order Number: order by title
- Production Date: 1976
- Format: VHS videotape
- Terms: Borrower pays return postage. Return 2 days after showing via United Parcel Service, insured. Book 2 weeks in advance.
  - Source: Center for South Asian Studies
  - University of Virginia
  - Video Library Coordinator
  - P. O. Box 400169, 110 Minor Hall
  - Charlottesville, VA 22904-4169
  - Phone: 1-434-924-8815
  - Email Address: southasia@virginia.edu

Annual Festivities and Ceremonies--Beliefs in Daily Life
While Japanese people, in general, have no fixed or exclusive religious affiliation, they do, at times, express belief very fervently, invoking the deity or creed appropriate to the situation or festivity, whether it be Buddhism, Christianity or one of the various Shinto deities. This video focuses on the belief as expressed in ceremonial occasions and annual celebrations.
- Availability: Schools, libraries, homeschoolers, and nursing homes in Connecticut (except Fairfield County), Maine, Massachusetts, New Hampshire, Rhode Island, and Vermont.
- Suggested Grade: 4-12
- Order Number: 451
- Production Date: 1991
- Format: VHS videotape
- Special Notes: No. 13 of the "Nippon the Land and Its People" series.
- Terms: Borrower pays return postage, including insurance. Return two weeks after receipt.
  - Source: Consulate General of Japan, Boston
  - Federal Reserve Plaza, 14th Floor
  - 600 Atlantic Avenue
  - Boston, MA 02210
  - Phone: 1-617-973-9772
  - Fax: 1-617-542-1329
  - World Wide Web URL:
  - http://www.boston.us.emb-japan.go.jp
  - Email Address: infocul@cgjbos.org

Annual Festivities and Ceremonies--Beliefs in Daily Life
Focuses on the belief as expressed in ceremonial occasions and annual celebrations, fervently invoking the deity or creed appropriate to the situation or festivity.
- Availability: Schools, libraries, and nursing homes in Oklahoma and Texas.
- Suggested Grade: 4-12
- Order Number: B12
- Production Date: 1991
- Format: VHS videotape
- Special Notes: No. 13 of the "Nippon the Land and Its People" series.
- Terms: Materials must be picked up in person. Under special circumstances, you may be able to have them shipped to you at your own expense (call for further details). Return within two weeks after scheduled showing. Videos must be registered with the U. S. Postal Service or returned by Priority Mail, Federal Express, or other registered shipping service.
  - Source: Consulate General of Japan, Houston
  - Cultural Affairs and Information Section
  - 909 Fannin Street, Suite 3000
  - Houston, TX 77010
  - Phone: 1-713-652-2977
  - Fax: 1-713-651-7822
  - World Wide Web URL:
  - http://www.houston.us.emb-japan.go.jp/en/culture/page1.htm
  - Email Address: info@cgjhouston.org

Annual Festivities and Ceremonies--Beliefs in Daily Life
While Japanese people, in general, have no fixed or exclusive religious affiliation, they do, at times, express belief very fervently, invoking the deity or creed appropriate to the situation or festivity, whether it be Buddhism, Christianity or one of the various Shinto deities. This video focuses on the belief as expressed in ceremonial occasions and annual celebrations.
- Availability: Schools, libraries, homeschoolers, and nursing homes in Nevada and northern California (zip codes beginning 932 and above, except 935).
- Suggested Grade: 4-12
- Order Number: order by title
- Production Date: 1991
- Format: VHS videotape
- Special Notes: No. 13 of the "Nippon the Land and Its People" series.
- Terms: Borrower pays return postage. Book two weeks in advance. Return within three weeks of date borrowed, via UPS, Federal Express or certified mail.
  - Source: Consulate General of Japan, San Francisco
  - 50 Fremont Street, Suite 2300
  - San Francisco, CA 94105-2236
  - Phone: 1-415-356-2564
  - Fax: 1-415-777-0518
  - World Wide Web URL: http://www.sf.us.emb-japan.go.jp/
  - Email Address: infoav@cgjsf.org

Bahia: Africa in the Americas
Discusses the impact on Brazil of African culture and the Candomble religion.
- Availability: Schools and libraries in Iowa, Illinois, Michigan, Minnesota, and Wisconsin.
- Suggested Grade: 6-12

All materials listed in this 2018-2019 edition are BRAND NEW!

RELIGION AND PHILOSOPHY

Order Number: AFRICABRAB14VHS
Production Date: 1991
Format: VHS videotape
Terms: Borrower pays return postage. Return 8 days after showing. Book 2 weeks in advance. Order may also be picked up for those near the Center.
**Source: Center for Latin American and Caribbean Studies
UW-Milwaukee
P. O. Box 413
Milwaukee, WI 53201
Phone: 1-414-229-5987**
World Wide Web URL: http://www.uwm.edu/Dept/CLACS
Email Address: audvis@usm.edu

Basic Christian Communities in Latin America
Two missionaries describe the functions of basic Christian communities in Brazil and Bolivia.
Availability: Schools in the United States.
Suggested Grade: 9-Adult
Order Number: order by title
Format: VHS videotape
Terms: Borrower pays return postage. Return 14 days after receipt, via USPS including insurance. All borrowers must have a current lending agreement on file with the Outreach program. This agreement is available via the web site or may be requested via phone or fax.
**Source: Center for Latin American Studies
University of Florida
319 Grinter Hall
P. O. Box 115530
Gainesville, FL 32611-5530
Phone: 1-352-392-0375
Fax: 1-352-392-7682**
World Wide Web URL: http://www.latam.ufl.edu/outreach
Email Address: maryr@ufl.edu

Buddhism and Black Belts
This video investigates how Buddhist practices influence daily life in modern Japan, looking at meditation, the tea ceremony, Ikebana (flower arranging), calligraphy, martial arts, and archery
Availability: Schools, libraries, and nursing homes in the United States and Canada.
Suggested Grade: 6-12
Order Number: JV077
Format: VHS videotape
Terms: Borrower pays return postage. Return with 14 days after scheduled showing, via UPS or U. S. Mail. All requests must included an educational institution affiliation, a current address, and phone number. Order through web site only.
Source: Cornell University East Asia Program
World Wide Web URL:
http://eap.einaudi.cornell.edu/lending_library
Email Address: east_asia1@cornell.edu

Buddhism: The Making of a Monk
Documents a young Tai man's entry into a Buddhist monastery. Describes his reasons and goals for becoming a monk and explains some of the basic aspects of monastic life. A sequence of the initiation ritual is shown and described within the context of the central Buddhist precepts.
Availability: Schools, libraries, homeschoolers, and nursing homes in the southeastern United States.
Suggested Grade: 7-12
Order Number: order by title
Production Date: 1999
Format: VHS videotape
Terms: Borrower pays return postage. Return 2 days after showing via United Parcel Service, insured. Book 2 weeks in advance.
**Source: Center for South Asian Studies
University of Virginia
Video Library Coordinator
P. O. Box 400169, 110 Minor Hall
Charlottesville, VA 22904-4169
Phone: 1-434-924-8815**
Email Address: southasia@virginia.edu

Buddhism: The Middle Way of Compassion
This video introduces the major concepts of the Buddhist religious tradition, including the Buddha, the concept of karma, the noble eightfold way, Theravada Buddhism, Mahayana Buddhism, and the relationship of Buddhism to Hinduism
Availability: Schools, libraries, and nursing homes in the United States and Canada.
Suggested Grade: 6-12
Order Number: EAV001
Format: VHS videotape
Terms: Borrower pays return postage. Return with 14 days after scheduled showing, via UPS or U. S. Mail. All requests must included an educational institution affiliation, a current address, and phone number. Order through web site only.
Source: Cornell University East Asia Program
World Wide Web URL:
http://eap.einaudi.cornell.edu/lending_library
Email Address: east_asia1@cornell.edu

Can These Bones Live?
Many centuries ago the prophet Ezekiel was given a vision of Israel's lost hope portrayed as a "valley of dry bones." Explores how this prediction has come to life and what may be yet to follow.
Availability: Schools, libraries, homeschoolers, churches, and nursing homes in the United States.
Suggested Grade: 6-Adult
Order Number: order by title
Format: DVD
Special Notes: May be retained permanently.
Terms: Book 2 to 3 weeks in advance.
**Source: Chicago Bible Students
Jeannine Farrell
310 South Lambert Road**

*All materials listed in this 2018-2019 edition are **BRAND NEW!***

RELIGION AND PHILOSOPHY

Glen Ellyn, IL 60137
Email Address: jean9farrell@aol.com

Common Ground, A
Produced by the American Institute for Islamic Affairs, this discusses the three Abrahamic faiths and the common ground between them.
- Availability: Schools, libraries, homeschoolers, and nursing homes in the United States.
- Suggested Grade: 7-12
- Order Number: order by title
- Production Date: 1987
- Format: VHS videotape
- Terms: Borrower pays return postage via any carrier with $400 insurance per parcel. Videos are loaned for 14 days; may be retained longer if requested in advance. Borrowers must complete a lending agreement.

  Source: Center for Middle Eastern Studies
  Outreach Coordinator
  University of Texas at Austin
  1 University Station, F9400
  Austin, TX 78712-0527
  World Wide Web URL:
  http://www.utexas.edu/cola/depts/mes/center/outreach/library-catalog.php
  Email Address: crose@mail.utexas.edu

Common Table: Basic Christian Communities in Latin America
Small groups of Christians integrate faith and life in the Latin American Church.
- Availability: Schools, libraries, and nursing homes in the United States.
- Suggested Grade: 6-12
- Order Number: RLA1-video
- Production Date: 1986
- Format: VHS videotape
- Terms: Borrowers must have a User's Agreement on file with this source--available by mail or via the Internet. Return postage is paid by borrower; return 12 days after showing. Book at least three weeks in advance. All borrowers are limited to a total of ten items per semester.

  Source: Latin American Resource Center
  Stone Center for Latin American Studies
  Tulane University, 100 Jones Hall
  New Orleans, LA 70118
  Phone: 1-504-862-3143
  Fax: 1-504-865-6719
  World Wide Web URL: http://stonecenter.tulane.edu/pages/detail/48/Lending-Library
  Email Address: crcrts@tulane.edu

Common Table: Central American Refugees--The Church Response
Efforts of churches to offer Biblical hospitality and challenges of immigration authority, as hundreds of thousands of Central Americans have sought refuge in the U. S.
- Availability: Schools, libraries, and nursing homes in the United States.
- Suggested Grade: 8-Adult
- Order Number: SICA5-video
- Production Date: 1987
- Format: VHS videotape
- Terms: Borrowers must have a User's Agreement on file with this source--available by mail or via the Internet. Return postage is paid by borrower; return 12 days after showing. Book at least three weeks in advance. All borrowers are limited to a total of ten items per semester.

  Source: Latin American Resource Center
  Stone Center for Latin American Studies
  Tulane University, 100 Jones Hall
  New Orleans, LA 70118
  Phone: 1-504-862-3143
  Fax: 1-504-865-6719
  World Wide Web URL: http://stonecenter.tulane.edu/pages/detail/48/Lending-Library
  Email Address: crcrts@tulane.edu

Confucianism and Taoism
Looks at the philosophy and rituals of Taoism and at how the philosophy and social doctrine have impacted Chinese culture.
- Availability: Schools, libraries, and nursing homes in the United States and Canada.
- Suggested Grade: 6-12
- Order Number: CV031
- Format: VHS videotape
- Terms: Borrower pays return postage. Return with 14 days after scheduled showing, via UPS or U. S. Mail. All requests must included an educational institution affiliation, a current address, and phone number. Order through web site only.

  Source: Cornell University East Asia Program
  World Wide Web URL:
  http://eap.einaudi.cornell.edu/lending_library
  Email Address: east_asia1@cornell.edu

Cycles of Independence
In Ladakh, Buddhist monks and lay families have a symbiotic relationship, evidenced especially in annual cycles of growing crops and festival dances of protector deities.
- Availability: Schools, libraries, homeschoolers, and nursing homes in the southeastern United States.
- Suggested Grade: 7-12
- Order Number: order by title
- Format: VHS videotape
- Terms: Borrower pays return postage. Return 2 days after showing via United Parcel Service, insured. Book 2 weeks in advance.

  Source: Center for South Asian Studies
  University of Virginia
  Video Library Coordinator
  P. O. Box 400169, 110 Minor Hall
  Charlottesville, VA 22904-4169

RELIGION AND PHILOSOPHY

    Phone: 1-434-924-8815
    Email Address: southasia@virginia.edu

Debate in the Tibetan Tradition
A presentation of some of the classic topics used in the study of logic and the practice of debate in Tibetan Buddhist Monastic universities in India, featuring Georges Dreyfus, the first Westerner to receive the geshey degree.
- Availability: Schools, libraries, homeschoolers, and nursing homes in the southeastern United States.
- Suggested Grade: 7-12
- Order Number: order by title
- Production Date: 1985
- Format: VHS videotape
- Terms: Borrower pays return postage. Return 2 days after showing via United Parcel Service, insured. Book 2 weeks in advance.
- Source: Center for South Asian Studies
    University of Virginia
    Video Library Coordinator
    P. O. Box 400169, 110 Minor Hall
    Charlottesville, VA 22904-4169
    Phone: 1-434-924-8815
    Email Address: southasia@virginia.edu

Father, Son and Holy War
Part 1: Sita's trial by ordeal in the Ramayana deals with a 1987 case of sati (the burning of a widow on her husband's funeral pyre), the fire rituals of the upper castes, and the communal fires in Bombay in 1993 contrasting burning violence with the the work of Hindu and Muslim "firefighters" working for women's rights and communal harmony. Part 2: Hero Pharmacy, examines constructions of masculinity among Hindus and Indian Muslims today and shows how they lead to violence, war, and genocide.
- Availability: Schools and libraries in the United States.
- Suggested Grade: 7-12
- Order Number: 67
- Production Date: 1994
- Format: Set of 2 VHS videotapes
- Terms: Borrower pays return postage. Return 3 days after showing via UPS. Book at least 2 weeks in advance.
- Source: Syracuse University, South Asia Center
    Video Library and Teaching Resources
    346F Eggers Hall
    The Maxwell School
    Syracuse, NY 13244

Fourth Stage, The: A Hindu's Quest for Release
A newly retired newspaper editor decides whether or not to enter the classical Hindu fourth stage of life and renounce the world.
- Availability: Schools, libraries, homeschoolers, and nursing homes in the southeastern United States.
- Suggested Grade: 7-12
- Order Number: order by title
- Production Date: 1984
- Format: VHS videotape
- Terms: Borrower pays return postage. Return 2 days after showing via United Parcel Service, insured. Book 2 weeks in advance.
- Source: Center for South Asian Studies
    University of Virginia
    Video Library Coordinator
    P. O. Box 400169, 110 Minor Hall
    Charlottesville, VA 22904-4169
    Phone: 1-434-924-8815
    Email Address: southasia@virginia.edu

Frontiers of Peace: Jainism in India
Interviews with laypeople, monks, and nuns reveal the teachings, history, and major observances of Jainism, and how modernism challenges Jain beliefs. The video opens in a Jain animal shelter, run in accordance with Jain principles of non-violence.
- Availability: Schools, libraries, homeschoolers, and nursing homes in the southeastern United States.
- Suggested Grade: 7-12
- Order Number: order by title
- Production Date: 1986
- Format: VHS videotape
- Terms: Borrower pays return postage. Return 2 days after showing via United Parcel Service, insured. Book 2 weeks in advance.
- Source: Center for South Asian Studies
    University of Virginia
    Video Library Coordinator
    P. O. Box 400169, 110 Minor Hall
    Charlottesville, VA 22904-4169
    Phone: 1-434-924-8815
    Email Address: southasia@virginia.edu

God's Millennium
A new day is dawning--the grand Millennial kingdom of God referred to in the last book of the Bible. Explores this experience that will be beyond man's expectations.
- Availability: Schools, libraries, homeschoolers, churches, and nursing homes in the United States.
- Suggested Grade: 6-Adult
- Order Number: order by title
- Format: DVD
- Special Notes: May be retained permanently.
- Terms: Book 2 to 3 weeks in advance.
- Source: Chicago Bible Students
    Jeannine Farrell
    310 South Lambert Road
    Glen Ellyn, IL 60137
    Email Address: jean9farrell@aol.com

Great Pyramid, The: Ancient Wonder, Modern Mystery
The Great Pyramid of Giza stands alone in its mystery, wonder and praise. See a unique biblical perspective on this

*All materials listed in this 2018-2019 edition are **BRAND NEW!***

RELIGION AND PHILOSOPHY

ancient wonder pointing to a message from God about the ultimate destiny of man.
- Availability: Schools, libraries, homeschoolers, churches, and nursing homes in the United States.
- Suggested Grade: 6-Adult
- Order Number: order by title
- Format: DVD
- Special Notes: May be retained permanently.
- Terms: Book 2 to 3 weeks in advance.

Source: Chicago Bible Students
Jeannine Farrell
310 South Lambert Road
Glen Ellyn, IL 60137
Email Address: jean9farrell@aol.com

Guadalupe: Mother of All Mexico
Explores the image of the Virgin Mary in Mexico from the time of the conquest to present day.
- Availability: Schools in the United States.
- Suggested Grade: 9-Adult
- Order Number: order by title
- Format: VHS videotape
- Terms: Borrower pays return postage. Return 14 days after receipt, via USPS including insurance. All borrowers must have a current lending agreement on file with the Outreach program. This agreement is available via the web site or may be requested via phone or fax.

Source: Center for Latin American Studies
University of Florida
319 Grinter Hall
P. O. Box 115530
Gainesville, FL 32611-5530
Phone: 1-352-392-0375
Fax: 1-352-392-7682
World Wide Web URL: http://www.latam.ufl.edu/outreach
Email Address: maryr@ufl.edu

Guests of God, The
Follow a German family who have converted to Islam as they perform the pilgrimage, or hajj, to Mecca and Medina.
- Availability: Schools, libraries, homeschoolers, and nursing homes in the United States.
- Suggested Grade: 7-12
- Order Number: order by title
- Production Date: 1991
- Format: VHS videotape
- Terms: Borrower pays return postage via any carrier with $400 insurance per parcel. Videos are loaned for 14 days; may be retained longer if requested in advance. Borrowers must complete a lending agreement.

Source: Center for Middle Eastern Studies
Outreach Coordinator
University of Texas at Austin
1 University Station, F9400
Austin, TX 78712-0527
World Wide Web URL:
http://www.utexas.edu/cola/depts/mes/center/outreach/library-catalog.php
Email Address: crose@mail.utexas.edu

Hail Umbanda
Insider's view of Brazil's fastest-growing religion.
- Availability: Schools, libraries, and nursing homes in the United States.
- Suggested Grade: 6-12
- Order Number: RBRA3-video
- Production Date: 1986
- Format: VHS videotape
- Terms: Borrowers must have a User's Agreement on file with this source--available by mail or via the Internet. Return postage is paid by borrower; return 12 days after showing. Book at least three weeks in advance. All borrowers are limited to a total of ten items per semester.

Source: Latin American Resource Center
Stone Center for Latin American Studies
Tulane University
100 Jones Hall
New Orleans, LA 70118
Phone: 1-504-862-3143
Fax: 1-504-865-6719
World Wide Web URL: http://stonecenter.tulane.edu/pages/detail/48/Lending-Library
Email Address: crcrts@tulane.edu

Hajj, The
This report follows an American Muslim who makes the Hajj (pilgrimage) to Mecca, and explains the significance.
- Availability: Schools, libraries, homeschoolers, and nursing homes in the United States.
- Suggested Grade: 7-12
- Order Number: order by title
- Production Date: 1997
- Format: VHS videotape
- Terms: Borrower pays return postage via any carrier with $400 insurance per parcel. Videos are loaned for 14 days; may be retained longer if requested in advance. Borrowers must complete a lending agreement.

Source: Center for Middle Eastern Studies
Outreach Coordinator
University of Texas at Austin
1 University Station, F9400
Austin, TX 78712-0527
World Wide Web URL:
http://www.utexas.edu/cola/depts/mes/center/outreach/library-catalog.php
Email Address: crose@mail.utexas.edu

Havana Nagila: The Jews in Cuba
History and presence of the Jewish community in Cuba and since the 1959 Revolution under Castro.
- Availability: Schools, libraries, and nursing homes in the United States.
- Suggested Grade: 6-12
- Order Number: RCUB2-video
- Production Date: 1995
- Format: VHS videotape
- Terms: Borrowers must have a User's Agreement on file with this source--available by mail or via the Internet. Return postage is paid by borrower; return 12 days after

All materials listed in this 2018-2019 edition are BRAND NEW!

RELIGION AND PHILOSOPHY

showing. Book at least three weeks in advance. All borrowers are limited to a total of ten items per semester.
Source: Latin American Resource Center
Stone Center for Latin American Studies
Tulane University
100 Jones Hall
New Orleans, LA 70118
Phone: 1-504-862-3143
Fax: 1-504-865-6719
World Wide Web URL: http://stonecenter.tulane.edu/pages/detail/48/Lending-Library
Email Address: crcrts@tulane.edu

Healer, The
An American missioner, who works among the Aymara Indians of Peru, finds God in an unexpected way. Contrasts ancient and traditional rites and customs.
Availability: Schools, libraries, and nursing homes in the United States.
Suggested Grade: 6-12
Order Number: RPER1-video
Production Date: 1975
Format: VHS videotape
Terms: Borrowers must have a User's Agreement on file with this source--available by mail or via the Internet. Return postage is paid by borrower; return 12 days after showing. Book at least three weeks in advance. All borrowers are limited to a total of ten items per semester.
Source: Latin American Resource Center
Stone Center for Latin American Studies
Tulane University, 100 Jones Hall
New Orleans, LA 70118
Phone: 1-504-862-3143
Fax: 1-504-865-6719
World Wide Web URL: http://stonecenter.tulane.edu/pages/detail/48/Lending-Library
Email Address: crcrts@tulane.edu

His Holiness the Dalai Lama
A series of lectures entitled "Emptiness and Great Compassion: The Psychology of Selflessness," in which the Dalai Lama teaches his synthesis of the entire Buddhist path to enlightenment. The lectures were delivered at Harvard University in 1981.
Availability: Schools, libraries, homeschoolers, and nursing homes in the southeastern United States.
Suggested Grade: 7-12
Order Number: order by title
Production Date: 1981
Format: Set of 8 VHS videotapes
Terms: Borrower pays return postage. Return 2 days after showing via United Parcel Service, insured. Book 2 weeks in advance.
Source: Center for South Asian Studies
University of Virginia
Video Library Coordinator
P. O. Box 400169, 110 Minor Hall
Charlottesville, VA 22904-4169
Phone: 1-434-924-8815
Email Address: southasia@virginia.edu

I Am a Sufi, I Am a Muslim
Travel to India, Pakistan, Turkey, and Macedonia to explore Sufism and observe how it is practiced in various parts of the world today. Also features Nusrat Fateh Ali Khan, a well-known performer of Qawali music.
Availability: Schools, libraries, homeschoolers, and nursing homes in the southeastern United States.
Suggested Grade: 7-12
Order Number: order by title
Production Date: 1996
Format: VHS videotape
Terms: Borrower pays return postage. Return 2 days after showing via United Parcel Service, insured. Book 2 weeks in advance.
Source: Center for South Asian Studies
University of Virginia
Video Library Coordinator
P. O. Box 400169, 110 Minor Hall
Charlottesville, VA 22904-4169
Phone: 1-434-924-8815
Email Address: southasia@virginia.edu

Introduction to East Asian Religions, An: Buddhism (Part I)
Cornell's H. Stanley Krusen Professor of World Religions, Jane Marie Law, presents a classroom lecture on Buddhism.
Availability: Schools, libraries, and nursing homes in the United States and Canada.
Suggested Grade: 6-Adult
Order Number: EAV012
Format: VHS videotape
Terms: Borrower pays return postage. Return with 14 days after scheduled showing, via UPS or U. S. Mail. All requests must included an educational institution affiliation, a current address, and phone number. Order through web site only.
Source: Cornell University East Asia Program
World Wide Web URL: http://eap.einaudi.cornell.edu/lending_library
Email Address: east_asia1@cornell.edu

Introduction to East Asian Religions, An: Confucianism (Part II)
Cornell's H. Stanley Krusen Professor of World Religions, Jane Marie Law, presents a classroom lecture on Confucianism.
Availability: Schools, libraries, and nursing homes in the United States and Canada.
Suggested Grade: 6-Adult
Order Number: EAV013
Format: VHS videotape
Terms: Borrower pays return postage. Return with 14 days after scheduled showing, via UPS or U. S. Mail. All requests must included an educational institution affiliation, a

RELIGION AND PHILOSOPHY

current address, and phone number. Order through web site only.
    Source: **Cornell University East Asia Program**
    World Wide Web URL:
    http://eap.einaudi.cornell.edu/lending_library
    Email Address: east_asia1@cornell.edu

Islam: Empire of Faith
Tells the story of the origins and rise of Islamic power during its first 1,000 years - from the birth of the prophet Muhammad to the peak of the Ottoman Empire under the reign of Suleiman the Magnificent.
Availability: Schools and libraries in the United States.
Suggested Grade: 7-12
Order Number: 123
Production Date: 2000
Format: VHS videotape
Terms: Borrower pays return postage. Return 3 days after showing via UPS. Book at least 2 weeks in advance.
    Source: **Syracuse University, South Asia Center**
    Video Library and Teaching Resources
    346F Eggers Hall
    The Maxwell School
    Syracuse, NY 13244

Islam in America
This is a discussion of Islam, as it is practiced in the United States today, and what American Muslims have in common with other Muslims around the world.
Availability: Schools, libraries, homeschoolers, and nursing homes in the United States.
Suggested Grade: 7-12
Order Number: order by title
Production Date: 1992
Format: VHS videotape
Terms: Borrower pays return postage via any carrier with $400 insurance per parcel. Videos are loaned for 14 days; may be retained longer if requested in advance. Borrowers must complete a lending agreement.
    Source: **Center for Middle Eastern Studies**
    Outreach Coordinator
    University of Texas at Austin
    1 University Station, F9400
    Austin, TX 78712-0527
    World Wide Web URL:
    http://www.utexas.edu/cola/depts/mes/center/outreach/library-catalog.php
    Email Address: crose@mail.utexas.edu

Israel: Born to Destiny
The pages of history would make it appear that Israel has been chosen for persecution, discrimination and exile. Is this the destiny for which Israel has been reborn? Trace prophecies that answer this question and the part they have in God's plan.
Availability: Schools, libraries, homeschoolers, churches, and nursing homes in the United States.
Suggested Grade: 6-Adult
Order Number: order by title
Format: DVD
Special Notes: May be retained permanently.
Terms: Book 2 to 3 weeks in advance.
    Source: **Chicago Bible Students**
    Jeannine Farrell
    310 South Lambert Road
    Glen Ellyn, IL 60137 Wide Web URL:
    Email Address: jean9farrell@aol.com

Jesus: His Life
This documentary details the life and times of Jesus of Galilee through interviews with scholars and theologians, and through archaeological evidence.
Availability: Schools, libraries, homeschoolers, and nursing homes in the United States.
Suggested Grade: 7-12
Order Number: order by title
Production Date: 1995
Format: VHS videotape
Terms: Borrower pays return postage via any carrier with $400 insurance per parcel. Videos are loaned for 14 days; may be retained longer if requested in advance. Borrowers must complete a lending agreement.
    Source: **Center for Middle Eastern Studies**
    Outreach Coordinator
    University of Texas at Austin
    1 University Station, F9400
    Austin, TX 78712-0527
    World Wide Web URL:
    http://www.utexas.edu/cola/depts/mes/center/outreach/library-catalog.php
    Email Address: crose@mail.utexas.edu

Kashmir Story, The
Describes the suffering and the aspirations of all Kashmiris--Sunni and Shia Muslims, Hindus and Buddhists, nomadic, children, their parents, boys with guns and the families whose loved ones are no more. Highlights the differences of religious perceptions that have overpowered peace in the state and the legacies of the Kashmiri tradition.
Availability: Schools and libraries in the United States.
Suggested Grade: 7-Adult
Order Number: SA43
Format: VHS videotape
Terms: Borrower pays return postage. Return 3 days after showing via UPS. Book at least 2 weeks in advance.
    Source: **Syracuse University, South Asia Center**
    Video Library and Teaching Resources
    346F Eggers Hall
    The Maxwell School
    Syracuse, NY 13244

King of Kings and Lord of Lords
Trace the scriptures that promise that because of the life and death of Jesus, every man, woman and child that has ever lived will be given an opportunity for everlasting life in God's Kingdom.

All materials listed in this 2018-2019 edition are BRAND NEW!

RELIGION AND PHILOSOPHY

Availability: Schools, libraries, homeschoolers, churches, and nursing homes in the United States.
Suggested Grade: 6-Adult
Order Number: order by title
Format: DVD
Special Notes: May be retained permanently.
Terms: Book 2 to 3 weeks in advance.
    Source: Chicago Bible Students
    Jeannine Farrell
    310 South Lambert Road
    Glen Ellyn, IL 60137
    Email Address: jean9farrell@aol.com

Loving Krishna
Two major festivals, the celebration of Krishna's birth and the great Chariot Festival, held in a small historic town where worship and daily life are intertwined, along with arts and crafts, and bazaar exchanges.
Availability: Schools, libraries, homeschoolers, and nursing homes in the southeastern United States.
Suggested Grade: 7-12
Order Number: order by title
Production Date: 1985
Format: VHS videotape
Terms: Borrower pays return postage. Return 2 days after showing via United Parcel Service, insured. Book 2 weeks in advance.
    Source: Center for South Asian Studies
    University of Virginia
    Video Library Coordinator
    P. O. Box 400169, 110 Minor Hall
    Charlottesville, VA 22904-4169
    Phone: 1-434-924-8815
    Email Address: southasia@virginia.edu

Message, The
An epic about the beginning of Islam and the story of the prophet Muhammad. The video requires some knowledge of the early history of Islam in order to understand what is going on in this feature. The making of an Epic, plus the original English and Arabic theatrical trailers are included.
Availability: Schools, libraries, homeschoolers, and nursing homes in the United States.
Suggested Grade: 9-12
Order Number: order by title
Production Date: 1976
Format: VHS videotape
Special Notes: Widescreen format, rated PG.
Terms: Borrower pays return postage via any carrier with $400 insurance per parcel. Videos are loaned for 14 days; may be retained longer if requested in advance. Borrowers must complete a lending agreement.
    Source: Center for Middle Eastern Studies
    Outreach Coordinator
    University of Texas at Austin
    1 University Station, F9400
    Austin, TX 78712-0527
    World Wide Web URL:
    http://www.utexas.edu/cola/depts/mes/center/outreach/library-catalog.php
    Email Address: crose@mail.utexas.edu

Messiah: The Biblical Message Behind the Musical Masterpiece
Many musical selections from Handel's Messiah accompany breathtaking scenes as the scriptures are explained in their greater context of God's plan.
Availability: Schools, libraries, homeschoolers, churches, and nursing homes in the United States.
Suggested Grade: 12-Adult
Order Number: order by title
Format: DVD
Special Notes: May be retained permanently.
Terms: Book 2 to 3 weeks in advance.
    Source: Chicago Bible Students
    Jeannine Farrell
    310 South Lambert Road
    Glen Ellyn, IL 60137
    Email Address: jean9farrell@aol.com

Mythology of Ancient Mexico
Development of successive pre-Columbian civilizations in Mexico and their religious beliefs and practices.
Availability: Schools, libraries, and nursing homes in the United States.
Suggested Grade: 6-12
Order Number: LPMEX1-video
Production Date: 1991
Format: VHS videotape
Terms: Borrowers must have a User's Agreement on file with this source--available by mail or via the Internet. Return postage is paid by borrower; return 12 days after showing. Book at least three weeks in advance. All borrowers are limited to a total of ten items per semester.
    Source: Latin American Resource Center
    Stone Center for Latin American Studies
    Tulane University
    100 Jones Hall
    New Orleans, LA 70118
    Phone: 1-504-862-3143
    Fax: 1-504-865-6719
    World Wide Web URL: http://stonecenter.tulane.edu/pages/detail/48/Lending-Library
    Email Address: crcrts@tulane.edu

Observing the Breath
An exposition of a traditional meditation technique from the Theravada school of Buddhism.
Availability: Schools, libraries, homeschoolers, and nursing homes in the southeastern United States.
Suggested Grade: 7-12
Order Number: order by title
Production Date: 1983
Format: VHS videotape

RELIGION AND PHILOSOPHY

Terms: Borrower pays return postage. Return 2 days after showing via United Parcel Service, insured. Book 2 weeks in advance.
Source: Center for South Asian Studies
University of Virginia
Video Library Coordinator
P. O. Box 400169, 110 Minor Hall
Charlottesville, VA 22904-4169
Phone: 1-434-924-8815
Email Address: southasia@virginia.edu

Sand Painting: Sacred Art of Tibetan Buddhism
Two Tibetan monks of Namgyal Monastery create the Kalachakra mandala at the Asian Art Museum of San Francisco.
Availability: Schools, libraries, homeschoolers, and nursing homes in the southeastern United States.
Suggested Grade: 7-12
Order Number: order by title
Production Date: 1991
Format: VHS videotape
Terms: Borrower pays return postage. Return 2 days after showing via United Parcel Service, insured. Book 2 weeks in advance.
Source: Center for South Asian Studies
University of Virginia
Video Library Coordinator
P. O. Box 400169, 110 Minor Hall
Charlottesville, VA 22904-4169
Phone: 1-434-924-8815
Email Address: southasia@virginia.edu

Sathya Sai Baba: Aura of Divinity
Five thousand years ago, the ancient scriptures of the Mahabharata prophesied that in this age of spiritual and moral decline, political corruption, crime and falsehood, a holy man would appear in order to put us all on the righteous path. Sri Sathya Si Baba claims to be such a man.
Availability: Schools, libraries, homeschoolers, and nursing homes in the southeastern United States.
Suggested Grade: 7-12
Order Number: order by title
Format: VHS videotape
Terms: Borrower pays return postage. Return 2 days after showing via United Parcel Service, insured. Book 2 weeks in advance.
Source: Center for South Asian Studies
University of Virginia
Video Library Coordinator
P. O. Box 400169, 110 Minor Hall
Charlottesville, VA 22904-4169
Phone: 1-434-924-8815
Email Address: southasia@virginia.edu

Shinto: Way of the Gods
According to Shinto, Japan's indigenous religion, divine spirits exist in all aspects of life, such as natural objects and other phenomena. This contains scenes of Shinto shrines and explores the role Shintoism plays in daily lives of the Japanese.
Availability: Schools, libraries, homeschoolers, and nursing homes in Connecticut (except Fairfield County), Maine, Massachusetts, New Hampshire, Rhode Island, and Vermont.
Suggested Grade: 9-Adult
Order Number: 501
Production Date: 1995
Format: VHS videotape
Special Notes: No. 2 of the "Nihon No Kokoro" series.
Terms: Borrower pays return postage, including insurance. Return two weeks after receipt.
Source: Consulate General of Japan, Boston
Federal Reserve Plaza, 14th Floor
600 Atlantic Avenue
Boston, MA 02210
Phone: 1-617-973-9772
Fax: 1-617-542-1329
World Wide Web URL:
http://www.boston.us.emb-japan.go.jp
Email Address: infocul@cgjbos.org

Shinto: Way of the Gods
According to Shinto, Japan's indigenous religion, divine spirits exist in all aspects of life, such as natural objects and other phenomena. This contains scenes of Shinto shrines and explores the role Shintoism plays in daily lives of the Japanese.
Availability: Schools, libraries, and nursing homes in Oklahoma and Texas.
Suggested Grade: 9-Adult
Order Number: K2
Production Date: 1995
Format: VHS videotape
Special Notes: No. 2 of the "Nihon No Kokoro" series.
Terms: Materials must be picked up in person. Under special circumstances, you may be able to have them shipped to you at your own expense (call for further details). Return within two weeks after scheduled showing. Videos must be registered with the U. S. Postal Service or returned by Priority Mail, Federal Express, or other registered shipping service.
Source: Consulate General of Japan, Houston
Cultural Affairs and Information Section
909 Fannin Street, Suite 3000
Houston, TX 77010
Phone: 1-713-652-2977
Fax: 1-713-651-7822
World Wide Web URL:
http://www.houston.us.emb-japan.go.jp/en/culture/page1.htm
Email Address: info@cgjhouston.org

Shinto: Way of the Gods
According to Shinto, Japan's indigenous religion, divine spirits exist in all aspects of life, such as natural objects and other phenomena. This contains scenes of Shinto shrines

All materials listed in this 2018-2019 edition are BRAND NEW!

RELIGION AND PHILOSOPHY

and explores the role Shintoism plays in daily lives of the Japanese.

Availability:	Schools, libraries, homeschoolers, and nursing homes in Nevada and northern California (zip codes beginning 932 and above, except 935).
Suggested Grade:	9-Adult
Order Number:	order by title
Production Date:	1995
Format:	VHS videotape
Special Notes:	No. 2 of the "Nihon No Kokoro" series.
Terms:	Borrower pays return postage. Book two weeks in advance. Return within three weeks of date borrowed, via UPS, Federal Express or certified mail.

Source: Consulate General of Japan, San Francisco
50 Fremont Street, Suite 2300
San Francisco, CA 94105-2236
Phone: 1-415-356-2564
Fax: 1-415-777-0518
World Wide Web URL: http://www.sf.us.emb-japan.go.jp/
Email Address: infoav@cgjsf.org

Story of Islam, The

Details the history and main tenets of the Islamic faith.

Availability:	Schools, libraries, homeschoolers, and nursing homes in the United States.
Suggested Grade:	7-12
Order Number:	order by title
Production Date:	1983
Format:	VHS videotape
Terms:	Borrower pays return postage via any carrier with $400 insurance per parcel. Videos are loaned for 14 days; may be retained longer if requested in advance. Borrowers must complete a lending agreement.

Source: Center for Middle Eastern Studies
Outreach Coordinator
University of Texas at Austin
1 University Station, F9400
Austin, TX 78712-0527
World Wide Web URL:
http://www.utexas.edu/cola/depts/mes/
center/outreach/library-catalog.php
Email Address: crose@mail.utexas.edu

Tales of Pabuji: A Rajasthani Tradition

Explores the 600 year tradition in Rajasthan of the epic of Lord Pabuji, patron saint of camel herders, and the everyday life of the Rebaris of Rajasthan.

Availability:	Schools, libraries, homeschoolers, and nursing homes in the southeastern United States.
Suggested Grade:	7-12
Order Number:	order by title
Production Date:	1996
Format:	VHS videotape
Terms:	Borrower pays return postage. Return 2 days after showing via United Parcel Service, insured. Book 2 weeks in advance.

Source: Center for South Asian Studies
University of Virginia
Video Library Coordinator
P. O. Box 400169, 110 Minor Hall
Charlottesville, VA 22904-4169
Phone: 1-434-924-8815
Email Address: southasia@virginia.edu

Tibetan Book of the Dead, The

A comprehensive examination of a Tibetan Buddhist text traditionally read aloud to dying persons. Part 1: A Way of Life gives a historical and cultural overview, including rituals performed for a recently deceased Ladakhi elder. It also includes an interview with the Dalai Lama. Part 2: The Great Liberation examines the content and teachings of the book in detail, through footage of a sequence of traditional rituals and through animation.

Availability:	Schools, libraries, homeschoolers, and nursing homes in the southeastern United States.
Suggested Grade:	7-12
Order Number:	order by title
Production Date:	1994
Format:	Set of 2 VHS videotapes
Terms:	Borrower pays return postage. Return 2 days after showing via United Parcel Service, insured. Book 2 weeks in advance.

Source: Center for South Asian Studies
University of Virginia
Video Library Coordinator
P. O. Box 400169, 110 Minor Hall
Charlottesville, VA 22904-4169
Phone: 1-434-924-8815
Email Address: southasia@virginia.edu

Trials of Telo Rinpoche

Tells the story of Eddie Omdaykow, an American from Philadelphia who was recognized by the Dalai Lama to be the reincarnation of Telo Rinpoche. Brought up as a Tibetan Buddhist monk, he has returned to his ancestral homeland in a southern Russian republic where he is revered as their spiritual leader and expected to revive the practice of Buddhism there.

Availability:	Schools, libraries, homeschoolers, and nursing homes in the southeastern United States.
Suggested Grade:	7-12
Order Number:	order by title
Production Date:	1994
Format:	VHS videotape
Terms:	Borrower pays return postage. Return 2 days after showing via United Parcel Service, insured. Book 2 weeks in advance.

Source: Center for South Asian Studies
University of Virginia
Video Library Coordinator
P. O. Box 400169, 110 Minor Hall
Charlottesville, VA 22904-4169

RELIGION AND PHILOSOPHY

Phone: 1-434-924-8815
Email Address: southasia@virginia.edu

Tribal Religions
Professor Hans Kung, a well-known Western theologian, first travels to Australia to investigate the beliefs of today's Aborigines through ceremonies involving body painting, music, and dance. He then travels to Africa to gain insights into tribal culture through modern rites that include torchlight processions, dance, and animal sacrifice.
Availability: Schools, libraries, and homeschoolers in the United States who serve the hearing impaired.
Suggested Grade: 10-12
Order Number: 11039
Production Date: 2001
Format: DVD
Special Notes: Also available as live streaming video over the Internet.
Terms: Sponsor pays all transportation costs. Return one week after receipt. Participation is limited to deaf or hard of hearing Americans, their parents, families, teachers, counselors, or others whose use would benefit a deaf or hard of hearing person. Only one person in the audience needs to be hearing impaired. You must register--which is free. These videos are all open-captioned--no special equipment is required for viewing.
Source: Described and Captioned Media Program
National Association of the Deaf
4211 Church Street Ext.
Roebuck, SC 29376
Phone: 1-800-237-6213
Fax: 1-800-538-5636
World Wide Web URL: http://www.dcmp.org

Two Tibetan Buddhist Nunneries
Documents life in the only two nunneries in the Tibetan exile community and examines the status of Tibetan Buddhist nunneries today and their possible preservation for the future.
Availability: Schools, libraries, homeschoolers, and nursing homes in the southeastern United States.
Suggested Grade: 7-12
Order Number: order by title
Production Date: 1986
Format: VHS videotape
Terms: Borrower pays return postage. Return 2 days after showing via United Parcel Service, insured. Book 2 weeks in advance.
Source: Center for South Asian Studies
University of Virginia
Video Library Coordinator
P. O. Box 400169, 110 Minor Hall
Charlottesville, VA 22904-4169
Phone: 1-434-924-8815
Email Address: southasia@virginia.edu

Valley of the Gods: Worship in Katmandu
Captures the celebration of religious traditions in elaborate ceremonies in Katmandu. Most of the population participates in these festivals, which stem from Hindu, Buddhist, and Muslim faiths and are sometimes intertwined.
Availability: Schools, libraries, homeschoolers, and nursing homes in the southeastern United States.
Suggested Grade: 7-12
Order Number: order by title
Production Date: 1995
Format: VHS videotape
Terms: Borrower pays return postage. Return 2 days after showing via United Parcel Service, insured. Book 2 weeks in advance.
Source: Center for South Asian Studies
University of Virginia
Video Library Coordinator
P. O. Box 400169, 110 Minor Hall
Charlottesville, VA 22904-4169
Phone: 1-434-924-8815
Email Address: southasia@virginia.edu

Vision of Juazeiro
Transformation of a small town in northeastern Brazil into a religious shrine, and analyzes economic and mystical aspects.
Availability: Schools, libraries, and nursing homes in the United States.
Suggested Grade: 6-12
Languages: Portuguese with English subtitles
Order Number: RBRA2-video
Production Date: 1969
Format: VHS videotape
Terms: Borrowers must have a User's Agreement on file with this source--available by mail or via the Internet. Return postage is paid by borrower; return 12 days after showing. Book at least three weeks in advance. All borrowers are limited to a total of ten items per semester.
Source: Latin American Resource Center
Stone Center for Latin American Studies
Tulane University
100 Jones Hall
New Orleans, LA 70118
Phone: 1-504-862-3143
Fax: 1-504-865-6719
World Wide Web URL: http://stonecenter.tulane.edu/pages/detail/48/Lending-Library
Email Address: crcrts@tulane.edu

Voices of the Orishas
Survival and strength of the Yoruba cultural and religious heritage of Caribbean African-Hispanics.
Availability: Schools and libraries in Iowa, Illinois, Michigan, Minnesota, and Wisconsin.
Suggested Grade: 6-12
Languages: English; Spanish with English subtitles
Order Number: AFRICACARV87VHS
Production Date: 1994

RELIGION AND PHILOSOPHY

Format: VHS videotape
Terms: Borrower pays return postage. Return 8 days after showing. Book 2 weeks in advance. Order may also be picked up for those near the Center.
Source: Center for Latin American and Caribbean Studies
UW-Milwaukee
P. O. Box 413
Milwaukee, WI 53201
Phone: 1-414-229-5987
World Wide Web URL: http://www.uwm.edu/Dept/CLACS
Email Address: audvis@usm.edu

Zen Temple
Every aspect of monks training including their meals, daily chores and free days, as well as their interviews with the NHK team is covered in this program.
Availability: Schools, libraries, homeschoolers, and nursing homes in Nevada and northern California (zip codes beginning 932 and above, except 935).
Suggested Grade: 7-Adult
Order Number: order by title
Format: VHS videotape
Terms: Borrower pays return postage. Book two weeks in advance. Return within three weeks of date borrowed, via UPS, Federal Express or certified mail.
Source: Consulate General of Japan, San Francisco
50 Fremont Street, Suite 2300
San Francisco, CA 94105-2236
Phone: 1-415-356-2564
Fax: 1-415-777-0518
World Wide Web URL: http://www.sf.us.emb-japan.go.jp/
Email Address: infoav@cgjsf.org

SCIENCE--ENVIRONMENTAL EDUCATION

Air Quality--Ozone
Discusses the importance of ozone and the harm of the deterioration that it is facing.
- Availability: Schools, libraries, and homeschoolers in Connecticut, Maine, Massachusetts, New Hampshire, Rhode Island, and Vermont.
- Suggested Grade: 9-12
- Order Number: C-98-12
- Production Date: 1998
- Format: VHS videotape
- Terms: Borrower pays return postage. Return within three weeks of receipt. If the tape you request is available, it will be mailed within 5 business days. If not, you will be notified that this video is already out on loan. No more than three titles may be borrowed by one requestor at a time. No reservations for a specific date will be accepted. It is most efficient to order via the web site.
- Source: U. S. Environmental Protection Agency, Region 1
  Customer Service Center
  One Congress Street, Suite 1100
  Boston, MA 02214
  World Wide Web URL: http://yosemite.epa.gov/r1/videolen.nsf/

Alternative Is Conservation
A documentary on water conservation with good examples of communities changing to water conservation techniques.
- Availability: Schools, libraries, and homeschoolers in Connecticut, Maine, Massachusetts, New Hampshire, Rhode Island, and Vermont.
- Suggested Grade: 7-12
- Order Number: VID 096
- Production Date: 1980
- Format: VHS videotape
- Terms: Borrower pays return postage. Return within three weeks of receipt. If the tape you request is available, it will be mailed within 5 business days. If not, you will be notified that this video is already out on loan. No more than three titles may be borrowed by one requestor at a time. No reservations for a specific date will be accepted. It is most efficient to order via the web site.
- Source: U. S. Environmental Protection Agency, Region 1
  Customer Service Center
  One Congress Street, Suite 1100
  Boston, MA 02214
  World Wide Web URL: http://yosemite.epa.gov/r1/videolen.nsf/

Amazonia - Minimum Critical Size of Ecosystems
Explores ecological complexity of the rainforest and the minimum area of undisturbed forest necessary to support each member of various species.
- Availability: Schools, libraries, and nursing homes in the United States.
- Suggested Grade: 6-12
- Order Number: GEBRA7-video
- Production Date: 1987
- Format: VHS videotape
- Terms: Borrowers must have a User's Agreement on file with this source--available by mail or via the Internet. Return postage is paid by borrower; return 12 days after showing. Book at least three weeks in advance. All borrowers are limited to a total of ten items per semester.
- Source: Latin American Resource Center
  Stone Center for Latin American Studies
  Tulane University
  100 Jones Hall
  New Orleans, LA 70118
  Phone: 1-504-862-3143
  Fax: 1-504-865-6719
  World Wide Web URL: http://stonecenter.tulane.edu/pages/detail/48/Lending-Library
  Email Address: crcrts@tulane.edu

Atmosphere: On the Air
A student-produced radio talk show discusses earth's atmosphere. Investigates its functions, layers, composition, movement, and the greenhouse effect. Time-lapse photography and computer graphics illustrate the information. The atmosphere protects the earth, supports life, and must be kept healthy for our survival.
- Availability: Schools, libraries, and homeschoolers in the United States who serve the hearing impaired.
- Suggested Grade: 5-10
- Order Number: 12814
- Production Date: 1993
- Format: DVD
- Special Notes: Produced by National Geographic Society.
- Terms: Sponsor pays all transportation costs. Return one week after receipt. Participation is limited to deaf or hard of hearing Americans, their parents, families, teachers, counselors, or others whose use would benefit a deaf or hard of hearing person. Only one person in the audience needs to be hearing impaired. You must register--which is free. These videos are all open-captioned--no special equipment is required for viewing.
- Source: Described and Captioned Media Program
  National Association of the Deaf
  4211 Church Street Ext.
  Roebuck, SC 29376
  Phone: 1-800-237-6213
  Fax: 1-800-538-5636
  World Wide Web URL: http://www.dcmp.org

Bentley Creek: A Story of an Urban Salt Marsh
Chronicles the degradation of Bentley creek and takes an inside look at the extraordinary restoration project that saved it.
- Availability: Schools, libraries, and homeschoolers in Connecticut, Maine, Massachusetts, New Hampshire, Rhode Island, and Vermont.
- Suggested Grade: 7-12
- Order Number: VID 358
- Production Date: 2000
- Format: VHS videotape

SCIENCE--ENVIRONMENTAL EDUCATION

Terms: Borrower pays return postage. Return within three weeks of receipt. If the tape you request is available, it will be mailed within 5 business days. If not, you will be notified that this video is already out on loan. No more than three titles may be borrowed by one requestor at a time. No reservations for a specific date will be accepted. It is most efficient to order via the web site.
Source: U. S. Environmental Protection Agency, Region 1
Customer Service Center
One Congress Street, Suite 1100
Boston, MA 02214
World Wide Web URL:
http://yosemite.epa.gov/r1/videolen.nsf/

Big Apple, Hot Apple
The emergency removal of radioactive/toxic waste at a site in a suburb of New York City is documented in this program. The United States Environmental Protection Agency is shown at work carrying out this procedure, and discussions as to how the public is educated about the environmental hazards of radioactive/toxic waste sites are presented.
Availability: Schools, libraries, and homeschoolers in Connecticut, Maine, Massachusetts, New Hampshire, Rhode Island, and Vermont.
Suggested Grade: Adult
Order Number: VID 041
Production Date: 1990
Format: VHS videotape
Terms: Borrower pays return postage. Return within three weeks of receipt. If the tape you request is available, it will be mailed within 5 business days. If not, you will be notified that this video is already out on loan. No more than three titles may be borrowed by one requestor at a time. No reservations for a specific date will be accepted. It is most efficient to order via the web site.
Source: U. S. Environmental Protection Agency, Region 1
Customer Service Center
One Congress Street, Suite 1100
Boston, MA 02214
World Wide Web URL:
http://yosemite.epa.gov/r1/videolen.nsf/

Biosphere, The
Discusses the features of the biosphere and explains how ecosystems can change through a process called succession.
Availability: Schools, libraries, and homeschoolers in the United States who serve the hearing impaired.
Suggested Grade: 7-10
Order Number: 11624
Production Date: 2002
Format: DVD
Special Notes: Also available as live streaming video over the Internet.
Terms: Sponsor pays all transportation costs. Return one week after receipt. Participation is limited to deaf or hard of hearing Americans, their parents, families, teachers, counselors, or others whose use would benefit a deaf or hard of hearing person. Only one person in the audience needs to be hearing impaired. You must register--which is free. These videos are all open-captioned--no special equipment is required for viewing.
Source: Described and Captioned Media Program
National Association of the Deaf
4211 Church Street Ext.
Roebuck, SC 29376
Phone: 1-800-237-6213
Fax: 1-800-538-5636
World Wide Web URL: http://www.dcmp.org

Bringing Environmental Technologies to the Marketplace
Discusses how EPA's Center for Environmental Industry and Technology brings cleaner, cheaper environmental technologies to the marketplace.
Availability: Schools, libraries, and homeschoolers in Connecticut, Maine, Massachusetts, New Hampshire, Rhode Island, and Vermont.
Suggested Grade: 9-12
Order Number: C-97-5
Production Date: 1997
Format: VHS videotape
Terms: Borrower pays return postage. Return within three weeks of receipt. If the tape you request is available, it will be mailed within 5 business days. If not, you will be notified that this video is already out on loan. No more than three titles may be borrowed by one requestor at a time. No reservations for a specific date will be accepted. It is most efficient to order via the web site.
Source: U. S. Environmental Protection Agency, Region 1
Customer Service Center
One Congress Street, Suite 1100
Boston, MA 02214
World Wide Web URL:
http://yosemite.epa.gov/r1/videolen.nsf/

Challenge of Global Warming, The
Scientifically looks at ways to dispose of air polluting carbon.
Availability: Schools, libraries, homeschoolers, and nursing homes in Connecticut (except Fairfield County), Maine, Massachusetts, New Hampshire, Rhode Island, and Vermont.
Suggested Grade: 6-12
Order Number: 557
Format: VHS videotape
Terms: Borrower pays return postage, including insurance. Return two weeks after receipt.
Source: Consulate General of Japan, Boston
Federal Reserve Plaza, 14th Floor
600 Atlantic Avenue
Boston, MA 02210
Phone: 1-617-973-9772
Fax: 1-617-542-1329
World Wide Web URL:
http://www.boston.us.emb-japan.go.jp
Email Address: infocul@cgjbos.org

SCIENCE--ENVIRONMENTAL EDUCATION

Challenge of Global Warming, The
Scientifically looks at ways to dispose of air polluting carbon.
Availability: Schools, libraries, and nursing homes in Hawaii.
Suggested Grade: 6-12
Order Number: NA-29
Format: VHS videotape
Terms: Borrower pays return postage. A maximum of 3 videos may be borrowed per person. Return within one week of date borrowed.
Source: Consulate General of Japan, Honolulu
1742 Nuuanu Avenue
Honolulu, HI 96817-3294
Phone: 1-808-543-3111
Fax: 1-808-543-3170
World Wide Web URL:
http://www.honolulu.us.emb-japan.go.jp

Close the Loop: Buy Recycled
A program to educate businesses, institutions, government, and consumers on how (and why) to purchase goods with recycled content.
Availability: Schools, libraries, and homeschoolers in Connecticut, Maine, Massachusetts, New Hampshire, Rhode Island, and Vermont.
Suggested Grade: 7-12
Order Number: RL9
Production Date: 1995
Format: VHS videotape
Terms: Borrower pays return postage. Return within three weeks of receipt. If the tape you request is available, it will be mailed within 5 business days. If not, you will be notified that this video is already out on loan. No more than three titles may be borrowed by one requestor at a time. No reservations for a specific date will be accepted. It is most efficient to order via the web site.
Source: U. S. Environmental Protection Agency, Region 1
Customer Service Center, One Congress Street, Suite 1100
Boston, MA 02214
World Wide Web URL:
http://yosemite.epa.gov/r1/videolen.nsf/

Coastal Growth: A Delicate Balance
Looks at the environmental, social, and economic impact of development of barrier islands and wetlands in Virginia.
Availability: Schools, libraries, and homeschoolers in Connecticut, Maine, Massachusetts, New Hampshire, Rhode Island, and Vermont.
Suggested Grade: 7-12
Order Number: VID 245
Format: VHS videotape
Terms: Borrower pays return postage. Return within three weeks of receipt. If the tape you request is available, it will be mailed within 5 business days. If not, you will be notified that this video is already out on loan. No more than three titles may be borrowed by one requestor at a time. No reservations for a specific date will be accepted. It is most efficient to order via the web site.
Source: U. S. Environmental Protection Agency, Region 1
Customer Service Center
One Congress Street, Suite 1100
Boston, MA 02214
World Wide Web URL:
http://yosemite.epa.gov/r1/videolen.nsf/

Complete the Circle: How to Buy Recycled
Focuses on how to buy recycled products and how/why to close the recycling loop. Features Joanne Woodward.
Availability: Schools, libraries, and homeschoolers in Connecticut, Maine, Massachusetts, New Hampshire, Rhode Island, and Vermont.
Suggested Grade: 7-Adult
Order Number: RL10
Production Date: 1995
Format: VHS videotape
Terms: Borrower pays return postage. Return within three weeks of receipt. If the tape you request is available, it will be mailed within 5 business days. If not, you will be notified that this video is already out on loan. No more than three titles may be borrowed by one requestor at a time. No reservations for a specific date will be accepted. It is most efficient to order via the web site.
Source: U. S. Environmental Protection Agency, Region 1
Customer Service Center
One Congress Street, Suite 1100
Boston, MA 02214
World Wide Web URL:
http://yosemite.epa.gov/r1/videolen.nsf/

Don't Throw It Away
Using a humorous gameshow format, this production is filled with information on waste reduction, recycling, and buying recycled products.
Availability: Schools, libraries, and homeschoolers in Connecticut, Maine, Massachusetts, New Hampshire, Rhode Island, and Vermont.
Suggested Grade: 7-Adult
Order Number: RL13
Production Date: 1991
Format: VHS videotape
Terms: Borrower pays return postage. Return within three weeks of receipt. If the tape you request is available, it will be mailed within 5 business days. If not, you will be notified that this video is already out on loan. No more than three titles may be borrowed by one requestor at a time. No reservations for a specific date will be accepted. It is most efficient to order via the web site.
Source: U. S. Environmental Protection Agency, Region 1
Customer Service Center
One Congress Street, Suite 1100
Boston, MA 02214
World Wide Web URL:
http://yosemite.epa.gov/r1/videolen.nsf/

Down in the Dumps
Describes what can be recycled, how the process works, and how a continual flow of trash impacts the environment.

All materials listed in this 2018-2019 edition are BRAND NEW!

SCIENCE--ENVIRONMENTAL EDUCATION

Provides some insight to some of the answers and creates a sense of urgency for addressing this issue.
- Availability: Schools, libraries, and homeschoolers in Connecticut, Maine, Massachusetts, New Hampshire, Rhode Island, and Vermont.
- Suggested Grade: 4-12
- Order Number: VID RL15
- Production Date: 1993
- Format: VHS videotape
- Terms: Borrower pays return postage. Return within three weeks of receipt. If the tape you request is available, it will be mailed within 5 business days. If not, you will be notified that this video is already out on loan. No more than three titles may be borrowed by one requestor at a time. No reservations for a specific date will be accepted. It is most efficient to order via the web site.

Source: U. S. Environmental Protection Agency, Region 1
Customer Service Center
One Congress Street, Suite 1100
Boston, MA 02214
World Wide Web URL: http://yosemite.epa.gov/r1/videolen.nsf/

Earth Revealed
This series shows the physical processes and human activities that shape our planet.
- Availability: All requesters
- Suggested Grade: 9-Adult
- Order Number: not applicable
- Production Date: 1992
- Format: Streaming Video
- Terms: A simple FREE registration is required to view videos.

Source: Annenberg Media
World Wide Web URL: http://www.learner.org/resources/browse.html

Emas Park
Examines animal and plant life found in this national park in the high plains of Brazil.
- Availability: Schools, libraries, and nursing homes in the United States.
- Suggested Grade: 6-12
- Order Number: GEBRA4-video
- Production Date: 1985
- Format: VHS videotape
- Terms: Borrowers must have a User's Agreement on file with this source--available by mail or via the Internet. Return postage is paid by borrower; return 12 days after showing. Book at least three weeks in advance. All borrowers are limited to a total of ten items per semester.

Source: Latin American Resource Center
Stone Center for Latin American Studies
Tulane University, 100 Jones Hall
New Orleans, LA 70118
Phone: 1-504-862-3143
Fax: 1-504-865-6719
World Wide Web URL: http://stonecenter.tulane.edu/pages/detail/48/Lending-Library
Email Address: crcrts@tulane.edu

Environmental Vision
Introduces Environmental Defense Fund Specialists and their work involving environmental issues. Focuses on DDT and the osprey population, acid rain, clean water, and energy efficiency.
- Availability: Schools, libraries, and homeschoolers in Connecticut, Maine, Massachusetts, New Hampshire, Rhode Island, and Vermont.
- Suggested Grade: 9-12
- Order Number: VID 224
- Production Date: 1990
- Format: VHS videotape
- Terms: Borrower pays return postage. Return within three weeks of receipt. If the tape you request is available, it will be mailed within 5 business days. If not, you will be notified that this video is already out on loan. No more than three titles may be borrowed by one requestor at a time. No reservations for a specific date will be accepted. It is most efficient to order via the web site.

Source: U. S. Environmental Protection Agency, Region 1
Customer Service Center
One Congress Street, Suite 1100
Boston, MA 02214
World Wide Web URL: http://yosemite.epa.gov/r1/videolen.nsf/

Environment Latest Approaches
Covers various aspects of preserving nature and the environment.
- Availability: Schools, libraries, homeschoolers, and nursing homes in Connecticut (except Fairfield County), Maine, Massachusetts, New Hampshire, Rhode Island, and Vermont.
- Suggested Grade: 6-12
- Order Number: 560
- Format: VHS videotape
- Terms: Borrower pays return postage, including insurance. Return two weeks after receipt.

Source: Consulate General of Japan, Boston
Federal Reserve Plaza, 14th Floor
600 Atlantic Avenue
Boston, MA 02210
Phone: 1-617-973-9772
Fax: 1-617-542-1329
World Wide Web URL: http://www.boston.us.emb-japan.go.jp
Email Address: infocul@cgjbos.org

Environment, The - New Global Concerns: Current Affairs
Destruction of Latin American rain forests, ozone depletion, green-house effect, and disposal of nuclear waste are all explored.
- Availability: Schools, libraries, and nursing homes in the United States.
- Suggested Grade: 6-12
- Order Number: GE19-video
- Production Date: 1989
- Format: VHS videotape

All materials listed in this 2018-2019 edition are BRAND NEW!

SCIENCE--ENVIRONMENTAL EDUCATION

Terms: Borrowers must have a User's Agreement on file with this source--available by mail or via the Internet. Return postage is paid by borrower; return 12 days after showing. Book at least three weeks in advance. All borrowers are limited to a total of ten items per semester.
Source: **Latin American Resource Center**
Stone Center for Latin American Studies
Tulane University, 100 Jones Hall
New Orleans, LA 70118
Phone: 1-504-862-3143
Fax: 1-504-865-6719
World Wide Web URL: http://stonecenter.tulane.edu/pages/detail/48/Lending-Library
Email Address: crcrts@tulane.edu

Environment Under Fire: Ecology and Politics in Central America

Central America's endangered natural environment means increased poverty among its people. Rainforest destruction, deadly pesticide use, the effects of cash cropping, and continuing conflict plague the region. Top Central American and U. S. environmentalists explore the issues and potential solution.
Availability: Schools and libraries in Iowa, Illinois, Michigan, Minnesota, and Wisconsin.
Suggested Grade: 9-Adult
Order Number: ENVCAEN8VHS
Production Date: 1988
Format: VHS videotape
Terms: Borrower pays return postage. Return 8 days after showing. Book 2 weeks in advance. Order may also be picked up for those near the Center.
Source: **Center for Latin American and Caribbean Studies**
UW-Milwaukee, P. O. Box 413
Milwaukee, WI 53201
Phone: 1-414-229-5987
World Wide Web URL: http://www.uwm.edu/Dept/CLACS
Email Address: audvis@usm.edu

Extreme Ice

An acclaimed photographer teams up with scientists to document the runaway melting of arctic glaciers.
Availability: All requesters
Suggested Grade: 7-Adult
Order Number: not applicable
Production Date: 2009
Format: Streaming Video
Source: **NOVA**
World Wide Web URL:
http://www.pbs.org/wgbh/nova/programs/index.html

Flight from the Marshes

Explores the fight to save the red-crested Japanese crane from extinction.
Availability: Schools, libraries, homeschoolers, and nursing homes in Connecticut (except Fairfield County), Maine, Massachusetts, New Hampshire, Rhode Island, and Vermont.
Suggested Grade: 6-12
Order Number: 120
Production Date: 1985
Format: VHS videotape
Terms: Borrower pays return postage, including insurance. Return two weeks after receipt.
Source: **Consulate General of Japan, Boston**
Federal Reserve Plaza, 14th Floor, 600 Atlantic Avenue
Boston, MA 02210
Phone: 1-617-973-9772
Fax: 1-617-542-1329
World Wide Web URL:
http://www.boston.us.emb-japan.go.jp
Email Address: infocul@cgjbos.org

Flight from the Marshes

Explores the fight to save the red-crested Japanese crane from extinction.
Availability: Schools, libraries, and nursing homes in Oklahoma and Texas.
Suggested Grade: 6-12
Order Number: I2
Production Date: 1984
Format: VHS videotape
Terms: Materials must be picked up in person. Under special circumstances, you may be able to have them shipped to you at your own expense (call for further details). Return within two weeks after scheduled showing. Videos must be registered with the U. S. Postal Service or returned by Priority Mail, Federal Express, or other registered shipping service.
Source: **Consulate General of Japan, Houston**
Cultural Affairs and Information Section
909 Fannin Street, Suite 3000
Houston, TX 77010
Phone: 1-713-652-2977
Fax: 1-713-651-7822
World Wide Web URL:
http://www.houston.us.emb-japan.go.jp/en/culture/page1.htm
Email Address: info@cgjhouston.org

Flight from the Marshes

Explores the fight to save the red-crested Japanese crane from extinction.
Availability: Schools, libraries, homeschoolers, and nursing homes in Arizona and California (zipcodes beginning 900-931 and 935).
Suggested Grade: 6-12
Order Number: 053
Production Date: 1984
Format: VHS videotape
Terms: Borrower pays postage both ways; you may call the number below to learn how much postage costs. Return within two weeks of date borrowed. An individual may borrow 2 items at one time. For non-profit and educational use only.
Source: **Consulate General of Japan, Los Angeles**
350 South Grand Avenue, Suite 1700
Los Angeles, CA 90071-3459

All materials listed in this 2018-2019 edition are BRAND NEW!

SCIENCE--ENVIRONMENTAL EDUCATION

Phone: 1-213-617-6700
Fax: 1-213-617-6727
World Wide Web URL: http://www.la.us.emb-japan.go.jp

Freshwater
Examines sources of freshwater, explains what groundwater is, and tells more about this vital resource.

Availability: Schools, libraries, and homeschoolers in the United States who serve the hearing impaired.
Suggested Grade: 5-10
Order Number: 11821
Production Date: 2002
Format: DVD
Special Notes: Also available as live streaming video over the Internet.
Terms: Sponsor pays all transportation costs. Return one week after receipt. Participation is limited to deaf or hard of hearing Americans, their parents, families, teachers, counselors, or others whose use would benefit a deaf or hard of hearing person. Only one person in the audience needs to be hearing impaired. You must register--which is free. These videos are all open-captioned--no special equipment is required for viewing.
Source: Described and Captioned Media Program
National Association of the Deaf
4211 Church Street Ext.
Roebuck, SC 29376
Phone: 1-800-237-6213
Fax: 1-800-538-5636
World Wide Web URL: http://www.dcmp.org

From the Heart of the World
Kogi Indians are convinced that modern culture is destroying the balance of life on earth. They attempt to teach us what they know about nature and the spiritual world.

Availability: Schools, libraries, and nursing homes in the United States.
Suggested Grade: 6-12
Order Number: GELA17-video
Production Date: 1991
Format: VHS videotape
Terms: Borrowers must have a User's Agreement on file with this source--available by mail or via the Internet. Return postage is paid by borrower; return 12 days after showing. Book at least three weeks in advance. All borrowers are limited to a total of ten items per semester.
Source: Latin American Resource Center
Stone Center for Latin American Studies
Tulane University
100 Jones Hall
New Orleans, LA 70118
Phone: 1-504-862-3143
Fax: 1-504-865-6719
World Wide Web URL: http://stonecenter.tulane.edu/pages/detail/48/Lending-Library
Email Address: crcrts@tulane.edu

Galapagos: My Fragile World
Evolutionary processes on the Galapagos Islands, both human and animal, as seen by a long-time resident.

Availability: Schools, libraries, and nursing homes in the United States.
Suggested Grade: 6-12
Order Number: GEECU1-video
Production Date: 1988
Format: VHS videotape
Terms: Borrowers must have a User's Agreement on file with this source--available by mail or via the Internet. Return postage is paid by borrower; return 12 days after showing. Book at least three weeks in advance. All borrowers are limited to a total of ten items per semester.
Source: Latin American Resource Center
Stone Center for Latin American Studies
Tulane University
100 Jones Hall
New Orleans, LA 70118
Phone: 1-504-862-3143
Fax: 1-504-865-6719
World Wide Web URL: http://stonecenter.tulane.edu/pages/detail/48/Lending-Library
Email Address: crcrts@tulane.edu

Gone With the Waste
Depicts the various solid waste alternatives including source reduction, consumer shopping, collection options, and recycling choices.

Availability: Schools, libraries, and homeschoolers in Connecticut, Maine, Massachusetts, New Hampshire, Rhode Island, and Vermont.
Suggested Grade: 6-12
Order Number: VIS RL23
Production Date: 1992
Format: VHS videotape
Terms: Borrower pays return postage. Return within three weeks of receipt. If the tape you request is available, it will be mailed within 5 business days. If not, you will be notified that this video is already out on loan. No more than three titles may be borrowed by one requestor at a time. No reservations for a specific date will be accepted. It is most efficient to order via the web site.
Source: U. S. Environmental Protection Agency, Region 1
Customer Service Center
One Congress Street, Suite 1100
Boston, MA 02214
World Wide Web URL:
http://yosemite.epa.gov/r1/videolen.nsf/

Helping Our Feathered Friends
Explores Japan's dedication to bird watching and the preservation of habitats.

Availability: Schools, libraries, homeschoolers, and nursing homes in Connecticut (except Fairfield County), Maine, Massachusetts, New Hampshire, Rhode Island, and Vermont.
Suggested Grade: 6-12
Order Number: 553

SCIENCE--ENVIRONMENTAL EDUCATION

Production Date: 1992
Format: VHS videotape
Terms: Borrower pays return postage, including insurance. Return two weeks after receipt.
Source: Consulate General of Japan, Boston
Federal Reserve Plaza, 14th Floor
600 Atlantic Avenue
Boston, MA 02210
Phone: 1-617-973-9772
Fax: 1-617-542-1329
World Wide Web URL:
http://www.boston.us.emb-japan.go.jp
Email Address: infocul@cgjbos.org

Helping Our Feathered Friends
Explores Japan's dedication to bird watching and the preservation of habitats.
Availability: Schools, libraries, homeschoolers, and nursing homes in Arizona and California (zipcodes beginning 900-931 and 935).
Suggested Grade: 6-12
Order Number: 192
Production Date: 1992
Format: VHS videotape
Terms: Borrower pays postage both ways; you may call the number below to learn how much postage costs. Return within two weeks of date borrowed. An individual may borrow 2 items at one time. For non-profit and educational use only.
Source: Consulate General of Japan, Los Angeles
350 South Grand Avenue, Suite 1700
Los Angeles, CA 90071-3459
Phone: 1-213-617-6700
Fax: 1-213-617-6727
World Wide Web URL: http://www.la.us.emb-japan.go.jp

Hiroshima, A New Threat--A-Bomb Water Dedication
A-Bomb Water Dedication is a ritual held at Peace Park in Hiroshima on August 6 each year. Spring and well waters from 16 sites in the city are collected for this ritual, and recently it has been discovered that they are so polluted they are not suitable for drinking. This introduces the important relationship between water and people.
Availability: Schools, libraries, homeschoolers, and nursing homes in Connecticut (except Fairfield County), Maine, Massachusetts, New Hampshire, Rhode Island, and Vermont.
Suggested Grade: 9-Adult
Order Number: 423
Production Date: 1990
Format: VHS videotape
Special Notes: No. 7 of the "Nippon Life" series.
Terms: Borrower pays return postage, including insurance. Return two weeks after receipt.
Source: Consulate General of Japan, Boston
Federal Reserve Plaza, 14th Floor
600 Atlantic Avenue
Boston, MA 02210
Phone: 1-617-973-9772
Fax: 1-617-542-1329
World Wide Web URL:
http://www.boston.us.emb-japan.go.jp
Email Address: infocul@cgjbos.org

Hiroshima, A New Threat--A-Bomb Water Dedication
A-Bomb Water Dedication is a ritual held at Peace Park in Hiroshima on August 6 each year. Spring and well waters from 16 sites in the city are collected for this ritual, and recently it has been discovered that they are so polluted they are not suitable for drinking. This introduces the important relationship between water and people.
Availability: Schools, libraries, and nursing homes in Oklahoma and Texas.
Suggested Grade: 9-Adult
Order Number: F7
Production Date: 1990
Format: VHS videotape
Special Notes: No. 7 of the "Nippon Life" series.
Terms: Materials must be picked up in person. Under special circumstances, you may be able to have them shipped to you at your own expense (call for further details). Return within two weeks after scheduled showing. Videos must be registered with the U. S. Postal Service or returned by Priority Mail, Federal Express, or other registered shipping service.
Source: Consulate General of Japan, Houston
Cultural Affairs and Information Section
909 Fannin Street, Suite 3000
Houston, TX 77010
Phone: 1-713-652-2977
Fax: 1-713-651-7822
World Wide Web URL:
http://www.houston.us.emb-japan.go.jp/en/culture/page1.htm
Email Address: info@cgjhouston.org

Hiroshima, A New Threat--A-Bomb Water Dedication
A-Bomb Water Dedication is a ritual held at Peace Park in Hiroshima on August 6 each year. Spring and well waters from 16 sites in the city are collected for this ritual, and recently it has been discovered that they are so polluted they are not suitable for drinking. This introduces the important relationship between water and people.
Availability: Schools, libraries, homeschoolers, and nursing homes in Arizona and California (zipcodes beginning 900-931 and 935).
Suggested Grade: 9-Adult
Order Number: 143
Production Date: 1990
Format: VHS videotape
Special Notes: No. 7 of the "Nippon Life" series.
Terms: Borrower pays postage both ways; you may call the number below to learn how much postage costs. Return within two weeks of date borrowed. An individual may borrow 2 items at one time. For non-profit and educational use only.

All materials listed in this 2018-2019 edition are BRAND NEW!

SCIENCE--ENVIRONMENTAL EDUCATION

Source: Consulate General of Japan, Los Angeles
350 South Grand Avenue, Suite 1700
Los Angeles, CA 90071-3459
Phone: 1-213-617-6700
Fax: 1-213-617-6727
World Wide Web URL: http://www.la.us.emb-japan.go.jp

Hiroshima, A New Threat--A-Bomb Water Dedication
A-Bomb Water Dedication is a ritual held at Peace Park in Hiroshima on August 6 each year. Spring and well waters from 16 sites in the city are collected for this ritual, and recently it has been discovered that they are so polluted they are not suitable for drinking. This introduces the important relationship between water and people.
- Availability: Schools, libraries, homeschoolers, and nursing homes in Nevada and northern California (zip codes beginning 932 and above, except 935).
- Suggested Grade: 9-Adult
- Order Number: order by title
- Production Date: 1990
- Format: Beta videotape; U-matic videotape; VHS videotape
- Special Notes: No. 7 of the "Nippon Life" series.
- Terms: Borrower pays return postage. Book two weeks in advance. Return within three weeks of date borrowed, via UPS, Federal Express or certified mail.

Source: Consulate General of Japan, San Francisco
50 Fremont Street, Suite 2300
San Francisco, CA 94105-2236
Phone: 1-415-356-2564
Fax: 1-415-777-0518
World Wide Web URL: http://www.sf.us.emb-japan.go.jp/
Email Address: infoav@cgjsf.org

How New England Environmental Assistance Team Helps Businesses Prevent Pollution
Discusses efforts to help New England businesses comply with environmental laws and prevent pollution--information is useful for all.
- Availability: Schools, libraries, and homeschoolers in Connecticut, Maine, Massachusetts, New Hampshire, Rhode Island, and Vermont.
- Suggested Grade: 9-12
- Order Number: C-97-2
- Production Date: 1997
- Format: VHS videotape
- Terms: Borrower pays return postage. Return within three weeks of receipt. If the tape you request is available, it will be mailed within 5 business days. If not, you will be notified that this video is already out on loan. No more than three titles may be borrowed by one requestor at a time. No reservations for a specific date will be accepted. It is most efficient to order via the web site.

Source: U. S. Environmental Protection Agency, Region 1
Customer Service Center, One Congress Street, Suite 1100
Boston, MA 02214
World Wide Web URL:
http://yosemite.epa.gov/r1/videolen.nsf/

How the Waste Was Won
Explains how to conquer waste disposal problems.
- Availability: Schools, libraries, and homeschoolers in Connecticut, Maine, Massachusetts, New Hampshire, Rhode Island, and Vermont.
- Suggested Grade: All ages
- Order Number: RL 29
- Production Date: 1990
- Format: VHS videotape
- Terms: Borrower pays return postage. Return within three weeks of receipt. If the tape you request is available, it will be mailed within 5 business days. If not, you will be notified that this video is already out on loan. No more than three titles may be borrowed by one requestor at a time. No reservations for a specific date will be accepted. It is most efficient to order via the web site.

Source: U. S. Environmental Protection Agency, Region 1
Customer Service Center
One Congress Street, Suite 1100
Boston, MA 02214
World Wide Web URL:
http://yosemite.epa.gov/r1/videolen.nsf/

IAQ Tools for Schools Walkthrough Video: 4 Schools Making a Difference
Shows the difference four schools are making in improving air quality.
- Availability: Schools, libraries, and homeschoolers in Connecticut, Maine, Massachusetts, New Hampshire, Rhode Island, and Vermont.
- Suggested Grade: All ages
- Order Number: VID 354
- Production Date: 2001
- Format: VHS videotape
- Terms: Borrower pays return postage. Return within three weeks of receipt. If the tape you request is available, it will be mailed within 5 business days. If not, you will be notified that this video is already out on loan. No more than three titles may be borrowed by one requestor at a time. No reservations for a specific date will be accepted. It is most efficient to order via the web site.

Source: U. S. Environmental Protection Agency, Region 1
Customer Service Center
One Congress Street, Suite 1100
Boston, MA 02214
World Wide Web URL:
http://yosemite.epa.gov/r1/videolen.nsf/

Indian Township Passamaquoddy Tribe: Composting Workshop
Presents a detailed demonstration of how to compost, including discussions of how compositing works and how to manage a compost pile at home.
- Availability: Schools, libraries, and homeschoolers in Connecticut, Maine, Massachusetts, New Hampshire, Rhode Island, and Vermont.
- Suggested Grade: 9-12
- Order Number: VID 314
- Production Date: 1998

SCIENCE--ENVIRONMENTAL EDUCATION

Format: VHS videotape
Terms: Borrower pays return postage. Return within three weeks of receipt. If the tape you request is available, it will be mailed within 5 business days. If not, you will be notified that this video is already out on loan. No more than three titles may be borrowed by one requestor at a time. No reservations for a specific date will be accepted. It is most efficient to order via the web site.
Source: U. S. Environmental Protection Agency, Region 1
Customer Service Center
One Congress Street, Suite 1100
Boston, MA 02214
World Wide Web URL:
http://yosemite.epa.gov/r1/videolen.nsf/

Jaguar Trax

This video provides an entertaining way of teaching young people the value of tropical rainforests, preserving biodiversity, and sustainably grown products.
Availability: Schools and libraries in Iowa, Illinois, Michigan, Minnesota, and Wisconsin.
Suggested Grade: 6-12
Order Number: ENVRFJ18VHS
Format: VHS videotape
Special Notes: Includes a study guide.
Terms: Borrower pays return postage. Return 8 days after showing. Book 2 weeks in advance. Order may also be picked up for those near the Center.
Source: Center for Latin American and Caribbean Studies
UW-Milwaukee
P. O. Box 413
Milwaukee, WI 53201
Phone: 1-414-229-5987
World Wide Web URL: http://www.uwm.edu/Dept/CLACS
Email Address: audvis@usm.edu

Jungle

Development and industrialization of the rain forests.
Availability: Schools, libraries, and nursing homes in the United States.
Suggested Grade: 6-12
Order Number: GESA5-video
Production Date: 1985
Format: VHS videotape
Terms: Borrowers must have a User's Agreement on file with this source--available by mail or via the Internet. Return postage is paid by borrower; return 12 days after showing. Book at least three weeks in advance. All borrowers are limited to a total of ten items per semester.
Source: Latin American Resource Center
Stone Center for Latin American Studies
Tulane University
100 Jones Hall
New Orleans, LA 70118
Phone: 1-504-862-3143
Fax: 1-504-865-6719
World Wide Web URL: http://stonecenter.tulane.edu/pages/detail/48/Lending-Library
Email Address: crcrts@tulane.edu

Lead in School Drinking Water

What you can do about lead in your school drinking water.
Availability: Schools, libraries, and homeschoolers in Connecticut, Maine, Massachusetts, New Hampshire, Rhode Island, and Vermont.
Suggested Grade: 7-12
Order Number: VID 156
Production Date: 1990
Format: VHS videotape
Terms: Borrower pays return postage. Return within three weeks of receipt. If the tape you request is available, it will be mailed within 5 business days. If not, you will be notified that this video is already out on loan. No more than three titles may be borrowed by one requestor at a time. No reservations for a specific date will be accepted. It is most efficient to order via the web site.
Source: U. S. Environmental Protection Agency, Region 1
Customer Service Center
One Congress Street, Suite 1100
Boston, MA 02214
World Wide Web URL:
http://yosemite.epa.gov/r1/videolen.nsf/

Lead Paint Poisoning: The Thief of Childhood

Profiles several families in and around the Boston area and their experiences with lead paint poisoning in the home. Information on prevention and removal of lead paint is provided by experts in the field.
Availability: Schools, libraries, and homeschoolers in Connecticut, Maine, Massachusetts, New Hampshire, Rhode Island, and Vermont.
Suggested Grade: 4-Adult
Order Number: VID 316
Production Date: 1995
Format: VHS videotape
Terms: Borrower pays return postage. Return within three weeks of receipt. If the tape you request is available, it will be mailed within 5 business days. If not, you will be notified that this video is already out on loan. No more than three titles may be borrowed by one requestor at a time. No reservations for a specific date will be accepted. It is most efficient to order via the web site.
Source: U. S. Environmental Protection Agency, Region 1
Customer Service Center
One Congress Street, Suite 1100
Boston, MA 02214
World Wide Web URL:
http://yosemite.epa.gov/r1/videolen.nsf/

Legal Winds of Change: Business and the New Clean Air Act

A conference held November 1990 on the Clean Air Act Amendments' effect on small business. It includes interviews with key Congressional, EPA and local air quality officials.
Availability: Schools, libraries, and homeschoolers in Connecticut, Maine, Massachusetts, New Hampshire, Rhode Island, and Vermont.
Suggested Grade: Adult

SCIENCE--ENVIRONMENTAL EDUCATION

Order Number: VID 004
Production Date: 1990
Format: VHS videotape
Terms: Borrower pays return postage. Return within three weeks of receipt. If the tape you request is available, it will be mailed within 5 business days. If not, you will be notified that this video is already out on loan. No more than three titles may be borrowed by one requestor at a time. No reservations for a specific date will be accepted. It is most efficient to order via the web site.
Source: U. S. Environmental Protection Agency, Region 1
Customer Service Center
One Congress Street, Suite 1100
Boston, MA 02214
World Wide Web URL:
http://yosemite.epa.gov/r1/videolen.nsf/

Madre Tierra
Nine beautiful animated films from South America, each with its own very special message about the environment and the importance of air, water, and earth.
Availability: Schools and libraries in Iowa, Illinois, Michigan, Minnesota, and Wisconsin.
Suggested Grade: 4-12
Order Number: ENVSAM26VHS
Production Date: 1993
Format: VHS videotape
Special Notes: No narration.
Terms: Borrower pays return postage. Return 8 days after showing. Book 2 weeks in advance. Order may also be picked up for those near the Center.
Source: Center for Latin American and Caribbean Studies
UW-Milwaukee, P. O. Box 413
Milwaukee, WI 53201
Phone: 1-414-229-5987
World Wide Web URL: http://www.uwm.edu/Dept/CLACS
Email Address: audvis@usm.edu

Merrimack River Watershed Protection
Discusses efforts being undertaken in this area to protect the watershed.
Availability: Schools, libraries, and homeschoolers in Connecticut, Maine, Massachusetts, New Hampshire, Rhode Island, and Vermont.
Suggested Grade: 9-Adult
Order Number: C-97-10
Production Date: 1997
Format: VHS videotape
Terms: Borrower pays return postage. Return within three weeks of receipt. If the tape you request is available, it will be mailed within 5 business days. If not, you will be notified that this video is already out on loan. No more than three titles may be borrowed by one requestor at a time. No reservations for a specific date will be accepted. It is most efficient to order via the web site.
Source: U. S. Environmental Protection Agency, Region 1
Customer Service Center
One Congress Street, Suite 1100
Boston, MA 02214
World Wide Web URL:
http://yosemite.epa.gov/r1/videolen.nsf/

New Superfund: What It Is, How It Works
Focuses on the emergency measures to be taken on superfund sites.
Availability: Schools, libraries, and homeschoolers in Connecticut, Maine, Massachusetts, New Hampshire, Rhode Island, and Vermont.
Suggested Grade: 9-Adult
Order Number: VID 028
Format: VHS videotape
Terms: Borrower pays return postage. Return within three weeks of receipt. If the tape you request is available, it will be mailed within 5 business days. If not, you will be notified that this video is already out on loan. No more than three titles may be borrowed by one requestor at a time. No reservations for a specific date will be accepted. It is most efficient to order via the web site.
Source: U. S. Environmental Protection Agency, Region 1
Customer Service Center
One Congress Street, Suite 1100
Boston, MA 02214
World Wide Web URL:
http://yosemite.epa.gov/r1/videolen.nsf/

1959: Endangered Planet
Presents a historical perspective of the rise of environmental concerns and movements.
Availability: Schools, libraries, and homeschoolers in the United States who serve the hearing impaired.
Suggested Grade: 9-Adult
Order Number: 13447
Production Date: 1999
Format: DVD
Terms: Sponsor pays all transportation costs. Return one week after receipt. Participation is limited to deaf or hard of hearing Americans, their parents, families, teachers, counselors, or others whose use would benefit a deaf or hard of hearing person. Only one person in the audience needs to be hearing impaired. You must register--which is free. These videos are all open-captioned--no special equipment is required for viewing.
Source: Described and Captioned Media Program
National Association of the Deaf
4211 Church Street Ext.
Roebuck, SC 29376
Phone: 1-800-237-6213
Fax: 1-800-538-5636
World Wide Web URL: http://www.dcmp.org

Our Hidden National Product
Describes hazardous waste generated by industrial processes used in making commonly used items. Visits facilities where recycling treatment and disposal are used and covers public hearings.
Availability: Schools, libraries, and homeschoolers in Connecticut, Maine, Massachusetts, New Hampshire, Rhode Island, and Vermont.

SCIENCE--ENVIRONMENTAL EDUCATION

Suggested Grade: 9-12
Order Number: VID 024
Production Date: 1979
Format: VHS videotape
Terms: Borrower pays return postage. Return within three weeks of receipt. If the tape you request is available, it will be mailed within 5 business days. If not, you will be notified that this video is already out on loan. No more than three titles may be borrowed by one requestor at a time. No reservations for a specific date will be accepted. It is most efficient to order via the web site.
Source: U. S. Environmental Protection Agency, Region 1
Customer Service Center
One Congress Street, Suite 1100
Boston, MA 02214
World Wide Web URL:
http://yosemite.epa.gov/r1/videolen.nsf/

Our Urban Wetlands: An Endangered Resource
Explains the nature of wetlands, their environmental benefits, related legislation, and ways of involving communities and schools in wetland preservation.
Availability: Schools, libraries, and homeschoolers in Connecticut, Maine, Massachusetts, New Hampshire, Rhode Island, and Vermont.
Suggested Grade: 7-Adult
Order Number: VID 278
Production Date: 1988
Format: VHS videotape
Terms: Borrower pays return postage. Return within three weeks of receipt. If the tape you request is available, it will be mailed within 5 business days. If not, you will be notified that this video is already out on loan. No more than three titles may be borrowed by one requestor at a time. No reservations for a specific date will be accepted. It is most efficient to order via the web site.
Source: U. S. Environmental Protection Agency, Region 1
Customer Service Center, One Congress Street, Suite 1100
Boston, MA 02214
World Wide Web URL:
http://yosemite.epa.gov/r1/videolen.nsf/

Our Water, Our Future: Saving Our Tribal Life Force Together
Documents the successful protection of water quality on Native American reservations.
Availability: Schools, libraries, and homeschoolers in Connecticut, Maine, Massachusetts, New Hampshire, Rhode Island, and Vermont.
Suggested Grade: 9-Adult
Order Number: VID 377
Format: VHS videotape
Terms: Borrower pays return postage. Return within three weeks of receipt. If the tape you request is available, it will be mailed within 5 business days. If not, you will be notified that this video is already out on loan. No more than three titles may be borrowed by one requestor at a time. No reservations for a specific date will be accepted. It is most efficient to order via the web site.

Source: U. S. Environmental Protection Agency, Region 1
Customer Service Center
One Congress Street, Suite 1100
Boston, MA 02214
World Wide Web URL:
http://yosemite.epa.gov/r1/videolen.nsf/

Poisoned Home, Poisoned People: CNN and Time on Special Assignment
Highlights "cotton poison" or methyl-parathion and its illegal use by exterminators inside homes.
Availability: Schools, libraries, and homeschoolers in Connecticut, Maine, Massachusetts, New Hampshire, Rhode Island, and Vermont.
Suggested Grade: 9-Adult
Order Number: VID 231
Production Date: 1997
Format: VHS videotape
Terms: Borrower pays return postage. Return within three weeks of receipt. If the tape you request is available, it will be mailed within 5 business days. If not, you will be notified that this video is already out on loan. No more than three titles may be borrowed by one requestor at a time. No reservations for a specific date will be accepted. It is most efficient to order via the web site.
Source: U. S. Environmental Protection Agency, Region 1
Customer Service Center
One Congress Street, Suite 1100
Boston, MA 02214
World Wide Web URL:
http://yosemite.epa.gov/r1/videolen.nsf/

Protecting Our Global Home--Japan's Ecological Contributions
The Japanese respect for nature is emphasized. The video talks about the endangered species and their protection, whale-watching, and the present push to control and diminish air pollution.
Availability: Schools, libraries, homeschoolers, and nursing homes in Connecticut (except Fairfield County), Maine, Massachusetts, New Hampshire, Rhode Island, and Vermont.
Suggested Grade: 6-12
Order Number: 551
Production Date: 1992
Format: VHS videotape
Terms: Borrower pays return postage, including insurance. Return two weeks after receipt.
Source: Consulate General of Japan, Boston
Federal Reserve Plaza, 14th Floor
600 Atlantic Avenue
Boston, MA 02210
Phone: 1-617-973-9772
Fax: 1-617-542-1329
World Wide Web URL:
http://www.boston.us.emb-japan.go.jp
Email Address: infocul@cgjbos.org

SCIENCE--ENVIRONMENTAL EDUCATION

Protecting Our Global Home--Japan's Ecological Contributions
The Japanese respect for nature is emphasized. The video talks about the endangered species and their protection, whale-watching, and the present push to control and diminish air pollution.
- Availability: Schools, libraries, homeschoolers, and nursing homes in Arizona and California (zipcodes beginning 900-931 and 935).
- Suggested Grade: 6-12
- Order Number: 197
- Format: VHS videotape
- Terms: Borrower pays postage both ways; you may call the number below to learn how much postage costs. Return within two weeks of date borrowed. An individual may borrow 2 items at one time. For non-profit and educational use only.
- Source: Consulate General of Japan, Los Angeles
  350 South Grand Avenue, Suite 1700
  Los Angeles, CA 90071-3459
  Phone: 1-213-617-6700
  Fax: 1-213-617-6727
  World Wide Web URL: http://www.la.us.emb-japan.go.jp

Protecting Our Habitat: Recycling at the Grassroots
Shows the different steps to recycling in Japan.
- Availability: Schools, libraries, homeschoolers, and nursing homes in Connecticut (except Fairfield County), Maine, Massachusetts, New Hampshire, Rhode Island, and Vermont.
- Suggested Grade: 6-12
- Order Number: 552
- Production Date: 1992
- Format: VHS videotape
- Terms: Borrower pays return postage, including insurance. Return two weeks after receipt.
- Source: Consulate General of Japan, Boston
  Federal Reserve Plaza, 14th Floor, 600 Atlantic Avenue
  Boston, MA 02210
  Phone: 1-617-973-9772
  Fax: 1-617-542-1329
  World Wide Web URL: http://www.boston.us.emb-japan.go.jp
  Email Address: infocul@cgjbos.org

Protecting Our Habitat: Recycling at the Grassroots
Shows the different steps to recycling in Japan.
- Availability: Schools, libraries, homeschoolers, and nursing homes in Arizona and California (zipcodes beginning 900-931 and 935).
- Suggested Grade: 6-12
- Order Number: 195
- Production Date: 1992
- Format: VHS videotape
- Terms: Borrower pays postage both ways; you may call the number below to learn how much postage costs. Return within two weeks of date borrowed. An individual may borrow 2 items at one time. For non-profit and educational use only.
- Source: Consulate General of Japan, Los Angeles
  350 South Grand Avenue, Suite 1700
  Los Angeles, CA 90071-3459
  Phone: 1-213-617-6700
  Fax: 1-213-617-6727
  World Wide Web URL: http://www.la.us.emb-japan.go.jp

Rain Forest
Problems of deforestation in the rain forests of Costa Rica and elsewhere.
- Availability: Schools, libraries, and nursing homes in the United States.
- Suggested Grade: 6-12
- Order Number: GECOS1-video
- Production Date: 1986
- Format: VHS videotape
- Terms: Borrowers must have a User's Agreement on file with this source--available by mail or via the Internet. Return postage is paid by borrower; return 12 days after showing. Book at least three weeks in advance. All borrowers are limited to a total of ten items per semester.
- Source: Latin American Resource Center
  Stone Center for Latin American Studies
  Tulane University
  100 Jones Hall
  New Orleans, LA 70118
  Phone: 1-504-862-3143
  Fax: 1-504-865-6719
  World Wide Web URL: http://stonecenter.tulane.edu/pages/detail/48/Lending-Library
  Email Address: crcrts@tulane.edu

Rainforests: Proving Their Worth
Shows how international marketing of renewable forest products may provide inhabitants with the means to protect their vanishing lands.
- Availability: Schools and libraries in Iowa, Illinois, Michigan, Minnesota, and Wisconsin.
- Suggested Grade: 6-12
- Order Number: ENVRFR13VHS
- Production Date: 1990
- Format: VHS videotape
- Terms: Borrower pays return postage. Return 8 days after showing. Book 2 weeks in advance. Order may also be picked up for those near the Center.
- Source: Center for Latin American and Caribbean Studies
  UW-Milwaukee
  P. O. Box 413
  Milwaukee, WI 53201
  Phone: 1-414-229-5987
  World Wide Web URL: http://www.uwm.edu/Dept/CLACS
  Email Address: audvis@usm.edu

Rainforests: Proving Their Worth
Shows how international marketing of renewable forest products may provide inhabitants with the means to protect their vanishing lands.
- Availability: Schools, libraries, and nursing homes in the United States.

*All materials listed in this 2018-2019 edition are **BRAND NEW!***

SCIENCE--ENVIRONMENTAL EDUCATION

Suggested Grade: 6-12
Order Number: GE9-video
Production Date: 1990
Format: VHS videotape
Terms: Borrowers must have a User's Agreement on file with this source--available by mail or via the Internet. Return postage is paid by borrower; return 12 days after showing. Book at least three weeks in advance. All borrowers are limited to a total of ten items per semester.
Source: Latin American Resource Center
Stone Center for Latin American Studies
Tulane University
100 Jones Hall
New Orleans, LA 70118
Phone: 1-504-862-3143
Fax: 1-504-865-6719
World Wide Web URL: http://stonecenter.tulane.edu/pages/detail/48/Lending-Library
Email Address: crcrts@tulane.edu

Recycle
Shows the successful recycling program created at Stonington High School in Pawcatuck, Connecticut.
Availability: Schools, libraries, and homeschoolers in Connecticut, Maine, Massachusetts, New Hampshire, Rhode Island, and Vermont.
Suggested Grade: 9-Adult
Order Number: VID 370
Production Date: 2001
Format: VHS videotape
Terms: Borrower pays return postage. Return within three weeks of receipt. If the tape you request is available, it will be mailed within 5 business days. If not, you will be notified that this video is already out on loan. No more than three titles may be borrowed by one requestor at a time. No reservations for a specific date will be accepted. It is most efficient to order via the web site.
Source: U. S. Environmental Protection Agency, Region 1
Customer Service Center, One Congress Street, Suite 1100
Boston, MA 02214
World Wide Web URL: http://yosemite.epa.gov/r1/videolen.nsf/

Reduce, Reuse, Recycle: The Bottom Line
Representatives of a few companies teach businesses how to reuse materials, source, and recycle.
Availability: Schools, libraries, and homeschoolers in Connecticut, Maine, Massachusetts, New Hampshire, Rhode Island, and Vermont.
Suggested Grade: 9-Adult
Order Number: VID RL48
Production Date: 1992
Format: VHS videotape
Terms: Borrower pays return postage. Return within three weeks of receipt. If the tape you request is available, it will be mailed within 5 business days. If not, you will be notified that this video is already out on loan. No more than three titles may be borrowed by one requestor at a time. No reservations for a specific date will be accepted. It is most efficient to order via the web site.
Source: U. S. Environmental Protection Agency, Region 1
Customer Service Center
One Congress Street, Suite 1100
Boston, MA 02214
World Wide Web URL: http://yosemite.epa.gov/r1/videolen.nsf/

Reviving Our Rain Forests--The Mission of Professor Akira Miyawaki
Professor Miyawaki was instrumental in developing a personal reforestation program in Japan; here is an interview with him.
Availability: Schools, libraries, homeschoolers, and nursing homes in Connecticut (except Fairfield County), Maine, Massachusetts, New Hampshire, Rhode Island, and Vermont.
Suggested Grade: 6-12
Order Number: 555
Production Date: 1992
Format: VHS videotape
Terms: Borrower pays return postage, including insurance. Return two weeks after receipt.
Source: Consulate General of Japan, Boston
Federal Reserve Plaza, 14th Floor
600 Atlantic Avenue
Boston, MA 02210
Phone: 1-617-973-9772
Fax: 1-617-542-1329
World Wide Web URL: http://www.boston.us.emb-japan.go.jp
Email Address: infocul@cgjbos.org

Reviving Our Rain Forests--The Mission of Professor Akira Miyawaki
Professor Miyawaki was instrumental in developing a personal reforestation program in Japan; here is an interview with him.
Availability: Schools, libraries, homeschoolers, and nursing homes in Arizona and California (zipcodes beginning 900-931 and 935).
Suggested Grade: 6-12
Order Number: 194
Production Date: 1992
Format: VHS videotape
Terms: Borrower pays postage both ways; you may call the number below to learn how much postage costs. Return within two weeks of date borrowed. An individual may borrow 2 items at one time. For non-profit and educational use only.
Source: Consulate General of Japan, Los Angeles
350 South Grand Avenue, Suite 1700
Los Angeles, CA 90071-3459
Phone: 1-213-617-6700
Fax: 1-213-617-6727
World Wide Web URL: http://www.la.us.emb-japan.go.jp

Rotten Truth, The
The PBS series "3-2-1 Contact" takes viewers on a visit to the fictitious "Museum of Modern Garbage" and to landfill

SCIENCE--ENVIRONMENTAL EDUCATION

sites to dramatize the mounting waste problem, and the need for consumers to change their habits.

Availability: Schools, libraries, and homeschoolers in Connecticut, Maine, Massachusetts, New Hampshire, Rhode Island, and Vermont.
Suggested Grade: All ages
Order Number: VID 130
Production Date: 1990
Format: VHS videotape
Terms: Borrower pays return postage. Return within three weeks of receipt. If the tape you request is available, it will be mailed within 5 business days. If not, you will be notified that this video is already out on loan. No more than three titles may be borrowed by one requestor at a time. No reservations for a specific date will be accepted. It is most efficient to order via the web site.
Source: **U. S. Environmental Protection Agency, Region 1**
Customer Service Center
One Congress Street, Suite 1100
Boston, MA 02214
World Wide Web URL:
http://yosemite.epa.gov/r1/videolen.nsf/

Serpent Fruits

Traces the effects of chemicals on the environment and on living creatures. Goes through an explanation of how chemicals are tested to see if they are carcinogenic.

Availability: Schools, libraries, and homeschoolers in Connecticut, Maine, Massachusetts, New Hampshire, Rhode Island, and Vermont.
Suggested Grade: 7-Adult
Order Number: VID 014
Production Date: 1979
Format: VHS videotape
Terms: Borrower pays return postage. Return within three weeks of receipt. If the tape you request is available, it will be mailed within 5 business days. If not, you will be notified that this video is already out on loan. No more than three titles may be borrowed by one requestor at a time. No reservations for a specific date will be accepted. It is most efficient to order via the web site.
Source: **U. S. Environmental Protection Agency, Region 1**
Customer Service Center
One Congress Street, Suite 1100
Boston, MA 02214
World Wide Web URL:
http://yosemite.epa.gov/r1/videolen.nsf/

Tramp in the Darien, A

Ecological, economic, and social conditions met while traveling by bus, boat, and foot through the Darien, a rainforest region near the Panama-Colombia border area.

Availability: Schools, libraries, and nursing homes in the United States.
Suggested Grade: 6-12
Order Number: GELA9-video
Production Date: 1989
Format: VHS videotape
Terms: Borrowers must have a User's Agreement on file with this source--available by mail or via the Internet. Return postage is paid by borrower; return 12 days after showing. Book at least three weeks in advance. All borrowers are limited to a total of ten items per semester.
Source: **Latin American Resource Center**
Stone Center for Latin American Studies
Tulane University
100 Jones Hall
New Orleans, LA 70118
Phone: 1-504-862-3143
Fax: 1-504-865-6719
World Wide Web URL: http://stonecenter.tulane.edu/pages/detail/48/Lending-Library
Email Address: crcrts@tulane.edu

Understanding Ecology: What Is a Food Chain?

Answers this question.

Availability: Schools, libraries, and homeschoolers in Connecticut, Maine, Massachusetts, New Hampshire, Rhode Island, and Vermont.
Suggested Grade: 9-Adult
Order Number: VID 276b
Format: VHS videotape
Terms: Borrower pays return postage. Return within three weeks of receipt. If the tape you request is available, it will be mailed within 5 business days. If not, you will be notified that this video is already out on loan. No more than three titles may be borrowed by one requestor at a time. No reservations for a specific date will be accepted. It is most efficient to order via the web site.
Source: **U. S. Environmental Protection Agency, Region 1**
Customer Service Center
One Congress Street, Suite 1100
Boston, MA 02214
World Wide Web URL:
http://yosemite.epa.gov/r1/videolen.nsf/

User's Guide to the Planet Earth, A: The American Environmental Test

Tom Selleck hosts this video that quizzes viewers on their environmental awareness. Celebrities ask a variety of questions regarding land, air, water, and energy issues, then explain the answers.

Availability: Schools, libraries, and homeschoolers in Connecticut, Maine, Massachusetts, New Hampshire, Rhode Island, and Vermont.
Suggested Grade: 7-Adult
Order Number: VID 037
Format: VHS videotape
Terms: Borrower pays return postage. Return within three weeks of receipt. If the tape you request is available, it will be mailed within 5 business days. If not, you will be notified that this video is already out on loan. No more than three titles may be borrowed by one requestor at a time. No reservations for a specific date will be accepted. It is most efficient to order via the web site.

SCIENCE--ENVIRONMENTAL EDUCATION

Source: U. S. Environmental Protection Agency, Region 1
Customer Service Center
One Congress Street, Suite 1100
Boston, MA 02214
World Wide Web URL:
http://yosemite.epa.gov/r1/videolen.nsf/

We Don't Have a Choice
Solid waste must be dealt with by a national strategy which includes source reduction, pollution prevention, and recycling.
- Availability: Schools, libraries, and homeschoolers in Connecticut, Maine, Massachusetts, New Hampshire, Rhode Island, and Vermont.
- Suggested Grade: 9-12
- Order Number: VID RL62
- Production Date: 1990
- Format: VHS videotape
- Terms: Borrower pays return postage. Return within three weeks of receipt. If the tape you request is available, it will be mailed within 5 business days. If not, you will be notified that this video is already out on loan. No more than three titles may be borrowed by one requestor at a time. No reservations for a specific date will be accepted. It is most efficient to order via the web site.

Source: U. S. Environmental Protection Agency, Region 1
Customer Service Center
One Congress Street, Suite 1100
Boston, MA 02214
World Wide Web URL:
http://yosemite.epa.gov/r1/videolen.nsf/

Whose Woods Are These?
Examination of the pattern of destruction in forests abroad and in the United States.
- Availability: Schools, libraries, and nursing homes in the United States.
- Suggested Grade: 6-12
- Order Number: GE10-video
- Production Date: 1992
- Format: VHS videotape
- Terms: Borrowers must have a User's Agreement on file with this source--available by mail or via the Internet. Return postage is paid by borrower; return 12 days after showing. Book at least three weeks in advance. All borrowers are limited to a total of ten items per semester.

Source: Latin American Resource Center
Stone Center for Latin American Studies
Tulane University
100 Jones Hall
New Orleans, LA 70118
Phone: 1-504-862-3143
Fax: 1-504-865-6719
World Wide Web URL: http://stonecenter.tulane.edu/pages/detail/48/Lending-Library
Email Address: crcrts@tulane.edu

Wings Above the Forest
Conservationist organization "Lighthawk," uses planes for environmental monitoring through North and Central America. They visit rain forests in Belize.
- Availability: Schools, libraries, and nursing homes in the United States.
- Suggested Grade: 9-Adult
- Order Number: GELA13-video
- Production Date: 1990
- Format: VHS videotape
- Terms: Borrowers must have a User's Agreement on file with this source--available by mail or via the Internet. Return postage is paid by borrower; return 12 days after showing. Book at least three weeks in advance. All borrowers are limited to a total of ten items per semester.

Source: Latin American Resource Center
Stone Center for Latin American Studies
Tulane University
100 Jones Hall
New Orleans, LA 70118
Phone: 1-504-862-3143
Fax: 1-504-865-6719
World Wide Web URL: http://stonecenter.tulane.edu/pages/detail/48/Lending-Library
Email Address: crcrts@tulane.edu

World Heritage--Shirakami Forest 1997
UNESCO certified Shirakami Mountain Forest, which borders Aomori and Akita prefectures, as a world heritage. This 17,000 hectacre forest area is among nature's most priceless treasures--a heritage that must be preserved for future generations.
- Availability: Schools, libraries, homeschoolers, and nursing homes in Connecticut (except Fairfield County), Maine, Massachusetts, New Hampshire, Rhode Island, and Vermont.
- Suggested Grade: 6-12
- Order Number: 556
- Format: VHS videotape
- Terms: Borrower pays return postage, including insurance. Return two weeks after receipt.

Source: Consulate General of Japan, Boston
Federal Reserve Plaza, 14th Floor
600 Atlantic Avenue
Boston, MA 02210
Phone: 1-617-973-9772
Fax: 1-617-542-1329
World Wide Web URL:
http://www.boston.us.emb-japan.go.jp
Email Address: infocul@cgjbos.org

World Heritage--Shirakami Forest 1997
UNESCO certified Shirakami Mountain Forest, which borders Aomori and Akita prefectures, as a world heritage. This 17,000 hectacre forest area is among nature's most priceless treasures--a heritage that must be preserved for future generations.
- Availability: Schools, libraries, and nursing homes in Hawaii.
- Suggested Grade: 6-12
- Order Number: NA-28

SCIENCE--ENVIRONMENTAL EDUCATION

Format: VHS videotape
Terms: Borrower pays return postage. A maximum of 3 videos may be borrowed per person. Return within one week of date borrowed.
Source: Consulate General of Japan, Honolulu
1742 Nuuanu Avenue
Honolulu, HI 96817-3294
Phone: 1-808-543-3111
Fax: 1-808-543-3170
World Wide Web URL:
http://www.honolulu.us.emb-japan.go.jp

You Can't Grow Home Again
Pre-teen takes viewers on a trip to the Costa Rican rainforest to examine issues of preservation.
Availability: Schools and libraries in Iowa, Illinois, Michigan, Minnesota, and Wisconsin.
Suggested Grade: 6-12
Order Number: ENVRFY8VHS
Production Date: 1990
Format: VHS videotape
Terms: Borrower pays return postage. Return 8 days after showing. Book 2 weeks in advance. Order may also be picked up for those near the Center.
Source: Center for Latin American and Caribbean Studies
UW-Milwaukee
P. O. Box 413
Milwaukee, WI 53201
Phone: 1-414-229-5987
World Wide Web URL: http://www.uwm.edu/Dept/CLACS
Email Address: audvis@usm.edu

You Can't Grow Home Again
Pre-teen takes viewers on a trip to the Costa Rican rainforest to examine issues of preservation.
Availability: Schools, libraries, and nursing homes in the United States.
Suggested Grade: 6-12
Order Number: GELA12-video
Production Date: 1990
Format: VHS videotape
Terms: Borrowers must have a User's Agreement on file with this source--available by mail or via the Internet. Return postage is paid by borrower; return 12 days after showing. Book at least three weeks in advance. All borrowers are limited to a total of ten items per semester.
Source: Latin American Resource Center
Stone Center for Latin American Studies
Tulane University
100 Jones Hall
New Orleans, LA 70118
Phone: 1-504-862-3143
Fax: 1-504-865-6719
World Wide Web URL: http://stonecenter.tulane.edu/pages/detail/48/Lending-Library
Email Address: crcrts@tulane.edu

Your Water, Your Life
Delivers a message: grassroots activism works! Alerts citizens to the problems of groundwater contamination and how they can change local policy and improve the environmental health of their communities.
Availability: Schools, libraries, and homeschoolers in Connecticut, Maine, Massachusetts, New Hampshire, Rhode Island, and Vermont.
Suggested Grade: 9-12
Order Number: VID 112
Production Date: 1998
Format: VHS videotape
Terms: Borrower pays return postage. Return within three weeks of receipt. If the tape you request is available, it will be mailed within 5 business days. If not, you will be notified that this video is already out on loan. No more than three titles may be borrowed by one requestor at a time. No reservations for a specific date will be accepted. It is most efficient to order via the web site.
Source: U. S. Environmental Protection Agency, Region 1
Customer Service Center
One Congress Street, Suite 1100
Boston, MA 02214
World Wide Web URL:
http://yosemite.epa.gov/r1/videolen.nsf/

SCIENCE--GENERAL SCIENCE

Amber Hunters
Amber--fossilized tree resin that often captures in its flow some form of life on earth millions of years ago. Prized for its rarity and beauty, amber is also sought by scientists for the potential discoveries of prehistoric life. Follow an amber hunter in a Dominican Republic marketplace and mine as he buys small quantities of this semiprecious jewel. Fellow scientists use modern technology to reveal the secrets of the encased fossil. Perhaps dinosaurs really can live again?
- Availability: Schools, libraries, and homeschoolers in the United States who serve the hearing impaired.
- Suggested Grade: 9-Adult
- Order Number: 13102
- Production Date: 1996
- Format: DVD
- Special Notes: Produced by Ambrose Video Publishing, Inc..
- Terms: Sponsor pays all transportation costs. Return one week after receipt. Participation is limited to deaf or hard of hearing Americans, their parents, families, teachers, counselors, or others whose use would benefit a deaf or hard of hearing person. Only one person in the audience needs to be hearing impaired. You must register--which is free. These videos are all open-captioned--no special equipment is required for viewing.

Source: Described and Captioned Media Program
National Association of the Deaf
4211 Church Street Ext.
Roebuck, SC 29376
Phone: 1-800-237-6213
Fax: 1-800-538-5636
World Wide Web URL: http://www.dcmp.org

Chemistry: The Basics
Provides a general introduction to basic chemistry. Begins with the atom as the building block of everything. Introduces the elements, explains the periodic table, identifies the three states of matter, and defines compound, mixture, and formula. Computer graphics illustrate atoms, ions, protons, neutrons, and isotopes. Ends with chemistry's impact on and importance to today's world.
- Availability: Schools, libraries, and homeschoolers in the United States who serve the hearing impaired.
- Suggested Grade: 9-12
- Format: DVD
- Special Notes: Produced by Allegro Productions.
- Terms: Sponsor pays all transportation costs. Return one week after receipt. Participation is limited to deaf or hard of hearing Americans, their parents, families, teachers, counselors, or others whose use would benefit a deaf or hard of hearing person. Only one person in the audience needs to be hearing impaired. You must register--which is free. These videos are all open-captioned--no special equipment is required for viewing.

Source: Described and Captioned Media Program
National Association of the Deaf
4211 Church Street Ext.
Roebuck, SC 29376
Phone: 1-800-237-6213
Fax: 1-800-538-5636
World Wide Web URL: http://www.dcmp.org

Energy Behind Finding Energy, The
A two-part video that gives an overview of exploration, drilling and production of oil and natural gas.
- Availability: Schools, libraries, and homeschoolers in OKLAHOMA only.
- Suggested Grade: All ages
- Order Number: order by title
- Format: DVD
- Special Notes: May be retained permanently.

Source: Oklahoma Energy Resources Board
Carla Zappola
3555 NW 58th, Suite 430
Oklahoma City, OK 73112
Phone: 1-405-942-5323
Fax: 1-405-942-3435
World Wide Web URL: http://www.oerb.com
Email Address: czappola@oerb.com

Flame in the Chemistry Lab
Tests the heat zones of a Bunsen burner and shows some elements' coloration when placed in the flame. Notes that chemistry is everywhere.
- Availability: Schools, libraries, and homeschoolers in the United States who serve the hearing impaired.
- Suggested Grade: 10-Adult
- Order Number: 11031
- Production Date: 2001
- Format: DVD
- Special Notes: Also available as streaming video.
- Terms: Sponsor pays all transportation costs. Return one week after receipt. Participation is limited to deaf or hard of hearing Americans, their parents, families, teachers, counselors, or others whose use would benefit a deaf or hard of hearing person. Only one person in the audience needs to be hearing impaired. You must register--which is free. These videos are all open-captioned--no special equipment is required for viewing.

Source: Described and Captioned Media Program
National Association of the Deaf
4211 Church Street Ext.
Roebuck, SC 29376
Phone: 1-800-237-6213
Fax: 1-800-538-5636
World Wide Web URL: http://www.dcmp.org

Hubble's Amazing Rescue
The unlikely story of how the world's most beloved telescope was saved.
- Availability: All requesters
- Suggested Grade: 7-Adult
- Order Number: not applicable
- Production Date: 2009
- Format: Streaming Video

Source: NOVA
World Wide Web URL:
http://www.pbs.org/wgbh/nova/programs/index.html

All materials listed in this 2018-2019 edition are BRAND NEW!

SCIENCE--GENERAL SCIENCE

Megabeasts' Sudden Death
Scientists propose a radical new idea of what killed off mammoths and other large animals at the end of the Ice Age.
Availability: All requesters
Suggested Grade: 7-Adult
Order Number: not applicable
Production Date: 2009
Format: Streaming Video
    Source: NOVA
   World Wide Web URL:
 http://www.pbs.org/wgbh/nova/programs/index.html

Periodic Table of Videos
Videos about each and everyone of the elements of the periodic table.
Availability: All requesters
Suggested Grade: 4-Adult
Order Number: not applicable
Format: Streaming video
    Source: Aldrich
   World Wide Web URL:
  http://www.periodicvideos.com/index.htm

School Testing--Behind the Numbers
A lively, humorous and thoughtful discussion of the meaning and impact of school testing.
Availability: All requesters
Suggested Grade: 7-Adult
Order Number: not applicable
Production Date: 2002
Format: Streaming Video
Terms: A simple FREE registration is required to view videos.
   Source: Annenberg Media
   World Wide Web URL:
  http://www.learner.org/resources/browse.html

Seasons of Life
These intriguing programs are an excellent introduction to developmental psychology from conception through old age.
Availability: All requesters
Suggested Grade: Adult
Order Number: not applicable
Production Date: 1990
Format: Streaming Video
Special Notes: May be purchased on DVD for $149.50.
Terms: A simple FREE registration is required to view videos.
   Source: Annenberg Media
   World Wide Web URL:
  http://www.learner.org/resources/browse.html

Where the Hot Stuff Is: Volcanoes of the Earth and Solar System
A recording of a webcast present on this topic.
Availability: All requesters
Suggested Grade: 9-12
Order Number: not applicable
Production Date: 2010
Format: Streaming Video
  Source: Smithsonian National Air and Space Museum
   World Wide Web URL:
  http://www.nasm.si.edu/webcasts/archive.cfm

SCIENCE--NATURE STUDY

Animals on the Ice Floe: Shiretoko in Mid-Winter
In winter, the sea along the Shiretoko peninsula in Hokkaido is surrounded with ice. This highlights some of the animals such as eagles and seals that live on the ice floe.
Availability: Schools, libraries, homeschoolers, and nursing homes in Connecticut (except Fairfield County), Maine, Massachusetts, New Hampshire, Rhode Island, and Vermont.
Suggested Grade: 4-Adult
Order Number: 166
Production Date: 1988
Format: VHS videotape
Special Notes: No. 11 of the "Document Japan" series.
Terms: Borrower pays return postage, including insurance. Return two weeks after receipt.
Source: Consulate General of Japan, Boston
Federal Reserve Plaza, 14th Floor
600 Atlantic Avenue
Boston, MA 02210
Phone: 1-617-973-9772
Fax: 1-617-542-1329
World Wide Web URL:
http://www.boston.us.emb-japan.go.jp
Email Address: infocul@cgjbos.org

Animals on the Ice Floe: Shiretoko in Mid-Winter
In winter, the sea along the Shiretoko peninsula in Hokkaido is surrounded with ice. This highlights some of the animals such as eagles and seals that live on the ice floe.
Availability: Schools, libraries, and nursing homes in Oklahoma and Texas.
Suggested Grade: 4-Adult
Order Number: C11
Production Date: 1988
Format: VHS videotape
Special Notes: No. 11 of the "Document Japan" series.
Terms: Materials must be picked up in person. Under special circumstances, you may be able to have them shipped to you at your own expense (call for further details). Return within two weeks after scheduled showing. Videos must be registered with the U. S. Postal Service or returned by Priority Mail, Federal Express, or other registered shipping service.
Source: Consulate General of Japan, Houston
Cultural Affairs and Information Section
909 Fannin Street, Suite 3000
Houston, TX 77010
Phone: 1-713-652-2977
Fax: 1-713-651-7822
World Wide Web URL:
http://www.houston.us.emb-japan.go.jp/en/culture/page1.htm
Email Address: info@cgjhouston.org

Animals on the Ice Floe: Shiretoko in Mid-Winter
In winter, the sea along the Shiretoko peninsula in Hokkaido is surrounded with ice. This highlights some of the animals such as eagles and seals that live on the ice floe.
Availability: Schools, libraries, homeschoolers, and nursing homes in Arizona and California (zipcodes beginning 900-931 and 935).
Suggested Grade: 4-Adult
Order Number: 110
Production Date: 1988
Format: VHS videotape
Special Notes: No. 11 of the "Document Japan" series.
Terms: Borrower pays postage both ways; you may call the number below to learn how much postage costs. Return within two weeks of date borrowed. An individual may borrow 2 items at one time. For non-profit and educational use only.
Source: Consulate General of Japan, Los Angeles
350 South Grand Avenue, Suite 1700
Los Angeles, CA 90071-3459
Phone: 1-213-617-6700
Fax: 1-213-617-6727
World Wide Web URL: http://www.la.us.emb-japan.go.jp

Animals on the Ice Floe: Shiretoko in Mid-Winter
In winter, the sea along the Shiretoko peninsula in Hokkaido is surrounded with ice. This highlights some of the animals such as eagles and seals that live on the ice floe.
Availability: Schools, libraries, homeschoolers, and nursing homes in Nevada and northern California (zip codes beginning 932 and above, except 935).
Suggested Grade: 4-Adult
Order Number: order by title
Production Date: 1988
Format: Beta videotape; U-matic videotape; VHS videotape
Special Notes: No. 11 of the "Document Japan" series.
Terms: Borrower pays return postage. Book two weeks in advance. Return within three weeks of date borrowed, via UPS, Federal Express or certified mail.
Source: Consulate General of Japan, San Francisco
50 Fremont Street, Suite 2300
San Francisco, CA 94105-2236
Phone: 1-415-356-2564
Fax: 1-415-777-0518
World Wide Web URL: http://www.sf.us.emb-japan.go.jp/
Email Address: infoav@cgjsf.org

Bird Dogs Afield
A complete video magazine for upland point dog enthusiasts and upland bird hunters.
Availability: All requesters
Suggested Grade: All ages
Order Number: not applicable
Format: Streaming Video
Source: Paul Fuller
World Wide Web URL:
http://www.birddogsafield.com/index.html

Carnivorous Plants
Animals usually eat plants, but where soil is poor and nutrients scarce, some plants have adapted and feed on

SCIENCE--NATURE STUDY

insects in order to survive. Excellent photography shows how these carnivorous plants trap and digest their food. Classifies the plants as a passive, semiactive, or active trap. Shows the cobra lily, pitcher plant, Cephalotus, sundew, Venus flytrap, and others. Notes that the "trap" is a modified leaf, not a flower.

Availability: Schools, libraries, and homeschoolers in the United States who serve the hearing impaired.
Suggested Grade: 6-10
Order Number: 13042
Production Date: 1993
Format: DVD
Special Notes: Produced by Stanton Films.
Terms: Sponsor pays all transportation costs. Return one week after receipt. Participation is limited to deaf or hard of hearing Americans, their parents, families, teachers, counselors, or others whose use would benefit a deaf or hard of hearing person. Only one person in the audience needs to be hearing impaired. You must register--which is free. These videos are all open-captioned--no special equipment is required for viewing.

Source: Described and Captioned Media Program
National Association of the Deaf
4211 Church Street Ext.
Roebuck, SC 29376
Phone: 1-800-237-6213
Fax: 1-800-538-5636
World Wide Web URL: http://www.dcmp.org

Extreme Cave Diving

A team of intrepid scientists journey into one of Earth's most dangerous and beautiful underwater frontiers.

Availability: All requesters
Suggested Grade: 7-Adult
Order Number: not applicable
Production Date: 2010
Format: Streaming Video

Source: NOVA
World Wide Web URL:
http://www.pbs.org/wgbh/nova/programs/index.html

Fight for Survival: The Fish Owl of Northern Japan

The Blakistons fish owl which lives in Hokkaido, Japan's northernmost island, is an endangered species. This program unveils the life of the fish owl.

Availability: Schools, libraries and homeschoolers in Alabama, Georgia, North Carolina, South Carolina, and Virginia.
Suggested Grade: 6-12
Order Number: 022
Production Date: 1993
Format: VHS videotape
Terms: Borrower pays return postage. Two tapes may be borrowed at a time. Return within 7 days after receipt. Reservations may be made by filling the application found on the web site.

Source: onsulate General of Japan, Atlanta
Japan Information Center,
One Alliance Center
3500 Lenox Road, Suite 1600
Atlanta, GA 30326
Phone: 1-404-365-9240
Fax: 1-404-240-4311
World Wide Web URL:
http://www.atlanta.us.emb-japan.go.jp
Email Address: info@cgjapanatlanta.org

Fight for Survival: The Fish Owl of Northern Japan

The Blakistons fish owl which lives in Hokkaido, Japan's northernmost island, is an endangered species. This program unveils the life of the fish owl.

Availability: Schools, libraries, homeschoolers, and nursing homes in Connecticut (except Fairfield County), Maine, Massachusetts, New Hampshire, Rhode Island, and Vermont.
Suggested Grade: 6-12
Order Number: 558
Production Date: 1993
Format: VHS videotape
Terms: Borrower pays return postage, including insurance. Return two weeks after receipt.

Source: Consulate General of Japan, Boston
Federal Reserve Plaza, 14th Floor
600 Atlantic Avenue
Boston, MA 02210
Phone: 1-617-973-9772
Fax: 1-617-542-1329
World Wide Web URL:
http://www.boston.us.emb-japan.go.jp
Email Address: infocul@cgjbos.org

Fight for Survival: The Fish Owl of Northern Japan

The Blakistons fish owl which lives in Hokkaido, Japan's northernmost island, is an endangered species. This program unveils the life of the fish owl.

Availability: Schools, libraries, and nursing homes in Hawaii.
Suggested Grade: 6-12
Order Number: NA-19
Production Date: 1993
Format: VHS videotape
Terms: Borrower pays return postage. A maximum of 3 videos may be borrowed per person. Return within one week of date borrowed.

Source: Consulate General of Japan, Honolulu
1742 Nuuanu Avenue
Honolulu, HI 96817-3294
Phone: 1-808-543-3111
Fax: 1-808-543-3170
World Wide Web URL:
http://www.honolulu.us.emb-japan.go.jp

Fight for Survival: The Fish Owl of Northern Japan

The Blakistons fish owl which live in Hokkaido, Japan's northernmost island, is an endangered species. This

SCIENCE--NATURE STUDY

program unveils the life of the fish owl.
Availability: Schools, libraries, homeschoolers, and nursing homes in Arizona and California (zipcodes beginning 900-931 and 935).
Suggested Grade: 6-12
Order Number: 198
Production Date: 1993
Format: VHS videotape
Terms: Borrower pays postage both ways; you may call the number below to learn how much postage costs. Return within two weeks of date borrowed. An individual may borrow 2 items at one time. For non-profit and educational use only.
Source: Consulate General of Japan, Los Angeles
350 South Grand Avenue, Suite 1700
Los Angeles, CA 90071-3459
Phone: 1-213-617-6700
Fax: 1-213-617-6727
World Wide Web URL: http://www.la.us.emb-japan.go.jp

Funny Crabs in the Mangrove, The
At least 70 species of crab live in the Iri-omote Island mangrove in Japan. This video looks at these animals and some of their strange and funny behaviors.
Availability: Schools, libraries and homeschoolers in Alabama, Georgia, North Carolina, South Carolina, and Virginia.
Suggested Grade: 4-12
Order Number: 028
Production Date: 1994
Format: VHS videotape
Terms: Borrower pays return postage. Two tapes may be borrowed at a time. Return within 7 days after receipt. Reservations may be made by filling the application found on the web site.
Source: Consulate General of Japan, Atlanta
Japan Information Center
One Alliance Center
3500 Lenox Road, Suite 1600
Atlanta, GA 30326
Phone: 1-404-365-9240
Fax: 1-404-240-4311
World Wide Web URL:
http://www.atlanta.us.emb-japan.go.jp
Email Address: info@cgjapanatlanta.org

Funny Crabs in the Mangrove, The
At least 70 species of crab live in the Iri-omote Island mangrove in Japan. This video looks at these animals and some of their strange and funny behaviors.
Availability: Schools, libraries, homeschoolers, and nursing homes in Connecticut (except Fairfield County), Maine, Massachusetts, New Hampshire, Rhode Island, and Vermont.
Suggested Grade: 4-12
Order Number: 548
Production Date: 1993
Format: VHS videotape
Terms: Borrower pays return postage, including insurance. Return two weeks after receipt.
Source: Consulate General of Japan, Boston
Federal Reserve Plaza, 14th Floor
600 Atlantic Avenue
Boston, MA 02210
Phone: 1-617-973-9772
Fax: 1-617-542-1329
World Wide Web URL:
http://www.boston.us.emb-japan.go.jp
Email Address: infocul@cgjbos.org

Funny Crabs in the Mangrove, The
At least 70 species of crab live in the Iri-omote Island mangrove in Japan. This video looks at these animals and some of their strange and funny behaviors.
Availability: Schools, libraries, and nursing homes in Hawaii.
Suggested Grade: 4-12
Order Number: NA-22
Production Date: 1993
Format: VHS videotape
Terms: Borrower pays return postage. A maximum of 3 videos may be borrowed per person. Return within one week of date borrowed.
Source: Consulate General of Japan, Honolulu
1742 Nuuanu Avenue
Honolulu, HI 96817-3294
Phone: 1-808-543-3111
Fax: 1-808-543-3170
World Wide Web URL:
http://www.honolulu.us.emb-japan.go.jp

Funny Crabs in the Mangrove, The
At least 70 species of crab live in the Iri-omote Island mangrove in Japan. This video looks at these animals and some of their strange and funny behaviors.
Availability: Schools, libraries, homeschoolers, and nursing homes in Arizona and California (zipcodes beginning 900-931 and 935).
Suggested Grade: 4-12
Order Number: 224
Production Date: 1993
Format: VHS videotape
Terms: Borrower pays postage both ways; you may call the number below to learn how much postage costs. Return within two weeks of date borrowed. An individual may borrow 2 items at one time. For non-profit and educational use only.
Source: Consulate General of Japan, Los Angeles
350 South Grand Avenue, Suite 1700
Los Angeles, CA 90071-3459
Phone: 1-213-617-6700
Fax: 1-213-617-6727
World Wide Web URL: http://www.la.us.emb-japan.go.jp

Galapagos of the East, The: Ogasawara Islands
Examines the creatures that live on these islands in the middle of the Pacific Ocean.

All materials listed in this 2018-2019 edition are BRAND NEW!

SCIENCE--NATURE STUDY

Availability: Schools, libraries and homeschoolers in Alabama, Georgia, North Carolina, South Carolina, and Virginia.
Suggested Grade: 4-12
Order Number: 030
Production Date: 1994
Format: VHS videotape
Terms: Borrower pays return postage. Two tapes may be borrowed at a time. Return within 7 days after receipt. Reservations may be made by filling the application found on the web site.
Source: Consulate General of Japan, Atlanta
Japan Information Center
One Alliance Center
3500 Lenox Road, Suite 1600
Atlanta, GA 30326
Phone: 1-404-365-9240
Fax: 1-404-240-4311
World Wide Web URL:
http://www.atlanta.us.emb-japan.go.jp
Email Address: info@cgjapanatlanta.org

Galapagos of the East, The: Ogasawara Islands
Examines the creatures that live on these islands in the middle of the Pacific Ocean.
Availability: Schools, libraries, homeschoolers, and nursing homes in Connecticut (except Fairfield County), Maine, Massachusetts, New Hampshire, Rhode Island, and Vermont.
Suggested Grade: 4-12
Order Number: 549
Production Date: 1993
Format: VHS videotape
Terms: Borrower pays return postage, including insurance. Return two weeks after receipt.
Source: Consulate General of Japan, Boston
Federal Reserve Plaza, 14th Floor
600 Atlantic Avenue
Boston, MA 02210
Phone: 1-617-973-9772
Fax: 1-617-542-1329
World Wide Web URL:
http://www.boston.us.emb-japan.go.jp
Email Address: infocul@cgjbos.org

Galapagos of the East, The: Ogasawara Islands
Examines the creatures that live on these islands in the middle of the Pacific Ocean.
Availability: Schools, libraries, and nursing homes in Hawaii.
Suggested Grade: 4-12
Order Number: NA-21
Production Date: 1993
Format: VHS videotape
Terms: Borrower pays return postage. A maximum of 3 videos may be borrowed per person. Return within one week of date borrowed.
Source: Consulate General of Japan, Honolulu
1742 Nuuanu Avenue
Honolulu, HI 96817-3294
Phone: 1-808-543-3111
Fax: 1-808-543-3170
World Wide Web URL:
http://www.honolulu.us.emb-japan.go.jp

Galapagos of the East, The: Ogasawara Islands
Examines the creatures that live on these islands in the middle of the Pacific Ocean.
Availability: Schools, libraries, homeschoolers, and nursing homes in Arizona and California (zipcodes beginning 900-931 and 935).
Suggested Grade: 4-12
Order Number: 225
Production Date: 1993
Format: VHS videotape
Terms: Borrower pays postage both ways; you may call the number below to learn how much postage costs. Return within two weeks of date borrowed. An individual may borrow 2 items at one time. For non-profit and educational use only.
Source: Consulate General of Japan, Los Angeles
350 South Grand Avenue, Suite 1700
Los Angeles, CA 90071-3459
Phone: 1-213-617-6700
Fax: 1-213-617-6727
World Wide Web URL: http://www.la.us.emb-japan.go.jp

Little Duck Tale, A
The drama of a spotbill duck family and their survival is filmed in the heart of Tokyo. A unique documentary on animal behavior.
Availability: Schools, libraries, homeschoolers, and nursing homes in Connecticut (except Fairfield County), Maine, Massachusetts, New Hampshire, Rhode Island, and Vermont.
Suggested Grade: All ages
Order Number: 438
Production Date: 1990
Format: VHS videotape
Terms: Borrower pays return postage, including insurance. Return two weeks after receipt.
Source: Consulate General of Japan, Boston
Federal Reserve Plaza, 14th Floor
600 Atlantic Avenue
Boston, MA 02210
Phone: 1-617-973-9772
Fax: 1-617-542-1329
World Wide Web URL:
http://www.boston.us.emb-japan.go.jp
Email Address: infocul@cgjbos.org

Little Duck Tale, A
The drama of a spotbill duck family and their survival is filmed in the heart of Tokyo. A unique documentary on animal behavior.
Availability: Schools, libraries, and nursing homes in Hawaii.
Suggested Grade: All ages
Order Number: NA-10

SCIENCE--NATURE STUDY

Production Date: 1990
Format: VHS videotape
Terms: Borrower pays return postage. A maximum of 3 videos may be borrowed per person. Return within one week of date borrowed.
Source: Consulate General of Japan, Honolulu
1742 Nuuanu Avenue
Honolulu, HI 96817-3294
Phone: 1-808-543-3111
Fax: 1-808-543-3170
World Wide Web URL:
http://www.honolulu.us.emb-japan.go.jp

Little Duck Tale, A
The drama of a spotbill duck family and their survival is filmed in the heart of Tokyo. A unique documentary on animal behavior.
Availability: Schools, libraries, homeschoolers, and nursing homes in Arizona and California (zipcodes beginning 900-931 and 935).
Suggested Grade: All ages
Order Number: 155
Production Date: 1990
Format: VHS videotape
Terms: Borrower pays postage both ways; you may call the number below to learn how much postage costs. Return within two weeks of date borrowed. An individual may borrow 2 items at one time. For non-profit and educational use only.
Source: Consulate General of Japan, Los Angeles
350 South Grand Avenue, Suite 1700
Los Angeles, CA 90071-3459
Phone: 1-213-617-6700
Fax: 1-213-617-6727
World Wide Web URL: http://www.la.us.emb-japan.go.jp

Lizard Kings
Meet the monitors, the largest, fiercest and craftiest lizards on Earth.
Availability: All requesters
Suggested Grade: 7-Adult
Order Number: not applicable
Production Date: 2009
Format: Streaming Video
Source: NOVA
World Wide Web URL:
http://www.pbs.org/wgbh/nova/programs/index.html

Rain Forest
Journey to the dense rain forests of Costa Rica and watch as leaf-cutting ants carry sections of leaves many times their weight to underground fungus gardens.
Availability: Schools in the United States.
Suggested Grade: All ages
Order Number: order by title
Production Date: 1983
Format: VHS videotape
Terms: Borrower pays return postage. Return 14 days after receipt, via USPS including insurance. All borrowers must have a current lending agreement on file with the Outreach program. This agreement is available via the web site or may be requested via phone or fax.
Source: Center for Latin American Studies
University of Florida
319 Grinter Hall
P. O. Box 115530
Gainesville, FL 32611-5530
Phone: 1-352-392-0375
Fax: 1-352-392-7682
World Wide Web URL: http://www.latam.ufl.edu/outreach
Email Address: maryr@ufl.edu

Sables in the Northern Land
The Sarobetsu Moor in northern Hokkaido is featured in this video--it is the habitat of the sable. This video documents these animals in Japan.
Availability: Schools, libraries and homeschoolers in Alabama, Georgia, North Carolina, South Carolina, and Virginia.
Suggested Grade: 6-12
Order Number: 029
Production Date: 1993
Format: VHS videotape
Terms: Borrower pays return postage. Two tapes may be borrowed at a time. Return within 7 days after receipt. Reservations may be made by filling the application found on the web site.
Source: Consulate General of Japan, Atlanta
Japan Information Center
One Alliance Center
3500 Lenox Road, Suite 1600
Atlanta, GA 30326
Phone: 1-404-365-9240
Fax: 1-404-240-4311
World Wide Web URL:
http://www.atlanta.us.emb-japan.go.jp
Email Address: info@cgjapanatlanta.org

Sables in the Northern Land
The Sarobetsu Moor in northern Hokkaido is featured in this video--it is the habitat of the sable. This video documents these animals in Japan.
Availability: Schools, libraries, homeschoolers, and nursing homes in Connecticut (except Fairfield County), Maine, Massachusetts, New Hampshire, Rhode Island, and Vermont.
Suggested Grade: 6-12
Order Number: 547
Production Date: 1993
Format: VHS videotape
Terms: Borrower pays return postage, including insurance. Return two weeks after receipt.
Source: Consulate General of Japan, Boston
Federal Reserve Plaza, 14th Floor
600 Atlantic Avenue
Boston, MA 02210
Phone: 1-617-973-9772
Fax: 1-617-542-1329

All materials listed in this 2018-2019 edition are BRAND NEW!

SCIENCE--NATURE STUDY

World Wide Web URL:
http://www.boston.us.emb-japan.go.jp
Email Address: infocul@cgjbos.org

Sables in the Northern Land
The Sarobetsu Moor in northern Hokkaido is featured in this video--it is the habitat of the sable. This video documents these animals in Japan.
Availability: Schools, libraries, and nursing homes in Hawaii.
Suggested Grade: 6-12
Order Number: NA-20
Production Date: 1993
Format: VHS videotape
Terms: Borrower pays return postage. A maximum of 3 videos may be borrowed per person. Return within one week of date borrowed.
Source: Consulate General of Japan, Honolulu
1742 Nuuanu Avenue
Honolulu, HI 96817-3294
Phone: 1-808-543-3111
Fax: 1-808-543-3170
World Wide Web URL:
http://www.honolulu.us.emb-japan.go.jp

Sables in the Northern Land
The Sarobetsu Moor in northern Hokkaido is featured in this video--it is the habitat of the sable. This video documents these animals in Japan.
Availability: Schools, libraries, homeschoolers, and nursing homes in Arizona and California (zipcodes beginning 900-931 and 935).
Suggested Grade: 6-12
Order Number: 223
Production Date: 1993
Format: VHS videotape
Terms: Borrower pays postage both ways; you may call the number below to learn how much postage costs. Return within two weeks of date borrowed. An individual may borrow 2 items at one time. For non-profit and educational use only.
Source: Consulate General of Japan, Los Angeles
350 South Grand Avenue, Suite 1700
Los Angeles, CA 90071-3459
Phone: 1-213-617-6700
Fax: 1-213-617-6727
World Wide Web URL: http://www.la.us.emb-japan.go.jp

Saving Inky
A documentary about Inky, a pygmy sperm whale who became ill when she ate plastic debris. The malnourishment caused her to beach herself in New Jersey. She was transported to the National Aquarium in Baltimore, rehabilitated, and set free.
Availability: Schools, libraries, and homeschoolers in Connecticut, Maine, Massachusetts, New Hampshire, Rhode Island, and Vermont.
Suggested Grade: 7-12
Order Number: VID 159
Production Date: 1984
Format: VHS videotape
Terms: Borrower pays return postage. Return within three weeks of receipt. If the tape you request is available, it will be mailed within 5 business days. If not, you will be notified that this video is already out on loan. No more than three titles may be borrowed by one requestor at a time. No reservations for a specific date will be accepted. It is most efficient to order via the web site.
Source: U. S. Environmental Protection Agency, Region 1
Customer Service Center
One Congress Street, Suite 1100
Boston, MA 02214
World Wide Web URL:
http://yosemite.epa.gov/r1/videolen.nsf/

Sea Turtles' Last Dance
Documents what little is known about the extraordinary Kemp's Ridley sea turtles who have been swimming the world's oceans since the time of the dinosaur. Rare archival footage shows 40,000 turtles nesting on the beaches of Mexico in 1947 in contrast to the few currently remaining.
Availability: Schools in the United States.
Suggested Grade: 9-Adult
Order Number: order by title
Production Date: 1988
Format: VHS videotape
Terms: Borrower pays return postage. Return 14 days after receipt, via USPS including insurance. All borrowers must have a current lending agreement on file with the Outreach program. This agreement is available via the web site or may be requested via phone or fax.
Source: Center for Latin American Studies
University of Florida
319 Grinter Hall
P. O. Box 115530
Gainesville, FL 32611-5530
Phone: 1-352-392-0375
Fax: 1-352-392-7682
World Wide Web URL: http://www.latam.ufl.edu/outreach
Email Address: maryr@ufl.edu

Vertebrates
A brief introduction to this classification of animals.
Availability: Schools, libraries, and homeschoolers in the United States who serve the hearing impaired.
Suggested Grade: 6-9
Order Number: 13431
Production Date: 1997
Format: DVD
Special Notes: Also available as live streaming video over the Internet.

SCIENCE--NATURE STUDY

Terms: Sponsor pays all transportation costs. Return one week after receipt. Participation is limited to deaf or hard of hearing Americans, their parents, families, teachers, counselors, or others whose use would benefit a deaf or hard of hearing person. Only one person in the audience needs to be hearing impaired. You must register--which is free. These videos are all open-captioned--no special equipment is required for viewing.

**Source: Described and Captioned Media Program
National Association of the Deaf
4211 Church Street Ext.
Roebuck, SC 29376
Phone: 1-800-237-6213
Fax: 1-800-538-5636
World Wide Web URL: http://www.dcmp.org**

Wild Birds of Taiwan
Located in the northwest Pacific, in tropical and subtropical zones, Taiwan is a common stopping-off point for migrating birds, and home to 400 species of birds, 14 endemic species found nowhere else. Chinese bulbuls like people and follow them from the lowlands to the highlands. Features splendid photography.

Availability: Schools, libraries, and nursing homes in the United States and Canada.
Suggested Grade: All ages
Order Number: TV013
Format: VHS videotape
Terms: Borrower pays return postage. Return with 14 days after scheduled showing, via UPS or U. S. Mail. All requests must included an educational institution affiliation, a current address, and phone number. Order through web site only.

**Source: Cornell University East Asia Program
World Wide Web URL:
http://eap.einaudi.cornell.edu/lending_library
Email Address: east_asia1@cornell.edu**

SOCIAL STUDIES--GEOGRAPHY--US

Adventure in Glen Canyon
On the Utah and Arizona border lies Glen Canyon, Lake Powell. Until 1950, Glen Canyon was largely unknown before the construction of Glen Canyon Dam. This is the story of the building of the Glen Canyon Dam.
- Availability: Schools, libraries, homeschoolers, nursing homes, and others in the United States and Canada.
- Suggested Grade: 4-12
- Order Number: order by title
- Format: VHS videotape
- Special Notes: May be copied for permanent retention. Cleared for TV broadcast with advance permission.
- Terms: Borrowers pay return postage. <u>Return 30 days after scheduled showing</u>, via U.S. Mail. Book 30 days in advance. Up to 2 videos will be sent out to one customer at a time. Your next order will be mailed as soon as you return previously borrowed tapes.

Source: **Bureau of Reclamation**
U.S. Department of the Interior
Attn: Kristi Thompson, Library, 84-21320
6th Avenue & Kipling Street, Building 67
Denver, CO 80225-0007
Phone: 1-303-445-2039
Fax: 1-303-445-6303
World Wide Web URL: http://www.usbr.gov/library
Email Address: library@do.usbr.gov

Arts of the Eskimo, The: An Arctic Adventure
Presents examples of Eskimo housing, clothing materials, amulets, and much more. Gives insight into Eskimo culture and religion.
- Availability: Schools, libraries, and homeschoolers in the United States who serve the hearing impaired.
- Suggested Grade: 5-13
- Order Number: 12887
- Production Date: 1995
- Format: DVD
- Special Notes: Also available as live streaming video over the Internet.
- Terms: Sponsor pays all transportation costs. Return one week after receipt. Participation is limited to deaf or hard of hearing Americans, their parents, families, teachers, counselors, or others whose use would benefit a deaf or hard of hearing person. Only one person in the audience needs to be hearing impaired. You must register--which is free. These videos are all open-captioned--no special equipment is required for viewing.

Source: **Described and Captioned Media Program**
National Association of the Deaf
4211 Church Street Ext.
Roebuck, SC 29376
Phone: 1-800-237-6213
Fax: 1-800-538-5636
World Wide Web URL: http://www.dcmp.org

Birth of Oroville Dam, The
Oroville Dam is the tallest dam in the United States. This video shows historic highlights of the dam's construction from ground breaking through its dedication by Ronald Reagan.
- Availability: Schools, libraries, homeschoolers, and nursing homes in the United States.
- Suggested Grade: 6-Adult
- Order Number: order by title
- Format: DVD
- Special Notes: A number of titles from this organization are included on this DVD.
- Terms: Borrower pays return postage. Return within 14 days after scheduled use, via UPS or Federal Express. Book at least 14 days in advance and include alternate date. Requests should include title(s), format, name of responsible person, organizational affiliation, phone, and complete delivery address. No part of any program can be used or duplicated without prior written permission. All programs are available for purchase at a nominal fee. May be available in other formats; inquire if interested. Online video previews are available.

Source: **California Department of Water Resources**
Attn: Video Library, Room 204-22
P. O. Box 942836
Sacramento, CA 94236-0001
Phone: 1-916-653-4893
Fax: 1-916-653-3310
World Wide Web URL: http://www.water.ca.gov/
Email Address: www.publicawillm@water.ca.gov

Build-Up on the Bighorn
Tells the history and the story of the construction of Yellowtail Dam in southeastern Montana.
- Availability: Schools, libraries, homeschoolers, nursing homes, and others in the United States and Canada.
- Suggested Grade: 6-12
- Order Number: order by title
- Format: VHS videotape
- Special Notes: May be copied for permanent retention. Cleared for TV broadcast with advance permission.
- Terms: Borrowers pay return postage. <u>Return 30 days after scheduled showing</u>, via U.S. Mail. Book 30 days in advance. Up to 2 videos will be sent out to one customer at a time. Your next order will be mailed as soon as you return previously borrowed tapes.

Source: **Bureau of Reclamation**
U.S. Department of the Interior
Attn: Kristi Thompson, Library, 84-21320
6th Avenue & Kipling Street, Building 67
Denver, CO 80225-0007
Phone: 1-303-445-2039
Fax: 1-303-445-6303
World Wide Web URL: http://www.usbr.gov/library
Email Address: library@do.usbr.gov

California Flooding
This documents the flooding situation that occurred in

*All materials listed in this 2018-2019 edition are **BRAND NEW!***

SOCIAL STUDIES--GEOGRAPHY--US

California during the late winter/early spring of 1986.
- Availability: Schools, libraries, homeschoolers, nursing homes, and others in the United States and Canada.
- Suggested Grade: 6-12
- Order Number: order by title
- Production Date: 1986
- Format: VHS videotape
- Special Notes: May be copied for permanent retention. Cleared for TV broadcast with advance permission.
- Terms: Borrowers pay return postage. <u>Return 30 days after scheduled showing</u>, via U.S. Mail. Book 30 days in advance. Up to 2 videos will be sent out to one customer at a time. Your next order will be mailed as soon as you return previously borrowed tapes.

Source: Bureau of Reclamation
U.S. Department of the Interior
Attn: Kristi Thompson, Library, 84-21320
6th Avenue & Kipling Street, Building 67
Denver, CO 80225-0007
Phone: 1-303-445-2039
Fax: 1-303-445-6303
World Wide Web URL: http://www.usbr.gov/library
Email Address: library@do.usbr.gov

California's Heritage: The Missions

Provides an overview of the 21 missions which represent a Spanish and Native American cross-cultural heritage.
- Availability: Schools, libraries, and homeschoolers in the United States who serve the hearing impaired.
- Suggested Grade: 7-Adult
- Order Number: 24063
- Production Date: 1999
- Format: DVD
- Special Notes: Also available as live streaming video over the Internet.
- Terms: Sponsor pays all transportation costs. Return one week after receipt. Participation is limited to deaf or hard of hearing Americans, their parents, families, teachers, counselors, or others whose use would benefit a deaf or hard of hearing person. Only one person in the audience needs to be hearing impaired. You must register--which is free. These videos are all open-captioned--no special equipment is required for viewing.

Source: Described and Captioned Media Program
National Association of the Deaf
4211 Church Street Ext.
Roebuck, SC 29376
Phone: 1-800-237-6213
Fax: 1-800-538-5636
World Wide Web URL: http://www.dcmp.org

California's State Water Project: Meeting the Challenge

California has one of the most sophisticated water delivery systems in the world, the State Water Project (SWP). This program presents a concise overview of the SWP including its history, location and operation.
- Availability: Schools, libraries, homeschoolers, and nursing homes in the United States.
- Suggested Grade: 6-Adult
- Order Number: order by title
- Production Date: 1997
- Format: VHS videotape
- Special Notes: Closed captioned.
- Terms: Borrower pays return postage. Return within 14 days after scheduled use, via UPS or Federal Express. Book at least 14 days in advance and include alternate date. Requests should include title(s), format, name of responsible person, organizational affiliation, phone, and complete delivery address. No part of any program can be used or duplicated without prior written permission. All programs are available for purchase at a nominal fee. May be available in other formats; inquire if interested. Online video previews are available.

Source: California Department of Water Resources
Attn: Video Library, Room 204-22
P. O. Box 942836
Sacramento, CA 94236-0001
Phone: 1-916-653-4893
Fax: 1-916-653-3310
World Wide Web URL: http://www.water.ca.gov/
Email Address: www.publicawillm@water.ca.gov

California Water Story, The

Over 200 years ago Native Americans and mission fathers created California's earliest irrigation systems. Today, vast engineering projects provide water for the state. This history of our water development is also the story of California's most important and sought after resource.
- Availability: Schools, libraries, homeschoolers, and nursing homes in the United States.
- Suggested Grade: 9-Adult
- Order Number: order by title
- Format: DVD
- Special Notes: A number of titles from this organization are included on this DVD.
- Terms: Borrower pays return postage. Return within 14 days after scheduled use, via UPS or Federal Express. Book at least 14 days in advance and include alternate date. Requests should include title(s), format, name of responsible person, organizational affiliation, phone, and complete delivery address. No part of any program can be used or duplicated without prior written permission. All programs are available for purchase at a nominal fee. May be available in other formats; inquire if interested. Online video previews are available.

Source: California Department of Water Resources
Attn: Video Library, Room 204-22
P. O. Box 942836
Sacramento, CA 94236-0001
Phone: 1-916-653-4893
Fax: 1-916-653-3310
World Wide Web URL: http://www.water.ca.gov/
Email Address: www.publicawillm@water.ca.gov

All materials listed in this 2018-2019 edition are BRAND NEW!

SOCIAL STUDIES--GEOGRAPHY--US

California Water Story, The
Over 200 years ago Native Americans and mission fathers created California's earliest irrigation systems. Today, vast engineering projects provide water for the state. This history of our water development is also the story of California's most important and sought after resource.
Availability: Schools, libraries, homeschoolers, and nursing homes in the United States.
Suggested Grade: 9-Adult
Order Number: order by title
Format: VHS videotape
Special Notes: Closed captioned.
Terms: Borrower pays return postage. Return within 14 days after scheduled use, via UPS or Federal Express. Book at least 14 days in advance and include alternate date. Requests should include title(s), format, name of responsible person, organizational affiliation, phone, and complete delivery address. No part of any program can be used or duplicated without prior written permission. All programs are available for purchase at a nominal fee. May be available in other formats; inquire if interested. Online video previews are available.
Source: California Department of Water Resources
Attn: Video Library, Room 204-22
P. O. Box 942836
Sacramento, CA 94236-0001
Phone: 1-916-653-4893
Fax: 1-916-653-3310
World Wide Web URL: http://www.water.ca.gov/
Email Address: www.publicawillm@water.ca.gov

Celebrating Hawaii's Cultures
Shows an exhibit from the Smithsonian Institution that depicts Hawaii's culture and history.
Availability: Schools, libraries, and homeschoolers in the United States who serve the hearing impaired.
Suggested Grade: 7-12
Order Number: 24998
Production Date: 1989
Format: DVD
Special Notes: Also available as live streaming video over the Internet.
Terms: Sponsor pays all transportation costs. Return one week after receipt. Participation is limited to deaf or hard of hearing Americans, their parents, families, teachers, counselors, or others whose use would benefit a deaf or hard of hearing person. Only one person in the audience needs to be hearing impaired. You must register--which is free. These videos are all open-captioned--no special equipment is required for viewing.
Source: Described and Captioned Media Program
National Association of the Deaf
4211 Church Street Ext.
Roebuck, SC 29376
Phone: 1-800-237-6213
Fax: 1-800-538-5636
World Wide Web URL: http://www.dcmp.org

Central Arizona Project--Lifeline to the Future
This program explains the history of the entire water project that covers large areas of Arizona and New Mexico. Fly-overs of the entire system are featured.
Availability: Schools, libraries, homeschoolers, nursing homes, and others in the United States and Canada.
Suggested Grade: 6-12
Order Number: order by title
Production Date: 1985
Format: VHS videotape
Special Notes: May be copied for permanent retention. Cleared for TV broadcast with advance permission.
Terms: Borrowers pay return postage. Return 30 days after scheduled showing, via U.S. Mail. Book 30 days in advance. Up to 2 videos will be sent out to one customer at a time. Your next order will be mailed as soon as you return previously borrowed tapes.
Source: Bureau of Reclamation
U.S. Department of the Interior
Attn: Kristi Thompson, Library, 84-21320
6th Avenue & Kipling Street, Building 67
Denver, CO 80225-0007
Phone: 1-303-445-2039
Fax: 1-303-445-6303
World Wide Web URL: http://www.usbr.gov/library
Email Address: library@do.usbr.gov

Central Utah Project
This program tells the history and benefits derived from the Bureau's project located in Utah.
Availability: Schools, libraries, homeschoolers, nursing homes, and others in the United States and Canada.
Suggested Grade: 6-12
Order Number: order by title
Format: VHS videotape
Special Notes: May be copied for permanent retention. Cleared for TV broadcast with advance permission.
Terms: Borrowers pay return postage. Return 30 days after scheduled showing, via U.S. Mail. Book 30 days in advance. Up to 2 videos will be sent out to one customer at a time. Your next order will be mailed as soon as you return previously borrowed tapes.
Source: Bureau of Reclamation
U.S. Department of the Interior
Attn: Kristi Thompson, Library, 84-21320
6th Avenue & Kipling Street, Building 67
Denver, CO 80225-0007
Phone: 1-303-445-2039
Fax: 1-303-445-6303
World Wide Web URL: http://www.usbr.gov/library
Email Address: library@do.usbr.gov

Drought Survival in California
This program shows how California survived the worst drought of the country by coordinating the efforts of all

SOCIAL STUDIES--GEOGRAPHY--US

parties involved.
Availability: Schools, libraries, homeschoolers, and nursing homes in the United States.
Suggested Grade: 6-12
English; Spanish in VHS only
Order Number: order by title
Format: DVD
Special Notes: A number of titles from this organization are included on this DVD.
Terms: Borrower pays return postage. Return within 14 days after scheduled use, via UPS or Federal Express. Book at least 14 days in advance and include alternate date. Requests should include title(s), format, name of responsible person, organizational affiliation, phone, and complete delivery address. No part of any program can be used or duplicated without prior written permission. All programs are available for purchase at a nominal fee. May be available in other formats; inquire if interested. Online video previews are available.
Source: California Department of Water Resources
Attn: Video Library, Room 204-22
P. O. Box 942836
Sacramento, CA 94236-0001
Phone: 1-916-653-4893
Fax: 1-916-653-3310
World Wide Web URL: http://www.water.ca.gov/
Email Address: www.publicawillm@water.ca.gov

Garcia Family, The: Puerto Rican Story
Story of three generations of a Puerto Rican family after moving to the U. S. mainland.
Availability: Schools, libraries, and nursing homes in the United States.
Suggested Grade: 6-12
Order Number: HISP43-video
Production Date: 1990
Format: VHS videotape
Terms: Borrowers must have a User's Agreement on file with this source--available by mail or via the Internet. Return postage is paid by borrower; return 12 days after showing. Book at least three weeks in advance. All borrowers are limited to a total of ten items per semester.
Source: Latin American Resource Center
Stone Center for Latin American Studies
Tulane University
100 Jones Hall
New Orleans, LA 70118
Phone: 1-504-862-3143
Fax: 1-504-865-6719
World Wide Web URL: http://stonecenter.tulane.edu/pages/detail/48/Lending-Library
Email Address: crcrts@tulane.edu

Good Place to Call Home, A: Maine Towns Creating Their Future
A documentary looking at Maine towns dealing with the threat to their natural resources and life style brought by unplanned development.

Availability: Schools, libraries, and homeschoolers in Connecticut, Maine, Massachusetts, New Hampshire, Rhode Island, and Vermont.
Suggested Grade: 9-Adult
Order Number: VID 268
Production Date: 1991
Format: VHS videotape
Terms: Borrower pays return postage. Return within three weeks of receipt. If the tape you request is available, it will be mailed within 5 business days. If not, you will be notified that this video is already out on loan. No more than three titles may be borrowed by one requestor at a time. No reservations for a specific date will be accepted. It is most efficient to order via the web site.
Source: U. S. Environmental Protection Agency, Region 1
Customer Service Center
One Congress Street, Suite 1100
Boston, MA 02214
World Wide Web URL: http://yosemite.epa.gov/r1/videolen.nsf/

High Water: The Record Floods of February 1986
This program chronicles the development of the huge storm of 1986 that caused levee breaks, extensive flooding and the evacuation of over 30,000 people in California. The Department of Water Resources' Division of Flood Management is shown mobilizing personnel and equipment to meet a flood emergency.
Availability: Schools, libraries, homeschoolers, and nursing homes in the United States.
Suggested Grade: 9-Adult
Order Number: order by title
Format: VHS videotape
Terms: Borrower pays return postage. Return within 14 days after scheduled use, via UPS or Federal Express. Book at least 14 days in advance and include alternate date. Requests should include title(s), format, name of responsible person, organizational affiliation, phone, and complete delivery address. No part of any program can be used or duplicated without prior written permission. All programs are available for purchase at a nominal fee. May be available in other formats; inquire if interested. Online video previews are available.
Source: California Department of Water Resources
Attn: Video Library, Room 204-22
P. O. Box 942836
Sacramento, CA 94236-0001
Phone: 1-916-653-4893
Fax: 1-916-653-3310
World Wide Web URL: http://www.water.ca.gov/
Email Address: www.publicawillm@water.ca.gov

History and Culture of Puerto Rico
Promotes an appreciation of the rich history and cultural traditions of Puerto Rico.
Availability: Schools in the United States.
Suggested Grade: 6-12
lANGUAGES: English; Spanish

All materials listed in this 2018-2019 edition are BRAND NEW!

SOCIAL STUDIES--GEOGRAPHY--US

Order Number: order by title
Production Date: 1989
Format: VHS videotape
Terms: Borrower pays return postage. Return 14 days after receipt, via USPS including insurance. All borrowers must have a current lending agreement on file with the Outreach program. This agreement is available via the web site or may be requested via phone or fax.

Source: Center for Latin American Studies
University of Florida
319 Grinter Hall
P. O. Box 115530
Gainesville, FL 32611-5530
Phone: 1-352-392-0375
Fax: 1-352-392-7682
World Wide Web URL: http://www.latam.ufl.edu/outreach
Email Address: maryr@ufl.edu

Hydropower

This video describes the Bureau of Reclamation's hydropower facilities.

Availability: Schools, libraries, homeschoolers, nursing homes, and others in the United States and Canada.
Suggested Grade: 6-12
Order Number: order by title
Format: VHS videotape
Special Notes: May be copied for permanent retention. Cleared for TV broadcast with advance permission.
Terms: Borrowers pay return postage. Return 30 days after scheduled showing, via U.S. Mail. Book 30 days in advance. Up to 2 videos will be sent out to one customer at a time. Your next order will be mailed as soon as you return previously borrowed tapes.

Source: Bureau of Reclamation
U.S. Department of the Interior
Attn: Kristi Thompson, Library, 84-21320
6th Avenue & Kipling Street, Building 67
Denver, CO 80225-0007
Phone: 1-303-445-2039
Fax: 1-303-445-6303
World Wide Web URL: http://www.usbr.gov/library
Email Address: library@do.usbr.gov

Journey Into Tradition

Traces the twelve-day journey of thirteen Penobscot Indians from Maine as they retraced a portion of the inland migratory routes of the Native People and a cultural exchange of Indians separated by 3,000 miles but with common interests and problems.

Availability: Schools, libraries, and homeschoolers in Connecticut, Maine, Massachusetts, New Hampshire, Rhode Island, and Vermont.
Suggested Grade: 7-Adult
Order Number: VID 402
Production Date: 1993
Format: VHS videotape
Terms: Borrower pays return postage. Return within three weeks of receipt. If the tape you request is available, it will be mailed within 5 business days. If not, you will be notified that this video is already out on loan. No more than three titles may be borrowed by one requestor at a time. No reservations for a specific date will be accepted. It is most efficient to order via the web site.

Source: U. S. Environmental Protection Agency, Region 1
Customer Service Center
One Congress Street, Suite 1100
Boston, MA 02214
World Wide Web URL:
http://yosemite.epa.gov/r1/videolen.nsf/

Lake Powell--Jewel of the Colorado

This program describes the historical background for building Glen Canyon Dam, Arizona. It takes you on a hike to see the beautiful scenery and on a boat ride to show you the recreational opportunities that were created with Lake Powell. It takes you into the dam, and you see Glen Canyon Dam in operation.

Availability: Schools, libraries, homeschoolers, nursing homes, and others in the United States and Canada.
Suggested Grade: 4-12
Order Number: order by title
Format: VHS videotape
Special Notes: May be copied for permanent retention. Cleared for TV broadcast with advance permission.
Terms: Borrowers pay return postage. Return 30 days after scheduled showing, via U.S. Mail. Book 30 days in advance. Up to 2 videos will be sent out to one customer at a time. Your next order will be mailed as soon as you return previously borrowed tapes.

Source: Bureau of Reclamation
U.S. Department of the Interior
Attn: Kristi Thompson, Library, 84-21320
6th Avenue & Kipling Street, Building 67
Denver, CO 80225-0007
Phone: 1-303-445-2039
Fax: 1-303-445-6303
World Wide Web URL: http://www.usbr.gov/library
Email Address: library@do.usbr.gov

Living Waters of the Colorado

This program starts the viewer in Colorado's San Juan Mountains, and takes you down the Colorado River. It provides an overview of the Colorado River Storage Project for Arizona, Colorado, New Mexico, Utah, and Wyoming.

Availability: Schools, libraries, homeschoolers, nursing homes, and others in the United States and Canada.
Suggested Grade: 6-12
Order Number: order by title
Format: VHS videotape
Special Notes: May be copied for permanent retention. Cleared for TV broadcast with advance permission.

All materials listed in this 2018-2019 edition are BRAND NEW!

SOCIAL STUDIES--GEOGRAPHY--US

Terms: Borrowers pay return postage. <u>Return 30 days after scheduled showing</u>, via U.S. Mail. Book 30 days in advance. Up to 2 videos will be sent out to one customer at a time. Your next order will be mailed as soon as you return previously borrowed tapes.
    Source: Bureau of Reclamation
    U.S. Department of the Interior
    Attn: Kristi Thompson, Library, 84-21320
    6th Avenue & Kipling Street, Building 67
    Denver, CO 80225-0007
    Phone: 1-303-445-2039
    Fax: 1-303-445-6303
    World Wide Web URL: http://www.usbr.gov/library
    Email Address: library@do.usbr.gov

Louisiana Wetlands: America's Coastal Crisis
Explains the problems of wetland losses in Louisiana and the steps that the state, citizens, and the EPA have undertaken to protect and restore them.
Availability: Schools, libraries, and homeschoolers in Connecticut, Maine, Massachusetts, New Hampshire, Rhode Island, and Vermont.
Suggested Grade: 9-12
Order Number: VID 232
Format: VHS videotape
Terms: Borrower pays return postage. Return within three weeks of receipt. If the tape you request is available, it will be mailed within 5 business days. If not, you will be notified that this video is already out on loan. No more than three titles may be borrowed by one requestor at a time. No reservations for a specific date will be accepted. It is most efficient to order via the web site.
Source: U. S. Environmental Protection Agency, Region 1
    Customer Service Center
    One Congress Street, Suite 1100
    Boston, MA 02214
    World Wide Web URL:
    http://yosemite.epa.gov/r1/videolen.nsf/

Miracle of Water
This video tells about the heritage of the Bureau, and explains the evolving and changing program that is required for a well-watered prosperous land. This program also shows why the Bureau built multi-purpose projects such as Central Valley Project in California.
Availability: Schools, libraries, homeschoolers, nursing homes, and others in the United States and Canada.
Suggested Grade: 5-Adult
Order Number: order by title
Format: VHS videotape
Special Notes: May be copied for permanent retention. Cleared for TV broadcast with advance permission.
Terms: Borrowers pay return postage. <u>Return 30 days after scheduled showing</u>, via U.S. Mail. Book 30 days in advance. Up to 2 videos will be sent out to one customer at a time. Your next order will be mailed as soon as you return previously borrowed tapes.

Source: Bureau of Reclamation
    U.S. Department of the Interior
    Attn: Kristi Thompson, Library, 84-21320
    6th Avenue & Kipling Street, Building 67
    Denver, CO 80225-0007
    Phone: 1-303-445-2039
    Fax: 1-303-445-6303
    World Wide Web URL: http://www.usbr.gov/library
    Email Address: library@do.usbr.gov

Mountain Skywater
The Story of the Colorado River Basin Pilot Project in the San Juan Mountains, Colorado, is presented in this program. An overview of the cloud seeding program is included.
Availability: Schools, libraries, homeschoolers, nursing homes, and others in the United States and Canada.
Suggested Grade: 5-Adult
Order Number: order by title
Format: VHS videotape
Special Notes: May be copied for permanent retention. Cleared for TV broadcast with advance permission.
Terms: Borrowers pay return postage. <u>Return 30 days after scheduled showing</u>, via U.S. Mail. Book 30 days in advance. Up to 2 videos will be sent out to one customer at a time. Your next order will be mailed as soon as you return previously borrowed tapes.
    Source: Bureau of Reclamation
    U.S. Department of the Interior
    Attn: Kristi Thompson, Library, 84-21320
    6th Avenue & Kipling Street, Building 67
    Denver, CO 80225-0007
    Phone: 1-303-445-2039
    Fax: 1-303-445-6303
    World Wide Web URL: http://www.usbr.gov/library
    Email Address: library@do.usbr.gov

Operation Glen Canyon
On the Colorado River you will see the first blast, the building of the world's highest steel bridge, and the construction of Glen Canyon Dam. The magnificent beauty of Glen Canyon is the backdrop for an achievement that serves a large community.
Availability: Schools, libraries, homeschoolers, nursing homes, and others in the United States and Canada.
Suggested Grade: All ages
Order Number: order by title
Format: VHS videotape
Special Notes: May be copied for permanent retention. Cleared for TV broadcast with advance permission.
Terms: Borrowers pay return postage. <u>Return 30 days after scheduled showing</u>, via U.S. Mail. Book 30 days in advance. Up to 2 videos will be sent out to one customer at a time. Your next order will be mailed as soon as you return previously borrowed tapes.

*All materials listed in this 2018-2019 edition are **BRAND NEW**!*

SOCIAL STUDIES--GEOGRAPHY--US

Source: Bureau of Reclamation
U.S. Department of the Interior
Attn: Kristi Thompson, Library, 84-21320
6th Avenue & Kipling Street, Building 67
Denver, CO 80225-0007
Phone: 1-303-445-2039
Fax: 1-303-445-6303
World Wide Web URL: http://www.usbr.gov/library
Email Address: library@do.usbr.gov

People of the Caribbean
Describes the heritage of United States immigrants with origins in the Caribbean.
Availability: Schools in the United States.
Suggested Grade: 6-12
English; Spanish
Order Number: order by title
Production Date: 1995
Format: VHS videotape
Terms: Borrower pays return postage. Return 14 days after receipt, via USPS including insurance. All borrowers must have a current lending agreement on file with the Outreach program. This agreement is available via the web site or may be requested via phone or fax.

Source: Center for Latin American Studies
University of Florida
319 Grinter Hall
P. O. Box 115530
Gainesville, FL 32611-5530
Phone: 1-352-392-0375
Fax: 1-352-392-7682
World Wide Web URL: http://www.latam.ufl.edu/outreach
Email Address: maryr@ufl.edu

Pipeline
After decades of anticipation, the arid central coast of California was finally connected to the State Water Project by the Coastal Branch, a one-hundred and forty-four mile pipeline. This dynamic program shows how and why this enormous task was completed.
Availability: Schools, libraries, homeschoolers, and nursing homes in the United States.
Suggested Grade: 9-12
Order Number: order by title
Production Date: 1997
Format: DVD
Special Notes: A number of titles from this organization are included on this DVD.
Terms: Borrower pays return postage. Return within 14 days after scheduled use, via UPS or Federal Express. Book at least 14 days in advance and include alternate date. Requests should include title(s), format, name of responsible person, organizational affiliation, phone, and complete delivery address. No part of any program can be used or duplicated without prior written permission. All programs are available for purchase at a nominal fee. May be available in other formats; inquire if interested. Online video previews are available.

Source: California Department of Water Resources
Attn: Video Library, Room 204-22
P. O. Box 942836
Sacramento, CA 94236-0001
Phone: 1-916-653-4893
Fax: 1-916-653-3310
World Wide Web URL: http://www.water.ca.gov/
Email Address: www.publicawillm@water.ca.gov

Pipeline
After decades of anticipation, the arid central coast of California was finally connected to the State Water Project by the Coastal Branch, a one-hundred and forty-four mile pipeline. This dynamic program shows how and why this enormous task was completed.
Availability: Schools, libraries, homeschoolers, and nursing homes in the United States.
Suggested Grade: 9-12
Order Number: order by title
Production Date: 1997
Format: VHS videotape
Terms: Borrower pays return postage. Return within 14 days after scheduled use, via UPS or Federal Express. Book at least 14 days in advance and include alternate date. Requests should include title(s), format, name of responsible person, organizational affiliation, phone, and complete delivery address. No part of any program can be used or duplicated without prior written permission. All programs are available for purchase at a nominal fee. May be available in other formats; inquire if interested. Online video previews are available.

Source: California Department of Water Resources
Attn: Video Library, Room 204-22
P. O. Box 942836
Sacramento, CA 94236-0001
Phone: 1-916-653-4893
Fax: 1-916-653-3310
World Wide Web URL: http://www.water.ca.gov/
Email Address: www.publicawillm@water.ca.gov

Place of the Falling Waters, The
A documentary history of the construction of a large hydro dam on Flathead Indian Reservation. Focuses more on the effects of the construction on Native culture than on the benefits of the dam itself.
Availability: Schools, libraries, and homeschoolers in Connecticut, Maine, Massachusetts, New Hampshire, Rhode Island, and Vermont.
Suggested Grade: 9-Adult
Order Number: VID 382
Format: VHS videotape
Terms: Borrower pays return postage. Return within three weeks of receipt. If the tape you request is available, it will be mailed within 5 business days. If not, you will be notified that this video is already out on loan. No more than three titles may be borrowed by one requestor at a time. No reservations for a specific date will be accepted. It is most efficient to order via the web site.

*All materials listed in this 2018-2019 edition are **BRAND NEW!***

SOCIAL STUDIES--GEOGRAPHY--US

Source: U. S. Environmental Protection Agency, Region 1
Customer Service Center
One Congress Street, Suite 1100
Boston, MA 02214
World Wide Web URL:
http://yosemite.epa.gov/r1/videolen.nsf/

Powering One Corner of the World
Shows the Grand Coulee Dam on the Columbia River and the many benefits it has brought to the west coast.
- Availability: Schools, libraries, homeschoolers, nursing homes, and others in the United States and Canada.
- Suggested Grade: 6-12
- Order Number: order by title
- Production Date: 1987
- Format: VHS videotape
- Special Notes: May be copied for permanent retention. Cleared for TV broadcast with advance permission.
- Terms: Borrowers pay return postage. Return 30 days after scheduled showing, via U.S. Mail. Book 30 days in advance. Up to 2 videos will be sent out to one customer at a time. Your next order will be mailed as soon as you return previously borrowed tapes.

Source: Bureau of Reclamation
U.S. Department of the Interior
Attn: Kristi Thompson, Library, 84-21320
6th Avenue & Kipling Street, Building 67
Denver, CO 80225-0007
Phone: 1-303-445-2039
Fax: 1-303-445-6303
World Wide Web URL: http://www.usbr.gov/library
Email Address: library@do.usbr.gov

Reversing the Tide
Details how and why Louisiana's coastal wetlands are eroding and its impact on the local environment and industry.
- Availability: Schools, libraries, and homeschoolers in Connecticut, Maine, Massachusetts, New Hampshire, Rhode Island, and Vermont.
- Suggested Grade: 9-Adult
- Order Number: VID 280
- Production Date: 1995
- Format: VHS videotape
- Terms: Borrower pays return postage. Return within three weeks of receipt. If the tape you request is available, it will be mailed within 5 business days. If not, you will be notified that this video is already out on loan. No more than three titles may be borrowed by one requestor at a time. No reservations for a specific date will be accepted. It is most efficient to order via the web site.

Source: U. S. Environmental Protection Agency, Region 1
Customer Service Center
One Congress Street, Suite 1100
Boston, MA 02214
World Wide Web URL:
http://yosemite.epa.gov/r1/videolen.nsf/

Rio Grande--Ribbon of Life
This program describes the 1,800 miles of the Rio Grande River system. It includes scenes of the Bureau's work, area farms, cities and scenery.
- Availability: Schools, libraries, homeschoolers, nursing homes, and others in the United States and Canada.
- Suggested Grade: All ages
- Order Number: order by title
- Production Date: 1986
- Format: VHS videotape
- Special Notes: May be copied for permanent retention. Cleared for TV broadcast with advance permission.
- Terms: Borrowers pay return postage. Return 30 days after scheduled showing, via U.S. Mail. Book 30 days in advance. Up to 2 videos will be sent out to one customer at a time. Your next order will be mailed as soon as you return previously borrowed tapes.

Source: Bureau of Reclamation
U.S. Department of the Interior
Attn: Kristi Thompson, Library, 84-21320
6th Avenue & Kipling Street, Building 67
Denver, CO 80225-0007
Phone: 1-303-445-2039
Fax: 1-303-445-6303
World Wide Web URL: http://www.usbr.gov/library
Email Address: library@do.usbr.gov

Snowfall to Sandstone
Presents the history and development of the Colorado River Basin.
- Availability: Schools, libraries, homeschoolers, nursing homes, and others in the United States and Canada.
- Suggested Grade: 4-12
- Order Number: order by title
- Format: VHS videotape
- Special Notes: May be copied for permanent retention. Cleared for TV broadcast with advance permission.
- Terms: Borrowers pay return postage. Return 30 days after scheduled showing, via U.S. Mail. Book 30 days in advance. Up to 2 videos will be sent out to one customer at a time. Your next order will be mailed as soon as you return previously borrowed tapes.

Source: Bureau of Reclamation
U.S. Department of the Interior
Attn: Kristi Thompson, Library, 84-21320
6th Avenue & Kipling Street, Building 67
Denver, CO 80225-0007
Phone: 1-303-445-2039
Fax: 1-303-445-6303
World Wide Web URL: http://www.usbr.gov/library
Email Address: library@do.usbr.gov

Southwest Region
Old photos, maps, graphics and more highlight the history, geography, capital, and more of four states--Arizona, New

SOCIAL STUDIES--GEOGRAPHY--US

Mexico, Oklahoma, and Texas.
- Availability: Schools, libraries, and homeschoolers in the United States who serve the hearing impaired.
- Suggested Grade: 3-9
- Order Number: 13556
- Production Date: 1998
- Format: DVD
- Special Notes: Also available as live streaming video over the Internet.
- Terms: Sponsor pays all transportation costs. Return one week after receipt. Participation is limited to deaf or hard of hearing Americans, their parents, families, teachers, counselors, or others whose use would benefit a deaf or hard of hearing person. Only one person in the audience needs to be hearing impaired. You must register--which is free. These videos are all open-captioned--no special equipment is required for viewing.

Source: Described and Captioned Media Program
National Association of the Deaf
4211 Church Street Ext.
Roebuck, SC 29376
Phone: 1-800-237-6213
Fax: 1-800-538-5636
World Wide Web URL: http://www.dcmp.org

Story of Hoover Dam, The

This program includes actual footage of the construction of Hoover Dam when it was being built in the 1930's.
- Availability: Schools, libraries, homeschoolers, nursing homes, and others in the United States and Canada.
- Suggested Grade: 4-12
- Order Number: order by title
- Format: VHS videotape
- Special Notes: May be copied for permanent retention. Cleared for TV broadcast with advance permission.
- Terms: Borrowers pay return postage. <u>Return 30 days after scheduled showing</u>, via U.S. Mail. Book 30 days in advance. Up to 2 videos will be sent out to one customer at a time. Your next order will be mailed as soon as you return previously borrowed tapes.

Source: Bureau of Reclamation
U.S. Department of the Interior
Attn: Kristi Thompson, Library, 84-21320
6th Avenue & Kipling Street, Building 67
Denver, CO 80225-0007
Phone: 1-303-445-2039
Fax: 1-303-445-6303
World Wide Web URL: http://www.usbr.gov/library
Email Address: library@do.usbr.gov

Sweet 15

The traditional 15th birthday celebration symbolically ushers a young Mexican girl into adulthood. When her father cancels the gala event, she accidentally uncovers her father's secret--he has never become a legal resident of the U. S.
- Availability: Schools and libraries in Iowa, Illinois, Michigan, Minnesota, and Wisconsin.
- Suggested Grade: 6-12
- Order Number: FFUSASW3.1VHS
- Production Date: 1990
- Format: VHS videotape
- Terms: Borrower pays return postage. Return 8 days after showing. Book 2 weeks in advance. Order may also be picked up for those near the Center.

Source: Center for Latin American and Caribbean Studies
UW-Milwaukee
P. O. Box 413
Milwaukee, WI 53201
Phone: 1-414-229-5987
World Wide Web URL: http://www.uwm.edu/Dept/CLACS
Email Address: audvis@usm.edu

Sweet 15

The traditional 15th birthday celebration symbolically ushers a young Mexican girl into adulthood. When her father cancels the gala event, she accidentally uncovers her father's secret--he has never become a legal resident of the U. S.
- Availability: Schools, libraries, and nursing homes in the United States.
- Suggested Grade: 6-12
- Order Number: SIHISP1-video
- Production Date: 1990
- Format: VHS videotape
- Terms: Borrowers must have a User's Agreement on file with this source--available by mail or via the Internet. Return postage is paid by borrower; return 12 days after showing. Book at least three weeks in advance. All borrowers are limited to a total of ten items per semester.

Source: Latin American Resource Center
Stone Center for Latin American Studies
Tulane University, 100 Jones Hall
New Orleans, LA 70118
Phone: 1-504-862-3143
Fax: 1-504-865-6719
World Wide Web URL: http://stonecenter.tulane.edu/pages/detail/48/Lending-Library
Email Address: crcrts@tulane.edu

Teton--Decision and Disaster

The Teton Range of the Rocky Mountains stretches from southeastern Idaho to northwestern Wyoming. It is truly the Grand Tetons. This videotape presentation details the background and reasons for the decision to build, and the disaster of Teton Dam, Idaho.
- Availability: Schools, libraries, homeschoolers, nursing homes, and others in the United States and Canada.
- Suggested Grade: 4-12
- Order Number: order by title
- Format: VHS videotape
- Special Notes: May be copied for permanent retention. Cleared for TV broadcast with advance permission.

*All materials listed in this 2018-2019 edition are **BRAND NEW!***

SOCIAL STUDIES--GEOGRAPHY--US

Terms: Borrowers pay return postage. <u>Return 30 days after scheduled showing</u>, via U.S. Mail. Book 30 days in advance. Up to 2 videos will be sent out to one customer at a time. Your next order will be mailed as soon as you return previously borrowed tapes.

  Source: Bureau of Reclamation
  U.S. Department of the Interior
  Attn: Kristi Thompson, Library, 84-21320
  6th Avenue & Kipling Street, Building 67
  Denver, CO 80225-0007
  Phone: 1-303-445-2039
  Fax: 1-303-445-6303
World Wide Web URL: http://www.usbr.gov/library
  Email Address: library@do.usbr.gov

Ties That Bind: Stories Behind the Immigration Controversy

Explores the human face of the debate of U.S. immigration policy from both sides of the Texas-Mexico border. Looks at why people choose to migrate, the politics of immigration policy, and how immigrants adjust to life in the United States.

Availability: Schools in the United States.
Suggested Grade: 9-Adult
Order Number: order by title
Format: VHS videotape
Terms: Borrower pays return postage. Return 14 days after receipt, via USPS including insurance. All borrowers must have a current lending agreement on file with the Outreach program. This agreement is available via the web site or may be requested via phone or fax.

  Source: Center for Latin American Studies
  University of Florida
  319 Grinter Hall
  P. O. Box 115530
  Gainesville, FL 32611-5530
  Phone: 1-352-392-0375
  Fax: 1-352-392-7682
World Wide Web URL: http://www.latam.ufl.edu/outreach
  Email Address: maryr@ufl.edu

Vermont Wetlands: A Natural Resource

Explains the nature of wetlands and their beneficial aspects, as well as the state and federal rules and regulations enacted to protect and govern Vermont's wetlands.

Availability: Schools, libraries, and homeschoolers in Connecticut, Maine, Massachusetts, New Hampshire, Rhode Island, and Vermont.
Suggested Grade: 7-Adult
Order Number: VID 221
Production Date: 1995
Format: VHS videotape
Terms: Borrower pays return postage. Return within three weeks of receipt. If the tape you request is available, it will be mailed within 5 business days. If not, you will be notified that this video is already out on loan. No more than three titles may be borrowed by one requestor at a time. No reservations for a specific date will be accepted. It is most efficient to order via the web site.

 Source: U. S. Environmental Protection Agency, Region 1
  Customer Service Center
  One Congress Street, Suite 1100
  Boston, MA 02214
  World Wide Web URL:
 http://yosemite.epa.gov/r1/videolen.nsf/

Wings Over Water

Through stunning aerial cinematography this program introduces the largest state-built, multipurpose water project in the United States, the California State Water Project, a system of reservoirs, aqueducts, power and pumping plants spanning two-thirds of California, from the mountainous regions of the Feather River in Northern California, south over the 600 miles to Lake Perris.

Availability: Schools, libraries, homeschoolers, and nursing homes in the United States.
Suggested Grade: 6-Adult
Order Number: order by title
Production Date: 1997
Format: VHS videotape
Terms: Borrower pays return postage. Return within 14 days after scheduled use, via UPS or Federal Express. Book at least 14 days in advance and include alternate date. Requests should include title(s), format, name of responsible person, organizational affiliation, phone, and complete delivery address. No part of any program can be used or duplicated without prior written permission. All programs are available for purchase at a nominal fee. May be available in other formats; inquire if interested. Online video previews are available.

  Source: California Department of Water Resources
  Attn: Video Library, Room 204-22
  P. O. Box 942836
  Sacramento, CA 94236-0001
  Phone: 1-916-653-4893
  Fax: 1-916-653-3310
World Wide Web URL: http://www.water.ca.gov/
Email Address: www.publicawillm@water.ca.gov

All materials listed in this 2018-2019 edition are BRAND NEW!

SOCIAL STUDIES--GEOGRAPHY--WORLD

Ache Moyuba Orisha
Explores the Santeria religion, unique to Cuba.
Availability: Schools, libraries, and nursing homes in the United States.
Suggested Grade: 6-12
Languages: Spanish with English subtitles
Order Number: RCUB3-video
Production Date: 1990
Format: VHS videotape
Terms: Borrowers must have a User's Agreement on file with this source--available by mail or via the Internet. Return postage is paid by borrower; return 12 days after showing. Book at least three weeks in advance. All borrowers are limited to a total of ten items per semester.
Source: Latin American Resource Center
Stone Center for Latin American Studies
Tulane University
100 Jones Hall
New Orleans, LA 70118
Phone: 1-504-862-3143
Fax: 1-504-865-6719
World Wide Web URL: http://stonecenter.tulane.edu/pages/detail/48/Lending-Library
Email Address: crcrts@tulane.edu

Adventure on the Way to the 21st Century
Explores Japan's continual preoccupation with change and newness and points to the origin of this thinking in the traditional culture and religion of the country.
Availability: Schools, libraries, homeschoolers, and nursing homes in Connecticut (except Fairfield County), Maine, Massachusetts, New Hampshire, Rhode Island, and Vermont.
Suggested Grade: 9-Adult
Order Number: 197
Production Date: 1989
Format: VHS videotape
Special Notes: No. 10 in the "Japan: Spirit and Form" series.
Terms: Borrower pays return postage, including insurance. Return two weeks after receipt.
Source: Consulate General of Japan, Boston
Federal Reserve Plaza, 14th Floor
600 Atlantic Avenue
Boston, MA 02210
Phone: 1-617-973-9772
Fax: 1-617-542-1329
World Wide Web URL:
http://www.boston.us.emb-japan.go.jp
Email Address: infocul@cgjbos.org

Adventure on the Way to the 21st Century
Explores Japan's continual preoccupation with change and newness and points to the origin of this thinking in the traditional culture and religion of the country.
Availability: Schools, libraries, and nursing homes in Oklahoma and Texas.
Suggested Grade: 9-Adult
Order Number: E10
Production Date: 1989
Format: VHS videotape
Special Notes: No. 10 in the "Japan: Spirit and Form" series.
Terms: Materials must be picked up in person. Under special circumstances, you may be able to have them shipped to you at your own expense (call for further details). Return within two weeks after scheduled showing. Videos must be registered with the U. S. Postal Service or returned by Priority Mail, Federal Express, or other registered shipping service.
Source: Consulate General of Japan, Houston
Cultural Affairs and Information Section
909 Fannin Street, Suite 3000
Houston, TX 77010
Phone: 1-713-652-2977
Fax: 1-713-651-7822
World Wide Web URL:
http://www.houston.us.emb-japan.go.jp/en/culture/page1.htm
Email Address: info@cgjhouston.org

Adventure on the Way to the 21st Century
Explores Japan's continual preoccupation with change and newness and points to the origin of this thinking in the traditional culture and religion of the country.
Availability: Schools, libraries, homeschoolers, and nursing homes in Nevada and northern California (zip codes beginning 932 and above, except 935).
Suggested Grade: 9-Adult
Order Number: order by title
Production Date: 1989
Format: Beta videotape; U-matic videotape; VHS videotape
Special Notes: No. 10 in the "Japan: Spirit and Form" series.
Terms: Borrower pays return postage. Book two weeks in advance. Return within three weeks of date borrowed, via UPS, Federal Express or certified mail.
Source: Consulate General of Japan, San Francisco
50 Fremont Street, Suite 2300
San Francisco, CA 94105-2236
Phone: 1-415-356-2564
Fax: 1-415-777-0518
World Wide Web URL: http://www.sf.us.emb-japan.go.jp/
Email Address: infoav@cgjsf.org

Africa's Child: Ethiopia: Festival of Fire
An Ethiopian teenager shares her life in Addis Ababa, the capital, as she talks about her religious life, schooling, foods, ambitions, and the Meskel Festival.
Availability: Schools, libraries, and homeschoolers in the United States who serve the hearing impaired.
Suggested Grade: 7-10
Order Number: 10960
Production Date: 2000
Format: DVD
Terms: Sponsor pays all transportation costs. Return one week after receipt. Participation is limited to deaf or hard of hearing Americans, their parents, families, teachers, counselors, or others whose use would benefit a deaf or

All materials listed in this 2018-2019 edition are BRAND NEW!

SOCIAL STUDIES--GEOGRAPHY--WORLD

hard of hearing person. Only one person in the audience needs to be hearing impaired. You must register--which is free. These videos are all open-captioned--no special equipment is required for viewing.

Source: Described and Captioned Media Program
National Association of the Deaf
4211 Church Street Ext.
Roebuck, SC 29376
Phone: 1-800-237-6213
Fax: 1-800-538-5636
World Wide Web URL: http://www.dcmp.org

Africa: South of the Sahara

Gives a broad overview of the countries of Africa that lie south of the Sahara desert.

Availability: Schools, libraries, and homeschoolers in the United States who serve the hearing impaired.
Suggested Grade: 7-10
Order Number: 12885
Production Date: 1999
Format: DVD
Special Notes: Also available as live streaming video over the Internet.
Terms: Sponsor pays all transportation costs. Return one week after receipt. Participation is limited to deaf or hard of hearing Americans, their parents, families, teachers, counselors, or others whose use would benefit a deaf or hard of hearing person. Only one person in the audience needs to be hearing impaired. You must register--which is free. These videos are all open-captioned--no special equipment is required for viewing.

Source: Described and Captioned Media Program
National Association of the Deaf
4211 Church Street Ext.
Roebuck, SC 29376
Phone: 1-800-237-6213
Fax: 1-800-538-5636
World Wide Web URL: http://www.dcmp.org

Almost a Woman

A young woman, her mother and six siblings move from Puerto Rico to New York. The young woman is determined to overcome all the new challenges in her life including her new identity as an immigrant.

Availability: Schools and libraries in Iowa, Illinois, Michigan, Minnesota, and Wisconsin.
Suggested Grade: 7-12
Languages: Portuguese with subtitles
Order Number: FFPRAL6VHS
Production Date: 2002
Format: VHS videotape
Terms: Borrower pays return postage. Return 8 days after showing. Book 2 weeks in advance. Order may also be picked up for those near the Center.

Source: Center for Latin American and Caribbean Studies
UW-Milwaukee
P. O. Box 413
Milwaukee, WI 53201
Phone: 1-414-229-5987
World Wide Web URL: http://www.uwm.edu/Dept/CLACS
Email Address: audvis@usm.edu

Amazon, The

History of the Amazon River from its discovery in 1637 to modern times, as well as effects of industry and development.

Availability: Schools, libraries, and nursing homes in the United States.
Suggested Grade: 6-12
Order Number: GESA7-video
Production Date: 1991
Format: VHS videotape
Terms: Borrowers must have a User's Agreement on file with this source--available by mail or via the Internet. Return postage is paid by borrower; return 12 days after showing. Book at least three weeks in advance. All borrowers are limited to a total of ten items per semester.

Source: Latin American Resource Center
Stone Center for Latin American Studies
Tulane University
100 Jones Hall
New Orleans, LA 70118
Phone: 1-504-862-3143
Fax: 1-504-865-6719
World Wide Web URL: http://stonecenter.tulane.edu/pages/detail/48/Lending-Library
Email Address: crcrts@tulane.edu

Americans 5: In Women's Hands: The Changing Roles of Women

Looks at how women in the Americas are adopting, by choice or necessity, new economic and political roles that break traditional stereotypes about gender and family. The spotlight is on Chile.

Availability: Schools in the United States.
Suggested Grade: 9-Adult
Order Number: order by title
Production Date: 1993
Format: VHS videotape
Terms: Borrower pays return postage. Return 14 days after receipt, via USPS including insurance. All borrowers must have a current lending agreement on file with the Outreach program. This agreement is available via the web site or may be requested via phone or fax.

Source: Center for Latin American Studies
University of Florida
319 Grinter Hall
P. O. Box 115530
Gainesville, FL 32611-5530
Phone: 1-352-392-0375
Fax: 1-352-392-7682
World Wide Web URL: http://www.latam.ufl.edu/outreach
Email Address: maryr@ufl.edu

Americas 1: Garden of Forking Paths: Dilemmas of National Development

Examines the 20th century development of the nations and

All materials listed in this 2018-2019 edition are BRAND NEW!

SOCIAL STUDIES--GEOGRAPHY--WORLD

national economies of the Americas. Focuses on Argentina.
- Availability: Schools in the United States.
- Suggested Grade: 9-Adult
- Order Number: order by title
- Production Date: 1993
- Format: VHS videotape
- Terms: Borrower pays return postage. Return 14 days after receipt, via USPS including insurance. All borrowers must have a current lending agreement on file with the Outreach program. This agreement is available via the web site or may be requested via phone or fax.
- Source: Center for Latin American Studies
University of Florida
319 Grinter Hall
P. O. Box 115530
Gainesville, FL 32611-5530
Phone: 1-352-392-0375
Fax: 1-352-392-7682
World Wide Web URL: http://www.latam.ufl.edu/outreach
Email Address: maryr@ufl.edu

Americas 2: Capital Sins: Authoritarianism and Democratization

Begins in the 1960s, when authoritarian governments swept the region. Focuses on Brazil.
- Availability: Schools in the United States.
- Suggested Grade: 9-Adult
- Order Number: order by title
- Production Date: 1993
- Format: VHS videotape
- Terms: Borrower pays return postage. Return 14 days after receipt, via USPS including insurance. All borrowers must have a current lending agreement on file with the Outreach program. This agreement is available via the web site or may be requested via phone or fax.
- Source: Center for Latin American Studies
University of Florida
319 Grinter Hall, P. O. Box 115530
Gainesville, FL 32611-5530
Phone: 1-352-392-0375
Fax: 1-352-392-7682
World Wide Web URL: http://www.latam.ufl.edu/outreach
Email Address: maryr@ufl.edu

Americas 3: Continent on the Move: Migration and Urbanization

Explores the causes and effects of one of the most important forces transforming the Americas: the migration of people within the region. Focuses on Mexico.
- Availability: Schools in the United States.
- Suggested Grade: 9-Adult
- Order Number: order by title
- Production Date: 1993
- Format: VHS videotape
- Terms: Borrower pays return postage. Return 14 days after receipt, via USPS including insurance. All borrowers must have a current lending agreement on file with the Outreach program. This agreement is available via the web site or may be requested via phone or fax.
- Source: Center for Latin American Studies
University of Florida
319 Grinter Hall
P. O. Box 115530
Gainesville, FL 32611-5530
Phone: 1-352-392-0375
Fax: 1-352-392-7682
World Wide Web URL: http://www.latam.ufl.edu/outreach
Email Address: maryr@ufl.edu

Americas 4: Mirrors of the Heart: Color, Class and Identity

Set on the island of Hispaniola and in Bolivia--examines how race, class, and ethnic identities continue to be redefined.
- Availability: Schools in the United States.
- Suggested Grade: 9-Adult
- Order Number: order by title
- Production Date: 1993
- Format: VHS videotape
- Terms: Borrower pays return postage. Return 14 days after receipt, via USPS including insurance. All borrowers must have a current lending agreement on file with the Outreach program. This agreement is available via the web site or may be requested via phone or fax.
- Source: Center for Latin American Studies
University of Florida
319 Grinter Hall
P. O. Box 115530
Gainesville, FL 32611-5530
Phone: 1-352-392-0375
Fax: 1-352-392-7682
World Wide Web URL: http://www.latam.ufl.edu/outreach
Email Address: maryr@ufl.edu

Americas 8: Get Up, Stand Up: The Problems of Sovereignty

Examines the ways in which nations struggle to maintain economic and cultural sovereignty in the face of strong pressures. Set in Colombia, Jamaica, and Panama, topics include guerrilla movements, drug lords, economic dependency, and foreign intervention.
- Availability: Schools in the United States.
- Suggested Grade: 9-Adult
- Order Number: order by title
- Production Date: 1993
- Format: VHS videotape
- Terms: Borrower pays return postage. Return 14 days after receipt, via USPS including insurance. All borrowers must have a current lending agreement on file with the Outreach program. This agreement is available via the web site or may be requested via phone or fax.
- Source: Center for Latin American Studies
University of Florida
319 Grinter Hall
P. O. Box 115530
Gainesville, FL 32611-5530
Phone: 1-352-392-0375
Fax: 1-352-392-7682

*All materials listed in this 2018-2019 edition are **BRAND NEW!***

SOCIAL STUDIES--GEOGRAPHY--WORLD

World Wide Web URL: http://www.latam.ufl.edu/outreach
Email Address: maryr@ufl.edu

Americas 9: Fire in the Mind: Revolutions and Revolutionaries
Looks at revolutionary movements in El Salvador and Peru, also examining earlier 20th century revolutions in Mexico, Cuba, and Nicaragua.
Availability: Schools in the United States.
Suggested Grade: 9-Adult
Order Number: order by title
Production Date: 1993
Format: VHS videotape
Terms: Borrower pays return postage. Return 14 days after receipt, via USPS including insurance. All borrowers must have a current lending agreement on file with the Outreach program. This agreement is available via the web site or may be requested via phone or fax.
Source: Center for Latin American Studies
University of Florida
319 Grinter Hall, P. O. Box 115530
Gainesville, FL 32611-5530
Phone: 1-352-392-0375
Fax: 1-352-392-7682
World Wide Web URL: http://www.latam.ufl.edu/outreach
Email Address: maryr@ufl.edu

Ancient Futures: Learning from Ladakh
Contrasts the harmonious agricultural society of Ladakh's countryside and the Westernized capital, Leh, with its problems of scarcity and crime. Based on a book by Helena Norberg-Hodge.
Availability: Schools and libraries in the United States.
Suggested Grade: 7-12
Order Number: 115
Production Date: 1994
Format: VHS videotape
Terms: Borrower pays return postage. Return 3 days after showing via UPS. Book at least 2 weeks in advance.
Source: Syracuse University, South Asia Center
Video Library and Teaching Resources
346F Eggers Hall
The Maxwell School
Syracuse, NY 13244

Archaeological Yucatan: Land of the Maya
Tourist guide to the Mayan ruins, followed by the travel, hotel, and restaurant segment.
Availability: Schools, libraries, and nursing homes in the United States.
Suggested Grade: 6-12
Order Number: MY25-video
Production Date: 1987
Format: VHS videotape
Terms: Borrowers must have a User's Agreement on file with this source--available by mail or via the Internet. Return postage is paid by borrower; return 12 days after showing. Book at least three weeks in advance. All borrowers are limited to a total of ten items per semester.
Source: Latin American Resource Center
Stone Center for Latin American Studies
Tulane University
100 Jones Hall
New Orleans, LA 70118
Phone: 1-504-862-3143
Fax: 1-504-865-6719
World Wide Web URL: http://stonecenter.tulane.edu/pages/detail/48/Lending-Library
Email Address: crcrts@tulane.edu

Argentina
Images of Argentina without narration, includes Buenos Aires, Patagonia, the coast, the highlands, Cuyo and Cordoba and the northeastern segment of Argentina.
Availability: Schools in the United States.
Suggested Grade: 7-12
Order Number: order by title
Production Date: 1988
Format: VHS videotape
Terms: Borrower pays return postage. Return 14 days after receipt, via USPS including insurance. All borrowers must have a current lending agreement on file with the Outreach program. This agreement is available via the web site or may be requested via phone or fax.
Source: Center for Latin American Studies
University of Florida
319 Grinter Hall
P. O. Box 115530
Gainesville, FL 32611-5530
Phone: 1-352-392-0375
Fax: 1-352-392-7682
World Wide Web URL: http://www.latam.ufl.edu/outreach
Email Address: maryr@ufl.edu

Argentina: Growth or Disappearance
Explains the current crisis in Argentina.
Availability: Schools and libraries in Iowa, Illinois, Michigan, Minnesota, and Wisconsin.
Suggested Grade: 9-Adult
Languages: Spanish with subtitles
Order Number: POL/SOCARGAR3VHS
Production Date: 2003
Format: VHS videotape
Terms: Borrower pays return postage. Return 8 days after showing. Book 2 weeks in advance. Order may also be picked up for those near the Center.
Source: Center for Latin American and Caribbean Studies
UW-Milwaukee
P. O. Box 413
Milwaukee, WI 53201
Phone: 1-414-229-5987
World Wide Web URL: http://www.uwm.edu/Dept/CLACS
Email Address: audvis@usm.edu

Around South America
Takes you on a journey around this continent to show culture and geography of different regions.
Availability: Schools in the United States.

SOCIAL STUDIES--GEOGRAPHY--WORLD

Suggested Grade: 7-12
Order Number: order by title
Production Date: 1987
Format: VHS videotape
Terms: Borrower pays return postage. Return 14 days after receipt, via USPS including insurance. All borrowers must have a current lending agreement on file with the Outreach program. This agreement is available via the web site or may be requested via phone or fax.
Source: Center for Latin American Studies
University of Florida
319 Grinter Hall
P. O. Box 115530
Gainesville, FL 32611-5530
Phone: 1-352-392-0375
Fax: 1-352-392-7682
World Wide Web URL: http://www.latam.ufl.edu/outreach
Email Address: maryr@ufl.edu

Arranged Marriages
A Westerner explores the institution of arranged marriages with her married Indian friends. She finds that there are many variations in the way these marriages are arranged, but in all cases, the marriage is a family matter, often used to reinforce the social standing of the family, and to preserve values from generation to generation.
Availability: Schools, libraries, homeschoolers, and nursing homes in the southeastern United States.
Suggested Grade: 7-12
Order Number: order by title
Production Date: 2003
Format: VHS videotape
Terms: Borrower pays return postage. Return 2 days after showing via United Parcel Service, insured. Book 2 weeks in advance.
Source: Center for South Asian Studies
University of Virginia
Video Library Coordinator
P. O. Box 400169, 110 Minor Hall
Charlottesville, VA 22904-4169
Phone: 1-434-924-8815
Email Address: southasia@virginia.edu

As Iwate Goes: Is Culture Local?
Focuses on the local culture of two small towns. One of the towns is famous for preserving its local legends-making it a well-known tourist attraction-while the other town strives instead to create new traditions.
Availability: Schools, libraries, homeschoolers, and nursing homes in Nevada and northern California (zip codes beginning 932 and above, except 935).
Suggested Grade: 6-12
Order Number: order by title
Format: VHS videotape
Terms: Borrower pays return postage. Book two weeks in advance. Return within three weeks of date borrowed, via UPS, Federal Express or certified mail.
Source: Consulate General of Japan, San Francisco
50 Fremont Street, Suite 2300
San Francisco, CA 94105-2236
Phone: 1-415-356-2564
Fax: 1-415-777-0518
World Wide Web URL: http://www.sf.us.emb-japan.go.jp/
Email Address: infoav@cgjsf.org

As Iwate Goes: Is Politics Local?
Introduces two small towns in northeastern Honshu as they struggle to reconcile local needs with national policies. Follows their struggle to combine economic development with environmental protection, in order to provide for a rapidly aging population.
Availability: Schools, libraries, homeschoolers, and nursing homes in Nevada and northern California (zip codes beginning 932 and above, except 935).
Suggested Grade: 6-12
Order Number: order by title
Production Date: 1992
Format: VHS videotape
Terms: Borrower pays return postage. Book two weeks in advance. Return within three weeks of date borrowed, via UPS, Federal Express or certified mail.
Source: Consulate General of Japan, San Francisco
50 Fremont Street, Suite 2300
San Francisco, CA 94105-2236
Phone: 1-415-356-2564
Fax: 1-415-777-0518
World Wide Web URL: http://www.sf.us.emb-japan.go.jp/
Email Address: infoav@cgjsf.org

Barbados
Tours the island of Barbados in the Caribbean. Shows the beautiful beaches and scenery as well as the various nightlife activities which visitors will enjoy.
Availability: Schools, libraries, and homeschoolers in the United States who serve the hearing impaired.
Suggested Grade: Adult
Order Number: 12487
Production Date: 1998
Format: DVD
Terms: Sponsor pays all transportation costs. Return one week after receipt. Participation is limited to deaf or hard of hearing Americans, their parents, families, teachers, counselors, or others whose use would benefit a deaf or hard of hearing person. Only one person in the audience needs to be hearing impaired. You must register--which is free. These videos are all open-captioned--no special equipment is required for viewing.
Source: Described and Captioned Media Program
National Association of the Deaf
4211 Church Street Ext.
Roebuck, SC 29376
Phone: 1-800-237-6213
Fax: 1-800-538-5636
World Wide Web URL: http://www.dcmp.org

All materials listed in this 2018-2019 edition are BRAND NEW!

SOCIAL STUDIES--GEOGRAPHY--WORLD

Carp Town, The
The town of Tsuwano in Shimane Prefecture in Western Japan is known for its carp kept in waterways that run in all directions through the town. The number of carp is reported to be five to ten times the total population of 9,000 people. The townspeople neither sell nor eat the carp, they simply take care of them for pleasure, as they have for 300 years.
Availability: Schools, libraries, homeschoolers, and nursing homes in Connecticut (except Fairfield County), Maine, Massachusetts, New Hampshire, Rhode Island, and Vermont.
Suggested Grade: 9-Adult
Order Number: 121
Production Date: 1985
Format: VHS videotape
Terms: Borrower pays return postage, including insurance. Return two weeks after receipt.
  Source: Consulate General of Japan, Boston
  Federal Reserve Plaza, 14th Floor
  600 Atlantic Avenue
  Boston, MA 02210
  Phone: 1-617-973-9772
  Fax: 1-617-542-1329
  World Wide Web URL:
  http://www.boston.us.emb-japan.go.jp
  Email Address: infocul@cgjbos.org

Carp Town, The
The town of Tsuwano in Shimane Prefecture in Western Japan is known for its carp kept in waterways that run in all directions through the town. The number of carp is reported to be five to ten times the total population of 9,000 people. The townspeople neither sell nor eat the carp, they simply take care of them for pleasure, as they have for 300 years.
Availability: Schools, libraries, and nursing homes in Hawaii.
Suggested Grade: 9-Adult
Order Number: CU-29
Production Date: 1985
Format: VHS videotape
Terms: Borrower pays return postage. A maximum of 3 videos may be borrowed per person. Return within one week of date borrowed.
  Source: Consulate General of Japan, Honolulu
  1742 Nuuanu Avenue
  Honolulu, HI 96817-3294
  Phone: 1-808-543-3111
  Fax: 1-808-543-3170
  World Wide Web URL:
  http://www.honolulu.us.emb-japan.go.jp

Carp Town, The
The town of Tsuwano in Shimane Prefecture in Western Japan is known for its carp kept in waterways that run in all directions through the town. The number of carp is reported to be five to ten times the total population of 9,000 people. The townspeople neither sell nor eat the carp, they simply take care of them for pleasure, as they have for 300 years.
Availability: Schools, libraries, and nursing homes in Oklahoma and Texas.
Suggested Grade: 9-Adult
Order Number: I5
Production Date: 1985
Format: VHS videotape
Terms: Materials must be picked up in person. Under special circumstances, you may be able to have them shipped to you at your own expense (call for further details). Return within two weeks after scheduled showing. Videos must be registered with the U. S. Postal Service or returned by Priority Mail, Federal Express, or other registered shipping service.
  Source: Consulate General of Japan, Houston
  Cultural Affairs and Information Section
  909 Fannin Street, Suite 3000
  Houston, TX 77010
  Phone: 1-713-652-2977
  Fax: 1-713-651-7822
  World Wide Web URL:
  http://www.houston.us.emb-japan.go.jp/en/culture/page1.htm
  Email Address: info@cgjhouston.org

Carp Town, The
The town of Tsuwano in Shimane Prefecture in Western Japan is known for its carp kept in waterways that run in all directions through the town. The number of carp is reported to be five to ten times the total population of 9,000 people. The townspeople neither sell nor eat the carp, they simply take care of them for pleasure, as they have for 300 years.
Availability: Schools, libraries, homeschoolers, and nursing homes in Arizona and California (zipcodes beginning 900-931 and 935).
Suggested Grade: 9-Adult
Order Number: 060
Production Date: 1985
Format: VHS videotape
Terms: Borrower pays postage both ways; you may call the number below to learn how much postage costs. Return within two weeks of date borrowed. An individual may borrow 2 items at one time. For non-profit and educational use only.
  Source: Consulate General of Japan, Los Angeles
  350 South Grand Avenue, Suite 1700
  Los Angeles, CA 90071-3459
  Phone: 1-213-617-6700
  Fax: 1-213-617-6727
  World Wide Web URL: http://www.la.us.emb-japan.go.jp

Carp Town, The
The town of Tsuwano in Shimane Prefecture in Western Japan is known for its carp kept in waterways that run in all directions through the town. The number of carp is reported to be five to ten times the total population of 9,000 people. The townspeople neither sell nor eat the carp, they simply take care of them for pleasure, as they have for 300 years.

SOCIAL STUDIES--GEOGRAPHY--WORLD

Availability: Schools, libraries, homeschoolers, and nursing homes in OREGON AND SOUTHERN IDAHO ONLY. Please make requests via the web site.
Suggested Grade: 9-Adult
Order Number: 206
Production Date: 1985
Format: VHS videotape
Terms: Borrower pays return postage. Return within three weeks after scheduled showing date. Book one month in advance if possible. Rewind the video and wrap securely for return. Be certain to indicate video number, date needed, name of your organization, and address to which video should be sent, along with phone number. Audience report enclosed with the video must be completed and returned.
Source: Consulate General of Japan, Oregon
Attn: Tamara, Video Library
1300 S. W. Fifth Avenue, Suite 2700
Portland, OR 97201
Phone: 1-503-221-1811, ext. 17
World Wide Web URL:
http://www.portland.us.emb-japan.go.jp/en/index.html
Email Address: tamara@cgjpdx.org

Caste at Birth
An exploration of the condition of the 150 million "untouchables," India's lowest caste, including government attempts to improve their condition, resistance among upper caste Hindus, and the work of leaders among the "untouchables" to bring about change
Availability: Schools and libraries in the United States.
Suggested Grade: 7-12
Order Number: 4
Production Date: 1990
Format: VHS videotape
Terms: Borrower pays return postage. Return 3 days after showing via UPS. Book at least 2 weeks in advance.
Source: Syracuse University, South Asia Center
Video Library and Teaching Resources
346F Eggers Hall
The Maxwell School
Syracuse, NY 13244

Celebrating the Seasons
Shows the color of Japan's changing seasons and seasonal festivals and traditional celebrations.
Availability: Schools, libraries and homeschoolers in Alabama, Georgia, North Carolina, South Carolina, and Virginia.
Suggested Grade: 6-Adult
Order Number: 222
Format: VHS videotape
Terms: Borrower pays return postage. Two tapes may be borrowed at a time. Return within 7 days after receipt. Reservations may be made by filling the application found on the web site.

Source: Consulate General of Japan, Atlanta
Japan Information Center
One Alliance Center
3500 Lenox Road, Suite 1600
Atlanta, GA 30326
Phone: 1-404-365-9240
Fax: 1-404-240-4311
World Wide Web URL:
http://www.atlanta.us.emb-japan.go.jp
Email Address: info@cgjapanatlanta.org

Central African Republic
The Central African Republic lies in the heart of Africa, remote and isolated. Briefly explores its geography, trade and transportation, and history. Shows the pygmy culture and the importance of the rain forest. Reviews government, religion, climate, exports, rulers, and population. Though rich in natural resources, the country's recent leadership has laid no plans for its brighter potential future. NOTE: some nudity.
Availability: Schools, libraries, and homeschoolers in the United States who serve the hearing impaired.
Suggested Grade: 7-12
Order Number: 12337
Production Date: 1994
Format: DVD
Special Notes: Produced by ACG/United Learning.
Terms: Sponsor pays all transportation costs. Return one week after receipt. Participation is limited to deaf or hard of hearing Americans, their parents, families, teachers, counselors, or others whose use would benefit a deaf or hard of hearing person. Only one person in the audience needs to be hearing impaired. You must register--which is free. These videos are all open-captioned--no special equipment is required for viewing.
Source: Described and Captioned Media Program
National Association of the Deaf
4211 Church Street Ext.
Roebuck, SC 29376
Phone: 1-800-237-6213
Fax: 1-800-538-5636
World Wide Web URL: http://www.dcmp.org

Central America Close-Up 1
Two portraits of contemporary youth in nations in conflict. Jeramias, a Guatemalan teen, and Flor, an El Salvadoran teen, both flee war in this video focusing on youth.
Availability: Schools in the United States.
Suggested Grade: 7-Adult
Order Number: order by title
Format: VHS videotape
Terms: Borrower pays return postage. Return 14 days after receipt, via USPS including insurance. All borrowers must have a current lending agreement on file with the Outreach program. This agreement is available via the web site or may be requested via phone or fax.

All materials listed in this 2018-2019 edition are BRAND NEW!

SOCIAL STUDIES--GEOGRAPHY--WORLD

Source: Center for Latin American Studies
University of Florida
319 Grinter Hall
P. O. Box 115530
Gainesville, FL 32611-5530
Phone: 1-352-392-0375
Fax: 1-352-392-7682
World Wide Web URL: http://www.latam.ufl.edu/outreach
Email Address: maryr@ufl.edu

Central America Close-Up 2
Carlos, an Honduran teen, reaches out to neighbors displaced by war; and Balty, a Nicaraguan medical student, works in a war zone.
Availability: Schools in the United States.
Suggested Grade: 7-Adult
Order Number: order by title
Format: VHS videotape
Terms: Borrower pays return postage. Return 14 days after receipt, via USPS including insurance. All borrowers must have a current lending agreement on file with the Outreach program. This agreement is available via the web site or may be requested via phone or fax.
Source: Center for Latin American Studies
University of Florida
319 Grinter Hall, P. O. Box 115530
Gainesville, FL 32611-5530
Phone: 1-352-392-0375
Fax: 1-352-392-7682
World Wide Web URL: http://www.latam.ufl.edu/outreach
Email Address: maryr@ufl.edu

Children in Towns & Villages
Depicts children's activities at school, at home and in their neighborhoods comparing life in urban and rural areas.
Availability: Schools, libraries, homeschoolers, and nursing homes in Arizona and California (zipcodes beginning 900-931 and 935).
Suggested Grade: All ages
Order Number: 114
Production Date: 1973
Format: VHS videotape
Terms: Borrower pays postage both ways; you may call the number below to learn how much postage costs. Return within two weeks of date borrowed. An individual may borrow 2 items at one time. For non-profit and educational use only.
Source: Consulate General of Japan, Los Angeles
350 South Grand Avenue, Suite 1700
Los Angeles, CA 90071-3459
Phone: 1-213-617-6700
Fax: 1-213-617-6727
World Wide Web URL: http://www.la.us.emb-japan.go.jp

Children of Japan, The
Focuses on school life for children, their hobbies, dancing, and interests.
Availability: Schools, libraries, and nursing homes in Hawaii.
Suggested Grade: 4-12
Order Number: CU-19
Format: VHS videotape
Terms: Borrower pays return postage. A maximum of 3 videos may be borrowed per person. Return within one week of date borrowed.
Source: Consulate General of Japan, Honolulu
1742 Nuuanu Avenue
Honolulu, HI 96817-3294
Phone: 1-808-543-3111
Fax: 1-808-543-3170
World Wide Web URL: http://www.honolulu.us.emb-japan.go.jp

Children of the Snow Country
Children are shown enjoying the snowbound winter months in the town of Nihonmatsu, approximately 3 hours north of Tokyo.
Availability: Schools, libraries, homeschoolers, and nursing homes in Arizona and California (zipcodes beginning 900-931 and 935).
Suggested Grade: All ages
Order Number: 077
Production Date: 1980
Format: VHS videotape
Terms: Borrower pays postage both ways; you may call the number below to learn how much postage costs. Return within two weeks of date borrowed. An individual may borrow 2 items at one time. For non-profit and educational use only.
Source: Consulate General of Japan, Los Angeles
350 South Grand Avenue, Suite 1700
Los Angeles, CA 90071-3459
Phone: 1-213-617-6700
Fax: 1-213-617-6727
World Wide Web URL: http://www.la.us.emb-japan.go.jp

China and the Forbidden City
Spell-binding tale captures life within China as it was in 1963 and had been for hundreds of years. Walk the streets and lanes of Beijing. Feel the excitement.
Availability: Schools, libraries, homeschoolers, and nursing homes in the United States and Canada.
Suggested Grade: 6-Adult
Order Number: order by title
Production Date: 1983
Format: VHS videotape
Terms: Postage is paid by borrower both ways--send $3.00 per tape to cover initial shipping to you--MONEY MUST BE SENT WITH REQUEST. Return 10 days after showing via U. S. Postal Service, library rate. Shipping is $5.00 to Canadian addresses.
Source: Center for Teaching About China
Kathleen Trescott
1214 West Schwartz
Carbondale, IL 62901
Phone: 1-618-549-1555
Email Address: trescott@midwest.net

All materials listed in this 2018-2019 edition are BRAND NEW!

SOCIAL STUDIES--GEOGRAPHY--WORLD

China and the Forbidden City: The Great Within
Cameras roam the Forbidden City in Beijing, the Emperor's Palace for hundreds of years.
- Availability: Schools, libraries, homeschoolers, and nursing homes in the United States and Canada.
- Suggested Grade: 6-Adult
- Order Number: order by title
- Production Date: 1995
- Format: VHS videotape
- Terms: Postage is paid by borrower both ways--send $3.00 per tape to cover initial shipping to you--MONEY MUST BE SENT WITH REQUEST. Return 10 days after showing via U. S. Postal Service, library rate. Shipping is $5.00 to Canadian addresses.
- Source: Center for Teaching About China
  Kathleen Trescott
  1214 West Schwartz
  Carbondale, IL 62901
  Phone: 1-618-549-1555
  Email Address: trescott@midwest.net

China Cry
The true story of two young people in love as they come in conflict with oppression and repression and flee to Hong Kong.
- Availability: Schools, libraries, homeschoolers, and nursing homes in the United States and Canada.
- Suggested Grade: 9-12
- Order Number: order by title
- Production Date: 1990
- Format: VHS videotape
- Terms: Postage is paid by borrower both ways--send $3.00 per tape to cover initial shipping to you--MONEY MUST BE SENT WITH REQUEST. Return 10 days after showing via U. S. Postal Service, library rate. Shipping is $5.00 to Canadian addresses.
- Source: Center for Teaching About China
  Kathleen Trescott
  1214 West Schwartz
  Carbondale, IL 62901
  Phone: 1-618-549-1555
  Email Address: trescott@midwest.net

Chinese Life Today
Emphasizes the way of life, work, play, and the family enjoyments, in a rather casual way.
- Availability: Schools, libraries, homeschoolers, and nursing homes in the United States and Canada.
- Suggested Grade: 9-12
- Order Number: order by title
- Format: VHS videotape
- Terms: Postage is paid by borrower both ways--send $3.00 per tape to cover initial shipping to you--MONEY MUST BE SENT WITH REQUEST. Return 10 days after showing via U. S. Postal Service, library rate. Shipping is $5.00 to Canadian addresses.
- Source: Center for Teaching About China
  Kathleen Trescott
  1214 West Schwartz
  Carbondale, IL 62901
  Phone: 1-618-549-1555
  Email Address: trescott@midwest.net

Christian Women in China
Shown at the UN World Conference on Women held in Beijing, 1995, this depicts the role of China's women in the rural and urban churches.
- Availability: Schools, libraries, homeschoolers, and nursing homes in the United States and Canada.
- Suggested Grade: 9-12
- Order Number: order by title
- Production Date: 1995
- Format: VHS videotape
- Terms: Postage is paid by borrower both ways--send $3.00 per tape to cover initial shipping to you--MONEY MUST BE SENT WITH REQUEST. Return 10 days after showing via U. S. Postal Service, library rate. Shipping is $5.00 to Canadian addresses.
- Source: Center for Teaching About China
  Kathleen Trescott
  1214 West Schwartz
  Carbondale, IL 62901
  Phone: 1-618-549-1555
  Email Address: trescott@midwest.net

Common Experiences: Different Visions
presents the different perceptions of the common experiences of two groups of high school students, one American from the state of Indiana, and the other Japanese from Kaminokawa High School in Tochigi Prefecture. Discusses how each group individually viewed the activities they jointly participated in such as athletic games, shopping, and camping.
- Availability: Schools, libraries, homeschoolers, and nursing homes in Nevada and northern California (zip codes beginning 932 and above, except 935).
- Suggested Grade: 6-12
- Order Number: order by title
- Production Date: 1994
- Format: VHS videotape
- Terms: Borrower pays return postage. Book two weeks in advance. Return within three weeks of date borrowed, via UPS, Federal Express or certified mail.
- Source: Consulate General of Japan, San Francisco
  50 Fremont Street, Suite 2300
  San Francisco, CA 94105-2236
  Phone: 1-415-356-2564
  Fax: 1-415-777-0518
  World Wide Web URL: http://www.sf.us.emb-japan.go.jp/
  Email Address: infoav@cgjsf.org

*All materials listed in this 2018-2019 edition are **BRAND NEW!***

SOCIAL STUDIES--GEOGRAPHY--WORLD

Cultural Journey Into Japan, A
A journey through Japan that touches upon the cultural aspects of this country. Depicts beautiful crafts such as gold leaf painting, obi making, and kimono silk painting as well as showing the beauty of classic rock gardens.
Availability: Schools, libraries, and nursing homes in Oklahoma and Texas.
Suggested Grade: 4-12
Order Number: J2
Production Date: 1984
Format: VHS videotape
Terms: Materials must be picked up in person. Under special circumstances, you may be able to have them shipped to you at your own expense (call for further details). Return within two weeks after scheduled showing. Videos must be registered with the U. S. Postal Service or returned by Priority Mail, Federal Express, or other registered shipping service.
Source: Consulate General of Japan, Houston
Cultural Affairs and Information Section
909 Fannin Street, Suite 3000
Houston, TX 77010
Phone: 1-713-652-2977
Fax: 1-713-651-7822
World Wide Web URL:
http://www.houston.us.emb-japan.go.jp/en/culture/page1.htm
Email Address: info@cgjhouston.org

Dadi and Her Family
Dadi is the grandmother who manages an extended family. The women in this film discuss family tensions, women's labor in the fields and at home, and the loneliness of being a stranger in the husband's family.
Availability: Schools, libraries, homeschoolers, and nursing homes in the southeastern United States.
Suggested Grade: 7-12
Order Number: order by title
Production Date: 1982
Format: VHS videotape
Terms: Borrower pays return postage. Return 2 days after showing via United Parcel Service, insured. Book 2 weeks in advance.
Source: Center for South Asian Studies
University of Virginia
Video Library Coordinator
P. O. Box 400169, 110 Minor Hall
Charlottesville, VA 22904-4169
Phone: 1-434-924-8815
Email Address: southasia@virginia.edu

Dadi and Her Family
Dadi is the grandmother who manages an extended family. The women in this film discuss family tensions, women's labor in the fields and at home, and the loneliness of being a stranger in the husband's family.
Availability: Schools and libraries in the United States.
Suggested Grade: 7-12
Order Number: 2
Production Date: 1979
Format: VHS videotape
Terms: Borrower pays return postage. Return 3 days after showing via UPS. Book at least 2 weeks in advance.
Source: Syracuse University, South Asia Center
Video Library and Teaching Resources
346F Eggers Hall
The Maxwell School
Syracuse, NY 13244

Day of the Dead
Presents the annual commemoration of the day of the Dead as it is celebrated on the island of La Picanda.
Availability: Schools in the United States.
Suggested Grade: 7-12
Spanish with English subtitles
Order Number: order by title
Format: VHS videotape
Special Notes: Produced by Films for the Humanities & Sciences--make this distinction when requesting as this source offers another video by the same name.
Terms: Borrower pays return postage. Return 14 days after receipt, via USPS including insurance. All borrowers must have a current lending agreement on file with the Outreach program. This agreement is available via the web site or may be requested via phone or fax.
Source: Center for Latin American Studies
University of Florida
319 Grinter Hall
P. O. Box 115530
Gainesville, FL 32611-5530
Phone: 1-352-392-0375
Fax: 1-352-392-7682
World Wide Web URL: http://www.latam.ufl.edu/outreach
Email Address: maryr@ufl.edu

Disaster Prevention
Shows some of the ways Japan copes with the constant threat of natural disasters.
Availability: Schools, libraries, homeschoolers, and nursing homes in Arizona and California (zipcodes beginning 900-931 and 935).
Suggested Grade: 6-Adult
Order Number: 072
Production Date: 1982
Format: VHS videotape
Terms: Borrower pays postage both ways; you may call the number below to learn how much postage costs. Return within two weeks of date borrowed. An individual may borrow 2 items at one time. For non-profit and educational use only.
Source: Consulate General of Japan, Los Angeles
350 South Grand Avenue, Suite 1700
Los Angeles, CA 90071-3459
Phone: 1-213-617-6700
Fax: 1-213-617-6727
World Wide Web URL: http://www.la.us.emb-japan.go.jp

SOCIAL STUDIES--GEOGRAPHY--WORLD

Discover Korea: Geography and Industry
A 12-year-old boy narrates a journey across South Korea.
- Availability: Schools, libraries, and nursing homes in the United States and Canada.
- Suggested Grade: All ages
- Order Number: KV002
- Format: VHS videotape
- Terms: Borrower pays return postage. Return with 14 days after scheduled showing, via UPS or U. S. Mail. All requests must included an educational institution affiliation, a current address, and phone number. Order through web site only.
  - Source: Cornell University East Asia Program
  - World Wide Web URL: http://eap.einaudi.cornell.edu/lending_library
  - Email Address: east_asia1@cornell.edu

District Nurse, A/Kangofu: The Japanese Nurse/The Battle Against Disease/Mobile Service/Floating Medical Clinic
Five topics include the daily routine of a district nurse in a small farming town; a nurse in the Kanagawa Prefectural Children's Medical Center; efforts of the Japanese government and the Japan Medical Association; a variety of mobile services available to people in remote areas; and a floating medical clinic administering to three remote islands.
- Availability: Schools, libraries, homeschoolers, and nursing homes in Connecticut (except Fairfield County), Maine, Massachusetts, New Hampshire, Rhode Island, and Vermont.
- Suggested Grade: 9-Adult
- Order Number: 136
- Format: VHS videotape
- Terms: Borrower pays return postage, including insurance. Return two weeks after receipt.
  - Source: Consulate General of Japan, Boston
  - Federal Reserve Plaza, 14th Floor
  - 600 Atlantic Avenue
  - Boston, MA 02210
  - Phone: 1-617-973-9772
  - Fax: 1-617-542-1329
  - World Wide Web URL: http://www.boston.us.emb-japan.go.jp
  - Email Address: infocul@cgjbos.org

Dominican Republic, Cradle of the Americas
Cultural, folklife and pre-Columbian art of the oldest country in America.
- Availability: Schools, libraries, and nursing homes in the United States.
- Suggested Grade: 6-12
- Order Number: IDOM2-video
- Production Date: 1975
- Format: VHS videotape
- Terms: Borrowers must have a User's Agreement on file with this source--available by mail or via the Internet. Return postage is paid by borrower; return 12 days after showing. Book at least three weeks in advance. All borrowers are limited to a total of ten items per semester.
  - Source: Latin American Resource Center
  - Stone Center for Latin American Studies
  - Tulane University
  - 100 Jones Hall
  - New Orleans, LA 70118
  - Phone: 1-504-862-3143
  - Fax: 1-504-865-6719
  - World Wide Web URL: http://stonecenter.tulane.edu/pages/detail/48/Lending-Library
  - Email Address: crcrts@tulane.edu

Eastern Canadian Provinces, The
Six provinces form Eastern Canada: New Brunswick, Newfoundland, Nova Scotia, Prince Edward Island, Quebec, and Ontario. Maps, photographs, graphics, and live photography help present a historical and geographic view of the region. Discusses each province, its size, population, industries, capital, points of interest, climate, history, and geographic regions. Eastern Canada remains an important gateway to the vast interior of North America.
- Availability: Schools, libraries, and homeschoolers in the United States who serve the hearing impaired.
- Suggested Grade: 6-10
- Order Number: 3600
- Production Date: 1998
- Format: DVD
- Special Notes: Produced by Film Ideas, Inc.
- Terms: Sponsor pays all transportation costs. Return one week after receipt. Participation is limited to deaf or hard of hearing Americans, their parents, families, teachers, counselors, or others whose use would benefit a deaf or hard of hearing person. Only one person in the audience needs to be hearing impaired. You must register--which is free. These videos are all open-captioned--no special equipment is required for viewing.
  - Source: Described and Captioned Media Program
  - National Association of the Deaf
  - 4211 Church Street Ext.
  - Roebuck, SC 29376
  - Phone: 1-800-237-6213
  - Fax: 1-800-538-5636
  - World Wide Web URL: http://www.dcmp.org

El Futuro Maya: Voces del Presente
Students, housewives, academics, community leaders, educators--provide perspectives on the meaning of the Maya Movement.
- Availability: Schools, libraries, and nursing homes in the United States.
- Suggested Grade: 6-12
- Languages: Spanish or Spanish with English subtitles
- Order Number: INDGUA5-video
- Production Date: 1998
- Format: VHS videotape
- Terms: Borrowers must have a User's Agreement on file with this source--available by mail or via the Internet. Return postage is paid by borrower; return 12 days after

SOCIAL STUDIES--GEOGRAPHY--WORLD

showing. Book at least three weeks in advance. All borrowers are limited to a total of ten items per semester.
Source: Latin American Resource Center
Stone Center for Latin American Studies
Tulane University
100 Jones Hall
New Orleans, LA 70118
Phone: 1-504-862-3143
Fax: 1-504-865-6719
World Wide Web URL: http://stonecenter.tulane.edu/pages/detail/48/Lending-Library
Email Address: crcrts@tulane.edu

End to Silence, Part 1: Paradise Is Under Your Mother's Foot
Explores how Muslim laws are applied in different countries.
Availability: Schools and libraries in the United States.
Suggested Grade: 9-Adult
Order Number: SA91
Production Date: 1994
Format: VHS videotape
Terms: Borrower pays return postage. Return 3 days after showing via UPS. Book at least 2 weeks in advance.
Source: Syracuse University, South Asia Center
Video Library and Teaching Resources
346F Eggers Hall
The Maxwell School
Syracuse, NY 13244

Europe: Southern Region
Compares the Mediterranean peninsular countries of southern Europe: Greece, Italy, Spain, and Portugal. Discusses geography, climates, cultures and life styles, industries, religions, and brief histories. Each country has an industrial, prosperous north and a poor, agricultural south. Though early civilizations flowed from this region, it is separate in many ways from the rest of Europe.
Availability: Schools, libraries, and homeschoolers in the United States who serve the hearing impaired.
Suggested Grade: 6-10
Order Number: 3242
Production Date: 1994
Format: DVD
Special Notes: Produced by Encyclopedia Britannica Educational Corporation.
Terms: Sponsor pays all transportation costs. Return one week after receipt. Participation is limited to deaf or hard of hearing Americans, their parents, families, teachers, counselors, or others whose use would benefit a deaf or hard of hearing person. Only one person in the audience needs to be hearing impaired. You must register--which is free. These videos are all open-captioned--no special equipment is required for viewing.
Source: Described and Captioned Media Program
National Association of the Deaf
4211 Church Street Ext.
Roebuck, SC 29376
Phone: 1-800-237-6213
Fax: 1-800-538-5636
World Wide Web URL: http://www.dcmp.org

Favelas
Shows the social reality of life in the shantytowns of Sao Paulo, Brazil.
Availability: Schools and libraries in Iowa, Illinois, Michigan, Minnesota, and Wisconsin.
Suggested Grade: 6-12
Order Number: CI/URBRAF27VHS
Production Date: 1989
Format: VHS videotape
Terms: Borrower pays return postage. Return 8 days after showing. Book 2 weeks in advance. Order may also be picked up for those near the Center.
Source: Center for Latin American and Caribbean Studies
UW-Milwaukee
P. O. Box 413
Milwaukee, WI 53201
Phone: 1-414-229-5987
World Wide Web URL: http://www.uwm.edu/Dept/CLACS
Email Address: audvis@usm.edu

Festival of India
Taped at the Festival of India, this video shows a series of folk performers invited to the U. S. Performances including juggling, puppetry, epic story telling, and various crafts people.
Availability: Schools and libraries in the United States.
Suggested Grade: 7-Adult
Order Number: SA18
Production Date: 1986
Format: VHS videotape
Terms: Borrower pays return postage. Return 3 days after showing via UPS. Book at least 2 weeks in advance.
Source: Syracuse University, South Asia Center
Video Library and Teaching Resources
346F Eggers Hall
The Maxwell School
Syracuse, NY 13244

Festivals in Taiwan
Features the festivals of Taiwan.
Availability: Schools, libraries, and nursing homes in the United States and Canada.
Suggested Grade: All ages
Order Number: TV003
Format: VHS videotape
Terms: Borrower pays return postage. Return with 14 days after scheduled showing, via UPS or U. S. Mail. All requests must included an educational institution affiliation, a current address, and phone number. Order through web site only.
Source: Cornell University East Asia Program
World Wide Web URL: http://eap.einaudi.cornell.edu/lending_library
Email Address: east_asia1@cornell.edu

All materials listed in this 2018-2019 edition are BRAND NEW!

SOCIAL STUDIES--GEOGRAPHY--WORLD

Firecracker: A Night to Remember in Yen-Shuei
Illustrates a special ceremony, steeped in history, that is believed to ward off the plague.
- Availability: Schools, libraries, and nursing homes in the United States and Canada.
- Suggested Grade: All ages
- Order Number: TV004
- Format: VHS videotape
- Terms: Borrower pays return postage. Return with 14 days after scheduled showing, via UPS or U. S. Mail. All requests must included an educational institution affiliation, a current address, and phone number. Order through web site only.
- Source: Cornell University East Asia Program
  World Wide Web URL:
  http://eap.einaudi.cornell.edu/lending_library
  Email Address: east_asia1@cornell.edu

Fire Fighters, The
This video tours the Tokyo Metropolitan Fire Department and its facilities.
- Availability: Schools, libraries, homeschoolers, and nursing homes in Arizona and California (zipcodes beginning 900-931 and 935).
- Suggested Grade: 6-Adult
- Order Number: 072
- Production Date: 1980
- Format: VHS videotape
- Terms: Borrower pays postage both ways; you may call the number below to learn how much postage costs. Return within two weeks of date borrowed. An individual may borrow 2 items at one time. For non-profit and educational use only.
- Source: Consulate General of Japan, Los Angeles
  350 South Grand Avenue, Suite 1700
  Los Angeles, CA 90071-3459
  Phone: 1-213-617-6700
  Fax: 1-213-617-6727
  World Wide Web URL: http://www.la.us.emb-japan.go.jp

Fishing in a Sea of Greed
Portrays the growing concern of local fish-workers in India and Bangladesh, as huge foreign factory ships decimate their fishing grounds and ruin their environment. Describes how a local union was transformed into a national movement, culminating in a blockade of Bombay's harbor and a joyous rally in a nearby fishing village.
- Availability: Schools, libraries, homeschoolers, and nursing homes in the southeastern United States.
- Suggested Grade: 7-12
- Order Number: order by title
- Production Date: 1998
- Format: VHS videotape
- Terms: Borrower pays return postage. Return 2 days after showing via United Parcel Service, insured. Book 2 weeks in advance.
- Source: Center for South Asian Studies
  University of Virginia, Video Library Coordinator
  P. O. Box 400169, 110 Minor Hall
  Charlottesville, VA 22904-4169
  Phone: 1-434-924-8815
  Email Address: southasia@virginia.edu

Four Seasons for Children
The passing year in Japan produces delicate changes as one season moves into another--from spring to summer, from autumn to winter, and then on again to spring. The sensitive moods of children respond to these changes, as they investigate nature and see new adventures.
- Availability: Schools, libraries, homeschoolers, and nursing homes in Arizona and California (zipcodes beginning 900-931 and 935).
- Suggested Grade: 4-Adult
- Order Number: 082
- Production Date: 1972
- Format: VHS videotape
- Terms: Borrower pays postage both ways; you may call the number below to learn how much postage costs. Return within two weeks of date borrowed. An individual may borrow 2 items at one time. For non-profit and educational use only.
- Source: Consulate General of Japan, Los Angeles
  350 South Grand Avenue, Suite 1700
  Los Angeles, CA 90071-3459
  Phone: 1-213-617-6700
  Fax: 1-213-617-6727
  World Wide Web URL: http://www.la.us.emb-japan.go.jp

Four Seasons in Japan, The
Shows the different seasons and how the lives of the people are affected by it.
- Availability: Schools, libraries, and nursing homes in Hawaii.
- Suggested Grade: All ages
- Order Number: TR-4
- Production Date: 1984
- Format: VHS videotape
- Terms: Borrower pays return postage. A maximum of 3 videos may be borrowed per person. Return within one week of date borrowed.
- Source: Consulate General of Japan, Honolulu
  1742 Nuuanu Avenue
  Honolulu, HI 96817-3294
  Phone: 1-808-543-3111
  Fax: 1-808-543-3170
  World Wide Web URL:
  http://www.honolulu.us.emb-japan.go.jp

Gardens of Japan
Various types of Japanese gardens, from a moss garden, to one devoid of trees and water, created of sand and rocks are shown in this video.
- Availability: Schools, libraries, homeschoolers, and nursing homes in Arizona and California (zipcodes beginning 900-931 and 935).

SOCIAL STUDIES--GEOGRAPHY--WORLD

Suggested Grade: 4-Adult
Order Number: 070
Production Date: 1964
Format: VHS videotape
Terms: Borrower pays postage both ways; you may call the number below to learn how much postage costs. Return within two weeks of date borrowed. An individual may borrow 2 items at one time. For non-profit and educational use only.
Source: Consulate General of Japan, Los Angeles
350 South Grand Avenue, Suite 1700
Los Angeles, CA 90071-3459
Phone: 1-213-617-6700
Fax: 1-213-617-6727
World Wide Web URL: http://www.la.us.emb-japan.go.jp

Ghosts of Machu Picchu
Why did the Incas abandon their city in the clouds?
Availability: All requesters
Suggested Grade: 7-Adult
Order Number: not applicable
Production Date: 2010
Format: Streaming Video
Source: NOVA
World Wide Web URL:
http://www.pbs.org/wgbh/nova/programs/index.html

Given to Dance
Based on Frederique Margolin's book The Wives of the God King, this film focuses on retired temple dancers connected with the cult of Jagannatha in Puri and Orissa, South India.
Availability: Schools, libraries, homeschoolers, and nursing homes in the southeastern United States.
Suggested Grade: 7-12
Order Number: order by title
Production Date: 1985
Format: VHS videotape
Terms: Borrower pays return postage. Return 2 days after showing via United Parcel Service, insured. Book 2 weeks in advance.
Source: Center for South Asian Studies
University of Virginia, Video Library Coordinator
P. O. Box 400169, 110 Minor Hall
Charlottesville, VA 22904-4169
Phone: 1-434-924-8815
Email Address: southasia@virginia.edu

Goddess of Mercy for Prevention of Senility
As the number of elderly increase in Japan, the number of senile people are also growing. People are making various prevention efforts, and statues of the Goddess of Mercy, who is said to prevent senility are being dedicated in greater numbers.
Availability: Schools, libraries, homeschoolers, and nursing homes in Connecticut (except Fairfield County), Maine, Massachusetts, New Hampshire, Rhode Island, and Vermont.

Suggested Grade: 9-Adult
Order Number: 422
Production Date: 1990
Format: VHS videotape
Special Notes: No. 6 of the "Nippon Life" series.
Terms: Borrower pays return postage, including insurance. Return two weeks after receipt.
Source: Consulate General of Japan, Boston
Federal Reserve Plaza, 14th Floor
600 Atlantic Avenue
Boston, MA 02210
Phone: 1-617-973-9772
Fax: 1-617-542-1329
World Wide Web URL:
http://www.boston.us.emb-japan.go.jp
Email Address: infocul@cgjbos.org

Goddess of Mercy for Prevention of Senility
As the number of elderly increase in Japan, the number of senile people are also growing. People are making various prevention efforts, and statues of the Goddess of Mercy, who is said to prevent senility, are being dedicated in greater numbers.
Availability: Schools, libraries, and nursing homes in Oklahoma and Texas.
Suggested Grade: 9-Adult
Order Number: F6
Production Date: 1990
Format: VHS videotape
Special Notes: No. 6 of the "Nippon Life" series.
Terms: Materials must be picked up in person. Under special circumstances, you may be able to have them shipped to you at your own expense (call for further details). Return within two weeks after scheduled showing. Videos must be registered with the U. S. Postal Service or returned by Priority Mail, Federal Express, or other registered shipping service.
Source: Consulate General of Japan, Houston
Cultural Affairs and Information Section
909 Fannin Street, Suite 3000
Houston, TX 77010
Phone: 1-713-652-2977
Fax: 1-713-651-7822
World Wide Web URL:
http://www.houston.us.emb-japan.go.jp/
en/culture/page1.htm
Email Address: info@cgjhouston.org

Goddess of Mercy for Prevention of Senility
As the number of elderly increase in Japan, the number of senile people are also growing. People are making various prevention efforts, and statues of the Goddess of Mercy, who is said to prevent senility are being dedicated in greater numbers.
Availability: Schools, libraries, homeschoolers, and nursing homes in Nevada and northern California (zip codes beginning 932 and above, except 935).
Suggested Grade: 9-Adult

SOCIAL STUDIES--GEOGRAPHY--WORLD

Order Number: order by title
Production Date: 1990
Format: Beta videotape; U-matic videotape; VHS videotape
Special Notes: No. 6 of the "Nippon Life" series.
Terms: Borrower pays return postage. Book two weeks in advance. Return within three weeks of date borrowed, via UPS, Federal Express or certified mail.
Source: Consulate General of Japan, San Francisco
50 Fremont Street, Suite 2300
San Francisco, CA 94105-2236
Phone: 1-415-356-2564
Fax: 1-415-777-0518
World Wide Web URL: http://www.sf.us.emb-japan.go.jp/
Email Address: infoav@cgjsf.org

Grateful Crane, A
This animated tale tells an old Japanese folktale of kindness and appreciation.
Availability: Schools, libraries, homeschoolers, and nursing homes in Arizona and California (zipcodes beginning 900-931 and 935).
Suggested Grade: 2-12
Order Number: 085
Production Date: 1981
Format: VHS videotape
Terms: Borrower pays postage both ways; you may call the number below to learn how much postage costs. Return within two weeks of date borrowed. An individual may borrow 2 items at one time. For non-profit and educational use only.
Source: Consulate General of Japan, Los Angeles
350 South Grand Avenue, Suite 1700
Los Angeles, CA 90071-3459
Phone: 1-213-617-6700
Fax: 1-213-617-6727
World Wide Web URL: http://www.la.us.emb-japan.go.jp

Harvesting the Sea
More and more fishermen are turning to modern methods of breeding and harvesting fish. See new applications of technology to meet the realities of supply and demand.
Availability: Schools, libraries, homeschoolers, and nursing homes in Arizona and California (zipcodes beginning 900-931 and 935).
Suggested Grade: 4-Adult
Order Number: 076
Format: VHS videotape
Terms: Borrower pays postage both ways; you may call the number below to learn how much postage costs. Return within two weeks of date borrowed. An individual may borrow 2 items at one time. For non-profit and educational use only.
Source: Consulate General of Japan, Los Angeles
350 South Grand Avenue, Suite 1700
Los Angeles, CA 90071-3459
Phone: 1-213-617-6700
Fax: 1-213-617-6727
World Wide Web URL: http://www.la.us.emb-japan.go.jp

Heart Within, The
An overview of the concepts, traditions, and cultural aspects of Japan.
Availability: Schools, libraries, and nursing homes in Oklahoma and Texas.
Suggested Grade: 6-12
Order Number: K1
Format: VHS videotape
Special Notes: Part of the "Nihon No Kokoro" series.
Terms: Materials must be picked up in person. Under special circumstances, you may be able to have them shipped to you at your own expense (call for further details). Return within two weeks after scheduled showing. Videos must be registered with the U. S. Postal Service or returned by Priority Mail, Federal Express, or other registered shipping service.
Source: Consulate General of Japan, Houston
Cultural Affairs and Information Section
909 Fannin Street, Suite 3000
Houston, TX 77010
Phone: 1-713-652-2977
Fax: 1-713-651-7822
World Wide Web URL:
http://www.houston.us.emb-japan.go.jp/
en/culture/page1.htm
Email Address: info@cgjhouston.org

High Technology in Japan
Focuses on the latest technological advances in Japan including new ceramics for automobiles, knives, and computer parts.
Availability: Schools, libraries, homeschoolers, and nursing homes in Connecticut (except Fairfield County), Maine, Massachusetts, New Hampshire, Rhode Island, and Vermont.
Suggested Grade: 6-Adult
Order Number: 565
Production Date: 1990
Format: VHS videotape
Terms: Borrower pays return postage, including insurance. Return two weeks after receipt.
Source: Consulate General of Japan, Boston
Federal Reserve Plaza, 14th Floor
600 Atlantic Avenue
Boston, MA 02210
Phone: 1-617-973-9772
Fax: 1-617-542-1329
World Wide Web URL:
http://www.boston.us.emb-japan.go.jp
Email Address: infocul@cgjbos.org

Holiday in Japan
Highlights of some popular tourist attractions in Japan are shown.
Availability: Schools, libraries, and nursing homes in Oklahoma and Texas.
Suggested Grade: 4-12
Order Number: J6
Format: VHS videotape

All materials listed in this 2018-2019 edition are BRAND NEW!

SOCIAL STUDIES--GEOGRAPHY--WORLD

Terms: Materials must be picked up in person. Under special circumstances, you may be able to have them shipped to you at your own expense (call for further details). Return within two weeks after scheduled showing. Videos must be registered with the U. S. Postal Service or returned by Priority Mail, Federal Express, or other registered shipping service.
Source: Consulate General of Japan, Houston
Cultural Affairs and Information Section
909 Fannin Street, Suite 3000
Houston, TX 77010
Phone: 1-713-652-2977
Fax: 1-713-651-7822
World Wide Web URL:
http://www.houston.us.emb-japan.go.jp/
en/culture/page1.htm
Email Address: info@cgjhouston.org

Hollow Harvest
Provides an overview of life in rural Japan over the past fifty years.
Availability: Schools, libraries, homeschoolers, and nursing homes in Nevada and northern California (zip codes beginning 932 and above, except 935).
Suggested Grade: 6-12
Order Number: order by title
Format: VHS videotape
Terms: Borrower pays return postage. Book two weeks in advance. Return within three weeks of date borrowed, via UPS, Federal Express or certified mail.
Source: Consulate General of Japan, San Francisco
50 Fremont Street, Suite 2300
San Francisco, CA 94105-2236
Phone: 1-415-356-2564
Fax: 1-415-777-0518
World Wide Web URL: http://www.sf.us.emb-japan.go.jp/
Email Address: infoav@cgjsf.org

Images of Korea, Volume 1
Shows Koryo Celadon, Seoul, Traditional Costumes, Folk Festivals and Games, Traditional Medicine, Masked Dancedrama, Traditional Wedding Ceremony, Traditional Architecture.
Availability: Schools, libraries, and nursing homes in the United States and Canada.
Suggested Grade: 6-Adult
Language: Korean
Order Number: KV015
Format: VHS videotape
Terms: Borrower pays return postage. Return with 14 days after scheduled showing, via UPS or U. S. Mail. All requests must included an educational institution affiliation, a current address, and phone number. Order through web site only.
Source: Cornell University East Asia Program
World Wide Web URL:
http://eap.einaudi.cornell.edu/lending_library
Email Address: east_asia1@cornell.edu

In Celebration of the Enthronement of His Majesty the Emperor of Japan
Details the ceremonial regalia and traditional costumes of the 1990 ceremony.
Availability: Schools, libraries, homeschoolers, and nursing homes in Connecticut (except Fairfield County), Maine, Massachusetts, New Hampshire, Rhode Island, and Vermont.
Suggested Grade: 6-12
Order Number: 544
Format: VHS videotape
Terms: Borrower pays return postage, including insurance. Return two weeks after receipt.
Source: Consulate General of Japan, Boston
Federal Reserve Plaza, 14th Floor
600 Atlantic Avenue
Boston, MA 02210
Phone: 1-617-973-9772
Fax: 1-617-542-1329
World Wide Web URL:
http://www.boston.us.emb-japan.go.jp
Email Address: infocul@cgjbos.org

India: Land of the Monsoon
A glimpse of how the people of India have learned to live with monsoons, which bring both needed rain and disastrous floods; includes a study of the different kinds of monsoons.
Availability: Schools and libraries in the United States.
Suggested Grade: 7-12
Order Number: 36
Production Date: 1991
Format: VHS videotape
Terms: Borrower pays return postage. Return 3 days after showing via UPS. Book at least 2 weeks in advance.
Source: Syracuse University, South Asia Center
Video Library and Teaching Resources
346F Eggers Hall
The Maxwell School
Syracuse, NY 13244

Indian Pilgrimage, An: Ramdevra
A folk pilgrimage by a group of Hindus to the grave of Ramdev, a medieval hero. Devotion, with little priestly instruction, guides their worship.
Availability: Schools, libraries, homeschoolers, and nursing homes in the southeastern United States.
Suggested Grade: 7-12
Order Number: order by title
Production Date: 1975
Format: VHS videotape
Terms: Borrower pays return postage. Return 2 days after showing via United Parcel Service, insured. Book 2 weeks in advance.
Source: Center for South Asian Studies
University of Virginia, Video Library Coordinator
P. O. Box 400169, 110 Minor Hall
Charlottesville, VA 22904-4169

All materials listed in this 2018-2019 edition are BRAND NEW!

SOCIAL STUDIES--GEOGRAPHY--WORLD

Phone: 1-434-924-8815
Email Address: southasia@virginia.edu

Inventive Young Minds
All over Japan there are public facilities designed to encourage the ingenuity and inventiveness of children. This video highlights one such facility, the Tokyo Metropolitan Children's Hall where youngsters from the third to sixth grade create toys and handicrafts from their own imagination.

Availability: Schools, libraries, homeschoolers, and nursing homes in Arizona and California (zipcodes beginning 900-931 and 935).
Suggested Grade: All ages
Order Number: 077
Production Date: 1980
Format: VHS videotape
Terms: Borrower pays postage both ways; you may call the number below to learn how much postage costs. Return within two weeks of date borrowed. An individual may borrow 2 items at one time. For non-profit and educational use only.

Source: Consulate General of Japan, Los Angeles
350 South Grand Avenue, Suite 1700
Los Angeles, CA 90071-3459
Phone: 1-213-617-6700
Fax: 1-213-617-6727
World Wide Web URL: http://www.la.us.emb-japan.go.jp

Jagriti (The Awakening)
Interviews with local politicians and administrators of international aid organizations--and students' satirical sketches of the same people--provide a record of the first year of a school for children in the poorest district of Delhi.

Availability: Schools, libraries, homeschoolers, and nursing homes in the southeastern United States.
Suggested Grade: 7-12
Order Number: order by title
Production Date: 1991
Format: VHS videotape
Terms: Borrower pays return postage. Return 2 days after showing via United Parcel Service, insured. Book 2 weeks in advance.

Source: Center for South Asian Studies
University of Virginia
Video Library Coordinator
P. O. Box 400169, 110 Minor Hall
Charlottesville, VA 22904-4169
Phone: 1-434-924-8815
Email Address: southasia@virginia.edu

Japanese Architecture: The Living Heritage
The genius of Japanese traditional architecture based on wood with its harmonious and valuable relationship to modern styles is explored. The concepts of "inside" and "outside" are examined.

Availability: Schools, libraries, and nursing homes in Illinois, Indiana, Iowa, Kansas, Minnesota, Missouri, Nebraska, North Dakota, South Dakota, and Wisconsin.
Suggested Grade: 6-Adult
Order Number: 02001
Production Date: 1982
Format: VHS videotape
Terms: Borrower pays return postage by U. S. Mail, UPS, or Federal Express, including insurance for "original" videos. Write, call, fax, or e-mail to request an application. An application form MUST be sent in one month in advance but not more than six months in advance. Include alternate titles and dates if provider can substitute titles. Send a SASE with request if you require confirmation. Return immediately after scheduled showing date. Videos may not be copied or broadcast without permission from the producer of the video. Borrower is responsible if video is lost or damaged.

Source: Consulate General of Japan at Chicago
Japan Information Center, Library
737 North Michigan Avenue, Suite 1000
Chicago, IL 60611
Phone: 1-312-280-0430
Fax: 1-312-280-6883
World Wide Web URL:
http://www.chicago.us.emb-japan.go.jp/jic.html
Email Address: jicchicago@webkddi.com

Japanese Architecture: A Living Heritage
The genius of Japanese traditional architecture based on wood with its harmonious and valuable relationship to modern styles is explored. The concepts of "inside" and "outside" are examined.

Availability: Schools, libraries, homeschoolers, and nursing homes in Arizona and California (zipcodes beginning 900-931 and 935).
Suggested Grade: 6-Adult
Order Number: 073
Production Date: 1982
Format: VHS videotape
Terms: Borrower pays postage both ways; you may call the number below to learn how much postage costs. Return within two weeks of date borrowed. An individual may borrow 2 items at one time. For non-profit and educational use only.

Source: Consulate General of Japan, Los Angeles
350 South Grand Avenue, Suite 1700
Los Angeles, CA 90071-3459
Phone: 1-213-617-6700
Fax: 1-213-617-6727
World Wide Web URL: http://www.la.us.emb-japan.go.jp

Japanese Culture: Cities; Entertainment; Architecture
Learn more about Japanese culture.

Availability: Schools, libraries and homeschoolers in Alabama, Georgia, North Carolina, South Carolina, and Virginia.

SOCIAL STUDIES--GEOGRAPHY--WORLD

Suggested Grade: 7-12
Order Number: 140
Format: VHS videotape
Special Notes: Part of the Japan Video Encyclopedia series.
Terms: Borrower pays return postage. Two tapes may be borrowed at a time. Return within 7 days after receipt. Reservations may be made by filling the application found on the web site.
Source: Consulate General of Japan, Atlanta
Japan Information Center
One Alliance Center
3500 Lenox Road, Suite 1600
Atlanta, GA 30326
Phone: 1-404-365-9240
Fax: 1-404-240-4311
World Wide Web URL:
http://www.atlanta.us.emb-japan.go.jp
Email Address: info@cgjapanatlanta.org

Japan: Journey of Discovery
Gives you the flavor of the cities and rural areas of Japan. Shows the scenic beauty of the temples, waterfalls, and other areas throughout Japan.
Availability: Schools, libraries, and nursing homes in Oklahoma and Texas.
Suggested Grade: All ages
Order Number: J1
Production Date: 1984
Format: VHS videotape
Terms: Materials must be picked up in person. Under special circumstances, you may be able to have them shipped to you at your own expense (call for further details). Return within two weeks after scheduled showing. Videos must be registered with the U. S. Postal Service or returned by Priority Mail, Federal Express, or other registered shipping service.
Source: Consulate General of Japan, Houston
Cultural Affairs and Information Section
909 Fannin Street, Suite 3000
Houston, TX 77010
Phone: 1-713-652-2977
Fax: 1-713-651-7822
World Wide Web URL:
http://www.houston.us.emb-japan.go.jp/en/culture/page1.htm
Email Address: info@cgjhouston.org

Japan Land of Enchantment
Provides an overall view of Japan through the seasons.
Availability: Schools, libraries, and nursing homes in Hawaii.
Suggested Grade: All ages
Order Number: TR-7
Format: VHS videotape
Terms: Borrower pays return postage. A maximum of 3 videos may be borrowed per person. Return within one week of date borrowed.
Source: Consulate General of Japan, Honolulu
1742 Nuuanu Avenue
Honolulu, HI 96817-3294
Phone: 1-808-543-3111
Fax: 1-808-543-3170
World Wide Web URL:
http://www.honolulu.us.emb-japan.go.jp

Japan Today
Portrays the multi-faceted life of today's Japanese people, focusing on combination of tradition and technical innovation.
Availability: Schools, libraries, and nursing homes in Oklahoma and Texas.
Suggested Grade: 7-Adult
Order Number: H
Production Date: 1991
Format: VHS videotape
Terms: Materials must be picked up in person. Under special circumstances, you may be able to have them shipped to you at your own expense (call for further details). Return within two weeks after scheduled showing. Videos must be registered with the U. S. Postal Service or returned by Priority Mail, Federal Express, or other registered shipping service.
Source: Consulate General of Japan, Houston
Cultural Affairs and Information Section
909 Fannin Street, Suite 3000
Houston, TX 77010
Phone: 1-713-652-2977
Fax: 1-713-651-7822
World Wide Web URL:
http://www.houston.us.emb-japan.go.jp/en/culture/page1.htm
Email Address: info@cgjhouston.org

Jing, a Chinese Girl
Features a typical Saturday and Sunday in the life of a fifth-grade student in Hangzhou, China.
Availability: Schools, libraries, and nursing homes in the United States and Canada.
Suggested Grade: All ages
Order Number: CV019
Format: VHS videotape
Terms: Borrower pays return postage. Return with 14 days after scheduled showing, via UPS or U. S. Mail. All requests must included an educational institution affiliation, a current address, and phone number. Order through web site only.
Source: Cornell University East Asia Program
World Wide Web URL:
http://eap.einaudi.cornell.edu/lending_library
Email Address: east_asia1@cornell.edu

Kalasha, The: Rites of Spring
A view of the threatened way of life of the Kalasha people, of the valleys of the Hindu Kush Mountains in northwest Pakistan.
Availability: Schools, libraries, homeschoolers, and nursing homes in the southeastern United States.
Suggested Grade: 7-12

SOCIAL STUDIES--GEOGRAPHY--WORLD

Order Number: order by title
Production Date: 1990
Format: VHS videotape
Terms: Borrower pays return postage. Return 2 days after showing via United Parcel Service, insured. Book 2 weeks in advance.
Source: Center for South Asian Studies
University of Virginia, Video Library Coordinator
P. O. Box 400169, 110 Minor Hall
Charlottesville, VA 22904-4169
Phone: 1-434-924-8815
Email Address: southasia@virginia.edu

Kangofu, The Japanese Nurse
Follow a nurse in the Kanagawa Prefectural Children's Medical Center on some of her daily rounds.
Availability: Schools, libraries, homeschoolers, and nursing homes in Arizona and California (zipcodes beginning 900-931 and 935).
Suggested Grade: 7-Adult
Order Number: 084
Production Date: 1983
Format: VHS videotape
Terms: Borrower pays postage both ways; you may call the number below to learn how much postage costs. Return within two weeks of date borrowed. An individual may borrow 2 items at one time. For non-profit and educational use only.
Source: Consulate General of Japan, Los Angeles
350 South Grand Avenue, Suite 1700
Los Angeles, CA 90071-3459
Phone: 1-213-617-6700
Fax: 1-213-617-6727
World Wide Web URL: http://www.la.us.emb-japan.go.jp

Kenyan Way of Life, The
Kenya is a country of contrasts, harmoniously blending the traditional and modern. Forty (40) different cultural groups and tribes, modern cities and villages, and industry and agriculture comprise today's Kenya. Looks at the country's economy, government, educational system, and historical development. Despite their diversity, Kenyans have lived peacefully together since their independence from Britain in 1963.
Availability: Schools, libraries, and homeschoolers in the United States who serve the hearing impaired.
Suggested Grade: 7-10
Order Number: 13048
Production Date: 1993
Format: DVD
Special Notes: Produced by Aims Multimedia.
Terms: Sponsor pays all transportation costs. Return one week after receipt. Participation is limited to deaf or hard of hearing Americans, their parents, families, teachers, counselors, or others whose use would benefit a deaf or hard of hearing person. Only one person in the audience needs to be hearing impaired. You must register--which is free. These videos are all open-captioned--no special equipment is required for viewing.
Source: Described and Captioned Media Program
National Association of the Deaf
4211 Church Street Ext.
Roebuck, SC 29376
Phone: 1-800-237-6213
Fax: 1-800-538-5636
World Wide Web URL: http://www.dcmp.org

Kenya: The Masai Homeland
Presents an overview of Kenya's main tribal and ethnic groups, focusing on their lives and traditions. Includes the legend of Kenya's beginning, its huge national parks, its animal life, and some tourist attractions. Focuses on the Masai and Turkana tribes.
Availability: Schools, libraries, and homeschoolers in the United States who serve the hearing impaired.
Suggested Grade: 6-10
Order Number: 13127
Production Date: 1998
Format: DVD
Special Notes: Produced by Ambrose Video Publishing, Inc..
Terms: Sponsor pays all transportation costs. Return one week after receipt. Participation is limited to deaf or hard of hearing Americans, their parents, families, teachers, counselors, or others whose use would benefit a deaf or hard of hearing person. Only one person in the audience needs to be hearing impaired. You must register--which is free. These videos are all open-captioned--no special equipment is required for viewing.
Source: Described and Captioned Media Program
National Association of the Deaf
4211 Church Street Ext.
Roebuck, SC 29376
Phone: 1-800-237-6213
Fax: 1-800-538-5636
World Wide Web URL: http://www.dcmp.org

Kisho Kurokawa: Architect
Some of the works of Japanese architect, Kisho Kurokawa.
Availability: Schools, libraries, homeschoolers, and nursing homes in Arizona and California (zipcodes beginning 900-931 and 935).
Suggested Grade: 7-Adult
Order Number: 073
Production Date: 1978
Format: VHS videotape
Terms: Borrower pays postage both ways; you may call the number below to learn how much postage costs. Return within two weeks of date borrowed. An individual may borrow 2 items at one time. For non-profit and educational use only.
Source: Consulate General of Japan, Los Angeles
350 South Grand Avenue, Suite 1700
Los Angeles, CA 90071-3459
Phone: 1-213-617-6700
Fax: 1-213-617-6727
World Wide Web URL: http://www.la.us.emb-japan.go.jp

All materials listed in this 2018-2019 edition are BRAND NEW!

SOCIAL STUDIES--GEOGRAPHY--WORLD

Kobe 1995--A Cruel Lesson
A documentary on the Great Hanshin Earthquake.
Availability: Schools, libraries, homeschoolers, and nursing homes in Connecticut (except Fairfield County), Maine, Massachusetts, New Hampshire, Rhode Island, and Vermont.
Suggested Grade: 6-12
Order Number: 526
Production Date: 1995
Format: VHS videotape
Terms: Borrower pays return postage, including insurance. Return two weeks after receipt.
Source: Consulate General of Japan, Boston
Federal Reserve Plaza, 14th Floor
600 Atlantic Avenue
Boston, MA 02210
Phone: 1-617-973-9772
Fax: 1-617-542-1329
World Wide Web URL:
http://www.boston.us.emb-japan.go.jp
Email Address: infocul@cgjbos.org

Kobe 1995--A Cruel Lesson
A documentary on the Great Hanshin Earthquake.
Availability: Schools, libraries, homeschoolers, and nursing homes in Arizona and California (zipcodes beginning 900-931 and 935).
Suggested Grade: 6-12
Order Number: 254
Production Date: 1995
Format: VHS videotape
Terms: Borrower pays postage both ways; you may call the number below to learn how much postage costs. Return within two weeks of date borrowed. An individual may borrow 2 items at one time. For non-profit and educational use only.
Source: Consulate General of Japan, Los Angeles
350 South Grand Avenue, Suite 1700
Los Angeles, CA 90071-3459
Phone: 1-213-617-6700
Fax: 1-213-617-6727
World Wide Web URL: http://www.la.us.emb-japan.go.jp

Kurashiki
An information tour of Kurashiki city.
Availability: Schools, libraries, and nursing homes in Hawaii.
Suggested Grade: 4-12
Order Number: TR-10
Format: VHS videotape
Terms: Borrower pays return postage. A maximum of 3 videos may be borrowed per person. Return within one week of date borrowed.
Source: Consulate General of Japan, Honolulu
1742 Nuuanu Avenue
Honolulu, HI 96817-3294
Phone: 1-808-543-3111
Fax: 1-808-543-3170
World Wide Web URL:
http://www.honolulu.us.emb-japan.go.jp

Kyoto--Scenes and Festivals
Shows scenes from the Kyoto Festival including dances and festivals.
Availability: Schools, libraries, and nursing homes in Illinois, Indiana, Iowa, Kansas, Minnesota, Missouri, Nebraska, North Dakota, South Dakota, and Wisconsin.
Suggested Grade: All ages
Order Number: 19205
Production Date: 1985
Format: VHS videotape
Terms: Borrower pays return postage by U. S. Mail, UPS, or Federal Express, including insurance for "original" videos. Write, call, fax, or e-mail to request an application. An application form MUST be sent in one month in advance but not more than six months in advance. Include alternate titles and dates if provider can substitute titles. Send a SASE with request if you require confirmation. Return immediately after scheduled showing date. Videos may not be copied or broadcast without permission from the producer of the video. Borrower is responsible if video is lost or damaged.
Source: Consulate General of Japan at Chicago
Japan Information Center
Library
737 North Michigan Avenue, Suite 1000
Chicago, IL 60611
Phone: 1-312-280-0430
Fax: 1-312-280-6883
World Wide Web URL: http://www.chicago.us.emb-japan.go.jp/jic.html
Email Address: jicchicago@webkddi.com

Kyoto--Scenes and Festivals
Shows scenes from the Kyoto Festival including dances and festivals.
Availability: Schools, libraries, homeschoolers, and nursing homes in Connecticut (except Fairfield County), Maine, Massachusetts, New Hampshire, Rhode Island, and Vermont.
Suggested Grade: All ages
Order Number: 111
Production Date: 1985
Format: VHS videotape
Terms: Borrower pays return postage, including insurance. Return two weeks after receipt.
Source: Consulate General of Japan, Boston
Federal Reserve Plaza, 14th Floor, 600 Atlantic Avenue
Boston, MA 02210
Phone: 1-617-973-9772
Fax: 1-617-542-1329
World Wide Web URL:
http://www.boston.us.emb-japan.go.jp
Email Address: infocul@cgjbos.org

Kyoto--Scenes and Festivals
Shows scenes from the Kyoto Festival including dances and festivals.

All materials listed in this 2018-2019 edition are BRAND NEW!

SOCIAL STUDIES--GEOGRAPHY--WORLD

Availability: Schools, libraries, and nursing homes in Oklahoma and Texas.
Suggested Grade: All ages
Order Number: I17
Format: VHS videotape
Terms: Materials must be picked up in person. Under special circumstances, you may be able to have them shipped to you at your own expense (call for further details). Return within two weeks after scheduled showing. Videos must be registered with the U. S. Postal Service or returned by Priority Mail, Federal Express, or other registered shipping service.
Source: Consulate General of Japan, Houston
Cultural Affairs and Information Section
909 Fannin Street, Suite 3000
Houston, TX 77010
Phone: 1-713-652-2977
Fax: 1-713-651-7822
World Wide Web URL:
http://www.houston.us.emb-japan.go.jp/en/culture/page1.htm
Email Address: info@cgjhouston.org

Lantern Festival, The
Provides a flavor of the rich and varied culture of China. Complete with anecdotes and folklore, this video outlines the ceremonies and traditions of the Chinese Lantern Festival, a colorful celebration of lights, food, music, and dance.
Availability: Schools, libraries, and nursing homes in the United States and Canada.
Suggested Grade: 6-Adult
Order Number: TV001
Format: VHS videotape
Terms: Borrower pays return postage. Return with 14 days after scheduled showing, via UPS or U. S. Mail. All requests must included an educational institution affiliation, a current address, and phone number. Order through web site only.
Source: Cornell University East Asia Program
World Wide Web URL:
http://eap.einaudi.cornell.edu/lending_library
Email Address: east_asia1@cornell.edu

Latitude and Longitude
How did early seafarers know where they were, or where they were going? How did they navigate? How do today's airplanes and ships know? What are latitude and longitude? How are they useful? Explains the development and use of latitude, longitude, sextant chronometer, the Prime Meridian, and other navigational systems from ancient to modern times.
Availability: Schools, libraries, and homeschoolers in the United States who serve the hearing impaired.
Suggested Grade: 7-12
Order Number: 13008
Production Date: 1994
Format: DVD
Special Notes: Produced by National Geographic Society.
Terms: Sponsor pays all transportation costs. Return one week after receipt. Participation is limited to deaf or hard of hearing Americans, their parents, families, teachers, counselors, or others whose use would benefit a deaf or hard of hearing person. Only one person in the audience needs to be hearing impaired. You must register--which is free. These videos are all open-captioned--no special equipment is required for viewing.
Source: Described and Captioned Media Program
National Association of the Deaf
4211 Church Street Ext.
Roebuck, SC 29376
Phone: 1-800-237-6213
Fax: 1-800-538-5636
World Wide Web URL: http://www.dcmp.org

Life from the Sea
Japan, a country whose people get 27% of their animal protein from fish, is noted for its fishermen who have refined the ancient art of fishing into a precise science. Fish today are caught with the help of research ships that study conditions in the ocean and help locate schools of fish.
Availability: Schools, libraries, homeschoolers, and nursing homes in Arizona and California (zipcodes beginning 900-931 and 935).
Suggested Grade: 4-Adult
Order Number: 076
Production Date: 1968
Format: VHS videotape
Terms: Borrower pays postage both ways; you may call the number below to learn how much postage costs. Return within two weeks of date borrowed. An individual may borrow 2 items at one time. For non-profit and educational use only.
Source: Consulate General of Japan, Los Angeles
350 South Grand Avenue, Suite 1700
Los Angeles, CA 90071-3459
Phone: 1-213-617-6700
Fax: 1-213-617-6727
World Wide Web URL: http://www.la.us.emb-japan.go.jp

Life in an Oasis
Portrays life at the Fachi oasis in Niger, Africa. Discusses its isolation; lack of modern conveniences; crops of dates, potatoes, and spices; and work in the salt pits. The Kanuri people of Fachi use their crops and salt to barter with the welcome caravans for needed supplies.
Availability: Schools, libraries, and homeschoolers in the United States who serve the hearing impaired.
Suggested Grade: 4-10
Order Number: 13051
Production Date: 1995
Format: DVD
Special Notes: Produced by Stanton Films.
Terms: Sponsor pays all transportation costs. Return one week after receipt. Participation is limited to deaf or hard of hearing Americans, their parents, families, teachers, counselors, or others whose use would benefit a deaf or hard of hearing person. Only one person in the audience

SOCIAL STUDIES--GEOGRAPHY--WORLD

needs to be hearing impaired. You must register--which is free. These videos are all open-captioned--no special equipment is required for viewing.

**Source: Described and Captioned Media Program
National Association of the Deaf
4211 Church Street Ext.
Roebuck, SC 29376
Phone: 1-800-237-6213
Fax: 1-800-538-5636
World Wide Web URL: http://www.dcmp.org**

Living Arts

A Japanese sixth-grade tells about how she and her two sisters and their family participate in the preservation of traditional arts while at the same time being "modern Japanese."

Availability: Schools, libraries, and nursing homes in the United States and Canada.
Suggested Grade: All ages
Order Number: JV014
Format: VHS videotape
Terms: Borrower pays return postage. Return with 14 days after scheduled showing, via UPS or U. S. Mail. All requests must included an educational institution affiliation, a current address, and phone number. Order through web site only.

**Source: Cornell University East Asia Program
World Wide Web URL:
http://eap.einaudi.cornell.edu/lending_library
Email Address: east_asia1@cornell.edu**

Magic of China/Children of China

Two documentaries are presented, about the magic and beauty of China and children in China.

Availability: Schools, libraries, homeschoolers, and nursing homes in the United States and Canada.
Suggested Grade: 9-12
Order Number: order by title
Production Date: 1988
Format: VHS videotape
Terms: Postage is paid by borrower both ways--send $3.00 per tape to cover initial shipping to you--MONEY MUST BE SENT WITH REQUEST. Return 10 days after showing via U. S. Postal Service, library rate. Shipping is $5.00 to Canadian addresses.

**Source: Center for Teaching About China
Kathleen Trescott
1214 West Schwartz
Carbondale, IL 62901
Phone: 1-618-549-1555
Email Address: trescott@midwest.net**

Marriages in Heaven

This illuminating documentary explores the ways in which globalization and modernization are affecting young people and changing the traditions of arranged marriages among Indians living both in India and in America.

Availability: Schools, libraries, homeschoolers, and nursing homes in the southeastern United States.
Suggested Grade: 7-12
Order Number: order by title
Production Date: 2001
Format: VHS videotape
Terms: Borrower pays return postage. Return 2 days after showing via United Parcel Service, insured. Book 2 weeks in advance.

**Source: Center for South Asian Studies
University of Virginia
Video Library Coordinator
P. O. Box 400169, 110 Minor Hall
Charlottesville, VA 22904-4169
Phone: 1-434-924-8815
Email Address: southasia@virginia.edu**

Masses and Murals

Murals and billboards connect Nicaragua's urban and rural areas through images and messages.

Availability: Schools and libraries in Iowa, Illinois, Michigan, Minnesota, and Wisconsin.
Suggested Grade: 9-Adult
Order Number: ART/FOLNICM37VHS
Production Date: 1986
Format: VHS videotape
Terms: Borrower pays return postage. Return 8 days after showing. Book 2 weeks in advance. Order may also be picked up for those near the Center.

**Source: Center for Latin American and Caribbean Studies
UW-Milwaukee
P. O. Box 413
Milwaukee, WI 53201
Phone: 1-414-229-5987
World Wide Web URL: http://www.uwm.edu/Dept/CLACS
Email Address: audvis@usm.edu**

Meeting the Third World Through Women's Perspectives

Global education unit introduces students to contemporary women in South Asia, Africa, and Latin America, to re-examine traditional concepts of family and work.

Availability: Schools, libraries, and nursing homes in the United States.
Suggested Grade: 8-Adult
Order Number: SI4-video
Production Date: 1988
Format: VHS videotape
Special Notes: Includes 120-page teachers guide, lesson plan, audiovisual guide, and reproducible handouts.
Terms: Borrowers must have a User's Agreement on file with this source--available by mail or via the Internet. Return postage is paid by borrower; return 12 days after showing. Book at least three weeks in advance. All borrowers are limited to a total of ten items per semester.

SOCIAL STUDIES--GEOGRAPHY--WORLD

Source: Latin American Resource Center
Stone Center for Latin American Studies
Tulane University
100 Jones Hall
New Orleans, LA 70118
Phone: 1-504-862-3143
Fax: 1-504-865-6719
World Wide Web URL: http://stonecenter.tulane.edu/pages/detail/48/Lending-Library
Email Address: crcrts@tulane.edu

Mercado, El
An introduction to the markets of Latin America--the hub of life in villages.
- Availability: Schools in the United States.
- Suggested Grade: All ages
- Language: Spanish
- Order Number: order by title
- Production Date: 1990
- Format: VHS videotape
- Terms: Borrower pays return postage. Return 14 days after receipt, via USPS including insurance. All borrowers must have a current lending agreement on file with the Outreach program. This agreement is available via the web site or may be requested via phone or fax.

Source: Center for Latin American Studies
University of Florida
319 Grinter Hall
P. O. Box 115530
Gainesville, FL 32611-5530
Phone: 1-352-392-0375
Fax: 1-352-392-7682
World Wide Web URL: http://www.latam.ufl.edu/outreach
Email Address: maryr@ufl.edu

Middle America: Mexico to Venezuela and the Caribbean Islands
Middle America is a cultural crossroads. Africa, Native American, and European influences are seen in its religions, foods, architecture, languages, and arts. Includes discussion of terrains and climates, food crops, cultural influences, regional economies, and tourism and environmental problems. Compares some of the Caribbean islands.
- Availability: Schools, libraries, and homeschoolers in the United States who serve the hearing impaired.
- Suggested Grade: 7-11
- Order Number: 12836
- Production Date: 1995
- Format: DVD
- Special Notes: Produced by Benchmark Media.
- Terms: Sponsor pays all transportation costs. Return one week after receipt. Participation is limited to deaf or hard of hearing Americans, their parents, families, teachers, counselors, or others whose use would benefit a deaf or hard of hearing person. Only one person in the audience needs to be hearing impaired. You must register--which is free. These videos are all open-captioned--no special equipment is required for viewing.

Source: Described and Captioned Media Program
National Association of the Deaf
4211 Church Street Ext.
Roebuck, SC 29376
Phone: 1-800-237-6213
Fax: 1-800-538-5636
World Wide Web URL: http://www.dcmp.org

Mini Series: Profile of a Nation
Presents 6 different videos in one that explore all aspects of Japan.
- Availability: Schools, libraries, and nursing homes in Hawaii.
- Suggested Grade: 4-12
- Order Number: CU-46
- Format: VHS videotape
- Terms: Borrower pays return postage. A maximum of 3 videos may be borrowed per person. Return within one week of date borrowed.

Source: Consulate General of Japan, Honolulu
1742 Nuuanu Avenue
Honolulu, HI 96817-3294
Phone: 1-808-543-3111
Fax: 1-808-543-3170
World Wide Web URL: http://www.honolulu.us.emb-japan.go.jp

Mini Series: Profile of a Nation
Presents 6 different videos in one that explore all aspects of Japan.
- Availability: Schools, libraries, and nursing homes in Hawaii.
- Suggested Grade: 4-12
- Order Number: CU-48
- Format: VHS videotape
- Terms: Borrower pays return postage. A maximum of 3 videos may be borrowed per person. Return within one week of date borrowed.

Source: Consulate General of Japan, Honolulu
1742 Nuuanu Avenue
Honolulu, HI 96817-3294
Phone: 1-808-543-3111
Fax: 1-808-543-3170
World Wide Web URL: http://www.honolulu.us.emb-japan.go.jp

Mini Series: Profile of a Nation
Presents 7 different videos in one that explore all aspects of Japan.
- Availability: Schools, libraries, and nursing homes in Hawaii.
- Suggested Grade: 4-12
- Order Number: CU-45
- Format: VHS videotape
- Terms: Borrower pays return postage. A maximum of 3 videos may be borrowed per person. Return within one week of date borrowed.

SOCIAL STUDIES--GEOGRAPHY--WORLD

Source: Consulate General of Japan, Honolulu
1742 Nuuanu Avenue
Honolulu, HI 96817-3294
Phone: 1-808-543-3111
Fax: 1-808-543-3170
World Wide Web URL:
http://www.honolulu.us.emb-japan.go.jp

Mobile Services
Depicts the variety of services available to people in remote areas who are in need of medical care.
Availability: Schools, libraries, homeschoolers, and nursing homes in Arizona and California (zipcodes beginning 900-931 and 935).
Suggested Grade: 7-Adult
Order Number: 084
Production Date: 1982
Format: VHS videotape
Terms: Borrower pays postage both ways; you may call the number below to learn how much postage costs. Return within two weeks of date borrowed. An individual may borrow 2 items at one time. For non-profit and educational use only.
Source: Consulate General of Japan, Los Angeles
350 South Grand Avenue, Suite 1700
Los Angeles, CA 90071-3459
Phone: 1-213-617-6700
Fax: 1-213-617-6727
World Wide Web URL: http://www.la.us.emb-japan.go.jp

Modern Brides: Arranged Marriage in South India
Describes two marriages that occur in Mysore, South India in 1983. One marriage is an arranged marriage and the other is a "love" marriage.
Availability: Schools and libraries in the United States.
Suggested Grade: 7-Adult
Order Number: SA9
Production Date: 1985
Format: VHS videotape
Terms: Borrower pays return postage. Return 3 days after showing via UPS. Book at least 2 weeks in advance.
Source: Syracuse University, South Asia Center
Video Library and Teaching Resources
346F Eggers Hall
The Maxwell School
Syracuse, NY 13244

Municipal Office and Its Services, The/Village Reborn, A/Toga: Village for the Theater
This three part tape begins with daily activities and functions of a typical municipal office. Shown is the story of how a dying village rejuvenates itself by converting from a one crop to a multi-crop system of agriculture. Toga village has recently undergone a renaissance thanks to its International Arts Festival and popularity of Tadashi Suzuki and his drama troupe.

Availability: Schools, libraries, homeschoolers, and nursing homes in Connecticut (except Fairfield County), Maine, Massachusetts, New Hampshire, Rhode Island, and Vermont.
Suggested Grade: 6-Adult
Order Number: 132
Format: VHS videotape
Terms: Borrower pays return postage, including insurance. Return two weeks after receipt.
Source: Consulate General of Japan, Boston
Federal Reserve Plaza, 14th Floor
600 Atlantic Avenue
Boston, MA 02210
Phone: 1-617-973-9772
Fax: 1-617-542-1329
World Wide Web URL:
http://www.boston.us.emb-japan.go.jp
Email Address: infocul@cgjbos.org

Munni (Little Girl): Childhood and Art in Mithila
An 11-year old girl in Jitwarpur, northeastern India, observes older women practicing traditional crafts.
Availability: Schools and libraries in the United States.
Suggested Grade: 7-12
Order Number: 14
Production Date: 1983
Format: VHS videotape
Terms: Borrower pays return postage. Return 3 days after showing via UPS. Book at least 2 weeks in advance.
Source: Syracuse University, South Asia Center
Video Library and Teaching Resources
346F Eggers Hall
The Maxwell School
Syracuse, NY 13244

Nature's Bounty: Flowers for the Japanese
Shows the beautiful flowers of Japan.
Availability: Schools, libraries, homeschoolers, and nursing homes in Arizona and California (zipcodes beginning 900-931 and 935).
Suggested Grade: 4-Adult
Order Number: 028
Production Date: 1969
Format: VHS videotape
Terms: Borrower pays postage both ways; you may call the number below to learn how much postage costs. Return within two weeks of date borrowed. An individual may borrow 2 items at one time. For non-profit and educational use only.
Source: Consulate General of Japan, Los Angeles
350 South Grand Avenue, Suite 1700
Los Angeles, CA 90071-3459
Phone: 1-213-617-6700
Fax: 1-213-617-6727
World Wide Web URL: http://www.la.us.emb-japan.go.jp

Neighborhood Tokyo
Theodor Bestor, an anthropologist has been studying a community of Mom-and Pop stores and small enterprises

SOCIAL STUDIES--GEOGRAPHY--WORLD

near the center of Tokyo for more than a decade. This program takes you into the streets of this town for a first hand look at an urban community

Availability: Schools, libraries, homeschoolers, and nursing homes in Nevada and northern California (zip codes beginning 932 and above, except 935).
Suggested Grade: 6-12
Order Number: order by title
Production Date: 1992
Format: VHS videotape
Terms: Borrower pays return postage. Book two weeks in advance. Return within three weeks of date borrowed, via UPS, Federal Express or certified mail.
Source: Consulate General of Japan, San Francisco
50 Fremont Street, Suite 2300
San Francisco, CA 94105-2236
Phone: 1-415-356-2564
Fax: 1-415-777-0518
World Wide Web URL: http://www.sf.us.emb-japan.go.jp/
Email Address: infoav@cgjsf.org

Nepal: Land of the Gods

A view of the mingling of Buddhist and pre-Buddhist customs in this Himalayan kingdom.

Availability: Schools, libraries, homeschoolers, and nursing homes in the southeastern United States.
Suggested Grade: 7-12
Order Number: order by title
Format: VHS videotape
Terms: Borrower pays return postage. Return 2 days after showing via United Parcel Service, insured. Book 2 weeks in advance.
Source: Center for South Asian Studies
University of Virginia, Video Library Coordinator
P. O. Box 400169, 110 Minor Hall
Charlottesville, VA 22904-4169
Phone: 1-434-924-8815
Email Address: southasia@virginia.edu

Night of Nine Tribes, The

Recommended for those with a particular interest in state-sponsored revivals of indigenous ritual ceremonies. This video chronicles the International Year of the Indigenous People, featuring the Tayal people of Wu Lai, and hosted by the Taiwan Cultural Ministry in cooperation with other government ministries and bureaus.

Availability: Schools, libraries, and nursing homes in the United States and Canada.
Suggested Grade: All ages
Languages: Chinese; subtitled in English
Order Number: TV007
Format: VHS videotape
Terms: Borrower pays return postage. Return with 14 days after scheduled showing, via UPS or U. S. Mail. All requests must included an educational institution affiliation, a current address, and phone number. Order through web site only.

Source: Cornell University East Asia Program
World Wide Web URL: http://eap.einaudi.cornell.edu/lending_library
Email Address: east_asia1@cornell.edu

No Longer Colonies: Hong Kong, 1997; Macau, 1999

Traces the history and prospects of the last European colonies in Chinese territory.

Availability: Schools, libraries, homeschoolers, and nursing homes in the United States and Canada.
Suggested Grade: 7-Adult
Order Number: order by title
Production Date: 1993
Format: VHS videotape
Terms: Postage is paid by borrower both ways--send $3.00 per tape to cover initial shipping to you--MONEY MUST BE SENT WITH REQUEST. Return 10 days after showing via U. S. Postal Service, library rate. Shipping is $5.00 to Canadian addresses.
Source: Center for Teaching About China
Kathleen Trescott
1214 West Schwartz
Carbondale, IL 62901
Phone: 1-618-549-1555
Email Address: trescott@midwest.net

No Longer Silent

This prize-winning documentary of the struggle of Indian women for equality provides an overview of women's organizations and resource centers, as well as profiles of activists seeking to correct current and traditional abuses.

Availability: Schools and libraries in the United States.
Suggested Grade: 7-12
Order Number: 61
Production Date: 1987
Format: VHS videotape
Terms: Borrower pays return postage. Return 3 days after showing via UPS. Book at least 2 weeks in advance.
Source: Syracuse University, South Asia Center
Video Library and Teaching Resources
346F Eggers Hall
The Maxwell School
Syracuse, NY 13244

Open to the World

An information video about Niigata Prefecture including plans for the expansion of the international airport.

Availability: Schools, libraries, and nursing homes in Hawaii.
Suggested Grade: 6-12
Order Number: TR-13
Format: VHS videotape
Terms: Borrower pays return postage. A maximum of 3 videos may be borrowed per person. Return within one week of date borrowed.
Source: Consulate General of Japan, Honolulu
1742 Nuuanu Avenue
Honolulu, HI 96817-3294

SOCIAL STUDIES--GEOGRAPHY--WORLD

Phone: 1-808-543-3111
Fax: 1-808-543-3170
World Wide Web URL:
http://www.honolulu.us.emb-japan.go.jp

Pakistan: Between the Chitralis and Pathans
This program looks at Pakistan's complex relations with Iran, India, and the United States and the contributions of its multicultural population.
Availability: Schools, libraries, homeschoolers, and nursing homes in the southeastern United States.
Suggested Grade: 7-12
Order Number: order by title
Production Date: 1999
Format: VHS videotape
Terms: Borrower pays return postage. Return 2 days after showing via United Parcel Service, insured. Book 2 weeks in advance.
Source: Center for South Asian Studies
University of Virginia
Video Library Coordinator
P. O. Box 400169, 110 Minor Hall
Charlottesville, VA 22904-4169
Phone: 1-434-924-8815
Email Address: southasia@virginia.edu

Parties, Pinatas and Plays: Mexican Christmas Traditions
Discusses and depicts the origins of the celebration of Christmas in Mexico.
Availability: Schools in the United States.
Suggested Grade: 6-12
Order Number: order by title
Format: VHS videotape
Terms: Borrower pays return postage. Return 14 days after receipt, via USPS including insurance. All borrowers must have a current lending agreement on file with the Outreach program. This agreement is available via the web site or may be requested via phone or fax.
Source: Center for Latin American Studies
University of Florida
319 Grinter Hall
P. O. Box 115530
Gainesville, FL 32611-5530
Phone: 1-352-392-0375
Fax: 1-352-392-7682
World Wide Web URL: http://www.latam.ufl.edu/outreach
Email Address: maryr@ufl.edu

Pie en la Marcha
Rural and urban poverty issues in Brazil.
Availability: Schools, libraries, and nursing homes in the United States.
Suggested Grade: 6-12
Language: Spanish
Order Number: DEVBRA4-video
Format: VHS videotape
Terms: Borrowers must have a User's Agreement on file with this source--available by mail or via the Internet. Return postage is paid by borrower; return 12 days after showing. Book at least three weeks in advance. All borrowers are limited to a total of ten items per semester.
Source: Latin American Resource Center
Stone Center for Latin American Studies
Tulane University
100 Jones Hall
New Orleans, LA 70118
Phone: 1-504-862-3143
Fax: 1-504-865-6719
World Wide Web URL: http://stonecenter.tulane.edu/pages/detail/48/Lending-Library
Email Address: crcrts@tulane.edu

Power of Compassion, The: Sakyadhita
This video gives an impression of the fourth international conference for Buddhist women held in Leh, Ladakh, India in August of 1995.
Availability: Schools, libraries, homeschoolers, and nursing homes in the southeastern United States.
Suggested Grade: 7-12
Order Number: order by title
Production Date: 1995
Format: VHS videotape
Terms: Borrower pays return postage. Return 2 days after showing via United Parcel Service, insured. Book 2 weeks in advance.
Source: Center for South Asian Studies
University of Virginia
Video Library Coordinator
P. O. Box 400169, 110 Minor Hall
Charlottesville, VA 22904-4169
Phone: 1-434-924-8815
Email Address: southasia@virginia.edu

Primary and Secondary Education in Japan
Japan's compulsory educational system is introduced by following the activities of various students. Also see a teacher of a group of third graders and student life introduced through profiles of three middle school students.
Availability: Schools, libraries, homeschoolers, and nursing homes in Arizona and California (zipcodes beginning 900-931 and 935).
Suggested Grade: 4-12
Order Number: 079
Production Date: 1985
Format: VHS videotape
Terms: Borrower pays postage both ways; you may call the number below to learn how much postage costs. Return within two weeks of date borrowed. An individual may borrow 2 items at one time. For non-profit and educational use only.
Source: Consulate General of Japan, Los Angeles
350 South Grand Avenue, Suite 1700
Los Angeles, CA 90071-3459

All materials listed in this 2018-2019 edition are BRAND NEW!

SOCIAL STUDIES--GEOGRAPHY--WORLD

        Phone: 1-213-617-6700
        Fax: 1-213-617-6727
World Wide Web URL: http://www.la.us.emb-japan.go.jp

Primary and Secondary Education in Japan/The Elementary School Teacher/School Days in Japan
Japan's compulsory educational system is introduced by following the activities of various students. Also see a teacher of a group of third graders and student life introduced through profiles of three middle school students.
- Availability: Schools, libraries, homeschoolers, and nursing homes in Connecticut (except Fairfield County), Maine, Massachusetts, New Hampshire, Rhode Island, and Vermont.
- Suggested Grade: 4-12
- Order Number: 009
- Production Date: 1985
- Format: VHS videotape
- Terms: Borrower pays return postage, including insurance. Return two weeks after receipt.

    Source: Consulate General of Japan, Boston
    Federal Reserve Plaza, 14th Floor
    600 Atlantic Avenue
    Boston, MA 02210
    Phone: 1-617-973-9772
    Fax: 1-617-542-1329
    World Wide Web URL:
    http://www.boston.us.emb-japan.go.jp
    Email Address: infocul@cgjbos.org

Primary and Secondary Education in Japan/The Elementary School Teacher
Japan's compulsory educational system is introduced by following the activities of various students. Also see a teacher of a group of third graders and student life introduced through profiles of three middle school students.
- Availability: Schools, libraries, homeschoolers, and nursing homes in Nevada and northern California (zip codes beginning 932 and above, except 935).
- Suggested Grade: 4-12
- Order Number: order by title
- Production Date: 1985
- Format: VHS videotape
- Terms: Borrower pays return postage. Book two weeks in advance. Return within three weeks of date borrowed, via UPS, Federal Express or certified mail.

    Source: Consulate General of Japan, San Francisco
    50 Fremont Street, Suite 2300
    San Francisco, CA 94105-2236
    Phone: 1-415-356-2564
    Fax: 1-415-777-0518
World Wide Web URL: http://www.sf.us.emb-japan.go.jp/
    Email Address: infoav@cgjsf.org

Producing Miracles Everyday
Focuses on the hard work and ingenuity of the Latin American labor force who work in the "informal economy."
- Availability: Schools, libraries, and nursing homes in the United States.
- Suggested Grade: 6-12
- Order Number: DEVLA12-video
- Production Date: 1990
- Format: VHS videotape
- Terms: Borrowers must have a User's Agreement on file with this source--available by mail or via the Internet. Return postage is paid by borrower; return 12 days after showing. Book at least three weeks in advance. All borrowers are limited to a total of ten items per semester.

    Source: Latin American Resource Center
    Stone Center for Latin American Studies
    Tulane University
    100 Jones Hall
    New Orleans, LA 70118
    Phone: 1-504-862-3143
    Fax: 1-504-865-6719
World Wide Web URL: http://stonecenter.tulane.edu/pages/detail/48/Lending-Library
    Email Address: crcrts@tulane.edu

Radha's Day: Hindu Family Life 5
Shows a girl in her late teens during a typical day. Abounds in ethnographic detail and in social and anthropological data that helps lead to a comprehension of Hindu family life in a middle-class, white-collar, urban setting.
- Availability: Schools and libraries in the United States.
- Suggested Grade: 7-Adult
- Order Number: SA54
- Production Date: 1969
- Format: VHS videotape
- Terms: Borrower pays return postage. Return 3 days after showing via UPS. Book at least 2 weeks in advance.

    Source: Syracuse University, South Asia Center
    Video Library and Teaching Resources
    346F Eggers Hall
    The Maxwell School
    Syracuse, NY 13244

Raise the Red Lantern
This recognized film has caught the attention of critics in both China and the United States as a daring new type of film.
- Availability: Schools, libraries, homeschoolers, and nursing homes in the United States and Canada.
- Suggested Grade: 9-12 Chinese
- Order Number: order by title
- Production Date: 1992
- Format: VHS videotape
- Terms: Postage is paid by borrower both ways--send $3.00 per tape to cover initial shipping to you--MONEY MUST BE SENT WITH REQUEST. Return 10 days after showing via U. S. Postal Service, library rate. Shipping is $5.00 to Canadian addresses.

All materials listed in this 2018-2019 edition are BRAND NEW!

SOCIAL STUDIES--GEOGRAPHY--WORLD

Source: Center for Teaching About China
Kathleen Trescott
1214 West Schwartz
Carbondale, IL 62901
Phone: 1-618-549-1555
Email Address: trescott@midwest.net

Recycling
See how the city of Machida in suburban Tokyo, has developed and put into operation a disposal system effective in recycling raw material and reducing sheer volume of daily waste.
Availability: Schools, libraries, homeschoolers, and nursing homes in Connecticut (except Fairfield County), Maine, Massachusetts, New Hampshire, Rhode Island, and Vermont.
Suggested Grade: 6-12
Order Number: 559
Production Date: 1982
Format: VHS videotape
Terms: Borrower pays return postage, including insurance. Return two weeks after receipt.
Source: Consulate General of Japan, Boston
Federal Reserve Plaza, 14th Floor,
600 Atlantic Avenue
Boston, MA 02210
Phone: 1-617-973-9772
Fax: 1-617-542-1329
World Wide Web URL:
http://www.boston.us.emb-japan.go.jp
Email Address: infocul@cgjbos.org

Recycling
See how the city of Machida in suburban Tokyo, has developed and put into operation a disposal system effective in recycling raw material and reducing sheer volume of daily waste.
Availability: Schools, libraries, homeschoolers, and nursing homes in Arizona and California (zipcodes beginning 900-931 and 935).
Suggested Grade: 6-12
Order Number: 068
Production Date: 1982
Format: VHS videotape
Terms: Borrower pays postage both ways; you may call the number below to learn how much postage costs. Return within two weeks of date borrowed. An individual may borrow 2 items at one time. For non-profit and educational use only.
Source: Consulate General of Japan, Los Angeles
350 South Grand Avenue, Suite 1700
Los Angeles, CA 90071-3459
Phone: 1-213-617-6700
Fax: 1-213-617-6727
World Wide Web URL: http://www.la.us.emb-japan.go.jp

Sabo: Erosion Control
Explores this highly advanced system of "sabo" or debris and erosion control necessary to help prevent natural disaster in Japan.
Availability: Schools, libraries, homeschoolers, and nursing homes in Arizona and California (zipcodes beginning 900-931 and 935).
Suggested Grade: 6-12
Order Number: 072
Production Date: 1982
Format: VHS videotape
Terms: Borrower pays postage both ways; you may call the number below to learn how much postage costs. Return within two weeks of date borrowed. An individual may borrow 2 items at one time. For non-profit and educational use only.
Source: Consulate General of Japan, Los Angeles
350 South Grand Avenue, Suite 1700
Los Angeles, CA 90071-3459
Phone: 1-213-617-6700
Fax: 1-213-617-6727
World Wide Web URL: http://www.la.us.emb-japan.go.jp

Saheri's Choice
Examines the custom of arranged marriages in India. The film follows the story of one girl and her family as they confront the reality of an impending marriage that was arranged when the girl was barely six years old.
Availability: Schools, libraries, homeschoolers, and nursing homes in the southeastern United States.
Suggested Grade: 7-12
Order Number: order by title
Production Date: 1998
Format: VHS videotape
Terms: Borrower pays return postage. Return 2 days after showing via United Parcel Service, insured. Book 2 weeks in advance.
Source: Center for South Asian Studies
University of Virginia
Video Library Coordinator
P. O. Box 400169, 110 Minor Hall
Charlottesville, VA 22904-4169
Phone: 1-434-924-8815
Fax: 1-434-982-3011 (ls)
World Wide Web URL:
Email Address: southasia@virginia.edu

Salaam Bombay
Presents the tribulations of life on the streets of Bombay, India through the eyes of a young, homeless boy.
Availability: Schools and libraries in the United States.
Suggested Grade: 7-Adult
Order Number: SA127
Production Date: 1988
Format: VHS videotape
Terms: Borrower pays return postage. Return 3 days after showing via UPS. Book at least 2 weeks in advance.
Source: Syracuse University, South Asia Center
Video Library and Teaching Resources
346F Eggers Hall, The Maxwell School
Syracuse, NY 13244

SOCIAL STUDIES--GEOGRAPHY--WORLD

School Days in Japan
Follow some middle school students through their school day in Japan.
Availability: Schools, libraries, homeschoolers, and nursing homes in Arizona and California (zipcodes beginning 900-931 and 935).
Suggested Grade: 6-12
Order Number: 080
Production Date: 1979
Format: VHS videotape
Terms: Borrower pays postage both ways; you may call the number below to learn how much postage costs. Return within two weeks of date borrowed. An individual may borrow 2 items at one time. For non-profit and educational use only.
    Source: Consulate General of Japan, Los Angeles
    350 South Grand Avenue, Suite 1700
    Los Angeles, CA 90071-3459
    Phone: 1-213-617-6700
    Fax: 1-213-617-6727
World Wide Web URL: http://www.la.us.emb-japan.go.jp

Seeds of Plenty, Seeds of Sorrow; Developing Stories 1
A documentary from India about the effects of the Green Revolution, from India's point of view.
Availability: Schools and libraries in the United States.
Suggested Grade: 7-Adult
Order Number: SA95
Production Date: 1992
Format: VHS videotape
Terms: Borrower pays return postage. Return 3 days after showing via UPS. Book at least 2 weeks in advance.
    Source: Syracuse University, South Asia Center
    Video Library and Teaching Resources
    346F Eggers Hall
    The Maxwell School
    Syracuse, NY 13244

Serial for Breakfast (Part I & II)
Explores the impact of global satellite television broadcasts on the Indian electronic mediascape.
Availability: Schools and libraries in the United States.
Suggested Grade: 7-Adult
Order Number: SA77
Production Date: 1998
Format: VHS videotape
Terms: Borrower pays return postage. Return 3 days after showing via UPS. Book at least 2 weeks in advance.
    Source: Syracuse University, South Asia Center
    Video Library and Teaching Resources
    346F Eggers Hall
    The Maxwell School
    Syracuse, NY 13244

Sixteen Decisions
Refers to a 16-point social charter developed by poor Bangladeshi women and instituted by the Grameen Bank to encourage fundamental community and personal change. This focuses on the everyday life of 18-year-old Selina, one of the 2.5 million impoverished women who are building a stronger rural economy through small businesses they start with loans from the Grameen Bank.
Availability: Schools, libraries, homeschoolers, and nursing homes in the southeastern United States.
Suggested Grade: 7-12
Order Number: order by title
Production Date: 2000
Format: VHS videotape
Terms: Borrower pays return postage. Return 2 days after showing via United Parcel Service, insured. Book 2 weeks in advance.
    Source: Center for South Asian Studies
    University of Virginia
    Video Library Coordinator
    P. O. Box 400169, 110 Minor Hall
    Charlottesville, VA 22904-4169
    Phone: 1-434-924-8815
    Email Address: southasia@virginia.edu

Sixteen Decisions
Refers to a 16-point social charter developed by poor Bangladeshi women and instituted by the Grameen Bank to encourage fundamental community and personal change. This focuses on the everyday life of 18-year-old Selina, one of the 2.5 million impoverished women who are building a stronger rural economy through small businesses they start with loans from the Grameen Bank.
Availability: Schools and libraries in the United States.
Suggested Grade: 7-12
Order Number: 97
Production Date: 2000
Format: VHS videotape
Terms: Borrower pays return postage. Return 3 days after showing via UPS. Book at least 2 weeks in advance.
    Source: Syracuse University, South Asia Center
    Video Library and Teaching Resources
    346F Eggers Hall, The Maxwell School
    Syracuse, NY 13244

Son of the Ocean
Join the passengers and crew of a riverboat for an exciting trip down the Yangtze River, through the heart of China. History and scenery are blended into this presentation.
Availability: Schools, libraries, homeschoolers, and nursing homes in the United States and Canada.
Suggested Grade: 9-12
Order Number: order by title
Production Date: 1979
Format: VHS videotape
Terms: Postage is paid by borrower both ways--send $3.00 per tape to cover initial shipping to you--MONEY MUST BE SENT WITH REQUEST. Return 10 days after showing via U. S. Postal Service, library rate. Shipping is $5.00 to Canadian addresses.

SOCIAL STUDIES--GEOGRAPHY--WORLD

Source: Center for Teaching About China
Kathleen Trescott
1214 West Schwartz
Carbondale, IL 62901
Phone: 1-618-549-1555
Email Address: trescott@midwest.net

South Africa: A Land Apart
Offers an overview of South Africa, a country with rich resources and a strong economy. Briefly mentions its history, natural resources, urban centers, European influences, and rural life. Agriculture, mining, and manufacturing are the basis for its economy. Reviews the struggle to overcome apartheid and the first democratic election.
Availability: Schools, libraries, and homeschoolers in the United States who serve the hearing impaired.
Suggested Grade: 7-12
Order Number: 13023
Production Date: 1994
Format: DVD
Special Notes: Produced by ACG/United Learning.
Terms: Sponsor pays all transportation costs. Return one week after receipt. Participation is limited to deaf or hard of hearing Americans, their parents, families, teachers, counselors, or others whose use would benefit a deaf or hard of hearing person. Only one person in the audience needs to be hearing impaired. You must register--which is free. These videos are all open-captioned--no special equipment is required for viewing.
Source: Described and Captioned Media Program
National Association of the Deaf
4211 Church Street Ext.
Roebuck, SC 29376
Phone: 1-800-237-6213
Fax: 1-800-538-5636
World Wide Web URL: http://www.dcmp.org

Splendid China: A Miniature Rendition in Florida
An overview of sights at the new Splendid China in Florida, filmed at its grand opening in 1995.
Availability: Schools, libraries, homeschoolers, and nursing homes in the United States and Canada.
Suggested Grade: 9-12
Order Number: order by title
Production Date: 1995
Format: VHS videotape
Terms: Postage is paid by borrower both ways--send $3.00 per tape to cover initial shipping to you--MONEY MUST BE SENT WITH REQUEST. Return 10 days after showing via U. S. Postal Service, library rate. Shipping is $5.00 to Canadian addresses.
Source: Center for Teaching About China
Kathleen Trescott
1214 West Schwartz
Carbondale, IL 62901
Phone: 1-618-549-1555
Email Address: trescott@midwest.net

Stirrings of Change
About a non governmental agency in rural India that has dramatically improved the life of women in particular and also the entire community through working with them to devise re-forestation, veterinary, health, and literacy programs.
Availability: Schools and libraries in the United States.
Suggested Grade: 7-Adult
Order Number: SA26
Production Date: 1990
Format: VHS videotape
Terms: Borrower pays return postage. Return 3 days after showing via UPS. Book at least 2 weeks in advance.
Source: Syracuse University, South Asia Center
Video Library and Teaching Resources
346F Eggers Hall
The Maxwell School
Syracuse, NY 13244

Taj Mahal: The Story of Muslim India
Identifies key influence of the Muslim culture upon the India sub-continent including this famous building.
Availability: Schools and libraries in the United States.
Suggested Grade: 7-Adult
Order Number: SA40
Production Date: 1991
Format: VHS videotape
Terms: Borrower pays return postage. Return 3 days after showing via UPS. Book at least 2 weeks in advance.
Source: Syracuse University, South Asia Center
Video Library and Teaching Resources
346F Eggers Hall
The Maxwell School
Syracuse, NY 13244

Tang, The: China's Cosmopolitan Age
The Tang Dynasty, 618-907 AD produced a wealth of art, music, government, religion, philosophy, and creativeness. This presentation is centered in the Xi'an area.
Availability: Schools, libraries, homeschoolers, and nursing homes in the United States and Canada.
Suggested Grade: 9-12
Order Number: order by title
Production Date: 1995
Format: VHS videotape
Terms: Postage is paid by borrower both ways--send $3.00 per tape to cover initial shipping to you--MONEY MUST BE SENT WITH REQUEST. Return 10 days after showing via U. S. Postal Service, library rate. Shipping is $5.00 to Canadian addresses.
Source: Center for Teaching About China
Kathleen Trescott
1214 West Schwartz
Carbondale, IL 62901
Phone: 1-618-549-1555
Email Address: trescott@midwest.net

SOCIAL STUDIES--GEOGRAPHY--WORLD

Tea Drinking in Taipei
For thousands of years, tea drinking has been appreciated by Chinese people as a means to promote health and friendship. This video describes the art of drinking tea, growing and processing tea, and tea's history in China.
- Availability: Schools, libraries, and nursing homes in the United States and Canada.
- Suggested Grade: 6-Adult
- Order Number: TV010
- Format: VHS videotape
- Terms: Borrower pays return postage. Return with 14 days after scheduled showing, via UPS or U. S. Mail. All requests must included an educational institution affiliation, a current address, and phone number. Order through web site only.

Source: Cornell University East Asia Program
World Wide Web URL:
http://eap.einaudi.cornell.edu/lending_library
Email Address: east_asia1@cornell.edu

Teyyam: The Annual Visit of the God Vishnumurti
Annual ritual in northern Kerala allow ritual specialists to take the shape of various gods worshiped during the Teyyam season (December through March). This video illustrates the honoring of the god Vishnumurti. This is one of the few occasions that brings different castes of the Hindu community together.
- Availability: Schools, libraries, homeschoolers, and nursing homes in the southeastern United States.
- Suggested Grade: 7-12
- Order Number: order by title
- Production Date: 1998
- Format: VHS videotape
- Terms: Borrower pays return postage. Return 2 days after showing via United Parcel Service, insured. Book 2 weeks in advance.

Source: Center for South Asian Studies
University of Virginia, Video Library Coordinator
P. O. Box 400169, 110 Minor Hall
Charlottesville, VA 22904-4169
Phone: 1-434-924-8815
Email Address: southasia@virginia.edu

This Other Haiti
Efforts by the Peasant Movement of Papay to bring about democratic social reform.
- Availability: Schools, libraries, and nursing homes in the United States.
- Suggested Grade: 8-Adult
- Order Number: HCHAI1-video
- Production Date: 1993
- Format: VHS videotape
- Terms: Borrowers must have a User's Agreement on file with this source--available by mail or via the Internet. Return postage is paid by borrower; return 12 days after showing. Book at least three weeks in advance. All borrowers are limited to a total of ten items per semester.

Source: Latin American Resource Center
Stone Center for Latin American Studies
Tulane University
100 Jones Hall
New Orleans, LA 70118
Phone: 1-504-862-3143
Fax: 1-504-865-6719
World Wide Web URL: http://stonecenter.tulane.edu/pages/detail/48/Lending-Library
Email Address: crcrts@tulane.edu

This Year We Went to Japan
Shows a young couple's first trip to Japan and takes you on an informal sightseeing tour throughout Japan.
- Availability: Schools, libraries, and nursing homes in Hawaii.
- Suggested Grade: 4-12
- Order Number: TR-5
- Format: VHS videotape
- Terms: Borrower pays return postage. A maximum of 3 videos may be borrowed per person. Return within one week of date borrowed.

Source: Consulate General of Japan, Honolulu
1742 Nuuanu Avenue
Honolulu, HI 96817-3294
Phone: 1-808-543-3111
Fax: 1-808-543-3170
World Wide Web URL:
http://www.honolulu.us.emb-japan.go.jp

Throw Me a Dime
Examines life in the poor Argentine village of Santa Fe. Culminates in a harrowing sequence where the children of Santa Fe run alongside the train as it passes by, begging for money from the passengers.
- Availability: Schools and libraries in Iowa, Illinois, Michigan, Minnesota, and Wisconsin.
- Suggested Grade: 9-12
- Languages: Spanish with English subtitles
- Order Number: DEV/ECUSAT41VHS
- Production Date: 1958
- Format: VHS videotape
- Terms: Borrower pays return postage. Return 8 days after showing. Book 2 weeks in advance. Order may also be picked up for those near the Center.

Source: Center for Latin American and Caribbean Studies
UW-Milwaukee, P. O. Box 413
Milwaukee, WI 53201
Phone: 1-414-229-5987
World Wide Web URL: http://www.uwm.edu/Dept/CLACS
Email Address: audvis@usm.edu

Tibet: The End of Time
This lost civilization, high in the Himalayan Mountains, is steeped in the Buddhist religion and captures the imagination and heart in this account of life there.
- Availability: Schools, libraries, homeschoolers, and nursing homes in the United States and Canada.

SOCIAL STUDIES--GEOGRAPHY--WORLD

Suggested Grade: 9-12
Order Number: order by title
Production Date: 1989
Format: VHS videotape
Terms: Postage is paid by borrower both ways--send $3.00 per tape to cover initial shipping to you--MONEY MUST BE SENT WITH REQUEST. Return 10 days after showing via U. S. Postal Service, library rate. Shipping is $5.00 to Canadian addresses.
  Source: **Center for Teaching About China**
Kathleen Trescott
1214 West Schwartz
Carbondale, IL 62901
Phone: 1-618-549-1555
Email Address: trescott@midwest.net

Tibet: Where Continents Collide
A video field trip, by David Howell of the U. S. Geological Survey, that blends geological history with glimpses of Tibetan culture.
Availability: Schools, libraries, homeschoolers, and nursing homes in the southeastern United States.
Suggested Grade: 7-12
Order Number: order by title
Production Date: 1989
Format: VHS videotape
Terms: Borrower pays return postage. Return 2 days after showing via United Parcel Service, insured. Book 2 weeks in advance.
  Source: **Center for South Asian Studies**
University of Virginia, Video Library Coordinator
P. O. Box 400169, 110 Minor Hall
Charlottesville, VA 22904-4169
Phone: 1-434-924-8815
Email Address: southasia@virginia.edu

To Live
Follows fortunes and misfortunes of a Chinese family through the civil war, the communist takeover, and the Cultural Revolution.
Availability: Schools, libraries, homeschoolers, and nursing homes in the United States and Canada.
Suggested Grade: 10-Adult
Order Number: order by title
Production Date: 1994
Format: VHS videotape
Terms: Postage is paid by borrower both ways--send $3.00 per tape to cover initial shipping to you--MONEY MUST BE SENT WITH REQUEST. Return 10 days after showing via U. S. Postal Service, library rate. Shipping is $5.00 to Canadian addresses.
  Source: **Center for Teaching About China**
Kathleen Trescott
1214 West Schwartz
Carbondale, IL 62901
Phone: 1-618-549-1555
Email Address: trescott@midwest.net

Trans-Tokyo Bay Road, The
Focuses on the enormous project of constructing the Trans-Tokyo Bay road between Kawasaki and Kisarazu, and its influence on the people.
Availability: Schools, libraries and homeschoolers in Alabama, Georgia, North Carolina, South Carolina, and Virginia.
Suggested Grade: 4-12
Order Number: 301
Production Date: 1990
Format: VHS videotape
Special Notes: No. 2 of the "Nippon Life" series.
Terms: Borrower pays return postage. Two tapes may be borrowed at a time. Return within 7 days after receipt. Reservations may be made by filling the application found on the web site.
  Source: **Consulate General of Japan, Atlanta**
Japan Information Center
One Alliance Center, 3500 Lenox Road, Suite 1600
Atlanta, GA 30326
Phone: 1-404-365-9240
Fax: 1-404-240-4311
World Wide Web URL:
http://www.atlanta.us.emb-japan.go.jp
Email Address: info@cgjapanatlanta.org

Trans-Tokyo Bay Road, The
Focuses on the enormous project of constructing the Trans-Tokyo Bay road between Kawasaki and Kisarazu, and its influence on the people.
Availability: Schools, libraries, and nursing homes in Oklahoma and Texas.
Suggested Grade: 4-12
Order Number: F2
Production Date: 1990
Format: VHS videotape
Special Notes: No. 2 of the "Nippon Life" series.
Terms: Materials must be picked up in person. Under special circumstances, you may be able to have them shipped to you at your own expense (call for further details). Return within two weeks after scheduled showing. Videos must be registered with the U. S. Postal Service or returned by Priority Mail, Federal Express, or other registered shipping service.
  Source: **Consulate General of Japan, Houston**
Cultural Affairs and Information Section
909 Fannin Street, Suite 3000
Houston, TX 77010
Phone: 1-713-652-2977
Fax: 1-713-651-7822
World Wide Web URL:
http://www.houston.us.emb-japan.go.jp/
en/culture/page1.htm
Email Address: info@cgjhouston.org

Trans-Tokyo Road, The
Focuses on the enormous project of constructing the Trans-Tokyo Bay road between Kawasaki and Kisarazu, and its influence on the people.

SOCIAL STUDIES--GEOGRAPHY--WORLD

Availability: Schools, libraries, homeschoolers, and nursing homes in Connecticut (except Fairfield County), Maine, Massachusetts, New Hampshire, Rhode Island, and Vermont.
Suggested Grade: 4-12
Order Number: 418
Production Date: 1990
Format: VHS videotape
Special Notes: No. 2 of the "Nippon Life" series.
Terms: Borrower pays return postage, including insurance. Return two weeks after receipt.
Source: Consulate General of Japan, Boston
Federal Reserve Plaza, 14th Floor
600 Atlantic Avenue
Boston, MA 02210
Phone: 1-617-973-9772
Fax: 1-617-542-1329
World Wide Web URL:
http://www.boston.us.emb-japan.go.jp
Email Address: infocul@cgjbos.org

Trans-Tokyo Road, The
Focuses on the enormous project of constructing the Trans-Tokyo Bay road between Kawasaki and Kisarazu, and its influence on the people.
Availability: Schools, libraries, and nursing homes in Hawaii.
Suggested Grade: 4-12
Order Number: BU-31
Production Date: 1990
Format: VHS videotape
Special Notes: No. 2 of the "Nippon Life" series.
Terms: Borrower pays return postage. A maximum of 3 videos may be borrowed per person. Return within one week of date borrowed.
Source: Consulate General of Japan, Honolulu
1742 Nuuanu Avenue
Honolulu, HI 96817-3294
Phone: 1-808-543-3111
Fax: 1-808-543-3170
World Wide Web URL:
http://www.honolulu.us.emb-japan.go.jp

Trans-Tokyo Road, The
Focuses on the enormous project of constructing the Trans-Tokyo Bay road between Kawasaki and Kisarazu, and its influence on the people.
Availability: Schools, libraries, homeschoolers, and nursing homes in OREGON AND SOUTHERN IDAHO ONLY. Please make requests via the web site.
Suggested Grade: 4-12
Order Number: 220
Production Date: 1990
Format: VHS videotape
Special Notes: No. 2 of the "Nippon Life" series.
Terms: Borrower pays return postage. Return within three weeks after scheduled showing date. Book one month in advance if possible. Rewind the video and wrap securely for return. Be certain to indicate video number, date needed, name of your organization, and address to which video should be sent, along with phone number. Audience report enclosed with the video must be completed and returned.
Source: Consulate General of Japan, Oregon
Attn: Tamara, Video Library
1300 S. W. Fifth Avenue, Suite 2700
Portland, OR 97201
Phone: 1-503-221-1811, ext. 17
World Wide Web URL:
http://www.portland.us.emb-japan.go.jp/en/index.html
Email Address: tamara@cgjpdx.org

Trans-Tokyo Road, The
Focuses on the enormous project of constructing the Trans-Tokyo Bay road between Kawasaki and Kisarazu, and its influence on the people.
Availability: Schools, libraries, homeschoolers, and nursing homes in Nevada and northern California (zip codes beginning 932 and above, except 935).
Suggested Grade: 4-12
Order Number: order by title
Production Date: 1990
Format: Beta videotape; U-matic videotape; VHS videotape
Special Notes: No. 2 of the "Nippon Life" series.
Terms: Borrower pays return postage. Book two weeks in advance. Return within three weeks of date borrowed, via UPS, Federal Express or certified mail.
Source: Consulate General of Japan, San Francisco
50 Fremont Street, Suite 2300
San Francisco, CA 94105-2236
Phone: 1-415-356-2564
Fax: 1-415-777-0518
World Wide Web URL: http://www.sf.us.emb-japan.go.jp/
Email Address: infoav@cgjsf.org

Travel Wise in Japan
Presents beautiful small towns and villages not often visited by tourists to Japan.
Availability: Schools, libraries and homeschoolers in Alabama, Georgia, North Carolina, South Carolina, and Virginia.
Suggested Grade: 4-12
Order Number: 322
Production Date: 1997
Format: VHS videotape
Terms: Borrower pays return postage. Two tapes may be borrowed at a time. Return within 7 days after receipt. Reservations may be made by filling the application found on the web site.
Source: Consulate General of Japan, Atlanta
Japan Information Center
One Alliance Center
3500 Lenox Road, Suite 1600
Atlanta, GA 30326
Phone: 1-404-365-9240

SOCIAL STUDIES--GEOGRAPHY--WORLD

Fax: 1-404-240-4311
World Wide Web URL:
http://www.atlanta.us.emb-japan.go.jp
Email Address: info@cgjapanatlanta.org

Travel Wise in Japan
Presents beautiful small towns and villages not often visited by tourists to Japan.
Availability: Schools, libraries, homeschoolers, and nursing homes in Connecticut (except Fairfield County), Maine, Massachusetts, New Hampshire, Rhode Island, and Vermont.
Suggested Grade: 4-12
Order Number: 564
Production Date: 1997
Format: VHS videotape
Terms: Borrower pays return postage, including insurance. Return two weeks after receipt.
Source: Consulate General of Japan, Boston
Federal Reserve Plaza, 14th Floor
600 Atlantic Avenue
Boston, MA 02210
Phone: 1-617-973-9772
Fax: 1-617-542-1329
World Wide Web URL:
http://www.boston.us.emb-japan.go.jp
Email Address: infocul@cgjbos.org

Travel Wise in Japan
Presents beautiful small towns and villages not often visited by tourists to Japan.
Availability: Schools, libraries, and nursing homes in Hawaii.
Suggested Grade: 4-12
Order Number: TR-21
Production Date: 1997
Format: VHS videotape
Terms: Borrower pays return postage. A maximum of 3 videos may be borrowed per person. Return within one week of date borrowed.
Source: Consulate General of Japan, Honolulu
1742 Nuuanu Avenue
Honolulu, HI 96817-3294
Phone: 1-808-543-3111
Fax: 1-808-543-3170
World Wide Web URL:
http://www.honolulu.us.emb-japan.go.jp

Travel Wise in Japan
Presents beautiful small towns and villages not often visited by tourists to Japan.
Availability: Schools, libraries, and nursing homes in Oklahoma and Texas.
Suggested Grade: 4-12
Order Number: A24
Production Date: 1997
Format: VHS videotape
Terms: Materials must be picked up in person. Under special circumstances, you may be able to have them shipped to you at your own expense (call for further details). Return within two weeks after scheduled showing. Videos must be registered with the U. S. Postal Service or returned by Priority Mail, Federal Express, or other registered shipping service.
Source: Consulate General of Japan, Houston
Cultural Affairs and Information Section
909 Fannin Street, Suite 3000
Houston, TX 77010
Phone: 1-713-652-2977
Fax: 1-713-651-7822
World Wide Web URL:
http://www.houston.us.emb-japan.go.jp/en/culture/page1.htm
Email Address: info@cgjhouston.org

Travel Wise in Japan
Presents beautiful small towns and villages not often visited by tourists to Japan.
Availability: Schools, libraries, homeschoolers, and nursing homes in OREGON AND SOUTHERN IDAHO ONLY. Please make requests via the web site.
Suggested Grade: 4-12
Order Number: 423
Production Date: 1997
Format: VHS videotape
Terms: Borrower pays return postage. Return within three weeks after scheduled showing date. Book one month in advance if possible. Rewind the video and wrap securely for return. Be certain to indicate video number, date needed, name of your organization, and address to which video should be sent, along with phone number. Audience report enclosed with the video must be completed and returned.
Source: Consulate General of Japan, Oregon
Attn: Tamara, Video Library
1300 S. W. Fifth Avenue, Suite 2700
Portland, OR 97201
Phone: 1-503-221-1811, ext. 17
World Wide Web URL:
http://www.portland.us.emb-japan.go.jp/en/index.html
Email Address: tamara@cgjpdx.org

Travel Wise in Japan
Presents beautiful small towns and villages not often visited by tourists to Japan.
Availability: Schools, libraries, homeschoolers, and nursing homes in Nevada and northern California (zip codes beginning 932 and above, except 935).
Suggested Grade: 4-12
Order Number: order by title
Production Date: 1997
Format: VHS videotape
Terms: Borrower pays return postage. Book two weeks in advance. Return within three weeks of date borrowed, via UPS, Federal Express or certified mail.

SOCIAL STUDIES--GEOGRAPHY--WORLD

Source: Consulate General of Japan, San Francisco
50 Fremont Street, Suite 2300
San Francisco, CA 94105-2236
Phone: 1-415-356-2564
Fax: 1-415-777-0518
World Wide Web URL: http://www.sf.us.emb-japan.go.jp/
Email Address: infoav@cgjsf.org

Tropical Kingdom of Belize
From mountaintop to barrier reef, the tiny Central American country of Belize features one of the most diverse natural environments in the world.
Availability: Schools in the United States.
Suggested Grade: All ages
Order Number: order by title
Production Date: 1986
Format: VHS videotape
Terms: Borrower pays return postage. Return 14 days after receipt, via USPS including insurance. All borrowers must have a current lending agreement on file with the Outreach program. This agreement is available via the web site or may be requested via phone or fax.
Source: Center for Latin American Studies
University of Florida
319 Grinter Hall
P. O. Box 115530
Gainesville, FL 32611-5530
Phone: 1-352-392-0375
Fax: 1-352-392-7682
World Wide Web URL: http://www.latam.ufl.edu/outreach
Email Address: maryr@ufl.edu

Tune in Korea: Legacy and Transformation
Explores the many facets of South Korea's history and culture by investigating such questions as: What is South Korea's place in the world today? Which world events led to the division of the Korean peninsula? How are North and South Korea poised for the future together?
Availability: Schools, libraries, and nursing homes in the United States and Canada.
Suggested Grade: 6-Adult
Order Number: KV067
Format: VHS videotape
Special Notes: Accompanied by a teacher's guide.
Terms: Borrower pays return postage. Return with 14 days after scheduled showing, via UPS or U. S. Mail. All requests must included an educational institution affiliation, a current address, and phone number. Order through web site only.
Source: Cornell University East Asia Program
World Wide Web URL:
http://eap.einaudi.cornell.edu/lending_library
Email Address: east_asia1@cornell.edu

Turquoise Coast via Istanbul, The
A travel video detailing Istanbul and the Agean Coast of Turkey.
Availability: Schools, libraries, homeschoolers, and nursing homes in the United States.
Suggested Grade: 7-12
Order Number: order by title
Production Date: 1988
Format: VHS videotape
Terms: Borrower pays return postage via any carrier with $400 insurance per parcel. Videos are loaned for 14 days; may be retained longer if requested in advance. Borrowers must complete a lending agreement.
Source: Center for Middle Eastern Studies
Outreach Coordinator
University of Texas at Austin
1 University Station, F9400
Austin, TX 78712-0527
World Wide Web URL:
http://www.utexas.edu/cola/depts/mes/
center/outreach/library-catalog.php
Email Address: crose@mail.utexas.edu

Twilight for a Coal Mining Town: The Tale of Takashima
Looks at the crisis this Japanese town faces and it's flourishing coal mine closed.
Availability: Schools, libraries and homeschoolers in Alabama, Georgia, North Carolina, South Carolina, and Virginia.
Suggested Grade: 6-12
Order Number: 509
Format: VHS videotape
Special Notes: Tape 9 of the "Document Japan" series.
Terms: Borrower pays return postage. Two tapes may be borrowed at a time. Return within 7 days after receipt. Reservations may be made by filling the application found on the web site.
Source: Consulate General of Japan, Atlanta
Japan Information Center
One Alliance Center
3500 Lenox Road, Suite 1600
Atlanta, GA 30326
Phone: 1-404-365-9240
Fax: 1-404-240-4311
World Wide Web URL:
http://www.atlanta.us.emb-japan.go.jp
Email Address: info@cgjapanatlanta.org

Twilight for a Coal-Mining Town: The Tale of Takashima
Recounts what happens when a town's main industry closes. A prosperous coal mine was closed in 1986. This program looks at the crisis Takashima and its people must confront.
Availability: Schools, libraries, homeschoolers, and nursing homes in Connecticut (except Fairfield County), Maine, Massachusetts, New Hampshire, Rhode Island, and Vermont.
Suggested Grade: 9-Adult
Order Number: 164
Production Date: 1988
Format: VHS videotape
Special Notes: Tape 9 of the "Document Japan" series.

SOCIAL STUDIES--GEOGRAPHY--WORLD

Terms: Borrower pays return postage, including insurance. Return two weeks after receipt.
Source: Consulate General of Japan, Boston
Federal Reserve Plaza, 14th Floor
600 Atlantic Avenue
Boston, MA 02210
Phone: 1-617-973-9772
Fax: 1-617-542-1329
World Wide Web URL:
http://www.boston.us.emb-japan.go.jp
Email Address: infocul@cgjbos.org

Twilight for a Coal Mining Town: The Tale of Takashima

Looks at the crisis this Japanese town faces and it's flourishing coal mine closed.
Availability: Schools, libraries, and nursing homes in Hawaii.
Suggested Grade: 6-12
Order Number: BU-27
Format: VHS videotape
Special Notes: Tape 9 of the "Document Japan" series.
Terms: Borrower pays return postage. A maximum of 3 videos may be borrowed per person. Return within one week of date borrowed.
Source: Consulate General of Japan, Honolulu
1742 Nuuanu Avenue
Honolulu, HI 96817-3294
Phone: 1-808-543-3111
Fax: 1-808-543-3170
World Wide Web URL:
http://www.honolulu.us.emb-japan.go.jp

Twilight for a Coal-Mining Town: The Tale of Takashima

Recounts what happens when a town's main industry closes. A prosperous coal mine was closed in 1986. This program looks at the crisis Takashima and its people must confront.
Availability: Schools, libraries, and nursing homes in Oklahoma and Texas.
Suggested Grade: 9-Adult
Order Number: C9
Production Date: 1988
Format: VHS videotape
Special Notes: Tape 9 of the "Document Japan" series.
Terms: Materials must be picked up in person. Under special circumstances, you may be able to have them shipped to you at your own expense (call for further details). Return within two weeks after scheduled showing. Videos must be registered with the U. S. Postal Service or returned by Priority Mail, Federal Express, or other registered shipping service.
Source: Consulate General of Japan, Houston
Cultural Affairs and Information Section
909 Fannin Street, Suite 3000
Houston, TX 77010
Phone: 1-713-652-2977
Fax: 1-713-651-7822
World Wide Web URL:
http://www.houston.us.emb-japan.go.jp/en/culture/page1.htm
Email Address: info@cgjhouston.org

Twilight for a Coal-Mining Town: The Tale of Takashima

Recounts what happens when a town's main industry closes. A prosperous coal mine was closed in 1986. This program looks at the crisis Takashima and its people must confront.
Availability: Schools, libraries, homeschoolers, and nursing homes in OREGON AND SOUTHERN IDAHO ONLY. Please make requests via the web site.
Suggested Grade: 9-Adult
Order Number: 509
Production Date: 1988
Format: VHS videotape
Special Notes: Tape 9 of the "Document Japan" series.
Terms: Borrower pays return postage. Return within three weeks after scheduled showing date. Book one month in advance if possible. Rewind the video and wrap securely for return. Be certain to indicate video number, date needed, name of your organization, and address to which video should be sent, along with phone number. Audience report enclosed with the video must be completed and returned.
Source: Consulate General of Japan, Oregon
Attn: Tamara, Video Library
1300 S. W. Fifth Avenue, Suite 2700
Portland, OR 97201
Phone: 1-503-221-1811, ext. 17
World Wide Web URL:
http://www.portland.us.emb-japan.go.jp/en/index.html
Email Address: tamara@cgjpdx.org

Twilight for a Coal-Mining Town: The Tale of Takashima

Recounts what happens when a town's main industry closes. A prosperous coal mine was closed in 1986. This program looks at the crisis Takashima and its people must confront.
Availability: Schools, libraries, homeschoolers, and nursing homes in Nevada and northern California (zip codes beginning 932 and above, except 935).
Suggested Grade: 9-Adult
Order Number: order by title
Production Date: 1988
Format: Beta videotape; U-matic videotape; VHS videotape
Special Notes: Tape 9 of the "Document Japan" series.
Terms: Borrower pays return postage. Book two weeks in advance. Return within three weeks of date borrowed, via UPS, Federal Express or certified mail.
Source: Consulate General of Japan, San Francisco
50 Fremont Street, Suite 2300
San Francisco, CA 94105-2236
Phone: 1-415-356-2564
Fax: 1-415-777-0518

SOCIAL STUDIES--GEOGRAPHY--WORLD

World Wide Web URL: http://www.sf.us.emb-japan.go.jp/
Email Address: infoav@cgjsf.org

Uganda: The Pearl of Africa
Photography displays the wealth of Uganda's natural beauty and abundant animal life. Pinpoints the country in the African continent and briefly notes its history, relationship with Britain, and its tribal cultures. Highlights the 1993 coronation of a king who has the title but no real power. Comments on the easing of ethnic tensions.
- Availability: Schools, libraries, and homeschoolers in the United States who serve the hearing impaired.
- Suggested Grade: 6-10
- Order Number: 12430
- Production Date: 1998
- Format: DVD
- Special Notes: Produced by Ambrose Video Publishing, Inc..
- Terms: Sponsor pays all transportation costs. Return one week after receipt. Participation is limited to deaf or hard of hearing Americans, their parents, families, teachers, counselors, or others whose use would benefit a deaf or hard of hearing person. Only one person in the audience needs to be hearing impaired. You must register--which is free. These videos are all open-captioned--no special equipment is required for viewing.

Source: Described and Captioned Media Program
National Association of the Deaf
4211 Church Street Ext.
Roebuck, SC 29376
Phone: 1-800-237-6213
Fax: 1-800-538-5636
World Wide Web URL: http://www.dcmp.org

Under the Same Sun
All the nations of the world develop and prosper as part of the earth. One sun provides the heat and light for all of them. Therefore, all nations must work together.
- Availability: Schools, libraries, homeschoolers, and nursing homes in the United States and Canada.
- Suggested Grade: 9-12
- Order Number: order by title
- Production Date: 1987
- Format: DVD
- Terms: Postage is paid by borrower both ways--send $3.00 per tape to cover initial shipping to you--MONEY MUST BE SENT WITH REQUEST. Return 10 days after showing via U. S. Postal Service, library rate. Shipping is $5.00 to Canadian addresses.

Source: Center for Teaching About China
Kathleen Trescott
1214 West Schwartz
Carbondale, IL 62901
Phone: 1-618-549-1555
Email Address: trescott@midwest.net

Venezuela: A Petroleum Powered Economy
Traces Venezuela's history to its present status as a major independent oil-producing nation.
- Availability: Schools, libraries, and nursing homes in the United States.
- Suggested Grade: 6-12
- Order Number: HCVEN1-video
- Production Date: 1994
- Format: VHS videotape
- Terms: Borrowers must have a User's Agreement on file with this source--available by mail or via the Internet. Return postage is paid by borrower; return 12 days after showing. Book at least three weeks in advance. All borrowers are limited to a total of ten items per semester.

Source: Latin American Resource Center
Stone Center for Latin American Studies
Tulane University
100 Jones Hall
New Orleans, LA 70118
Phone: 1-504-862-3143
Fax: 1-504-865-6719
World Wide Web URL: http://stonecenter.tulane.edu/pages/detail/48/Lending-Library
Email Address: crcrts@tulane.edu

Village Man, City Man
Views of the daily life of a young mill worker in Delhi and his return visit to his native village suggest that the dichotomous modern/traditional model of change may not apply in India.
- Availability: Schools, libraries, homeschoolers, and nursing homes in the southeastern United States.
- Suggested Grade: 7-12
- Order Number: order by title
- Production Date: 1975
- Format: VHS videotape
- Terms: Borrower pays return postage. Return 2 days after showing via United Parcel Service, insured. Book 2 weeks in advance.

Source: Center for South Asian Studies
University of Virginia
Video Library Coordinator
P. O. Box 400169, 110 Minor Hall
Charlottesville, VA 22904-4169
Phone: 1-434-924-8815
Email Address: southasia@virginia.edu

Voices of the Sierra Tarahumara
This documentary focuses on the Tarahumara, a group of people who live in the mountains and canyons of the Sierra Tarahumara of Mexico.
- Availability: Schools in the United States.
- Suggested Grade: 10-Adult
- Order Number: order by title
- Format: VHS videotape
- Terms: Borrower pays return postage. Return 14 days after receipt, via USPS including insurance. All borrowers must have a current lending agreement on file with the Outreach program. This agreement is available via the web site or may be requested via phone or fax.

SOCIAL STUDIES--GEOGRAPHY--WORLD

Source: Center for Latin American Studies
University of Florida
319 Grinter Hall
P. O. Box 115530
Gainesville, FL 32611-5530
Phone: 1-352-392-0375
Fax: 1-352-392-7682
World Wide Web URL: http://www.latam.ufl.edu/outreach
Email Address: maryr@ufl.edu

Water is Ours, The
Documents the fallout from the privatization of water rights in the city of Cochabamba, Bolivia.
Availability: Schools and libraries in Iowa, Illinois, Michigan, Minnesota, and Wisconsin.
Suggested Grade: 9-12
Languages: Spanish with English subtitles
Order Number: DEV/ECBOLW29VHS
Production Date: 2000
Format: VHS videotape
Terms: Borrower pays return postage. Return 8 days after showing. Book 2 weeks in advance. Order may also be picked up for those near the Center.
Source: Center for Latin American and Caribbean Studies
UW-Milwaukee
P. O. Box 413
Milwaukee, WI 53201
Phone: 1-414-229-5987
World Wide Web URL: http://www.uwm.edu/Dept/CLACS
Email Address: audvis@usm.edu

We Are Guatemalans
Talks to the people of Guatemala who left refugee camps in Mexico to return to their homeland in the Ixcan jungle.
Availability: Schools in the United States.
Suggested Grade: 7-Adult
Order Number: order by title
Format: VHS videotape
Terms: Borrower pays return postage. Return 14 days after receipt, via USPS including insurance. All borrowers must have a current lending agreement on file with the Outreach program. This agreement is available via the web site or may be requested via phone or fax.
Source: Center for Latin American Studies
University of Florida
319 Grinter Hall
P. O. Box 115530
Gainesville, FL 32611-5530
Phone: 1-352-392-0375
Fax: 1-352-392-7682
World Wide Web URL: http://www.latam.ufl.edu/outreach
Email Address: maryr@ufl.edu

Wedding of the Goddess
Part 1 gives the historical background of the Chittirai festival of the city of Madurai, South India, in which the marriage of the goddess Minakshi to the god Sundaresshvara (the "beautiful Lord," Shiva), is re-enacted yearly. Part II follows the events of the nineteen-day festival, including the re-enactment of the goddess's coronation and marriage. There are scenes of public and private worship as well as interviews.
Availability: Schools, libraries, homeschoolers, and nursing homes in the southeastern United States.
Suggested Grade: 7-12
Order Number: order by title
Production Date: 1976
Format: VHS videotape
Terms: Borrower pays return postage. Return 2 days after showing via United Parcel Service, insured. Book 2 weeks in advance.
Source: Center for South Asian Studies
University of Virginia
Video Library Coordinator
P. O. Box 400169, 110 Minor Hall
Charlottesville, VA 22904-4169
Phone: 1-434-924-8815
Email Address: southasia@virginia.edu

Western Europe: Our Legacy
Ancient Greece and Rome made significant contributions to the world, and their presence in western Europe permanently impacted its society. After the Reformation, European immigrants to the American colonies brought those influences of philosophy, democracy, laws, language, and militarism with them. Though many cultures have contributed to American society, that from western Europe remains the most significant.
Availability: Schools, libraries, and homeschoolers in the United States who serve the hearing impaired.
Suggested Grade: 6-11
Order Number: 1450
Production Date: 1995
Format: DVD
Special Notes: Produced by Benchmark Media.
Terms: Sponsor pays all transportation costs. Return one week after receipt. Participation is limited to deaf or hard of hearing Americans, their parents, families, teachers, counselors, or others whose use would benefit a deaf or hard of hearing person. Only one person in the audience needs to be hearing impaired. You must register--which is free. These videos are all open-captioned--no special equipment is required for viewing.
Source: Described and Captioned Media Program
National Association of the Deaf
4211 Church Street Ext.
Roebuck, SC 29376
Phone: 1-800-237-6213
Fax: 1-800-538-5636
World Wide Web URL: http://www.dcmp.org

Yellow River, The
See the most important river in China, the lifeline into the interior, full of sorrow and joy.

SOCIAL STUDIES--GEOGRAPHY--WORLD

Availability: Schools, libraries, homeschoolers, and nursing homes in the United States and Canada.
Suggested Grade: 9-12
Order Number: order by title
Format: Set of 2 VHS videotapes
Terms: Postage is paid by borrower both ways--send $3.00 per tape to cover initial shipping to you--MONEY MUST BE SENT WITH REQUEST. Return 10 days after showing via U. S. Postal Service, library rate. Shipping is $5.00 to Canadian addresses.

Source: Center for Teaching About China
Kathleen Trescott
1214 West Schwartz
Carbondale, IL 62901
Phone: 1-618-549-1555
Email Address: trescott@midwest.net

SOCIAL STUDIES--HISTORY

Ahmedabad--Life of a City in India
Historical vignettes depict the struggles of the working class under Hindu, Moslem, and British rule. Includes footage of an uprising led by Gandhi.
Availability: Schools, libraries, homeschoolers, and nursing homes in the southeastern United States.
Suggested Grade: 7-12
Order Number: order by title
Production Date: 1983
Format: VHS videotape
Terms: Borrower pays return postage. Return 2 days after showing via United Parcel Service, insured. Book 2 weeks in advance.
Source: Center for South Asian Studies
University of Virginia
Video Library Coordinator
P. O. Box 400169, 110 Minor Hall
Charlottesville, VA 22904-4169
Phone: 1-434-924-8815
Email Address: southasia@virginia.edu

Anatomy of a Coup: Crisis in Iran
Broadcast on the History Channel this looks at the CIA involvement in the 1953 coup that toppled Iranian prime minister Mohammad Mossadegh and restored Shah Mohammad Reza Pahlavi. Basic information and archival footage of Iran in the 1950's.
Availability: Schools, libraries, homeschoolers, and nursing homes in the United States.
Suggested Grade: 7-12
Order Number: order by title
Production Date: 2000
Format: VHS videotape
Terms: Borrower pays return postage via any carrier with $400 insurance per parcel. Videos are loaned for 14 days; may be retained longer if requested in advance. Borrowers must complete a lending agreement.
Source: Center for Middle Eastern Studies
Outreach Coordinator
University of Texas at Austin
1 University Station, F9400
Austin, TX 78712-0527
World Wide Web URL:
http://www.utexas.edu/cola/depts/mes/center/outreach/library-catalog.php
Email Address: crose@mail.utexas.edu

Ancient Arabia: Legacy of Ancient Civilizations
Imagine a society based on the fragrant wealth of perfume, spices, and incense. As goods were carried vast distances from the Far East, all the way to Rome, Arabia stood proudly at the crossroads.
Availability: Schools, libraries, homeschoolers, and nursing homes in the United States.
Suggested Grade: 7-12
Order Number: order by title
Production Date: 1999
Format: VHS videotape
Terms: Borrower pays return postage via any carrier with $400 insurance per parcel. Videos are loaned for 14 days; may be retained longer if requested in advance. Borrowers must complete a lending agreement.
Source: Center for Middle Eastern Studies
Outreach Coordinator
University of Texas at Austin
1 University Station, F9400
Austin, TX 78712-0527
World Wide Web URL:
http://www.utexas.edu/cola/depts/mes/center/outreach/library-catalog.php
Email Address: crose@mail.utexas.edu

Ancient Religions of the Mediterranean
As the world's largest sea, the Mediterranean has nourished various civilizations for centuries. Discover the mythologies, gods, and rituals that played an important role in the social and political lives of these ancient peoples.
Availability: Schools, libraries, homeschoolers, and nursing homes in the United States.
Suggested Grade: 7-12
Order Number: order by title
Production Date: 1998
Format: VHS videotape
Terms: Borrower pays return postage via any carrier with $400 insurance per parcel. Videos are loaned for 14 days; may be retained longer if requested in advance. Borrowers must complete a lending agreement.
Source: Center for Middle Eastern Studies
Outreach Coordinator, University of Texas at Austin
1 University Station, F9400
Austin, TX 78712-0527
World Wide Web URL:
http://www.utexas.edu/cola/depts/mes/center/outreach/library-catalog.php
Email Address: crose@mail.utexas.edu

Ann-Ping Chin: "Four Sisters of Hofei: Culture and Change in Early Modern China"
Ann-ping Chin of Yale University speaks at Cornell University on November 21, 1997 about four sisters' lives to illustrate the cultural, social, and political history of 20th-century China.
Availability: Schools, libraries, and nursing homes in the United States and Canada.
Suggested Grade: 9-Adult
Order Number: CV027
Format: VHS videotape
Terms: Borrower pays return postage. Return with 14 days after scheduled showing, via UPS or U. S. Mail. All requests must included an educational institution affiliation, a current address, and phone number. Order through web site only.
Source: Cornell University East Asia Program
World Wide Web URL:
http://eap.einaudi.cornell.edu/lending_library
Email Address: east_asia1@cornell.edu

All materials listed in this 2018-2019 edition are BRAND NEW!

SOCIAL STUDIES--HISTORY

Arabian Seafarers: In the Wake of Sinbad
In the Middle Ages, the Arabs emerged as a nation of brilliant navigators. This program follows the old sea route to East Africa, Sri Lanka and India.
- Availability: Schools, libraries, homeschoolers, and nursing homes in the United States.
- Suggested Grade: 7-12
- Order Number: order by title
- Production Date: 1994
- Format: VHS videotape
- Terms: Borrower pays return postage via any carrier with $400 insurance per parcel. Videos are loaned for 14 days; may be retained longer if requested in advance. Borrowers must complete a lending agreement.
- Source: Center for Middle Eastern Studies
  Outreach Coordinator
  University of Texas at Austin
  1 University Station, F9400
  Austin, TX 78712-0527
  World Wide Web URL:
  http://www.utexas.edu/cola/depts/mes/center/outreach/library-catalog.php
  Email Address: crose@mail.utexas.edu

Assassination of King Tut
In 1323 B.C. Egypt's young king Tutankhamun died under mysterious circumstances. Hastily mummified, he was placed in a tomb until his sensational discovery in 1922. So, how and why did he die? Two U.S. homicide detectives say evidence points to conspiracy, cover-up and murder. A fascinating study.
- Availability: Schools, libraries, homeschoolers, and nursing homes in the United States.
- Suggested Grade: 7-12
- Order Number: order by title
- Production Date: 2002
- Format: VHS videotape
- Terms: Borrower pays return postage via any carrier with $400 insurance per parcel. Videos are loaned for 14 days; may be retained longer if requested in advance. Borrowers must complete a lending agreement.
- Source: Center for Middle Eastern Studies
  Outreach Coordinator
  University of Texas at Austin
  1 University Station, F9400
  Austin, TX 78712-0527
  World Wide Web URL:
  http://www.utexas.edu/cola/depts/mes/center/outreach/library-catalog.php
  Email Address: crose@mail.utexas.edu

Between Wars: Latin America: Intervention in Our Own Backyard
The Monroe Doctrine and all of its negative ramifications are made evident in this use of old film clips which illustrate U.S. intentions to dictate policy in this hemisphere and the accommodations of such latter day initiatives as the Good Neighbor Policy and Alliance for Progress.
- Availability: Schools in the United States.
- Suggested Grade: 9-Adult
- Order Number: order by title
- Format: VHS videotape
- Terms: Borrower pays return postage. Return 14 days after receipt, via USPS including insurance. All borrowers must have a current lending agreement on file with the Outreach program. This agreement is available via the web site or may be requested via phone or fax.
- Source: Center for Latin American Studies
  University of Florida
  319 Grinter Hall
  P. O. Box 115530
  Gainesville, FL 32611-5530
  Phone: 1-352-392-0375
  Fax: 1-352-392-7682
  World Wide Web URL: http://www.latam.ufl.edu/outreach
  Email Address: maryr@ufl.edu

Breaking the History of Silence
Survivors finally speaking out; Prosecutors accusing Japan's highest-ranking officials of war crimes; Veterans admitting to rape; Expert witnesses revealing the structure of the sexual slavery system; and more.
- Availability: Schools, libraries, and nursing homes in the United States and Canada.
- Suggested Grade: 9-Adult
- Order Number: JV083
- Format: VHS videotape
- Terms: Borrower pays return postage. Return with 14 days after scheduled showing, via UPS or U. S. Mail. All requests must included an educational institution affiliation, a current address, and phone number. Order through web site only.
- Source: Cornell University East Asia Program
  World Wide Web URL:
  http://eap.einaudi.cornell.edu/lending_library
  Email Address: east_asia1@cornell.edu

Byzantium: The Lost Empire
Relive the powerful legacy of ancient Greece and Rome, the first Christian Empire and the last flowering of classical civilization before it fell to the Ottoman Turks.
- Availability: Schools, libraries, homeschoolers, and nursing homes in the United States.
- Suggested Grade: 7-12
- Order Number: order by title
- Production Date: 1997
- Format: VHS videotape
- Terms: Borrower pays return postage via any carrier with $400 insurance per parcel. Videos are loaned for 14 days; may be retained longer if requested in advance. Borrowers must complete a lending agreement.
- Source: Center for Middle Eastern Studies
  Outreach Coordinator
  University of Texas at Austin
  1 University Station, F9400
  Austin, TX 78712-0527

All materials listed in this 2018-2019 edition are BRAND NEW!

SOCIAL STUDIES--HISTORY

World Wide Web URL:
http://www.utexas.edu/cola/depts/mes/
center/outreach/library-catalog.php
Email Address: crose@mail.utexas.edu

Chiapas: The Inside Story
This documentary examines the 30-year rebellion and conflict between the Mexican government and the indigenous population in Chiapas through interviews with village residents, journalists, politicians, and rebel Zapatista leaders.

Availability: Schools in the United States.
Suggested Grade: 11-Adult
Order Number: order by title
Production Date: 1999
Format: VHS videotape
Terms: Borrower pays return postage. Return 14 days after receipt, via USPS including insurance. All borrowers must have a current lending agreement on file with the Outreach program. This agreement is available via the web site or may be requested via phone or fax.

Source: Center for Latin American Studies
University of Florida
319 Grinter Hall
P. O. Box 115530
Gainesville, FL 32611-5530
Phone: 1-352-392-0375
Fax: 1-352-392-7682
World Wide Web URL: http://www.latam.ufl.edu/outreach
Email Address: maryr@ufl.edu

Chicano! History of the Mexican American Civil Rights Movement
Educators kid includes four videos (and much more) from this PBS television series.

Availability: Schools in the United States.
Suggested Grade: 9-Adult
Order Number: order by title
Production Date: 1996
Format: Set of 4 VHS videotapes
Terms: Borrower pays return postage. Return 14 days after receipt, via USPS including insurance. All borrowers must have a current lending agreement on file with the Outreach program. This agreement is available via the web site or may be requested via phone or fax.

Source: Center for Latin American Studies
University of Florida
319 Grinter Hall
P. O. Box 115530
Gainesville, FL 32611-5530
Phone: 1-352-392-0375
Fax: 1-352-392-7682
World Wide Web URL: http://www.latam.ufl.edu/outreach
Email Address: maryr@ufl.edu

Columbus and the Age of Discovery
Seven part series: A. Columbus' World; Sets stage for Columbus's adventure. B. Idea Takes Shape, An; Examines motivations and advances in navigation that made trip possible. C. Crossing, The; Full scale replicas of the Nina, Pinta, and Santa Maria. D Worlds Found and Lost; Modern sailboat and crew retrace route of Columbus's first voyage. E. Sword and the Cross, The; Explores interests of the conquistadors and the church. F. Columbian Exchange, The; Interchange of horses, cattle, corn, potatoes, an sugar cane between the Old World and the New. G. In Search of Columbus; Follows the path of his fourth and final voyage, and how different nations perceive him.

Availability: Schools, libraries, and nursing homes in the United States.
Suggested Grade: 6-12
Order Number: HLA29-video
Production Date: 1991
Format: VHS videotape
Special Notes: Please specify program when ordering. Seasonal for October.
Terms: Borrowers must have a User's Agreement on file with this source--available by mail or via the Internet. Return postage is paid by borrower; return 12 days after showing. Book at least three weeks in advance. All borrowers are limited to a total of ten items per semester.

Source: Latin American Resource Center
Stone Center for Latin American Studies
Tulane University
100 Jones Hall
New Orleans, LA 70118
Phone: 1-504-862-3143
Fax: 1-504-865-6719
World Wide Web URL: http://stonecenter.tulane.edu/pages/detail/48/Lending-Library
Email Address: crcrts@tulane.edu

Cuba: In the Shadow of Doubt
Historical overview of U. S.-Cuban relations and then a picture of everyday Cuban life.

Availability: Schools, libraries, and nursing homes in the United States.
Suggested Grade: 6-12
Order Number: HCCUB14-video
Production Date: 1986
Format: VHS videotape
Terms: Borrowers must have a User's Agreement on file with this source--available by mail or via the Internet. Return postage is paid by borrower; return 12 days after showing. Book at least three weeks in advance. All borrowers are limited to a total of ten items per semester.

Source: Latin American Resource Center
Stone Center for Latin American Studies
Tulane University
100 Jones Hall
New Orleans, LA 70118
Phone: 1-504-862-3143
Fax: 1-504-865-6719
World Wide Web URL: http://stonecenter.tulane.edu/pages/detail/48/Lending-Library
Email Address: crcrts@tulane.edu

SOCIAL STUDIES--HISTORY

Dark Light of Dawn, The
Examines recent years of conflict in Guatemala. Includes depictions of human rights violations against the Indian population.
Availability: Schools, libraries, and nursing homes in the United States.
Suggested Grade: 8-Adult
Order Number: SIGUA2-video
Production Date: 1986
Format: VHS videotape
Terms: Borrowers must have a User's Agreement on file with this source--available by mail or via the Internet. Return postage is paid by borrower; return 12 days after showing. Book at least three weeks in advance. All borrowers are limited to a total of ten items per semester.
Source: Latin American Resource Center
Stone Center for Latin American Studies
Tulane University
100 Jones Hall
New Orleans, LA 70118
Phone: 1-504-862-3143
Fax: 1-504-865-6719
World Wide Web URL: http://stonecenter.tulane.edu/pages/detail/48/Lending-Library
Email Address: crcrts@tulane.edu

Earth Day: The Future Remembered
In commemoration of the 30th anniversary of Earth Day, look back on the great environmental movement of the 70's and 80's.
Availability: Schools, libraries, and homeschoolers in Connecticut, Maine, Massachusetts, New Hampshire, Rhode Island, and Vermont.
Suggested Grade: All ages
Order Number: VID 116
Production Date: 1990
Format: VHS videotape
Terms: Borrower pays return postage. Return within three weeks of receipt. If the tape you request is available, it will be mailed within 5 business days. If not, you will be notified that this video is already out on loan. No more than three titles may be borrowed by one requestor at a time. No reservations for a specific date will be accepted. It is most efficient to order via the web site.
Source: U. S. Environmental Protection Agency, Region 1
Customer Service Center
One Congress Street, Suite 1100
Boston, MA 02214
World Wide Web URL: http://yosemite.epa.gov/r1/videolen.nsf/

Egypt: Beyond the Pyramids
Examine recent archeological discoveries that have altered our understanding of the Kingdom of the Nile, uncovering long-lost temples, tombs and treasures.
Availability: Schools, libraries, homeschoolers, and nursing homes in the United States.
Suggested Grade: 7-12
Order Number: order by title
Production Date: 2000
Format: VHS videotape
Terms: Borrower pays return postage via any carrier with $400 insurance per parcel. Videos are loaned for 14 days; may be retained longer if requested in advance. Borrowers must complete a lending agreement.
Source: Center for Middle Eastern Studies
Outreach Coordinator
University of Texas at Austin
1 University Station, F9400
Austin, TX 78712-0527
World Wide Web URL: http://www.utexas.edu/cola/depts/mes/center/outreach/library-catalog.php
Email Address: crose@mail.utexas.edu

Enchanted Travels of Benjamin of Tudela, The
This animated video brings to life the travels of Benjamin as he traveled the Jewish world during the 12th century, visiting the Mediterranean as well as the Near East.
Availability: Schools, libraries, homeschoolers, and nursing homes in the United States.
Suggested Grade: 1-12
Order Number: order by title
Format: VHS videotape
Terms: Borrower pays return postage via any carrier with $400 insurance per parcel. Videos are loaned for 14 days; may be retained longer if requested in advance. Borrowers must complete a lending agreement.
Source: Center for Middle Eastern Studies
Outreach Coordinator
University of Texas at Austin
1 University Station, F9400
Austin, TX 78712-0527
World Wide Web URL: http://www.utexas.edu/cola/depts/mes/center/outreach/library-catalog.php
Email Address: crose@mail.utexas.edu

Films from the Raj
Shows British India during 15 years before independence. Compiled from silent home movies taken by British families in India, plus letters, diaries, and photographs.
Availability: Schools, libraries, homeschoolers, and nursing homes in the southeastern United States.
Suggested Grade: 7-12
Order Number: order by title
Production Date: 1977
Format: VHS videotape
Special Notes: Black and white.
Terms: Borrower pays return postage. Return 2 days after showing via United Parcel Service, insured. Book 2 weeks in advance.
Source: Center for South Asian Studies
University of Virginia
Video Library Coordinator
P. O. Box 400169, 110 Minor Hall
Charlottesville, VA 22904-4169

All materials listed in this 2018-2019 edition are BRAND NEW!

SOCIAL STUDIES--HISTORY

Phone: 1-434-924-8815
Email Address: southasia@virginia.edu

Great Pharaohs of Egypt, The: Volume 1
Describes the beginnings of Egyptian civilization and the legendary first pharaoh, Narmer, as well as the Old Kingdom builders of the pyramids.
Availability: Schools, libraries, homeschoolers, and nursing homes in the United States.
Suggested Grade: 7-12
Order Number: order by title
Production Date: 1997
Format: VHS videotape
Terms: Borrower pays return postage via any carrier with $400 insurance per parcel. Videos are loaned for 14 days; may be retained longer if requested in advance. Borrowers must complete a lending agreement.
Source: Center for Middle Eastern Studies
Outreach Coordinator
University of Texas at Austin
1 University Station, F9400
Austin, TX 78712-0527
World Wide Web URL:
http://www.utexas.edu/cola/depts/mes/center/outreach/library-catalog.php
Email Address: crose@mail.utexas.edu

Great Pharaohs of Egypt, The: Volume 2
Describes the end of the Old Kingdom, the First Intermediate Period, and the rise of the New Kingdom under the reign of several strong military leaders, as well as Hatshepsut, a woman who ruled as King.
Availability: Schools, libraries, homeschoolers, and nursing homes in the United States.
Suggested Grade: 7-12
Order Number: order by title
Production Date: 1997
Format: VHS videotape
Terms: Borrower pays return postage via any carrier with $400 insurance per parcel. Videos are loaned for 14 days; may be retained longer if requested in advance. Borrowers must complete a lending agreement.
Source: Center for Middle Eastern Studies
Outreach Coordinator
University of Texas at Austin
1 University Station, F9400
Austin, TX 78712-0527
World Wide Web URL:
http://www.utexas.edu/cola/depts/mes/center/outreach/library-catalog.php
Email Address: crose@mail.utexas.edu

Guazapa: The Face of War in El Salvador
Documentary about an FMLN-controlled area of El Salvador during the mid-1980's.
Availability: Schools, libraries, and nursing homes in the United States.
Suggested Grade: 6-12
Order Number: HCELS8-video
Production Date: 1990
Format: VHS videotape
Terms: Borrowers must have a User's Agreement on file with this source--available by mail or via the Internet. Return postage is paid by borrower; return 12 days after showing. Book at least three weeks in advance. All borrowers are limited to a total of ten items per semester.
Source: Latin American Resource Center
Stone Center for Latin American Studies
Tulane University
100 Jones Hall
New Orleans, LA 70118
Phone: 1-504-862-3143
Fax: 1-504-865-6719
World Wide Web URL: http://stonecenter.tulane.edu/pages/detail/48/Lending-Library
Email Address: crcrts@tulane.edu

Hiroshima: City of Peace
Recounts tragic detail from August 6, 1945, when the world's first atomic bomb was dropped on the city of Hiroshima. This video tells a tale of the city's rebirth into what has come to be known as the City of Peace.
Availability: Schools, libraries, and nursing homes in Illinois, Indiana, Iowa, Kansas, Minnesota, Missouri, Nebraska, North Dakota, South Dakota, and Wisconsin.
Suggested Grade: 9-Adult
Order Number: 15007
Production Date: 1995
Format: VHS videotape
Special Notes: No. 7 of the "Nihon No Kokoro" series.
Terms: Borrower pays return postage by U. S. Mail, UPS, or Federal Express, including insurance for "original" videos. Write, call, fax, or e-mail to request an application. An application form MUST be sent in one month in advance but not more than six months in advance. Include alternate titles and dates if provider can substitute titles. Send a SASE with request if you require confirmation. Return immediately after scheduled showing date. Videos may not be copied or broadcast without permission from the producer of the video. Borrower is responsible if video is lost or damaged.
Source: Consulate General of Japan at Chicago
Japan Information Center
Library
737 North Michigan Avenue, Suite 1000
Chicago, IL 60611
Phone: 1-312-280-0430
Fax: 1-312-280-6883
World Wide Web URL:
http://www.chicago.us.emb-japan.go.jp/jic.html
Email Address: jicchicago@webkddi.com

Hiroshima: City of Peace
Recounts tragic detail from August 6, 1945, when the world's first atomic bomb was dropped on the city of Hiroshima. This video tells a tale of the city's rebirth into

SOCIAL STUDIES--HISTORY

what has come to be known as the City of Peace.
- Availability: Schools, libraries and homeschoolers in Alabama, Georgia, North Carolina, South Carolina, and Virginia.
- Suggested Grade: 9-Adult
- Order Number: 540
- Production Date: 1995
- Format: VHS videotape
- Special Notes: No. 7 of the "Nihon No Kokoro" series. A Japanese version is available.
- Terms: Borrower pays return postage. Two tapes may be borrowed at a time. Return within 7 days after receipt. Reservations may be made by filling the application found on the web site.

Source: Consulate General of Japan, Atlanta
Japan Information Center
One Alliance Center
3500 Lenox Road, Suite 1600
Atlanta, GA 30326
Phone: 1-404-365-9240
Fax: 1-404-240-4311
World Wide Web URL:
http://www.atlanta.us.emb-japan.go.jp
Email Address: info@cgjapanatlanta.org

Hiroshima: City of Peace
Recounts tragic detail from August 6, 1945, when the world's first atomic bomb was dropped on the city of Hiroshima. This video tells a tale of the city's rebirth into what has come to be known as the City of Peace.
- Availability: Schools, libraries, homeschoolers, and nursing homes in Connecticut (except Fairfield County), Maine, Massachusetts, New Hampshire, Rhode Island, and Vermont.
- Suggested Grade: 9-Adult
  English; Japanese
- Order Number: 503
- Production Date: 1995
- Format: VHS videotape
- Special Notes: No. 7 of the "Nihon No Kokoro" series.
- Terms: Borrower pays return postage, including insurance. Return two weeks after receipt.

Source: Consulate General of Japan, Boston
Federal Reserve Plaza, 14th Floor
600 Atlantic Avenue
Boston, MA 02210
Phone: 1-617-973-9772
Fax: 1-617-542-1329
World Wide Web URL:
http://www.boston.us.emb-japan.go.jp
Email Address: infocul@cgjbos.org

Hiroshima: City of Peace
Recounts tragic detail from August 6, 1945, when the world's first atomic bomb was dropped on the city of Hiroshima. This video tells a tale of the city's rebirth into what has come to be known as the City of Peace.
- Availability: Schools, libraries, and nursing homes in Hawaii.
- Suggested Grade: 9-Adult
- Order Number: TR-14
- Production Date: 1995
- Format: VHS videotape
- Special Notes: No. 7 of the "Nihon No Kokoro" series.
- Terms: Borrower pays return postage. A maximum of 3 videos may be borrowed per person. Return within one week of date borrowed.

Source: Consulate General of Japan, Honolulu
1742 Nuuanu Avenue
Honolulu, HI 96817-3294
Phone: 1-808-543-3111
Fax: 1-808-543-3170
World Wide Web URL:
http://www.honolulu.us.emb-japan.go.jp

Hiroshima: City of Peace
Recounts tragic detail from August 6, 1945, when the world's first atomic bomb was dropped on the city of Hiroshima. This video tells a tale of the city's rebirth into what has come to be known as the City of Peace.
- Availability: Schools, libraries, and nursing homes in Oklahoma and Texas.
- Suggested Grade: 9-Adult
- Order Number: K8
- Production Date: 1995
- Format: VHS videotape
- Special Notes: No. 7 of the "Nihon No Kokoro" series.
- Terms: Materials must be picked up in person. Under special circumstances, you may be able to have them shipped to you at your own expense (call for further details). Return within two weeks after scheduled showing. Videos must be registered with the U. S. Postal Service or returned by Priority Mail, Federal Express, or other registered shipping service.

Source: Consulate General of Japan, Houston
Cultural Affairs and Information Section
909 Fannin Street, Suite 3000
Houston, TX 77010
Phone: 1-713-652-2977
Fax: 1-713-651-7822
World Wide Web URL:
http://www.houston.us.emb-japan.go.jp/en/culture/page1.htm
Email Address: info@cgjhouston.org

Hiroshima: City of Peace
Recounts tragic detail from August 6, 1945, when the world's first atomic bomb was dropped on the city of Hiroshima. This video tells a tale of the city's rebirth into what has come to be known as the City of Peace.
- Availability: Schools, libraries, homeschoolers, and nursing homes in OREGON AND SOUTHERN IDAHO ONLY. Please make requests via the web site.
- Suggested Grade: 9-Adult
- Order Number: 357
- Production Date: 1995
- Format: VHS videotape

*All materials listed in this 2018-2019 edition are **BRAND NEW!***

SOCIAL STUDIES--HISTORY

Special Notes: No. 7 of the "Nihon No Kokoro" series.
Terms: Borrower pays return postage. Return within three weeks after scheduled showing date. Book one month in advance if possible. Rewind the video and wrap securely for return. Be certain to indicate video number, date needed, name of your organization, and address to which video should be sent, along with phone number. Audience report enclosed with the video must be completed and returned.
Source: Consulate General of Japan, Oregon
Attn: Tamara, Video Library
1300 S. W. Fifth Avenue, Suite 2700
Portland, OR 97201
Phone: 1-503-221-1811, ext. 17
World Wide Web URL:
http://www.portland.us.emb-japan.go.jp/en/index.html
Email Address: tamara@cgjpdx.org

Hiroshima: City of Peace
Recounts tragic detail from August 6, 1945, when the world's first atomic bomb was dropped on the city of Hiroshima. This video tells a tale of the city's rebirth into what has come to be known as the City of Peace.
Availability: Schools, libraries, homeschoolers, and nursing homes in Nevada and northern California (zip codes beginning 932 and above, except 935).
Suggested Grade: 9-Adult
Languages: English; Japanese
Order Number: order by title
Production Date: 1995
Format: VHS videotape
Special Notes: No. 7 of the "Nihon No Kokoro" series.
Terms: Borrower pays return postage. Book two weeks in advance. Return within three weeks of date borrowed, via UPS, Federal Express or certified mail.
Source: Consulate General of Japan, San Francisco
50 Fremont Street, Suite 2300
San Francisco, CA 94105-2236
Phone: 1-415-356-2564
Fax: 1-415-777-0518
World Wide Web URL: http://www.sf.us.emb-japan.go.jp/
Email Address: infoav@cgjsf.org

History Channel II: Change in Heaven
Tells how the communists regrouped after the Long March, and how they planned the defeat of two enemies: the Japanese and the nationalists
Availability: Schools, libraries, and nursing homes in the United States and Canada.
Suggested Grade: 9-Adult
Order Number: CV033
Format: VHS videotape
Terms: Borrower pays return postage. Return with 14 days after scheduled showing, via UPS or U. S. Mail. All requests must included an educational institution affiliation, a current address, and phone number. Order through web site only.
Source: Cornell University East Asia Program
World Wide Web URL:
http://eap.einaudi.cornell.edu/lending_library
Email Address: east_asia1@cornell.edu

Hunt for Pancho Villa, The
Blending picture postcards, archival footage and interviews with survivors, this documentary creates a picture of the violent life on the border in the years before World War I.
Availability: Schools in the United States.
Suggested Grade: 9-12
Order Number: order by title
Production Date: 1993
Format: VHS videotape
Terms: Borrower pays return postage. Return 14 days after receipt, via USPS including insurance. All borrowers must have a current lending agreement on file with the Outreach program. This agreement is available via the web site or may be requested via phone or fax.
Source: Center for Latin American Studies
University of Florida
319 Grinter Hall
P. O. Box 115530
Gainesville, FL 32611-5530
Phone: 1-352-392-0375
Fax: 1-352-392-7682
World Wide Web URL: http://www.latam.ufl.edu/outreach
Email Address: maryr@ufl.edu

Imperial Wedding, The--The Crown Prince and Princess of Japan
Shows the wedding ceremonies and the various matrimonial rites which occurred as Crown Prince Naruhito was married.
Availability: Schools, libraries and homeschoolers in Alabama, Georgia, North Carolina, South Carolina, and Virginia.
Suggested Grade: 4-12
Order Number: 025
Production Date: 1993
Format: VHS videotape
Terms: Borrower pays return postage. Two tapes may be borrowed at a time. Return within 7 days after receipt. Reservations may be made by filling the application found on the web site.
Source: Consulate General of Japan, Atlanta
Japan Information Center
One Alliance Center
3500 Lenox Road, Suite 1600
Atlanta, GA 30326
Phone: 1-404-365-9240
Fax: 1-404-240-4311
World Wide Web URL:
http://www.atlanta.us.emb-japan.go.jp
Email Address: info@cgjapanatlanta.org

Imperial Wedding, The--The Crown Prince and Princess of Japan
Shows the wedding ceremonies and the various matrimonial

SOCIAL STUDIES--HISTORY

rites which occurred as Crown Prince Naruhito was married.
- Availability: Schools, libraries, homeschoolers, and nursing homes in Connecticut (except Fairfield County), Maine, Massachusetts, New Hampshire, Rhode Island, and Vermont.
- Suggested Grade: 4-12
- Order Number: 539
- Format: VHS videotape
- Terms: Borrower pays return postage, including insurance. Return two weeks after receipt.
- Source: Consulate General of Japan, Boston
  Federal Reserve Plaza, 14th Floor
  600 Atlantic Avenue
  Boston, MA 02210
  Phone: 1-617-973-9772
  Fax: 1-617-542-1329
  World Wide Web URL:
  http://www.boston.us.emb-japan.go.jp
  Email Address: infocul@cgjbos.org

Imperial Wedding, The--The Crown Prince and Princess of Japan
Shows the wedding ceremonies and the various matrimonial rites which occurred as Crown Prince Naruhito was married.
- Availability: Schools, libraries, and nursing homes in Hawaii.
- Suggested Grade: 4-12
- Order Number: CU-3
- Format: VHS videotape
- Terms: Borrower pays return postage. A maximum of 3 videos may be borrowed per person. Return within one week of date borrowed.
- Source: Consulate General of Japan, Honolulu
  1742 Nuuanu Avenue
  Honolulu, HI 96817-3294
  Phone: 1-808-543-3111
  Fax: 1-808-543-3170
  World Wide Web URL:
  http://www.honolulu.us.emb-japan.go.jp

Imperial Wedding, The--The Crown Prince and Princess of Japan
Shows the wedding ceremonies and the various matrimonial rites which occurred as Crown Prince Naruhito was married.
- Availability: Schools, libraries, homeschoolers, and nursing homes in Arizona and California (zipcodes beginning 900-931 and 935).
- Suggested Grade: 4-12
- Order Number: 206
- Format: VHS videotape
- Terms: Borrower pays postage both ways; you may call the number below to learn how much postage costs. Return within two weeks of date borrowed. An individual may borrow 2 items at one time. For non-profit and educational use only.
- Source: Consulate General of Japan, Los Angeles
  350 South Grand Avenue, Suite 1700
  Los Angeles, CA 90071-3459
  Phone: 1-213-617-6700
  Fax: 1-213-617-6727
  World Wide Web URL: http://www.la.us.emb-japan.go.jp

Incas Remembered, The
Centuries ago they performed technical brain surgery, built irrigation canals, and ruled half of South America.
- Availability: Schools, libraries, and nursing homes in the United States.
- Suggested Grade: 6-12
- Order Number: INC12-video
- Production Date: 1986
- Format: VHS videotape
- Terms: Borrowers must have a User's Agreement on file with this source--available by mail or via the Internet. Return postage is paid by borrower; return 12 days after showing. Book at least three weeks in advance. All borrowers are limited to a total of ten items per semester.
- Source: Latin American Resource Center
  Stone Center for Latin American Studies
  Tulane University
  100 Jones Hall
  New Orleans, LA 70118
  Phone: 1-504-862-3143
  Fax: 1-504-865-6719
  World Wide Web URL: http://stonecenter.tulane.edu/pages/detail/48/Lending-Library
  Email Address: crcrts@tulane.edu

India Unveiled
A PBS presentation of the history of India from the time of Mahatma Gandhi to the time of Rajiv Gandhi.
- Availability: Schools, libraries, homeschoolers, and nursing homes in the southeastern United States.
- Suggested Grade: 7-12
- Order Number: order by title
- Production Date: 1986
- Format: VHS videotape
- Terms: Borrower pays return postage. Return 2 days after showing via United Parcel Service, insured. Book 2 weeks in advance.
- Source: Center for South Asian Studies
  University of Virginia
  Video Library Coordinator
  P. O. Box 400169, 110 Minor Hall
  Charlottesville, VA 22904-4169
  Phone: 1-434-924-8815
  Email Address: southasia@virginia.edu

Indus: The Unvoiced Civilization
Shrouded in mystery, the details of the Indus Valley civilization are slowly being extracted from the archaeological record. In this program, experts investigate the language, customs, and beliefs of the inhabitants of Mohenjoy-daro, Harappa, Dholavira, and Kalibangan.

SOCIAL STUDIES--HISTORY

Availability: Schools, libraries, homeschoolers, and nursing homes in the southeastern United States.
Suggested Grade: 7-12
Order Number: order by title
Production Date: 2001
Format: VHS videotape
Terms: Borrower pays return postage. Return 2 days after showing via United Parcel Service, insured. Book 2 weeks in advance.
Source: Center for South Asian Studies
University of Virginia
Video Library Coordinator
P. O. Box 400169, 110 Minor Hall
Charlottesville, VA 22904-4169
Phone: 1-434-924-8815
Email Address: southasia@virginia.edu

Inn of Sixth Happiness
True story of an American missionary woman in China. Her greatest feat was to lead a group of 100 homeless children through Japanese lines to safety.
Availability: Schools, libraries, homeschoolers, and nursing homes in the United States and Canada.
Suggested Grade: 9-12
Order Number: order by title
Production Date: 1958
Format: VHS videotape
Special Notes: Based on the book "The Small Woman by Allan Burgess.
Terms: Postage is paid by borrower both ways--send $3.00 per tape to cover initial shipping to you--MONEY MUST BE SENT WITH REQUEST. Return 10 days after showing via U. S. Postal Service, library rate. Shipping is $5.00 to Canadian addresses.
Source: Center for Teaching About China
Kathleen Trescott
1214 West Schwartz
Carbondale, IL 62901
Phone: 1-618-549-1555
Email Address: trescott@midwest.net

In the Footsteps of Alexander the Great
Part I follows Alexander the Great through Asia Minor (modern day Turkey), Lebanon, Israel, Gaza, and into Egypt. Part II continues to Iraq and Iran observing similarities between ancient and modern Persian culture. Part III from shell-shocked Kabul, Afghanistan into former Soviet Central Asia. Part IV follows Alexander's route into Pakistan and India, and then on his return route his untimely demise in Babylon.
Availability: Schools, libraries, homeschoolers, and nursing homes in the United States.
Suggested Grade: 7-12
Order Number: order by title
Production Date: 1997
Format: VHS videotape
Special Notes: A study guide is available upon request.

Terms: Borrower pays return postage via any carrier with $400 insurance per parcel. Videos are loaned for 14 days; may be retained longer if requested in advance. Borrowers must complete a lending agreement.
Source: Center for Middle Eastern Studies
Outreach Coordinator
University of Texas at Austin
1 University Station, F9400
Austin, TX 78712-0527
World Wide Web URL:
http://www.utexas.edu/cola/depts/mes/center/outreach/library-catalog.php
Email Address: crose@mail.utexas.edu

Iraq: The Cradle of Civilization
The first cities were built 5000 years ago on the banks of the Euphrates in Southern Iraq, and urban life soon transformed the human race. This video shows how ancient civilizations of Iraq still affect life in the region today.
Availability: Schools, libraries, homeschoolers, and nursing homes in the United States.
Suggested Grade: 7-12
Order Number: order by title
Format: VHS videotape
Terms: Borrower pays return postage via any carrier with $400 insurance per parcel. Videos are loaned for 14 days; may be retained longer if requested in advance. Borrowers must complete a lending agreement.
Source: Center for Middle Eastern Studies
Outreach Coordinator
University of Texas at Austin
1 University Station, F9400
Austin, TX 78712-0527
World Wide Web URL:
http://www.utexas.edu/cola/depts/mes/center/outreach/library-catalog.php
Email Address: crose@mail.utexas.edu

June 4, 1989
Television news coverage from China, Hong Kong, Taiwan, and the United States, of the Tien an Men Square "incident" is extensive.
Availability: Schools, libraries, homeschoolers, and nursing homes in the United States and Canada.
Suggested Grade: 9-12
Mostly English, some is in Chinese with English subtitles
Order Number: order by title
Format: VHS videotape
Terms: Postage is paid by borrower both ways--send $3.00 per tape to cover initial shipping to you--MONEY MUST BE SENT WITH REQUEST. Return 10 days after showing via U. S. Postal Service, library rate. Shipping is $5.00 to Canadian addresses.
Source: Center for Teaching About China
Kathleen Trescott
1214 West Schwartz
Carbondale, IL 62901

SOCIAL STUDIES--HISTORY

Phone: 1-618-549-1555
Email Address: trescott@midwest.net

Khyber
A study, by anthropologists Akbar Ahmed and Louis Depree, of the sensitive region on the border of Pakistan and Afghanistan, where Pathans killed 17,000 British soldiers, women and children in 1842.
- Availability: Schools, libraries, homeschoolers, and nursing homes in the southeastern United States.
- Suggested Grade: 7-12
- Order Number: order by title
- Production Date: 1979
- Format: VHS videotape
- Terms: Borrower pays return postage. Return 2 days after showing via United Parcel Service, insured. Book 2 weeks in advance.

Source: Center for South Asian Studies
University of Virginia
Video Library Coordinator
P. O. Box 400169, 110 Minor Hall
Charlottesville, VA 22904-4169
Phone: 1-434-924-8815
Email Address: southasia@virginia.edu

Killer Subs in Pearl Habor
Beneath the waves, discover an untold story of a day that lives in infamy.
- Availability: All requesters
- Suggested Grade: 7-Adult
- Order Number: not applicable
- Production Date: 2010
- Format: Streaming Video

Source: NOVA
World Wide Web URL:
http://www.pbs.org/wgbh/nova/programs/index.html

Mexico
Covers over 4,000 years of Mexican cultural history.
- Availability: Schools, libraries, and nursing homes in the United States.
- Suggested Grade: 6-12
- Order Number: HMEX12-video
- Production Date: 1997
- Format: VHS videotape
- Terms: Borrowers must have a User's Agreement on file with this source--available by mail or via the Internet. Return postage is paid by borrower; return 12 days after showing. Book at least three weeks in advance. All borrowers are limited to a total of ten items per semester.

Source: Latin American Resource Center
Stone Center for Latin American Studies
Tulane University
100 Jones Hall
New Orleans, LA 70118
Phone: 1-504-862-3143
Fax: 1-504-865-6719
World Wide Web URL: http://stonecenter.tulane.edu/pages/detail/48/Lending-Library
Email Address: crcrts@tulane.edu

Mission, The
Depicts the conflicts between Jesuit priests and slavery traders from the colonial empires of Spain and Portugal during the 18th century in their battle to shield a South American Indian tribe from brutal subjugation.
- Availability: Schools in the United States.
- Suggested Grade: 10-Adult
- Order Number: order by title
- Production Date: 1986
- Format: VHS videotape
- Terms: Borrower pays return postage. Return 14 days after receipt, via USPS including insurance. All borrowers must have a current lending agreement on file with the Outreach program. This agreement is available via the web site or may be requested via phone or fax.

Source: Center for Latin American Studies
University of Florida
319 Grinter Hall
P. O. Box 115530
Gainesville, FL 32611-5530
Phone: 1-352-392-0375
Fax: 1-352-392-7682
World Wide Web URL: http://www.latam.ufl.edu/outreach
Email Address: maryr@ufl.edu

Official Story, The
An Academy award winning film, teachers may find this useful for lessons about the military dictatorships in Latin America and the aftershocks of these regimes.
- Availability: Schools in the United States.
- Suggested Grade: 9-Adult
  Spanish with English subtitles
- Order Number: order by title
- Production Date: 1985
- Format: VHS videotape
- Terms: Borrower pays return postage. Return 14 days after receipt, via USPS including insurance. All borrowers must have a current lending agreement on file with the Outreach program. This agreement is available via the web site or may be requested via phone or fax.

Source: Center for Latin American Studies
University of Florida
319 Grinter Hall
P. O. Box 115530
Gainesville, FL 32611-5530
Phone: 1-352-392-0375
Fax: 1-352-392-7682
World Wide Web URL: http://www.latam.ufl.edu/outreach
Email Address: maryr@ufl.edu

Peru: Inca Heritage
Explore the majestic ruins in Cuzco and the modern-day culture of the Quechua Indians.
- Availability: Schools, libraries, and nursing homes in the United States.

SOCIAL STUDIES--HISTORY

Suggested Grade: 7-Adult
Order Number: INC14-video
Production Date: 1970
Format: VHS videotape
Terms: Borrowers must have a User's Agreement on file with this source--available by mail or via the Internet. Return postage is paid by borrower; return 12 days after showing. Book at least three weeks in advance. All borrowers are limited to a total of ten items per semester.
Source: Latin American Resource Center
Stone Center for Latin American Studies
Tulane University
100 Jones Hall
New Orleans, LA 70118
Phone: 1-504-862-3143
Fax: 1-504-865-6719
World Wide Web URL: http://stonecenter.tulane.edu/pages/detail/48/Lending-Library
Email Address: crcrts@tulane.edu

Pu Yi, China's Last Emperor
Wonderful historic footage of Pu-Yi and of China in the 1930's, 1940's, and 1950's.
Availability: Schools, libraries, homeschoolers, and nursing homes in the United States and Canada.
Suggested Grade: 9-12
Order Number: order by title
Format: VHS videotape
Terms: Postage is paid by borrower both ways--send $3.00 per tape to cover initial shipping to you--MONEY MUST BE SENT WITH REQUEST. Return 10 days after showing via U. S. Postal Service, library rate. Shipping is $5.00 to Canadian addresses.
Source: Center for Teaching About China
Kathleen Trescott
1214 West Schwartz
Carbondale, IL 62901
Phone: 1-618-549-1555
Email Address: trescott@midwest.net

Rebels vs. the Raj: India During World War II
Profiles Subas Chandra Bose, from 1939 to 1947 Independence, and his Indian National Army in their joint attempt with the Japanese to invade British India from Burma. Contains rare film footage.
Availability: Schools, libraries, homeschoolers, and nursing homes in the southeastern United States.
Suggested Grade: 7-12
Order Number: order by title
Production Date: 1986
Format: VHS videotape
Terms: Borrower pays return postage. Return 2 days after showing via United Parcel Service, insured. Book 2 weeks in advance.
Source: Center for South Asian Studies
University of Virginia
Video Library Coordinator
P. O. Box 400169, 110 Minor Hall
Charlottesville, VA 22904-4169
Phone: 1-434-924-8815
Email Address: southasia@virginia.edu

Riddles of the Sphinx
A marvel of ancient engineering is vanishing. Can it be saved?
Availability: All requesters
Suggested Grade: 7-Adult
Order Number: not applicable
Production Date: 2010
Format: Streaming Video
Source: NOVA
World Wide Web URL:
http://www.pbs.org/wgbh/nova/programs/index.html

Roots in the Sand
A multi-generational portrait of pioneering Punjabi-Mexican families who settled, a century ago, in Southern California's Imperial Valley.
Availability: Schools and libraries in the United States.
Suggested Grade: 7-Adult
Order Number: SA127
Production Date: 1998
Format: VHS videotape
Terms: Borrower pays return postage. Return 3 days after showing via UPS. Book at least 2 weeks in advance.
Source: Syracuse University, South Asia Center
Video Library and Teaching Resources
346F Eggers Hall
The Maxwell School
Syracuse, NY 13244

Satya: A Prayer for the Enemy
Testimonies by Tibetan nuns who have led in the resistance to the Chinese occupation of Tibet and suffered brutal treatment as political prisoners, yet adhere strictly to the principles of nonviolence.
Availability: Schools, libraries, homeschoolers, and nursing homes in the southeastern United States.
Suggested Grade: 7-12
Order Number: order by title
Production Date: 1993
Format: VHS videotape
Terms: Borrower pays return postage. Return 2 days after showing via United Parcel Service, insured. Book 2 weeks in advance.
Source: Center for South Asian Studies
University of Virginia
Video Library Coordinator
P. O. Box 400169, 110 Minor Hall
Charlottesville, VA 22904-4169
Phone: 1-434-924-8815
Email Address: southasia@virginia.edu

All materials listed in this 2018-2019 edition are BRAND NEW!

SOCIAL STUDIES--HISTORY

Scroll of Time, The: A Visual History of Japan
General introduction to the history of Japan, using art and artifacts as well as scenes from actual scrolls to depict life in various historical periods.
- Availability: Schools, libraries, homeschoolers, and nursing homes in OREGON AND SOUTHERN IDAHO ONLY. Please make requests via the web site.
- Suggested Grade: 8-Adult
- Order Number: 409
- Production Date: 1995
- Format: VHS videotape
- Terms: Borrower pays return postage. Return within three weeks after scheduled showing date. Book one month in advance if possible. Rewind the video and wrap securely for return. Be certain to indicate video number, date needed, name of your organization, and address to which video should be sent, along with phone number. Audience report enclosed with the video must be completed and returned.
  - Source: Consulate General of Japan, Oregon
    Attn: Tamara, Video Library
    1300 S. W. Fifth Avenue, Suite 2700
    Portland, OR 97201
    Phone: 1-503-221-1811, ext. 17
    World Wide Web URL:
    http://www.portland.us.emb-japan.go.jp/en/index.html
    Email Address: tamara@cgjpdx.org

Shikoku: An Island in Time
Presents the dignity and charge of Japanese history by introducing Shikoku which is known as an island of pilgrimage.
- Availability: Schools, libraries and homeschoolers in Alabama, Georgia, North Carolina, South Carolina, and Virginia.
- Suggested Grade: 6-12
- Order Number: 320
- Format: VHS videotape
- Terms: Borrower pays return postage. Two tapes may be borrowed at a time. Return within 7 days after receipt. Reservations may be made by filling the application found on the web site.
  - Source: Consulate General of Japan, Atlanta
    Japan Information Center
    One Alliance Center
    3500 Lenox Road, Suite 1600
    Atlanta, GA 30326
    Phone: 1-404-365-9240
    Fax: 1-404-240-4311
    World Wide Web URL:
    http://www.atlanta.us.emb-japan.go.jp
    Email Address: info@cgjapanatlanta.org

Shikoku: An Island in Time
Presents the dignity and charge of Japanese history by introducing Shikoku which is known as an island of pilgrimage.
- Availability: Schools, libraries, homeschoolers, and nursing homes in Connecticut (except Fairfield County), Maine, Massachusetts, New Hampshire, Rhode Island, and Vermont.
- Suggested Grade: 6-12
- Order Number: 562
- Production Date: 1997
- Format: VHS videotape
- Terms: Borrower pays return postage, including insurance. Return two weeks after receipt.
  - Source: Consulate General of Japan, Boston
    Federal Reserve Plaza, 14th Floor
    600 Atlantic Avenue
    Boston, MA 02210
    Phone: 1-617-973-9772
    Fax: 1-617-542-1329
    World Wide Web URL:
    http://www.boston.us.emb-japan.go.jp
    Email Address: infocul@cgjbos.org

Shikoku: An Island in Time
Presents the dignity and charge of Japanese history by introducing Shikoku which is known as an island of pilgrimage.
- Availability: Schools, libraries, and nursing homes in Hawaii.
- Suggested Grade: 6-12
- Order Number: TR-20
- Production Date: 1997
- Format: VHS videotape
- Terms: Borrower pays return postage. A maximum of 3 videos may be borrowed per person. Return within one week of date borrowed.
  - Source: Consulate General of Japan, Honolulu
    1742 Nuuanu Avenue
    Honolulu, HI 96817-3294
    Phone: 1-808-543-3111
    Fax: 1-808-543-3170
    World Wide Web URL:
    http://www.honolulu.us.emb-japan.go.jp

Shikoku: An Island in Time
Presents the dignity and charge of Japanese history by introducing Shikoku which is known as an island of pilgrimage.
- Availability: Schools, libraries, and nursing homes in Oklahoma and Texas.
- Suggested Grade: 6-12
- Order Number: A22
- Production Date: 1997
- Format: VHS videotape
- Terms: Materials must be picked up in person. Under special circumstances, you may be able to have them shipped to you at your own expense (call for further details). Return within two weeks after scheduled showing. Videos must be registered with the U. S. Postal Service or returned by Priority Mail, Federal Express, or other registered shipping service.

SOCIAL STUDIES--HISTORY

Source: Consulate General of Japan, Houston
Cultural Affairs and Information Section
909 Fannin Street, Suite 3000
Houston, TX 77010
Phone: 1-713-652-2977
Fax: 1-713-651-7822
World Wide Web URL:
http://www.houston.us.emb-japan.go.jp/en/culture/page1.htm
Email Address: info@cgjhouston.org

Shikoku: An Island in Time
Presents the dignity and charge of Japanese history by introducing Shikoku which is known as an island of pilgrimage.
Availability: Schools, libraries, homeschoolers, and nursing homes in OREGON AND SOUTHERN IDAHO ONLY. Please make requests via the web site.
Suggested Grade: 6-12
Order Number: 421
Production Date: 1996
Format: VHS videotape
Terms: Borrower pays return postage. Return within three weeks after scheduled showing date. Book one month in advance if possible. Rewind the video and wrap securely for return. Be certain to indicate video number, date needed, name of your organization, and address to which video should be sent, along with phone number. Audience report enclosed with the video must be completed and returned.
Source: Consulate General of Japan, Oregon
Attn: Tamara, Video Library
1300 S. W. Fifth Avenue, Suite 2700
Portland, OR 97201
Phone: 1-503-221-1811, ext. 17
World Wide Web URL:
http://www.portland.us.emb-japan.go.jp/en/index.html
Email Address: tamara@cgjpdx.org

Shikoku: An Island in Time
Presents the dignity and charge of Japanese history by introducing Shikoku which is known as an island of pilgrimage.
Availability: Schools, libraries, homeschoolers, and nursing homes in Nevada and northern California (zip codes beginning 932 and above, except 935).
Suggested Grade: 6-12
Order Number: order by title
Format: VHS videotape
Terms: Borrower pays return postage. Book two weeks in advance. Return within three weeks of date borrowed, via UPS, Federal Express or certified mail.
Source: Consulate General of Japan, San Francisco
50 Fremont Street, Suite 2300
San Francisco, CA 94105-2236
Phone: 1-415-356-2564
Fax: 1-415-777-0518
World Wide Web URL: http://www.sf.us.emb-japan.go.jp/
Email Address: infoav@cgjsf.org

Somos Mas
Documents a march by women in Santiago, Chile, in 1984 in demand of democracy and justice.
Availability: Schools, libraries, and nursing homes in the United States.
Suggested Grade: 6-12
Order Number: HCCHI6-video
Production Date: 1984
Format: VHS videotape
Terms: Borrowers must have a User's Agreement on file with this source--available by mail or via the Internet. Return postage is paid by borrower; return 12 days after showing. Book at least three weeks in advance. All borrowers are limited to a total of ten items per semester.
Source: Latin American Resource Center
Stone Center for Latin American Studies
Tulane University
100 Jones Hall
New Orleans, LA 70118
Phone: 1-504-862-3143
Fax: 1-504-865-6719
World Wide Web URL: http://stonecenter.tulane.edu/pages/detail/48/Lending-Library
Email Address: crcrts@tulane.edu

SOCIAL STUDIES--WORLD AFFAIRS

Afghanistan: The Lost Generation
Filmed after the rise of the Taliban and before the events of September 2001, this film looks at the effects of 20 years of war.
Availability: Schools, libraries, homeschoolers, and nursing homes in the United States.
Suggested Grade: 7-12
Order Number: order by title
Production Date: 2000
Format: VHS videotape
Terms: Borrower pays return postage via any carrier with $400 insurance per parcel. Videos are loaned for 14 days; may be retained longer if requested in advance. Borrowers must complete a lending agreement.
Source: Center for Middle Eastern Studies
Outreach Coordinator
University of Texas at Austin
1 University Station, F9400
Austin, TX 78712-0527
World Wide Web URL:
http://www.utexas.edu/cola/depts/mes/center/outreach/library-catalog.php
Email Address: crose@mail.utexas.edu

Charcoal People, The
Explores the lives of sixty thousand laborers employed in cutting down forests in the Amazon and producing charcoal for the multinational pig-iron industry. The laborers and their families discuss the backbreaking and dangerous work as we witness the toll it takes on their own health and the global environment.
Availability: Schools and libraries in Iowa, Illinois, Michigan, Minnesota, and Wisconsin.
Suggested Grade: 9-Adult
Languages: Portuguese with English subtitles
Order Number: ENVAMZC37VHS
Production Date: 1999
Format: VHS videotape
Terms: Borrower pays return postage. Return 8 days after showing. Book 2 weeks in advance. Order may also be picked up for those near the Center.
Source: Center for Latin American and Caribbean Studies
UW-Milwaukee
P. O. Box 413
Milwaukee, WI 53201
Phone: 1-414-229-5987
World Wide Web URL: http://www.uwm.edu/Dept/CLACS
Email Address: audvis@usm.edu

Children in Debt
Discusses debt crisis and poverty in Bolivia, Argentina, and Peru from a Latin American viewpoint.
Availability: Schools and libraries in Iowa, Illinois, Michigan, Minnesota, and Wisconsin.
Suggested Grade: 6-12
Languages: Spanish with English subtitles
Order Number: CHISAC43VHS
Production Date: 1987
Format: VHS videotape
Terms: Borrower pays return postage. Return 8 days after showing. Book 2 weeks in advance. Order may also be picked up for those near the Center.
Source: Center for Latin American and Caribbean Studies
UW-Milwaukee
P. O. Box 413
Milwaukee, WI 53201
Phone: 1-414-229-5987
World Wide Web URL: http://www.uwm.edu/Dept/CLACS
Email Address: audvis@usm.edu

Coca Mama--The War on Drugs
Millions of U. S. tax dollars are being spent to eradicate drug production in South America, but there is little evidence that this money will diminish supply. Filmed over a year in four coutnries, this documentary examines the "war on drugs" and its various participants including the coca-growing peasants, anti-narcotic patrols, and American lawmakers.
Availability: Schools in the United States.
Suggested Grade: 10-Adult
Order Number: order by title
Format: VHS videotape
Terms: Borrower pays return postage. Return 14 days after receipt, via USPS including insurance. All borrowers must have a current lending agreement on file with the Outreach program. This agreement is available via the web site or may be requested via phone or fax.
Source: Center for Latin American Studies
University of Florida
319 Grinter Hall
P. O. Box 115530
Gainesville, FL 32611-5530
Phone: 1-352-392-0375
Fax: 1-352-392-7682
World Wide Web URL: http://www.latam.ufl.edu/outreach
Email Address: maryr@ufl.edu

Controversia
A serious subject, not only in Cuba, but throughout Latin America--machismo and the role of women today.
Availability: Schools, libraries, and nursing homes in the United States.
Suggested Grade: 6-12
Languages: Spanish with English subtitles
Order Number: SILA5-video
Production Date: 1975
Format: VHS videotape
Terms: Borrowers must have a User's Agreement on file with this source--available by mail or via the Internet. Return postage is paid by borrower; return 12 days after showing. Book at least three weeks in advance. All borrowers are limited to a total of ten items per semester.
Source: Latin American Resource Center
Stone Center for Latin American Studies
Tulane University
100 Jones Hall
New Orleans, LA 70118
Phone: 1-504-862-3143

SOCIAL STUDIES--WORLD AFFAIRS

Fax: 1-504-865-6719
World Wide Web URL: http://stonecenter.tulane.edu/pages/
detail/48/Lending-Library
Email Address: crcrts@tulane.edu

Crisis in Iran: The Death of the Shah and the Hostage Crisis

This looks at the rule of the Shah and the problems that led to the revolution of 1978-79, and the subsequent seige of the U.S. Embassy in Tehran and the hostage crisis.

Availability: Schools, libraries, homeschoolers, and nursing homes in the United States.
Suggested Grade: 7-12
Order Number: order by title
Production Date: 1994
Format: VHS videotape
Terms: Borrower pays return postage via any carrier with $400 insurance per parcel. Videos are loaned for 14 days; may be retained longer if requested in advance. Borrowers must complete a lending agreement.
Source: Center for Middle Eastern Studies
Outreach Coordinator
University of Texas at Austin
1 University Station, F9400
Austin, TX 78712-0527
World Wide Web URL:
http://www.utexas.edu/cola/depts/mes/
center/outreach/library-catalog.php
Email Address: crose@mail.utexas.edu

Cuba and Human Rights

Explores perceptions of human rights in Cuba by U.S. policymakers, Cuban policymakers, and Cubans. The video includes interviews with the U.S. Under Secretary of State and follows Emmy Award winning filmmaker Jon Alpert into Cuba to gauge popular sentiment.

Availability: Schools in the United States.
Suggested Grade: 7-Adult
Order Number: order by title
Production Date: 1997
Format: VHS videotape
Terms: Borrower pays return postage. Return 14 days after receipt, via USPS including insurance. All borrowers must have a current lending agreement on file with the Outreach program. This agreement is available via the web site or may be requested via phone or fax.
Source: Center for Latin American Studies
University of Florida
319 Grinter Hall
P. O. Box 115530
Gainesville, FL 32611-5530
Phone: 1-352-392-0375
Fax: 1-352-392-7682
World Wide Web URL: http://www.latam.ufl.edu/outreach
Email Address: maryr@ufl.edu

Dance of Hope*

Key issues of social policy and human rights in Chile, against the backdrop of the 1988 plebiscite which led to the defeat of Pinochet's government. British pop singer Sting is featured.

Availability: Schools, libraries, and nursing homes in the United States.
Suggested Grade: 6-12
Interviews in Spanish with English subtitles
Order Number: SICHI1-video
Production Date: 1989
Format: VHS videotape
Terms: Borrowers must have a User's Agreement on file with this source--available by mail or via the Internet. Return postage is paid by borrower; return 12 days after showing. Book at least three weeks in advance. All borrowers are limited to a total of ten items per semester.
Source: Latin American Resource Center
Stone Center for Latin American Studies
Tulane University
100 Jones Hall
New Orleans, LA 70118
Phone: 1-504-862-3143
Fax: 1-504-865-6719
World Wide Web URL: http://stonecenter.tulane.edu/pages/
detail/48/Lending-Library
Email Address: crcrts@tulane.edu

Displaced in the New South

Explores cultural collision between Asian and Hispanic immigrants and the suburban communities near Atlanta, Georgia, where they have settled.

Availability: Schools, libraries, and nursing homes in the United States.
Suggested Grade: 6-12
Order Number: HISP68-video
Production Date: 1995
Format: VHS videotape
Terms: Borrowers must have a User's Agreement on file with this source--available by mail or via the Internet. Return postage is paid by borrower; return 12 days after showing. Book at least three weeks in advance. All borrowers are limited to a total of ten items per semester.
Source: Latin American Resource Center
Stone Center for Latin American Studies
Tulane University
100 Jones Hall
New Orleans, LA 70118
Phone: 1-504-862-3143
Fax: 1-504-865-6719
World Wide Web URL: http://stonecenter.tulane.edu/pages/
detail/48/Lending-Library
Email Address: crcrts@tulane.edu

Dreams of Tibet

Looks at how the uncertain fate of Tibet has become a phenomenon of popular culture. Correspondent and China-watcher Orville Schell explores the West's intense interest in Tibet and the growing awareness of an endangered religious and cultural in the face of Chinese repression.

SOCIAL STUDIES--WORLD AFFAIRS

Availability: Schools, libraries, and nursing homes in the United States and Canada.
Suggested Grade: 9-Adult
Order Number: TBV001
Format: VHS videotape
Terms: Borrower pays return postage. Return with 14 days after scheduled showing, via UPS or U. S. Mail. All requests must included an educational institution affiliation, a current address, and phone number. Order through web site only.
Source: **Cornell University East Asia Program**
World Wide Web URL:
http://eap.einaudi.cornell.edu/lending_library
Email Address: east_asia1@cornell.edu

Families of Israel
This video focuses on two Israeli children, one who lives on a kibbutz in the Negev desert, one who lives in Jerusalem.
Availability: Schools, libraries, homeschoolers, and nursing homes in the United States.
Suggested Grade: 5-12
Order Number: order by title
Format: VHS videotape
Terms: Borrower pays return postage via any carrier with $400 insurance per parcel. Videos are loaned for 14 days; may be retained longer if requested in advance. Borrowers must complete a lending agreement.
Source: **Center for Middle Eastern Studies**
Outreach Coordinator
University of Texas at Austin
1 University Station, F9400
Austin, TX 78712-0527
Fax: 1-512-471-7834 (ls)
World Wide Web URL:
http://www.utexas.edu/cola/depts/mes/center/outreach/library-catalog.php
Email Address: crose@mail.utexas.edu

Five Months That Changed a Nation
Documents the massive literacy campaign in Nicaragua which reduced illiteracy from over 50% to less than 13% of the population.
Availability: Schools and libraries in Iowa, Illinois, Michigan, Minnesota, and Wisconsin.
Suggested Grade: 9-Adult
Order Number: DEV/ECNICF58VHS
Format: VHS videotape
Terms: Borrower pays return postage. Return 8 days after showing. Book 2 weeks in advance. Order may also be picked up for those near the Center.
Source: **Center for Latin American and Caribbean Studies**
UW-Milwaukee
P. O. Box 413
Milwaukee, WI 53201
Phone: 1-414-229-5987
Fax: 1-414-229-2879 (ls)
World Wide Web URL: http://www.uwm.edu/Dept/CLACS
Email Address: audvis@usm.edu

From the Burning Embers
This documentary deals with one case of sati (widow immolation) in Rajasthan and the ensuing religious and political controversy over the issue. Provides historical and contemporary perspectives from the point view of different people.
Availability: Schools and libraries in the United States.
Suggested Grade: 9-Adult
Order Number: SA15
Format: VHS videotape
Terms: Borrower pays return postage. Return 3 days after showing via UPS. Book at least 2 weeks in advance.
Source: **Syracuse University, South Asia Center**
Video Library and Teaching Resources
346F Eggers Hall
The Maxwell School
Syracuse, NY 13244
Fax: 1-315-443-9085 (ls)
World Wide Web URL:

From the Other Side
Explores the hardships that are endured by the many people who wait to come into the United States illegally. Their journey is hard and dangerous, perusing the mountains and deserts of southern Arizona.
Availability: Schools and libraries in Iowa, Illinois, Michigan, Minnesota, and Wisconsin.
Suggested Grade: 9-Adult
Spanish with subtitles
Order Number: POL/SOCUSA/MEXF92VHS
Production Date: 2002
Format: VHS videotape
Terms: Borrower pays return postage. Return 8 days after showing. Book 2 weeks in advance. Order may also be picked up for those near the Center.
Source: **Center for Latin American and Caribbean Studies**
UW-Milwaukee
P. O. Box 413
Milwaukee, WI 53201
Phone: 1-414-229-5987
Fax: 1-414-229-2879 (ls)
World Wide Web URL: http://www.uwm.edu/Dept/CLACS
Email Address: audvis@usm.edu

Hiroshima and Nagasaki
This examination of the decision to drop the atom bomb on Hiroshima provides a vehicle for students to learn many things about modern international relations.
Availability: Schools, libraries, and nursing homes in the United States and Canada.
Suggested Grade: 9-Adult
Order Number: JV008
Format: VHS videotape
Terms: Borrower pays return postage. Return with 14 days after scheduled showing, via UPS or U. S. Mail. All requests must included an educational institution affiliation, a current address, and phone number. Order through web site only.

*All materials listed in this 2018-2019 edition are **BRAND NEW!***

SOCIAL STUDIES--WORLD AFFAIRS

Source: Cornell University East Asia Program
World Wide Web URL:
http://eap.einaudi.cornell.edu/lending_library
Email Address: east_asia1@cornell.edu

Human Rights: The Rights of the Child
Children's rights, as defined by the United Nations, and violations of them are shown. Offers UNICEF's action programs as a solution.

Availability: Schools, libraries, and nursing homes in the United States.
Suggested Grade: 8-Adult
Order Number: SI7-video
Production Date: 1991
Format: VHS videotape
Special Notes: Teachers may want to preview intense footage.
Terms: Borrowers must have a User's Agreement on file with this source--available by mail or via the Internet. Return postage is paid by borrower; return 12 days after showing. Book at least three weeks in advance. All borrowers are limited to a total of ten items per semester.
Source: Latin American Resource Center
Stone Center for Latin American Studies
Tulane University
100 Jones Hall
New Orleans, LA 70118
Phone: 1-504-862-3143
Fax: 1-504-865-6719
World Wide Web URL: http://stonecenter.tulane.edu/pages/detail/48/Lending-Library
Email Address: crcrts@tulane.edu

If the Mango Tree Could Speak
A documentary about children and war in Central America. Children talk about peace, justice, ethnic identity, friendship, and marriage.

Availability: Schools and libraries in Iowa, Illinois, Michigan, Minnesota, and Wisconsin.
Suggested Grade: 4-12
Order Number: CHLA1F1.1VHS
Production Date: 1993
Format: VHS videotape
Terms: Borrower pays return postage. Return 8 days after showing. Book 2 weeks in advance. Order may also be picked up for those near the Center.
Source: Center for Latin American and Caribbean Studies
UW-Milwaukee
P. O. Box 413
Milwaukee, WI 53201
Phone: 1-414-229-5987
World Wide Web URL: http://www.uwm.edu/Dept/CLACS
Email Address: audvis@usm.edu

If the Mango Tree Could Speak: A Documentary About Children and War in Central America
Portrait of ten boys and girls, ages 12 to 15, growing up in the midst of war in Guatemala and El Salvador.

Availability: Schools, libraries, and nursing homes in the United States.
Suggested Grade: 6-12
Order Number: SICA8-video
Production Date: 1993
Format: VHS videotape
Special Notes: Includes 30 page study guide.
Terms: Borrowers must have a User's Agreement on file with this source--available by mail or via the Internet. Return postage is paid by borrower; return 12 days after showing. Book at least three weeks in advance. All borrowers are limited to a total of ten items per semester.
Source: Latin American Resource Center
Stone Center for Latin American Studies
Tulane University
100 Jones Hall
New Orleans, LA 70118
Phone: 1-504-862-3143
Fax: 1-504-865-6719
World Wide Web URL: http://stonecenter.tulane.edu/pages/detail/48/Lending-Library
Email Address: crcrts@tulane.edu

Immigration Policy in the United States
Looks at various waves of immigrants who came to the United States, why they came and how they reacted to their new country. Good introduction to immigration.

Availability: Schools, libraries, and nursing homes in the United States.
Suggested Grade: 8-Adult
Order Number: SIUS6-video
Production Date: 1992
Format: VHS videotape
Terms: Borrowers must have a User's Agreement on file with this source--available by mail or via the Internet. Return postage is paid by borrower; return 12 days after showing. Book at least three weeks in advance. All borrowers are limited to a total of ten items per semester.
Source: Latin American Resource Center
Stone Center for Latin American Studies
Tulane University
100 Jones Hall
New Orleans, LA 70118
Phone: 1-504-862-3143
Fax: 1-504-865-6719
World Wide Web URL: http://stonecenter.tulane.edu/pages/detail/48/Lending-Library
Email Address: crcrts@tulane.edu

Immigration Reform
Two immigration reform activists answer questions from an audience of high school students.

Availability: Schools, libraries, and nursing homes in the United States.
Suggested Grade: 6-12
Order Number: SILA6-video
Production Date: 1987
Format: VHS videotape

SOCIAL STUDIES--WORLD AFFAIRS

Terms: Borrowers must have a User's Agreement on file with this source--available by mail or via the Internet. Return postage is paid by borrower; return 12 days after showing. Book at least three weeks in advance. All borrowers are limited to a total of ten items per semester.
Source: Latin American Resource Center
Stone Center for Latin American Studies
Tulane University
100 Jones Hall
New Orleans, LA 70118
Phone: 1-504-862-3143
Fax: 1-504-865-6719
World Wide Web URL: http://stonecenter.tulane.edu/pages/detail/48/Lending-Library
Email Address: crcrts@tulane.edu

Interview with Daniel Ortega
Discusses U. S. defiance of international law, repression, Soviet support and Nicaraguan desire for better relations with the U. S.
Availability: Schools, libraries, and nursing homes in the United States.
Suggested Grade: 6-12
Order Number: HCNIC11-video
Production Date: 1986
Format: VHS videotape
Special Notes: From the TV show, Nightline.
Terms: Borrowers must have a User's Agreement on file with this source--available by mail or via the Internet. Return postage is paid by borrower; return 12 days after showing. Book at least three weeks in advance. All borrowers are limited to a total of ten items per semester.
Source: Latin American Resource Center
Stone Center for Latin American Studies
Tulane University
100 Jones Hall
New Orleans, LA 70118
Phone: 1-504-862-3143
Fax: 1-504-865-6719
World Wide Web URL: http://stonecenter.tulane.edu/pages/detail/48/Lending-Library
Email Address: crcrts@tulane.edu

Interview with Guatemalan President Cerezo
Problems running a democracy when military coups are a threat.
Availability: Schools, libraries, and nursing homes in the United States.
Suggested Grade: 6-12
Order Number: HCGUA4-video
Production Date: 1986
Format: VHS videotape
Special Notes: A CBS Sixty Minuts episode.
Terms: Borrowers must have a User's Agreement on file with this source--available by mail or via the Internet. Return postage is paid by borrower; return 12 days after showing. Book at least three weeks in advance. All borrowers are limited to a total of ten items per semester.
Source: Latin American Resource Center
Stone Center for Latin American Studies
Tulane University
100 Jones Hall
New Orleans, LA 70118
Phone: 1-504-862-3143
Fax: 1-504-865-6719
World Wide Web URL: http://stonecenter.tulane.edu/pages/detail/48/Lending-Library
Email Address: crcrts@tulane.edu

Introduction to the Arab World
Introduces people and places of the region, and addresses important concerns confronting the Arab World today
Availability: Schools, libraries, homeschoolers, and nursing homes in the United States.
Suggested Grade: 7-12
Order Number: order by title
Production Date: 1991
Format: VHS videotape
Special Notes: An annotated script, timelines, maps, classroom exercises, and handouts may be borrowed. (Please specify this in your request).
Terms: Borrower pays return postage via any carrier with $400 insurance per parcel. Videos are loaned for 14 days; may be retained longer if requested in advance. Borrowers must complete a lending agreement.
Source: Center for Middle Eastern Studies
Outreach Coordinator
University of Texas at Austin
1 University Station, F9400
Austin, TX 78712-0527
World Wide Web URL:
http://www.utexas.edu/cola/depts/mes/center/outreach/library-catalog.php
Email Address: crose@mail.utexas.edu

Iran: Adventure Divas
An intriguing look at women in modern Iran, and their fierce independence and self-assertion despite living in a conservative, restrictive society.
Availability: Schools, libraries, homeschoolers, and nursing homes in the United States.
Suggested Grade: 7-12
Order Number: order by title
Format: VHS videotape
Terms: Borrower pays return postage via any carrier with $400 insurance per parcel. Videos are loaned for 14 days; may be retained longer if requested in advance. Borrowers must complete a lending agreement.
Source: Center for Middle Eastern Studies
Outreach Coordinator
University of Texas at Austin
1 University Station, F9400
Austin, TX 78712-0527
http://www.utexas.edu/cola/depts/mes/center/outreach/library-catalog.php
Email Address: crose@mail.utexas.edu

SOCIAL STUDIES--WORLD AFFAIRS

Isle of Flowers
Darkly comic look at the eating hierarchy of a Brazilian island where pigs are fed first.
- Availability: Schools, libraries, and nursing homes in the United States.
- Suggested Grade: 6-12
- Order Number: GEBRA11-video
- Production Date: 1990
- Format: VHS videotape
- Terms: Borrowers must have a User's Agreement on file with this source--available by mail or via the Internet. Return postage is paid by borrower; return 12 days after showing. Book at least three weeks in advance. All borrowers are limited to a total of ten items per semester.
- Source: Latin American Resource Center
  Stone Center for Latin American Studies
  Tulane University
  100 Jones Hall
  New Orleans, LA 70118
  Phone: 1-504-862-3143
  Fax: 1-504-865-6719
  World Wide Web URL: http://stonecenter.tulane.edu/pages/detail/48/Lending-Library
  Email Address: crcrts@tulane.edu

Jerusalem: Within These Walls
Jerusalem's Old City is a tiny enclave where some of history's greatest dramas have been enacted. Busy and colorful, it is the fountainhead of three major religions. This is a view of the city and its people as they are today.
- Availability: Schools, libraries, homeschoolers, and nursing homes in the United States.
- Suggested Grade: 7-12
- Order Number: order by title
- Production Date: 1986
- Format: VHS videotape
- Terms: Borrower pays return postage via any carrier with $400 insurance per parcel. Videos are loaned for 14 days; may be retained longer if requested in advance. Borrowers must complete a lending agreement.
- Source: Center for Middle Eastern Studies
  Outreach Coordinator
  University of Texas at Austin
  1 University Station, F9400
  Austin, TX 78712-0527
  World Wide Web URL:
  http://www.utexas.edu/cola/depts/mes/center/outreach/library-catalog.php
  Email Address: crose@mail.utexas.edu

Kashmir: Valley of Despair
Provides a history and thorough analysis of the political, religious, and ethnic causes of the Kashmir conflict--as Kashmir struggles to seek independence, India and Pakistan deny it.
- Availability: Schools and libraries in the United States.
- Suggested Grade: 7-Adult
- Order Number: SA112
- Production Date: 1998
- Format: VHS videotape
- Terms: Borrower pays return postage. Return 3 days after showing via UPS. Book at least 2 weeks in advance.
- Source: Syracuse University, South Asia Center
  Video Library and Teaching Resources
  346F Eggers Hall
  The Maxwell School
  Syracuse, NY 13244

La Operacion
Discusses the historical, controversial policy of mass sterilization of women in Puerto Rico.
- Availability: Schools in the United States.
- Suggested Grade: 11-Adult
- Order Number: order by title
- Production Date: 1982
- Format: VHS videotape
- Terms: Borrower pays return postage. Return 14 days after receipt, via USPS including insurance. All borrowers must have a current lending agreement on file with the Outreach program. This agreement is available via the web site or may be requested via phone or fax.
- Source: Center for Latin American Studies
  University of Florida
  319 Grinter Hall
  P. O. Box 115530
  Gainesville, FL 32611-5530
  Phone: 1-352-392-0375
  Fax: 1-352-392-7682
  World Wide Web URL: http://www.latam.ufl.edu/outreach
  Email Address: maryr@ufl.edu

Los Ninos Abandonados
Classically realistic story made in the streets of a small Colombian city, with a cast of abandoned children.
- Availability: Schools and libraries in Iowa, Illinois, Michigan, Minnesota, and Wisconsin.
- Suggested Grade: 8-Adult
  Spanish with English subtitles
- Order Number: CHICOLN62VHS
- Production Date: 1975
- Format: VHS videotape
- Terms: Borrower pays return postage. Return 8 days after showing. Book 2 weeks in advance. Order may also be picked up for those near the Center.
- Source: Center for Latin American and Caribbean Studies
  UW-Milwaukee
  P. O. Box 413
  Milwaukee, WI 53201
  Phone: 1-414-229-5987
  World Wide Web URL: http://www.uwm.edu/Dept/CLACS
  Email Address: audvis@usm.edu

Los Olvidados
Some abandoned children live in the streets and rob and even commit murder in order to survive in a violent society.
- Availability: Schools and libraries in Iowa, Illinois, Michigan, Minnesota, and Wisconsin.
- Suggested Grade: 6-12

SOCIAL STUDIES--WORLD AFFAIRS

Languages: Spanish with English subtitles
Order Number: FFMEXOL9VHS
Production Date: 1950
Format: VHS videotape
Terms: Borrower pays return postage. Return 8 days after showing. Book 2 weeks in advance. Order may also be picked up for those near the Center.
Source: Center for Latin American and Caribbean Studies
UW-Milwaukee
P. O. Box 413
Milwaukee, WI 53201
Phone: 1-414-229-5987
World Wide Web URL: http://www.uwm.edu/Dept/CLACS
Email Address: audvis@usm.edu

Mayan Voices: American Lives
Illustrates issues of identity, cultural integration, migration, and social change, as the Maya of Guatemala impact a small agricultural community in Florida.
Availability: Schools, libraries, and nursing homes in the United States.
Suggested Grade: 6-12
Order Number: HISP62-video
Production Date: 1994
Format: VHS videotape
Terms: Borrowers must have a User's Agreement on file with this source--available by mail or via the Internet. Return postage is paid by borrower; return 12 days after showing. Book at least three weeks in advance. All borrowers are limited to a total of ten items per semester.
Source: Latin American Resource Center
Stone Center for Latin American Studies
Tulane University
100 Jones Hall
New Orleans, LA 70118
Phone: 1-504-862-3143
Fax: 1-504-865-6719
World Wide Web URL: http://stonecenter.tulane.edu/pages/detail/48/Lending-Library
Email Address: crcrts@tulane.edu

Mickey Mouse Goes to Haiti: Walt Disney and the Science of Exploitation
Discusses the use of Haitian labor--paid low wages in terrible conditions--to produce items for the Disney empire.
Availability: Schools in the United States.
Suggested Grade: 7-Adult
Order Number: order by title
Production Date: 1996
Format: VHS videotape
Terms: Borrower pays return postage. Return 14 days after receipt, via USPS including insurance. All borrowers must have a current lending agreement on file with the Outreach program. This agreement is available via the web site or may be requested via phone or fax.
Source: Center for Latin American Studies
University of Florida
319 Grinter Hall, P. O. Box 115530
Gainesville, FL 32611-5530
Phone: 1-352-392-0375
Fax: 1-352-392-7682
World Wide Web URL: http://www.latam.ufl.edu/outreach
Email Address: maryr@ufl.edu

Miles from the Border
Twenty years after immigrating, the Aparicio family shares experiences of dislocation and difficulties of crossing cultures.
Availability: Schools, libraries, and nursing homes in the United States.
Suggested Grade: 6-12
Order Number: HISP60-video
Format: VHS videotape
Terms: Borrowers must have a User's Agreement on file with this source--available by mail or via the Internet. Return postage is paid by borrower; return 12 days after showing. Book at least three weeks in advance. All borrowers are limited to a total of ten items per semester.
Source: Latin American Resource Center
Stone Center for Latin American Studies
Tulane University
100 Jones Hall
New Orleans, LA 70118
Phone: 1-504-862-3143
Fax: 1-504-865-6719
World Wide Web URL: http://stonecenter.tulane.edu/pages/detail/48/Lending-Library
Email Address: crcrts@tulane.edu

Miss Universe in Peru
Juxtaposes the glamour of the pageant with the realities of Peruvian women's lives.
Availability: Schools, libraries, and nursing homes in the United States.
Suggested Grade: 6-12
Languages: Spanish with English subtitles
Order Number: SIPER1-video
Production Date: 1986
Format: VHS videotape
Terms: Borrowers must have a User's Agreement on file with this source--available by mail or via the Internet. Return postage is paid by borrower; return 12 days after showing. Book at least three weeks in advance. All borrowers are limited to a total of ten items per semester.
Source: Latin American Resource Center
Stone Center for Latin American Studies
Tulane University
100 Jones Hall
New Orleans, LA 70118
Phone: 1-504-862-3143
Fax: 1-504-865-6719
World Wide Web URL: http://stonecenter.tulane.edu/pages/detail/48/Lending-Library
Email Address: crcrts@tulane.edu

Mujer Negra Habla
Interviews with women from the Atlantic Coast of Costa Rica as they speak out on their situation.

SOCIAL STUDIES--WORLD AFFAIRS

Availability: Schools, libraries, and nursing homes in the United States.
Suggested Grade: 6-12
Language: Spanish
Order Number: AFLACOS1-video
Production Date: 1993
Format: VHS videotape
Terms: Borrowers must have a User's Agreement on file with this source--available by mail or via the Internet. Return postage is paid by borrower; return 12 days after showing. Book at least three weeks in advance. All borrowers are limited to a total of ten items per semester.
Source: Latin American Resource Center
Stone Center for Latin American Studies
Tulane University
100 Jones Hall
New Orleans, LA 70118
Phone: 1-504-862-3143
Fax: 1-504-865-6719
World Wide Web URL: http://stonecenter.tulane.edu/pages/detail/48/Lending-Library
Email Address: crcrts@tulane.edu

Multi-Racial Crosstalk
Looks at difficulties of Indians in communicating ideas with the English because of cultural assumptions.
Availability: Schools, libraries, and nursing homes in the United States.
Suggested Grade: 6-12
Order Number: EC21-video
Production Date: 1970
Format: VHS videotape
Terms: Borrowers must have a User's Agreement on file with this source--available by mail or via the Internet. Return postage is paid by borrower; return 12 days after showing. Book at least three weeks in advance. All borrowers are limited to a total of ten items per semester.
Source: Latin American Resource Center
Stone Center for Latin American Studies
Tulane University
100 Jones Hall
New Orleans, LA 70118
Phone: 1-504-862-3143
Fax: 1-504-865-6719
World Wide Web URL: http://stonecenter.tulane.edu/pages/detail/48/Lending-Library
Email Address: crcrts@tulane.edu

NAFTA and the New Economic Frontier: Life Along the U. S./Mexico Border
ABC news correspondent Judy Muller reports on the quality of life along the international border between El Paso and Juarez since the implemantion of NAFTA.
Availability: Schools and libraries in Iowa, Illinois, Michigan, Minnesota, and Wisconsin.
Suggested Grade: 9-Adult
Order Number: DEV/ECMEXN13VHS
Production Date: 2002
Format: VHS videotape
Terms: Borrower pays return postage. Return 8 days after showing. Book 2 weeks in advance. Order may also be picked up for those near the Center.
Source: Center for Latin American and Caribbean Studies
UW-Milwaukee
P. O. Box 413
Milwaukee, WI 53201
Phone: 1-414-229-5987
World Wide Web URL: http://www.uwm.edu/Dept/CLACS
Email Address: audvis@usm.edu

New Generation, The
Born after the 1960's, this "new race" grew up in the midst of Japanese prosperity and never experienced war. Are they changing Japan's social and economic values?
Availability: Schools, libraries and homeschoolers in Alabama, Georgia, North Carolina, South Carolina, and Virginia.
Suggested Grade: 6-Adult
Order Number: 405
Production Date: 1988
Format: VHS videotape
Special Notes: Part of the "Faces of Japan" series.
Terms: Borrower pays return postage. Two tapes may be borrowed at a time. Return within 7 days after receipt. Reservations may be made by filling the application found on the web site.
Source: Consulate General of Japan, Atlanta
Japan Information Center
One Alliance Center
3500 Lenox Road, Suite 1600
Atlanta, GA 30326
Phone: 1-404-365-9240
Fax: 1-404-240-4311
World Wide Web URL: http://www.atlanta.us.emb-japan.go.jp
Email Address: info@cgjapanatlanta.org

New Generation, The
Born after the 1960's, this "new race" grew up in the midst of Japanese prosperity and never experienced war. Are they changing Japan's social and economic values?
Availability: Schools, libraries, homeschoolers, and nursing homes in Connecticut (except Fairfield County), Maine, Massachusetts, New Hampshire, Rhode Island, and Vermont.
Suggested Grade: 6-Adult
Order Number: 173
Production Date: 1988
Format: VHS videotape
Special Notes: Part of the "Faces of Japan" series.
Terms: Borrower pays return postage, including insurance. Return two weeks after receipt.
Source: Consulate General of Japan, Boston
Federal Reserve Plaza, 14th Floor
600 Atlantic Avenue
Boston, MA 02210
Phone: 1-617-973-9772
Fax: 1-617-542-1329

SOCIAL STUDIES--WORLD AFFAIRS

World Wide Web URL:
http://www.boston.us.emb-japan.go.jp
Email Address: infocul@cgjbos.org

New Generation, The
Born after the 1960's, this "new race" grew up in the midst of Japanese prosperity and never experienced war. Are they changing Japan's social and economic values?
Availability: Schools, libraries, and nursing homes in Oklahoma and Texas.
Suggested Grade: 6-Adult
Order Number: D5
Production Date: 1988
Format: VHS videotape
Special Notes: Part of the "Faces of Japan" series.
Terms: Materials must be picked up in person. Under special circumstances, you may be able to have them shipped to you at your own expense (call for further details). Return within two weeks after scheduled showing. Videos must be registered with the U. S. Postal Service or returned by Priority Mail, Federal Express, or other registered shipping service.
Source: Consulate General of Japan, Houston
Cultural Affairs and Information Section
909 Fannin Street, Suite 3000
Houston, TX 77010
Phone: 1-713-652-2977
Fax: 1-713-651-7822
World Wide Web URL:
http://www.houston.us.emb-japan.go.jp/en/culture/page1.htm
Email Address: info@cgjhouston.org

New Generation, The
Born after the 1960's, this "new race" grew up in the midst of Japanese prosperity and never experienced war. Are they changing Japan's social and economic values?
Availability: Schools, libraries, homeschoolers, and nursing homes in OREGON AND SOUTHERN IDAHO ONLY. Please make requests via the web site.
Suggested Grade: 6-Adult
Order Number: 518
Production Date: 1988
Format: VHS videotape
Special Notes: Part of the "Faces of Japan" series.
Terms: Borrower pays return postage. Return within three weeks after scheduled showing date. Book one month in advance if possible. Rewind the video and wrap securely for return. Be certain to indicate video number, date needed, name of your organization, and address to which video should be sent, along with phone number. Audience report enclosed with the video must be completed and returned.
Source: Consulate General of Japan, Oregon
Attn: Tamara, Video Library
1300 S. W. Fifth Avenue, Suite 2700
Portland, OR 97201
Phone: 1-503-221-1811, ext. 17

World Wide Web URL:
http://www.portland.us.emb-japan.go.jp/en/index.html
Email Address: tamara@cgjpdx.org

New Generation, The
Born after the 1960's, this "new race" grew up in the midst of Japanese prosperity and never experienced war. Are they changing Japan's social and economic values?
Availability: Schools, libraries, homeschoolers, and nursing homes in Nevada and northern California (zip codes beginning 932 and above, except 935).
Suggested Grade: 6-Adult
Order Number: order by title
Production Date: 1988
Format: VHS videotape
Special Notes: Part of the "Faces of Japan" series.
Terms: Borrower pays return postage. Book two weeks in advance. Return within three weeks of date borrowed, via UPS, Federal Express or certified mail.
Source: Consulate General of Japan, San Francisco
50 Fremont Street, Suite 2300
San Francisco, CA 94105-2236
Phone: 1-415-356-2564
Fax: 1-415-777-0518
World Wide Web URL: http://www.sf.us.emb-japan.go.jp/
Email Address: infoav@cgjsf.org

Nowhere Else to Live
Depicts the plight of the urban poor in Mexico City.
Availability: Schools and libraries in Iowa, Illinois, Michigan, Minnesota, and Wisconsin.
Suggested Grade: 6-12
Order Number: CI/URMEXN86VHS
Production Date: 1998
Format: VHS videotape
Terms: Borrower pays return postage. Return 8 days after showing. Book 2 weeks in advance. Order may also be picked up for those near the Center.
Source: Center for Latin American and Caribbean Studies
UW-Milwaukee
P. O. Box 413
Milwaukee, WI 53201
Phone: 1-414-229-5987
World Wide Web URL: http://www.uwm.edu/Dept/CLACS
Email Address: audvis@usm.edu

Oaxacalifornia
Three generations of the Mejia family experience changing realities of living between the U. S. and Mexico.
Availability: Schools, libraries, and nursing homes in the United States.
Suggested Grade: 6-12
Order Number: HISP65-video
Production Date: 1995
Format: VHS videotape
Terms: Borrowers must have a User's Agreement on file with this source--available by mail or via the Internet. Return postage is paid by borrower; return 12 days after

SOCIAL STUDIES--WORLD AFFAIRS

showing. Book at least three weeks in advance. All borrowers are limited to a total of ten items per semester.
Source: Latin American Resource Center
Stone Center for Latin American Studies
Tulane University
100 Jones Hall
New Orleans, LA 70118
Phone: 1-504-862-3143
Fax: 1-504-865-6719
World Wide Web URL: http://stonecenter.tulane.edu/pages/detail/48/Lending-Library
Email Address: crcrts@tulane.edu

Price of Change, The
Examines how Egyptian women now have a choice to work outside the home and they do not necessarily experience this as a liberating choice. Pioneering women using and dispensing birth control devices is reviewed.
Availability: Schools, libraries, homeschoolers, and nursing homes in the United States.
Suggested Grade: 9-12
Order Number: order by title
Production Date: 1982
Format: VHS videotape
Terms: Borrower pays return postage via any carrier with $400 insurance per parcel. Videos are loaned for 14 days; may be retained longer if requested in advance. Borrowers must complete a lending agreement.
Source: Center for Middle Eastern Studies
Outreach Coordinator
University of Texas at Austin
1 University Station, F9400
Austin, TX 78712-0527
World Wide Web URL:
http://www.utexas.edu/cola/depts/mes/center/outreach/library-catalog.php
Email Address: crose@mail.utexas.edu

Queen Noor: Between Two Realms
This program documents the life of Queen Noor of Jordan, her childhood in the United States, her marriage to King Hussein, and her role in Jordanian society.
Availability: Schools, libraries, homeschoolers, and nursing homes in the United States.
Suggested Grade: 7-12
Order Number: order by title
Production Date: 1999
Format: VHS videotape
Terms: Borrower pays return postage via any carrier with $400 insurance per parcel. Videos are loaned for 14 days; may be retained longer if requested in advance. Borrowers must complete a lending agreement.
Source: Center for Middle Eastern Studies
Outreach Coordinator
University of Texas at Austin
1 University Station, F9400
Austin, TX 78712-0527
World Wide Web URL:
http://www.utexas.edu/cola/depts/mes/center/outreach/library-catalog.php
Email Address: crose@mail.utexas.edu

Racial Profiling and Law Enforcement: America in Black and White
An ABC News "Nightline" special on racial profiling and law enforcement in the United States.
Availability: Schools in the United States.
Suggested Grade: Adult
Order Number: order by title
Production Date: 1999
Format: VHS videotape
Terms: Borrower pays return postage. Return 14 days after receipt, via USPS including insurance. All borrowers must have a current lending agreement on file with the Outreach program. This agreement is available via the web site or may be requested via phone or fax.
Source: Center for Latin American Studies
University of Florida
319 Grinter Hall
P. O. Box 115530
Gainesville, FL 32611-5530
Phone: 1-352-392-0375
Fax: 1-352-392-7682
World Wide Web URL: http://www.latam.ufl.edu/outreach
Email Address: maryr@ufl.edu

Saludos Hispanos
Profiles of successful Hispanic personalities and discussions of critical issues, emphasizing the importance of education in attaining goals.
Availability: Schools, libraries, and nursing homes in the United States.
Suggested Grade: 7-12
English or Spanish
Order Number: HISP57-video
Production Date: 1989
Format: VHS videotape
Special Notes: Includes study guide.
Terms: Borrowers must have a User's Agreement on file with this source--available by mail or via the Internet. Return postage is paid by borrower; return 12 days after showing. Book at least three weeks in advance. All borrowers are limited to a total of ten items per semester.
Source: Latin American Resource Center
Stone Center for Latin American Studies
Tulane University
100 Jones Hall
New Orleans, LA 70118
Phone: 1-504-862-3143
Fax: 1-504-865-6719
World Wide Web URL: http://stonecenter.tulane.edu/pages/detail/48/Lending-Library
Email Address: crcrts@tulane.edu

Seca
A look at hard lives of impoverished Brazilians in the

SOCIAL STUDIES--WORLD AFFAIRS

northeast, played as pawns during election years.
Availability: Schools, libraries, and nursing homes in the United States.
Suggested Grade: 8-Adult
Languages: Portuguese with English subtitles
Order Number: SIBRA6-video
Production Date: 1991
Format: VHS videotape
Terms: Borrowers must have a User's Agreement on file with this source--available by mail or via the Internet. Return postage is paid by borrower; return 12 days after showing. Book at least three weeks in advance. All borrowers are limited to a total of ten items per semester.
Source: Latin American Resource Center
Stone Center for Latin American Studies
Tulane University
100 Jones Hall
New Orleans, LA 70118
Phone: 1-504-862-3143
Fax: 1-504-865-6719
World Wide Web URL: http://stonecenter.tulane.edu/pages/detail/48/Lending-Library
Email Address: crcrts@tulane.edu

Secuestro: Story of a Kidnapping
Complex problem of kidnapping in Colombia, where the disparity between rich and poor has turned kidnapping for ransom into a virtual business.
Availability: Schools, libraries, and nursing homes in the United States.
Suggested Grade: 8-Adult
Languages: Spanish with English subtitles
Order Number: SICOL5-video
Production Date: 1993
Format: VHS videotape
Terms: Borrowers must have a User's Agreement on file with this source--available by mail or via the Internet. Return postage is paid by borrower; return 12 days after showing. Book at least three weeks in advance. All borrowers are limited to a total of ten items per semester.
Source: Latin American Resource Center
Stone Center for Latin American Studies
Tulane University
100 Jones Hall
New Orleans, LA 70118
Phone: 1-504-862-3143
Fax: 1-504-865-6719
World Wide Web URL: http://stonecenter.tulane.edu/pages/detail/48/Lending-Library
Email Address: crcrts@tulane.edu

Story of Qiu Ju, The
The wife demands an apology from the village chief for the kick in the groin he gave her husband. The chief refused, so the wife appealed higher and higher, until the sweet/sour victory.
Availability: Schools, libraries, homeschoolers, and nursing homes in the United States and Canada.
Suggested Grade: 9-12
Languages: Chinese with English subtitles
Order Number: order by title
Production Date: 1993
Format: VHS videotape
Terms: Postage is paid by borrower both ways--send $3.00 per tape to cover initial shipping to you--MONEY MUST BE SENT WITH REQUEST. Return 10 days after showing via U. S. Postal Service, library rate. Shipping is $5.00 to Canadian addresses.
Source: Center for Teaching About China
Kathleen Trescott
1214 West Schwartz
Carbondale, IL 62901
Phone: 1-618-549-1555
Email Address: trescott@midwest.net

Struggle and Success: The African American Experience in Japan
The first documentary to thoroughly examine the complex relationships of African Americans and Japanese people, produced by Reggie Life, the recipient of many awards. This is the culmination of two years of research, development and production in Japan and the United States.
Availability: Schools, libraries and homeschoolers in Alabama, Georgia, North Carolina, South Carolina, and Virginia.
Suggested Grade: 6-Adult
Languages: English; Japanese
Order Number: 213
Production Date: 1993
Format: VHS videotape
Terms: Borrower pays return postage. Two tapes may be borrowed at a time. Return within 7 days after receipt. Reservations may be made by filling the application found on the web site.
Source: Consulate General of Japan, Atlanta
Japan Information Center
One Alliance Center
3500 Lenox Road, Suite 1600
Atlanta, GA 30326
Phone: 1-404-365-9240
Fax: 1-404-240-4311
World Wide Web URL: http://www.atlanta.us.emb-japan.go.jp
Email Address: info@cgjapanatlanta.org

Struggle and Success: The African American Experience in Japan
The first documentary to thoroughly examine the complex relationships of African Americans and Japanese people, produced by Reggie Life, the recipient of many awards. This is the culmination of two years of research, development and production in Japan and the United States.
Availability: Schools, libraries, homeschoolers, and nursing homes in Connecticut (except Fairfield County), Maine, Massachusetts, New Hampshire, Rhode Island, and Vermont.
Suggested Grade: 6-Adult

All materials listed in this 2018-2019 edition are **BRAND NEW!**

SOCIAL STUDIES--WORLD AFFAIRS

Language: English; Japanese
Order Number: 463
Production Date: 1993
Format: VHS videotape
Terms: Borrower pays return postage, including insurance. Return two weeks after receipt.
    Source: Consulate General of Japan, Boston
    Federal Reserve Plaza, 14th Floor
    600 Atlantic Avenue
    Boston, MA 02210
    Phone: 1-617-973-9772
    Fax: 1-617-542-1329
    World Wide Web URL:
    http://www.boston.us.emb-japan.go.jp
    Email Address: infocul@cgjbos.org

Syria, Jordan and Lebanon
Travel from Jordan's Wadi Rum to the cities of Beirut and Damascus, the Golan Heights of Syria, and into the desert monasteries near Aleppo.
Availability: Schools, libraries, homeschoolers, and nursing homes in the United States.
Suggested Grade: 7-12
Order Number: order by title
Production Date: 1999
Format: VHS videotape
Terms: Borrower pays return postage via any carrier with $400 insurance per parcel. Videos are loaned for 14 days; may be retained longer if requested in advance. Borrowers must complete a lending agreement.
    Source: Center for Middle Eastern Studies
    Outreach Coordinator
    University of Texas at Austin
    1 University Station, F9400
    Austin, TX 78712-0527
    World Wide Web URL:
    http://www.utexas.edu/cola/depts/mes/center/outreach/library-catalog.php
    Email Address: crose@mail.utexas.edu

They Shoot Children Don't They?
Documents the lives of street children in Guatemala City and those that try to help them survive. It gives a horrifying picture of the human rights violations committed against those children and how some agencies that are designed to protect actually hinder the process.
Availability: Schools and libraries in Iowa, Illinois, Michigan, Minnesota, and Wisconsin.
Suggested Grade: 6-12
Order Number: CHIGUAT34VHS
Format: VHS videotape
Terms: Borrower pays return postage. Return 8 days after showing. Book 2 weeks in advance. Order may also be picked up for those near the Center.
    Source: Center for Latin American and Caribbean Studies
    UW-Milwaukee
    P. O. Box 413
    Milwaukee, WI 53201
    Phone: 1-414-229-5987
    World Wide Web URL: http://www.uwm.edu/Dept/CLACS
    Email Address: audvis@usm.edu

To Be a Mother in Latin America
Documents healthcare issues such as childbirth, abortion, and forced sterilization as well as other topics including the effect of poverty.
Availability: Schools in the United States.
Suggested Grade: Adult
Order Number: order by title
Production Date: 1997
Format: VHS videotape
Special Notes: Includes a graphic segment on childbirth and surgery.
Terms: Borrower pays return postage. Return 14 days after receipt, via USPS including insurance. All borrowers must have a current lending agreement on file with the Outreach program. This agreement is available via the web site or may be requested via phone or fax.
    Source: Center for Latin American Studies
    University of Florida
    319 Grinter Hall
    P. O. Box 115530
    Gainesville, FL 32611-5530
    Phone: 1-352-392-0375
    Fax: 1-352-392-7682
    World Wide Web URL: http://www.latam.ufl.edu/outreach
    Email Address: maryr@ufl.edu

Troubled Harvest
Examines lives of women migrant workers from Mexico and Central America, as they work in grape, strawberry, and cherry harvests in California and the Pacific Northwest.
Availability: Schools, libraries, and nursing homes in the United States.
Suggested Grade: 8-Adult
Order Number: SIUS5-video
Production Date: 1990
Format: VHS videotape
Terms: Borrowers must have a User's Agreement on file with this source--available by mail or via the Internet. Return postage is paid by borrower; return 12 days after showing. Book at least three weeks in advance. All borrowers are limited to a total of ten items per semester.
    Source: Latin American Resource Center
    Stone Center for Latin American Studies
    Tulane University
    100 Jones Hall
    New Orleans, LA 70118
    Phone: 1-504-862-3143
    Fax: 1-504-865-6719
    World Wide Web URL: http://stonecenter.tulane.edu/pages/detail/48/Lending-Library
    Email Address: crcrts@tulane.edu

Unheard Voices
Interviews with Salvadoran children orphaned by internal war. They ask for world peace and an end to their suffering and the violence.

SOCIAL STUDIES--WORLD AFFAIRS

Availability: Schools, libraries, and nursing homes in the United States.
Suggested Grade: 8-Adult
Order Number: SIELS4-video
Production Date: 1990
Format: VHS videotape
Special Notes: Graphic images. May not be appropriate for young audiences.
Terms: Borrowers must have a User's Agreement on file with this source--available by mail or via the Internet. Return postage is paid by borrower; return 12 days after showing. Book at least three weeks in advance. All borrowers are limited to a total of ten items per semester.
Source: **Latin American Resource Center**
Stone Center for Latin American Studies
Tulane University
100 Jones Hall
New Orleans, LA 70118
Phone: 1-504-862-3143
Fax: 1-504-865-6719
World Wide Web URL: http://stonecenter.tulane.edu/pages/detail/48/Lending-Library
Email Address: crcrts@tulane.edu

War and Peace
Filmed over three years in India, Pakistan, Japan and the United States, after the 1998 nuclear tests on the Indian subcontinent, this film documents the current, epic journey of peace activism in the face of global militarism and war.
Availability: Schools, libraries, homeschoolers, and nursing homes in the southeastern United States.
Suggested Grade: 7-12
Order Number: order by title
Production Date: 2001
Format: VHS videotape
Terms: Borrower pays return postage. Return 2 days after showing via United Parcel Service, insured. Book 2 weeks in advance.
Source: **Center for South Asian Studies**
University of Virginia
Video Library Coordinator
P. O. Box 400169, 110 Minor Hall
Charlottesville, VA 22904-4169
Phone: 1-434-924-8815
Email Address: southasia@virginia.edu

War on Nicaragua
Explores why the U. S. was involved in Nicaragua in the 1980's and Reagan's policy leading to that involvement.
Availability: Schools, libraries, and nursing homes in the United States.
Suggested Grade: 6-12
Order Number: HCNIC5-video
Production Date: 1987
Format: VHS videotape
Terms: Borrowers must have a User's Agreement on file with this source--available by mail or via the Internet. Return postage is paid by borrower; return 12 days after showing. Book at least three weeks in advance. All borrowers are limited to a total of ten items per semester.
Source: **Latin American Resource Center**
Stone Center for Latin American Studies
Tulane University
100 Jones Hall
New Orleans, LA 70118
Phone: 1-504-862-3143
Fax: 1-504-865-6719
World Wide Web URL: http://stonecenter.tulane.edu/pages/detail/48/Lending-Library
Email Address: crcrts@tulane.edu

Washington/Peru: We Ain't Winning
Difficulties of forming international policy and introducing alternative crops to areas where coca is presently harvested, as the U. S. is dedicated to eradicating drug-dealers at the source.
Availability: Schools, libraries, and nursing homes in the United States.
Suggested Grade: 8-Adult
Order Number: SIUS3-video
Production Date: 1992
Format: VHS videotape
Terms: Borrowers must have a User's Agreement on file with this source--available by mail or via the Internet. Return postage is paid by borrower; return 12 days after showing. Book at least three weeks in advance. All borrowers are limited to a total of ten items per semester.
Source: **Latin American Resource Center**
Stone Center for Latin American Studies
Tulane University
100 Jones Hall
New Orleans, LA 70118
Phone: 1-504-862-3143
Fax: 1-504-865-6719
World Wide Web URL: http://stonecenter.tulane.edu/pages/detail/48/Lending-Library
Email Address: crcrts@tulane.edu

We Aren't Asking for the Moon
Women garment workers in Mexico City struggle to form a union and cooperative.
Availability: Schools, libraries, and nursing homes in the United States.
Suggested Grade: 6-12
Order Number: HCMEX8-video
Production Date: 1986
Format: VHS videotape
Terms: Borrowers must have a User's Agreement on file with this source--available by mail or via the Internet. Return postage is paid by borrower; return 12 days after showing. Book at least three weeks in advance. All borrowers are limited to a total of ten items per semester.
Source: **Latin American Resource Center**
Stone Center for Latin American Studies
Tulane University
100 Jones Hall
New Orleans, LA 70118

SOCIAL STUDIES--WORLD AFFAIRS

        Phone: 1-504-862-3143
        Fax: 1-504-865-6719
World Wide Web URL: http://stonecenter.tulane.edu/pages/
        detail/48/Lending-Library
        Email Address: crcrts@tulane.edu

Where There Is Hatred
Analyzes successful protest movements in Chile and the Philippines using non-violent tactics.
- Availability: Schools, libraries, and nursing homes in the United States.
- Suggested Grade: 6-12
- Order Number: HC3-video
- Production Date: 1990
- Format: VHS videotape
- Terms: Borrowers must have a User's Agreement on file with this source--available by mail or via the Internet. Return postage is paid by borrower; return 12 days after showing. Book at least three weeks in advance. All borrowers are limited to a total of ten items per semester.

    Source: Latin American Resource Center
    Stone Center for Latin American Studies
    Tulane University
    100 Jones Hall
    New Orleans, LA 70118
    Phone: 1-504-862-3143
    Fax: 1-504-865-6719
World Wide Web URL: http://stonecenter.tulane.edu/pages/
    detail/48/Lending-Library
    Email Address: crcrts@tulane.edu

World Beat: U. S. Foreign Policy
Made at the end of the Reagan administration, this newsmagazine-style show examines U. S. support of the Nicaraguan contras.
- Availability: Schools, libraries, and nursing homes in the United States.
- Suggested Grade: 6-12
- Order Number: HCUS4-video
- Production Date: 1986
- Format: VHS videotape
- Terms: Borrowers must have a User's Agreement on file with this source--available by mail or via the Internet. Return postage is paid by borrower; return 12 days after showing. Book at least three weeks in advance. All borrowers are limited to a total of ten items per semester.

    Source: Latin American Resource Center
    Stone Center for Latin American Studies
    Tulane University
    100 Jones Hall
    New Orleans, LA 70118
    Phone: 1-504-862-3143
    Fax: 1-504-865-6719
World Wide Web URL: http://stonecenter.tulane.edu/pages/
    detail/48/Lending-Library
    Email Address: crcrts@tulane.edu

Yitzhak Rabin
Documents the life of Yitzhak Rabin from his days in the Haganah to Prime Minister and the signing of the Oslo Accords, to his assassination in 1995.
- Availability: Schools, libraries, homeschoolers, and nursing homes in the United States.
- Suggested Grade: 7-12
- Order Number: order by title
- Production Date: 1995
- Format: VHS videotape
- Terms: Borrower pays return postage via any carrier with $400 insurance per parcel. Videos are loaned for 14 days; may be retained longer if requested in advance. Borrowers must complete a lending agreement.

    Source: Center for Middle Eastern Studies
    Outreach Coordinator
    University of Texas at Austin
    1 University Station, F9400
    Austin, TX 78712-0527
    World Wide Web URL:
http://www.utexas.edu/cola/depts/mes/
    center/outreach/library-catalog.php
    Email Address: crose@mail.utexas.edu

Young Voices from the Arab World: The Lives and Times of Five Teenagers
Everyday aspects of Arab culture and society are conveyed through the lives of five young people from Jordan, Lebanon, Egypt, Kuwait, and Morocco.
- Availability: Schools, libraries, homeschoolers, and nursing homes in the United States.
- Suggested Grade: 5-12
- Order Number: order by title
- Format: VHS videotape
- Special Notes: A teacher's guide is available upon request.
- Terms: Borrower pays return postage via any carrier with $400 insurance per parcel. Videos are loaned for 14 days; may be retained longer if requested in advance. Borrowers must complete a lending agreement.

    Source: Center for Middle Eastern Studies
    Outreach Coordinator
    University of Texas at Austin
    1 University Station, F9400
    Austin, TX 78712-0527
    World Wide Web URL:
http://www.utexas.edu/cola/depts/mes/
    center/outreach/library-catalog.php
    Email Address: crose@mail.utexas.edu

*All materials listed in this 2018-2019 edition are **BRAND NEW!***

TITLE INDEX

-A-

Ache Moyuba Orisha	154
Acres of Oysters	1
Adelante	96
Adventure in Glen Canyon	144
Adventure on the Way to the 21st Century	154
Afghanistan: The Lost Generation	206
Africa's Child: Ethiopia: Festival of Fire	154
Africa: South of the Sahara	155
Against All the Odds	6
Ahmedabad--Life of a City in India	193
Air Quality--Ozone	119
Alabama, the Place for Aquaculture!	1
Alias, La Gringa	21
Almost a Woman	155
Alsino and the Condor	21
Altar of Fire	107
Alternative Is Conservation	119
Amazonia - Minimum Critical Size of Ecosystems	119
Amazon, The	155
Amber Hunters	135
American Impressionist, An: William Merritt Chase at Shinnecock	38
Americans 5: In Women's Hands: The Changing Roles of Women	155
Americas 1: Garden of Forking Paths: Dilemmas of National Development	155
Americas 2: Capital Sins: Authoritarianism and Democratization	156
Americas 3: Continent on the Move: Migration and Urbanization	156
Americas 4: Mirrors of the Heart: Color, Class and Identity	156
Americas 8: Get Up, Stand Up: The Problems of Sovereignty	156
Americas 9: Fire in the Mind: Revolutions and Revolutionaries	157
Ana Mendieta: Fuego de Tierra	28
Anatomy of a Coup: Crisis in Iran	193
Ancient Arabia: Legacy of Ancient Civilizations	193
Ancient Chinese Paintings	38
Ancient Futures: Learning from Ladakh	157
Ancient Religions of the Mediterranean	193
Anemia: The Silent Shadow	76
Animals on the Ice Floe: Shiretoko in Mid-Winter	137
Animation in the Classroom	38
Ann-Ping Chin: Four Sisters of Hofei: Culture and Change in Early Modern China	193
Annual Festivities and Ceremonies– Beliefs in Daily Life	107
Anuncios Comerciales	96
Apaissionata	21
Aquaculture and the Rural African Farmer/Pictorial Modelling	1
Arabian Seafarers: In the Wake of Sinbad	194
Archaeological Yucatan: Land of the Maya	157
Argentina	157
Argentina: Growth or Disappearance	157
Around South America	157
Arranged Marriages	158
Arruza	28
Art and Meaning of Ikebana, The	38
Art and Revolution in Mexico	38
Art From Asia	39
Art: Ikebana--Flower Arrangement	39
Artist, The	28
Art of Haiti, The	39
Art of Romare Bearden, The	40
Arts of the Eskimo, The: An Arctic Adventure	144
Asi es Mi Tierra	21
As Iwate Goes: Is Culture Local?	158
As Iwate Goes: Is Politics Local?	158
Assassination of King Tut	194
Atmosphere: On the Air	119
Awareness Series: American Art	40
Awareness Series: Old Masters	40

-B-

Baby Shower for Betsy, A	80

TITLE INDEX

Bahia: Africa in the Americas	107
Banana Split	6
Banking on Life and Debt	6
Barbados	158
Basic Christian Communities in Latin America	108
Battle Against Disease, The	76
Beauticians	16
Beauty of Famous Paintings In the National Palace Museum, The	41
Beekeeping in Northern Climates	1
Behavior Success	16
Bellas Damas, Las	62
Benazir Bhutto: Walking the Tightrope	28
Benedita da Silva	28
Bentley Creek: A Story of an Urban Salt Marsh	119
Between Heaven and Earth: The Temple of Taiwan	62
Between Wars: Latin America: Intervention in Our Own Backyard	194
Big Apple, Hot Apple	120
Biosphere, The	120
Biotechnology & Agriculture	2
Bird Dogs Afield	137
Birth of an Empire	29
Birth of Oroville Dam, The	144
Black Orpheus	22
Body Image for Boys	80
Bolivar Soy Yo	22
Borderline Cases	6
Brazilian Music	62
Breaking Barriers: Foreign Companies That Succeed in Japan	6
Breaking Barriers: Foreign Companies That Succeed in Japan	7
Breaking the History of Silence	194
Bringing Environmental Technologies to the Marketplace	120
Buddhism and Black Belts	108
Buddhism: The Making of a Monk	108
Buddhism: The Middle Way of Compassion	108
Budo: The Martial Arts/The Art of Karate	100
Buena Vista Social Club	62
Build-Up on the Bighorn	144
Bunraku Puppet Theatre of Japan	63
Business Savvy	7
Byzantium: The Lost Empire	194

-C-

Cairo: 1001 Years of Art and Architecture	41
California Flooding	144
California's Heritage: The Missions	145
California's State Water Project: Meeting the Challenge	145
California Water Story, The	145
California Water Story, The	146
Can These Bones Live?	108
Career Close-Ups: School Teacher	16
Carlos Fuentes	29
Carmen Miranda: Bananas Is My Business	29
Carnivorous Plants	137
Carp Town, The	15
Cartoon Magic With Fran	41
Caste at Birth	160
Celebrating Hawaii's Cultures	146
Celebrating the Seasons	160
Central African Republic	160
Central America Close-Up #1	160
Central America Close-Up #2	161
Central Arizona Project--Lifeline to the Future	146
Central Utah Project	146
Ceramics: Basic Throwing Skills with Alleghany Meadows	41
Ceramics Handbuilding: Pinch and Coil Construction with Mollie Favour	41
Challenge of Global Warming, The	120
Challenge of Global Warming, The	121
Chancay, the Forgotten Art	42
Changing Attitude Toward Food, A	2
Charcoal People, The	206
Chemistry: The Basics	135
Chiapas: The Inside Story	195

TITLE INDEX

Christian Laettner: The Power Forward	101
Christian Women in China	162
Christmas Story in Art, The	42
Chulas Fronteras	63
City of Cathay, A	42
Close the Loop: Buy Recycled	121
Coastal Growth: A Delicate Balance	121
Coca Mama--The War on Drugs	206
Coffee: A Sack Full of Power	7
Columbus	29
Columbus and the Age of Discovery	195
Commodities: Black Market	8
Common Experiences: Different Visions	162
Common Ground, A	109
Common Table: Basic Christian Communities in Latin America	109
Common Table: Central American Refugees--The Church Response	109
Communication Gap	8
Communication Success	16
Compassion in Exile: The Story of the 14th Dalai Lama	30
Complete the Circle: How to Buy Recycled	121
Confucianism and Taoism	109
Controversia	206
Courtly Art of Ancient Maya	42
Cover Letter Training	16
Covert Bailey's Fit or Fat	76
Crafting in the USA: Appalachia Region	43
Crafting in the USA: Folklore	43
Crafting in the USA: Hawaii	43
Crafts in Less than 10 Minutes Vol. 1	43
Creating Abstract Art	44
Crisis in Iran: The Death of the Shah and the Hostage Crisis	207
Cuba and Human Rights	207
Cuba: In the Shadow of Doubt	195
Cultural Journey Into Japan, A	163
Cycles of Independence	109

-D-

Dadi and Her Family	163
Dalai Lama: The Soul of Tibet	30
Dalda 13: A Talented Woman History Forgot	30
Dance of Hope*	207
Dark Light of Dawn, The	196
Day in Shrishnagar, A	2
Day of the Dead	163
Dealing with Illegal Questions	17
Debate in the Tibetan Tradition	110
Deep Fat Frying and Pan Frying	85
Depending on Heaven: The Desert	2
Desert Agriculture	2
Devil Gave Us Oil, The	8
Dialogo Entre Augusto Roa Bastos y Fernando Alegria	30
Diary of a Police Post	17
Diego Rivera in the United States	44
Dinner's Served: A Food Safety Program	85
Disaster Prevention	163
Discover Korea: Geography and Industry	164
Displaced in the New South	207
District Nurse, A	18
District Nurse, A/Kangofu: The Japanese Nurse/The Battle Against Disease/Mobile Service/Floating Medical Clinic	164
Doll Master and His Apprentice, The	44
Dominican Republic, Cradle of the Americas	164
Don Segundo Sombra	22
Don't Throw It Away	121
Down in the Dumps	121
Drawing With Pastels	45
Dream Across Time and Place, A--The Legacy of Tsuda Umeko	30
Dreams of Tibet	207
Dream Window: Reflections on the Japanese Garden	45
Drought Survival in California	146
Dust to Dust	22

-E-

Earth Day: The Future Remembered	196
Earth Revealed	122

223

TITLE INDEX

Earth: The Changing Environment	8
Eastern Canadian Provinces, The	164
Eating Disorders	76
Eating for Life	85
Eating, Teens and Calcium	80
Eating Well, Increasing Fiber	85
Economics	8
Economics Classroom, The: Growth & Entrepreneurship	9
Economics Classroom, The: How Economists Think	9
Economics Classroom, The: Learning, Earning, Saving	9
Economics Classroom, The: Monetary & Fiscal Policy	9
Economics Classroom, The: The Building Blocks of Macroeconomics	10
Economics Classroom, The: Trading Globally	10
Eddie's Last Fight: The Old Trainer/19 Year Old Champion	101
Edouard Vuillard	31
Egypt: Beyond the Pyramids	196
Elementary School Teacher, An	18
El Futuro Maya: Voces del Presente	164
El Norte	23
El Peregrinaje de las Flores	23
El Tango en Broadway	23
Emas Park	122
Emerging Powers: Mexico	10
Enchanted Travels of Benjamin of Tudela, The	196
End to Silence, Part 1: Paradise Is Under Your Mother's Foot	165
Energy Behind Finding Energy, The	135
Ennosuke Ichikawa III: Kabuki Actor	63
Ennosuke Ichikawa III: Kabuki Actor	64
Environmental Vision	122
Environment Latest Approaches	122
Environment, The - New Global Concerns: Current Affairs	122
Environment Under Fire: Ecology and Politics in Central America	123
Ernesto Che Guevara: Restless Revolutionary	31
Ernesto Che Guevara: The Bolivian Diary	31
Ethics in America	72
Europe: Southern Region	165
Evita: The Woman Behind the Myth	31
Evita: The Woman Behind the Myth	32
Expanding Canon, The: Teaching Multicultural Literature in High School	96
Extreme Cave Diving	138
Extreme Ice	123
Eye of Thomas Jefferson, The	32

-F-

Families of Israel	208
Famous Deaf Americans--Part I	32
Famous Deaf Americans--Part II	32
Farming in All Seasons	3
Father, Son and Holy War	110
Fats of Life, The	86
Favelas	165
Fervor! The Giant Kite Battle of Ensyu	101
Fervor! The Giant Kite Battle of Ensyu	102
Fervor! The Giant Kite Battle of Ensyu	103
Festival of India	165
Festivals in Taiwan	165
Fetal Alcohol Syndrome: Prenatal Drug and Alcohol Use and Its Effects	76
Fidel Castro: El Comandante	33
Fight for Survival: The Fish Owl of Northern Japan	138
Films from the Raj	196
Firecracker: A Night to Remember in Yen-Shuei	166
Fire Fighters, The	166
First Foods: Lily Feeds Her Baby	80
Fishing in a Sea of Greed	166
Five Months That Changed a Nation	208
Flame in the Chemistry Lab	135
Flexibility	103
Flight from the Marshes	123
Food: A Multi-Cultural Feast	86
Food and Agriculture in Contemporary Japan	3
Footholds	3

TITLE INDEX

Four Seasons for Children	166
Four Seasons in Japan, The	166
14 Steps to Better Breastfeeding	81
Fourth Stage, The: A Hindu's Quest for Release	110
Freshwater	124
Frida	33
Frida Kahlo	33
From Impressionism to Modernism: The Chester Dale Collection	45
From the Burning Embers	208
From the Heart of the World	124
From the Other Side	208
Frontiers of Peace: Jainism in India	110
Funny Crabs in the Mangrove, The	139

-G-

Gabriel Garcia Marquez: Magic and Reality	33
Gagaku: The Court Music of Japan	64
Galapagos: My Fragile World	124
Galapagos of the East, The: Ogasawara Islands	139
Galapagos of the East, The: Ogasawara Islands	140
Garcia Family, The: Puerto Rican Story	147
Gardens of Japan	166
Ghosts of Machu Picchu	167
Ginevra's Story	45
Given to Dance	167
Global Assembly Line, The	10
Goal Away: Setting and Achieving Goals: Turning Dreams Into Reality	72
Goddess of Mercy for Prevention of Senility	167
God's Millennium	110
Gone With the Waste	124
Good Earth, The	96
Good Place to Call Home, A: Maine Towns Creating Their Future	147
Grateful Crane, A	168
Great Food Mixes You Can Make at Home	86
Great Pharaohs of Egypt, The: Volume 1	197
Great Pharaohs of Egypt, The: Volume 2	197
Great Pyramid, The: Ancient Wonder, Modern Mystery	110
Growing Old in a New Age	72
Grupo Corpo--Brazilian Dance Theatre	64
Guadalupe: Mother of All Mexico	111
Guazapa: The Face of War in El Salvador	197
Guests of God, The	111
Guide to Your Healthy Heart	77

-H-

Hail Umbanda	111
Hajari Bhand of Rajasthan: Jester Without Court	64
Hajj, The	111
Hamburger: Jungle Burger	3
Handling of Pigs	3
Harder They Come, The	23
Harvesting New Songs - Brazil	64
Harvesting the Sea	168
Havana Nagila: The Jews in Cuba	111
Healer, The	112
Health During Pregnancy: Lily Looks Back	81
Healthy Dividends: A Plan for Balancing Your Fat Budget	86
Healthy Eating for a Healthy Baby	81
Healthy Foods, Healthy Baby	81
Healthy Japanese Diet, The	87
Healthy Japanese Diet, The	88
Heart Within, The	168
Heated Competition: Jonkara-Bushi	65
Helping Our Feathered Friends	124
Helping Our Feathered Friends	125
Henri Rousseau: Jungles in Paris	46
Henry Moore: A Life in Sculpture	33
Hepatitis-The Silent Epidemic	77
Hernan Cortes	34
High Five: Nutrition Program for High School Youth	88
High Technology in Japan	168

TITLE INDEX

High Water: The Record Floods of February 1986	147
Hiroshima and Nagasaki	208
Hiroshima, A New Threat--A-Bomb Water Dedication	125
Hiroshima, A New Threat--A-Bomb Water Dedication	126
Hiroshima: City of Peace	197
Hiroshima: City of Peace	198
Hiroshima: City of Peace	199
His Holiness the Dalai Lama	112
History and Culture of Puerto Rico	147
History Channel II: Change in Heaven	199
Holiday in Japan	168
Hollow Harvest	169
Hollow Harvest	4
Home Plate	88
Hour of the Star	23
How New England Environmental Assistance Team Helps Businesses Prevent Pollution	126
How Safe Is Your Food?	89
How the Waste Was Won	126
How to Deal With the Jerks In Your Life and Earn the Respect of Your Friends	72
How to Lower Your Cholesterol: A Simple Dietary Approach	89
How to Read the New Food Label	77
How to Read the New Food Label for Persons with Diabetes	89
Hubble's Amazing Rescue	135
Human Geography: People, Places, Change	11
Human Relations in Japan	11
Human Rights: The Rights of the Child	209
Hunt for Pancho Villa, The	199
Hydropower	148

-I-

I Am a Sufi, I Am a Muslim	112
IAQ Tools for Schools Walkthrough Video: 4 Schools Making a Difference	126
If the Mango Tree Could Speak	209
If the Mango Tree Could Speak: A Documentary About Children and War in Central America	209
I Love Sushi	89
Images of Kingdoms	46
Images of Korea, Volume 1	169
Immigration Policy in the United States	209
Immigration Reform	209
Imperial Wedding, The--The Crown Prince and Princess of Japan	199
Imperial Wedding, The--The Crown Prince and Princess of Japan	200
Incas Remembered, The	200
In Celebration of the Enthronement of His Majesty the Emperor of Japan	169
India: Land of the Monsoon	169
Indian Pilgrimage, An: Ramdevra	169
Indian Township Passamaquoddy Tribe: Composting Workshop	126
India Unveiled	200
Indus: The Unvoiced Civilization	200
Inn of Sixth Happiness	201
Inside My Mom	82
Interview with Daniel Ortega	210
Interview with Guatemalan President Cerezo	210
In the Footsteps of Alexander the Great	201
Introducing Mexico: Part One, The Land	4
Introduction to Diabetes: The Game Plan	77
Introduction to East Asian Religions, An: Buddhism (Part I)	112
Introduction to East Asian Religions, An: Confucianism (Part II)	112
Introduction to European Art in the National Gallery of Art	46
Introduction to Let's Learn Japanese Basic I	96
Introduction to Let's Learn Japanese Basic II	96
Introduction to the Arab World	210
Inventive Young Minds	170
Iran: Adventure Divas	210
Iraq: The Cradle of Civilization	201
Islam: Empire of Faith	113

TITLE INDEX

Islam in America 113
Isle of Flowers 211
Israel: Born to Destiny 113

-J-

Jagriti (The Awakening) 170
Jaguar Trax 127
James McNeill Whistler: His Etchings 46
James McNeill Whistler: The Lyrics of Art 47
Japan Arts and Crafts 47
Japanese and Rice Cultivation, The 4
Japanese Architecture: A Living Heritage 170
Japanese Architecture: The Living Heritage 170
Japanese Cooking--A Taste for All Seasons 90
Japanese Culture: Cities; Entertainment; Architecture 170
Japan: Journey of Discovery 171
Japan Land of Enchantment 171
Japan's Distribution System 11
Japan's Leading Edge Agricultural Technology at Work in Biotechnology 4
Japan Today 171
Japan Video Encyclopedia--Japanese Industry & Economy 11
Jerico 23
Jerusalem: Within These Walls 211
Jesus: His Life 113
Jing, a Chinese Girl 171
Job Search Preparation 18
Jongara Bushi Competition--The Tsugaru Jamisen National Contest 66
Journey Into Tradition 148
Journey Within a Journey, A 66
June 4, 1989 201
Jungle 127

-K-

Kabuki: Classic Theater of Japan/Noh, Drama, Bunraku: The Puppet Theater of Japan 66
Kaguya Hime: Princess of the Moon 97
Kalasha, The: Rites of Spring 171
Kangofu, The Japanese Nurse 172
Kashmir: Valley of Despair 211
Kashmir Story, The 113
Kendo 103
Kendo 104
Kenyan Way of Life, The 172
Kenya: The Masai Homeland 172
Keys to Success in the Japanese Market 11
Khyber 202
Killer Subs in Pearl Habor 202
King of Kings and Lord of Lords 113
Kings, Lovers, and Thieves 66
Kings, Lovers, and Thieves 67
Kisho Kurokawa: Architect 172
Knife Skills: Vegetables 91
Kobe 1995--A Cruel Lesson 173
Korean Treasures 47
Kurashiki 173
Kyoto--Scenes and Festivals 173

-L-

Lake Powell--Jewel of the Colorado 148
Landscape Gardener 47
Landscapes of Frederic Edwin Church, The 48
Langston Hughes: The Dream Keeper 34
Lantern Festival, The 173
La Operacion 211
La Piramide de la Alimentacion 91
Last of the Khans, The 34
Latino Artists: Pushing Artistic Boundaries 48
Latitude and Longitude 173
Lead in School Drinking Water 127
Lead Paint Poisoning: The Thief of Childhood 127
L.E.A.R.: League of Revolutionary Artists and Writers 48

TITLE INDEX

Learning a Trade	18
Leaving School	72
Legal Winds of Change: Business and the New Clean Air Act	127
Legends of the American West: Part Two	34
Leonardo: To Know How to See	48
Leo Tolstoy	35
Less Is More: Pollution Prevention Is Good Business	12
Let's Learn Japanese: Basic I	97
Life from the Sea	173
Life in an Oasis	173
Linnea In Monet's Garden	49
Little Duck Tale, A	140
Little Duck Tale, A	141
Living Arts	175
Living Waters of the Colorado	148
Lizard Kings	141
Look Who's Eating	82
Loosening the Mold	73
Loosing the Mold	73
Lo Que Comes: Por Ti Y Tu Bebe	78
Los Murales de la Cuidad de Mexico: El Muro de las Celebraciones	49
Los Ninos Abandonados	211
Los Olvidados	211
Louisiana Wetlands: America's Coastal Crisis	149
Loving Krishna	114

-M-

Madre Tierra	128
Magic of China/Children of China	175
Man Facing Southeast	24
Maquila: A Tale of Two Mexicos	12
Maria Candelaria	24
Mario Benedetti	35
Marriages in Heaven	175
Martin Chambi and the Heirs of the Incas	49
Martin Fierro	24
Masses and Murals	175
Masterpieces of Chinese Painting and Calligraphy at the National Palace Museum	49
Masters of the Wok	91
Mayan Voices: American Lives	212
Maysa Matarazzo	35
Meal Planning: Eating Right for People with Diabetes	91
Meeting the Third World Through Women's Perspectives	175
Megabeasts' Sudden Death	136
Meinung's Oiled Paper Umbrellas	50
Mercado, El	176
Merrimack River Watershed Protection	128
Message, The	114
Messiah: The Biblical Message Behind the Musical Masterpiece	114
Mexican Sign Language	97
Mexico	202
Mickey Mouse Goes to Haiti: Walt Disney and the Science of Exploitation	212
Middle America: Mexico to Venezuela and the Caribbean Islands	176
Miles from the Border	212
Mini Series: Profile of a Nation	176
Miracle of Water	149
Mirror in My Mind, The: Body Image & Self-Esteem	78
Missing	24
Mission, The	202
Miss Mary	24
Miss Universe in Peru	212
Mobile Services	177
Modern Brides: Arranged Marriage in South India	177
Molly's Pilgrim	97
Mountain Music in Peru	67
Mountain Skywater	149
Mujer Negra Habla	212
Multi-Racial Crosstalk	213
Municipal Office and Its Services, The/Village Reborn, A/Toga: Village for the Theater	177
Munni (Little Girl): Childhood and Art in Mithila	177
Music of Bunraku	67
Music of Latin America	67

TITLE INDEX

Music of Modern Japan/Kitaro, Synthesizer Musician   67
Mythology of Ancient Mexico   114

-N-

NAFTA and the New Economic Frontier: Life Along the U. S./Mexico Border   213
Naginata   104
Narrative Writing 1: Structures--What is a Narrative?   98
National Gallery of Art, A Treasury of Masterpieces   50
Nature's Bounty: Flowers for the Japanese   177
Neighborhood Tokyo   177
Nepal: Land of the Gods   178
Neputa Painter, The   50
Neputa Painter, The   51
New Generation, The   213
New Generation, The   214
New Superfund: What It Is, How It Works   128
Night of Nine Tribes, The   178
1959: Endangered Planet   128
Noh Drama, Kabuki, Bunraku--Classical Theater in Japan   68
No Longer Colonies: Hong Kong, 1997; Macau, 1999   178
No Longer Silent   178
Nowhere Else to Live   214

-O-

Oaxacalifornia   214
Oaxacan Woodcarving: Innovation Meets Tradition   51
Observing the Breath   114
Ocean of Wisdom   35
Official Story, The   202
Of Time, Tombs, and Treasure: The Treasures of Tutankhamun   51
One World, One Economy   12
On Top of the Whale   25
Open to the World   178
Operation Glen Canyon   149
Origami   52
Our Hidden National Product   128
Our Mexican-American Musical Heritage   68
Our Urban Wetlands: An Endangered Resource   129
Our Water, Our Future: Saving Our Tribal Life Force Together   129

-P-

Pablo Neruda Present   35
Pakistan: Between the Chitralis and Pathans   179
Para una Tumba sin Nombre   25
Parties, Pinatas and Plays: Mexican Christmas Traditions   179
Past, Present and Future: Washi--Unique Japanese Paper Culture   52
Past, Present and Future: Washi--Unique Japanese Paper Culture   53
People of the Caribbean   150
Periodic Table of Videos   136
Peru: Inca Heritage   202
Picasso and His Time   36
Picasso: The Early Years   53
Pie en la Marcha   179
Pipeline   150
Pixote   25
Place of the Falling Waters, The   150
Place to Be, A: The Construction of the East Building of the National Gallery of Art   53
Plunder   54
Poaching and Steaming   92
Poisoned Home, Poisoned People: CNN and Time on Special Assignment   129
Popol Vuh: The Creation Myth of the Maya   98
Popular Hispanic Culture   54
Powering One Corner of the World   151
Power of Compassion, The: Sakyadhita   179
Pregnant Teens Taking Care   82

TITLE INDEX

Price of Change, The	215
Primary and Secondary Education in Japan	179
Primary and Secondary Education in Japan/The Elementary School Teacher	180
Primary and Secondary Education in Japan/The Elementary School Teacher/School Days in Japan	180
Producer Through Consumer--Partners to a Safe Food Supply	92
Producing Miracles Everyday	180
Protecting Our Global Home--Japan's Ecological Contributions	129
Protecting Our Global Home--Japan's Ecological Contributions	130
Protecting Our Habitat: Recycling at the Grassroots	130
Punctuation: Program 6--Introduction to Punctuation and the End Marks	98
Pu Yi, China's Last Emperor	203
Pyramids of the Sun and Moon	54

-Q-

Quality Control, An American Idea Takes Root in Japan	12
Quality Control, An American Idea Takes Root in Japan	13
Quality Control and the Q.C. Circle	13
Queen Noor: Between Two Realms	215
Querido Diario	25
Quiet Collector, The: Andrew W. Mellon Remembered	54
Quincas Berro D'Agua	25

-R-

Racial Profiling and Law Enforcement: America in Black and White	215
Radha's Day: Hindu Family Life #5	180
Raices Del Pueblo: Cantos y Danzas de Veracruz	68
Rain Forest	130
Rain Forest	141
Rainforests: Proving Their Worth	130
Raise the Red Lantern	180
Raphael and the American Collector	55
Real People Coping with Eating Disorders	73
Rebels vs. the Raj: India During World War II	203
Recreating Taste in Low Fat Cooking	92
Recycle	131
Recycling	181
Reduce, Reuse, Recycle: The Bottom Line	131
Reflections: The Story of The Treasure Houses of Britain	55
Reproductive Systems	82
R-E-S-P-E-C-T	73
Reversing the Tide	151
Reviving Our Rain Forests--The Mission of Professor Akira Miyawaki	131
Rewarding Employment: How to Get a Really Good Job	18
Riddles of the Sphinx	203
Rimpa School Crosses the Ocean	55
Rimpa School Crosses the Ocean	56
Rio Grande--Ribbon of Life	151
Rivera: Portrait of an Artist	56
Roasting	92
Rockin' Hand Washin' Report, The	78
Roji Koie-Potter	57
Roots in the Sand	203
Roots of Rhythm	68
Roots, Rock, Reggae: Inside the Jamaican Music Scene	68
Rotten Truth, The	131
Rotund World of Botero, The	36
Routes of Rhythm--Part II	69
Routes of Rhythm--Part III	69

-S-

Sabina Sanchez - The Art of Embroidery	57
Sables in the Northern Land	141
Sables in the Northern Land	142
Sabo: Erosion Control	181
Safe Food, Healthy Children	93
Saheri's Choice	181
Salaam Bombay	181

TITLE INDEX

Saludos Hispanos	215
Sand Painting: Sacred Art of Tibetan Buddhism	115
Sathya Sai Baba: Aura of Divinity	115
Satya: A Prayer for the Enemy	203
Saving Inky	142
School Days in Japan	182
School Testing--Behind the Numbers	136
Scroll of Time, The: A Visual History of Japan	204
Seasons of Life	136
Sea Turtles' Last Dance	142
Seca	215
Secuestro: Story of a Kidnapping	216
Seeds of Plenty, Seeds of Sorrow; Developing Stories 1	182
Seeing Color: Object, Light, Observer	57
Selected Songs by Famous Singers	69
Serial for Breakfast (Part I & II)	182
Serpent Fruits	132
Shacho, The--A Japanese President & His Company	13
Shacho, The--A Japanese President & His Company	14
Shadows of Turkey/The Witches	69
Shaw Memorial, The: The Power and Glory of Public Art	58
Shikoku: An Island in Time	204
Shikoku: An Island in Time	205
Shingo Kojima--Cabinetmaker	58
Shingo Kojima--Cabinetmaker	59
Shinto: Way of the Gods	115
Shogyo Ohba's Challenge--Lacquerer	59
Shopping for Health: Smart Choices at the Supermarket	93
Shopping for Heart Health: Lower Your Blood Cholesterol and Reduce Your Risk of Coronary Artery Disease	93
Sixteen Decisions	182
Snowfall to Sandstone	151
Sokui-no-Rei, The	36
Somos Mas	205
Son of the Ocean	182
Sound Nutrition for Teenage Mothers-to-Be	83
South Africa: A Land Apart	183
South America: The Southern Plains	14
Southwest Region	151
So You Want to Be? Teacher/Make-Up Artist	19
Spirit of Edo Firemen, The--Alive in Tokyo Today	19
Splendid China: A Miniature Rendition in Florida	183
Starting Solid Foods: Lily Helps Ana	83
Stirrings of Change	183
Story of Hoover Dam, The	152
Story of Islam, The	116
Story of Noriko, The	14
Story of Noriko, The	15
Story of Qiu Ju, The	216
Struggle and Success: The African American Experience in Japan	216
Student Workshop: All About Respect	74
Sugar Cane Alley	26
Sumo	104
Sweet 15	152
Syria, Jordan and Lebanon	217

-T-

Taj Mahal: The Story of Muslim India	183
Taking Blessings Door to Door	69
Taking Blessings Door to Door	70
Tale of the Heike, The: Biwa Concern at Cornell University	70
Tales of Pabuji: A Rajasthani Tradition	116
Tango Bar	26
Tango Is Also History	70
Tango: Our Dance	70
Tang, The: China's Cosmopolitan Age	183
Taste of Japan, The: A Tradition of Hospitality	93
Taste of Japan, The: A Tradition of Hospitality	94
Tea Drinking in Taipei	184
Teenage Nutrition: Prevention of Obesity	79
Teen Breastfeeding: The Natural Choice	83

TITLE INDEX

Ten Who Dared - Alexander von Humboldt 36
Ten Who Dared: Francisco Pizzarro 36
Teton--Decision and Disaster 152
Teyyam: The Annual Visit of the
    God Vishnumurti 184
Theater Lives, The 71
They Shoot Children Don't They? 217
This Other Haiti 184
This Year We Went to Japan 184
Throw Me a Dime 184
Tibetan Book of the Dead, The 116
Tibet: The End of Time 184
Tibet: Where Continents Collide 185
Ties That Bind: Stories Behind the
    Immigration Controversy 153
To Be a Mother in Latin America 217
To Live 185
To Live in a Multi-Cultural World 74
Toulouse-Lautrec and Montmartre 59
Tour of the Prado, A 59
Traditional Japanese Culture: Japanese
    Cuisine 94
Traditional Japanese Culture: Japanese
    Cuisine 95
Traditional Sports: Karatedo 105
Traditional Sports: Kendo 105
Traditional Sports: Sumo 105
Tramp in the Darien, A 132
Trans-Tokyo Bay Road, The 185
Trans-Tokyo Road, The 185
Trans-Tokyo Road, The 186
Travel Wise in Japan 186
Travel Wise in Japan 187
Trials of Telo Rinpoche 116
Tribal Religions 117
Tropical Kingdom of Belize 88
Troubled Harvest 217
Tsukuba Academic New Town 15
Tune in Korea: Legacy and
    Transformation 88
Turquoise Coast via Istanbul, The 88
Twilight for a Coal Mining Town:
    The Tale of Takashima 88
Twilight for a Coal-Mining Town:
    The Tale of Takashima 88
Twilight for a Coal Mining Town:
    The Tale of Takashima 189
Twilight for a Coal-Mining Town:
    The Tale of Takashima 189
Two Tibetan Buddhist Nunneries 117

-U-

Uganda: The Pearl of Africa 190
Umm Kulthum: A Voice Like Egypt 71
Understanding Ecology: What Is
    a Food Chain? 132
Under the Same Sun 190
Unheard Voices 217
U. S., Mexico, and NAFTA 15
User's Guide to the Planet Earth, A:
    The American Environmental
    Test 132

-V-

Valley of the Gods: Worship in
    Katmandu 117
Venezuela: A Petroleum Powered
    Economy 190
Vermont Wetlands: A Natural Resource 153
Vertebrates 142
Village Man, City Man 190
Visiones del Pueblo: The Folk Art of
    Latin America 60
Vision of Juazeiro 117
Viva Zapata 26
Vocational Training 19
Voice from Heaven, A: Nusrat Fateh
    Ali Khan 71
Voices of Latin America 98
Voices of the Orishas 117
Voices of the Sierra Tarahumara 190

-W-

Waiapi Instrumental Music 71
Wake Up Call 74
War and Peace 218
War on Nicaragua 218

TITLE INDEX

Washington/Peru: We Ain't Winning	218
Wash Those Hands!	79
Water for Agricultural Progress	4
Water is Ours, The	191
Way of Life in Japan, The: Mastery of the Chef's Blade	19
Way of Life in Japan, The: Mastery of the Chef's Blade	20
We Are Guatemalans	191
We Aren't Asking for the Moon	218
Wedding of the Goddess	191
We Don't Have a Choice	133
Weight: Maintaining a Healthy Balance	79
Well Baby Check Ups: From Infants to Tots	83
Western Europe: Our Legacy	191
Where the Hot Stuff Is: Volcanoes of the Earth and Solar System	136
Where There Is Hatred	219
Whose Woods Are These?	133
Wild Birds of Taiwan	143
William Wordsworth	98
Wings Above the Forest	133
Wings Over Water	153
Win-Win	74
Women in Dental Research	75
Women in Ukiyo-E	60
Women Scientists with Disabilities	75
World Beat: U. S. Foreign Policy	219
World Heritage--Shirakami Forest 1997	133
Wuthering Heights	27

-X-Y-Z-

Yaro Civilization, The	61
Yellow River, The	191
Yitzhak Rabin	219
You Can't Grow Home Again	134
Young Baseball Heroes	105
Young Baseball Heroes	106
Young Family, A	84
Young Voices from the Arab World: The Lives and Times of Five Teenagers	219
Your Body, Your Diet, and Cholesterol	95
You're in Charge: Teens With Asthma	79
Your Water, Your Life	134
Zen Temple	118
Zoot Suit	27

SUBJECT INDEX

ACID RAIN
Environmental Vision 122
ADOLESCENCE
Body Image for Boys 80
Eating, Teens and Calcium 80
Healthy Foods, Healthy Baby 81
High Five: Nutrition Program for High School Youth 88
Leaving School 72
Mirror in My Mind, The: Body Image & Self-Esteem 78
Pregnant Teens Taking Care 82
Sound Nutrition for Teenage Mothers-to-Be 83
Teenage Nutrition: Prevention of Obesity 79
Teen Breastfeeding: The Natural Choice 83
AEROSPACE EDUCATION
Hubble's Amazing Rescue 135
Where the Hot Stuff Is: Volcanoes of the Earth and Solar System 136
AFGHANISTAN
Afghanistan: The Lost Generation 206
In the Footsteps of Alexander the Great 201
Khyber 202
AFRICA
Africa's Child: Ethiopia: Festival of Fire 154
Africa: South of the Sahara 155
Aquaculture and the Rural African Farmer/Pictorial Modelling 1
Central African Republic 160
Kenyan Way of Life, The 172
Kenya: The Masai Homeland 172
Life in an Oasis 173
South Africa: A Land Apart 183
Tribal Religions 117
Uganda: The Pearl of Africa 190
AFRICAN AMERICANS
Struggle and Success: The African American Experience in Japan 216
AFRICAN INFLUENCE
Mujer Negra Habla 212
AGING
Growing Old in a New Age 72
AGRICULTURE
Acres of Oysters 1
Biotechnology & Agriculture 2
Changing Attitude Toward Food, A 2
Day in Shrishnagar, A 2
Depending on Heaven: The Desert 2
Desert Agriculture 2
Devil Gave Us Oil, The 8
Farming in All Seasons 3
Food and Agriculture in Contemporary Japan 3
Footholds 3
Handling of Pigs 3

AGRICULTURE   (continued)
Hollow Harvest 4
Introducing Mexico: Part One, The Land 4
Japanese and Rice Cultivation, The 4
Japan's Leading Edge Agricultural Technology at Work in Biotechnology 4
Water for Agricultural Progress 4
AIR POLLUTION
Atmosphere: On the Air 119
Challenge of Global Warming, The 120
Challenge of Global Warming, The 121
IAQ Tools for Schools Walkthrough Video: 4 Schools Making a Difference 126
Legal Winds of Change: Business and the New Clean Air Act 127
Protecting Our Global Home--Japan's Ecological Contributions 129
Protecting Our Global Home--Japan's Ecological Contributions 130
ALABAMA
Alabama, the Place for Aquaculture! 1
ALCOHOL AND ALCOHOL ABUSE
Fetal Alcohol Syndrome: Prenatal Drug and Alcohol Use and Its Effects 76
ALEXANDER THE GREAT
In the Footsteps of Alexander the Great 201
AMAZON
Amazon, The 155
Charcoal People, The 206
ANCIENT GREECE
Byzantium: The Lost Empire 194
ANCIENT HISTORY
Megabeasts' Sudden Death 136
Riddles of the Sphinx 203
ANCIENT ROME
Byzantium: The Lost Empire 194
ANCIENT SCRIPTURES
Sathya Sai Baba: Aura of Divinity 115
ANEMIA
Anemia: The Silent Shadow 76
ANIMALS
Emas Park 122
Galapagos: My Fragile World 124
Sables in the Northern Land 141
Sables in the Northern Land 142
Sea Turtles' Last Dance 142
Vertebrates 142
ANIMATION
Grateful Crane, A 168
Kaguya Hime: Princess of the Moon 97

SUBJECT INDEX

ANOREXIA
   Eating Disorders 76
   Real People Coping with Eating Disorders 73

ANTHROPOLOGY
   Khyber 202
   Pyramids of the Sun and Moon 54

AQUACULTURE
   Alabama, the Place for Aquaculture! 1
   Aquaculture and the Rural African Farmer/Pictorial Modelling 1

ARABIA
   Ancient Arabia: Legacy of Ancient Civilizations 193
   Arabian Seafarers: In the Wake of Sinbad 194

ARAB WORLD
   Introduction to the Arab World 210

ARCHAEOLOGY
   Archaeological Yucatan: Land of the Maya 157
   Chancay, the Forgotten Art 42
   Egypt: Beyond the Pyramids 196
   Indus: The Unvoiced Civilization 200
   Plunder 54
   Popol Vuh: The Creation Myth of the Maya 98
   Yaro Civilization, The 61

ARCHITECTURE
   Cairo: 1001 Years of Art and Architecture 41
   Japanese Architecture: A Living Heritage 170
   Japanese Architecture: The Living Heritage 170
   Kisho Kurokawa: Architect 172
   Korean Treasures 47
   Place to Be, A: The Construction of the East Building of the National Gallery of Art 53

ARGENTINA
   Americas 1: Garden of Forking Paths: Dilemmas of National Development 155
   Argentina 157
   Argentina: Growth or Disappearance 157
   Children in Debt 206
   Don Segundo Sombra 22
   El Tango en Broadway 23
   Evita: The Woman Behind the Myth 32
   Man Facing Southeast 24
   Martin Fierro 24
   Miss Mary 24
   Tango Bar 26
   Tango Is Also History 70
   Tango: Our Dance 70
   Throw Me a Dime 184

ARIZONA
   Adventure in Glen Canyon 144
   Central Arizona Project--Lifeline to the Future 146
   Southwest Region 151

ART HISTORY
   Ancient Chinese Paintings 38
   Beauty of Famous Paintings In the National Palace Museum, The 41
   Los Murales de la Cuidad de Mexico: El Muro de las Celebraciones 49
   Tour of the Prado, A 59

ARTISTS
   American Impressionist, An: William Merritt Chase at Shinnecock 38
   Ana Mendieta: Fuego de Tierra 28
   Art of Romare Bearden, The 40
   Diego Rivera in the United States 44
   Edouard Vuillard 31
   Frida Kahlo 33
   Henri Rousseau: Jungles in Paris 46
   Henry Moore: A Life in Sculpture 33
   Linnea In Monet's Garden 49
   Picasso and His Time 36
   Picasso: The Early Years 53
   Quiet Collector, The: Andrew W. Mellon Remembered 54
   Raphael and the American Collector 55
   Rivera: Portrait of an Artist 56
   Rotund World of Botero, The 36
   Seeing Color: Object, Light, Observer 57
   Toulouse-Lautrec and Montmartre 59
   Tour of the Prado, A 59

ARTS AND CRAFTS
   Ancient Chinese Paintings 38
   Animation in the Classroom 38
   Art From Asia 39
   Arts of the Eskimo, The: An Arctic Adventure 144
   Awareness Series: American Art 40
   Awareness Series: Old Masters 40
   Beauty of Famous Paintings In the National Palace Museum, The 41
   Cartoon Magic With Fran 41
   Ceramics: Basic Throwing Skills with Alleghany Meadows 41
   Ceramics Handbuilding: Pinch and Coil Construction with Mollie Favour 41
   Christmas Story in Art, The 42
   City of Cathay, A 42
   Courtly Art of Ancient Maya 42
   Crafting in the USA: Appalachia Region 43
   Crafting in the USA: Folklore 43
   Crafting in the USA: Hawaii 43
   Crafts in Less than 10 Minutes Vol. 1 43
   Creating Abstract Art 44
   Cultural Journey Into Japan, A 163
   Drawing With Pastels 45
   Eye of Thomas Jefferson, The 32

SUBJECT INDEX

ARTS AND CRAFTS (continued)
From Impressionism to Modernism: The
    Chester Dale Collection 45
Ginevra's Story 45
Introduction to European Art in the National
    Gallery of Art 46
James McNeill Whistler: His Etchings 46
James McNeill Whistler: The Lyrics of Art 47
Japan Arts and Crafts 47
Landscapes of Frederic Edwin Church, The 48
Leonardo: To Know How to See 48
Loving Krishna 114
Meinung's Oiled Paper Umbrellas 50
Munni (Little Girl): Childhood and Art in Mithila 177
National Gallery of Art, A Treasury of Masterpieces 50
Oaxacan Woodcarving: Innovation Meets Tradition 51
Of Time, Tombs, and Treasure: The Treasures of
    Tutankhamun 51
Origami 52
Past, Present and Future: Washi--Unique Japanese
    Paper Culture 52
Past, Present and Future: Washi--Unique Japanese
    Paper Culture 53
Place to Be, A: The Construction of the East
    Building of the National Gallery of Art 53
Popular Hispanic Culture 54
Reflections: The Story of The Treasure Houses
    of Britain 55
Sand Painting: Sacred Art of Tibetan Buddhism 115
Seeing Color: Object, Light, Observer 57
Shaw Memorial, The: The Power and Glory
    of Public Art 58
Shingo Kojima--Cabinetmaker 58
Shingo Kojima--Cabinetmaker 59
Visiones del Pueblo: The Folk Art of Latin America 60

ASIA
Adventure on the Way to the 21st Century 154
Art From Asia 39
As Iwate Goes: Is Culture Local? 158
As Iwate Goes: Is Politics Local? 158
Between Heaven and Earth: The Temple of Taiwan 62
China and the Forbidden City 161
China and the Forbidden City: The Great Within 162
China Cry 162
Chinese Folk Arts 42
Chinese Life Today 162
Chinese Musical Instruments: Parts I and II 63
Chinese Musical Instruments: Parts III and IV 63
Christian Women in China 162
Common Experiences: Different Visions 162
Depending on Heaven: The Desert 2
Discover Korea: Geography and Industry 164
Dreams of Tibet 207

ASIA (continued)
Elementary School Teacher, An 18
Festivals in Taiwan 165
Firecracker: A Night to Remember in
    Yen-Shuei 166
Gardens of Japan 166
Hollow Harvest 169
In Celebration of the Enthronement of His
    Majesty the Emperor of Japan 169
Inn of Sixth Happiness 201
Japanese Culture: Cities; Entertainment;
    Architecture 170
Jing, a Chinese Girl 171
June 4, 1989 201
Kabuki: Classic Theater of Japan/Noh, Drama,
    Bunraku: The Puppet Theater of Japan 66
Kashmir: Valley of Despair 211
Living Arts 175
Magic of China/Children of China 175
Modern Brides: Arranged Marriage in South India 177
Music of Modern Japan/Kitaro, Synthesizer
    Musician 67
Neighborhood Tokyo 177
Noh Drama, Kabuki, Bunraku--Classical Theater
    in Japan 68
No Longer Colonies: Hong Kong, 1997;
    Macau, 1999 178
Primary and Secondary Education in Japan 179
Primary and Secondary Education in Japan/The
    Elementary School Teacher 180
Primary and Secondary Education in Japan/The
    Elementary School Teacher/School Days in
    Japan 180
Pu Yi, China's Last Emperor 203
Raise the Red Lantern 180
Salaam Bombay 181
School Days in Japan 182
Seeds of Plenty, Seeds of Sorrow; Developing
    Stories 1 182
Selected Songs by Famous Singers 69
Son of the Ocean 182
Splendid China: A Miniature Rendition in Florida 183
Stirrings of Change 183
Story of Qiu Ju, The 216
Taj Mahal: The Story of Muslim India 183
Tang, The: China's Cosmopolitan Age 183
Theater Lives, The 71
Tibet: The End of Time 184
Traditional Sports: Karatedo 105
Tsukuba Academic New Town 15
Tune in Korea: Legacy and Transformation 88
Under the Same Sun 190
Yellow River, The 191

SUBJECT INDEX

ASTHMA
You're in Charge: Teens With Asthma   79
ATOMIC BOMB
Hiroshima: City of Peace   197
Hiroshima: City of Peace   198
Hiroshima: City of Peace   199
AUSTRALIA
Tribal Religions   117
AZTECS
Pyramids of the Sun and Moon   54
BANGLADESH
Fishing in a Sea of Greed   166
Sixteen Decisions   182
BANKS AND BANKING
Banking on Life and Debt   6
BARBADOS
Barbados   158
BEARDEN, ROMARE
Art of Romare Bearden, The   40
BEES AND BEEKEEPING
Beekeeping in Northern Climates   1
BELIZE
Tropical Kingdom of Belize   88
Wings Above the Forest   133
BIBLE
Can These Bones Live?   108
Great Pyramid, The: Ancient Wonder, Modern Mystery   110
Israel: Born to Destiny   113
King of Kings and Lord of Lords   113
Messiah: The Biblical Message Behind the Musical Masterpiece   114
BIODIVERSITY
Jaguar Trax   127
BIOGRAPHIES
Ana Mendieta: Fuego de Tierra   28
Arruza   28
Benedita da Silva   28
Birth of an Empire   29
Carlos Fuentes   29
Carmen Miranda: Bananas Is My Business   29
Christian Laettner: The Power Forward   101
Columbus   29
Compassion in Exile: The Story of the 14th Dalai Lama   30
Dalai Lama: The Soul of Tibet   30
Dalda 13: A Talented Woman History Forgot   30
Dialogo Entre Augusto Roa Bastos y Fernando Alegria   30
Edouard Vuillard   31
Ernesto Che Guevara: Restless Revolutionary   31

BIOGRAPHIES (continued)
Ernesto Che Guevara: The Bolivian Diary   31
Evita: The Woman Behind the Myth   31
Evita: The Woman Behind the Myth   32
Famous Deaf Americans--Part I   32
Famous Deaf Americans--Part II   32
Fidel Castro: El Comandante   33
Frida   33
Frida Kahlo   33
Henry Moore: A Life in Sculpture   33
Hernan Cortes   34
Langston Hughes: The Dream Keeper   34
Last of the Khans, The   34
Legends of the American West: Part Two   34
Leo Tolstoy   35
Mario Benedetti   35
Ocean of Wisdom   35
Pablo Neruda Present   35
Picasso and His Time   36
Ten Who Dared: Francisco Pizarro   36
BIOLOGY
Reproductive Systems   82
Seasons of Life   136
BIOTECHNOLOGY
Biotechnology & Agriculture   2
Japan's Leading Edge Agricultural Technology at Work in Biotechnology   4
BIRDS
Flight from the Marshes   123
Helping Our Feathered Friends   124
Helping Our Feathered Friends   125
Wild Birds of Taiwan   143
BOLIVIA
Americas 4: Mirrors of the Heart: Color, Class and Identity   156
Basic Christian Communities in Latin America   108
Children in Debt   206
Ernesto Che Guevara: The Bolivian Diary   31
Water is Ours, The   191
BOTANY
Rain Forest   141
BOXING
Eddie's Last Fight: The Old Trainer/19 Year Old Champion   101
BRAZIL
Amazonia - Minimum Critical Size of Ecosystems   119
Americas 2: Capital Sins: Authoritarianism and Democratization   156
Apaissionata   21
Bahia: Africa in the Americas   107
Basic Christian Communities in Latin America   108
Benedita da Silva   28

SUBJECT INDEX

BRAZIL (continued)
Black Orpheus 22
Brazilian Music 62
Carmen Miranda: Bananas Is My Business 29
Coffee: A Sack Full of Power 7
Emas Park 122
Favelas 165
Grupo Corpo--Brazilian Dance Theatre 64
Hail Umbanda 111
Harvesting New Songs - Brazil 64
Hour of the Star 23
Isle of Flowers 211
Maysa Matarazzo 35
Pie en la Marcha 179
Pixote 25
Quincas Berro D'Agua 25
Seca 215
Vision of Juazeiro 117
Waiapi Instrumental Music 71

BREAKFAST
Health During Pregnancy: Lily Looks Back 81

BREASTFEEDING
Baby Shower for Betsy, A 80
14 Steps to Better Breastfeeding 81

BRITISH INDIA
Films from the Raj 196

BUDDHISM
Buddhism and Black Belts 108
Buddhism: The Making of a Monk 108
Buddhism: The Middle Way of Compassion 108
Debate in the Tibetan Tradition 110
His Holiness the Dalai Lama 112
Introduction to East Asian Religions, An: Buddhism (Part I) 112
Introduction to East Asian Religions, An: Confucianism (Part II) 112
Observing the Breath 114
Ocean of Wisdom 35
Power of Compassion, The: Sakyadhita 179
Sand Painting: Sacred Art of Tibetan Buddhism 115
Satya: A Prayer for the Enemy 203
Tibetan Book of the Dead, The 116
Trials of Telo Rinpoche 116
Two Tibetan Buddhist Nunneries 117
Valley of the Gods: Worship in Katmandu 117

BULIMIA
Eating Disorders 76
Real People Coping with Eating Disorders 73

BYZANTIUM EMPIRE
Byzantium: The Lost Empire 194

CAIRO
Cairo: 1001 Years of Art and Architecture 41

CALIFORNIA
Birth of Oroville Dam, The 144
California Flooding 144
California's Heritage: The Missions 145
California's State Water Project: Meeting the Challenge 145
California Water Story, The 145
California Water Story, The 146
Drought Survival in California 146
High Water: The Record Floods of February 1986 147
Miracle of Water 149
Pipeline 150
Wings Over Water 153

CANADA
Eastern Canadian Provinces, The 164

CAREERS
Beauticians 16
Behavior Success 16
Career Close-Ups: School Teacher 16
Communication Success 16
Cover Letter Training 16
Dealing with Illegal Questions 17
Diary of a Police Post 17
Job Search Preparation 18
Learning a Trade 18
So You Want to Be? Teacher/Make-Up Artist 19
Spirit of Edo Firemen, The--Alive in Tokyo Today 19
Vocational Training 19
Way of Life in Japan, The: Mastery of the Chef's Blade 19
Way of Life in Japan, The: Mastery of the Chef's Blade 20
Women in Dental Research 75
Women Scientists with Disabilities 75

CARIBBEAN
Sugar Cane Alley 26

CARTOONS
Cartoon Magic With Fran 41

CASTES
Caste at Birth 160
Teyyam: The Annual Visit of the God Vishnumurti 184

CASTRO, FIDEL
Fidel Castro: El Comandante 33

CATHOLICISM
Healer, The 112

CAVES
Extreme Cave Diving 138

CENTRAL AMERICA
Common Table: Central American Refugees--The Church Response 109
Environment Under Fire: Ecology and Politics in Central America 123

SUBJECT INDEX

CENTRAL AMERICA (continued)
If the Mango Tree Could Speak 209
If the Mango Tree Could Speak: A Documentary About Children and War in Central America 209
Middle America: Mexico to Venezuela and the Caribbean Islands 176
Troubled Harvest 217

CEREMONIES
Imperial Wedding, The--The Crown Prince and Princess of Japan 199
Imperial Wedding, The--The Crown Prince and Princess of Japan 200
Sokui-no-Rei, The 36
Tea Drinking in Taipei 184

CHASE, WILLIAM MERRIT
American Impressionist, An: William Merritt Chase at Shinnecock 38

CHEMISTRY
Chemistry: The Basics 135
Flame in the Chemistry Lab 135

CHILD CARE
Safe Food, Healthy Children 93

CHILD LABOR
Mickey Mouse Goes to Haiti: Walt Disney and the Science of Exploitation 212

CHILDREN'S RIGHTS
Human Rights: The Rights of the Child 209

CHILE
Americans 5: In Women's Hands: The Changing Roles of Women 155
Dance of Hope* 207
Footholds 3
On Top of the Whale 25
Somos Mas 205
Where There Is Hatred 219

CHINA
Ancient Chinese Paintings 38
Ann-Ping Chin: Four Sisters of Hofei: Culture and Change in Early Modern China 193
Art From Asia 39
Beauty of Famous Paintings In the National Palace Museum, The 41
Between Heaven and Earth: The Temple of Taiwan 62
China and the Forbidden City 161
China and the Forbidden City: The Great Within 162
China Cry 162
Chinese Folk Arts 42
Chinese Life Today 162
Chinese Musical Instruments: Parts I and II 63
Chinese Musical Instruments: Parts III and IV 63
Christian Women in China 162

CHINA (continued)
City of Cathay, A 42
Confucianism and Taoism 109
Dreams of Tibet 207
Human Geography: People, Places, Change 11
Inn of Sixth Happiness 201
Jing, a Chinese Girl 171
June 4, 1989 201
Magic of China/Children of China 175
Masterpieces of Chinese Painting and Calligraphy at the National Palace Museum 49
Masters of the Wok 91
Meinung's Oiled Paper Umbrellas 50
Night of Nine Tribes, The 178
No Longer Colonies: Hong Kong, 1997; Macau, 1999 178
Pu Yi, China's Last Emperor 203
Raise the Red Lantern 180
Satya: A Prayer for the Enemy 203
Son of the Ocean 182
Splendid China: A Miniature Rendition in Florida 183
Story of Qiu Ju, The 216
Tang, The: China's Cosmopolitan Age 183
Tea Drinking in Taipei 184
Tibet: The End of Time 184
To Live 185
Under the Same Sun 190
Yellow River, The 191

CHINESE
Beauty of Famous Paintings In the National Palace Museum, The 41
Chinese Musical Instruments: Parts I and II 63
Chinese Musical Instruments: Parts III and IV 63
June 4, 1989 201
Night of Nine Tribes, The 178
Raise the Red Lantern 180
Selected Songs by Famous Singers 69
Story of Qiu Ju, The 216

CHOLESTEROL
Fats of Life, The 86
How to Lower Your Cholesterol: A Simple Dietary Approach 89
Shopping for Heart Health: Lower Your Blood Cholesterol and Reduce Your Risk of Coronary Artery Disease 93
Your Body, Your Diet, and Cholesterol 95

CHRISTMAS
Christmas Story in Art, The 42

CHURCH, FREDERIC EDWIN
Landscapes of Frederic Edwin Church, The 48

CIA
Anatomy of a Coup: Crisis in Iran 193

SUBJECT INDEX

CIVIL WAR
    Shaw Memorial, The: The Power
        and Glory of Public Art 58
COLOMBIA
    Americas 8: Get Up, Stand Up: The
        Problems of Sovereignty 156
    Footholds 3
    Gabriel Garcia Marquez: Magic and Reality 33
    Los Ninos Abandonados 211
    Secuestro: Story of a Kidnapping 216
COLORADO RIVER
    Adventure in Glen Canyon 144
    Central Arizona Project--Lifeline to the Future 146
    Lake Powell--Jewel of the Colorado 148
    Living Waters of the Colorado 148
    Mountain Skywater 149
    Operation Glen Canyon 149
    Snowfall to Sandstone 151
    Story of Hoover Dam, The 152
COLUMBIA RIVER
    Powering One Corner of the World 151
COLUMBUS, CHRISTOPHER
    Columbus 29
    Columbus and the Age of Discovery 195
COMMUNICATION
    Communication Success 16
COMMUNICATIONS
    Serial for Breakfast (Part I & II) 182
COMMUNITY PROJECTS
    Your Water, Your Life 134
COMPOSTING
    Indian Township Passamaquoddy Tribe:
        Composting Workshop 126
CONFLICT RESOLUTION
    Win-Win 74
CONSERVATION
    Alternative Is Conservation 119
    Environment Latest Approaches 122
    Jaguar Trax 127
    Louisiana Wetlands: America's Coastal Crisis 149
    Madre Tierra 128
    Protecting Our Habitat: Recycling at the Grassroots 130
    Rainforests: Proving Their Worth 130
    Understanding Ecology: What Is a Food Chain? 132
    Whose Woods Are These? 133
CONSUMER EDUCATION
    Close the Loop: Buy Recycled 121
    Shopping for Heart Health: Lower Your Blood
        Cholesterol and Reduce Your Risk of Coronary
        Artery Disease 93

CONTEMPORARY HISTORY
    Carlos Fuentes 29
    Cuba: In the Shadow of Doubt 195
COOKING
    High Five: Nutrition Program for High School Youth 88
    I Love Sushi 89
    Japanese Cooking--A Taste for All Seasons 90
COSTA RICA
    Coffee: A Sack Full of Power 7
    Hamburger: Jungle Burger 3
    Mujer Negra Habla 212
    Rain Forest 130
    Rain Forest 141
    You Can't Grow Home Again 134
CRAFTSMANSHIP
    Doll Master and His Apprentice, The 44
CREATIONISM
    King of Kings and Lord of Lords 113
CUBA
    Ache Moyuba Orisha 154
    Americas 9: Fire in the Mind: Revolutions and
        Revolutionaries 157
    Buena Vista Social Club 62
    Cuba and Human Rights 207
    Cuba: In the Shadow of Doubt 195
    Havana Nagila: The Jews in Cuba 111
    Routes of Rhythm--Part II 69
    Voices of the Orishas 117
CULTURE
    Ancient Religions of the Mediterranean 193
    Families of Israel 208
    Iran: Adventure Divas 210
    Jerusalem: Within These Walls 211
    Price of Change, The 215
    Queen Noor: Between Two Realms 215
    Syria, Jordan and Lebanon 217
    Tibet: Where Continents Collide 185
    Young Voices from the Arab World:
        The Lives and Times of Five Teenagers 219
DALAI LAMA
    Compassion in Exile: The Story of the 14th
        Dalai Lama 30
    Dalai Lama: The Soul of Tibet 30
    His Holiness the Dalai Lama 112
    Ocean of Wisdom 35
    Trials of Telo Rinpoche 116
DAMS
    Adventure in Glen Canyon 144
    Birth of Oroville Dam, The 144
    Build-Up on the Bighorn 144
    Hydropower 148
    Lake Powell--Jewel of the Colorado 148

SUBJECT INDEX

DAMS (continued)
Operation Glen Canyon 149
Place of the Falling Waters, The 150
Story of Hoover Dam, The 152
Teton--Decision and Disaster 152

DANCES AND FESTIVALS
Annual Festivities and Ceremonies--Beliefs in Daily Life 107
Arruza 28
El Peregrinaje de las Flores 23
Festivals in Taiwan 165
Firecracker: A Night to Remember in Yen-Shuei 166
Grupo Corpo--Brazilian Dance Theatre 64
Kyoto--Scenes and Festivals 173
Lantern Festival, The 173
Loving Krishna 114
Night of Nine Tribes, The 178
Parties, Pinatas and Plays: Mexican Christmas Traditions 179
Raices Del Pueblo: Cantos y Danzas de Veracruz 68
Tango Is Also History 70
Tango: Our Dance 70
Valley of the Gods: Worship in Katmandu 117
Wedding of the Goddess 191

DA VINCI, LEONARDO
Ginevra's Story 45
Leonardo: To Know How to See 48

DEATH AND DYING
Tibetan Book of the Dead, The 116

DENTISTRY
Women in Dental Research 75

DIABETES
How to Read the New Food Label for Persons with Diabetes 89
Introduction to Diabetes: The Game Plan 77
Meal Planning: Eating Right for People with Diabetes 91

DIETARY FAT
Fats of Life, The 86
Healthy Dividends: A Plan for Balancing Your Fat Budget 86
How to Lower Your Cholesterol: A Simple Dietary Approach 89
Recreating Taste in Low Fat Cooking 92
Your Body, Your Diet, and Cholesterol 95

DIETARY FIBER
Eating Well, Increasing Fiber 85

DINOSAURS
Megabeasts' Sudden Death 136

DISABILITIES
Women Scientists with Disabilities 75

DISCRIMINATION
Breaking the History of Silence 194

DISEASE PREVENTION
Dinner's Served: A Food Safety Program 85

DISEASES
Guide to Your Healthy Heart 77
Hepatitis-The Silent Epidemic 77
How to Read the New Food Label for Persons with Diabetes 89
Introduction to Diabetes: The Game Plan 77
Meal Planning: Eating Right for People with Diabetes 91
You're in Charge: Teens With Asthma 79

DOMINICAN REPUBLIC
Americas 4: Mirrors of the Heart: Color, Class and Identity 156
Dominican Republic, Cradle of the Americas 164

DRAMA
Hajari Bhand of Rajasthan: Jester Without Court 64
Music of Bunraku 67
Taking Blessings Door to Door 69
Taking Blessings Door to Door 70

DROUGHT
Drought Survival in California 146

DRUGS AND DRUG ABUSE
Coca Mama--The War on Drugs 206

EARTH DAY
Earth Day: The Future Remembered 196

EARTHQUAKES
Earth Revealed 122
Kobe 1995--A Cruel Lesson 173

EARTH SCIENCE
Atmosphere: On the Air 119
Earth Revealed 122

EAST AFRICA
Arabian Seafarers: In the Wake of Sinbad 194

EATING DISORDERS
Eating Disorders 76
Real People Coping with Eating Disorders 73

ECOLOGY
Biosphere, The 120
Understanding Ecology: What Is a Food Chain? 132

ECONOMIC DEVELOPMENT
Children in Debt 206
Good Place to Call Home, A: Maine Towns Creating Their Future 147

ECONOMICS
Against All the Odds 6
Banking on Life and Debt 6
Commodities: Black Market 8
Earth: The Changing Environment 8

SUBJECT INDEX

ECONOMICS (continued)
Economics 8
Economics Classroom, The: Growth & Entrepreneurship 9
Economics Classroom, The: How Economists Think 9
Economics Classroom, The: Learning, Earning, Saving 9
Economics Classroom, The: Monetary & Fiscal Policy 9
Economics Classroom, The: The Building Blocks of Macroeconomics 10
Economics Classroom, The: Trading Globally 10
Emerging Powers: Mexico 10
Hollow Harvest 4
Human Geography: People, Places, Change 11
Japan's Distribution System 11
Japan Video Encyclopedia--Japanese Industry & Economy 11
One World, One Economy 12
Sixteen Decisions 182
U. S., Mexico, and NAFTA 15

ECUADOR
Footholds 3
Galapagos: My Fragile World 124

EDUCATION
Elementary School Teacher, An 18
Primary and Secondary Education in Japan 179
Primary and Secondary Education in Japan/The Elementary School Teacher 180
Primary and Secondary Education in Japan/The Elementary School Teacher/School Days in Japan 180
School Days in Japan 182

EGYPT
Assassination of King Tut 194
Egypt: Beyond the Pyramids 196
Great Pharaohs of Egypt, The: Volume 1 197
Great Pharaohs of Egypt, The: Volume 2 197
In the Footsteps of Alexander the Great 201
Price of Change, The 215
Riddles of the Sphinx 203
Umm Kulthum: A Voice Like Egypt 71
Young Voices from the Arab World: The Lives and Times of Five Teenagers 219

ELDERLY
Goddess of Mercy for Prevention of Senility 167

EL SALVADOR
Americas 9: Fire in the Mind: Revolutions and Revolutionaries 157
Central America Close-Up #1 160
Guazapa: The Face of War in El Salvador 197
Unheard Voices 217

ENDANGERED SPECIES
Fight for Survival: The Fish Owl of Northern Japan 138
Flight from the Marshes 123
Protecting Our Global Home--Japan's Ecological Contributions 129
Protecting Our Global Home--Japan's Ecological Contributions 130

ENERGY
Environmental Vision 122
User's Guide to the Planet Earth, A: The American Environmental Test 132

ENTERTAINMENT
Bolivar Soy Yo 22
Dust to Dust 22
Zoot Suit 27

ENVIRONMENTAL EDUCATION
Amazonia - Minimum Critical Size of Ecosystems 119
Amazon, The 155
Bentley Creek: A Story of an Urban Salt Marsh 119
Borderline Cases 6
Bringing Environmental Technologies to the Marketplace 120
Coastal Growth: A Delicate Balance 121
Disaster Prevention 163
Earth Day: The Future Remembered 196
Environmental Vision 122
Environment, The - New Global Concerns: Current Affairs 122
Fire Fighters, The 166
Indian Township Passamaquoddy Tribe: Composting Workshop 126
Lead in School Drinking Water 127
Less Is More: Pollution Prevention Is Good Business 12
1959: Endangered Planet 128
Recycling 181
Sabo: Erosion Control 181
Serpent Fruits 132
User's Guide to the Planet Earth, A: The American Environmental Test 132
Vermont Wetlands: A Natural Resource 153

EQUALITY
No Longer Silent 178

EROSION
Reversing the Tide 151

ESKIMOS
Arts of the Eskimo, The: An Arctic Adventure 144

ETHICS
Ethics in America 72
Goal Away: Setting and Achieving Goals: Turning Dreams Into Reality 72

ETHNIC CUISINE
Food: A Multi-Cultural Feast 86

243

SUBJECT INDEX

ETHNIC CUISINE (continued)
Healthy Japanese Diet, The 87
Healthy Japanese Diet, The 88
I Love Sushi 89
Japanese Cooking--A Taste for All Seasons 90
Taste of Japan, The: A Tradition of Hospitality 94
Traditional Japanese Culture: Japanese Cuisine 94
Traditional Japanese Culture: Japanese Cuisine 95

EUROPE
Europe: Southern Region 165
Introduction to European Art in the National Gallery of Art 46
Western Europe: Our Legacy 191

EXPLORERS AND EXPLORATION
Columbus 29

FAITH
Can These Bones Live? 108
King of Kings and Lord of Lords 113
Messiah: The Biblical Message Behind the Musical Masterpiece 114

FAMILY
Dadi and Her Family 163
Dadi and Her Family 163

FAMILY LIFE
Families of Israel 208
Young Family, A 84

FAMOUS PEOPLE
Ahmedabad--Life of a City in India 193
Ana Mendieta: Fuego de Tierra 28
Arruza 28
Benazir Bhutto: Walking the Tightrope 28
Benedita da Silva 28
Birth of an Empire 29
Carlos Fuentes 29
Carmen Miranda: Bananas Is My Business 29
Christian Laettner: The Power Forward 101
Columbus 29
Compassion in Exile: The Story of the 14th Dalai Lama 30
Dalai Lama: The Soul of Tibet 30
Dalda 13: A Talented Woman History Forgot 30
Dialogo Entre Augusto Roa Bastos y Fernando Alegria 30
Edouard Vuillard 31
Ernesto Che Guevara: Restless Revolutionary 31
Ernesto Che Guevara: The Bolivian Diary 31
Evita: The Woman Behind the Myth 31
Evita: The Woman Behind the Myth 32
Famous Deaf Americans--Part I 32
Famous Deaf Americans--Part II 32
Fidel Castro: El Comandante 33
Frida 33

FAMOUS PEOPLE (continued)
Frida Kahlo 33
Henry Moore: A Life in Sculpture 33
Hernan Cortes 34
Langston Hughes: The Dream Keeper 34
Last of the Khans, The 34
Legends of the American West: Part Two 34
Leo Tolstoy 35
Mario Benedetti 35
Ocean of Wisdom 35
Pablo Neruda Present 35
Picasso and His Time 36
Umm Kulthum: A Voice Like Egypt 71

FISH AND FISHING
Fishing in a Sea of Greed 166
Harvesting the Sea 168
Life from the Sea 173

FLOODS AND FLOODING
California Flooding 144
High Water: The Record Floods of February 1986 147

FOLK ART
Chinese Folk Arts 42
Festival of India 165
Journey Within a Journey, A 66
Sabina Sanchez - The Art of Embroidery 57

FOLKLORE
Crafting in the USA: Folklore 43

FOLK MUSIC
Buena Vista Social Club 62

FOLK OPERA
Kings, Lovers, and Thieves 66
Kings, Lovers, and Thieves 67

FOLK SONGS
Grupo Corpo--Brazilian Dance Theatre 64

FOLK TALES
Tale of the Heike, The: Biwa Concern at Cornell University 70

FOOD GUIDE PYRAMID
Health During Pregnancy: Lily Looks Back 81
How to Read the New Food Label for Persons with Diabetes 89
Introduction to Diabetes: The Game Plan 77
La Piramide de la Alimentacion 91
Meal Planning: Eating Right for People with Diabetes 91

FOOD LABELS
Fats of Life, The 86
How to Read the New Food Label 77
How to Read the New Food Label for Persons with Diabetes 89

SUBJECT INDEX

FOOD PREPARATION
  Deep Fat Frying and Pan Frying 85
  Dinner's Served: A Food Safety Program 85
  Knife Skills: Vegetables 91
  Poaching and Steaming 92
  Roasting 92

FOODS
  Masters of the Wok 91

FOOD SAFETY
  Dinner's Served: A Food Safety Program 85
  How Safe Is Your Food? 89
  Producer Through Consumer--Partners to a Safe Food Supply 92
  Safe Food, Healthy Children 93

FOREIGN LANGUAGES
  Ache Moyuba Orisha 154
  Adelante 96
  Alias, La Gringa 21
  Almost a Woman 155
  Alsino and the Condor 21
  Ana Mendieta: Fuego de Tierra 28
  Anemia: The Silent Shadow 76
  Anuncios Comerciales 96
  Apaissionata 21
  Argentina: Growth or Disappearance 157
  Asi es Mi Tierra 21
  Beauty of Famous Paintings In the National Palace Museum, The 41
  Bellas Damas, Las 62
  Benedita da Silva 28
  Black Orpheus 22
  Bolivar Soy Yo 22
  Brazilian Music 62
  Buena Vista Social Club 62
  Carmen Miranda: Bananas Is My Business 29
  Charcoal People, The 206
  Children in Debt 206
  Chinese Musical Instruments: Parts I and II 63
  Chinese Musical Instruments: Parts III and IV 63
  Controversia 206
  Dance of Hope* 207
  Day of the Dead 163
  Dialogo Entre Augusto Roa Bastos y Fernando Alegria 30
  Don Segundo Sombra 22
  Dream Across Time and Place, A--The Legacy of Tsuda Umeko 30
  Drought Survival in California 146
  Dust to Dust 22
  El Futuro Maya: Voces del Presente 164
  El Norte 23
  El Peregrinaje de las Flores 23
  El Tango en Broadway 23

FOREIGN LANGUAGES (continued)
  Fetal Alcohol Syndrome: Prenatal Drug and Alcohol Use and Its Effects 76
  14 Steps to Better Breastfeeding 81
  From the Other Side 208
  Health During Pregnancy: Lily Looks Back 81
  Healthy Eating for a Healthy Baby 81
  Hiroshima: City of Peace 197
  Hiroshima: City of Peace 198
  Hiroshima: City of Peace 199
  History and Culture of Puerto Rico 147
  Hour of the Star 23
  How to Read the New Food Label 77
  Images of Korea, Volume 1 169
  Inside My Mom 82
  Introduction to Let's Learn Japanese Basic I 96
  Introduction to Let's Learn Japanese Basic II 96
  Jerico 23
  June 4, 1989 201
  Kaguya Hime: Princess of the Moon 97
  La Piramide de la Alimentacion 91
  Let's Learn Japanese: Basic I 97
  Look Who's Eating 82
  Lo Que Comes: Por Ti Y Tu Bebe 78
  Los Ninos Abandonados 211
  Los Olvidados 211
  Man Facing Southeast 24
  Maria Candelaria 24
  Martin Fierro 24
  Maysa Matarazzo 35
  Mercado, El 176
  Mexican Sign Language 97
  Miss Universe in Peru 212
  Mountain Music in Peru 67
  Mujer Negra Habla 212
  Night of Nine Tribes, The 178
  Oaxacan Woodcarving: Innovation Meets Tradition 51
  Official Story, The 202
  Para una Tumba sin Nombre 25
  People of the Caribbean 150
  Pie en la Marcha 179
  Pixote 25
  Querido Diario 25
  Quincas Berro D'Agua 25
  Raices Del Pueblo: Cantos y Danzas de Veracruz 68
  Raise the Red Lantern 180
  Saludos Hispanos 215
  Seca 215
  Secuestro: Story of a Kidnapping 216
  Selected Songs by Famous Singers 69
  Starting Solid Foods: Lily Helps Ana 83
  Story of Qiu Ju, The 216
  Struggle and Success: The African American Experience in Japan 216

245

SUBJECT INDEX

FOREIGN LANGUAGES (continued)
　Sugar Cane Alley 26
　Tale of the Heike, The: Biwa Concern at
　　　Cornell University 70
　Tango Bar 26
　Tango: Our Dance 70
　Throw Me a Dime 184
　Vision of Juazeiro 117
　Voices of the Orishas 117
　Water is Ours, The 191
　Wuthering Heights 27

FOREIGN POLICY
　Unheard Voices 217
　Washington/Peru: We Ain't Winning 218
　World Beat: U. S. Foreign Policy 219

FOREIGN TRADE
　Breaking Barriers: Foreign Companies That Succeed
　　　in Japan 6
　Breaking Barriers: Foreign Companies That Succeed
　　　in Japan 7
　Human Relations in Japan 11
　Keys to Success in the Japanese Market 11
　NAFTA and the New Economic Frontier: Life Along
　　　the U. S./Mexico Border 213

FORESTS AND FORESTRY
　Earth: The Changing Environment 8
　Rainforests: Proving Their Worth 130
　Reviving Our Rain Forests--The Mission
　　　of Professor Akira Miyawaki 131
　Whose Woods Are These? 133
　World Heritage--Shirakami Forest 1997 133

FRENCH
　Sugar Cane Alley 26

GALAPAGOS ISLANDS
　Galapagos: My Fragile World 124

GANDHI, MAHATMA
　Ahmedabad--Life of a City in India 193
　India Unveiled 200

GANDHI, RAJIV
　India Unveiled 200

GARDENS AND GARDENING
　Dream Window: Reflections on the Japanese Garden 45
　Gardens of Japan 166

GENDER
　Americans 5: In Women's Hands: The Changing
　　　Roles of Women 155

GEOGRAPHY
　Amazonia - Minimum Critical Size of Ecosystems 119
　Amazon, The 155
　Borderline Cases 6
　Earth Revealed 122
　Extreme Cave Diving 138

GEOGRAPHY (continued)
　From the Heart of the World 124
　Ghosts of Machu Picchu 167
　Jungle 127
　Place of the Falling Waters, The 150
　Rain Forest 130
　Southwest Region 151
　Tramp in the Darien, A 132
　Whose Woods Are These? 133
　Wings Above the Forest 133
　You Can't Grow Home Again 134

GEOLOGY
　Freshwater 124
　Life in an Oasis 173

GHANA
　One World, One Economy 12

GLACIERS
　Extreme Ice 123

GLOBAL WARMING
　Challenge of Global Warming, The 120
　Challenge of Global Warming, The 121

GOVERNMENT
　Seca 215
　Where There Is Hatred 219

GROUNDWATER
　Freshwater 124
　Your Water, Your Life 134

GUATEMALA
　Central America Close-Up #1 160
　Dark Light of Dawn, The 196
　El Futuro Maya: Voces del Presente 164
　Interview with Guatemalan President Cerezo 210
　They Shoot Children Don't They? 217
　We Are Guatemalans 191

GUIDANCE
　How to Deal With the Jerks In Your Life and
　　　Earn the Respect of Your Friends 72
　R-E-S-P-E-C-T 73

HAITI
　Americas 4: Mirrors of the Heart: Color, Class
　　　and Identity 156
　Art of Haiti, The 39
　Mickey Mouse Goes to Haiti: Walt Disney and
　　　the Science of Exploitation 212
　This Other Haiti 184

HAWAII
　Celebrating Hawaii's Cultures 146
　Crafting in the USA: Hawaii 43

HAZARDOUS WASTE
　Big Apple, Hot Apple 120
　New Superfund: What It Is, How It Works 128

SUBJECT INDEX

HEARING IMPAIRED
　Mexican Sign Language 97
HEART
　Guide to Your Healthy Heart 77
HIMALAYAS
　Nepal: Land of the Gods 178
HINDUISM
　Fourth Stage, The: A Hindu's Quest for Release 110
　Kashmir Story, The 113
　Radha's Day: Hindu Family Life #5 180
　Teyyam: The Annual Visit of the God Vishnumurti 184
　Valley of the Gods: Worship in Katmandu 117
HINDU KUSH MOUNTAINS
　Kalasha, The: Rites of Spring 171
HIROSHIMA
　Hiroshima and Nagasaki 208
HISPANICS
　Chicano! History of the Mexican American Civil Rights Movement 195
　Displaced in the New South 207
　Garcia Family, The: Puerto Rican Story 147
　Latino Artists: Pushing Artistic Boundaries 48
　Popular Hispanic Culture 54
　Saludos Hispanos 215
HISTORIC SITES
　Ghosts of Machu Picchu 167
HISTORY
　Amber Hunters 135
　Americas 1: Garden of Forking Paths: Dilemmas of National Development 155
　Anatomy of a Coup: Crisis in Iran 193
　Ancient Arabia: Legacy of Ancient Civilizations 193
　Ancient Religions of the Mediterranean 193
　Ann-Ping Chin: Four Sisters of Hofei: Culture and Change in Early Modern China 193
　Assassination of King Tut 194
　Benazir Bhutto: Walking the Tightrope 28
　Between Wars: Latin America: Intervention in Our Own Backyard 194
　Breaking the History of Silence 194
　Cairo: 1001 Years of Art and Architecture 41
　California's Heritage: The Missions 145
　Chiapas: The Inside Story 195
　Chicano! History of the Mexican American Civil Rights Movement 195
　Columbus 29
　Columbus and the Age of Discovery 195
　Great Pharaohs of Egypt, The: Volume 1 197
　Great Pharaohs of Egypt, The: Volume 2 197
　Hiroshima and Nagasaki 208
　History and Culture of Puerto Rico 147
　History Channel II: Change in Heaven 199

HISTORY   (continued)
　Hunt for Pancho Villa, The 199
　Images of Kingdoms 46
　Imperial Wedding, The--The Crown Prince and Princess of Japan 199
　Imperial Wedding, The--The Crown Prince and Princess of Japan 200
　Introduction to European Art in the National Gallery of Art 46
　Iraq: The Cradle of Civilization 201
　Islam: Empire of Faith 113
　Jerusalem: Within These Walls 211
　Jesus: His Life 113
　Legends of the American West: Part Two 34
　Masterpieces of Chinese Painting and Calligraphy at the National Palace Museum 49
　Message, The 114
　Missing 24
　Querido Diario 25
　Roots in the Sand 203
　Shaw Memorial, The: The Power and Glory of Public Art 58
　Sokui-no-Rei, The 36
　Story of Islam, The 116
　Tango Is Also History 70
　Ten Who Dared - Alexander von Humboldt 36
　Tibet: Where Continents Collide 185
　To Live 185
　Yaro Civilization, The 61
HOBBIES
　Beekeeping in Northern Climates 1
　Bird Dogs Afield 137
HOLIDAYS
　Christmas Story in Art, The 42
　Day of the Dead 163
HOMELESS
　Salaam Bombay 181
HONDURAS
　Banana Split 6
HOOVER DAM
　Story of Hoover Dam, The 152
HUBBLE TELESCOPE
　Hubble's Amazing Rescue 135
HUGHES, LANGSTON
　Langston Hughes: The Dream Keeper 34
HUMAN RIGHTS
　Cuba and Human Rights 207
　They Shoot Children Don't They? 217
HUNTING
　Bird Dogs Afield 137
HYDRO POWER
　Hydropower 148

SUBJECT INDEX

HYGIENE
Rockin' Hand Washin' Report, The 78
Wash Those Hands! 79

IDAHO
Teton--Decision and Disaster 152

IKEBANA
Art and Meaning of Ikebana, The 38
Art: Ikebana--Flower Arrangement 39

IMMIGRANTS
Almost a Woman 155
From the Other Side 208
People of the Caribbean 150
Roots in the Sand 203
Ties That Bind: Stories Behind the
    Immigration Controversy 153

IMMIGRATION
Immigration Policy in the United States 209
Immigration Reform 209

INCAS
Ghosts of Machu Picchu 167
Incas Remembered, The 200
Peru: Inca Heritage 202

INDIA
Ahmedabad--Life of a City in India 193
Altar of Fire 107
Ancient Futures: Learning from Ladakh 157
Arabian Seafarers: In the Wake of Sinbad 194
Arranged Marriages 158
Caste at Birth 160
Dalda 13: A Talented Woman History Forgot 30
Day in Shrishnagar, A 2
End to Silence, Part 1: Paradise Is Under Your
    Mother's Foot 165
Father, Son and Holy War 110
Festival of India 165
Films from the Raj 196
Fishing in a Sea of Greed 166
From the Burning Embers 208
Frontiers of Peace: Jainism in India 110
Given to Dance 167
I Am a Sufi, I Am a Muslim 112
India: Land of the Monsoon 169
Indian Pilgrimage, An: Ramdevra 169
India Unveiled 200
In the Footsteps of Alexander the Great 201
Jagriti (The Awakening) 170
Journey Within a Journey, A 66
Kashmir: Valley of Despair 211
Kings, Lovers, and Thieves 66
Kings, Lovers, and Thieves 67
Marriages in Heaven 175
Modern Brides: Arranged Marriage in South India 177

INDIA (continued)
Munni (Little Girl): Childhood and Art in Mithila 177
No Longer Silent 178
Pakistan: Between the Chitralis and Pathans 179
Power of Compassion, The: Sakyadhita 179
Radha's Day: Hindu Family Life #5 180
Rebels vs. the Raj: India During World War II 203
Saheri's Choice 181
Salaam Bombay 181
Seeds of Plenty, Seeds of Sorrow; Developing
    Stories 1 182
Serial for Breakfast (Part I & II) 182
Stirrings of Change 183
Taj Mahal: The Story of Muslim India 183
Village Man, City Man 190
War and Peace 218
Wedding of the Goddess 191

INDONESIA
Art From Asia 39

INDUS VALLEY
Indus: The Unvoiced Civilization 200

INFANTS
Baby Shower for Betsy, A 80
Fetal Alcohol Syndrome: Prenatal Drug and Alcohol
    Use and Its Effects 76
First Foods: Lily Feeds Her Baby 80
14 Steps to Better Breastfeeding 81
Healthy Eating for a Healthy Baby 81
Look Who's Eating 82
Starting Solid Foods: Lily Helps Ana 83
Well Baby Check Ups: From Infants to Tots 83

IRAN
Anatomy of a Coup: Crisis in Iran 193
Crisis in Iran: The Death of the Shah
    and the Hostage Crisis 207
In the Footsteps of Alexander the Great 201
Iran: Adventure Divas 210
Pakistan: Between the Chitralis and Pathans 179

IRAQ
In the Footsteps of Alexander the Great 201
Iraq: The Cradle of Civilization 201

ISLAM
Guests of God, The 111
Hajj, The 111
Islam: Empire of Faith 113
Islam in America 113
Message, The 114
Story of Islam, The 116

ISRAEL
Families of Israel 208
In the Footsteps of Alexander the Great 201
Israel: Born to Destiny 113

SUBJECT INDEX

JAINISM
   Frontiers of Peace: Jainism in India 110

JAMAICA
   Americas 8: Get Up, Stand Up: The Problems of Sovereignty 156
   Harder They Come, The 23
   Roots, Rock, Reggae: Inside the Jamaican Music Scene 68

JAPAN
   Adventure on the Way to the 21st Century 154
   Against All the Odds 6
   Animals on the Ice Floe: Shiretoko in Mid-Winter 137
   Annual Festivities and Ceremonies--Beliefs in Daily Life 107
   Art and Meaning of Ikebana, The 38
   Art From Asia 39
   Art: Ikebana--Flower Arrangement 39
   As Iwate Goes: Is Culture Local? 158
   As Iwate Goes: Is Politics Local? 158
   Battle Against Disease, The 76
   Beauticians 16
   Biotechnology & Agriculture 2
   Breaking Barriers: Foreign Companies That Succeed in Japan 6
   Breaking Barriers: Foreign Companies That Succeed in Japan 7
   Breaking the History of Silence 194
   Buddhism and Black Belts 108
   Budo: The Martial Arts/The Art of Karate 100
   Bunraku Puppet Theatre of Japan 63
   Business Savvy 7
   Carp Town, The 15
   Celebrating the Seasons 160
   Changing Attitude Toward Food, A 2
   Children in Towns & Villages 161
   Children of Japan, The 161
   Children of the Snow Country 161
   Commodities: Black Market 8
   Common Experiences: Different Visions 162
   Communication Gap 8
   Cultural Journey Into Japan, A 163
   Depending on Heaven: The Desert 2
   Desert Agriculture 2
   Diary of a Police Post 17
   Disaster Prevention 163
   District Nurse, A 18
   District Nurse, A/Kangofu: The Japanese Nurse/The Battle Against Disease/Mobile Service/Floating Medical Clinic 164
   Doll Master and His Apprentice, The 44
   Dream Across Time and Place, A--The Legacy of Tsuda Umeko 30
   Dream Window: Reflections on the Japanese Garden 45

JAPAN (continued)
   Eddie's Last Fight: The Old Trainer/19 Year Old Champion 101
   Elementary School Teacher, An 18
   Ennosuke Ichikawa III: Kabuki Actor 63
   Ennosuke Ichikawa III: Kabuki Actor 64
   Farming in All Seasons 3
   Fervor! The Giant Kite Battle of Ensyu 101
   Fervor! The Giant Kite Battle of Ensyu 102
   Fervor! The Giant Kite Battle of Ensyu 103
   Fire Fighters, The 166
   Flight from the Marshes 123
   Food and Agriculture in Contemporary Japan 3
   Four Seasons for Children 166
   Four Seasons in Japan, The 166
   Funny Crabs in the Mangrove, The 139
   Gagaku: The Court Music of Japan 64
   Gardens of Japan 166
   Goddess of Mercy for Prevention of Senility 167
   Grateful Crane, A 168
   Harvesting the Sea 168
   Healthy Japanese Diet, The 87
   Healthy Japanese Diet, The 88
   Heart Within, The 168
   Heated Competition: Jonkara-Bushi 65
   Helping Our Feathered Friends 124
   Helping Our Feathered Friends 125
   High Technology in Japan 168
   Hiroshima, A New Threat--A-Bomb Water Dedication 125
   Hiroshima, A New Threat--A-Bomb Water Dedication 126
   Hiroshima: City of Peace 197
   Hiroshima: City of Peace 198
   Hiroshima: City of Peace 199
   Holiday in Japan 168
   Hollow Harvest 169
   Hollow Harvest 4
   Human Relations in Japan 11
   Imperial Wedding, The--The Crown Prince and Princess of Japan 199
   Imperial Wedding, The--The Crown Prince and Princess of Japan 200
   In Celebration of the Enthronement of His Majesty the Emperor of Japan 169
   Inventive Young Minds 170
   Japan Arts and Crafts 47
   Japanese and Rice Cultivation, The 4
   Japanese Architecture: A Living Heritage 170
   Japanese Architecture: The Living Heritage 170
   Japanese Cooking--A Taste for All Seasons 90
   Japanese Culture: Cities; Entertainment; Architecture 170
   Japan: Journey of Discovery 171

SUBJECT INDEX

JAPAN (continued)
- Japan Land of Enchantment 171
- Japan's Distribution System 11
- Japan's Leading Edge Agricultural Technology at Work in Biotechnology 4
- Japan Today 171
- Japan Video Encyclopedia--Japanese Industry & Economy 11
- Jongara Bushi Competition--The Tsugaru Jamisen National Contest 66
- Kabuki: Classic Theater of Japan/Noh, Drama, Bunraku: The Puppet Theater of Japan 66
- Kangofu, The Japanese Nurse 172
- Kendo 103
- Kendo 104
- Keys to Success in the Japanese Market 11
- Kisho Kurokawa: Architect 172
- Kobe 1995--A Cruel Lesson 173
- Kurashiki 173
- Kyoto--Scenes and Festivals 173
- Landscape Gardener 47
- Learning a Trade 18
- Life from the Sea 173
- Living Arts 175
- Loosening the Mold 73
- Loosing the Mold 73
- Mini Series: Profile of a Nation 176
- Mobile Services 177
- Municipal Office and Its Services, The/Village Reborn, A/Toga: Village for the Theater 177
- Music of Bunraku 67
- Music of Modern Japan/Kitaro, Synthesizer Musician 67
- Naginata 104
- Nature's Bounty: Flowers for the Japanese 177
- Neighborhood Tokyo 177
- Neputa Painter, The 50
- Neputa Painter, The 51
- New Generation, The 213
- New Generation, The 214
- Noh Drama, Kabuki, Bunraku--Classical Theater in Japan 68
- Open to the World 178
- Origami 52
- Past, Present and Future: Washi--Unique Japanese Paper Culture 52
- Past, Present and Future: Washi--Unique Japanese Paper Culture 53
- Primary and Secondary Education in Japan 179
- Primary and Secondary Education in Japan/The Elementary School Teacher 180
- Primary and Secondary Education in Japan/The Elementary School Teacher/School Days in Japan 180

JAPAN (continued)
- Protecting Our Global Home--Japan's Ecological Contributions 129
- Protecting Our Global Home--Japan's Ecological Contributions 130
- Protecting Our Habitat: Recycling at the Grassroots 130
- Quality Control, An American Idea Takes Root in Japan 12
- Quality Control, An American Idea Takes Root in Japan 13
- Quality Control and the Q.C. Circle 13
- Recycling 181
- Reviving Our Rain Forests--The Mission of Professor Akira Miyawaki 131
- Rimpa School Crosses the Ocean 55
- Rimpa School Crosses the Ocean 56
- Roji Koie-Potter 57
- Sables in the Northern Land 141
- Sables in the Northern Land 142
- Sabo: Erosion Control 181
- School Days in Japan 182
- Scroll of Time, The: A Visual History of Japan 204
- Shacho, The--A Japanese President & His Company 13
- Shacho, The--A Japanese President & His Company 14
- Shikoku: An Island in Time 204
- Shikoku: An Island in Time 205
- Sokui-no-Rei, The 36
- Spirit of Edo Firemen, The--Alive in Tokyo Today 19
- Story of Noriko, The 14
- Story of Noriko, The 15
- Struggle and Success: The African American Experience in Japan 216
- Sumo 104
- Taking Blessings Door to Door 69
- Taking Blessings Door to Door 70
- Taste of Japan, The: A Tradition of Hospitality 93
- Taste of Japan, The: A Tradition of Hospitality 94
- Theater Lives, The 71
- This Year We Went to Japan 184
- Traditional Japanese Culture: Japanese Cuisine 94
- Traditional Japanese Culture: Japanese Cuisine 95
- Traditional Sports: Karatedo 105
- Traditional Sports: Kendo 105
- Traditional Sports: Sumo 105
- Trans-Tokyo Bay Road, The 185
- Trans-Tokyo Road, The 185
- Trans-Tokyo Road, The 186
- Travel Wise in Japan 186
- Travel Wise in Japan 187
- Tsukuba Academic New Town 15
- Twilight for a Coal Mining Town: The Tale of Takashima 88
- Twilight for a Coal Mining Town: The Tale of Takashima 189

SUBJECT INDEX

JAPAN (continued)
    Twilight for a Coal-Mining Town: The
        Tale of Takashima 88
    Twilight for a Coal-Mining Town: The
        Tale of Takashima 189
    Vocational Training 19
    War and Peace 218
    Water for Agricultural Progress 4
    Way of Life in Japan, The: Mastery of
        the Chef's Blade 19
    Way of Life in Japan, The: Mastery of the
        Chef's Blade 20
    Women in Ukiyo-E 60
    World Heritage--Shirakami Forest 1997 133
    Young Family, A 84
    Zen Temple 118

JAPANESE
    Beauty of Famous Paintings In the
        National Palace Museum, The 41
    Dream Across Time and Place, A--The Legacy of
        Tsuda Umeko 30
    Hiroshima: City of Peace 197
    Hiroshima: City of Peace 198
    Hiroshima: City of Peace 199
    Introduction to Let's Learn Japanese Basic I 96
    Introduction to Let's Learn Japanese Basic II 96
    Kaguya Hime: Princess of the Moon 97
    Let's Learn Japanese: Basic I 97
    Struggle and Success: The African American Experience
        in Japan 216
    Tale of the Heike, The: Biwa Concern at
        Cornell University 70

JEFFERSON, PRESIDENT THOMAS
    Eye of Thomas Jefferson, The 32

JERUSALEM
    Jerusalem: Within These Walls 211

JESUS
    Jesus: His Life 113

JEWELRY AND JEWELRY MAKING
    Shogyo Ohba's Challenge--Lacquerer 59

JORDAN
    Queen Noor: Between Two Realms 215
    Syria, Jordan and Lebanon 217
    Young Voices from the Arab World: The Lives
        and Times of Five Teenagers 219

KABUKI
    Kabuki: Classic Theater of Japan/Noh, Drama, Bunraku:
        The Puppet Theater of Japan 66
    Noh Drama, Kabuki, Bunraku--Classical Theater in
        Japan 68

KAHLO, FRIDA
    Frida 33

KARATE
    Budo: The Martial Arts/The Art of Karate 100
    Naginata 104

KASHMIR
    Kashmir: Valley of Despair 211

KHAN, GENGHIS
    Birth of an Empire 29

KHAN, KUBLAI
    Last of the Khans, The 34

KING TUT
    Assassination of King Tut 194

KITES AND KITE FLYING
    Fervor! The Giant Kite Battle of Ensyu 101
    Fervor! The Giant Kite Battle of Ensyu 102
    Fervor! The Giant Kite Battle of Ensyu 103

KOREA
    Discover Korea: Geography and Industry 164
    Images of Korea, Volume 1 169
    Korean Treasures 47
    Tune in Korea: Legacy and Transformation 88

KOREAN
    Images of Korea, Volume 1 169

KUWAIT
    Young Voices from the Arab World:
        The Lives and Times of Five Teenagers 219

LABOR
    Producing Miracles Everyday 180
    We Aren't Asking for the Moon 218

LADAKH
    Ancient Futures: Learning from Ladakh 157
    Cycles of Independence 109

LANGUAGE ARTS
    Good Earth, The 96
    Narrative Writing 1: Structures--What is a Narrative? 98
    Punctuation: Program 6--Introduction to Punctuation
        and the End Marks 98
    Voices of Latin America 98
    William Wordsworth 98

LATIN AMERICA
    Between Wars: Latin America: Intervention in Our
        Own Backyard 194
    Carlos Fuentes 29
    Common Table: Basic Christian Communities in
        Latin America 109
    Controversia 206
    Environment, The - New Global Concerns:
        Current Affairs 122
    From the Heart of the World 124
    Mercado, El 176
    Music of Latin America 67
    Official Story, The 202

SUBJECT INDEX

LATIN AMERICA (continued)
  Popular Hispanic Culture 54
  Roots of Rhythm 68
  Ten Who Dared - Alexander von Humboldt 36
  To Be a Mother in Latin America 217
  Voices of Latin America 98

LAW ENFORCEMENT
  Racial Profiling and Law Enforcement: America in Black and White 215

LEAD POISONING
  Lead Paint Poisoning: The Thief of Childhood 127

LEBANON
  In the Footsteps of Alexander the Great 201
  Syria, Jordan and Lebanon 217
  Young Voices from the Arab World: The Lives and Times of Five Teenagers 219

LIFE CYCLE
  Seasons of Life 136

LITERACY
  Five Months That Changed a Nation 208

LITERATURE
  Dialogo Entre Augusto Roa Bastos y Fernando Alegria 30
  Gabriel Garcia Marquez: Magic and Reality 33
  Good Earth, The 96
  Martin Fierro 24
  Molly's Pilgrim 97
  Pablo Neruda Present 35
  Para una Tumba sin Nombre 25
  Voices of Latin America 98

LOUISIANA
  Louisiana Wetlands: America's Coastal Crisis 149
  Reversing the Tide 151

MAINE
  Good Place to Call Home, A: Maine Towns Creating Their Future 147

MANUFACTURING PROCESSES
  Our Hidden National Product 128

MAPS AND MAPMAKING
  Latitude and Longitude 173

MARINE LIFE
  Funny Crabs in the Mangrove, The 139

MARRIAGE
  Arranged Marriages 158
  Marriages in Heaven 175
  Saheri's Choice 181

MARTIAL ARTS
  Budo: The Martial Arts/The Art of Karate 100
  Kendo 103
  Kendo 104
  Naginata 104

MARTIAL ARTS (continued)
  Sumo 104
  Traditional Sports: Karatedo 105
  Traditional Sports: Kendo 105
  Traditional Sports: Sumo 105

MASSACHUSETTS
  Shaw Memorial, The: The Power and Glory of Public Art 58

MASS MEDIA
  Serial for Breakfast (Part I & II) 182

MAYA
  Courtly Art of Ancient Maya 42

MAYANS
  Archaeological Yucatan: Land of the Maya 157
  Popol Vuh: The Creation Myth of the Maya 98

MEDITATION
  Observing the Breath 114

MEDITERRANEAN
  Ancient Religions of the Mediterranean 193
  Enchanted Travels of Benjamin of Tudela, The 196

MEXICO
  Americas 3: Continent on the Move: Migration and Urbanization 156
  Americas 9: Fire in the Mind: Revolutions and Revolutionaries 157
  Anuncios Comerciales 96
  Arruza 28
  Art and Revolution in Mexico 38
  Asi es Mi Tierra 21
  Borderline Cases 6
  Chiapas: The Inside Story 195
  Courtly Art of Ancient Maya 42
  Day of the Dead 163
  Devil Gave Us Oil, The 8
  Diego Rivera in the United States 44
  El Peregrinaje de las Flores 23
  Emerging Powers: Mexico 10
  Global Assembly Line, The 10
  Guadalupe: Mother of All Mexico 111
  Hernan Cortes 34
  Hunt for Pancho Villa, The 199
  Introducing Mexico: Part One, The Land 4
  L.E.A.R.: League of Revolutionary Artists and Writers 48
  Los Murales de la Cuidad de Mexico: El Muro de las Celebraciones 49
  Los Olvidados 211
  Maquila: A Tale of Two Mexicos 12
  Maria Candelaria 24
  Mexico 202
  Middle America: Mexico to Venezuela and the Caribbean Islands 176

SUBJECT INDEX

MEXICO (continued)
  Miles from the Border 212
  Mythology of Ancient Mexico 114
  Nowhere Else to Live 214
  Oaxacan Woodcarving: Innovation Meets Tradition 51
  One World, One Economy 12
  Our Mexican-American Musical Heritage 68
  Parties, Pinatas and Plays: Mexican Christmas Traditions 179
  Querido Diario 25
  Raices Del Pueblo: Cantos y Danzas de Veracruz 68
  Rivera: Portrait of an Artist 56
  Sabina Sanchez - The Art of Embroidery 57
  Troubled Harvest 217
  Viva Zapata 26
  Voices of the Sierra Tarahumara 190
  We Aren't Asking for the Moon 218
  Wuthering Heights 27

MIDDLE EAST
  Israel: Born to Destiny 113

MODERN ART
  Art and Revolution in Mexico 38
  Art of Haiti, The 39
  Diego Rivera in the United States 44
  L.E.A.R.: League of Revolutionary Artists and Writers 48
  Martin Chambi and the Heirs of the Incas 49
  Masses and Murals 175
  Rivera: Portrait of an Artist 56

MONASTERY
  Buddhism: The Making of a Monk 108
  Zen Temple 118

MONET, CLAUDE
  Linnea In Monet's Garden 49

MONSOONS
  India: Land of the Monsoon 169

MOROCCO
  Young Voices from the Arab World: The Lives and Times of Five Teenagers 219

MOUNTAINS
  Teton--Decision and Disaster 152

MUHAMMAD
  Message, The 114

MULTICULTURAL EDUCATION
  Expanding Canon, The: Teaching Multicultural Literature in High School 96
  Mayan Voices: American Lives 212
  Miles from the Border 212
  Multi-Racial Crosstalk 213
  Oaxacalifornia 214

MUSIC
  Bellas Damas, Las 62

MUSIC (continued)
  Brazilian Music 62
  Carmen Miranda: Bananas Is My Business 29
  Chinese Musical Instruments: Parts I and II 63
  Chinese Musical Instruments: Parts III and IV 63
  Chulas Fronteras 63
  Gagaku: The Court Music of Japan 64
  Heated Competition: Jonkara-Bushi 65
  I Am a Sufi, I Am a Muslim 112
  Jongara Bushi Competition--The Tsugaru Jamisen National Contest 66
  Maysa Matarazzo 35
  Our Mexican-American Musical Heritage 68
  Popular Hispanic Culture 54
  Roots of Rhythm 68
  Roots, Rock, Reggae: Inside the Jamaican Music Scene 68
  Routes of Rhythm--Part II 69
  Routes of Rhythm--Part III 69
  Selected Songs by Famous Singers 69
  Tango Is Also History 70
  Voice from Heaven, A: Nusrat Fateh Ali Khan 71
  Waiapi Instrumental Music 71

MUSICAL INSTRUMENTS
  Music of Modern Japan/Kitaro, Synthesizer Musician 67

MUSLIM
  End to Silence, Part 1: Paradise Is Under Your Mother's Foot 165
  Islam: Empire of Faith 113
  Islam in America 113
  Kashmir Story, The 113
  Taj Mahal: The Story of Muslim India 183
  Valley of the Gods: Worship in Katmandu 117

NAFTA
  U. S., Mexico, and NAFTA 15

NATIONAL PARKS
  Emas Park 122

NATIVE AMERICANS
  Journey Into Tradition 148
  Legends of the American West: Part Two 34
  Multi-Racial Crosstalk 213
  Our Water, Our Future: Saving Our Tribal Life Force Together 129
  Place of the Falling Waters, The 150

NATURAL RESOURCES
  Birth of Oroville Dam, The 144
  Build-Up on the Bighorn 144
  California's State Water Project: Meeting the Challenge 145
  California Water Story, The 145
  California Water Story, The 146
  Central Arizona Project--Lifeline to the Future 146

SUBJECT INDEX

NATURAL RESOURCES (continued)
- Central Utah Project 146
- Energy Behind Finding Energy, The 135
- Good Place to Call Home, A: Maine Towns Creating Their Future 147
- Hydropower 148
- Living Waters of the Colorado 148
- Miracle of Water 149
- Mountain Skywater 149
- Operation Glen Canyon 149
- Pipeline 150
- Powering One Corner of the World 151
- Snowfall to Sandstone 151
- Story of Hoover Dam, The 152
- Wings Over Water 153

NATURE STUDY
- Bird Dogs Afield 137
- Environmental Vision 122
- Extreme Cave Diving 138
- Funny Crabs in the Mangrove, The 139
- Galapagos of the East, The: Ogasawara Islands 139
- Galapagos of the East, The: Ogasawara Islands 140
- Lizard Kings 141
- Sables in the Northern Land 141
- Sables in the Northern Land 142
- Sea Turtles' Last Dance 142

NEAR EAST
- Enchanted Travels of Benjamin of Tudela, The 196

NEPAL
- Nepal: Land of the Gods 178

NERUDA, PABLO
- Pablo Neruda Present 35

NEW MEXICO
- Southwest Region 151

NICARAGUA
- Alsino and the Condor 21
- Americas 9: Fire in the Mind: Revolutions and Revolutionaries 157
- Central America Close-Up #2 161
- Five Months That Changed a Nation 208
- Interview with Daniel Ortega 210
- Masses and Murals 175
- War on Nicaragua 218
- World Beat: U. S. Foreign Policy 219

NUTRITION
- Anemia: The Silent Shadow 76
- Covert Bailey's Fit or Fat 76
- Eating for Life 85
- Eating, Teens and Calcium 80
- First Foods: Lily Feeds Her Baby 80
- Healthy Eating for a Healthy Baby 81
- Look Who's Eating 82

NUTRITION (continued)
- Starting Solid Foods: Lily Helps Ana 83
- Teenage Nutrition: Prevention of Obesity 79

OCEAN LIFE
- Saving Inky 142

OKLAHOMA
- Southwest Region 151

OPERA
- Selected Songs by Famous Singers 69

ORIGAMI
- Origami 52

ORTEGA, DANIEL
- Interview with Daniel Ortega 210

OSLO ACCORDS
- Yitzhak Rabin 219

OZONE
- Air Quality--Ozone 119

PAINTERS
- Ginevra's Story 45

PAINTINGS
- Beauty of Famous Paintings In the National Palace Museum, The 41
- Masterpieces of Chinese Painting and Calligraphy at the National Palace Museum 49
- Women in Ukiyo-E 60

PAKISTAN
- Benazir Bhutto: Walking the Tightrope 28
- Kalasha, The: Rites of Spring 171
- Kashmir: Valley of Despair 211
- Khyber 202
- Pakistan: Between the Chitralis and Pathans 179
- War and Peace 218

PALEONTOLOGY
- Amber Hunters 135

PANAMA
- Americas 8: Get Up, Stand Up: The Problems of Sovereignty 156

PARAGUAY
- Dialogo Entre Augusto Roa Bastos y Fernando Alegria 30
- Footholds 3

PARENTS AND PARENTING
- Baby Shower for Betsy, A 80
- First Foods: Lily Feeds Her Baby 80
- 14 Steps to Better Breastfeeding 81
- Healthy Eating for a Healthy Baby 81
- Home Plate 88
- Lead Paint Poisoning: The Thief of Childhood 127
- Look Who's Eating 82
- Starting Solid Foods: Lily Helps Ana 83
- Well Baby Check Ups: From Infants to Tots 83

SUBJECT INDEX

PEACE
War and Peace 218

PEARL HARBOR
Killer Subs in Pearl Habor 202

PERIODIC TABLE OF THE ELEMENTS
Periodic Table of Videos 136

PERON, EVA
Evita: The Woman Behind the Myth 31

PERU
Alias, La Gringa 21
Americas 9: Fire in the Mind: Revolutions and Revolutionaries 157
Chancay, the Forgotten Art 42
Children in Debt 206
Footholds 3
Healer, The 112
Martin Chambi and the Heirs of the Incas 49
Miss Universe in Peru 212
Mountain Music in Peru 67
Peru: Inca Heritage 202
Plunder 54
Ten Who Dared: Francisco Pizzarro 36
Washington/Peru: We Ain't Winning 218

PESTICIDES
Poisoned Home, Poisoned People: CNN and Time on Special Assignment 129
Serpent Fruits 132

PETROLEUM
Devil Gave Us Oil, The 8

PHILIPPINES
Global Assembly Line, The 10
Where There Is Hatred 219

PHOTOJOURNALISM
Dalda 13: A Talented Woman History Forgot 30

PHYSICAL FITNESS
Covert Bailey's Fit or Fat 76
Flexibility 103

PICASSO, PABLO
Picasso and His Time 36
Picasso: The Early Years 53

PILGRIMAGE
Indian Pilgrimage, An: Ramdevra 169

POETRY
William Wordsworth 98

POISON PREVENTION
Lead Paint Poisoning: The Thief of Childhood 127
Poisoned Home, Poisoned People: CNN and Time on Special Assignment 129

POLAND
One World, One Economy 12

POLLUTION
Bentley Creek: A Story of an Urban Salt Marsh 119
Down in the Dumps 121
Environmental Vision 122
Environment Under Fire: Ecology and Politics in Central America 123
How New England Environmental Assistance Team Helps Businesses Prevent Pollution 126
Lead in School Drinking Water 127
Legal Winds of Change: Business and the New Clean Air Act 127
Less Is More: Pollution Prevention Is Good Business 12
Rotten Truth, The 131
Saving Inky 142
User's Guide to the Planet Earth, A: The American Environmental Test 132

PORTUGUESE
Almost a Woman 155
Apaissionata 21
Benedita da Silva 28
Black Orpheus 22
Brazilian Music 62
Carmen Miranda: Bananas Is My Business 29
Charcoal People, The 206
Hour of the Star 23
Maysa Matarazzo 35
Pixote 25
Quincas Berro D'Agua 25
Seca 215
Vision of Juazeiro 117

POTTERY
Roji Koie-Potter 57

POVERTY
Environment Under Fire: Ecology and Politics in Central America 123

PREGNANCY
Eating, Teens and Calcium 80
Fetal Alcohol Syndrome: Prenatal Drug and Alcohol Use and Its Effects 76
Healthy Foods, Healthy Baby 81
Inside My Mom 82
Lo Que Comes: Por Ti Y Tu Bebe 78
Pregnant Teens Taking Care 82
Sound Nutrition for Teenage Mothers-to-Be 83
Teen Breastfeeding: The Natural Choice 83

PRESIDENTS OF THE UNITED STATES
Eye of Thomas Jefferson, The 32

PUERTO RICO
History and Culture of Puerto Rico 147
La Operacion 211
Latino Artists: Pushing Artistic Boundaries 48

SUBJECT INDEX

PUPPETRY
  Music of Bunraku 67
PURCHASING
  Complete the Circle: How to Buy Recycled 121
  Shopping for Health: Smart Choices at the Supermarket 93
QUALITY CONTROL
  Quality Control, An American Idea Takes Root in Japan 12
  Quality Control, An American Idea Takes Root in Japan 13
  Quality Control and the Q.C. Circle 13
QUEEN NOOR OF JORDAN
  Queen Noor: Between Two Realms 215
RABIN, YITZHAK
  Yitzhak Rabin 219
RACISM AND PREJUDICE
  Racial Profiling and Law Enforcement: America in Black and White 215
RADIOACTIVITY
  Big Apple, Hot Apple 120
RAINFORESTS
  Charcoal People, The 206
  Earth: The Changing Environment 8
  Environment, The - New Global Concerns: Current Affairs 122
  Environment Under Fire: Ecology and Politics in Central America 123
  Jaguar Trax 127
  Jungle 127
  Rain Forest 130
  Rain Forest 141
  Rainforests: Proving Their Worth 130
  Reviving Our Rain Forests--The Mission of Professor Akira Miyawaki 131
  Tramp in the Darien, A 132
  Wings Above the Forest 133
  You Can't Grow Home Again 134
RAPHAEL
  Raphael and the American Collector 55
RECIPES
  Great Food Mixes You Can Make at Home 86
  Healthy Japanese Diet, The 87
  Healthy Japanese Diet, The 88
  High Five: Nutrition Program for High School Youth 88
  I Love Sushi 89
  Japanese Cooking--A Taste for All Seasons 90
  Recreating Taste in Low Fat Cooking 92
  Taste of Japan, The: A Tradition of Hospitality 93
  Taste of Japan, The: A Tradition of Hospitality 94
RECREATION
  Bird Dogs Afield 137

RECYCLING
  Close the Loop: Buy Recycled 121
  Complete the Circle: How to Buy Recycled 121
  Don't Throw It Away 121
  Down in the Dumps 121
  Gone With the Waste 124
  How the Waste Was Won 126
  Protecting Our Habitat: Recycling at the Grassroots 130
  Recycle 131
  Reduce, Reuse, Recycle: The Bottom Line 131
  We Don't Have a Choice 133
REFORESTATION
  Reviving Our Rain Forests--The Mission of Professor Akira Miyawaki 131
REFUGEES
  We Are Guatemalans 191
RELIGION
  Ache Moyuba Orisha 154
  Altar of Fire 107
  Ancient Religions of the Mediterranean 193
  Bahia: Africa in the Americas 107
  Basic Christian Communities in Latin America 108
  Buddhism and Black Belts 108
  Buddhism: The Middle Way of Compassion 108
  Common Ground, A 109
  Common Table: Basic Christian Communities in Latin America 109
  Confucianism and Taoism 109
  End to Silence, Part 1: Paradise Is Under Your Mother's Foot 165
  From the Burning Embers 208
  God's Millennium 110
  Guadalupe: Mother of All Mexico 111
  Guests of God, The 111
  Hajj, The 111
  I Am a Sufi, I Am a Muslim 112
  Images of Korea, Volume 1 169
  Introduction to East Asian Religions, An: Buddhism (Part I) 112
  Introduction to East Asian Religions, An: Confucianism (Part II) 112
  Jesus: His Life 113
  Kashmir Story, The 113
  Night of Nine Tribes, The 178
  Roots, Rock, Reggae: Inside the Jamaican Music Scene 68
  Shinto: Way of the Gods 115
  Taj Mahal: The Story of Muslim India 183
  Tribal Religions 117
  Vision of Juazeiro 117
  Voices of the Orishas 117
RENAISSANCE
  Artist, The 28

SUBJECT INDEX

RENAISSANCE (continued)
  Leonardo: To Know How to See 48
  Picasso: The Early Years 53
  Raphael and the American Collector 55
REPTILES
  Lizard Kings 141
RESPECT
  R-E-S-P-E-C-T 73
  Student Workshop: All About Respect 74
RIO GRANDE RIVER
  Rio Grande--Ribbon of Life 151
RIVERA, DIEGO
  Diego Rivera in the United States 44
  Rivera: Portrait of an Artist 56
ROCKY MOUNTAINS
  Teton--Decision and Disaster 152
SCULPTURE
  Henry Moore: A Life in Sculpture 33
  Shaw Memorial, The: The Power and
      Glory of Public Art 58
SELF ESTEEM
  Body Image for Boys 80
SELF IMAGE
  Mirror in My Mind, The: Body Image & Self-Esteem 78
SEX AND SEX EDUCATION
  Reproductive Systems 82
SEXUAL ABUSE
  Wake Up Call 74
SHADOW PUPPETS
  Shadows of Turkey/The Witches 69
SHINTOISM
  Shinto: Way of the Gods 115
SIGN LANGUAGE
  Mexican Sign Language 97
SNACKS AND SNACKING
  Home Plate 88
SOCIAL ISSUES
  Benedita da Silva 28
  Common Table: Central American
      Refugees--The Church Response 109
  Controversia 206
  Dance of Hope* 207
  Dark Light of Dawn, The 196
  Sweet 15 152
SOLAR SYSTEM
  Where the Hot Stuff Is: Volcanoes of the Earth
      and Solar System 136
SOLID WASTE
  Don't Throw It Away 121
  We Don't Have a Choice 133

SOUTH AFRICA
  South Africa: A Land Apart 183
SOUTH AMERICA
  Amazon, The 155
  Around South America 157
  Coca Mama--The War on Drugs 206
  Earth: The Changing Environment 8
  Jungle 127
  Madre Tierra 128
  Middle America: Mexico to Venezuela and
      the Caribbean Islands 176
  Mission, The 202
  South America: The Southern Plains 14
SPAIN
  Tour of the Prado, A 59
SPANISH
  Ache Moyuba Orisha 154
  Adelante 96
  Alias, La Gringa 21
  Alsino and the Condor 21
  Ana Mendieta: Fuego de Tierra 28
  Anemia: The Silent Shadow 76
  Anuncios Comerciales 96
  Argentina: Growth or Disappearance 157
  Asi es Mi Tierra 21
  Bellas Damas, Las 62
  Bolivar Soy Yo 22
  Buena Vista Social Club 62
  Children in Debt 206
  Controversia 206
  Dance of Hope* 207
  Day of the Dead 163
  Dialogo Entre Augusto Roa Bastos y Fernando
      Alegria 30
  Don Segundo Sombra 22
  Drought Survival in California 146
  Dust to Dust 22
  El Futuro Maya: Voces del Presente 164
  El Norte 23
  El Peregrinaje de las Flores 23
  El Tango en Broadway 23
  Fetal Alcohol Syndrome: Prenatal Drug and
      Alcohol Use and Its Effects 76
  14 Steps to Better Breastfeeding 81
  From the Other Side 208
  Health During Pregnancy: Lily Looks Back 81
  Healthy Eating for a Healthy Baby 81
  History and Culture of Puerto Rico 147
  How to Read the New Food Label 77
  Inside My Mom 82
  Jerico 23
  La Piramide de la Alimentacion 91
  Look Who's Eating 82

SUBJECT INDEX

SPANISH (continued)
- Lo Que Comes: Por Ti Y Tu Bebe 78
- Los Ninos Abandonados 211
- Los Olvidados 211
- Man Facing Southeast 24
- Maria Candelaria 24
- Martin Fierro 24
- Mercado, El 176
- Mexican Sign Language 97
- Miss Universe in Peru 212
- Mountain Music in Peru 67
- Mujer Negra Habla 212
- Oaxacan Woodcarving: Innovation Meets Tradition 51
- Official Story, The 202
- Para una Tumba sin Nombre 25
- People of the Caribbean 150
- Pie en la Marcha 179
- Querido Diario 25
- Raices Del Pueblo: Cantos y Danzas de Veracruz 68
- Saludos Hispanos 215
- Secuestro: Story of a Kidnapping 216
- Starting Solid Foods: Lily Helps Ana 83
- Tango Bar 26
- Tango: Our Dance 70
- Throw Me a Dime 184
- Voices of the Orishas 117
- Water is Ours, The 191
- Wuthering Heights 27

SPORTS
- Christian Laettner: The Power Forward 101
- Young Baseball Heroes 105
- Young Baseball Heroes 106

SRI LANKA
- Arabian Seafarers: In the Wake of Sinbad 194

STEREOTYPES AND STEREOTYPING
- To Live in a Multi-Cultural World 74

SWINE
- Handling of Pigs 3

SYRIA
- Syria, Jordan and Lebanon 217

TAIWAN
- Between Heaven and Earth: The Temple of Taiwan 62
- Festivals in Taiwan 165
- Firecracker: A Night to Remember in Yen-Shuei 166
- Lantern Festival, The 173
- Wild Birds of Taiwan 143

TALIBAN
- Afghanistan: The Lost Generation 206

TEACHER REFERENCE
- Economics Classroom, The: Growth & Entrepreneurship 9
- Economics Classroom, The: How Economists Think 9

TEACHER REFERENCE (continued)
- Economics Classroom, The: Learning, Earning, Saving 9
- Economics Classroom, The: Monetary & Fiscal Policy 9
- Economics Classroom, The: The Building Blocks of Macroeconomics 10
- Economics Classroom, The: Trading Globally 10
- Expanding Canon, The: Teaching Multicultural Literature in High School 96
- School Testing--Behind the Numbers 136
- Seasons of Life 136

TEACHER'S GUIDES
- Lo Que Comes: Por Ti Y Tu Bebe 78
- Oaxacan Woodcarving: Innovation Meets Tradition 51
- Shopping for Health: Smart Choices at the Supermarket 93
- Tune in Korea: Legacy and Transformation 88

TECHNOLOGY
- Tsukuba Academic New Town 15

TECHNOLOGY EDUCATION
- High Technology in Japan 168

TESTS AND TESTING
- School Testing--Behind the Numbers 136

TEXAS
- Southwest Region 151

THEATER
- Bunraku Puppet Theatre of Japan 63
- Kabuki: Classic Theater of Japan/Noh, Drama, Bunraku: The Puppet Theater of Japan 66
- Noh Drama, Kabuki, Bunraku--Classical Theater in Japan 68
- Theater Lives, The 71

THIRD WORLD COUNTRIES
- Meeting the Third World Through Women's Perspectives 175

TIBET
- Ancient Futures: Learning from Ladakh 157
- Debate in the Tibetan Tradition 110
- Dreams of Tibet 207
- Sand Painting: Sacred Art of Tibetan Buddhism 115
- Satya: A Prayer for the Enemy 203
- Tibetan Book of the Dead, The 116
- Tibet: Where Continents Collide 185
- Trials of Telo Rinpoche 116
- Two Tibetan Buddhist Nunneries 117

TOLSTOY, LEO
- Leo Tolstoy 35

TRADITIONS
- Heart Within, The 168
- Tales of Pabuji: A Rajasthani Tradition 116

SUBJECT INDEX

TRANSPORTATION
South America: The Southern Plains 14

TURKEY
Shadows of Turkey/The Witches 69
Turquoise Coast via Istanbul, The 88

TUTANKHAMUN
Of Time, Tombs, and Treasure: The Treasures of Tutankhamun 51

UNITED STATES
Arts of the Eskimo, The: An Arctic Adventure 144
El Norte 23
Extreme Cave Diving 138
Food: A Multi-Cultural Feast 86
Immigration Policy in the United States 209
Immigration Reform 209
Islam in America 113
Missing 24
NAFTA and the New Economic Frontier: Life Along the U. S./Mexico Border 213
Pakistan: Between the Chitralis and Pathans 179
Roots in the Sand 203
Routes of Rhythm--Part III 69
Southwest Region 151
Unheard Voices 217
War and Peace 218
War on Nicaragua 218
Washington/Peru: We Ain't Winning 218
Whose Woods Are These? 133
World Beat: U. S. Foreign Policy 219

UTAH
Adventure in Glen Canyon 144
Central Utah Project 146

VENEZUELA
Jerico 23
Venezuela: A Petroleum Powered Economy 190

VERMONT
Vermont Wetlands: A Natural Resource 153

VIOLENCE AND VIOLENCE PREVENTION
Father, Son and Holy War 110
Win-Win 74

VOCATIONAL GUIDANCE
Beauticians 16
Behavior Success 16
Career Close-Ups: School Teacher 16
Communication Success 16
Cover Letter Training 16
Dealing with Illegal Questions 17
Diary of a Police Post 17
Job Search Preparation 18
Learning a Trade 18

VOCATIONAL GUIDANCE (continued)
Rewarding Employment: How to Get a Really Good Job 18
So You Want to Be? Teacher/Make-Up Artist 19
Spirit of Edo Firemen, The--Alive in Tokyo Today 19
Vocational Training 19
Way of Life in Japan, The: Mastery of the Chef's Blade 19
Way of Life in Japan, The: Mastery of the Chef's Blade 20
Women in Dental Research 75
Women Scientists with Disabilities 75

VOLCANOES
Earth Revealed 122

WARS
Afghanistan: The Lost Generation 206
Hiroshima: City of Peace 197
Hiroshima: City of Peace 198
Hiroshima: City of Peace 199

WASTE DISPOSAL
Big Apple, Hot Apple 120
Don't Throw It Away 121
Down in the Dumps 121
Gone With the Waste 124
How the Waste Was Won 126
Rotten Truth, The 131
Saving Inky 142
We Don't Have a Choice 133

WATER
Alternative Is Conservation 119
Birth of Oroville Dam, The 144
Build-Up on the Bighorn 144
California's State Water Project: Meeting the Challenge 145
California Water Story, The 145
California Water Story, The 146
Central Arizona Project--Lifeline to the Future 146
Central Utah Project 146
Drought Survival in California 146
Freshwater 124
Hiroshima, A New Threat--A-Bomb Water Dedication 125
Hiroshima, A New Threat--A-Bomb Water Dedication 126
Hydropower 148
Living Waters of the Colorado 148
Miracle of Water 149
Mountain Skywater 149
Operation Glen Canyon 149
Our Water, Our Future: Saving Our Tribal Life Force Together 129
Pipeline 150
Place of the Falling Waters, The 150

SUBJECT INDEX

WATER (continued)
Powering One Corner of the World 151
Snowfall to Sandstone 151
Story of Hoover Dam, The 152
Water for Agricultural Progress 4
Wings Over Water 153

WATER POLLUTION
Our Water, Our Future: Saving Our Tribal Life Force Together 129
Your Water, Your Life 134

WATERSHEDS
Merrimack River Watershed Protection 128

WEIGHT MANAGEMENT
Weight: Maintaining a Healthy Balance 79

WELLNESS
High Five: Nutrition Program for High School Youth 88

WETLANDS
Louisiana Wetlands: America's Coastal Crisis 149
Our Urban Wetlands: An Endangered Resource 129
Vermont Wetlands: A Natural Resource 153

WHALES
Protecting Our Global Home--Japan's Ecological Contributions 129
Protecting Our Global Home--Japan's Ecological Contributions 130
Saving Inky 142

WHISTLER, JAMES MCNEILL
James McNeill Whistler: His Etchings 46
James McNeill Whistler: The Lyrics of Art 47

WILDLIFE
Animals on the Ice Floe: Shiretoko in Mid-Winter 137
Fight for Survival: The Fish Owl of Northern Japan 138
Galapagos: My Fragile World 124
Galapagos of the East, The: Ogasawara Islands 139
Galapagos of the East, The: Ogasawara Islands 140
Little Duck Tale, A 140
Little Duck Tale, A 141
Wild Birds of Taiwan 143

WOMEN
Americans 5: In Women's Hands: The Changing Roles of Women 155
Breaking the History of Silence 194
Christian Women in China 162
From the Burning Embers 208
Iran: Adventure Divas 210
Meeting the Third World Through Women's Perspectives 175
Miss Universe in Peru 212
Mujer Negra Habla 212
No Longer Silent 178
Power of Compassion, The: Sakyadhita 179
Sixteen Decisions 182
Somos Mas 205
Stirrings of Change 183
Story of Noriko, The 14
Story of Noriko, The 15
To Be a Mother in Latin America 217
Troubled Harvest 217
We Aren't Asking for the Moon 218
Women in Dental Research 75
Women Scientists with Disabilities 75

WORLD AFFAIRS
Coca Mama--The War on Drugs 206
Global Assembly Line, The 10

WORLD WAR II
Hiroshima and Nagasaki 208
Killer Subs in Pearl Habor 202
Rebels vs. the Raj: India During World War II 203

WRITING
Narrative Writing 1: Structures--What is a Narrative? 98
Punctuation: Program 6--Introduction to Punctuation and the End Marks 98

WYOMING
Teton--Decision and Disaster 152

SOURCE INDEX

The SOURCE INDEX is an alphabetical list of the organizations from which the materials listed in the EDUCATORS GUIDE TO FREE VIDEOS–SECONDARY EDUCATION may be obtained. There are 31 sources listed in this Sixty-Fifth Edition of the GUIDE, **10 of which are new**. The numbers following each listing are the page numbers on which the materials from each source are annotated in the body of the GUIDE.

When requesting materials via mail or fax, please use a letter of request similar to the sample shown in the front part of the GUIDE. When requesting via telephone, please have the name of the material you desire in front of you (along with the order number if necessary). Please read each listing carefully to be certain that the material you are requesting is available via the method through which you choose to order.

Bold type indicates a source that is new in the 2018-2019 edition. Complete addresses for each source are found following the description of the material in the body of the GUIDE.

Aldrich   136

Annenberg Media   72, 96, 122, 136

Bureau of Reclamation   144, 145, 146, 148, 149, 150, 151, 152, 153

California Department of Water Resources   144, 145, 146, 147, 150, 153

Center for Latin American and Caribbean Studies   6, 8, 12, 21, 22, 23, 24, 25, 26, 27, 29, 33, 36, 39, 46, 48, 49, 51, 56, 60, 64, 70, 74, 108, 118, 123, 127, 128, 130, 134, 152, 155, 157, 165, 175, 184, 191, 206, 208, 209, 211, 212, 213, 214, 217

Center for Latin American Studies   3, 4, 6, 8, 10, 14, 15, 28, 31, 33, 35, 49, 54, 62, 63, 68, 69, 96, 98, 108, 111, 141, 142, 148, 150,1 53, 155, 156, 157, 158, 161, 163, 176, 179, 188, 191, 193, 194, 199, 202, 206, 207, 211, 212, 215, 217

Center for Middle Eastern Studies   41, 69, 71, 109, 111, 113, 114, 116, 188, 192, 193, 194, 195, 196, 201, 206, 207, 208, 210, 211, 215, 217, 219

Center for South Asian Studies   28, 30, 35, 64, 66, 67, 71, 107, 108, 109, 110, 112, 114, 115, 116, 117, 158, 163, 166, 167, 169, 170, 172, 175, 178, 179, 181, 182, 184, 185, 190, 191, 192, 196, 200, 201, 202, 203, 218

Center for Teaching About China   161, 162, 175, 178, 181, 183, 162, 175, 178, 181, 183, 185, 190, 192, 201, 203, 216

Chicago Bible Students   108, 110, 111, 113, 114

SOURCE INDEX

Consulate General of Japan at Chicago   2, 47, 52, 59, 103, 104, 105, 170, 173, 196

Consulate General of Japan, Atlanta   7, 19, 50, 87, 90, 100, 102, 103, 105, 138, 139, 140, 141, 160, 171, 185, 186, 188, 198, 199, 204, 213, 216

Consulate General of Japan, Boston   6, 12, 13, 14, 17, 20, 36, 45, 50, 52, 56, 57, 58, 60, 63, 65, 70, 71, 73, 87, 90, 94, 95, 96, 97, 100, 101, 102, 106, 107, 115, 120, 122, 123, 125, 129. 130, 131, 133, 137, 138, 139, 140, 141, 154, 159, 164, 167, 168, 169, 173, 177, 180, 181, 186, 187, 189, 198, 200, 204, 213, 217

Consulate General of Japan, Honolulu   8, 11, 19, 20, 66, 87, 90, 100, 102, 104, 121, 134, 138, 139, 140, 141, 142, 159, 161, 166, 171, 173, 176, 177, 178, 184, 186, 187, 189, 198, 200, 204

Consulate General of Japan, Houston   7, 13, 14, 15, 17, 44, 51, 52, 56, 58, 60, 64, 65, 70, 73, 87, 90, 94, 95, 97, 101, 102, 106, 107, 115, 123, 125, 137, 154, 159, 163, 167, 168, 169, 171, 174, 185, 187, 189, 198, 205, 214

Consulate General of Japan, Los Angeles   2, 3, 4, 5, 7, 13, 14, 15, 16, 18, 19, 38, 45, 48, 53, 56, 57, 59, 60, 63, 64, 65, 68, 76, 88, 90, 94, 97, 123, 125, 126, 130, 131, 137, 139, 140, 141, 142, 159, 161, 163, 166, 167, 168, 170, 172, 173, 174, 177, 179, 181, 182, 200

Consulate General of Japan, Oregon   3, 11, 20, 39, 51, 66, 88, 91, 101, 103, 104, 106, 160, 186, 187, 189, 199, 204, 205, 214

Consulate General of Japan, San Francisco   7, 11, 13, 14, 15, 17, 51, 53, 56, 57, 59, 61, 65, 68, 70, 73, 84, 88, 94, 95, 100, 101, 103, 105, 106, 107, 116, 118, 126, 137, 154, 158, 162, 168, 169, 178, 180, 186, 188, 189, 199, 205, 214

Cornell University East Asia Program   2, 4, 6, 8, 11, 29, 30, 31, 34, 38, 41, 42, 47, 49, 50, 63, 64, 67, 69, 70, 91, 96, 108, 109, 112, 113, 143, 164, 165, 166, 169, 171, 174, 175, 178, 184, 188, 193, 199, 208, 209

SOURCE INDEX

Described and Captioned Media Program   9, 10, 16, 17, 18, 19, 28, 32, 34, 35,3 6, 38, 41, 42, 43, 44, 45, 49, 72, 74, 75, 76, 77, 78, 79, 80, 84, 85, 86, 97, 98, 99, 101, 103, 117, 119, 120, 124, 128, 135, 138, 143, 144, 145, 146, 152, 155, 158, 160, 164, 165, 172, 174, 175, 176, 183, 190, 191

Latin American Resource Center   3, 6, 10, 12, 21, 22, 23, 24, 25, 26, 27, 28, 29, 30, 31, 32, 33, 34, 35, 36, 37, 39, 42, 44, 48, 54, 57, 60, 61, 62, 65, 67, 68, 69, 71, 96, 98, 109, 111, 112, 114, 117, 119, 122, 123, 124, 127, 130, 131, 132, 133, 134, 147, 152, 154, 164, 165, 176, 179, 180, 184, 190, 194, 195, 196, 200, 202, 203, 205, 206, 207, 209, 210, 211, 212, 213, 215, 216, 217, 218, 219

National Agricultural Library   1, 2, 4, 73, 76, 77, 78, 79, 80, 82, 83, 85, 86, 87, 88, 89, 91, 92, 93, 95

National Gallery of Art   31, 32, 34, 38, 39, 40, 42, 43, 45, 46, 47, 48, 49, 50, 51, 53, 54, 55, 58, 59

National Institutes of Health, Office of Science Education   75

NOVA   123, 135, 136, 138, 141, 167, 202, 203

Oklahoma Energy Resources Board   135

Paul Fuller   137

Smithsonian National Air and Space Museum   136

Syracuse University, South Asia Center   2, 67, 110, 113, 157, 160, 163, 165, 169, 177, 178, 180, 181, 182, 183, 203, 208, 211

Taipei Economic and Cultural Office in New York   62

U. S. Environmental Protection Agency, Region 1   12, 79, 119, 120, 121, 122, 124, 126, 127, 128, 129, 131, 132, 133, 134, 142, 147, 148, 149, 151, 153, 195